ENCYCLOPEDIA OF AMERICAN HISTORY

Postwar United States
1946 to 1968

VOLUME IX

ENCYCLOPEDIA OF AMERICAN HISTORY

ENCYCLOPEDIA OF AMERICAN HISTORY

Postwar United States
1946 to 1968

VOLUME IX

Allan M. Winkler, Editor
Susan V. Spellman, Associate Editor
Gary B. Nash, General Editor

☑®

Facts On File, Inc.

Encyclopedia of American History:
Postwar United States (1946 to 1968)

Editorial Director: Laurie E. Likoff
Editor in Chief: Owen Lancer
Chief Copy Editor: Michael G. Laraque
Associate Editor: Dorothy Cummings
Production Director: Olivia McKean
Production Associates: Rachel L. Berlin and Theresa Montoya
Art Director: Cathy Rincon
Interior Designer: Joan M. Toro
Desktop Designers: Erika K. Arroyo and David C. Strelecky
Maps and Illustrations: Dale E. Williams and Jeremy Eagle

Facts On File, Inc.
132 West 31st Street
New York NY 10001

Library of Congress Cataloging-in-Publication Data

Encyclopedia of American history / Gary B. Nash, general editor.
p. cm.
Includes bibliographical references and indexes.
Contents: v. 1. Three worlds meet — v. 2. Colonization and settlement —
v. 3. Revolution and new nation — v. 4. Expansion and reform — v. 5. Civil War
and Reconstruction — v. 6. The development of the industrial United States —
v. 7. The emergence of modern America — v. 8. The Great Depression and
World War II — v. 9. Postwar United States — v. 10. Contemporary
United States. — v. 11 Comprehensive index
ISBN 0-8160-4371-X (set)   ISBN 0-8160-4369-8 (v. 9)
1. United States—History—Encyclopedias. 1. Nash, Gary B.
E174 .E53 2002
973′.03—dc21   2001051278

Contents

List of Entries

About the Editors

General Editor: Gary B. Nash received a Ph.D from Princeton University. He is currently director of the National Center for History in the Schools at the University of California, Los Angeles, where he teaches American history of the colonial and Revolutionary era. He is a published author of college and precollegiate history texts. Among his best-selling works is *The American People: Creating a Nation and Society* (Addison Wesley, Longman), now in its fifth edition.

Nash is an elected member of the Society of American Historians, American Academy of Arts and Sciences, and the American Philosophical Society. He has served as past president of the Organization of American Historians, 1994–95, and was a founding member of the National Council for History Education, 1990.

Volume Editor: Allan M. Winkler, Miami University of Ohio, received a Ph.D from Yale University. He is the author of several books, including *Life Under a Cloud: American Anxiety about the Atom* (Oxford University Press, 1993) and a best-selling textbook, *The American People: Creating a Nation and Society* (with Gary Nash), now in its fifth edition.

Acknowledgments

This book depended on the good work of the dozens of contributors who met deadlines, rewrote entries as requested, and kept the venture moving forward. Their names appear at the end of each entry. Gary Nash played an important role in conceptualizing the entire project, and in helping define how this volume, the ninth of 10, fit into the overall plan. He was equally helpful in reading and critiquing drafts of the table of contents and the entries themselves. My thanks go to Miami University's Graduate School for providing a fellowship for a graduate student to assist me with this book. Susan V. Spellman, who accepted that fellowship, played a major role in keeping track of contributors, doing a first edit of all entries, and performing all of the other assignments that had to be done, and she richly deserves the designation of associate editor of this volume.

— Allan M. Winkler
Miami University
Oxford, Ohio

Foreword

The Encyclopedia of American History series is designed as a handy reference to the most important individuals, events, and topics in U.S. history. In 10 volumes, the encyclopedia covers the period from the 15th century, when European explorers first made their way across the Atlantic Ocean to the Americas, to the present day. The encyclopedia is written for precollegiate as well as college students, for parents of young learners in the schools, and for the general public. The volume editors are distinguished historians of American history. In writing individual entries, each editor has drawn upon the expertise of scores of specialists. This ensures the scholarly quality of the entire series. Articles contributed by the various volume editors are uncredited.

This 10-volume encyclopedia of "American history" is broadly conceived to include the historical experience of the various peoples of North America. Thus, in the first volume, many essays treat the history of a great range of indigenous people before contact with Europeans. In the same vein, readers will find essays in the first several volumes that sketch Spanish, Dutch, and French explorers and colonizers who opened up territories for European settlement that later would become part of the United States. The venues and cast of characters in the American historical drama are thus widened beyond traditional encyclopedias.

In creating the eras of American history that define the chronological limits of each volume, and in addressing major topics in each era, the encyclopedia follows the architecture of *The National Standards for United States History, Revised Edition* (Los Angeles: National Center for History in the Schools, 1996). Mandated by the U.S. Congress, the national standards for U.S. history have been widely used by states and school districts in organizing curricular frameworks and have been followed by many other curriculum-building efforts.

Entries are cross-referenced, when appropriate, with *See also* citations at the end of articles. At the end of most entries, a listing of articles and books allows readers to turn to specialized sources and historical accounts. In each volume, an array of maps provide geographical context, while numerous illustrations help vivify the material covered in the text. A time line is included to provide students with a chronological reference to major events occurring in the given era. The selection of historical documents in the back of each volume gives students experience with the raw documents that historians use when researching history. A comprehensive index to each volume also facilitates the reader's access to particular information.

In each volume, long entries are provided for major categories of American historical experience. These categories may include: African Americans, agriculture, art and architecture, business, economy, education, family life, foreign policy, immigration, labor, Native Americans, politics, population, religion, urbanization, and women. By following these essays from volume to volume, the reader can access what might be called a mini-history of each broad topic, for example, family life, immigration, or religion.

— Gary B. Nash
University of California, Los Angeles

Introduction

★ ───────────────────────────────────

The United States changed dramatically in the post–World War II years. The economic boom based on wartime spending continued and made the nation richer than ever before. Large corporations dominated the business world, but unions grew too, and most American workers saw their lives improve. Some Americans, however, still found themselves left out. Huge gaps still existed between rich and poor, and millions of people were still part of what one critic called "the other America." Building on a start made during the war, African Americans and members of other minority groups began to mobilize to change American society. In time, the Civil Rights movement encouraged other movements for reform.

Meanwhile the United States found itself in the midst of a new kind of international conflict. The cold war, which stemmed from divergent views about the shape of the postwar world, pitted the United States against the Soviet Union in a competitive struggle that had ramifications around the globe. Strong and secure after its successful involvement in World War II, the United States sought to spread the values of liberty, equality, and democracy that provided the underpinning of the American dream, and to create a world where American enterprise could thrive. When those aims and values came into conflict with Soviet insistence on a different kind of security and stability, the cold war was the result.

This volume, part of a 10-volume *Encyclopedia of American History*, charts the changes that occurred in the decades following World War II. It seeks to provide easy access to the social and political developments of the postwar years, highlighting social, cultural, and economic issues as well as political and diplomatic affairs. Taken together, the entries provide a good overview of the shifts of the postwar years.

— Allan M. Winkler
Miami University
Oxford, Ohio

ENTRIES
A TO Z

A

Acheson, Dean (1892–1971)

Secretary of state when Communist forces drove Jiang Jieshi off the Chinese mainland, Dean Acheson found himself labeled "The Red Dean" and the man who "lost" China by critics of presidents Franklin D. Roosevelt and HARRY S. TRUMAN.

Acheson, born in Middletown, Connecticut, on April 11, 1893, was the eldest son in a distinguished family with Scots-Irish roots. His father, Episcopal bishop of Connecticut, preached hope, charity, and good works. His mother, Eleanor Gooderham, was the daughter of a prominent Toronto whiskey distiller and banker. His father insisted the young Acheson attend all the finest schools—Groton, Yale, and later Harvard Law School. Although he found Groton to be a harsh environment, Acheson developed a fierce independent streak, which he found invaluable in maintaining his composure later in life. At Harvard Law, Felix Frankfurter took him under his wing and Acheson bloomed. After a year clerking for Supreme Court Justice Louis Brandeis, at Frankfurter's recommendation, Acheson joined a Washington law firm and quickly made a name for himself in financial law.

Perhaps at Frankfurter's suggestion, newly elected president Franklin D. Roosevelt asked Acheson to serve as undersecretary of the treasury. Unfortunately, Acheson and Roosevelt disagreed on fiscal policy. When Roosevelt took the nation off the gold standard, Acheson resigned in protest at what he thought was an unwise action. His loyalties, however, remained with the DEMOCRATIC PARTY, and he never fully cut ties with the Roosevelt administration.

In 1941, Roosevelt called upon Acheson to serve as assistant secretary of state, and within four years he was promoted to undersecretary. In 1949, President Harry S. Truman chose him to succeed GEORGE C. MARSHALL at the State Department. Acheson believed that the SOVIET UNION was the major threat to the United States and felt the nation's first priority was to contain Soviet expansion into Eastern Europe. To accomplish this, he was convinced American allies would have to be strengthened both economically and militarily. Acheson helped draft the blueprint for European economic recovery, the MARSHALL PLAN, and the military alliance that evolved into the NORTH ATLANTIC TREATY ORGANIZATION (NATO). Although ASIA

Dean Acheson *(Library of Congress)*

was a secondary concern to Acheson, he also negotiated the Japanese Peace Treaty.

More controversial was Acheson's involvement in framing the National Security Council's new foreign policy document, NSC-68, which called for an increased military buildup to contain the Soviet Union in the way diplomat GEORGE F. KENNAN had counseled. During Acheson's tenure as secretary of state, the COLD WAR held center stage and the way Acheson and the Truman administration dealt with it came increasingly under fire. Equally controversial was Acheson's role in the KOREAN WAR. He encouraged American intervention and advised Truman to go to the United Nations rather than Congress for approval. The Republican-controlled Congress thereby acquired the ammunition to label Korea "Truman's War," but Republicans before the attack also accused Acheson of giving the North Koreans a green light when he remarked in a Washington speech that the peninsula was not within the U.S. defense sphere.

While many criticized Acheson, JOHN F. KENNEDY consulted him during the CUBAN MISSILE CRISIS and both Kennedy and LYNDON B. JOHNSON sought his advice on the VIETNAM WAR. Initially hawkish, Acheson encouraged intervention because he was certain the United States would win the war. As the struggle dragged on, Acheson, ever the pragmatist, became convinced the war could not be won and urged the withdrawal of troops. Acheson died in 1971.

Further reading: Dean Acheson, *Present at the Creation* (New York: W. W. Norton, 1969); Walter Isaacson and Evan Thomas, *The Wise Men: Six Friends and the World They Made* (New York: Simon & Schuster, 1986).

— Gisela Abels

advertising

Advertising encouraged Americans to buy all kinds of new products in the increasingly materialistic consumer society of the post–World War II years.

Advertising, which came of age in the 1920s, changed significantly with the advent of TELEVISION in the 1950s. New ads now appeared not just in newspapers and on the radio but on television screens as well. Advertising agencies jumped at the opportunity to use audio and visual components together in creative combinations. Many companies rushed to find ad agencies that specialized in TV promotions. In 1957, *Variety* magazine reported that, during a typical week, an average viewer encountered 420 commercials, totaling five hours, eight minutes. By year's end, ad expenditures in radio and TV crossed the $2 billion mark.

In the 1950s, advertising agencies concentrated on simple themes, with slogans that were repeated over and

Man wrestles with manual razor in television commercial
(Library of Congress)

over again. One candy manufacturer told consumers that "M&M's melt in your mouth, not in your hands," while a toothpaste company proclaimed "Colgate cleans your breath while it cleans your teeth." The theory that a consumer could only retain one strong claim from an ad lay behind the simplistic ads of the 1950s. Rather than being original, advertisements were all alike in their format and style.

The 1950s also saw a rise in consumerism with the end of the war, and advertising promoted a host of new goods and products. Mass housing was developed, as were supermarkets and shopping malls. There was a rise in RECREATION, where families took yearly vacations and generally went outside the home for entertainment to events such as baseball games and the theater. Families also became increasingly materialistic, buying up new products such as dishwashers, blenders, and freezers. Ad agencies played to middle-class families during such popular television shows as *I Love Lucy* and *Leave It to Beaver.* Ad companies knew these were popular sitcoms, with millions of Americans tuning in each week. Ad agencies vied with one another for commercial time during these shows.

The 1960s produced a creative wave in the advertising world. Ad agencies began to use brighter images, and to shy away from short slogans. The Avis car-rental company told customers in a highly effective campaign: "Avis is only No. 2 in rent-a-cars. So why go with us?" The answer: "We try harder. (When you're not the biggest, you have to.) . . . We can't afford to take you for granted. Go with us next time. The line at our counter is shorter."

Political advertising also became more commonplace. In 1964, negative political TV advertising began with the "Daisy" commercial. It appeared in LYNDON B. JOHNSON's presidential campaign, and cast Republican candidate BARRY GOLDWATER as a warmonger who might start a nuclear war. It showed a little girl counting while pulling the petals off a daisy. As she finished, the ad showed a nuclear explosion dissolving into a mushroom cloud behind her. It caused such controversy that it only appeared once nationwide.

Consumers were not always pleased with the ads they saw. The American Association of Advertising released a study in 1965 on what consumers thought of ads. The survey included television, radio, newspaper, magazine, and outdoor advertising. It found that only 35 percent of those interviewed thought that advertisements were informative. Consumers believed that some ads were misleading or made statements that they thought were false. In the same study, however, consumers acknowledged they were more likely to accept information from television than from a printed ad. These criticisms notwithstanding, advertising remained an important part of American culture.

Further reading: Stephen Fox, *The Mirror Makers: A History of American Advertising and Its Creators* (New York: William Morrow, 1984); Roland Marchand, *Advertising the American Dream: Making Way for Modernity, 1920–1940* (Berkeley: University of California Press, 1985).
— Megan D. Wessel

Africa (and foreign policy)

World War II marked an important watershed in American-African relations because the United States established a new relationship with Africa, which had been closely identified in the past with its European allies, such as Great Britain and France, which had colonies on that continent.

In the immediate post–World War II years, U.S. dealings with Africa were largely driven by two key determinants: decolonization of European colonies and the need to contain the spread of COMMUNISM. In principle, successive postwar American administrations referred to the Atlantic Charter of 1941 to insist that the "right of all peoples to choose the form of government under which they will live" must be extended to all European colonies in Africa and

not just countries then occupied by the Axis powers. The United States also believed that the spread of communism to EUROPE and regions like Africa, where decolonization was becoming increasingly likely, would run contrary to its vision of a global economy under American leadership. Africa, potentially, could serve American geostrategic, political, and economic interests.

American preoccupation with containing expansionism by the SOVIET UNION meant that, by the early 1950s, American policymakers still considered the future of European colonies in Africa important only insofar as how U.S. attitudes toward colonial issues would affect U.S. relations with its European allies. State Department officials therefore carefully weighed the practical advantages of strengthening the NORTH ATLANTIC TREATY ORGANIZATION (NATO) alliance against what would accrue from granting self-government to European colonies in Africa. Not only was the United States cautious not to alienate its European allies but it also still recognized Africa as a "special European responsibility." Thus, in spite of its official rhetoric in support of self-determination for all peoples of the world, American support for African independence was tempered by its desire to maintain strong ties with its European allies.

From the mid-1950s onward, the Soviet Union became more actively engaged in debates in the United Nations calling for African independence and established friendly relations with newly independent African states, including Ghana (1957) and Guinea (1958). In spite of this obvious Soviet drive to extend its influence in Africa, the American response to African affairs was slow and ambivalent, reflecting the dilemma of supporting decolonization while not pushing it at a pace that would alienate European allies of the United States.

Ghana's independence served as a catalyst for rapid decolonization in the rest of Africa, prompting Americans to rethink their position about the continent. An independent Bureau of African Affairs was created in the State Department in 1958. A number of American consulates in Africa were replaced by fully operational embassies. The United States realized that it could lure the votes of the newly independent African states in the United Nations to strengthen its global dominance.

A significant milestone in American-African relations came with the accession of JOHN F. KENNEDY to the presidency in 1961. In Kennedy's view, anticolonialism could serve the United States and guard against growing Soviet influence in Africa. Furthermore, his administration realized that Africa could serve American military and nonmilitary needs with products such as uranium and copper. American aid to Africa thus expanded during this period. More than any other presidency before it, the Kennedy administration became more directly involved in African affairs. In 1961, for example, the United States provided some covert financial support for rebel Holden Roberto's Frente Nacional de Libertação de Angola (FNLA), a revolutionary independence movement then fighting a guerrilla war against the Portuguese-controlled Angolan government. Also, in the aftermath of the 1960 Sharpeville riot in Johannesburg, during which South African police opened fire at black protesters, killing 67, Kennedy not only criticized apartheid but also announced that the United States would discontinue its arms trade with South Africa after 1963.

The administration of LYNDON B. JOHNSON went one step further. In June 1964, the United States endorsed a UN Security Council resolution to establish a special committee of experts to study the feasibility of sanctions against South Africa. While most Africans welcomed such developments, American involvement in the Congo was considered less palatable. During the Congo civil war, on November 24, 1964, American planes transported Belgian paratroopers to Stanleyville in an apparent move to rescue hostages from the rebel forces of the Congolese National Liberation Council. Many Africans, however, viewed the Stanleyville airlift as a cover for a military operation to assist the central government then headed by the largely unpopular Moise Tshombe against the rebels. On a more positive note, on October 27, 1966, the United States supported the UN General Assembly resolution terminating the South African mandate in Namibia.

In spite of some significant changes in the 1960s, American policy toward Africa continued to be predicated on the need to support only moderate and constitutional demands from African nationalists and also to prevent Soviet influence from spreading throughout the continent. Rather than being regarded as important in their own right, African countries were generally perceived by United States policymakers as a means of preventing the spread of Soviet communism.

Further reading: Peter Duigan and L. H. Gann, *The United States and Africa: A History* (Cambridge: Cambridge University Press, 1984); Peter J. Schraeder, *United States Foreign Policy toward Africa: Incrementalism, Crisis and Change* (Cambridge: Cambridge University Press, 1994).

— Tamba M'Bayo

African-American movement

The post–World War II period brought immeasurable advances for African Americans, as the Civil Rights movement helped to guarantee blacks equal status under the law, and the coupling of the black arts movement and rise in black nationalism during the 1960s cultivated a sense of African-American pride.

During World War II, large numbers of African-American men served the United States in the armed forces, fighting the threat of fascism in Europe and the Pacific. They returned home in 1945, however, to a country where blacks still suffered from legal SEGREGATION and discrimination in the South, and were relegated to squalid ghettos of de facto segregation in the North.

Though most northern states had adopted public policies that outlawed racial discrimination, the South in the 1940s was still guided by a collection of policies referred to as "Jim Crow laws" that reinforced segregation practices. The segregation principle in the South subjected African Americans to second-class public transportation, schools, parks, theaters, restaurants, and even cemeteries. Those blacks who violated the social norms laid out by Jim Crow risked the threat of lynching, a form of vigilante justice, which persisted from the Reconstruction era through the mid-20th century, despite pleas from the NATIONAL ASSOCIATION FOR THE ADVANCEMENT OF COLORED PEOPLE (NAACP) to President Franklin D. Roosevelt to make the practice a federal crime.

The hostile racial tensions of the South prompted large numbers of African Americans to migrate during the early 20th century to northern urban centers such as New York, Chicago, Detroit, Philadelphia, Cleveland, and Pittsburgh, in a population shift known as the Great Migration. Living conditions in the North for migrants were incredibly poor, however, and many black families in large cities were relegated to one-room tenement style apartments known as "kitchenettes." Unfair housing and employment practices served to segregate blacks from whites in northern cities, creating predominantly African-American communities. The flood of migrants from the South overwhelmed many African-American communities such as the Bronzeville neighborhood of Chicago and Harlem in New York, which prior to the war had become thriving and economically diverse centers of black culture and business. By the 1940s, many African-American neighborhoods in the North had deteriorated into urban ghettos.

Efforts to end legalized racial discrimination in the South and to improve the quality of life for northern blacks were spearheaded by the NAACP Legal Defense and Education Fund, which was independently established in 1939 as the legal arm of the NAACP. The earliest successes in the Civil Rights movement came as a result of the war effort, with the outlawing of discrimination in defense industries in 1941 and the desegregation of the armed forces in 1948. In the early 1950s, the NAACP legal team began pressing a series of civil rights–related cases before the U.S. Supreme Court in which the lawyers argued that segregation affirmed inherently unequal educational and other public facilities for African Americans. The landmark Supreme Court decision in *BROWN V. BOARD OF EDUCATION*

(1954), in which the majority opinion declared that separate, segregated educational facilities were unequal and unconstitutional, was a tremendous victory for the NAACP, and sparked a mass movement among African Americans and liberal whites to end segregation and racially unjust practices across the country.

Protest took other forms as well. In 1955, ROSA PARKS, an African-American seamstress in Montgomery, Alabama, was arrested for refusing to give up her seat and move to the black section at the back of a city bus. Parks's arrest prompted a one-day boycott of the Montgomery bus system, and the boycott movement then continued under the leadership of a young Montgomery minister, MARTIN LUTHER KING, JR., until Montgomery felt the economic pressure and capitulated. The SOUTHERN CHRISTIAN LEADERSHIP CONFERENCE (SCLC), founded in 1957 by King, brought the resistance movement to cities across the South. The passive acts of CIVIL DISOBEDIENCE advocated by King and the SCLC aimed to undermine the system of segregation and racial discrimination through nonviolent means.

The early 1960s brought a new practice of resistance in the form of SIT-INS. African-American college students in Greensboro, North Carolina, staged the first sit-in at a local lunch counter that did not serve blacks. Despite verbal and physical harassment, the students demanded service, and they refused to leave. Similar sit-ins were carried out at restaurants, theaters, and department stores across the nation, largely under the leadership of the STUDENT NON-VIOLENT COORDINATING COMMITTEE (SNCC). In the summer of 1961, the CONGRESS OF RACIAL EQUALITY (CORE) expanded the sit-in movement by coordinating a group of "freedom riders" who traveled across the South, testing segregation policies in interstate transportation. More than 70,000 young people, both white and African-American, participated in the FREEDOM RIDES. The nonviolent protests of the early 1960s prompted the desegregation of a wide range of private businesses, and fueled the optimism of the Civil Rights movement.

Perhaps the most dramatic moment of the movement came in August 1963, as hundreds of thousands of people rallied in the nation's capital for the MARCH ON WASHINGTON, a sign of support for the major civil rights legislation that was pending in Congress. The passage of that legislation, in the form of the CIVIL RIGHTS ACT OF 1964, which prohibited discrimination in public accommodations, and the VOTING RIGHTS ACT OF 1965, which outlawed prejudicial voter registration tactics, marked the climax of the movement for equality and integration.

The effects of the growing sense of black identity found their way into the African-American artistic and literary landscape as well. While black writers in the 1930s and 1940s, such as *Native Son* author Richard Wright, focused on LITERATURE as a means of protesting racial injustice, the progress of the Civil Rights movement and the decline of segregation tended, in the words of writer Arthur P. Davis, "to destroy the protest element in Negro writing." James Baldwin and Ralph Ellison, who were both protégés of Wright, broke away from the tradition of the protest novel and called for a body of literature that more completely reflected the complexity of the African-American experience. Baldwin's novel *Go Tell It on the Mountain* (1953) portrayed the experiences of migrant blacks in Harlem and the role of the black church in their lives. Ellison drew on a variety of subjects ranging from segregated education to competing political ideologies in his deeply resonant novel *Invisible Man* (1952). In 1959, playwright Lorraine Hansberry became the first African-American woman to have a play produced on Broadway with *Raisin in the Sun,* her depiction of the struggles of a working-class black family living in Chicago.

Prior to World War II, even the playing fields of professional SPORTS had been divided along segregated lines. Though black athletes such as boxer Joe Louis and Olympian Jesse Owens had achieved national popularity in the 1930s, they were exceptions to the rule, and most African Americans, such as the stars of the Negro baseball leagues, played in relative anonymity, excluded from all-white professional leagues. The racial line was crossed in 1947, however, when JACKIE ROBINSON became the first black player in modern major league baseball, signing a contract with general manager BRANCH RICKEY of the Brooklyn Dodgers. Robinson endured steady abuse from white spectators and opposing players, but, spurred on by the support of his white teammates, he won the 1947 Rookie of the Year Award and helped carry the Dodgers to the National League championship. The success of Robinson paved the way for other black baseball players such as Willie Mays and Henry (Hank) Aaron, who, starring during the 1950s and 1960s, became household names and beloved national icons.

As more and more African-American athletes achieved stardom, some, such as heavyweight boxer MUHAMMAD ALI (formerly known as Cassius Clay), used their status to address racial injustice and take a political stand. Ali first attracted notice by winning the gold medal at the 1960 Olympic Games in Rome, and he subsequently became the world heavyweight champion by defeating Sonny Liston in 1964. That same year, he joined the Nation of Islam and changed his name from Cassius Clay to Muhammad Ali. Ali adored the spotlight and became famous for his proclamations of invincibility, often delivered in poetic verse, and his personal slogan "I am the greatest!" The image of an articulate and boastful black athlete angered many whites, and his taunting of black opponents, often calling upon slave stereotypes such as stupid and illiterate, drew the ire of many in the black community. Nonetheless, Ali's popularity was unmatched by any black athlete of his time, and he fascinated the media and public alike, even more so in 1967, when he refused induction into the U.S. Army on the basis of his religious convictions. Ali called upon other blacks to refuse induction rather than fight in the VIETNAM WAR for a country that oppressed them. He was convicted of violating the Selective Service Act and stripped of his heavyweight title, though the U.S. Supreme Court overturned his conviction in 1971.

The sense of promise that the early years of the Civil Rights movement brought African Americans gradually declined into disappointment, frustration, and unrest during the mid-1960s as it became clear that the overall political and economic welfare of blacks had been changed little by civil rights legislation. Younger blacks sparked a sense of radicalism in the movement; they grew impatient with the slow rate of progress and called for a more militant approach in demanding change. Violent riots in Harlem during the summer of 1964 were followed by sim-

ilar demonstrations in predominantly black urban ghettos across the country over the next two years. In addition, the tragic murders of civil rights activist Medgar Evers in Mississippi and four young black girls in a church bombing in Birmingham, Alabama, shocked many African Americans into rethinking the established principles of the Civil Rights movement.

Notions of nonviolence and racial harmony were increasingly replaced by ideas such as BLACK POWER and "separatism" during the middle and late 1960s. STOKELY CARMICHAEL, a longtime civil rights activist who became the chair of SNCC in 1966, became frustrated with the nonviolence doctrine and, while leading a march in Mississippi in 1966, he rallied demonstrators around the concept of "Black Power." Carmichael associated black power with self-defense, the ability to defend the black community, political and economic power, and racial pride. African-American leaders who had been critical of King's pragmatic and nonviolent methods, such as Black Muslim leader MALCOLM X, found an alert national audience calling for black separatism, pride, and self-dependence. Malcolm X had

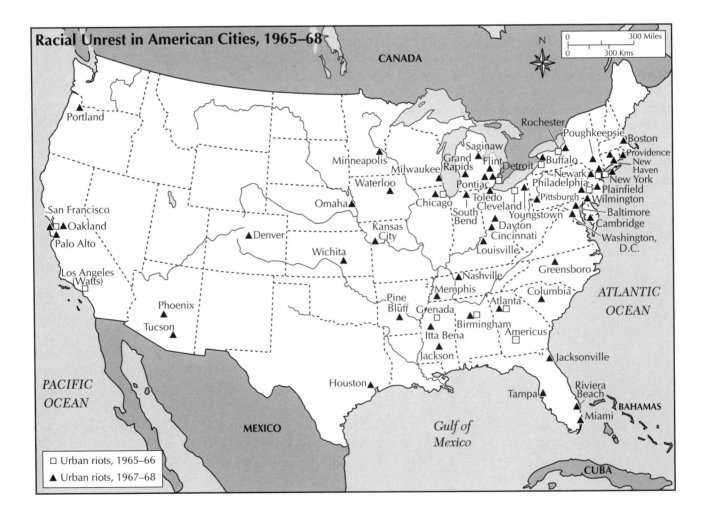

Racial Unrest in American Cities, 1965–68

□ Urban riots, 1965–66
▲ Urban riots, 1967–68

risen to power within ELIJAH MUHAMMAD's Nation of Islam before breaking off and establishing his own organization. His assassination in 1965 was followed soon after by publication of *The Autobiography of Malcolm X* by Alex Haley, which became an inspiration for numerous young black radicals.

In 1966, African-American activists Huey P. Newton and Bobby Seale founded the BLACK PANTHERS in Oakland, California, a militant organization that epitomized the separatist movement. The Black Panthers advocated the use of violence to protect African-American communities from police brutality. The party gradually developed into a Marxist political organization, calling for all blacks to arm themselves and demanding that African-American prisoners be released from jail.

A sense of black nationalism pervaded the artistic world by way of the Black Arts movement, which was characterized by dramatic artistic and literary development during the 1960s. Proponents of the movement called for the destruction of traditional eurocentric cultural norms and the creation of a "black aesthetic." The Black Arts movement encouraged African Americans to embrace their cultural ancestry and helped coin familiar slogans, such as "black is beautiful," in the desire to cultivate a sense of racial pride. Adherents to the movement broke away from traditionally white artistic institutions and established African-American publishing houses, theater troupes, and even repertory schools. Author and playwright Leroi Jones, who changed his name to Amiri Baraka in 1968, was a leader in the movement. Baraka's play *Dutchman* (1964) appeared off-Broadway and drew considerable critical acclaim. The play focused around the interaction between a white woman and a black intellectual, highlighting the anger of African Americans toward the dominant white culture. In 1965, Baraka founded the Black Arts Repertory Theatre in Harlem, which encouraged young black playwrights to create a stronger black aesthetic in theater.

Further reading: Henry Louis Gates, Jr. and Cornel West, *The African-American Century: How Black Americans Have Shaped Our Country* (New York: Free Press, 2000).

— Guy R. Temple

agriculture

American agriculture in the post–World War II years underwent a massive transition from labor-based to mechanized farming and from traditional small family farms to large corporate establishments. Although the federal government sought to protect farmers from the economic risks of free enterprise, American farmers struggled throughout the postwar years for an income competitive with the national average.

While the productivity of American agriculture continually rose throughout the postwar period due to technological advances, the number of American farmers fell. In 1940, there were over 6 million farms in the United States operated by a farmer population that exceeded 30 million. By 1973, the number of farms had declined to 2.8 million, and the farmer population had dropped by nearly 10 million. The American farm had a new face, one characterized by the presence of more tractors and fewer farmhands, by electricity, chemical fertilizers, hybrid crops and livestock, and greater size.

Between 1940 and 1970, farms increased in average size from 138 to 385 acres, as mechanization and automation increased the farmer's staple crop production rates per acre and per man-hour. In 1940, one farm worker could supply 11 people with the agricultural products they required; by 1970, one worker was able to supply 47 people. From 1910 to 1970, tractors increased from fewer than 1,000 to 5.5 million, as horses and mules decreased from 25 million to approximately 2.4 million. Interest in the scientific aspects of farming increased, as scientists and researchers developed techniques that could increase production. Soil analysis became widely employed to determine the elements needed by a particular soil to maintain or restore its fertility. Farmers learned to combat the loss of soil by erosion with strip cropping, which involved sowing strips of dense-rooted plants to serve as water-breaks or windbreaks in fields of plants with loose-root systems, the use of cover crops which were quick-growing plants with dense root systems to bind soil, and contour plowing, in which the furrows followed the contour of the land and ran parallel to hills instead of up and down them, thus providing channels for runoff water. After the first hybrids appeared in the 1930s, research in the field of selective breeding continued, producing improved strains of both farm animals and crop plants. More farms received electrification, mail service, telephone lines, and consolidated schooling, services that were predominantly traits of urban life prior to the 1950s.

Agricultural transport also underwent changes during the postwar period. The improvement of trucks that increased their range and payloads, as well as the construction of the highway network that came as a result of the INTERSTATE HIGHWAY ACT OF 1956, greatly added to the efficiency of agricultural transport. By 1967, 51 percent of foods and kindred products were transported by trucks, 47 percent by rail, and 2 percent by water. Trucks hauled most of the perishable crops, while railroads continued to transport grains and other semiperishables.

Tenant farmers or sharecroppers, historically always large providers of agricultural labor, decreased in number after 1940, largely due to the many changes resulting from the revolution in farming methods that nearly eliminated marginal farms and drastically reduced labor requirements. In the 1930s, tenant farmers made up 62 percent of the South's farmer population and 42 percent of the farmer populations elsewhere in the United States. By 1969, the number of farms worked by tenants dropped to 11.7 percent in the South and 12.9 percent in the other farming regions. Tenant farmers either migrated to urban centers or became owners or part-owner operators. Sharecropping was lowest for livestock farming and highest in the cash-crop fields of cotton and tobacco. The primary shift in tenant farming after 1940 was toward part-ownership. The number of farms in this group remained small, however, in terms of acreage operated and percentage of farm production. Part owners had become the largest group by 1969, leasing farmland mainly on a cash basis. Between 1940 and 1969, the percentage of farms owned by part owners increased from 10.1 percent to 24.6 percent.

Farmer organization during the 20th century was inconsistent compared to other labor fields, as farmers generally only organized when there was a mutual advantage to be had or the circumstances warranted it. Popular during the 1950s was the National Farmers Union, founded by Newt Gresham at Point, Texas, in 1902. Although the union first grew in the South, it gained notable strength after 1910, as it moved into the wheat-growing states of the West. By 1974, its national membership included about 250,000 farm families. Its policies were generally aimed at preserving family farms, increasing bargaining power with the federal government, and gaining special assistance for low-income farmers. Also popular during the mid-20th century was the American Farm Bureau Federation, formed in 1920 by a coalition of state representatives seeking a body of farmer representation in Congress to fight falling prices after World War I. After World War II, overproduction became a major problem, and, in 1947, the American Farm Bureau Federation began to advocate a reduction in the use of public funds to increase farm productive capacity, returning to policies that allowed prices to respond to supply and demand. By the 1970s, the American Farm Bureau Federation was the largest American farmers' organization, with a national membership of more than 2 million families. The National Farmers Organization (NFO), however, was perhaps the most significant farmers' organization during the postwar period. The NFO was formed in Iowa in 1955 to protest low farm prices, and within a few months it became an organization of approximately 71,000 members. The NFO sought to establish a collective bargaining system whereby farmers set prices for their produce. To accomplish this end, it initiated a system of withholding products from market until prices were met. During the 1960s, NFO membership figures were not released, but estimates vary from 115,000 to 270,000.

A persistent problem of American agriculture in the 20th century has been the tendency of farm income to fall behind increases in the costs of production. Government policies to protect farmers from the economic risks of a free enterprise system began most notably during the New Deal of the 1930s under President Franklin D. Roosevelt with a concept called parity, in which the federal government established a level for farm-product prices. When actual prices fell below that level, government would augment farmer income to ensure farmers maintained economic stability during price depressions. The Agricultural Adjustment Act of 1933 established quotas limiting production of basic agricultural commodities. The Supreme Court found the act unconstitutional in 1936, but after several new justices were appointed to the Supreme Court, it became law again in the Agricultural Adjustment Act of 1938, based on the same quota system. Throughout the postwar period, the act was amended several times, the basic aims being formation of a price-support program to bring farm income into balance with national income.

World War II drove farm-product prices back up, although cost of production was also up, which meant actual farmer income did not increase, and thus government parity payments remained in place. Federal costs for supporting the ongoing parity payments at a fixed rate became too expensive, as some commodities were being sold at prices much less than those paid to farmers. To reduce the government costs of maintaining farming support programs, the administration of President DWIGHT D. EISENHOWER proposed that flexible, or variable, price supports replace the rigid 90 percent of parity in force. Congress enacted a bill authorizing a sliding scale of payments at 82.5 percent to 90 percent of parity on the basic commodities in 1954. Another measure in 1956 established the soil-bank program, which was designed to reduce surpluses by removing land from production. The soil-bank program authorized federal payments to farmers if they reduced production of certain crops. A subsidy plan was formulated to pay farmers for converting part of their cropland to soil-conserving uses. In practice, farmers shared the costs of planting trees or grasses, receiving annual payments that compensated them for economic loss incurred by the removal of some of their land from crop production. In 1959, Congress terminated the acreage reserve section of the soil-bank program, but left the conservation reserve program in effect until 1965, when the entire act was repealed by passage of the Food and Agriculture Act of 1965.

The Department of Agriculture in the administrations of Presidents JOHN F. KENNEDY and LYNDON B. JOHNSON during the 1960s made control of overproduction a primary goal of farm policy. Farmers were offered payments in what amounted to a rental for part of their land, which would be taken out of production the following year. At the same time, measures were implemented to expand export markets for agricultural products. During this period, the ratio of a farmer's per capita income to that of a nonfarm person increased from about 50 percent to about 75 percent. The Food and Agriculture Act of 1965 established a long-term land-retirement policy, as well as a new four-year price-adjustment program. In 1966, the federal minimum wage was extended to farmer workers and the President's Committee on Rural Poverty was established.

The national agricultural policy in the postwar years also included improvement of the standard of living for nonfarming Americans. Some significant legislation passed under this intent included the National School Lunch Act of 1946, a provision for food distribution to the needy in 1961, and the Food Stamp Act of 1964, an allocation of funding for the purchase of groceries for needy people. In 1967 and 1968, legislation provided food packages for expectant mothers as well as special food services for children. During the 1970s, the Department of Agriculture, through its extension service, began to expand nutrition and 4-H programs into urban areas of the nation.

Further reading: Willard W. Cochrane, *The Development of American Agriculture* (Minneapolis: University of Minnesota Press, 1993).

— Jason Reed

Muhammad Ali, formerly Cassius Clay, 1964
(Library of Congress)

Ali, Muhammad (1942–)

One of the greatest heavyweight boxers of all time, Muhammad Ali was also one of the most important and controversial cultural figures of the 1960s, a symbol of the racial, cultural, and ideological conflicts of the decade.

Born Cassius Marcellus Clay, Jr., on January 17, 1942, in Louisville, Kentucky, Ali began boxing when he was 12 and quickly established himself as an elite athlete, winning national Amateur Athletic Union and Golden Gloves championships. His skills gained a wider audience in the 1960 Summer Olympics in Rome, where he defeated a Soviet boxer to win the gold medal in the light-heavyweight division.

As a handsome, accomplished athlete who also was skilled in the arts of self-promotion, Clay seemed destined to become a star. He began his professional boxing career in October 1960, and during the next three years won all 19 of his fights, 15 of them by knockout. Then, and throughout his career, Clay attracted attention as much for his actions and words outside of the ring as for his victories in it, often using playful rhymes to predict exactly when his opponents would fall and then backing up his boasts. Despite his claims that he already was the "greatest," when Clay challenged Sonny Liston for the heavyweight championship in February 1964, he entered the ring as a 7-1 underdog.

When Liston stayed in his corner at the beginning of the seventh round, Clay had his first championship belt.

The next day, after he announced his membership in the controversial Nation of Islam, the American public had another reason to discuss Clay. During the mid-1960s, the adherents of the Black Muslim faith frightened and threatened much of white America. In March 1964, Clay drew more attention to his conversion by rejecting his given name and accepting Muhammad Ali, a name given to him by ELIJAH MUHAMMAD, the leader of the Nation of Islam. With his new name, his conscious rejection of Christianity, and his increasingly controversial statements about American race relations, Ali lost most of his support from mainstream America even as he continued dominating the heavyweight division.

By March 1967, Ali had a 29-0 record, but battles more significant than those in any ring helped define his professional boxing career. After stating in 1966 that he had "no quarrel with them Viet Cong," referring to the VIETNAM WAR, in 1967 Ali officially became a conscientious objector to the draft. In the face of a five-year prison sentence and a $10,000 fine, he refused to join the military. Because of this decision, governing boards stripped Ali of his titles, and he did not fight for more than three years. Ali's refusal to enlist drew the maximum sentence from a judge, the hatred of many older and more traditional Americans, and the adulation of a new generation of Americans, white and black, who were beginning to protest the war in Vietnam. Throughout the late 1960s and early 1970s, Ali was a highly visible symbol of the nation's growing division over the war.

In October 1970, Ali resumed his boxing career, knocking out two opponents in a seven-week span. In March 1971, in the first of three classic bouts, Ali met Joe Frazier in New York City, suffering his first loss in a titanic 15-round struggle. Within months, Ali won a more significant victory when the U.S. Supreme Court overturned his conviction for draft evasion.

Ali won 12 out of his next 13 fights, losing only to Ken Norton, before the 1974 "Rumble in the Jungle" in Kinshasa, Zaire, against heavily favored George Foreman. Using a new tactic, the "rope-a-dope," Ali fought defensively for several rounds, absorbing Foreman's punches and wearing him out. When Ali attacked, Foreman had no energy left, and Ali became the second heavyweight champion to regain his belt. By this time, as many others had come to share Ali's views on the war, he became one of the most popular athletes in the nation and around the world.

After several other legendary fights, Ali lost his title in February 1975 to Leon Spinks. Ali defeated Spinks a mere seven months later, regaining the title for the final time and becoming history's first three-time heavyweight champion. After retiring as champion, Ali returned for two more fights, losing them both and leaving him with a final professional record of 56 wins, five losses, and 37 knockouts.

Although Ali no longer boxed, he remained in the public eye. Still widely hailed as the greatest boxer and SPORTS showman of all time, Ali remains one of the most recognizable humans on earth. The onset of Parkinson's disease in the mid-1980s has reduced the number of his public appearances and has tempered his ability to speak out on issues, but it has not dampened his wit or his desire to contribute to society. In 1990, he met with Saddam Hussein, the ruler of Iraq, in an attempt to forestall war in the Persian Gulf. Ali created the Muhammad Ali Community and Economic Development Corporation in Chicago to teach job skills to low-income public-housing residents. In 1996, 36 years after his original Olympic glory, he lit the flame at the Summer Olympics in Atlanta, reminding billions around the world that he could still perform when the spotlight was on him.

Further reading: Elliott J. Gorn, ed. *Muhammad Ali, The People's Champ* (Urbana: University of Illinois Press,

1995); Thomas Hauser, *Muhammad Ali: His Life and Times* (New York: Simon & Schuster. 1991).
— Brad Austin and William L. Glankler

Alliance for Progress

A regional reform program created during the administration of JOHN F. KENNEDY, the Alliance for Progress, or Alianza para el Progreso, promised economic aid to Latin American countries in return for political and social reforms.

Kennedy outlined the new program in a speech to Latin American diplomats in March 1961. The United States pledged large amounts of economic aid to Latin American countries, and in return those leaders would institute land and tax reforms, improve health care, education, and housing, streamline bureaucratic procedures, and undertake other changes to benefit the poor and middle classes. The Kennedy administration promised $20 billion in public and private capital over the next 10 years, as well as an additional $80 billion in internal investment. The first congressional appropriation for the Alliance was $500 million in 1961.

This influx of foreign money was designed to double the economic growth rate in LATIN AMERICA, raise literacy rates and living standards, cut infant mortality in half, and provide every school-age child access to primary education. Kennedy and his advisers believed that poverty and repression left Latin America vulnerable to instability, agitation, and revolutionary communist movements, both internal and Soviet-directed. The experience of the MARSHALL PLAN and new social science models, especially modernization theory dealing with the process of moving into the industrial age, influenced these policymakers and caused them to underestimate the difficulties ahead. They also overestimated the communist threat to the region.

The Alliance for Progress failed to meaningfully transform Latin American societies. The annual economic growth rate held at a paltry 1.5 percent throughout the 1960s; the number of unemployed persons rose; annual per capita income did not change; and agricultural production per person declined. The population growth rate was 3 percent, the highest in the world. Societies remained inequitable with a sharp division between rich and poor, and political instability continued. Adult literacy and infant mortality did improve, but not as much as expected.

One major contribution to the program's failure was the desire for short-term stability, which clashed with the need for long-term permanent change. The U.S. government continued to support right-wing dictators, like the Somozas in Nicaragua, because they were reliable allies and maintained stability. Congress, less enthusiastic about the Alliance than the executive branch, did not order U.S. funds to be used to carry out land redistribution, the heart of the program, because doing so smacked too much of socialism. Latin American oligarchs often pocketed the Alliance money and ignored implementing reforms. Even moderate politicians came from families that would be disadvantaged by progressive taxation or land reforms, and the only other alternative internal source of funds would be to nationalize foreign enterprises, a step that would not have met with approval in the United States.

Economic factors also played a key role. The balance of payments problem—whereby more money was going out than coming in—exacerbated Kennedy administration concerns about the standing of the United States in the world economy and meant that less funds were available than during the heady days of the Marshall Plan. Latin American economies depended on exports, and while export income grew steadily throughout the 1960s, it was not enough to keep up with global trade during that prosperous decade. The prices of primary products that most Latin American countries exported, especially coffee, fluctuated wildly. The region also faced new competition from Western Europe and Japan, now fully recovered from World War II, and emerging Asian and African nations.

Cultural differences also hampered the Alliance for Progress. American policymakers hoped to replicate their Marshall Plan success, but the Western European nations they rebuilt had social and political arrangements remarkably similar to those in the United States. Most Latin American societies, on the other hand, were characterized by Iberian and Amerindian traditions, including planned economies, strong central governments, and the organization of society into corporate groups, all unfamiliar to American policymakers. In addition, the modernization theories that required Latin Americans to copy the Western European and North American models implicitly disparaged Latin American traditions and culture and met with resentment.

The Alliance withered away during the administration of LYNDON B. JOHNSON. Congress found itself even less likely to appropriate the necessary funds due to intensifying problems in Vietnam. Much of the money that was available went to military goals, such as training and funding internal security forces.

Further reading: Stephen G. Rabe, *The Most Dangerous Area in the World: John F. Kennedy Confronts Communist Revolution in Latin America* (Chapel Hill: University of North Carolina Press, 1999).

— Jennifer Walton

American Federation of Labor (AFL)

The AFL was an important skilled trade organization that helped mobilize organized labor, and bolstered the union movement in the decades after the 1930s.

A precursor to the AFL was the Federation of Organized Trades and Labor Unions, which began in 1881. In 1886, a reorganization led by Samuel Gompers, a cigarmaker, created the AFL to protect the legislative interests of craft unions. Unifying the American labor movement for nearly half a century, the AFL coordinated activities of nearly 100 national and international unions, which maintained autonomy and controlled their own immediate affairs. Membership grew with a booming ECONOMY. But even though the organization did a good job in settling disputes among member unions, it had a hard time negotiating with BUSINESS owners. Without legal recognition of the right to bargain collectively, the AFL, like the union movement in general, had a tough time.

When Franklin D. Roosevelt was elected president in 1933, labor enjoyed a more sympathetic political climate. Unprecedented opportunities to organize and to bargain collectively led to the formation of the AFL's main competition, the CONGRESS OF INDUSTRIAL ORGANIZATIONS (CIO), organized in 1935, which sought to do for industrial unions in mass-production industries like steel, rubber, and motorcars what the AFL did for the skilled trades.

As labor grew stronger in the 1940s and began to use its political support, conservatives passed the TAFT-HARTLEY ACT in 1947, which circumscribed the right to strike, limited political activity, and demanded that union leaders sign anticommunist oaths. Initially, some AFL unions found the Taft-Hartley Act advantageous to them in their rivalry with CIO affiliates. For example, few AFL leaders balked at signing non-communist affidavits, therefore permitting them to challenge nonsigning CIO organizations for the upper hand in labor circles.

Although the Taft-Hartley Act created some tension between the AFL and the CIO, they both agreed on the need for the federal government to stimulate economic growth. Labor leaders, such as George Meany of the AFL and Emil Rieve, Phillip Murray, and WALTER REUTHER of the CIO, agreed that there needed to be improvements in workmen's compensation, Social Security, EDUCATION, and health care for its lower-income members. As a result, the AFL and CIO began to work together to ensure a greater governmental role in economic matters.

In 1955, the two organizations merged into the AFL-CIO. Despite conflicting personalities, Walter Reuther, head of the United Auto Workers (UAW) and president of the CIO, agreed to work with former AFL president George Meany. Meany's personality and ideology were very different from those of Reuther, who espoused socialist principles. Icy relations between the conservative Meany and the liberal Reuther made working together difficult.

The AFL, like the CIO, recognized the need to uphold ethical standards. In the 1950s, the Central and Southern

States Pension Fund, controlled by Teamster president Jimmy Hoffa, accumulated hundreds of millions of dollars for a wide variety of investments. Teamster money was not available for social projects, but rather flowed to hotels, nightclubs, and casinos, helping to underwrite the development of Las Vegas. In 1957, the AFL expelled the TEAMSTERS UNION, the largest union at the time, after disclosures of corruption and labor racketeering. Governmental probes resulted in Hoffa's imprisonment in 1967 for jury tampering, pension fund fraud, and conspiracy.

Meanwhile, relations between the AFL and the CIO deteriorated. Meany relied, at one point, on distorted information supplied by the Federal Bureau of Investigation, to accuse antiwar spokesmen in the CIO of being dupes for the Communist Party of the United States (CPUSA) and of the SOVIET UNION. Emil Mazey, Reuther's close associate and secretary treasurer, accused Meany of character assassination. In 1968, Meany succeeded in getting Reuther and several others expelled from the executive board, and as a result, Reuther's UAW promptly withdrew from the AFL-CIO. Reuther angrily declared that Meany was forcing labor to become "a complacent custodian of the status quo."

Yet prospects for the future depended on working together. Despite friction, the AFL had a far more powerful voice as a result of its link to the CIO.

Further reading: Robert H. Zieger, *American Workers, American Unions, 1920–1985* (Baltimore: Johns Hopkins University Press, 1986).

— John E. Bibish IV

American Indian Movement (AIM)

The American Indian Movement (AIM), founded in 1968, was an activist Indian group concerned with the civil rights of Native Americans.

Founded in Minneapolis, Minnesota, by Dennis Banks, Clyde Bellecourt, Eddie Benton Banai, and George Mitchell, AIM's original purpose was to help Native Americans deal with discriminatory practices of and harassment by the police in the arrest of Indians in the urban ghettos of Minneapolis and Saint Paul. AIM gave expression to the anger and agitation building up in Native Americans over centuries of mistreatment by the government. In a time when there existed many groups clamoring for social change, AIM embodied the Native American battle cry of "Red Power."

Although primarily an urban phenomenon, the appeal of this social movement spread quickly and as a result, chapters formed all over the United States. AIM also became involved in tribal affairs on Indian reservations, established "survival schools" in urban areas, and sponsored international conferences on several Lakota Sioux reservations,

resulting in the 1977 International Treaty Conferences with the United Nations in Geneva, Switzerland.

AIM first turned its attentions to aiding Native Americans living in urban ghettos, who faced problems as a result of the TERMINATION POLICY of DWIGHT D. EISENHOWER's administration, which led to urban relocation in the 1950s. Many Indian people found themselves facing poor housing conditions, including overcrowding, high rents, discrimination in the renting process, and a sense of displacement. AIM sought to foster a feeling of community and tradition in these urban areas and provide protection and support against mistreatment by landlords and law enforcement officials.

In time, AIM's ambitions began to grow. At its height, the group's demands encompassed economic independence, revitalization of traditional culture, protection of legal rights, and, most especially, autonomy over tribal lands and areas and the restoration of lands that Indians believed the U.S. government illegally seized in the past.

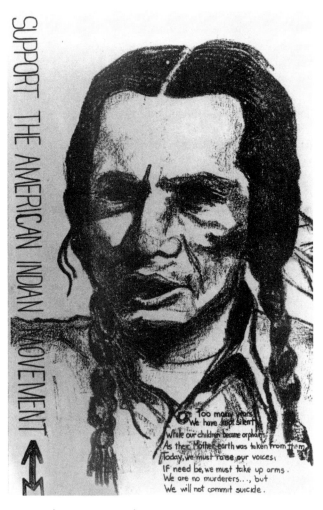

Support the American Indian Movement poster
(Library of Congress)

Joining in the wave of militancy prevalent in many activist groups, such as the BLACK PANTHERS, AIM, too, took militant action. In 1969, AIM seized and occupied the defunct federal prison of Alcatraz in San Francisco Bay, symbolically protesting the inefficiency of the Bureau of Indian Affairs (BIA) in handling Indian welfare issues. The group converted the prison into an Indian education and cultural center until forced by government officials in 1971 to abandon the enterprise. In November 1972, AIM was instrumental in the weeklong occupation by Native Americans of the BIA building in Washington, D.C., and, in early 1973, the group took over the village of Wounded Knee, South Dakota, for 10 weeks. The occupation of Wounded Knee came almost a century after the massacre of Native Americans at the site by the U.S. Cavalry in 1890. Protestors gathered to remember the massacre and protest contemporary Native American injustices as well as the numerous treaties made with Native American tribes that were broken by the U.S. government.

Involved in much highly publicized protest, AIM was thought too militant by many, generally older, Native Americans who believed change could occur through peaceful means and who sought to distance themselves from the movement. This caused a division between the older and younger generations who felt that their elders had "sold out" to the white establishment. With many of its leaders in prison and rife with internal dissention, AIM's national leadership disbanded in 1978, although local chapters continue to function.

Further reading: Vine Deloria, *Custer Died for Your Sins: An Indian Manifesto* (New York: Macmillan, 1969); Paul Chaat Smith, *Like a Hurricane: The Indian Movement from Alcatraz to Wounded Knee* (New York: New Press, 1996).

— Nichole Suzanne Prescott

Americans for Democratic Action (ADA)

Favoring liberal domestic and foreign policies and ANTI-COMMUNISM, the Americans for Democratic Action (ADA) worked to bring a strong liberal approach to American government.

Founded in 1947, the Americans for Democratic Action brought together a coalition of anti-communist liberals during the COLD WAR. The organization was born out of Franklin D. Roosevelt's fragile political coalition, the developing global conflict, and the burgeoning Civil Rights movement. The ADA, recognizing the postwar era as a time of both opportunity and danger, promoted pragmatic liberalism and anticommunism.

President HARRY S. TRUMAN presided over America's difficult transition from ghastly war to unstable peace. The years 1946–48 were marred by industrial strikes, a housing crisis, and fears of a renewed depression. In foreign affairs, Americans perceived a communist threat at home and abroad. At times, Truman's foreign policy appeared erratic, ranging from genial negotiation to blustery bullying, and his domestic policy was equally inconsistent. *The Nation* labeled the president a "weak, baffled, angry man." For many of his fellow Democrats, Truman appeared ill-prepared to face the daunting challenges that lay ahead, a marked contrast from his savvy predecessor.

By 1948, the DEMOCRATIC PARTY threatened to fracture. On the left, HENRY A. WALLACE, the former vice president and commerce secretary, enjoyed support from progressives who favored accommodation with the SOVIET UNION. Disagreeing publicly with Wallace in September 1946, Truman fired Wallace from his cabinet post. In response, Wallace formed his own rival political organization, initiated a nationwide speaking tour, and waged a presidential campaign.

On the right, conservative southern Democrats bristled over Truman's domestic agenda, particularly its civil rights components. Many openly preferred South Carolina governor Strom Thurmond. Furthermore, after the 1946 midterm elections, Truman's Republican opponents controlled Congress, thwarted many of his domestic policies, and eagerly awaited the 1948 presidential election.

In January 1947, in part as a response to Truman's perceived weakness and Wallace's high-profile defiance, 130 former New Dealers and other prominent liberals organized the ADA with the ultimate purpose of finding an alternative to Truman in the next election. Although small, the membership rolls included influential public figures such as economist JOHN KENNETH GALBRAITH, historian Arthur Schlesinger, Jr., Minneapolis mayor HUBERT H. HUMPHREY, former first lady Eleanor Roosevelt, theologian Reinhold Niebuhr, black newspaper publisher John Stengstacke, attorney Joseph Rauh, labor leader WALTER REUTHER, and journalists Joseph and Stewart Alsop. Later, the Hollywood chapter included Ronald Reagan, Frank Sinatra, and Bette Davis.

In domestic affairs, the ADA defended Roosevelt's NEW DEAL programs that provided a government-sponsored "safety net" for all Americans. Members also promoted the extension of civil rights and protection of civil liberties. In general, their domestic agenda resembled Henry Wallace's, but whereas Wallace advocated a centralized government role and insisted on "full employment," ADA members argued for, in Schlesinger's words, "the necessity of political compromise" and pragmatism. They favored "doers" over "utopians" and put their faith in "the limited state."

In foreign affairs, the ADA rejected Wallace's accommodationist approach toward the Soviet Union. They viewed COMMUNISM as a vital threat to world peace and

American security. In particular, Niebuhr, Rauh, and Roosevelt expressed alarm over Soviet expansion in EUROPE and frustration over Soviet intransigence in the United Nations. Humphrey, Reuther, and the Alsops envisioned political rewards for liberals espousing anticommunism. For these reasons, ADA members embraced both internationalism and containment.

Despite holding similar political opinions, Truman never joined the ADA, and the ADA pursued DWIGHT D. EISENHOWER as an alternative to Truman in 1948. Once the popular general declined to run, the ADA reluctantly supported the incumbent against New York governor THOMAS E. DEWEY in the election. At the 1948 Democratic convention, Humphrey sponsored the civil rights plank that sparked the Thurmond-led DIXIECRAT PARTY walkout. ADA members reasoned that the plank not only supported liberal ideals but also attracted a neglected constituency. Meanwhile, they resisted Henry Wallace's PROGRESSIVE PARTY campaign for the presidency. Throughout the fall, Truman and the ADA marginalized the Wallace and Thurmond candidacies and stressed Truman's anticommunist credentials. Rather than suffering defeat, Truman's storied campaign triumphed. Together, Truman and the ADA successfully designed a political blueprint for future Democrats to follow.

In later years, the ADA repeatedly faced the troublesome dilemma of balancing its liberal ideals with its anticommunist crusade. During the 1950s Red Scare, members struggled to reconcile their fight against communism with their protection of civil liberties. While they expressed distaste for JOSEPH R. MCCARTHY's anticommunist witch-hunt tactics, many members feared the political consequences of appearing "too soft" on communism. Later, as the VIETNAM WAR intensified, the ADA membership split. Some members portrayed the war as another ideological contest with communism and appealed for escalation; others emphasized American imperialism and argued for withdrawal.

Internal divisions over Vietnam, the GREAT SOCIETY's end, and the conservatives' rise to power proved insurmountable to the small, underfunded organization. While important in its early years, the ADA's influence waned.

Further reading: Steven M. Gillon, *Politics and Vision* (New York: Oxford University Press, 1987); Richard H. Pells, *The Liberal Mind in a Conservative Age* (Middletown, Conn.: Wesleyan University Press, 1985).

— Andrew J. Falk

anticommunism

The primary force behind the COLD WAR, anticommunism constituted both popular attitude and government policy after World War II.

FOREIGN POLICY was one obvious area that anticommunism affected greatly. Despite a wartime hiatus, anticommunism dominated the tone of America's relations with the Soviets. Although divisive geopolitical issues existed between the United States and the SOVIET UNION, American anticommunist attitudes made these disagreements seem much more dangerous.

The cold war's anticommunist atmosphere led the United States to view radical political movements across the globe as threats. These movements ranged from the far left political parties of America's European allies to anti-imperialist national liberation movements and, of course, to any group that openly espoused COMMUNISM. Americans saw the world as divided into two hostile camps. They gauged a nation's friendliness to the United States by the degree of its opposition to communism.

This attitude had negative consequences for America's relationship to many other nations. It drove some nationalist leaders, including Egypt's president Gamal Abdel Nasser and Cuban dictator Fidel Castro, into greater cooperation with the Soviet Union than they might otherwise have contemplated. Also, the United States felt compelled to send troops to several places around the world to oppose perceived communist expansion directly. The KOREAN WAR and the VIETNAM WAR were the most significant examples of this intervention. In the eyes of much of the non-Western world, America's insistence that other nations adopt its commitment to anti-communism resembled the domineering demands of the European colonial powers in the past. This undermined American efforts to establish constructive relations with the nations that were freeing themselves from European colonial rule.

Anticommunism also affected American society and domestic politics, mainly by making people feel insecure and paranoid about a communist takeover. The Red Scare of the late 1940s and early 1950s was perhaps the most dramatic manifestation. The federal government helped start this hysteria with the FEDERAL EMPLOYEE LOYALTY PROGRAM, which sought to remove communists from government employ. Such actions caused many Americans to believe that there was a serious problem with communist traitors in the United States. Congress also contributed to this climate when it passed the MCCARRAN ACT (1950). This highly publicized law openly stated that a communist conspiracy existed that was bent on overthrowing the constitutionally established government of the United States. The HOUSE UN-AMERICAN ACTIVITIES COMMITTEE (HUAC) treated witnesses aggressively in its effort to determine whether they were now or had ever been members of the Communist Party. Several highly publicized and sensational spy trials, including those of ALGER HISS and JULIUS AND ETHEL ROSENBERG, confirmed this in the eyes of much of the American public.

The culmination of this anticommunist paranoia came in the early 1950s. Although only a minuscule number of actual subversives and spies were uncovered by Wisconsin senator JOSEPH R. MCCARTHY, his scare tactics created such hysteria and outrage in the American public that hundreds of those accused of being communists lost careers in government, education, and entertainment. In terms of policymaking, this climate compelled politicians and government officials to take hard-line positions to avoid later accusations of being soft on communism. This often made American diplomacy inflexible and uncreative.

Fear of communist takeover made many Americans uneasy. One effect of this was to intensify an existing postwar trend of seeking comfort and stability in the traditional American family and Judeo-Christian values. This led to a zealous emphasis on conformity reflected in clothing, housing, and living styles, as well as thought. Those who challenged established traditions were often labeled as communist subversives. People became extremely willing to support almost any plan that was aimed at protecting the United States from communism. One popular way to get support for an idea was to link it to fighting communism. Conversely, people began to label policies they opposed as communist inspired, regardless of their actual ideological origins.

Further reading: David Caute, *The Great Fear: The Anti-Communist Purge under Truman and Eisenhower* (New York: Simon & Schuster, 1979); Thomas Patterson, *Meeting the Communist Threat: Truman to Reagan* (New York: Oxford University Press, 1988).

— Dave Price

antiwar movement   See Volume X

Appalachian Regional Development Act

The Appalachian Regional Development Act sought to identify and restructure the economically disadvantaged mountainous regions of the United States.

The centerpiece of LYNDON B. JOHNSON'S WAR ON POVERTY, the Appalachian Regional Development Act, passed by Congress in 1965, created the Appalachian Regional Commission, a federal-state partnership designed to funnel federal money to programs serving an especially depressed part of the country. The Appalachian Regional Commission was an exploratory body created by JOHN F. KENNEDY in 1963 that studied Appalachian conditions and made extensive recommendations for economic restructuring, to be implemented by a permanent body. The 1965 measure originally defined the Appalachian region to include all or parts of 11 states from Pennsylvania to Alabama; two years later, in 1967, Congress added counties in New York and Mississippi to the list.

The impetus for the Appalachian Regional Development Act came from a procession of nationally transmitted media exposés of the region's intense poverty. Focusing mostly on coal-mining counties in Kentucky and West Virginia, these magazine articles and TELEVISION documentaries presented Appalachia as a place out of step with the recent history of the United States, a place that postwar progress had passed by. While some depictions investigated the collapse of the coal industry as a source of poverty, most placed the blame on geographic isolation and a culture of poverty among Appalachian people.

The attention on isolation allowed national audiences to maintain their faith in American ideals and institutions. Instead of seeing poverty as a failure of industrial development, it was now viewed as a result of inaccessibility. The region's poverty represented simply a lag in progress behind the rest of the nation. For a nation that advertised its prosperity to the third world in its competition with international COMMUNISM, the discovery of poverty was a potential embarrassment. The isolation interpretation, however, gave the Kennedy and Johnson administrations an opportunity to demonstrate what the United States could accomplish for underdeveloped regions while leaving the reputation of industrial capitalism intact.

In step with the media portrayals, the Appalachian Regional Commission based its policies on the assumption that isolation, particularly economic isolation, caused poverty in mountain regions. Economic isolation meant that the region was incompletely linked to national labor markets, capital markets, and consumer networks. The Appalachian Regional Commission pursued economic development by replacing isolation with integration, primarily through the creation of modern infrastructure and transportation. To that end, the great bulk of the commission's funds—over 80 percent of early budgets—went to finance road construction, a necessary precursor to any other kind of development. Ultimately, the goal was less to solve immediate and individual experiences of poverty than to create tools for long-term planning and restructuring. The Johnson administration left emergency relief, the human side of the War on Poverty, to agencies such as the Office of Economic Opportunity.

The policies of the Appalachian Regional Commission reflected a common scholarly conviction that uncommercialized rural living, in settlements far from modern amenities such as EDUCATION, health care, and secure employment, could not provide an acceptable American standard of living. To many of the creators of the War on Poverty, moreover, isolated rural living implied narrow-mindedness, ignorance, and racial violence. Only urban life, with its libraries, museums, and other cultural perks, could provide the foundation necessary for both economic security and personal growth. Appalachia, which contained few substantial towns or cities, posed an especially difficult problem.

Consequently, the organization concentrated its funds on creating or supplementing urban "growth centers" in the mountains. It defined growth centers as places whose economic base was sufficiently diversified to allow continued expansion and development. As providers of employment and cultural opportunities, growth centers would act as magnets, drawing in the rural population from the hinterlands. For the depopulated countryside, the Appalachian Regional Commission worked with the U.S. Forest Service and the U.S. Army Corps of Engineers, providing money for conservation, reforestation, flood control, and, as a consequence, the development of a tourism and recreation industry.

Throughout its history, the Appalachian Regional Commission has received criticism from many directions. Fiscal conservatives have considered it a cauldron of federal pork; during the Ronald Reagan administration, Congress reduced the organization's funding by over 40 percent. Only the election of several Republican congressmen from Appalachian districts kept the agency alive in the age of budget cuts. Left-leaning critics have argued that, by neglecting the political and economic dominance of the coal and timber industries, the commission failed to tackle the true roots of regional poverty.

Supporters of the agency, on the other hand, point to the organization's accomplishments. It has funded health care facilities, environmental projects, and thousands of miles of roads, successfully breaking down Appalachia's physical isolation. Most of the counties labeled distressed in 1965 no longer bear that designation, and some parts of the mountains currently enjoy a prosperity that exceeds national averages. Moreover, the important role played by state government in the agency, working closely with numerous local development districts, spurs the promise of additional activity at a time when many federal programs have fallen out of public favor.

Further reading: Michael Bradshaw, *The Appalachian Regional Commission: Twenty-five Years of Government Policy* (Lexington: University Press of Kentucky, 1992); Monroe Newman, *The Political Economy of Appalachia: A Case Study in Regional Integration* (Lexington, Mass.: D.C. Heath, 1972); David Whisnant, *Modernizing the Mountaineer* (Boone, N.C.: Appalachian Consortium Press, 1980).

— Robert Weise

arms race

The arms race refers to the buildup of nuclear weapons by the United States and the SOVIET UNION during the COLD WAR, a buildup that provoked fear of global destruction in the already tense standoff between the two most powerful nations in the post–World War II era.

The arms race began in 1949, when the Soviet Union successfully tested its first ATOMIC BOMB. The United States

had naively assumed it would have a monopoly for 15 years after the war. Now it found itself in competition to build bigger and better bombs. The American decision to create a HYDROGEN BOMB in 1950, with the expectation that the Soviets would do the same, escalated the arms race.

Then in 1957, the Soviet Union launched its first satellite, *Sputnik*. This meant that the Russians now had the missile capability to launch nuclear warheads as well. Competition developed in the missile area. President DWIGHT D. EISENHOWER offered intermediate-range ballistic missiles to NORTH ATLANTIC TREATY ORGANIZATION (NATO) allies, and by 1958, Great Britain, Italy, and Turkey all deployed American missiles on their territory. Additionally, Eisenhower pushed for the development of long-range intercontinental ballistic missiles (ICBMs) and created the NATIONAL AERONAUTICS AND SPACE ADMINISTRATION (NASA) to coordinate the advancement of missile TECHNOLOGY. As the Eisenhower administration came to a close in 1961, the arms race was well underway and the president had good reason to decry the advent of a MILITARY-INDUSTRIAL COMPLEX in his farewell address.

The arms race further accelerated during the administration of JOHN F. KENNEDY. The NEW FRONTIER, Kennedy's call for a more assertive and revitalized America both at home and abroad, included an ambitious arms buildup. Consequently, nuclear confrontation reached new heights and came to a head as the two superpowers confronted one another over Cuba in October 1962. Only in the aftermath of the CUBAN MISSILE CRISIS did Kennedy attempt to reduce tensions between the United States and the Soviet Union. The result was the LIMITED TEST BAN TREATY OF 1963, negotiated with both Great Britain and the Soviet Union. This treaty banned detonations aboveground, an effort to curb atmospheric pollution with radioactivity. It was a first, small step toward reining in the arms race.

It fell to Richard M. Nixon to achieve significant reduction in the arms race. Nixon's efforts at détente with the Soviet Union culminated in the Strategic Arms Limitation Talks (SALT). The SALT agreement of 1972 limited the number of ICBMs in the possession of each nation, and limited the construction of antiballistic missile systems.

President Jimmy Carter attempted to follow Nixon's lead. Carter renewed talks with the USSR to further bring the arms race under control. SALT II, initiated in 1978, placed limits on the number of bombers and missiles on both sides and on the development of new weapons systems. Carter's efforts, however, satisfied no one at home. Liberals charged that the SALT II agreement did not go far enough to reduce the arms race. Conservatives believed Carter had surrendered a decisive advantage to the Soviet Union in terms of the number of missiles, and the agreement was never ratified.

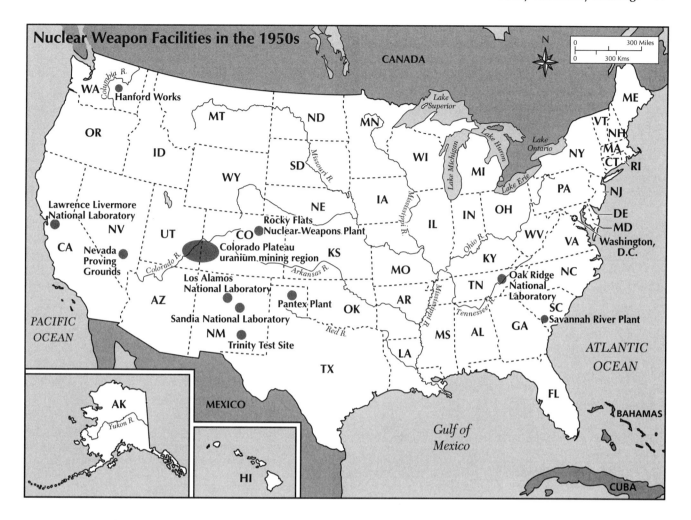

Nuclear Weapon Facilities in the 1950s

Carter's successor, Ronald Reagan, assumed office in 1980 and, in language reminiscent of Kennedy 20 years before, declared that a "missile gap" existed between the United States and Soviet Union. The results were similar as well. The arms race was renewed in earnest as the United States embarked on a major military buildup. Reagan's tone changed, however, during his second term in office, and he attempted to negotiate an arms agreement with Soviet premier Mikhail Gorbachev. In December 1987, Reagan and Gorbachev signed a treaty to eliminate intermediate-range nuclear forces. The treaty was a significant accomplishment, marking the first time that the two rival nations had agreed to destroy a whole class of weapon system. Additional agreements followed during the administration of George H.W. Bush.

While the arms race that dominated the cold war era ended with the collapse of the Soviet Union, the world still faces the threat of nuclear proliferation, as more and more nations develop nuclear weapons.

Further reading: Sheldon Ungar, *The Rise and Fall of Nuclearism* (University Park: Pennsylvania State University Press, 1992).

— Matthew Flynn

Army-McCarthy hearings

The Army-McCarthy Hearings of 1954 began as an attempt to oust alleged Communist Party members from the U.S. Army, but instead exposed the brutal tactics of Senator JOSEPH R. MCCARTHY.

During the years following the close of World War II, anticommunist sentiment swept the United States. McCarthy, elected to the Senate as a Republican from Wisconsin, began, in the 1950s, an effort aimed at purging alleged communists from the government of the United States, which came to be known as McCarthyism. He gained considerable support from both the REPUBLICAN PARTY and the American public.

In late 1953 and early 1954, McCarthy concentrated his attacks on the U.S. Army. David Schine, one of his assistants, was drafted into the army. Because of McCarthy's clout, Schine became a highly privileged recruit, receiving weekend passes and relief from unpleasant duties. Even so, McCarthy felt the army was not taking sufficient action, and so he decided to investigate the army itself for alleged sympathies to communism.

McCarthy accused army members of communist affiliations. He claimed that Captain Irving Peress, an army dentist, was guilty of communist activity. When Peress invoked the Fifth Amendment, which gave him the right not to speak about the charges against him, he received an honorable discharge from the army, and McCarthy immediately began questioning General Ralph Zwicker about the discharge. When Zwicker could not provide answers to these questions, McCarthy accused him of evading the

truth. This type of brutal attack on the general made other senators question McCarthy and his accusations.

In the midst of the hearings, McCarthy displayed a carbon copy of a letter from J. EDGAR HOOVER, the director of the Federal Bureau of Investigation (FBI), to a member of Army Intelligence. The letter supposedly listed communists within the army stationed at Fort Monmouth, New Jersey. This piece of evidence led others to question how McCarthy had obtained the letter, and if his methods were within the parameters of the law.

The climax of the hearings occurred when McCarthy attacked Fred Fisher, a member of the law firm of Joseph Welch, attorney for the army, for having belonged to an organization with communist sympathies. Welch, angered because Roy Cohn, McCarthy's assistant, had agreed not to raise this issue, lashed out at McCarthy, "Until this moment, Senator, I think I never really gauged your cruelty

Senator Joseph McCarthy offers to give reporters a list of State Department employees he says are undergoing a security-loyalty check   *(Library of Congress)*

or your recklessness . . . Let us not assassinate this lad further, Senator. You have done enough. Have you no sense of decency, sir, at long last? Have you left no sense of decency?" Applause followed Welch's remarks, but McCarthy still continued his relentless attacks.

Although no legal verdict resulted from the Army-McCarthy hearings, the American public was, for the first time, exposed to the brutal inquisition method used by McCarthy. TELEVISION played an important role in the hearings over the course of the weeks they took place. The public could both see and hear McCarthy make his attacks, and his lack of hard evidence became obvious. While American viewers may have missed the constitutional significance (civil liberties such as freedom of speech and the right not to testify guaranteed by the First and Fifth Amendments) of the hearings, focusing instead on the emotions of the event coming out of the images they were watching, the impact was still powerful. Television stations even played unedited versions of the hearings in order to portray the harshness of McCarthy.

The hearings also had a tremendous impact on McCarthy's popularity. According to the GALLUP POLL, McCarthy had a 50 percent approval rating in January 1954. By June, his approval had dropped to 34 percent. The percentages of those people who outrightly opposed him increased significantly as well. Republicans and Democrats also began to grow more weary of McCarthy. A backlash resulted, involving such people as President DWIGHT D. EISENHOWER and members of the Senate. As head of the Permanent Subcommittee on Investigations, McCarthy was put under tighter restrictions in his efforts, and many bills he attempted to push through the Senate were adamantly opposed. The Senate resisted censuring McCarthy, but in December 1954, the Senate voted 67-22 to condemn McCarthy because of his abuse of senatorial power. This was only the third time in 165 years that this punishment had occurred.

The Army-McCarthy hearings became the climax of the age of McCarthyism. The once popular and powerful senator now dropped out of the public scene, and he died of alcohol-related ailments only three years later in 1957. These hearings enabled Americans, through the medium of television, to witness McCarthy for the first time in the midst of his attacks. After seeing and experiencing McCarthyism first hand, the public stopped supporting McCarthy and his tactics.

Further reading: Richard M. Fried, *Men against McCarthy* (New York: Columbia University Press, 1976); Arthur Herman, *Joseph McCarthy: Reexamining the Life and Legacy of America's Most Hated Senator* (New York: Free Press, 2000); David Oshinsky, *A Conspiracy So Immense: The World of Joe McCarthy* (New York: Free Press, 1983).

— Jennifer Parson

art and architecture

Art and architecture, including paintings, buildings, sculptures, and furniture, changed dramatically in the United States in the 1950s and 1960s.

Building had slowed during the Great Depression, but resumed in the post–World War II years. Architecture in the 1940s used glass-curtain walls to make up the body of the structures. The most successful architect was Ludwig Mies van der Rohe, who used this technique in many of his buildings in Chicago, Illinois. He designed buildings for the Illinois Institute of Technology, using designs described by other architects as "a celebration of American power and wealth." The influence of Mies van der Rohe continued into the 1950s. Along with architect Philip Johnson, Mies van der Rohe designed the Seagram Building in New York. Their design utilized open space, simple form, and rich materials (such as topaz-gray tinted glass with bronze frames decorating the outside of the building), which quickly became the favorite approach of the architectural community in the 1950s and served as a symbol of corporate America.

Also important in the 1950s was the mass production of homes in the United States. WILLIAM J. LEVITT, using his assembly-line techniques, built houses more quickly and efficiently than ever before. His homes featured large picture windows and a two-car garage. The houses were exact replicas of each other, forming rows and rows of identical homes in developments that came to be known as Levittowns. Levitt and his techniques forever changed the way houses were designed and built.

In the 1960s, architecture began using more simple, geometric shapes, in odd combinations. Circles, squares, and rectangles made up many of the designs, but they were constructed differently than they had been before. For example, *Habitat,* designed by Moshe Safdie in 1967, utilized rectangular boxes made of concrete, stacked randomly on top and next to one another. Each box comprised its own room, and the result was a structure with no apparent organization that ignored the traditional approaches to architecture that had been used in earlier years. Brightly colored canvas tarps were stretched over organic or angular shapes, creating a tented structure, also popular in the 1960s.

Art, especially painting, took on many new forms in the 1950s and 1960s. Jackson Pollock became famous in the late 1940s for his drip-painting method, in which he walked around a large canvas dripping and swirling paint. The pictures seemed to have no organization or structure. abstract expressionism, which used seemingly unorganized collections of shapes to create a painting, dominated the artistic world in the 1950s. The images were sometimes recognizable, and other times were not; the traditional portraits and pictures were left behind. Mark Rothko, an artist during this time, used intensely colored blocks with soft edges, set in a light or dark background, in his abstract paintings. Other artists, such as Helen Frankenthaler, used techniques similar to those of Jackson Pollock, but let the paint soak into the canvas, instead of simply resting on top of it. Perhaps the artist who best represented abstract expressionism was Willem de Kooning. His painting *Excavation* was the preeminent work of the period. *Excavation* featured bits and pieces of anatomical parts, all in black or gray, spread across the canvas like a jigsaw puzzle. De Kooning then began painting abstract women in pictures that became tremendously controversial. Joan Mitchell, another artist of the period, brought abstract expressionism closer to impressionism and the works of artists like Claude Monet by using abstract techniques to paint what appeared to be landscapes. Jasper Johns, another artist, expressed defiance for the ideas of abstract expressionism. He painted the American flag as an abstract pattern, and used hot wax to bind the paint, which was an old technique.

In the 1960s, painting in the United States took a much different turn. Pop art, which used everyday objects and images as the subjects of works, invaded American culture. The imagery was immediately recognizable, unlike

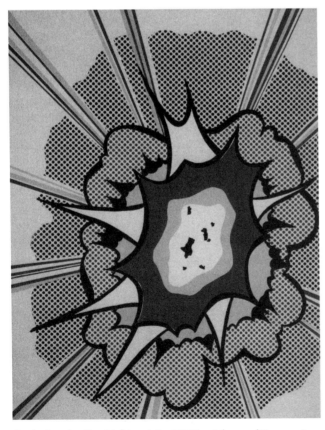

Explosion, by Roy Lichtenstein, 1967   *(Library of Congress)*

that of abstract expressionism. Pop artists aimed to identify the essence of Americanism in their works. Pop art also interested people who were previously uninterested in art.

Roy Lichtenstein was one of the highly visible artists from this period. His paintings used enlarged frames from comic strips and involved hard lines, flat color, and lettering to describe explosions. *Whaam!* is probably his best work, depicting a fighter jet shooting down an opponent. Lichtenstein's work was largely based on comic books, which became increasingly popular in the 1950s and 1960s.

Andy Warhol was perhaps the most notable artist of the time period. He accepted popular heroes and habits instead of rejecting them. His work *Marilyn Monroe* used a series of pictures of the starlet, each with a different color background. Warhol also painted a Campbell's soup can, using the same technique of different colored backgrounds behind each image. Warhol also used photographs in his paintings. *Race Riot* used an enlarged photograph, which Warhol then silk-screened onto canvas.

Another form, called op art, also became popular in the 1960s. Op artists moved away from the flowing, chaotic techniques of abstract expressionism by creating designs featuring sharply defined circles, squares, and other geometric shapes, along with vibrant colors, creating a feeling of disillusionment for the viewer.

Sculpture also took on many different characteristics in the 1950s and 1960s. In the 1950s, sculptors like David Smith welded pieces of metal together to create works of the abstract expressionist movement sweeping the United States. His sculptures seemed to resemble figures, but with no real feeling of volume or depth. Louise Nevelson, another sculptor, used fragments of architecture and furniture to create large artistic pieces. Nevelson was the first woman to be recognized as a Modernist sculptor. In the 1960s, two different kinds of sculpture developed. Minimal forms involved using simple shapes, such as rectangular boxes, to create sculptures. Pop sculpture involved re-creating everyday objects as sculptures, such as Claes Oldenburg's vinyl stuffed hamburgers. The sculpture during this time, like the paintings, used immediately recognizable images and objects.

Furniture in the 1950s and 1960s also followed the traditions of abstract expressionism and pop art. In the 1950s, most furniture designers were trained architects, and in the early 1950s they used simple traditional designs, such as that of the plain, steel bar-framed sofas. Gradually designers moved on to more innovative designs, and experimented with new materials. Round, Plexiglas chairs were popular, as were cup-like chairs. The traditional furniture patterns of the 1940s and early 1950s gave way to the new patterns of the 1960s. The Globe chair, for example, used a hollow globe with a section cut out in which to sit. Designs on the furniture involved bright colors and organic or angular shapes.

Also taking place during the 1960s was the Black Arts movement. It began as an effort to put down the stereotypes of African-American inferiority in the United States. For example, Jeff Donaldson's *Aunt Jemima and the Pillsbury Doughboy* portrayed the feeling of oppression during the time. The painting used images of the Doughboy (symbolic of the white community) standing over Aunt Jemima (symbolic of the African-American community), restraining her. Aunt Jemima, however, was depicted as much larger and stronger, even though she lay beneath the Doughboy. Black artists used their paintings to illustrate the ongoing oppression of the time.

The artistic movements of the 1950s and 1960s reflected larger developments in American society. In the 1950s, architects and artists, whose work reflected the turbulence to come in the 1960s, were challenging cultural patterns that were widely accepted. The audience, however, was small, and often included those who were directly involved or who had been involved for many years. In the 1960s, the United States was in a state of upheaval, with the ANTIWAR MOVEMENT and the Civil Rights movement in full swing, and the art reflected the coldness and indifference that had come out of the many years of conflict.

Further reading: Lesley Jackson, *The New Look: Design in the Fifties* (New York: Thames & Hudson, 1998); Edward Lucie-Smith, *Visual Arts in the Twentieth Century* (New York: Harry N. Abrams, 1996).

— Jennifer Parson

Asia (and foreign policy)

After World War II, the United States became increasingly interested in areas bordering on the Pacific Ocean, and, as a result of the COLD WAR, Asia became the site of a number of conflicts.

Following the defeat of the Japanese by American forces in World War II, the United States occupied Japan. Reforms included a new constitution, war crime trials, women's rights, the dismantling of the feudal landownership system, and American censorship of Japanese films, so that Emperor Hirohito was not depicted as a god but as a constitutional monarch.

As a more pacifist culture replaced militarism in Japan, the cold war became more contentious in China, where Mao Zedong led his forces to victory in a triumph of COMMUNISM. Feeling threatened by a revived Japan, the SOVIET UNION was sympathetic to Mao, while it was at the same time anxious about American expansion in Asian markets.

Mao came to power in 1949. The communists defeated the Guomindang, the corruption-riddled Nationalist government led by Jiang Jieshi (Chiang Kai-shek), and drove him and his supporters to the island of Taiwan. The U.S. government then issued the China WHITE PAPER, a lengthy document offering reasons why the United States was unable to alter the result of the communist victory. In his "Letter of Transmittal," or brief summary of the situation, Secretary of State DEAN ACHESON wrote to President HARRY S. TRUMAN saying, "nothing that this country [the United States] did or could have done within the reasonable limits of its capabilities could have changed the result." As Nationalists retreated to Taiwan, the United States refused to recognize the People's Republic of China. Because Mao needed an ally, he negotiated with Soviet leader Joseph Stalin to obtain a treaty of friendship and alliance, declaring that each nation would come to the other's aid if attacked by a third party.

Soon after the Chinese Revolution, the United States found itself involved in Korea. The nation had been divided at the end of World War II along the 38th parallel, with American troops accepting surrenders in the North, and the Soviet Union doing the same in the South. Soviet and American occupation forces clashed when the communist North invaded the South in 1950, triggering the KOREAN WAR. Truman readied American naval and air forces and directed General DOUGLAS MACARTHUR in Japan to supply South Korea. The United States went to the UN Security Council to secure a unanimous resolution branding North Korea the aggressor, and another resolution calling on UN members to assist South Korea. When the United Nations intervened and repulsed the North Korean troops, Communist China became involved. A stalemate resulted, in part because of Truman's decision to conduct only a limited war, provoking a bitter struggle between MacArthur and Truman, which culminated in Truman firing the general for insubordination. The Korean War led to the election of a Republican administration in 1952, and helped fuel fear of communist subversion in the United States.

No Asian country was untouched by the ideological confrontation between the United States and the Soviet Union. Vietnam became another trouble spot. During the VIETNAM WAR, Communist forces won in Vietnam when China and the Soviet Union aided North Vietnam in the defeat of the United States–supported South Vietnam in 1975. From 1946 to 1954, the Vietnamese had struggled for their independence from France, the colonial power for much of the century, during the First Indochina War. After the Vietnamese defeated the French, the country was divided into North and South Vietnam. Ho Chi Minh, the communist leader in the North, hoped to bring all Vietnam under his control. The United States became involved because it believed that if Vietnam fell under communist rule, then all of Southeast Asia could fall as well. This "domino theory" triggered U.S. support of the South Vietnamese government, first through aid and then through military involvement. The United States failed to achieve its goal of preventing the collapse of the South Vietnamese government. In 1975, unified under communist control, the nation became the Socialist Republic of Vietnam. During the conflict, millions of Vietnamese lost their lives.

Other areas faced similar turbulence. On the Indian subcontinent, religious separatism caused a continuing rift between Muslim Pakistan and Hindu India after partition and independence in 1947.

Further reading: Fredrik Logevall, *Choosing War* (Berkeley: University of California Press, 1999); Qiang Zhai, *The Dragon, the Lion and the Eagle* (Kent, Ohio.: Kent State University Press, 1994).

— John E. Bibish IV

Asian-American movement

As an integral part of the Civil Rights movement, the Asian-American movement played an important role in the formation of an Asian-American identity.

The movement was born in the late 1960s as some radical Asian-American youths, especially college students, participated in the ANTIWAR MOVEMENT and became aware of the need to unite and struggle for racial equality, social justice, and political empowerment in their own lives. Emulating the AFRICAN-AMERICAN MOVEMENT, they focused their efforts on establishing a pan-Asian identity and targeted racial discrimination that had long excluded them from mainstream society. The history of Asian Americans fighting against oppression and racial discrimination differed from ethnic group to ethnic group because of the existing cultural and class diversity, but the movement represented the first time in American history that combined action was taken in the name of Asian Americans rather than of Chinese Americans or Japanese Americans.

Asian Americans had been historically discriminated against and oppressed in American society. From the mid-19th century onward, the entry of Chinese immigrants, the earliest Asian immigrant group, was restricted by harsh legislation, which culminated in the 1882 Chinese Exclusion Act. From the 1860s onward, a series of local and federal laws driven by anti-Chinese sentiment consistently denied the rights of Chinese immigrants to become citizens, own certain kinds of property, attend first class schools, or marry outside of their race. These laws later affected other Asian immigrants as well. The incarceration of Japanese Americans during World War II was an extreme case of how war hysteria and racial discrimination could lead American society to deviate from its ideology of democracy and equality.

During World War II, however, images of Asian Americans, particularly Chinese and Filipinos, were enhanced because of both their contributions to America's war effort and the contributions of their countries of origin. In the postwar era, the racially based immigration and naturalization laws against Asians were gradually lifted, and the number of Asian Americans entering professional fields appreciably increased. However, the situation of Asian Americans in the postwar era still called for improvement. When soldiers were fighting Asians in the KOREAN WAR in the 1950s and in the VIETNAM WAR in the 1960s and 1970s, some Asian Americans feared the possibility of being unjustly treated as the Japanese Americans had been in World War II. In addition, although Asian Americans were stereotypically depicted as members of a "model minority," problems such as unequal employment opportunities and media stereotypes still negatively affected them.

Early activities of the movement copied what other radical Americans did in the turbulent antiwar protests. Meetings, demonstrations, and the publication of leaflets and broadsides of radical ideas argued the participants' case. Activists also formed various study groups to discuss the problems that plagued their ethnic communities. These activities enabled them to reassess their position in American society and address issues that in their belief resulted from racial discrimination, class oppression, imperialism, and sexism. Their activities brought profound changes to the ideology of the Asian Americans. From the late 1960s onward, Asian Americans were more active and united in struggling for their interests than ever before.

The second stage of the movement in the 1970s included a turn to communist ideology. Even though the conservative tone in the Asian-American community remained strong, a small number of college students adopted ideology from communist countries such as China. They believed in a total facelift of the American social system to change the fate of the country and its people. They formed communist study groups to promulgate COMMUNISM and prepare for a proletariat revolution. The revolution they expected never materialized.

Currently, the Asian-American movement is marked by Asian Americans' active participation in electoral politics. Although Asian Americans have a history of success in electoral politics, they wanted a more decisive voice. From the 1980s onward, more Asian Americans have become actively involved in running for public office.

The movement did not directly engender substantial changes in terms of the economic and political situation of the Asian-American community, but it did promote class and ethnic consciousness. The movement gave birth to a new field of higher learning in colleges—Asian-American studies—and created a network of organizations and activists dedicated to the betterment of the Asian-American community.

Further reading: William Wei. *The Asian American Movement* (Philadelphia: Temple University Press, 1993).

— Mingyi Weng

The USS *Nautilus* (SS-571), the navy's first atomic-powered submarine, on its initial sea trials   *(Library of Congress)*

atomic bomb   See Volume VIII

Atomic Energy Commission (AEC)

The Atomic Energy Commission (AEC) was a civilian agency created to explore, promote, and regulate the uses of nuclear energy.

Established by the Atomic Energy Act of 1946, the AEC inherited the central task of the Manhattan Project, which created the first ATOMIC BOMB, developing fissionable weapons for military purposes, but also sought to create peacetime applications of atomic power. President HARRY S. TRUMAN appointed the commission's five civilian members, only one of whom was a scientist (Robert F. Bacher). The first chairman was David E. Lilienthal, former head of the Tennessee Valley Authority. Protected under tight security and privileged with a virtual monopoly on nuclear matters,

the AEC and its constituent labs invested resources heavily on classified research and weapons production.

The mounting COLD WAR tensions of the late 1940s and the early 1950s resulted in a massive rearmament campaign, one that included the HYDROGEN BOMB project, that began with the decision to move ahead with this new weapon in 1950. The AEC tested all weapons, beginning with tests in the Bikini atoll in the Pacific Ocean in 1946, and continuing with other tests in subsequent years both in the Pacific and at the Nevada Test Site, near Las Vegas, that opened in 1950. Between 1951 and 1963, the United States conducted approximately 106 tests at this site. As tests around the world showered fallout—residual radioactive debris produced by the weapons being tested—over people everywhere, concern mounted about the health dangers. The AEC, responsible for both development and control, went out of its way to minimize the danger fallout posed.

At the same time, the AEC hoped to ease public fears by promoting the atom in peace-minded terms. Lilienthal, whom the press dubbed "Mr. Atom," routinely wrote and spoke about the benevolent promises of atomic energy. Research institutions under contract with the commission, such as Brookhaven National Laboratory in Long Island, New York, actively publicized the nonmilitary benefits of nuclear science. President DWIGHT D. EISENHOWER further voiced the optimistic uses of the atom. In his "Atoms for Peace" speech delivered at the United Nations on December 8, 1953, the Republican president called for the international control of atomic energy and underscored its possibilities in fostering global peace.

The Atomic Energy Act of 1954 assured a continuation and expansion of the AEC's activities. The new act called for further development of atomic weapons, renewed discourse about the "peaceful atom," and encouraged the implementation of nuclear reactors through the assistance of private companies. AEC members believed that commercial power plants would not only provide for an alternative energy source but also would exemplify the peacetime potential of atomic power and help restore the nation's preponderant status in nuclear technology (once broken by the Soviets' successful testing of their A-bomb in 1949).

The first breakthrough came when Admiral Hyman G. Rickover directed the development of the first nuclear-powered submarine, launched in 1954. The submarine provided a model for a reactor on land. In 1957, Rickover, presided over the development of a reactor that went online in Shippingport, Pennsylvania. Nuclear power, while expensive, was a reality.

The AEC did all it could to promote atomic power. It offered previously classified information, technical assistance, financial support, and a number of other inducements to private businesses. Even though the operation and maintenance costs of the early reactors were considerably higher than those of fossil fuel plants, by August 1955, five companies announced their interest in running nuclear power plants. The breakthrough construction of the Oyster Creek power plant of the Jersey Central Power and Light Company in 1963—a facility that was almost fully financed by General Electric (GE)—ushered in a booming phase in the reactor industry. Competition intensified among private entities, particularly between GE and Westinghouse. Applications for power plants increased in number, the size of plants grew, and the electrical capacity of fissionable sources multiplied. In 1966 and 1967, utilities ordered about 50 plants. Between 1970 and 1974, they ordered more than a hundred additional facilities.

Meanwhile, reactor development raised serious medical and environmental concerns. The bombs dropped on Hiroshima and Nagasaki, as well as nuclear testing of the early post–World War II years, sparked the fear of nuclear fallout and prompted scientists of the National Committee on Radiation Protection (and other groups) to assess the dangers of radiological contamination. The fallout debate quickly spread to the general public; in an effort to prevent disastrous consequences, the AEC decided to tighten its radiation standards for power plants and elaborate on safety procedures. The Price-Anderson Act of 1957 further granted compensations for damages caused by power plant accidents. Despite these new agendas and policies, professional and public apprehensions continued to surface over such issues as thermal pollution, waste disposal, and core meltdown.

The growing concern about the environment and safety issues revealed the difficulties in appropriating atomic power for peacetime uses. Eventually, the AEC found itself more than fully occupied with the task of both development and regulation of nuclear energy. In 1974, Congress passed the Energy Reorganization Act, which divided the AEC into the Energy Research and Development Administration and the Nuclear Regulatory Commission. The act went into effect in January 1975.

Further reading: George T. Mazuzan and J. Samuel Walker, *Controlling the Atom: The Beginning of Nuclear Regulation 1946–1972* (Berkeley: University of California Press, 1985); J. Samuel Walker, *Containing the Atom: Nuclear Regulation in a Changing Environment, 1963–1971* (Berkeley: University of California Press, 1992).

— Hiroshi Kitamura

automobile industry

The decades after World War II saw automotive production in the United States rise to unparalleled heights, as American machines set the global standard for style and quality.

The postwar period marked the golden age for American car producers, at least for those that survived in the competitive industry. Dozens of firms produced cars in the 1940s, but only four remained by 1968: General Motors, Ford, Chrysler, and American Motors. In time, each would be rocked by foreign competition, environmental critiques, and consumer safety concerns.

The end of World War II found the industry primed for profits. After years of war and depression, the nation possessed a nearly insatiable automotive appetite. Numerous independent firms joined the Big Three (General Motors, Chrysler, and Ford) in the race to supply America's automotive needs, but, to the misfortune of many of these ambitious concerns, the demand for parts and labor in the initial postwar years was nearly insatiable as well. Labor disputes and shortages of vital materials plagued the nation's return to peace, forcing automakers to pay dearly for both supplies and workers. Union employees made great strides in this tight labor market, and, in 1947, the United Auto Workers won promises from the Big Three tying wage increases to the Labor Department's cost-of-living index. Ford guaranteed retirement wages for workers with three decades of service the following year, and similar packages quickly became the industry standard. Independent car manufacturers could hardly afford such premiums, and though their market share reached nearly 18 percent in 1948, few survived the 1950s.

When the federal government lifted the KOREAN WAR's price controls and production restrictions in 1953, America's largest automakers began their period of greatest prosperity and their famed infatuation with large cars. Unburdened by war, depression, labor strife, or material shortages for the first time in a quarter-century, the Big Three began producing vehicles of unprecedented size. Cars in America had never been merely for transportation; to many, they represented their owner's status and visible prosperity. With cheap gasoline prices and prosperity visible everywhere, style and power drove design as never before. Large amounts of chrome adorned models whose dimensions seemed to stretch with every passing year, and features once considered luxuries, such as air conditioning, automatic transmission, and power brakes and steering, all became standard equipment. Not until 1959 did the Big Three even offer a compact model.

Style and size mattered in the 1950s, not only because Americans were generally prosperous but also because they spent more time in their cars. SUBURBANIZATION forced motorists into longer commutes. The INTERSTATE HIGHWAY ACT OF 1956, arguably the largest civil engineering project in human history, encouraged this trend, promising drivers coast-to-coast transit along over 42,000 miles of federally funded highways. The interstate system, supported by DWIGHT D. EISENHOWER, also provided civil defense planners with easy means to evacuate the nation's largest cities, should the COLD WAR ever turn hot.

By 1960, the market dominance of the Big Three and their large machines began to crack. Even though imported cars amounted to less than 2 percent of the American domestic market in 1953, by 1959 their market share had reached double figures and was rapidly growing. Chief among the foreign imports was the Volkswagen Beetle, a fuel-efficient compact automobile whose diminutive stature made it a natural pick for consumers eager to snub the conventions of the 1950s. Of greater future importance was the growing availability of Japanese models, including Toyota and Nissan, which appeared in America's marketplace in 1957 and 1958. Already buffeted by these imports, America's auto industry came under assault from consumer and environmental advocates as well. In 1965, attorney RALPH NADER published *Unsafe at Any Speed,* a critique of the industry's safety record that claimed faulty vehicle design was a major factor in highway accidents. Public furor over Nader's revelations helped spawn the NATIONAL TRAFFIC AND MOTOR VEHICLE SAFETY ACT OF 1966 and

A 1956 Ford Crown Victoria automobile   *(Library of Congress)*

Woman demonstrates benefits of wearing automobile seat belt, 1955   *(Library of Congress)*

the Highway Safety Act, which mandated that safety devices, such as seat belts, become standard on every American car. The industry also suffered from environmental criticisms during these years, especially after scientists reported that 70 percent of Los Angeles's famous smog was produced by automobile exhausts. California lowered acceptable emissions levels in 1960, and five years later Congress passed similar legislation. Such standards have been part of automotive design ever since.

By the end of the 1960s, the heyday of America's automotive industry was indeed over. Its image tarnished by consumer and environmental complaints and its market share weakened by foreign pressure, the industry's ability to ward off these threats suffered under the weight of the lucrative labor packages signed during the heady 1940s. Worse days were yet to come, particularly with the oil shortages of the 1970s. Increased competition in subsequent years ultimately made cars cleaner, safer, and more fuel-efficient.

Further reading: John B. Rae, *The American Automobile Industry* (Boston: Twayne Publishers, 1984); Rude Volti, "A Century of Automobility," *Technology and Culture*, 37, no. 4 (October 1996): 663–685.

— Jeffrey A. Engel

aviation

Aviation provided Americans with a new and exciting form of transportation that became more accessible in the post–World War II years.

An exciting new epoch in American aviation began in 1946, a time when many of the dreams of the industry's first pioneers would come true. Millions took their first flights, as passenger travel grew at unprecedented rates. Jet aviation, which made its theoretical debut before World War II and its military appearance during the conflict, blossomed in the war's aftermath for both civilian airliners and warplanes alike. Test pilots challenged and broke the sound barrier (the speed at which sound travels) in the late 1940s, and a scant 15 years later, Great Britain and France committed to jointly produce the Concorde, a commercial jet promising twice that speed.

The postwar world was primed for a vast expansion in commercial aviation. Engineering knowledge gained from wartime bomber developments easily transferred to civilian use, as airlines offered services spanning the Atlantic and the vast expanse of America. Passengers could fly coast-to-coast, with stops along the way, in less than 11 hours. Unfortunately for aircraft manufacturers, the immediate postwar years were lean ones, as war-surplus planes saturated the market. Although impressive new machines rolled off their assembly lines (such as Lockheed's Constellation or Douglas's DC-6), few companies made profits during these years of military cutbacks.

These new aircraft, however, transformed commercial service, combining unprecedented range with the comfort of pressurized flight at high altitudes, far above turbulent weather. Passenger traffic doubled once wartime travel restrictions were removed in 1946, and with the introduction of "coach" or tourist class by Capital Airlines in 1948, commercial travel grew by nearly 15 percent. Indeed, by 1956, the nation's four largest domestic carriers—American, Eastern, United, and Trans World Airlines—were each larger than the entire industry had been only a decade before. Such growth heavily taxed the country's airports and its inadequate air-traffic control system. Federal and local officials struggled throughout the 1950s to coordinate so many new flights and to develop airports capable of handling progressively larger and noisier aircraft. Radar and other advanced means of communication, coupled with the federal government's increasing willingness to help finance airport construction, eventually helped ease the nation's aviation growing pains.

To assist in the regulation and safety of civil aviation, the U.S. government established the Federal Aviation

Aerial view of a Boeing B-47 Stratojet taking on a load of jet fuel from a Boeing KC-97 Stratofreighter tanker-transport
(*Library of Congress*)

Administration (FAA) as part of the Federal Aviation Act of 1958. The FAA encouraged and developed civil aeronautics, including new aviation TECHNOLOGY, and the agency created a common system of air-traffic control and navigation for both civil and military aircraft. With the help of the FAA, the aviation industry continued to grow and prosper throughout the 1960s.

As the industry grew, so too did its aircraft. The first commercial jet airliner appeared in 1952, a British plane called the Comet. Passengers flocked to this innovative craft's lure of comfortable and speedy jet travel. Unfortunately, the first Comets met with disaster, as several exploded in 1954 due to unforeseen problems of metal fatigue. Great Britain's lead in the blossoming field of jet aviation never fully recovered. By the close of the decade, American manufacturers such as Boeing (with its 707) and Douglas (with its DC-8) led the way. Their planes could transport nearly 200 passengers at more than 600 miles per hour. Before the end of the 1960s, Boeing offered airlines its famed 747, capable of flying nearly 400 travelers even greater distances. Innovation did not always lead to profit, however, in this cutthroat industry. Many companies' commercial operations teetered on the brink of failure by the close of the decade, including both Douglas and Lockheed, and even the success of the 747 could not insulate Boeing from major layoffs.

Though commercial aviation made great strides in the 1950s and 1960s, the industry was truly propelled by its military role. COLD WAR expenditures boosted aviation manufacturing from its post–World War II slump, and the superpower conflict made the development of increasingly advanced aircraft and avionics a vital necessity. Military requirements advanced helicopter development, as witnessed by the craft's extensive use in both the KOREAN WAR and the VIETNAM WAR. Frequently these military developments aided commercial projects, as with Boeing's 707, developed in conjunction with a U.S. Air Force jet tanker. As technological development broached the earth's atmosphere, aviation itself became aerospace, since advances in rocketry enabled humanity's initial forays into outer space during this period. The first human-made satellite, a Soviet-developed model named *Sputnik,* made its first successful orbit in 1957, and five years later, men orbited the earth. To further U.S. advancement in SPACE EXPLORATION, the NATIONAL AERONAUTICS AND SPACE ADMINISTRATION (NASA) was created in 1958. By the close of the decade, Americans walked on the moon. America's military used these advances in rocketry to develop ballistic missiles, capable of propelling nuclear weapons into the earth's atmosphere and then back down onto targets halfway across the globe. It was the great irony of this innovative age that many of the same companies that strove to bring the world closer together through travel and space exploration also gave policymakers the means by which to destroy it.

Across the entire breadth of the field, the aviation industry's technological achievements were breathtaking. With the use of airborne tankers, American bombers circled the globe while its most advanced spy plane (the SR-71 Blackbird) flew at more than three times the speed of sound with a cruising altitude above 80,000 feet.

Further reading: Charles D. Bright, *The Jet Makers: The Aerospace Industry from 1945–1972* (Lawrence: University of Kansas Press; 1985).

— Jeffrey A. Engel

B

baby boom

The baby boom, a large and sustained increase in births in the United States between 1946 and 1964, created a generation that became a major engine for social change in America and momentarily reversed a decades-long trend in the United States and other industrial countries toward lower fertility rates.

American birthrates, low in the 1920s, fell even further during the Great Depression of the 1930s before rising again in 1940. In 1942, more Americans married than in any year since 1920, and in 1943, the birthrate reached its highest level since 1927. The real increases, however, began with the end of World War II. In 1945, for example, the median age at marriage for women fell to its lowest level of the century while the proportion of women who were married reached a high point. Nine months after the end of World War II, birthrates began to rise quickly, climbing to record heights in October 1946. By the end of 1946, 3.4 million children had been born, 20 percent more than in 1945.

The booming birthrate proved to have remarkable longevity, constituting much more than just a statistical anomaly following the war. In 1947, total births rose to 3.8 million, and, in 1952, they reached 3.9 million; by 1954, total births passed the 4 million mark, where they remained through 1964, before declining. Measured by birthrate, or the number of births per thousand of population, the boom peaked in 1947 at 26.6, the highest rate since 1921. This rate declined slowly, remaining at 24.0 or higher through 1959, and falling only to 21.0 by 1964, after which it plunged to levels comparable to those of the 1930s. By 1964, a full 40 percent of the nation's population had been born since 1946—76.4 million births altogether.

The baby boom occurred in the context of unprecedented and sustained economic expansion, exceptional American influence abroad, and rapid expansion of the country's already broad middle classes. As the economic hard times of the 1930s became little more than a bad memory, Americans moved in increasing numbers to new homes in the suburbs, attended colleges and universities in record numbers, and purchased an extraordinary range of consumer goods, from toasters and blenders to automobiles and televisions. With only 7 percent of the world's population, the United States possessed half of the world's manufacturing output, consistently low levels of unemployment, and the world's highest standard of living. Home ownership, EDUCATION, and seemingly secure employment within the reach of increasing numbers of Americans made settling down and forming a family a higher priority for more and more people.

Demographically, several factors served as important components of the marked increase in births of the period. First, many older couples who had delayed marriage during the hard times of the Great Depression decided to marry and have children once the ECONOMY began to turn around in the 1940s, particularly after the end of World War II. Second, more Americans in their late teens and early twenties chose to marry and have children than had their parents, driving down the average age at marriage for both men and women. Not only did more young people decide to get married—the percentage of women over 30 who had never been married fell from 15 percent in 1940 to only 7 percent by 1960—but more chose to have children—92 percent of all families in the 1950s, as compared to only 85 percent in the 1930s. Finally, the divorce rate, which spiked to record highs in 1945 and 1946, fell quickly thereafter and remained low until the mid-1960s.

The demographic bulge of the period had important consequences, reflecting a temporary reversal of long-term trends in the country toward lower birth rates, later (and shorter) marriages, and smaller families. Socially and culturally, the term "baby boom generation" quickly became a phrase journalists and social critics used to characterize the postwar era's large-scale changes. From the emergence of an enormous new youth market to the fascination with juvenile delinquency in the 1950s to the social upheavals of

Birth and Population Rates, 1900–70

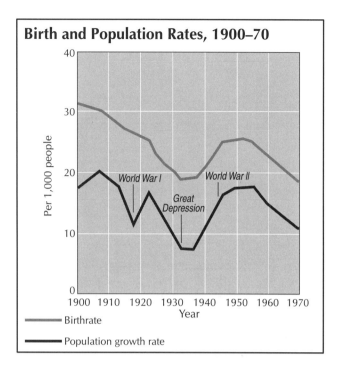

Birthrate

Population growth rate

the 1960s, the baby boom has often helped explain new developments and social trends. Traditional social distinctions of race, class, gender, age, and region still divided the baby boomers themselves, however, revealing the limits of the phrase's explanatory power and underlining the fact that the popular image of cozy domesticity of the period contains as much myth as reality.

Further reading: Landon Jones, *Great Expectations: America and the Baby Boom Generation* (New York: Coward, McCann, and Geoghegan, 1980).

— Christopher W. Wells

Baker, Ella Josephine (1903–1986)

Ella Baker was a grass-roots organizer and leader of African-American progressive political and social movements during the Civil Rights movement.

From the 1940s through the 1960s, Baker was involved in behind-the-scenes organizing and held leadership roles in such key civil rights organizations as the NATIONAL ASSOCIATION FOR THE ADVANCEMENT OF COLORED PEOPLE (NAACP), the SOUTHERN CHRISTIAN LEADERSHIP CONFERENCE (SCLC), the STUDENT NONVIOLENT COORDINATING COMMITTEE (SNCC), and the MISSISSIPPI FREEDOM DEMOCRATIC PARTY (MFDP). Throughout Baker's political life, she strove to inspire ordinary people to empower themselves.

Born in Norfolk, Virginia, on December 13, 1903, and raised in Littleton, North Carolina, Baker's early years were spent within a strong black community. Her father was a waiter on the Norfolk to Washington, D.C., ferry and her mother, who cared for sick and needy neighbors, was a schoolteacher prior to marriage. Both her parents were educated children of former slaves. Baker's maternal grandfather, a farmer and Baptist preacher, purchased tracts of North Carolina land which he had worked as a slave. He then parceled out the land to family members and shared crops and livestock with the entire community. Baker grew up with two siblings in this extended family. In 1918 she left home to attend secondary school and college at Shaw University in Raleigh, North Carolina.

After earning her B.A. in 1927, Baker hoped to attend the University of Chicago for graduate study in sociology and to pursue a career as a medical missionary. Lacking financial support, Baker moved to New York City to live with relatives, arriving during the Harlem Renaissance. She waitressed and took sociology courses at Columbia University. During the Great Depression, Baker joined the editorial staff of the *American West Indian News,* and then managed the newspaper offices of leading black intellectual George Schuyler's *Negro National News.* She became active in the consumers' cooperative movement, and, along with Schuyler, she founded and led the Young Negroes' Cooperative League. In 1934, she joined the staff of the New York Public Library, where she was involved in the Works Progress Administration's (WPA) Library Project. This led to a teaching position with the WPA's Consumer Education Project.

In 1941, Baker began organizing for the NAACP. As a field secretary, she traveled the South recruiting members, raising funds, and creating a network of southern contacts. She was highly successful and soon became director of branches. Often at odds with its leadership, Baker worked to democratize the NAACP, insisting on larger, more active roles for local, rank-and-file members. In 1946, Baker resigned as director of branches, frustrated with the NAACP's bureaucracy. Baker then began work with the New York City NAACP on school desegregation. In 1952, she became that chapter's first woman president. The next year, she ran unsuccessfully for New York City Council as a Liberal Party candidate.

Baker's attention returned to the South by the mid-1950s. She helped Bayard Rustin and Stanley Levison to found In Friendship, a northern organization that raised money for the expanding southern civil rights struggle, aiding the Montgomery Improvement Association's bus boycott in 1955–56 among other actions. When the Southern Christian Leadership Conference (SCLC) was formed in 1957, Rustin and Levison convinced Baker to set up the Atlanta headquarters and to organize the SCLC's Crusade for Citizenship, a voter registration campaign. Baker served as the first acting director of the SCLC. Just as she disagreed with the NAACP's strategies, however, Baker took issue with the SCLC's top-down leadership style and narrow focus of its charismatic president, MARTIN LUTHER KING, JR. Baker's philosophy was that "strong people don't need strong leaders." She argued for decentralized leadership and local decision making in the SCLC.

When hundreds of students led SIT-INS to protest segregated lunch counters in 1960, Baker organized a conference to foster student leadership and plan strategies. From this meeting the Student Nonviolent Coordinating Committee (SNCC) emerged. More radical than other civil rights organizations, SNCC utilized mass direct action and practiced nonviolent resistance in the fight for civil rights. Baker left the SCLC to focus on SNCC, where she mentored many students. In 1964, SNCC helped to launch the Mississippi Freedom Democratic Party (MFDP), an alternative to the party's all-white delegation to the Democratic National Convention. Baker managed the party's national office and delivered the keynote address at its state convention. During the 1960s, Baker also worked for the National Student Young Women's Christian Association and the interracial Southern Conference Education Fund. She continued her political activism through the early 1980s in the Coalition of Concerned Black Americans, the Puerto Rican Solidarity Committee, and other organizations. Baker died in New York City in 1986.

Further reading: Ellen Cantarow, *Moving the Mountain: Women Working for Social Change* (New York: The Feminist Press, 1980); Joanne Grant. *Ella Baker: Freedom Bound* (New York: John Wiley & Sons, 1998).

— Lori Creed

Baker v. Carr (1962)

Baker v. Carr was a landmark Supreme Court decision in the early 1960s that aided the breakdown of SEGREGATION and discrimination in the South and furthered the role of the federal government in helping to advance the Civil Rights movement.

In March 1962, the Supreme Court, under the direction of Chief Justice EARL WARREN, ruled in favor of Charles Baker, a Tennessee voter, that his state was electing members of the state legislature based on district boundaries that were too old to represent accurately the distribution of the population. As a result, the sparse rural population of the state maintained its grip on the state government, while the growing urban population possessed but a muted voice.

With this ruling, the WARREN COURT determined that legislative apportionment by the states was now subject to the scrutiny of the federal courts. The final decision was six-to-two. Justices Hugo L. Black, William J. Brennan, Tom C. Clark, William O. Douglas, and Potter Stewart joined Warren in support of the ruling, while Justices Felix Frankfurter and John Marshal Harlan dissented. This final margin, however, did not reveal the considerable internal debate and dissension within the Court that made this final tally closer than it appeared. One justice, Charles E. Whittaker, was forced to abstain from casting his vote due to his hospitalization. Had he been able to vote, Whittaker made it clear that he would have been a dissenting voice. Similarly, Clark had initially opposed the ruling. He was, in fact, originally chosen by Frankfurter to write the dissent. Clark, however, decided to switch his vote after preparing a draft of his statement. During this process he came to the conclusion that the federal courts were the only recourse open to the people of Tennessee to enact apportionment reform, the state legislature having proved itself unwilling to implement change. In Tennessee, the last time the district lines had been redrawn was 1900.

Warren asked Brennan to write the momentous opinion. Brennan did so, keeping in mind the tenuous support of a number of justices. Stewart, in fact, only backed the ruling on the grounds that it indicated the Court's willingness to hear cases about the apportionment of state legislatures. Brennan wrote his opinion to reflect Stewart's concern. Once drafted, it did little more than rule that Baker's complaint was now within the federal court's jurisdiction. Still to be decided were questions of enforcement and apportionment standards as required by the Constitution. Despite these limitations, *Baker v. Carr* was momentous in its own right. It chipped away at state's rights by overriding the Court's previous stand that state apportionment was a political question, one to be considered by the legislative branch only and not the judicial branch of the state or federal government. This was a reversal of the view of the Court reached in an earlier decision, that of *Colegrove v. Green* (1946).

Primarily for this reason, Warren considered *Baker v. Carr* "the most important case of my tenure on the Court." His statement contains much validity. Following this ruling, judicial activism was more the norm, and political activists, religious dissenters, and civil rights workers could expect new forms of legal protection. Additionally, and predictably, in the politically charged 1960s, this ruling rapidly became a racial one. Since blacks populated many southern cities in great numbers, they were effectively stymied by whites from flexing their true voting power under the old system of election that ignored population centers in favor of rural areas. With *Baker v. Carr*, this inequity was dismantled.

Consequently this ruling heralded the Supreme Court's lead in the civil rights crusade. This was a great surprise considering that Warren, the three-time governor of California, had supported the internment of Japanese Americans during World War II and, after this conflict, had attacked the administration of HARRY S. TRUMAN for "coddling" communists. The Warren court, however, proved more liberal than conservative, prompting DWIGHT D. EISENHOWER to remark that appointing Warren to the Supreme Court was the "biggest damn fool mistake I ever made."

Not surprisingly, *Baker v. Carr* had to endure a number of legal challenges. Foremost among these were efforts undertaken in the House of Representatives, which passed a bill to deny federal court jurisdiction over state apportionment. But the Senate refused to concur and the bill failed. Meanwhile, in 1964, in *Wesberry v. Sanders*, the Supreme Court reaffirmed and encouraged the implementation of *Baker v. Carr*, underscoring the principle of equal representation, according to a system of "one man, one vote." In the same year, with REYNOLDS V. SIMS, the Court again extended its ruling, declaring that both houses of a legislature had to be apportioned on the basis of population, the sole exception being the U.S. Senate. These guidelines had to be followed even if the people of a state had approved a different system of representation.

Further reading: Bernard Schwartz, *Super Chief: Earl Warren and His Supreme Court—A Judicial Biography* (New York: New York University Press, 1983).

— Matthew Flynn

Baldwin, James (1924–1987)

James Baldwin was an African-American novelist, essayist, playwright, and poet, whose passion and eloquence on the subject of sexual identity and race relations in the United States made him a leading spokesperson of the Civil Rights movement.

Baldwin was born on August 2, 1924, into poverty in Harlem, in New York City, where he was raised by his mother and stepfather, David Baldwin, a Pentecostal minister. He began writing as a child, but at 14 his literary interests were put on hold when he became a junior minister in a Harlem storefront church. Although Baldwin left the ministry and Christianity three years later, his writings reflected biblical cadences and imagery throughout his career.

In 1943, Baldwin's literary career began in earnest when the death of his stepfather and the outbreak of the Harlem riots within a 24-hour period spurred him to concentrate on his writing. During the winter of 1944–45, Baldwin met *Native Son* author Richard Wright, who became a mentor and helped him to win the 1945 Eugene Saxton Fellowship to allow him to write. Baldwin was soon

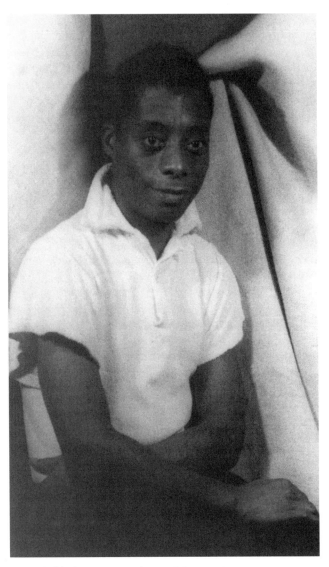

James Baldwin, 1955 *(Library of Congress)*

publishing essays and reviews in the *Nation, New Leader, Commentary,* and *Partisan Review.* In 1948, Baldwin won a Rosenwald Fellowship, which he used to travel to Paris, where he hoped to escape the racial and sexual prejudices that prevailed in the United States. Baldwin denied that he was an expatriate, referring to himself in his later years as a "transatlantic commuter," but he maintained his residency in France for the rest of his life.

In his early career, Baldwin saw himself primarily as a novelist, but his fiction's forthright portrayals of homosexuality disturbed many critics. In 1953, he published his first novel, *Go Tell It on the Mountain,* a partly autobiographical account of his teenage years that received widespread praise. But his later works of fiction received mixed reviews. In particular, the novels *Giovanni's Room* (1956) and

Another Country (1962), whose protagonists struggled to define sexual, racial, and national identities amidst frank depictions of homosexual relationships, drew criticism from inside and outside the Civil Rights movement. The latter work prompted a famous response from BLACK PANTHERS leader Eldridge Cleaver, who declared that the novel exposed Baldwin's "agonizing, total hatred of black people."

Baldwin's essays, however, which focused for the most part on race relations, won him critical acclaim as an astute and prophetic commentator on racial discrimination and identity. Pieces such as "Everybody's Protest Novel" (1949) and "Many Thousands Gone" (1951) established him as an important voice in the Civil Rights movement, though the criticism of Wright contained in the essays produced a lasting break between the two writers. Baldwin's most important collections of essays, *Notes of a Native Son* (1955), *Nobody Knows My Name* (1961), and *The Fire Next Time* (1963), were published as the Civil Rights movement exploded across the American South. As one critic explained, they "won Baldwin a popularity and acclaim as the 'conscience of the nation,'" whose "knife-edged criticism of the failed promises of American democracy, and the consequent social injustices, is unrelenting and demonstrates a piercing understanding of the function of blacks in the white racial imagination."

In 1957, Baldwin returned to the United States to take part directly in the Civil Rights movement, organizing protests, lecturing, and speaking out at forums while continuing to write. In America, the slow pace of change tempered his initial optimism. In his earlier essays, Baldwin called for reconciliation between whites and blacks, attributing racial prejudice to the insecurities of whites, who made scapegoats of African Americans to assuage their own feelings of powerlessness. In *The Fire Next Time*, however, Baldwin argued prophetically that American race relations were in danger of erupting into violence. Still, he concluded the essay with a note of optimism, suggesting that "if we [blacks and whites] do not falter in our duty now, we may be able . . . to end the racial nightmare, and achieve our country, and change the history of the world."

Despite increasing criticism from more radical, separatist civil rights leaders and a general lessening of interest in his work, Baldwin continued to write until his death. His other works included the plays *The Amen Corner* (1955) and *Blues for Mr. Charlie* (1964); the short story collection *Going to Meet the Man* (1965); the essay collections *No Name in the Street* (1972), *The Evidence of Things Not Seen* (1985), and *The Price of the Ticket: Collected Nonfiction, 1948–1985* (1985); and the novels *Tell Me How Long the Train's Been Gone* (1968), *If Beale Street Could Talk* (1974) and *Just Above My Head* (1979). When Baldwin died of stomach cancer in France, he was working on a play and a biography of MARTIN LUTHER KING, JR.

Further reading: James Campbell, *Talking at the Gates: A Life of James Baldwin* (New York: Viking, 1991); David Leeming, *James Baldwin: A Biography* (New York: H. Holt, 1995).

— Kevin D. Smith

Bay of Pigs

Located on the southern coast of Cuba, the Bay of Pigs marks the site of a failed invasion of Cuban exile forces trained by the CENTRAL INTELLIGENCE AGENCY (CIA) in April 1961. The operation was designed to overthrow the regime of Fidel Castro, considered a dangerous communist by the American government.

By the late 1950s, North Americans owned most of the mines, cattle ranches, and sugar plantations in Cuba and the U.S. government propped up the corrupt and dictatorial regime of General Fulgencio Batista. After a three-year campaign, a group of revolutionaries and peasants led by Fidel Castro marched into Havana and overthrew the Batista government on New Year's Day, 1959. Castro had received little help from the Cuban Communist Party during his struggle, although he soon took control of it. He launched his own brand of reform program that involved massive land redistribution, seizure of U.S.–owned oil companies, and confiscation of other privately owned firms. In response, President DWIGHT D. EISENHOWER halted American imports of Cuban sugar and cut off all trade to Cuba except for medicine and some food staples. Castro turned to Premier Nikita Khrushchev for economic assistance, and the Soviets bought increasing amounts of Cuban sugar. Convinced that Castro was a puppet of the Soviets and that this invasion was the first step toward communist control of the Caribbean, the Eisenhower administration prepared plans to overthrow the new Cuban leader.

CIA chief Allen Dulles dispatched agents to Guatemala to train a group of Cuban exiles to invade their homeland. The CIA believed that a small invasion force would trigger a large internal uprising, but it underestimated the depth of the Cuban public's support for Castro.

When JOHN F. KENNEDY became president and learned of the operation, he agreed to support it. He had made Cuba a major issue in the 1960 campaign by criticizing the Eisenhower administration for "losing" a country in America's backyard to the communists. Kennedy had promised to take action against Castro and believed that his political credibility was at stake. Like Eisenhower, Kennedy also subscribed to the domino theory and argued that if Castro was not defeated, he would launch a series of leftist revolutions culminating in the communization of LATIN AMERICA. He overestimated the degree of Cuban interference in the internal affairs of its neighbors, at least at that time. Because he viewed COMMU-

NISM as a monolithic movement, Kennedy thought of Cuba as a Soviet satellite, a picture that was not entirely accurate. Castro approved all Soviet decisions about economic or military aid to Cuba. Kennedy's view of Castro contributed to his decision to approve the invasion, named Operation Zapata.

Concerned about American prestige, Kennedy wanted to hide U.S. involvement as much as possible. Less than a month before the invasion, he revised the plan so that the landing site was more isolated and the landing would occur at night. He also inserted a stipulation that there would be no direct U.S. military participation, including air cover. These changes proved to be disastrous.

The invasion began on April 17, 1961, and in less than two days it was over. Of the more than 1,450 men, 114 died and the rest were captured and imprisoned. Because the Bay of Pigs is a swampy area, easily cut off from the rest of the island, Castro's army quickly surrounded the invasion force and sank the ship transporting the reserve ammunition. Even if the commandos had somehow managed to

evade Castro's forces, they would have had to cross the wetlands to reach the Escambray Mountains where they were supposed to meet up with internal anti-Castro allies, recoup their losses, and launch guerrilla operations from the mountainsides. More critical, the expedition failed to trigger an internal uprising. The exile army's fate was sealed when Kennedy canceled a planned second strike by American planes. Eventually, Kennedy authorized a payment of $53 million in pharmaceuticals and food to the Cuban government in exchange for the release of the surviving prisoners.

The CIA's role in the operation soon became public knowledge and the United States suffered international condemnation. Although Kennedy publicly accepted sole responsibility for the invasion, he privately believed that his advisers had failed him and that the CIA and the military had misled him. He shook up the CIA, replacing Dulles with John McCone, and rearranged the national security bureaucracy to have more authority in the White House. The Kennedy administration also intensified its campaign

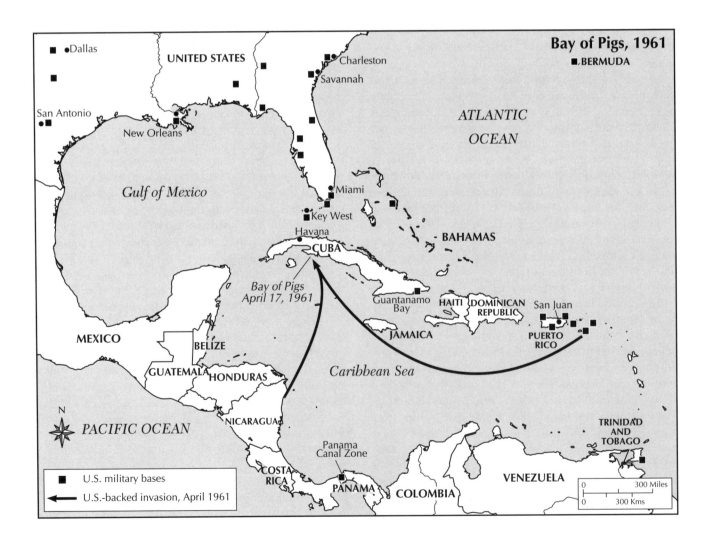

against the Cuban government by tightening the economic blockade and instituting OPERATION MONGOOSE, an inter-agency task force designed to overthrow the Castro regime by fomenting discord, sabotaging economic targets in Cuba, and, if necessary, assassinating Castro himself. These covert operations led Castro to seek military assistance from the SOVIET UNION, precipitating the CUBAN MISSILE CRISIS in 1962.

Further reading: Peter Wyden, *Bay of Pigs* (New York: Simon & Schuster, 1979).

— Jennifer Walton

Beat Generation

The Beat Generation was a group of poets, authors, and artists who challenged and actively rebelled against the homogenization of American culture in the 1950s. Led by writers William S. Burroughs, ALLEN GINSBERG, and JACK KEROUAC, the group's defiant need to reject the predomi-nant status quo, personified by uninhibited drug experi-mentation, helped sow the seeds of a COUNTERCULTURE that came into its own during the mid to late 1960s.

In 1944, Ginsberg, a student at Columbia University, and Kerouac, a former Columbia student, met Burroughs through their mutual friend Lucien Carr. Although they were a study in differences—Ginsberg was Jewish, a rather awkward and unassuming intellectual, Kerouac was a Catholic French-Canadian, attending Columbia on a foot-ball scholarship, and Burroughs was a polished upper-class Anglo-Saxon Protestant whose connections in New York's underworld helped support a rabid drug habit—they soon became fast friends and moved into a communal apartment in the city.

The three became part of a larger Bohemian commu-nity later christened by Kerouac as the Beats. It included John Clellon Holmes, whose 1952 work *Go* was the first true Beat novel, Gary Snyder, a naturalist thought of as his era's Henry David Thoreau, and Gregory Corso, the Beat poet considered second only to Ginsberg. Enjoying the sex-ual and cultural freedom of New York's Greenwich Vil-lage—both Burroughs and Ginsberg were openly gay—the group held a passion for living life raw and free, happily rejecting the affluence and passive accommodation of the Truman and Eisenhower eras. More important, these men were writers who desperately wanted to capture their emotions and experiences using the most nakedly honest words possible.

Kerouac, the man who many felt personified the Beats, was driven by a need to record the unpolished pace of a truly free life filled with action and adventure. Unsuccess-ful with the 1950 publication of his traditional novel *The Town and the City,* Kerouac shifted gears in 1951, writing

On the Road in three weeks on one long roll of typing paper. At first Kerouac's masterpiece, based on travels in the West he took with friend Neal Cassady, amounted to a single extended paragraph with little punctuation; it remained unpublished until 1957. Ginsberg's 1955 free-form poem, *Howl,* which continued Kerouac's stream-of-consciousness style, was the first Beat success story. The considerable clout Ginsberg gained from *Howl* allowed him to promote the works of his friends.

Just as *Howl* and *On the Road* broke new ground in both form and content, Burroughs's novel, *Naked Lunch,* published in 1962, was one of the most innovative works of Beat literature. Devoid of a single protagonist and stub-bornly nonlinear in its style and plot, the book took most of its material from Burroughs's travels through South Amer-ica and North Africa on a quest mainly for men and more potent drugs. Critics took Burroughs, like they did Gins-berg for *Howl,* to court on charges of obscenity.

By the late 1950s, the Beats were too well known and well read to be restrained by lawsuits or even bad reviews. As these men moved about the country, the movement spread to San Francisco as well as Kansas City and Chicago, and it reached college campuses nation-wide. *On the Road, Howl,* and other Beat works quickly became a clarion call to a vast subculture of devoted fol-lowers. Their adoption of the slang of urban blacks (including words like "dig," "hip," "square," "swing," "cool," and "man") led novelist Norman Mailer in 1957 to reflect on the social connection in his essay, "The White Negro." Notorious for crowding into nightclubs to read poetry in the style of their heroes, the group also received the title of "Beatniks" and were precursors of the hippies of the 1960s.

As the counterculture emerged, Ginsberg took his newfound celebrity in stride, quickly becoming the Beats' most prominent spokesman, befriending such 1960s icons as Ken Kesey, TIMOTHY LEARY, and BOB DYLAN. Kerouac, at heart a rather conservative man, was discouraged by the attention his writing received as a blueprint for rebellion. He withdrew from his friends and turned instead to alco-hol, living in seclusion in Florida. In the 1960s, he pub-lished a few books on Buddhism, particularly *The Dharma Bums,* which helped to popularize the religion during the period. By 1969, however, embittered that his life never truly lived up to his myth, he died of internal hemorrhaging brought on by his alcoholism. With Kerouac gone and Cas-sady dead a year earlier, the Beats, overtaken by a more mainstream counterculture they helped to create, faded into relative obscurity.

Both Ginsberg and Burroughs enjoyed long careers that lasted well into the 1990s, reuniting in 1982 with almost all of their Beat colleagues to celebrate the 25th anniversary of *On the Road.* Ginsberg died at 70 of liver cancer in April 1997, and Burroughs died, at 83, of natural causes in August of the same year.

Further reading: Bruce Cook, *The Beat Generation* (New York: Quill, 1971, 1994); Edward Halsey Foster, *Understanding The Beats* (Columbia: University of South Carolina Press, 1992); John Tytell, *Paradise Outlaws: Remembering the Beats* (New York: William Morrow, 1999).

— Adam B. Vary

Beatles

A British ROCK AND ROLL band, the Beatles brought their music and their enigmatic personalities to America in the 1960s and became a voice for COUNTERCULTURE youth.

The Beatles were formed in 1957 by John Lennon, Paul McCartney, and George Harrison in Liverpool, England. In 1962, the group replaced then drummer Pete Best with Ringo Starr (Richard Starkey), uniting the quartet that revolutionized popular MUSIC in the 1960s. The band went through several name changes, including the "Quarrymen," "Johnny and the Moondogs" and the "Silver Beetles," before settling on "Beatles," a name (and spelling) that came to Lennon in a dream. Influenced by American rock and roll musicians of the late 1950s, the Beatles' early repertoire included Carl Perkins, Chuck Berry, and Buddy Holly songs.

The group gained popularity in England by playing clubs such as the Cavern, a local Liverpool nightspot, as they sang their own songs composed primarily by Lennon and McCartney. The upbeat melodies, harmony vocals, and simple lyrics that characterized early Beatles's songs such as "Love Me Do," "P.S. I Love You," and "Please Please Me," combined with the high-spirited personalities and boyish good looks of the band members, propelled the Beatles to

Ed Sullivan and the Beatles   *(Library of Congress)*

stardom in England. By 1963, crowds of hysterical fans thronged Beatles' performances attempting to catch a glimpse of the foursome and "Beatlemania" was born. That same year, their single, "From Me to You," went to number one on the British charts, followed by "She Loves You," which became the biggest-selling single in British history.

Yet in the United States, the "Fab Four" continued to remain relatively unknown. It was not until February 7, 1964, that the Beatles stepped off a plane at New York's Kennedy Airport and stepped into American POPULAR CULTURE history. Their February 9, 1964, appearance on "The Ed Sullivan Show" marked the first time most Americans got a glimpse of the band, and proved to be a watershed moment in TELEVISION history. Seventy-three million people tuned in to watch the Beatles perform five songs, shattering the previous record for the largest American television viewing audience. Their mop-topped heads, clean-cut appearance, and cheeky sense of humor won over American audiences, catapulting the Beatles into mainstream culture in a short time.

An aggressive merchandising campaign brought Beatles wigs, clothes, and dolls to the market, and fans flocked to stores to buy the latest Beatles magazine or album. In April 1964, the band held the top five positions on *Billboard* magazine's singles chart with "Can't Buy Me Love," "Twist and Shout," "She Loves You," "I Want to Hold Your Hand," and "Please Please Me." The Beatles quickly became four of the most recognizable men in America. When John Lennon commented in 1966 that the Beatles were "more popular than Jesus Christ," the tarnish from their popularity faded momentarily, but their resilient nature outlasted the bonfires some outraged fans lighted to destroy their Beatles albums.

While delighted with their early recording efforts, the Beatles experimented with innovative sounds and more complex lyrical arrangements in later works. Their album *Sgt. Pepper's Lonely Hearts Club Band* (1967), considered by many to be the first concept album, incorporated elements of electronically altered sounds, exotic instruments, and enigmatic musical verse. Songs such as "Lucy in the Sky with Diamonds" and "A Day in the Life" were carefully examined by listeners for hidden messages and meanings. The Beatles extended their creative talents to MOVIES, a form they had explored previously with the release of *A Hard Day's Night* (1964) and *Help!* (1965), producing *Magical Mystery Tour* (1967), a film panned by critics but representative of their creative talents and manifold countercultural influences. A brief encounter with transcendental meditation and the Maharishi Mahesh Yogi influenced their musical style, as Indian rhythms and instruments combined with experimental electronic sounds to create innovative music. Albums produced in this period, *The Beatles* (referred to as the White Album) (1968), *Abbey*

Road (1969), and *Let It Be* (1970) reflected the band's ability to expand the scope of its musical style, and influenced a generation of musicians who tried to copy its sound and techniques.

The Beatles broke up in 1970 and each member pursued a career in music, either as a solo act or with other bands. While all found success in their endeavors, rumors of a Beatles reunion persisted until the shooting death of John Lennon on December 8, 1980, outside his New York City apartment building. The Beatles were inducted into the Rock and Roll Hall of Fame in 1988.

Further reading: Walter Everett, *The Beatles as Musicians: Revolver through the Anthology* (New York: Oxford University Press, 1999); Michael Bryan Kelly, *The Beatle Myth: The British Invasion of American Popular Music, 1956–1969* (Jefferson, N.C.: McFarland, 1991).

— Susan V. Spellman

Berlin blockade

The Soviet blockade of West Berlin, and the subsequent allied airlift that supplied the beleaguered city, signaled the first major crisis of the COLD WAR.

Following the surrender of Nazi Germany in May 1945, the United States, Great Britain, the SOVIET UNION, and later France, divided the vanquished nation into four occupation zones, with each responsible for administering its own zone. Deeply embedded in the Soviet zone, Berlin was treated as a special case because of its symbolic significance as the former capital of the Third Reich, and was also split into four parts. These divisions were intended to be a temporary military measure with the eventual goal of rebuilding a unified, neutral Germany. During the years immediately following the war, however, schisms appeared in the relationship between the occupying powers, rendering powerless such organs of unity as the Allied Control Council (the Council created to head a unified Germany) and the Kommandatura (the similar body intended for coordinated control of Berlin).

By 1948, international events had elevated tensions between the United States and the Soviet Union to the breaking point. In Germany, the American and Soviet occupying forces crossed swords over virtually every issue. The once mutually agreed upon goal of creating a unified neutral Germany was cast aside, as both the Americans and the Soviets sought to implement their own programs. Fearing the revival of a strong Germany, the Soviet Union maintained a punishing reparations program geared toward ensuring the continued weakness of the German people. Believing that this program would prevent Western European recovery, the United States, along with Great Britain and France, sought to rehabilitate West Germany. These strategic differences eventually culminated in the blockade of Berlin.

The final straw was the American effort to introduce currency reform in the Western occupation zones. Americans perceived the currency reform as a necessary measure to restore stability to the Western zone, whereas Soviets believed currency reform to signal the West determination to rebuild West Germany and permanently divide the Germans. From March to June 1948, the Soviets progressively closed off access to Berlin. On June 24, the Soviet Union announced that four-power administration of the city had ended and suspended all land traffic from the West into Berlin. Faced with this provocation, the administration of HARRY S. TRUMAN considered a number of options. Offered everything from bombing Soviet troops to sending an armored column to Berlin in defiance of the Soviet decree, Truman ultimately decided upon a more flexible and less hostile airlift.

On June 26, the United States and Great Britain began to supply West Berlin with food and other vital supplies by air. Although it began slowly at first, the airlift became increasingly efficient under the direction of General Curtis Lemay. The airlift kept Berlin supplied for 11 months until the Soviet Union lifted the blockade on May 12, 1949. Together, the United States and Great Britain made 300,000 flights along just three air corridors. The airlift delivered 2,323,738 tons of food, fuel, machinery, and other supplies at a total cost of $224,000,000. The Soviet Union ultimately lifted the blockade because it failed to drive the Western powers out of Berlin, induced the West to initiate an embargo on all strategic exports to the Eastern Bloc, and sullied the Soviets' hard-won international prestige.

The blockade hastened the establishment of the Federal Republic of Germany, spurred the creation of the NORTH ATLANTIC TREATY ORGANIZATION (NATO), and solidified the division of Berlin, Germany, EUROPE, and the world. The Berlin Blockade also helped transform the perception of Germans in the West. The ostensible courage of West Berliners in standing firm in the face of Soviet intimidation and stoically enduring months of difficult living conditions helped convince Americans that West Germans were dependable democrats and not nascent Nazis.

Further reading: Thomas Parrish. *Berlin in the Balance: The Blockade, the Airlift, the First Major Battle of the Cold War* (Reading, Mass.: Addison-Wesley, 1998); Ann Tusa and John Tusa, *The Berlin Blockade* (London: Hodder and Stoughton, 1988).

— Brian Etheridge

Birmingham (Alabama) confrontation

The Birmingham confrontation, launched by the SOUTH-ERN CHRISTIAN LEADERSHIP CONFERENCE (SCLC) and MARTIN LUTHER KING, JR., in 1963, was a major effort to force desegregation in one of the most racially divided cities in the United States.

In spring 1963, the Reverend Fred Shuttlesworth invited King and the SCLC to Birmingham. Many civil rights activists nicknamed the city "Bombingham" because the metropolis was the site of 18 unsolved bombings in black neighborhoods and a vicious mob attack on people involved in the FREEDOM RIDES to desegregate interstate transportation on Mother's Day, 1961. King had come to Birmingham in the midst of political upheaval in the city GOVERNMENT. Voters had decided to eliminate the three-man city commission and instead elect a mayor. This was done to force Eugene "Bull" Connor, the commissioner of public safety and the man responsible for the attack on the freedom riders, to step down. Connor refused to leave, however, and Birmingham housed two city administrations until the courts could adjudicate the matter.

During this time of political turmoil, the SCLC decided to launch "Project C" (for Confrontation). On April 3, 1963, "B Day" (for Birmingham), the SCLC staged SIT-INS. On April 6, police arrested 45 protestors who were marching from the Sixteenth Street Baptist Church to City Hall. The next day, Palm Sunday, even more protestors were arrested and two police dogs attacked 19-year-old protester Leroy Allen. In response to the protests, Judge W. A. Jenkins, Jr., issued an order preventing 133 of the city's civil rights leaders, King, and his fellow SCLC leaders Ralph Abernathy and Shuttlesworth from organizing more demonstrations in the city. "Project C," however, planned for King to be arrested on April 12, Good Friday. King did manage to get himself arrested and he was placed in solitary confinement. While in jail, King read an advertisement in the *Birmingham News,* taken out by white ministers, calling him a troublemaker. He responded by writing in the margins of the newspaper and on toilet paper a long essay that was published as his famous "Letter from Birmingham Jail": "While confined here in the Birmingham City Jail, I came across your recent statement calling our present activities "unwise and untimely." . . . Frankly I have yet to engage in a direct action movement that was 'well timed' in the view of those who have not suffered unduly from the disease of segregation."

King was released from the city jail on April 20. While he was in jail, the SCLC planned "D Day," which was to include demonstrations by children. On May 2, children ranging in age from six to 18 gathered at Kelly Ingram Park, and around 1 P.M., 15 of the children began to march downtown singing "We Shall Overcome." The children were arrested and put into police vans. In the same manner, children left the park in groups and were arrested by the police. Three hours later, the police had arrested 959 children and put them in jail. The next day, over a thousand children stayed out of school and gathered again in Kelly Igram Park. "Bull" Connor was determined not to let the children march downtown, but he had no room left in the jails for them. Instead, he ordered firefighters out and turned hoses that shot water at high pressure at the children. The water was strong enough to break bones and many of the protesters rolled down the street as the water hit them. In addition, Connor also ordered police dogs to attack protesters as they tried to enter the Sixteenth Street Baptist Church, which was located across the street from the park. Reporters took pictures of the confrontation and the media portrayed the horror of children being attacked by dogs and high-pressure fire hoses.

The demonstrations only escalated and the jails became more overcrowded. On May 12, 1963, the home of King's brother was bombed along with the A. G. Gaston Motel, which served as black integrationist headquarters. With the escalating violence, President JOHN F. KENNEDY ordered the National Guard to Birmingham and federalized the Alabama National Guard to bring order to the city. Finally, the BUSINESS community in Birmingham agreed to integrate lunch counters and hire more African Americans over the objections of city officials.

Further reading: Dan T. Carter, *The Politics of Rage* (Baton Rouge: Louisiana State University Press, 2000).
— Sarah Brenner

Black Panthers

Dedicated to the improvement of the African-American community, the Black Panthers' commitment to armed self-defense and revolutionary politics led to violent conflicts with local, state, and national authorities.

The Black Panthers were formed on October 15, 1966, in Oakland, California, by Huey P. Newton and Bobby Seale. Students at Merritt College in Oakland, Newton and Seale were heavily influenced by the teachings of black activist MALCOLM X. In forming the Black Panthers, both men advocated the arming of the black community for self-defense.

Members of the Black Panthers were easily identified by their uniform, which consisted of a black beret, black pants, a powder blue shirt, black shoes, and a black leather jacket. As slogans the Panthers often proclaimed "Power to the People" and "Off the Pigs," referring to the overthrowing of police authority. The symbol of the panther was adopted from the Lowndes County Freedom Party in Alabama. It was chosen because the Panther never attacks unless cornered, and the African-American community of the 1960s felt cornered.

The founding of the Black Panthers reflected a major shift in the African-American struggle for equality and justice from a national to an international focus. The African-

American community began to look toward those African nations that used force to gain independence from colonial powers, and they saw a need for a more militant approach to gaining equality. They also questioned the legitimacy of the existing social, economic, and political systems more actively in the 1960s.

Newton and Seale created a 10-point program called "What We Want," which reflected a new nationalist thrust aimed at the average African American, not a black member of the middle class. The "What We Want" program called for freedom, full employment, the end of white destruction of the black community, decent housing, and equal EDUCATION. It also demanded exemption for all African Americans from military service and called for an end to police brutality and murder. The Panthers further demanded freedom for African Americans from federal, state, county, and city prisons, and for all African Americans to be tried by a jury of other African Americans. Newton and Seale said "We want land, bread, housing, education, clothing, justice, and peace." The 10-point program reflected influences of revolutionaries such as Malcolm X, Frantz Fanon, the Chinese dictator Mao Zedong, and Argentinian revolutionary Che Guevara. Newton saw himself as the heir to Malcolm X, and the Black Panthers as a continuation of Malcolm's Afro-American Unity organization.

The Panthers attempted a coalition with the STUDENT NONVIOLENT COORDINATING COMMITTEE (SNCC) in 1968, and it appeared that an alliance had been forged at a rally in February 1968. Due to differences between the two groups and interference on the part of the Federal Bureau of Investigation (FBI), the alliance was never brought to fruition. Members of SNCC believed that the Black Panther organization was too militant and sexist and they did not want to accept the Panther's 10-point program. The FBI also began calling SNCC leaders and their families, threatening them in the name of the Black Panthers.

From the years 1967 to 1970, Huey P. Newton was imprisoned, leaving Eldridge Cleaver as the main ideological figurehead of the Black Panthers. Cleaver began pushing alliances with white militant organizations, causing ideological disagreements with the imprisoned Newton. The Panthers no longer spoke of self-defense against police, but rather they began advocating the increased use of unprovoked attacks on police. Cleaver took the Black Panthers in a more openly revolutionary direction from the reformist position Newton envisioned.

Between 1968 and 1969, violence between the Panthers and police escalated due to Cleaver's increased emphasis on the use of guns. On April 6, 1968, police killed Panther leader Bobby Hutton in a shootout. During this period, J. EDGAR HOOVER and the FBI named the Black Panthers as the most dangerous black "extremist" organization in America. The FBI used counterintelligence pro-

Poster for the Black Panther Party   *(Library of Congress)*

grams against the Panthers. The goal of these programs was to destroy the Panthers from the inside as well as the outside. The FBI fabricated and distributed fake propaganda, created front groups, and gave misinformation. The violence of the period reached its peak in Chicago on December 4, 1969, when Black Panther members Fred Hampton and Mark Clark were murdered during a police raid.

Beginning in 1969, the Black Panthers began a major reorganization at both national and local levels. This reorganization became public by 1971 when the Panthers officially expelled Cleaver in the February 20 issue of the *Black Panther*, the organization's newspaper.

Despite many internal and external struggles, the Black Panthers were one of the first organizations to forge new post–civil rights agendas and tactics in the struggle to gain equality for the African-American community.

Further reading: Charles E. Jones, *The Black Panther Party Reconsidered* (Baltimore: Black Classic Press, 1998);

Jennifer B. Smith, *An International History of the Black Panther Party* (New York: Garland, 1999).

— Sarah Brenner

Black Power

Coined by STOKELY CARMICHAEL on a march in Greenwood, Mississippi, in 1966, the phrase Black Power constituted an African-American call-to-action in cultural, racial, and political spheres.

In 1966, the mainstream Civil Rights movement lost much of its momentum. Following the passage of the CIVIL RIGHTS ACT OF 1964 and the VOTING RIGHTS ACT OF 1965, many of the original goals of the movement had been achieved. Yet racism and discrimination persisted, and young African-American radicals continued pressing for further change. One such activist was Stokely Carmichael, the head of the STUDENT NONVIOLENT COORDINATING COMMITTEE (SNCC). Carmichael had become disenchanted with the notions of nonviolence as a tactic in the struggle for civil rights. As civil rights workers sometimes faced deadly violence, he felt they had to respond. Furthermore, he believed that integration as a goal was "a subterfuge for the maintenance of white supremacy."

Following his arrest for trying to erect a tent city on an African-American school playground for SNCC supporters, Carmichael reached the breaking point. Addressing those in attendance at the Greenwood march about his arrest in the African-American schoolyard, he said, "Everybody owns our neighborhoods except us. . . . Now we're going to get something and we're going to get some representing. We ain't going to worry about whether it's white-maybe black. Don't be ashamed. We been saying 'Freedom' for six years and we ain't got nothin.' What we gonna start saying now is Black Power!" Carmichael believed that Black Power meant "smashing everything Western Civilization has created." In addition to his opposition to integration, Carmichael also advocated the need for African Americans to take power for themselves, both politically and culturally. Perhaps the most important aspect of this call-to-arms was the notion that African Americans needed to take pride in their blackness.

Following Carmichael's proclamation, the notion of Black Power spread like wildfire. On the West Coast in October 1966, two African Americans in Oakland, California, founded the BLACK PANTHERS, a paramilitary organization. The group advocated the expansion of Black Power ideals. It sought self-determination for the African-American community, better housing, better education, and an end to police brutality. Black Panther members donned black leather jackets and black berets as symbols of unity, and they carried firearms.

The Black Power slogan was a perfect way for militant young African Americans to express their frustration with the nonviolent, church-based movement of MARTIN LUTHER KING, JR. These young radicals wished to mold their communities into strong, cohesive units that reflected their racial consciousness. Politically they wanted nothing to do with patronizing white liberals, who had been active in the movement in the past.

The Black Power movement had a significant impact upon the AFRICAN-AMERICAN MOVEMENT as a whole. Soon African Americans were highlighting the black aesthetic in the arts and literature. Many African Americans adopted a natural "Afro" look, leaving complex hair-straightening techniques behind. Many individuals chose to wear traditional African clothing and use a traditional black dialect. The terms *black* and *Afro-American* took the place of *Negro* in referring to African Americans.

The extent of the Black Power movement found its way into the world of SPORTS as well. At the 1968 Summer

Poster showing John Carlos and Tommie Smith bowing their heads and raising their black-gloved fists in the air, a traditional symbol of Black Power, at the 1968 Summer Olympic games in Mexico   *(Library of Congress)*

Olympic games in Mexico City, African-American sprinters Tommie Smith and John Carlos lowered their heads and raised black-gloved fists as the "Star-Spangled Banner" played during the medal ceremony. A traditional symbol of Black Power, the act aroused both pride in some circles and anger in others.

With all of the positive aspects the Black Power movement brought to African Americans, it had its setbacks as well. Although the movement proclaimed to want to help all African Americans, women were often left out of the picture. When asked about the role of women, Stokely Carmichael once remarked with a sexual allusion as he declared that "the only position for women in SNCC is prone." African-American women, angered by that statement, became increasingly involved in the black feminist movement. Meanwhile, the Black Power movement horrified white America, which still clung to hopes of nonviolence. In the end, the Black Power movement lost political momentum in the 1970s, but it left a legacy of cultural pride.

Further reading: Stokely Carmichael and Charles V. Hamilton, *Black Power: The Politics of Liberation in America* (New York: Random House, 1967); William L. Van Deburg, *New Day in Babylon: The Black Power Movement and American Culture, 1965–1975* (Chicago: University of Chicago Press; 1992).

— Clayton Douglas

braceros

Providing agricultural labor, the braceros were Mexican workers (literally "arms" in Spanish) imported by the U.S. government during the mid-20th century.

As early as 1942, as the United States plunged into World War II, critical labor shortages threatened farm production. In response to this dilemma, the U.S. government arranged for braceros to work in the fields. Between 1942 and 1947, these workers made the difference between lost production and harvested crops first in the Southwest and then in other parts of the nation. With immense pressure on an already labor-starved agricultural economy due to the war, the program became institutionalized among many farms across the nation.

In these early years of the program, braceros signed contracts in Mexico and then migrated to American farms to assist in crop cultivation and harvesting. During the period between 1942 and 1947, more than 20,000 braceros entered the United States, working on farms in 24 states, with the most employed in California. Other Mexicans, however, pejoratively called "wetbacks," a name given to those who swam the Rio Grande, entered the United States illegally. The initial group consisted of both legal and illegal

workers at the mercy of an oppressive labor system and unable to look out for themselves.

Between 1948 and 1951, the original bracero agreement devolved into the Mexican Labor Program. With government interference declining, the primary contractor was no longer the U.S. government, but rather the individual American farmer who now had more responsibility than before. The employer alone bore the cost of transporting the worker from his Mexican home into the United States, and then back again to Mexico at the end of the contracted time. Between 1948 and 1950, farmers imported more than 200,000 legally contracted braceros into the United States.

On July 12, 1951, however, the program changed again. Congress established a precedent by granting specific legislative authority for contracting this foreign labor on a government-to-government basis. President HARRY S. TRUMAN signed a joint resolution on August 16, 1951, to fund the bracero program, yet he hoped that "Congress would comply with his recommendations for strengthening the program's penalty provisions," thereby complying with the Mexican government's position stating that "either punitive legislation aimed at halting the wetback flow would be enacted by Congress, or there would be no *bracero* program." The Mexican government feared losing its own laborers. The "wetback bill," signed by Truman on March 20, 1952, made it "a felony punishable by fine not exceeding two thousand dollars or by imprisonment for not more than five years, or both, to aid anyone entering the country illegally or harboring or concealing [an] illegal entrant."

The period from 1952 to 1959 helped stabilize the bracero program. While continually negotiating compromises and amendments that improved arrangements for both the workers and the farmers, the two governments repeatedly extended the program. In a compromise document signed in 1954, the program was extended to December 31, 1955, under specific conditions that declared that the American secretary of labor determined wages, although the Mexican government retained the right to request a review. Furthermore, the bracero had the benefit of both nonoccupational and occupational insurance. Both the U.S. and Mexican governments determined places of unacceptable employment, and the Mexican government set up a new recruitment depot. Finally, employers were not required to pay full transportation and subsistence cost if the contract was not completed by their hired bracero; only payment in proportion to services rendered by the bracero was required. During this time a push for unionization of migrant farm workers began. Drives to unionize the braceros started in the 1960s, due in part to the efforts of César Chávez, a migrant farm worker and organizer of the National Farm Workers Association.

Following a period of congressional hearings and rising Senate opposition, the bracero program was terminated on December 31, 1964. The acceleration of agriculture mechanization, increasing uneasiness about the morality of the bracero program, and mounting burdens associated with bracero contracting, coupled with growing frustration among farm groups with the administration of the program, contributed to the end of the 22-year-long Mexican labor program.

Further reading: Richard Craig, *The Bracero Program* (London: University of Texas Press, 1971); Ernesto Galarza, *Merchants of Labor: The Mexican Bracero Story; An Account of the Managed Migration of Mexican Farmworkers in California, 1942–1960* (Santa Barbara, Calif.: McNally & Loftin, 1964).

— Susan F. Yates

Bridges, Harry   See Volume VIII

Brown Berets   See Young Chicanos for Community Action

Brown v. Board of Education (1954)

One of the most important Supreme Court decisions of the 20th century, *Brown v. Board of Education* desegregated schools, reversing the Court's 1896 decision in *Plessy v. Ferguson.*

Plessy had established the "separate but equal" principle, which allowed individual states to provide separate public facilities for blacks as long as the facilities were equal to those provided for whites. The court thus decided that Jim Crow laws—state-mandated statutes establishing racial SEGREGATION in public accommodations and education—did not violate the Fourteenth Amendment's Equal Protection Clause. *Plessy* also declared that using separate facilities carried with it "no badge of inferiority." Southern states used the ruling to further entrench Jim Crow.

Brown marked the culmination of a decades-long litigation campaign against racial segregation organized by the NATIONAL ASSOCIATION FOR THE ADVANCEMENT OF COLORED PEOPLE (NAACP) and its legal arm, the NAACP Legal Defense and Education Fund. Filing suits in state and federal courts, which challenged Jim Crow, the NAACP's strategy was to chip away at the *Plessy* decision. By the early 1950s, the NAACP had secured several major victories against segregation, including *Shelley v. Kraemer* (1948) in which the Court declared that restrictive covenants were unconstitutional, and *Sweatt v. Painter* (1950), which rejected segregation in law schools.

After these successful precedents, the NAACP fought segregation in public elementary and secondary schools, fil-

ing suits against school boards across the nation. A Kansas suit involved Oliver Brown, a black minister who wanted to enroll his young daughter Linda in a public elementary school located just blocks from his home. The Topeka school board refused since a state segregation law required black children to attend an all-black school located across town. Brown, backed by the NAACP, sought relief. By 1952, the Supreme Court had agreed to hear Brown's case combined with four others involving segregated public education in Delaware, South Carolina, Virginia, and Washington, D.C.

Led by THURGOOD MARSHALL, NAACP lawyers argued in *Brown* that separate schools could never be equal, regardless of the comparative quality of the facilities, and that segregated schools violated the Fourteenth Amendment. They used social scientific evidence to show that segregation socially and psychologically handicapped black children. In a series of studies conducted by psychologists Kenneth and Mamie Clark, northern and southern black children were shown two dolls—one black, one white—and asked which doll they liked. The Clarks found that a preponderance of the black children preferred the white doll. When asked which doll was most like them, many children became upset when they chose the black doll they had rejected. The Clarks concluded that black children, especially those educated under Jim Crow, had internalized a sense of inferiority. These tests and other social science data served as proof that school segregation in itself was damaging. The NAACP lawyers urged the court to consider these deeper negative effects of segregation.

Prominent constitutional lawyer John W. Davis represented the school boards. He argued that the Fourteenth Amendment did not apply to segregation in public schools. Davis also denied that the court had the power to force desegregation in school systems on the basis of controversial sociological evidence.

The court was leaning toward desegregation by mid 1953, but members remained undecided on the question of relief. During this stalemate, Chief Justice Fred Vinson died. He was replaced by EARL WARREN, who ended the stalemate by calling for rearguments and suggesting that a separate opinion be handed down regarding relief.

On May 17, 1954, the Supreme Court unanimously struck down *Plessy*'s separate but equal doctrine, outlawing segregated public schools. In the Court's opinion, Warren cited social science evidence and wrote that "separate educational facilities are inherently unequal" and were responsible for a "feeling of inferiority" in black children "as to their status in the community that may affect their hearts and minds in a way unlikely ever to be undone." Therefore, the Court ruled that segregation in public schools denied blacks equal protection as guaranteed under the Fourteenth Amendment. This decision is referred to as *Brown I.* In 1955, after rearguments, the Court handed down *Brown II,* which dealt with implementation. In this second decision, the justices set no firm deadlines or guidelines for desegregation. Instead, *Brown II* equivocally called for communities to desegregate their schools "with all deliberate speed."

After *Brown,* school desegregation proceeded slowly and met with resistance. While some communities quickly complied with *Brown,* many segregationists used violence or other means to prevent integration. In 1957 in Little Rock, Arkansas, Governor ORVAL FAUBUS barred nine black students from Central High School. President DWIGHT D. EISENHOWER reluctantly sent federal troops to protect the black students' rights. Meanwhile, civil rights activists fought for integration in public facilities. *Brown* did not end the school desegregation battle; enforcement issues were debated in the nation's courts into the 1970s.

Further reading: Waldo E. Martin, Jr., ed. *Brown v. Board of Education: A Brief History with Documents* (New York: Bedford/St. Martin's, 1998); James T. Patterson, *Brown v. Board of Education: A Civil Rights Milestone and Its Troubled Legacy* (New York: Oxford University Press, 2001).

— Lori Creed

Bunche, Ralph (1904–1971)

Serving his country in a variety of areas, Ralph Bunche was a political scientist, government official, and United Nations official, who won the Nobel Peace Prize in 1950 for mediating the conflict between Israel and Arab countries.

Born in Detroit, Michigan, on August 7, 1904, Bunche was the descendant of both African Americans and Native American Indians. Orphaned at the age of 13, he moved to Los Angeles, California, and into the care of his maternal grandmother. He worked his way through the University of California at Los Angeles and graduated summa cum laude in 1927. During these years, Bunche developed an interest in race relations. He earned a Ph.D. from Harvard in government and international relations in 1934. Following graduation, Bunche became chief assistant from 1938 to 1940 to Gunnar Myrdal, the Swedish sociologist who wrote a study on African Americans titled *An American Dilemma.*

During World War II, Bunche worked in the Office of Strategic Services as a senior social science analyst and expert on colonial areas and peoples. He then moved to the State Department in 1944, and, in 1946, he joined the Trusteeship Council of the United Nations (UN), an organization he helped establish. As problems developed in the Middle East, Bunche, now a member of the UN Secretariat, flew to Palestine in 1947 and formed the Palestine

Dr. Kwame Nkrumah, prime minister of Ghana (right), chats with United Nations official Ralph Bunche, 1958 *(Library of Congress)*

Implementation Commission to partition Israel and Palestine. As the first Arab-Israeli war broke out following the establishment of the state of Israel, the then acting chief mediator, Count Folke Bernadotte, was assassinated. Bunche took on the position of mediator himself. By negotiating separately with Israel and each Arab country, Bunche exercised extreme patience and diplomatic skills in breaking down resistance to peace and pushing for compromise. Following months of 18- to 20-hour days, an armistice was signed. For his work in mediation, Bunche received the Nobel Peace Prize in 1950, the first black man to do so.

Bunche faced difficulties during the anticommunist crusade of the 1950s. A loyalty investigation, under the authority of Henry Cabot Lodge, the ambassador representing the United States at the United Nations, and executed by the Federal Bureau of Investigation (FBI), began in 1953. Later, the administration of DWIGHT D. EISENHOWER created the International Organizations Employees Loyalty Board to continue the investigation. When it came to public attention in May 1954 that Bunche was under investigation, Eisenhower sent Maxwell Rabb, a presidential assistant, to warn Bunche and offer support. Bunche, however, chose to stand alone at the hearing, as two ex-communist witnesses who had worked for the Justice Department accused him of having communist connections. After two days of testimony, Bunche was unanimously cleared of all charges.

Serving as deputy secretary general of the United Nations, Bunche held the highest position by an American in the organization. Much of his work in the 1950s involved settling continuing disputes in the Middle East. In the 1960s, he turned his attention to AFRICA, trying to end violence and make peace in the Congo.

Bunche continued to serve both the United Nations and the United States throughout the 1960s. He flew to Yemen in 1963 to try to prevent a possible civil war, and to Cyprus in 1964 to direct troops for peacekeeping. He was also a participant in the Civil Rights movement and on the Board of Directors of the NATIONAL ASSOCIATION FOR THE ADVANCEMENT OF COLORED PEOPLE (NAACP), and spoke at the 1963 MARCH ON WASHINGTON.

Further reading: Jean G. Cornell *Ralph Bunche: Champion of Peace* (Champaign, Ill.: Garrard Publishing Company, 1976).

— Katherine R. Yarosh

business

The period from 1945 to 1968 was one in which American business made great strides materially and laid the foundation for the highest standard of living in the world, but such prosperity carried substantial costs, both to the nation's psyche and to its environment.

During World War II, economic policy had placed business activity firmly under government control. Ending these controls and dealing with their effects were top priorities for the business community when the war ended. The government had favored large firms for war contracts to such an extent that the 100 largest manufacturing firms accounted for over 70 percent of the nation's industrial production during the war compared with only 30 percent before the war. Although the share of smaller business increased slightly in the years after the war, the war effort established that the nation's largest firms would conduct the lion's share of economic activity. In 1969, the Federal Trade Commission concluded that the trend in American business organization since World War II had been "centralizing and consolidating corporate control and decision-making among a relatively few vast companies." The negative effects of this consolidation on small business and the public interest were apparent as the nation's largest home appliance manufacturers and steel producers were convicted of price fixing and other anticompetitive practices in the 1960s.

The wartime experience of individual industries and firms varied greatly. Entire industries, such as watchmaking, abandoned production for the domestic market to meet military needs. American watchmakers soon discovered that the public grew accustomed to imported Swiss watches during the war. Until the COLD WAR re-created demand for explosive timers, the American watch industry floundered. There were businesses, however, that turned wartime production into postwar opportunities. With contracts to supply soldiers with its product, Coca-Cola penetrated overseas markets wherever American forces went.

When the war was over, the process of reconversion to a civilian economy began almost immediately. The government sold production facilities and a variety of surplus equipment and materials to private business for nominal fees. War contracts were abruptly cancelled and government controls on resource allocation were hastily abandoned. For a few months immediately following the war, unemployment was high, strikes were common, and there were shortages of almost everything.

After these initial hardships American business stabilized and inaugurated a period of sustained prosperity, interrupted by only four brief, mild recessions from 1945 through the 1960s. The sheer scale of America's economic growth was impressive. Even when adjusted for inflation, the nation's gross national product (GNP) grew dramatically, nearly doubling between 1946 and 1968. More important, the GNP rose in all but three years in this period, making this prosperity remarkably steady.

Initially, the growth was spurred by pent-up demand for housing and consumer goods. Out of economic necessity during the Great Depression and because of their unavailability during the war, products Americans desired were often hard to find. Americans were eager to end that deprivation, and $140 billion in personal savings during the war gave them the financial means to do so. This consumption stimulated production and employment. Before this demand was satisfied, defense policy dictated high levels of military spending. This spending provided a solid base of demand for business that was independent of the fluctuations of consumer spending.

In this larger postwar American ECONOMY, business differed in several respects from its previous operation. Government spending played a noticeably greater role. President Franklin D. Roosevelt's peacetime budgets averaged 9.2 percent of the GNP. Government spending between 1945 and 1968 was double that on average. Meanwhile the SERVICE SECTOR grew while manufacturing remained steady at a little over 28 percent of GNP; professional and financial services increased their share of America's GNP to more than 24 percent by the late 1960s, up from less than 19 percent in the years immediately after World War II.

The American workforce experienced even greater changes. After World War II, clerical workers and blue-collar laborers each comprised slightly more than 20 percent of the workforce. By the late 1960s, clerical and kindred workers made up over one-third of the labor force, while the percentage of blue-collar workers fell. The percentage of workers in service industries rose from a little over 11 percent to almost 17 percent by the late 1960s. Manufacturing still accounted for roughly the same amount of economic activity as it did in the late 1940s and was still the single biggest component of the economy. Nevertheless, clerical positions had greatly expanded and the service industries produced a larger share of the nation's GNP and employed more of the nation's workforce in the 1960s than they had in the 1940s. Mining and AGRICULTURE saw the greatest decline in the percentage of the nation's economic activity.

Business activity spread out from the urban areas of the Northeast and West Coast during this period as well.

The Sunbelt areas of the South and West recruited defense contractors to serve the military bases located in the regions. Soon, they began to draw manufacturing enterprises. Service and transportation industries quickly followed. The nation's business activities were spreading into areas previously dominated by agriculture and extractive industries, such as timber and mining, giving the Sunbelt a more diverse economic structure.

Following World War II, the United States dominated the global economy. This created many new opportunities for American businesses in both exporting and importing. Multinational corporations became a major factor in the world's economy. Increasingly, large American firms established overseas subsidiaries. This gave businesses more direct access to raw materials, markets, and labor outside the United States. The amount of America's economic activity that rested on international trade nearly quadrupled from 1946 to 1968. The U.S. government eagerly facilitated this increase in American overseas economic activity through programs such as the MARSHALL PLAN and POINT

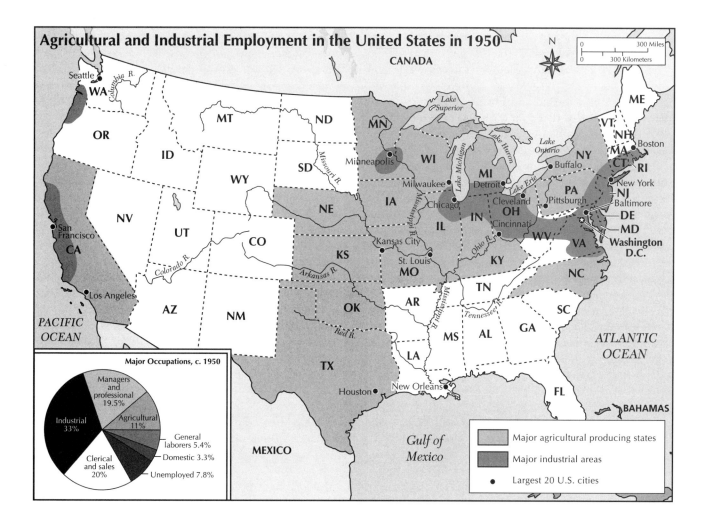

FOUR PROGRAM and by supporting institutions like the International Monetary Fund (IMF) and World Bank and inaugurating tariff reductions through the General Agreement on Tariffs and Trade (GATT).

The UNION MOVEMENT emerged from the war very strong. Unions and their leadership, once considered a threat, were co-opted by business. Business leaders began dealing with union leaders more as equals than as adversaries. They relied on union leadership to help solicit government contracts and to keep the union rank and file from making extreme demands. Union leaders found themselves with their own vested interests and positions to protect, often making them more natural allies of management than the membership of their own unions. While some union members criticized the close relationship between unions and business leaders, they, too, were being placated into passivity. Work contracts began to include many provisions desirable to workers, including medical coverage, paid vacations, guaranteed annual wages, and an automatic COST-OF-LIVING ADJUSTMENT (COLA). With leadership more sympathetic to management and a workforce complacent following the material improvement in its condition, unions did little to shake the foundations of business in the 1950s and 1960s.

Beginning in the 1960s, the CONSUMER MOVEMENT and its most vocal spokesperson, author RALPH NADER, did shake up business. Nader and others, such as author and environmentalist RACHEL CARSON, alerted the country to how irresponsible business had been while creating the material prosperity that many Americans enjoyed. In response to public pressure generated from publicizing the negative effects of business activity, Congress embarked on a whole new series of regulations of business practices. Some hazardous products were banned or severely restricted, and laws such as the Water Quality Act, Clean Air Act, and the NATIONAL TRAFFIC AND MOTOR VEHICLE SAFETY ACT OF 1966 were passed to insure that business was attentive to consumer safety and to minimizing its destruction of the environment. This was the beginning of the most comprehensive round of business regulation since the Progressive era in the early 20th century.

A negative aspect of American business during this period was the effect increasingly larger and more bureaucratized work structures had on employees. Several authors, including sociologists C. WRIGHT MILLS and David Riesman and novelist Sloan Wilson, explained how the new scale and structure of business organization made white-collar and clerical employees "cogs in a machine," just as assembly-line production had done to blue-collar workers generations earlier. These critics charged that this imposed a dehumanizing conformity on almost every business employee. As author VANCE PACKARD pointed out, people were told to seek solace from this emotional emptiness by consuming more goods, reinforcing the materialist emphasis of American capitalism and stimulating sales and production of more goods. While businesses stripped away the humanity and individuality of their employees, their increasingly pervasive ADVERTISING told the workers not to worry, but instead to go shopping.

From a material standpoint, American business was in better shape between 1946 and 1968 than it had ever been. American businesses were growing in size and were spreading throughout the noncommunist world. Their ability to fulfill the desires of American consumers seemed limitless. One could reasonably ask, as critics did, at what price had this prosperity come? To a generation that grew up in the deprivation of the Great Depression and World War II, answers to that question were perhaps not that important. The public expressed its desire to be protected from businesses that were unconcerned about the safety of their products and environmental destruction, but few outside the COUNTERCULTURE expressed skepticism of capitalist materialism. Unions became docile and most Americans continued their consumptive race to "keep up with the Joneses." As the BABY BOOM generation came of age, however, business would have to work harder to convince these younger Americans to accept the practices and dynamics of the American system of business that had been created after World War II, or, failing that, to adjust the system to the new generation's ideals and expectations.

Further reading: John Kenneth Galbraith, *The Affluent Society* (Boston: Houghton-Mifflin, 1958); Thomas McGraw, *American Business, 1920–2000: How It Worked* (Wheeling, Ill: Harlan-Davidson, 2000); Sloan Wilson, *The Man in the Gray Flannel Suit* (New York: Simon & Schuster, 1955).

— Dave Price

C

Carmichael, Stokely (1941–1998)

Stokely Carmichael was head of the STUDENT NONVIO-LENT COORDINATING COMMITTEE (SNCC) and a prominent member of the BLACK PANTHERS during the 1960s.

Carmichael was born in Port of Spain, Trinidad, to Mabel and Adolphus Carmichael, a carpenter, in 1941. Stokely's parents moved to the United States when he was still very young, leaving the child in the care of relatives. Stokely and his three sisters joined their parents in New York City in 1952, settling in Harlem and later the Bronx.

Carmichael excelled as a student and gained admittance to the Bronx High School of Science, where he was one of only two black students in his class. He rejected a number of scholarships to predominantly white colleges and universities and entered historically black Howard University in 1960 as a premedical student, although he eventually graduated with a degree in philosophy. While at Howard, Carmichael joined the CONGRESS OF RACIAL EQUALITY (CORE) and became involved in a number of anti-SEGREGATION efforts from SIT-INS to voter education campaigns in the South. On a 1961 FREEDOM RIDE through Mississippi, Carmichael was arrested for violating state segregation laws and endured 53 days in deplorable conditions at the state's infamous Parchman Penitentiary, an experience that apparently only strengthened his resolve to fight for African-American rights.

Carmichael graduated from Howard in 1964 and joined SNCC, the major student-organized civil rights organization of the 1960s. In Lowndes County, Mississippi, Carmichael played an integral part in the evolution of the Lowndes County Freedom Organization, formed as a separate political party for African Americans. He rapidly became known for his talent for working effectively with college-educated activists, working-class blacks, and white supporters.

By 1966 fissures were appearing in SNCC over what role whites should play in the organization. Although Carmichael rejected the view of a minority of SNCC work-ers that whites be excluded, he took advantage of the climate of divisiveness and ran for SNCC chairman. Carmichael hoped to shape SNCC into an organization like the Lowndes County body, providing more power to working-class African Americans with less stress on nonviolence. In the election, Carmichael defeated JOHN LEWIS, who had led SNCC since 1963, and he began pointing the group in a more militant direction. During the summer of 1966, Carmichael spearheaded SNCC's efforts to complete the march across Mississippi begun by activist JAMES MEREDITH, who had been shot and wounded before completing the trek. During this march Carmichael first began using the phrase that soon became identified with him (although he was not the first to use it)—"BLACK POWER." Carmichael's use of the phrase only codified a long-brewing shift toward militancy for SNCC. The slogan of "Black Power" galvanized white support for the Civil Rights movement and boldly called for an increasingly black nationalist agenda for younger civil rights activists.

In subsequent years Carmichael continued to move toward Black Nationalism instead of relying on white leadership and nonviolence. Black Power appealed to many within SNCC because it awakened a sense of pride and confidence in a uniquely black aesthetic dormant in more conservative forms of black protest. Carmichael still did not preclude interracial cooperation, but he stressed the need for self-determination and unity among people of color. The move toward black power further damaged the already fragile unity between SNCC and more conservative civil rights organizations.

Carmichael continued to call for Black Power throughout his time at the head of SNCC, but his support soon waned. The more radical SNCC became, the faster northern financial support disappeared. Likewise, many working-class southern African Americans did not relate to calls for Black Nationalism, and the issue of what role whites should play continued to divide SNCC. By the spring of

Stokely Carmichael addressing an audience, 1966
(Library of Congress)

1967, it was clear that Carmichael's time at the head of SNCC was up, and he resigned as chairman.

In June 1967, Carmichael joined the Black Panther Party. That same summer he went on a tour that included Cuba, China, North Vietnam, and Guinea (among other countries). During the trip he further cemented his ties to left-wing radicalism and pan-Africanism. Carmichael's open willingness to associate with foreign leftists angered many Americans but only enhanced his prestige among black power advocates. Carmichael had become too radical for SNCC, though, and he was expelled in August 1968. The expulsion meant little to Carmichael, since he had not attended a staff meeting since his return from abroad and now worked primarily with the Black Panthers.

Facing increased pressure from Federal Bureau of Investigation (FBI) surveillance and feeling dissatisfied with his role with the Black Panther Party, Carmichael began spending time in Guinea and soon took up permanent residence there. In 1978 he changed his name to Kwame Toure. He died in 1998, having never stopped working toward his pan-African vision.

Further reading: Clayborne Carson, *In Struggle: SNCC and the Black Awakening of the 1960s* (Cambridge, Mass.: Harvard University Press, 1981).

— Kevin P. Bower

Carson, Rachel (1907–1964)

Biologist and author of the 1962 book *Silent Spring*, Rachel Carson is credited with founding the modern ENVIRON-MENTAL MOVEMENT in the United States.

The publication of *Silent Spring* led to public outcry over the use of chemical insecticides such as DDT. Congressional hearings were held to look into the effects of the chemical and a grass-roots movement began calling for stricter environmental protection. The result was the establishment of the Environmental Protection Agency (EPA) in 1970 and the ban on DDT.

Born in Springdale, Pennsylvania, on May 27, 1907, Carson acquired an appreciation for the natural world from her mother. Carson attended the Pennsylvania College for Women (now Chatham College) where she agonized over whether to study English or biology. She changed her major to biology, but remained devoted to literary activity for the rest of her life. Carson studied zoology in graduate school at Johns Hopkins University, received her M.A. in 1932, and taught at the University of Maryland from 1931 to 1936. Family responsibilities kept Carson from pursuing her doctorate, but she did manage to spend her summers studying at the Marine Biological Laboratory in Woods Hole, Massachusetts. Although Carson loved the sea, her trip to Woods Hole marked the first time she had ever seen it. Carson became enchanted with the ocean and vowed to devote her life to the study of marine biology.

After her father's death in 1935, Carson began writing radio scripts on SCIENCE issues for the U.S. Bureau of Fisheries (the forerunner of the Fish and Wildlife Service) in Maryland. A year later she was appointed aquatic biologist. Her first book, *Under the Sea Wind* (1941) was an extension of a widely acclaimed article she published in the *Atlantic Monthly*. Carson's flowing prose and her dramatic representation of sea life made science accessible to the public in a way that had not been done before. The book went unnoticed by critics, however, and Carson devoted more time to her work at the Bureau of Fisheries, where she drafted conservation bulletins, wrote a series of pamphlets on wildlife refuges, and edited scientific reports. By 1949, Carson had been promoted to chief editor of publications.

Carson's second book, *The Sea Around Us* (1951), dealt with the geological processes that formed the earth and the oceans. It became a best seller and won both the John Burroughs Medal and a National Book Award. Financial success accompanied her literary acclaim, allowing Carson to retire from her position at the Bureau of Fisheries and devote herself to writing full time. She purchased a cottage on the coast of Maine and began work on her third book, *The Edge of the Sea* (1955), about the seashores of the world and their communities of plants and animals.

Carson had been concerned about the effects of insecticides on the environment since the mid-1940s. Chemical pesticides such as DDT were being used by the government to combat mosquitoes in Massachusetts, the gypsy moth on Long Island, and fire ants in the southern United States. Carson and other scientists realized that these pesticides were having catastrophic effects on many of the plants and animals in the affected ecosystems. When Carson heard that DDT and other harmful insecticide compounds were about to be approved for public use by the Department of Agriculture, she reluctantly abandoned her writing about the sea to warn the public of the dangers associated with insecticides.

The publication of *Silent Spring* (1962) sparked an international debate on the use of chemical insecticides. Carson was attacked by the chemical industry as a "hysterical woman" who misunderstood the scientific processes she wrote about. *Silent Spring* was officially endorsed by President JOHN F. KENNEDY's Science Advisory Committee, and sparked a grass-roots movement for a clean environment. Carson testified before Congress in 1963, encouraging legislators to institute environmentally responsible policies to protect human health and wildlife. When the Environmental Protection Agency was created in 1970, DDT was the first chemical to be banned.

Rachel Carson died of breast cancer at the age of 56. Her final book, *The Sense of Wonder* (1965), explained the importance of cultivating a child's natural curiosity about the environment.

Further reading: Linda Lear, *Rachel Carson: Witness for Nature* (New York: Henry Holt, 1997); Philip Sterling, *Sea and Earth: The Life of Rachel Carson* (New York: Crowell, 1970).

— Angela K. O'Neal

Central Intelligence Agency (CIA)

The best known of the American intelligence agencies, the Central Intelligence Agency (CIA) was created to coordinate the government's intelligence operations and give the president quick, clear information for the conduct of domestic and FOREIGN POLICY.

The CIA had its origins in intelligence operations during World War II. In the aftermath of Pearl Harbor, the fledgling American intelligence community was criticized for not disseminating vital information that could have prepared the U.S. Navy for the surprise Japanese attack in 1941. Government officials believed that a central clearinghouse responsible for coordinating intelligence-gathering operations and the distribution of vital information would prevent another Pearl Harbor. The Office of Strategic Services (OSS), the American intelligence corps that carried out intelligence-gathering activities as well as covert operations behind enemy lines, provided a further example of the need for and possible benefits of having a permanent government agency assigned to carry out these tasks after the war.

As the uneasy alliance between the Allies degenerated into Soviet-American confrontation, President HARRY S. TRUMAN supported the need for an intelligence agency to coordinate the acquisition and dissemination of needed information on potential foes. The NATIONAL SECURITY ACT OF 1947 created the Central Intelligence Agency.

In theory, the CIA was originally intended to oversee the entire American intelligence establishment, which included the separate intelligence branches of the armed services as well as the Federal Bureau of Investigation. In practice the various intelligence-gathering components within the United States government were not willing to cooperate to the extent envisioned by Truman, especially as the intelligence community dramatically expanded in later years. Instead of coordinating intelligence activities, the CIA concentrated primarily on espionage, also known as HUMINT (human intelligence), and since its inception, it has carried out covert operations.

Rachel Carson speaking before a Senate Government Operations subcommittee studying pesticide spraying, 1963 *(Library of Congress)*

The two most important divisions within the CIA are the Directorate of Intelligence and the Directorate of Operations. The intelligence section is responsible for placing and/or recruiting spies within foreign governments and using them to gather information vital to American national security. The operations section carries out secret operations against foreign governments sometimes in tandem with but often independent of intelligence collection. The director of Central Intelligence oversees both aspects of the CIA's operations and acts as the primary liaison between the president and the intelligence community. The agency focuses its attentions on foreign governments, especially those deemed threats to American national security.

The history of the CIA has been inextricably linked with the COLD WAR. The chief target of the CIA's activities from the very beginning was the SOVIET UNION. The CIA spent much time and money infiltrating various Soviet government organizations, including the Soviet Army and the KGB (the Soviet counterpart of the CIA), and the agency provided much valuable information about Soviet intentions, troop strength, and nuclear missile capability to American foreign policymakers.

More controversial were the activities of the CIA in the Third World, which comprised the primary battlefield of the COLD WAR. Most of the agency's covert operations were aimed at governments in the developing world that American policymakers feared were leaning toward the Soviet bloc. The administration of DWIGHT D. EISENHOWER placed a good deal of emphasis on covert operations, especially as they were more effective than diplomacy and much cheaper (and less risky in the nuclear age) than all-out war, despite their dubious legality. Eisenhower authorized the CIA to undertake operations that destabilized and overthrew democratically elected governments in Guatemala and Iran. President JOHN F. KENNEDY authorized the CIA to carry out a coup attempt against Fidel Castro's Cuba in 1961 using CIA-trained and -funded Cuban émigrés, but the BAY OF PIGS initiative failed disastrously. As a result of these and other controversial activities, the CIA came under increased congressional oversight and various presidents have prohibited covert operations that include activities such as assassination.

The end of the cold war in the late 1980s and early 1990s caused the CIA to dramatically change direction. Although some questioned the need for the agency at all, the CIA rapidly made the transition from cold war concerns to such issues as the war on drugs, nuclear nonproliferation, and combating international terrorism.

Further reading: Rhodri Jeffreys-Jones, *The CIA and American Democracy* (New Haven, Conn.: Yale University Press, 1988); Loch Johnson, *America's Secret Power: The CIA in a Democratic Society* (New York: Oxford University Press, 1989).

— Matthew M. Davis

Chambers, Whittaker (1901–1961)

Whittaker Chambers's significance stems almost exclusively from his involvement in the ALGER HISS perjury trial in 1948.

Hiss became an infamous target of the HOUSE UN-AMERICAN ACTIVITIES COMMITTEE (HUAC), a congressional committee originally convened in 1947 to ferret out communist infiltration of the film industry, a mandate later extended to track down communists from all walks of life. The accusation that Hiss was a communist agent came from Chambers.

Chambers's past was a checkered one. Born on April 1, 1901, in Philadelphia, and reared in New York, he came from a troubled upbringing. As a youth he had been dismissed from Columbia University. A writer of some talent, Chambers eked out an existence for a number of years as a journalist, all the while flirting with a radicalism he found appealing in the bohemian underworld of New York City. A confessed communist agent in the 1920s and into the 1930s, Chambers claimed that he had grown disillusioned with COMMUNISM in the late 1930s. After the Nazi-Soviet pact of 1939, his break with the party became total. In the 1940s, he continued his journalism career and became an editor for two notable publications, *Time* and the *National Review,* marking his total about-face from communist agent to conservative reactionary.

Chambers testified before HUAC that, in the late 1930s, Hiss had been a member of the Communist Party. He claimed that he had collected party dues from both Hiss and his wife. Hiss denied that he knew Chambers and that he had had any past affiliation with the Communist Party. Under continued and relentless questioning from HUAC member Richard M. Nixon, Hiss was forced to admit that he had known Chambers, even acknowledging that he had let him use his car and live in his apartment, although Hiss insisted that Chambers had used a different name at the time, that of George Crosley. Still, Hiss denied ever being a communist, and challenged Chambers to repeat his accusations outside of Congress where Congressional immunity would lapse and Hiss could sue Chambers for libel.

In response, Chambers went on the radio program *Meet the Press* and labeled Hiss a communist. Hiss sued. Chambers then revealed additional information. He testified that Hiss had passed him secret State Department documents to be turned over to the Soviet Union. Chambers dramatically produced microfilms of the documents he claimed to have received from Hiss, documents that were typed copies of State Department records reproduced on a Woodstock model typewriter once owned by Hiss. These were the famous "pumpkin papers," so called because Chambers said he had kept them hidden in a pumpkin in his vegetable garden.

Unable to be tried for espionage because the statute of limitations had run out, Hiss was tried for perjury. His first trial ended in a hung jury in July 1949. But on January 21, 1950, at the conclusion of a second trial, Hiss was convicted of two counts of perjury for having lied about his communist connections in the 1930s. He spent almost four years in prison.

The exchange between Chambers and Hiss embodied the larger confrontation between NEW DEAL LIBERALISM and resurgent CONSERVATISM underlying the COLD WAR and carried with it far-ranging ramifications. Hiss's past service in the State Department cast further suspicion upon a body already suspected of harboring communists. From a more general perspective, the Hiss-Chambers confrontation aided and abetted the growing tide of McCarthyism, unleashed upon America in the early 1950s.

Whittaker Chambers in courthouse corridor, 1949
(*Library of Congress*)

In the years after the Hiss case, Chambers slid into obscurity. Unable to revive his journalism career, he contented himself with publishing his memoirs telling his side of the controversial Hiss trial. He died in 1961.

Further reading: Sam Tanenhaus, *Whittaker Chambers: A Biography* (Random House: New York, 1997).
— Matthew Flynn

Chávez, César   See United Farm Workers

Chicano movement   See Latino movement

cities and urban life

The changes that occurred in American cities after World War II significantly altered patterns of living in the 1950s and 1960s and beyond.

Beginning in the 1950s, manufacturing centers in the Northeast and Midwest declined in population, as industries moved out of these regions. An urban stretch extending across this part of the country became known as the Rust Belt because of all the abandoned factories. Industries such as steel and automobile manufacturing moved overseas or to other parts of the United States, as some failed to keep up with technological advancements and others were plagued with high costs and taxes. Rather than invest millions of dollars in updating existing machinery and employing high-wage union help, many corporations found it cheaper and easier to reestablish their businesses elsewhere. Areas affected by such moves experienced a significant loss of population. Major industrial cities such as Detroit, Michigan; Gary, Indiana; Cleveland, Ohio; Pittsburgh, Pennsylvania; and Buffalo, New York, were among the hardest hit.

While cities in the Northeast and Midwest bore the brunt of industrial relocation, areas in the South and West benefited in the years following World War II when corporations began investing in these warmer regions. Cities such as Los Angeles, Miami, Atlanta, Dallas, Houston, and Phoenix experienced substantial growth and prosperity. Referred to as the Sun Belt, for their temperate climate and plentiful sunshine, these cities exploded in population as Americans followed manufacturing industries and jobs, leaving behind difficult times and cold weather. Lower taxes and a more modest cost of living also helped attract workers and industry. Sun Belt cities profited from increased defense spending, high-tech industrial development, and greater interest in RECREATION, as millions moved to sunny areas to relax and retire.

The relocation of industries had a ripple effect on people and institutions in many cities throughout the nation. As the number of manufacturing jobs declined, lower paying SERVICE SECTOR jobs multiplied and unemployment rates increased. Increasing poverty contributed to growing crime rates.

Racial tensions intensified as large numbers of African Americans moved into northern and western cities, continuing the rural to urban migration started in previous decades. As whites moved to the suburbs, African Americans began to move out of traditionally black neighborhoods and closer to all-white areas, sometimes escalating friction between the two groups. At the same time, other groups from rural backgrounds moved into the cities, including migrants from Appalachia and immigrants from Puerto Rico, Mexico, and other parts of Latin America. Between 1940 and 1960, the Puerto Rican population of New York City increased from 70,000 to over 600,000. In the West, between 1950 and 1960, the Mexican population of Los Angeles doubled, from 300,000 to 600,000. After passage of the IMMIGRATION ACT OF 1965, IMMIGRATION to American cities from Asia increased as well. This influx of immigrants changed the appearance of the cities, making them more culturally diverse in their makeup. Though these changes resulted in different neighborhood composition, cities remained largely segregated by race with most less fortunate inhabitants having little prospect of moving to the suburbs.

In the 1960s, riots in cities such as Los Angeles, New York, Detroit, and Chicago reflected tensions resulting from social, economic, and racial segregation that reached a breaking point. The proliferation of images of urban violence on TELEVISION served to reinforce the notion that cities were unsafe, creating a further divide between cities and suburbs.

One response to the growing social, political, and economic inequality of urban America was the creation of government agencies and programs. Under President LYNDON B. JOHNSON, Congress passed the Housing and Urban Development Act of 1965. The measure allocated almost $3 billion for the rehabilitation of existing housing and the creation of new public housing. New business also began to develop, bringing a boom in the construction of high-rise office buildings. Some cities saw the redevelopment of previously abandoned or run-down blocks. In Boston, during the 1960s, the city tore down old buildings and built a new city hall and office buildings in an effort to revitalize the downtown area. Other regions experienced a revival in architecture and urban planning, as city managers sought new ways to cope with expanding populations. The infusion of new groups of minorities into a number of areas brought with it a mix of cultures resulting in a blending of art, music, and traditions. Many cities experienced a cultural renaissance during the 1960s that continued into the 1970s and beyond.

Other parts of Johnson's WAR ON POVERTY, particularly the COMMUNITY ACTION PROGRAM (CAP) and MODEL CITIES PROGRAM, were intended to help the revitalization of cities by allowing residents to have a voice in public policy. Although the programs had many problems from the beginning, including conflicts between local government and community organizations, they did give some, particularly African Americans, the opportunity to practice political leadership.

Further reading: Randall Bartlett, *The Crisis of America's Cities* (New York: M.E. Sharpe, 1998); Jon C. Teaford, *The Twentieth-Century American City* (Baltimore: Johns Hopkins University Press, 1993).

— Heather L. Tompkins

civil defense

As the commitment to atomic weaponry increased after World War II, the issue of civil defense received considerable attention, as national politicians and scientific and military authorities debated the extent to which the United States should prepare for the immediate protection of civilian lives and property in case of a nuclear attack.

Influenced by German attacks on the English homefront during World War II, President Franklin D. Roosevelt created the Office of Civilian Defense (OCD) on May 20, 1941. The OCD's efforts to mobilize air raid warning systems, wardens, bomb shelters, rescue workers, and fire-fighting units, however, produced only victory gardens and physical-fitness programs, as the likelihood of an air attack on the U.S. homefront diminished. On June 30, 1945, President HARRY S. TRUMAN abolished the OCD. Although Truman resisted significant funding for civil defense, preferring to save money for weapons, the KOREAN WAR and the SOVIET UNION's development of an ATOMIC BOMB provided the impetus for the return of civil defense in 1950. The development of civil defense during the postwar period was erratic, as leaders continued debating its very necessity. The military community questioned its role in civil defense, the American public resisted spending too much money on questionable shelters, and high government officials failed to agree on the direction and form that civil defense should take.

In 1950, the Truman administration set up the Federal Civil Defense Administration (FCDA) as an independent agency responsible for administering a national civil defense program. During this period of American civil defense history, funding was the most debated issue, as Congress continually cut FCDA funding requests by at least half. Much civil defense actually consisted of a propaganda campaign that produced a series of booklets, films, TELEVISION shows, and media stories aimed at convincing Americans that they could survive a nuclear attack with only the most basic preparations. It was during this time that atomic air-raid drills became common practice in public schools where children were instructed to "Duck and Cover" by dropping to their knees, covering their heads, and so protecting themselves from an atomic attack.

During the presidency of DWIGHT D. EISENHOWER, civil defense changed. Because blast shelters were expensive, the nation began to consider evacuation. The INTERSTATE HIGHWAY ACT OF 1965 was justified on the grounds that it could offer a means of escape after a nuclear attack. With the discovery of fallout, the radioactive matter left in the atmosphere after an atomic blast, fallout shelters became popular. The FCDA distributed free literature on building such structures, usually in basements. The building of fallout shelters flourished during the Eisenhower years, particularly after the American public became increasingly aware of atomic capability as the government conducted regular tests and eventually developed the HYDROGEN BOMB. These developments, however, instilled gradually in the American public a belief that civil defense was useless against the effects of weapons that might wipe out entire cities. Eisenhower understood that only a catastrophic result could come from an exchange of nuclear weapons with the Soviets. In 1958, ignoring calls for a greater, more expensive civil defense program from the FCDA's director, Eisenhower cut civil defense funding and shut down the FCDA. The FCDA, together with the Office of Defense Mobilization, was merged into the Office of Civil and Defense Mobilization. The Office of Civil and Defense Mobilization was placed under the Executive Office of the president in order to centralize nonmilitary defense functions in a single agency responsible directly to the president.

Presidential support for a civil defense program peaked in 1961 under President JOHN F. KENNEDY. In 1960, a thorough review of the civil defense program prompted Kennedy to reorganize it in 1961 by setting up a new Office of Civil Defense (OCD) under the secretary of defense, who was given the task of implementing a system of fallout shelters and emergency communications, as well as assisting state and local communities in establishing their own systems for maintaining order and safety after an attack.

During the debate over the fate of Berlin between Kennedy and Soviet leader Nikita Khrushchev, Kennedy asked Congress to increase its defense effort as well as allocate an additional $207.6 million for an expanded shelter program. After the LIMITED TEST BAN TREATY OF 1963 prohibited atmospheric testing, however, civil defense fell dormant and was not resurrected again until the late 1970s. In 1964, the OCD was transferred to the Office of the Secretary of the Army. After the establishment of the OCD,

the Office of Civil and Defense Mobilization became the Office of Emergency Planning, coordinating emergency activities such as the use of manpower and materials and the provision of disaster assistance to states, counties, and local communities.

Further reading: Thomas J. Kerr, *Civil Defense in the U.S.: Bandaid for a Holocaust?* (Boulder, Colo.: Westview Press, 1983); Kenneth Rose, *One Nation Underground: The Fallout Shelter in American Culture* (New York: New York University Press, 2001). Allan M. Winkler, *Life under a Cloud: American Anxiety about the Atom* (New York: Oxford University Press, 1993).

— Jason Reed

civil disobedience

Civil disobedience, the symbolic and illustrative violation of existing laws, gained considerable popularity as a form of protest in the 20th-century civil rights, labor, and antiwar movements in the United States and around the world.

Civil disobedience involves knowingly breaking a law that the protestor believes to be reprehensible. Since such an act is a crime, the civil disobedient then submits to punishment in the hopes of setting a moral example that will provoke those in GOVERNMENT to enact meaningful change. As an extralegal and moralistic approach, civil disobedience in principle should be nonviolent and used only as a last avenue for change.

Deeply rooted in Western philosophy, civil disobedience was championed by thinkers such as Cicero, John Locke, Thomas Aquinas, Thomas Jefferson, and most notably, American author Henry David Thoreau. Thoreau's 1849 essay "Civil Disobedience" called men to "break the law [and] let your life be counter friction to stop the machine," if government is "of such a nature that it requires injustice." In his advocacy of civil disobedience, Thoreau glorified the ability of the individual, acting on good conscience, to bring a system of government to its knees. In India in the mid-20th century, Mohandas Gandhi developed the philosophy of *satyagraha*, meaning "truth force" in Hindi, as a guiding philosophy for the Indian people in their fight to overthrow the British colonial government in India. *Satyagraha* prohibited the use of violence in opposition to evil, and required practitioners to disclose their intentions to the opposition, forbidding secrecy to be used as a tactic. Gandhi employed his philosophy through a series of nonviolent individual and group protests, which included hunger strikes, boycotts, and organized noncooperation with British government structures.

Though critics claimed that the philosophy of *satyagraha* assumed the opposition held a certain level of morality that could be appealed to, Gandhi maintained that civil disobedience would prevail anywhere because it had the power to convert anyone.

The concept of nonviolent protest and civil disobedience was popularized in the United States by civil rights leader MARTIN LUTHER KING, JR. King was first introduced to Gandhi's philosophy while attending the Crozer Theological Seminary in Chester, Pennsylvania. The SOUTHERN CHRISTIAN LEADERSHIP CONFERENCE (SCLC), which King later organized, made contact with Gandhi's followers, and as a result of their discussion about the *satyagraha* philosophy, in 1959, King and the SCLC were received by Indian prime minister Jawaharlal Nehru, himself a veteran of the nonviolent movement in India.

Using the tactics of active nonviolence, King was able to energize blacks and gain the allegiance of liberal whites in the Civil Rights movement. King advocated the use of nonviolent actions such as SIT-INS and boycotts as a means to expose the injustice faced by blacks. Twice he was arrested and jailed. While participating in a student-organized lunch counter sit-in in Atlanta, in 1960, he was arrested along with 33 students and sentenced to Reidsville State Prison Farm, causing a public outcry that ended only when presidential candidate JOHN F. KENNEDY arranged for his release. Later, in the spring of 1963, while leading a march in Birmingham, Alabama, King was jailed along with large numbers of supporters, including numerous schoolchildren. While incarcerated, King composed his famous "Letter from Birmingham Jail," in which he answered the criticisms of both blacks and whites who discouraged his advocacy of civil disobedience. "You may well ask: 'Why direct action? Why sit-ins, marches and so forth?'" said King. "Nonviolent direct action seeks to create such a crisis and foster such a tension that a community which has constantly refused to negotiate is forced to confront the issue. It seeks so to dramatize the issue that it can no longer be ignored. . . . We know through painful experience that freedom is never voluntarily given by the oppressor; it must be demanded by the oppressed."

King's eloquent trumpet call for nonviolent protest made civil disobedience popular not only in the movement to secure civil rights for blacks but also in the antiwar movement, which gained momentum in its opposition to the VIETNAM WAR in the late 1960s. Many acts of civil disobedience in opposition to the war occurred on college campuses, beginning with the rise of the FREE SPEECH MOVEMENT on the campus of the University of California at Berkeley. Student activists protested continued escalation of the war effort by occupying university buildings, invoking passionate rhetoric in their heated confrontations with the administration. In December 1964, over 800 students were arrested for occupying the Berkeley administration building. Movement leader MARIO SAVIO gave an impassioned speech moments before the sit-in, proclaim-

ing, "There is a time when the operation of the machine becomes so odious . . . you've got to indicate to the people who own it . . . that unless you're free, the machine will be prevented from working at all." The sit-ins progressed into mass rallies known as "teach-ins," and soon appeared on campuses across the country, continuing to employ the principles of nonviolent protest and attempting to pressure the administration of President LYNDON B. JOHNSON to slow the escalating conflict in Vietnam.

Further reading: Carl Cohen, *Civil Disobedience: Conscience, Tactics, and the Law* (New York: Columbia University Press, 1971); Martin Luther King, Jr., *Letter from Birmingham Jail* (San Francisco: Harper, 1994).

— Guy R. Temple

Civil Rights Act of 1957

The Civil Rights Act of 1957 represented an important landmark in civil rights legislation, albeit primarily as a symbol, providing hope for future progress in the Civil Rights movement.

The 1957 act, passed 82 years after the last civil rights legislation, was the first attempt to deal with civil rights since Reconstruction. The new legislation, however, was limited by the context in which it developed. In particular, the DEMOCRATIC PARTY and the REPUBLICAN PARTY were battling for electoral support in the southern states. Republicans looked to protect President DWIGHT D. EISENHOWER's gains in the South in the election of 1956, and they feared that too close an association with the cause of civil rights would threaten these gains. Southern Democrats also tried to distance their party from civil rights issues, fearing further Republican gains in the South.

Despite this shared fear of addressing civil rights issues in both parties, Eisenhower called for civil rights legislation in his State of the Union Message in 1957. Pushed forward in particular by opposition to the Montgomery bus boycott, the public indignation that it raised, and the Supreme Court's ruling in 1956 that Alabama's separate but equal law for transportation was unconstitutional, the House of Representatives passed a bill in 1957 that included all of the suggestions made in Eisenhower's address. The House bill proposed the creation of a Commission on Civil Rights, a bipartisan and independent agency within the executive branch, designed to investigate and recommend remedies for unconstitutional discrimination. The bill also proposed creating a Civil Rights Division within the Department of Justice. Title III, which met immediate opposition in the Senate, authorized the federal government to seek court injunctions whenever an individual's civil rights were violated. Finally, the House bill sought to enforce the Fifteenth Amendment by authorizing the Department of

Justice to investigate voting rights violations and to seek court injunctions against illegal interference with the right to vote.

Senator majority leader LYNDON B. JOHNSON, a skilled political negotiator with presidential ambitions, played a key role in the Senate's debate of the House bill. With Eisenhower's help, Johnson convinced enough northern senators to support the deletion of Title III in its entirety from the Senate's version of the bill. Johnson worked to remove Title III, a broad measure that was seen as a way for the federal government to sue for school desegregation, with broad language implying a much wider scope for the Attorney General's activities, to assure southern support for the revised bill in the Senate. The Senate further diluted the revised bill by attaching an amendment to it that required a trial by jury in all cases arising from the voting rights section of the proposed bill. This amendment, promoted in part by Johnson's appeals for moderation and pragmatism, further appeased wary southern Democrats who believed that local white juries would prove less threatening than federal judges in such cases. The Senate version of the bill eventually became the Civil Rights Act of 1957.

The deletion of Title III allowed many southerners to view the Civil Rights Act of 1957 as a victory. They argued, correctly, that the 1957 act was closely limited to voting rights. They also pointed out that they had prevented federal government intervention in favor of school desegregation, an especially threatening possibility from their point of view in light of the Supreme Court's BROWN V. BOARD OF EDUCATION (1954) decision which ruled school SEGREGATION unconstitutional.

Liberal Democrats were less pleased with the 1957 act, viewing its reliance on due process as expensive and time-consuming. They had advocated moving beyond the federal government's voluntary model with weak enforcement mechanisms to a more aggressive use of federal government power. Title III had thus been central to the 1957 act for them, a symbol of the enlightened use of the power of the federal government to help those too poor, intimidated, or unenlightened to help themselves. Civil rights leaders likewise expressed disappointment with the 1957 act. It was used only once in its first 16 months, in a suit against the election registrars of Terrell County, Georgia. Many African-American spokesmen felt betrayed by the legislation.

The disappointing results achieved in the short term by the Civil Rights Act of 1957, however, proved to be less important than the act's long-term meaning. The Commission on Civil Rights would investigate and publicize civil rights issues. The disappointment generated by the deletion of Title III and the weakness of the 1957 act also helped galvanize a movement for stronger civil rights legislation. The federal government had become actively involved in civil rights, and its involvement would continue to grow in the CIVIL RIGHTS ACT OF 1960, the CIVIL RIGHTS ACT OF 1964, and the VOTING RIGHTS ACT OF 1965.

Further reading: Carl M Brauer, *John F. Kennedy and the Second Reconstruction* (New York: Columbia University Press, 1977).

— Allan Wesley Austin

Civil Rights Act of 1960

As frustration with the lack of progress under the CIVIL RIGHTS ACT OF 1957 continued to build, Congress passed new legislation in 1960 to aid blacks in registering to vote.

Critics of the 1957 act could demonstrate its impotence by pointing out widespread violations involving the denial of suffrage documented by the commission on civil rights. Despite the 1957 act's intentions to end such violations, only one case involving the denial of the right to vote came before the courts in the law's first 16 months. The 1958 elections increased northern liberal representation in Congress, and this development encouraged civil rights advocates to push for stronger measures. In particular, these advocates sought legislation that authorized the federal government to seek court injunctions whenever an individual's civil rights were violated (a provision that had been cut from the 1957 act prior to its passage).

A number of factors resulted in a new law that encompassed slight changes to the voting rights provisions of the 1957 act: delaying tactics in the House of Representatives, the longest filibuster in Senate history, efforts by the administration of DWIGHT D. EISENHOWER to limit the scope of the proposed legislation, and the disorganized efforts of liberals. The 1960 act did not address the issue of school desegregation or other SEGREGATION issues under protest at SIT-INS throughout the South.

Although civil rights advocates now possessed greater legal, ideological, and political resources than they had in the past, they still proved unable to defeat their opponents. Eisenhower's lack of commitment to the cause of civil rights resulted in a passive administration stance that did not press for significant change in the 1960 act. The Eisenhower administration met renewed pressure for civil rights legislation with a modest plan to create a system of voting referees that would be used by the courts to register African-American voters. This proposal marked a step back from the proposal of the Commission on Civil Rights, which would have allowed the referees to register voters without court action. Southern Democrats in Congress shared the Eisenhower administration's reluctance to try to effect racial change in the South. The dominance of racial moderation in the 1950s, when even many of those favorable toward civil rights hesitated to act, continued to limit the achievements of civil rights legislation.

While a filibuster in the Senate prevented action on a proposed civil rights bill, the House produced a measure with four key provisions. The first three addressed voting issues. State election officials were ordered to retain registration and qualification records of voters in federal elections. The bill also proposed allowing federal courts to declare individuals eligible to vote, enabling the federal government to address violations of voting rights based on race. In addition, the bill proposed endowing federal courts with the power to appoint voting referees who would collect evidence and provide the courts with reports on how African-American voters were treated. The final provision of the bill provided criminal penalties for bombing and mob action that obstructed court orders. This section also made it a federal crime to cross state borders to avoid prosecution for such actions.

The Civil Rights Act of 1960, as many civil rights advocates feared, proved largely ineffective. The federal district judges charged with hearing voting violations cases were often unsympathetic to issues of civil rights and racial justice. They moved slowly and frequently acted to obfuscate the 1960 act. Southern judges in particular at times failed to appoint voting referees, despite the act's provisions. Recalcitrant judges could also delay the process in a variety of ways. Incorrect and insufficient rulings, unjustified dismissals, and other tactics of procrastination could make the process more expensive in terms of both time and money. The federal government appealed such decisions and often won but faced delayed results. Even decisions in favor of the federal government did not always bring about immediate progress; unsympathetic judges at times moved slowly to enforce rulings in the federal government's favor. African-American voter registration was little affected by the 1960 act. At best, token registration occurred.

The 16 months of debate, maneuver, and compromise that marked the passage of the Civil Rights Act of 1960 produced much weaker legislation, similar to that which had happened with the Civil Rights Act of 1957, and left both friends and foes of the new act exhausted. In spite of some hyperbole from both sides, the 1960 act provoked little response from most involved in the lengthy debate. This lack of rancor resulted in part from the limited nature of the relatively innocuous 1960 act as well as the hopes it stirred for progress in the future.

Further reading: Daniel M. Berman, *A Bill Becomes a Law: Congress Enacts Civil Rights Legislation* (New York: Macmillan, 1966); Carl M. Brauer, *John F. Kennedy and the Second Reconstruction* (New York: Columbia University Press, 1977).

— Allan Wesley Austin

Civil Rights Act of 1964

The Civil Rights Act of 1964 was the most comprehensive civil rights legislation yet passed, helping to initiate widespread changes in the racial patterns of American society.

The Civil Rights Act of 1964 developed under forceful presidential leadership and bipartisan congressional support in an effort to avoid continued bloodshed and upheaval in the United States. The passage of the first effective civil rights law since Reconstruction was spurred by events of the BIRMINGHAM CONFRONTATION, where the police turned high-pressure fire hoses and snarling dogs on demonstrators, and by ugly episodes elsewhere. President JOHN F. KENNEDY sent Congress a broad civil rights bill in June 1963 that clearly represented a new and more comprehensive approach to the issue of civil rights designed to avoid the limited nature and ineffective results of the CIVIL RIGHTS ACT OF 1957 and the CIVIL RIGHTS ACT OF 1960.

President LYNDON B. JOHNSON committed himself to the passage of the civil rights bill in the aftermath of Kennedy's assassination. A cloture petition to terminate debate on the 1964 act was circulated in the Senate in an attempt to defeat southern resistance. A similar tactic had failed to garner the necessary two-thirds vote in 1960, but the cloture petition succeeded with votes to spare in 1964 because the uncompromising posture of southern hard-liners alienated many senators who had been undecided about the 1964 act and because Johnson used his considerable persuasive skills to rally support. Senator Everett M. Dirksen, the Republican Senate minority leader, also played an important role in the approval of cloture and passage of the 1964 act.

Johnson signed the Civil Rights Act of 1964 into law on July 2, 1964, describing it as promoting "a more abiding commitment to freedom, a more constant pursuit of justice, and a deeper respect for human dignity." The Johnson administration acted with considerable speed to enforce the provisions of the act. The president, Congress, and the courts worked in concert to promote civil rights following the passage of the measure.

The sweeping scope of the 1964 act covered a number of issues. Titles I and VIII addressed voting rights. Title I prohibited the denial of the right to vote in national elections on the basis of race, color, religion, or national origin. It also limited the use of literacy tests to determine voter eligibility. Title VIII directed the Bureau of the Census to gather statistics from elections for the House of Representatives since 1960 concerning race, color, and national origin in districts selected by the Commission on Civil Rights.

Title II provided injunctive relief against discrimination in public accommodations. One of the 1964 act's boldest provisions, Title II faced opposition from southerners who based their arguments on the rhetoric of states' rights,

Cartoon showing an African-American family watching fireworks. The fireworks represent the Civil Rights Bill *(Library of Congress)*

little attention during debates over the 1964 act. It became, however, a very powerful weapon for the executive branch with its permission to terminate federal funding to programs in violation of the new act. This title continues to affect educational institutions that receive federal funding today.

Title VII, another very important provision of the measure, established the EQUAL EMPLOYMENT OPPORTUNITY COMMISSION (EEOC). The title prohibited discrimination by companies with 25 or more employees on the basis of race, color, religion, gender, and national origin. Opponents of the bill had inserted the clause on gender in hopes of derailing the bill; the tactic failed but led to revolutionary changes in the legal status of female workers.

The Civil Rights Act of 1964 represented a watershed in civil rights legislation. It destroyed many southern defenses and cleared the way for the VOTING RIGHTS ACT OF 1965. It also ended the paralysis of school desegregation that had followed the *BROWN v. BOARD OF EDUCATION* (1954) decision. Although discrimination was not eliminated by the act, it helped to alter attitudes among the public and at the workplace.

Further reading: Hugh Davis Graham, *The Civil Rights Era: Origins and Development of National Policy, 1960–1972* (New York: Oxford University Press, 1990).

— Allan Wesley Austin

Civil Rights movement   See African-American movement

cold war

The cold war is the term that defines the all-encompassing struggle during the last half of the 20th century between the SOVIET UNION and the United States.

Coined by financier Bernard Baruch and popularized by journalist Walter Lippmann, the term "cold war" characterized this struggle as a political, ideological, and economic conflict that rarely included direct military confrontation. Consisting of propaganda battles, economic warfare, proxy wars, and an ARMS RACE, the cold war touched virtually every corner of the globe in the years after World War II.

American participation in the cold war represented a sharp break in the history of American foreign relations. Before World War II, most American presidents followed the advice laid out in George Washington's farewell address, and avoided political and military participation in the world. After World War II, the presidential administration of HARRY S. TRUMAN believed that global conditions demanded greater American participation. His advisers

mythic memories of Reconstruction, and fears of federal tyranny betraying the ideals of the founding fathers. They pleaded instead for gradualism and voluntarism, but their pleas failed to rally support in light of TELEVISION coverage of events in Birmingham and elsewhere.

Titles III and IV permitted the Department of Justice to file suit to desegregate public facilities and public education. Such suits could be brought only upon receipt of a written complaint from an individual too poor or too threatened to undertake such a suit. The measure also empowered various agencies to work on civil rights issues. Title V extended the life of the Commission on Civil Rights through 1969 and authorized it to serve as a clearinghouse for civil rights information and to investigate alleged vote frauds. Title X established a Community Relations Service within the Department of Commerce to help states and communities resolve disputes based in allegedly discriminatory practices.

Title VI, prohibiting discrimination in federally assisted programs, drew bipartisan support and attracted believed that world stability was predicated on peace and prosperity, and that peace and prosperity, in turn, depended on the expansion of American ideals abroad. Democracy, free enterprise, and the protection of individual liberties—together these beliefs constituted the core of the American ideology that, if adopted by other countries, would lay the groundwork for a wealthy and peaceful global economic and political system. The Truman administration also believed that the U.S. ECONOMY needed to import raw materials and export finished goods to remain healthy. At every turn, the Soviet Union represented a threat to this strategy.

Different concerns animated the conduct of Soviet foreign policy. Believing that its continued existence rested on securing its boundaries against renewed German and/or capitalist aggression, the Soviet Union focused on acquiring stable borders and friendly neighbors. Joseph Stalin, leader of the Soviet Union, also sought to reconstruct the Soviet Union's industrial base, maintain a strong army, and present the Soviet Union and COMMUNISM as a shining alternative to the capitalist system. Although the Soviet Union often preached world revolution, it proved to be very cautious and pragmatic in its foreign policy.

Despite its overall caution, however, the Soviet Union, in light of its strategic objectives, sought to establish a buffer zone in Eastern Europe. In Poland, Stalin insisted that the new Polish government cohere around a group of communist exiles known as the Lublin Poles, claiming that Poland had served as a "corridor" for German advances in the past, proving that Soviet influence in Poland was necessary. For added protection, the Soviet Union reabsorbed the states of Estonia, Latvia, and Lithuania. In 1947, the Soviet Union overthrew the democratically elected noncommunist government of Hungary. The following year, it helped communists seize power in Czechoslovakia. With communist states also in Romania, Bulgaria, and Yugoslavia, the Soviets succeeded in establishing a large bloc of pro-Soviet states that was institutionalized in the Warsaw Pact of 1955.

Fearful that the Soviet Union sought to extend its sphere of influence farther, the United States attempted to rebuild Western Europe as a bulwark against communism. In February 1946, GEORGE F. KENNAN, a U.S. diplomat in Moscow, wrote a "Long Telegram" that urged American policymakers to realize the severity of the communist threat, arguing that the Soviet Union blended Russia's historic sense of insecurity with an expansive political ideology. To meet this danger, Kennan articulated what became known as the "containment" policy, which stated that the United States should "contain" the Soviet Union within its present boundaries; such a policy, Kennan believed, would ultimately enable the internal contradictions of communist ideology to unravel. In 1947, the Truman administration, in response to perceived communist aggression in Turkey and Greece, announced the TRUMAN DOCTRINE, which stated that the United States would provide economic and military aid to these nations and would assist any nation attempting to resist communist subjugation. A year later, the United States offered the MARSHALL PLAN, which outlined an aid package for reconstructing Western Europe. In 1949, the United States broke with tradition and entered the NORTH ATLANTIC TREATY ORGANIZATION (NATO), a permanent alliance with Canada and Western European states designed to deter Soviet aggression, in which an attack against one member nation was considered an attack against all, to be met with force.

The vanquished nation of Germany became a microcosm of the burgeoning cold war. After the defeat of Nazi Germany in May 1945, the United States, Great Britain, France, and the Soviet Union partitioned the country into four zones, with the understanding that this division constituted a temporary military measure. Because of its special symbolic significance as the former capital of Nazi Germany, Berlin was also divided into four parts. Over time, as the Soviet Union and the United States began to pursue conflicting policies in their respective occupation zones of Germany, the division of Germany hardened and finally crystallized when the Soviet Union initiated the BERLIN BLOCKADE in 1948, cutting off supply lines to the German capital. In response to the Berlin blockade, the United States and the other Western powers established the Federal Republic of Germany in 1949.

As Europe divided itself along a new ideological fault line, so too did the major powers of ASIA. In Japan, Americans, despite Soviet objections, assumed sole responsibility for Japanese occupation and reconstruction. At first hoping to reform Japan, the United States switched gears as events in EUROPE deteriorated, moving to establish a strong Japan as an Asian bulwark against communism. Under the leadership of DOUGLAS MACARTHUR, the United States abandoned efforts to break up Japanese business conglomerates, reinstated former imperial leaders, and funneled massive amounts of aid to Japan. In China, the civil war that raged between Mao Zedong's communist army and Jiang Jieshi's Nationalist army came to an end in 1949, when the Nationalists fled to Formosa and Mao proclaimed the People's Republic on October 1. American aid had propped up Jiang's regime for several years, but Jiang's incompetence and reactionary policies finally convinced many American observers that the Nationalist cause was a lost one and the United States withdrew support.

With the fall of China to communism in 1949, the developing countries gradually emerged as the focus of the cold war. Much of the developing world had existed for centuries as colonies of Asian and European powers; with the conclusion of World War II, these colonial powers had

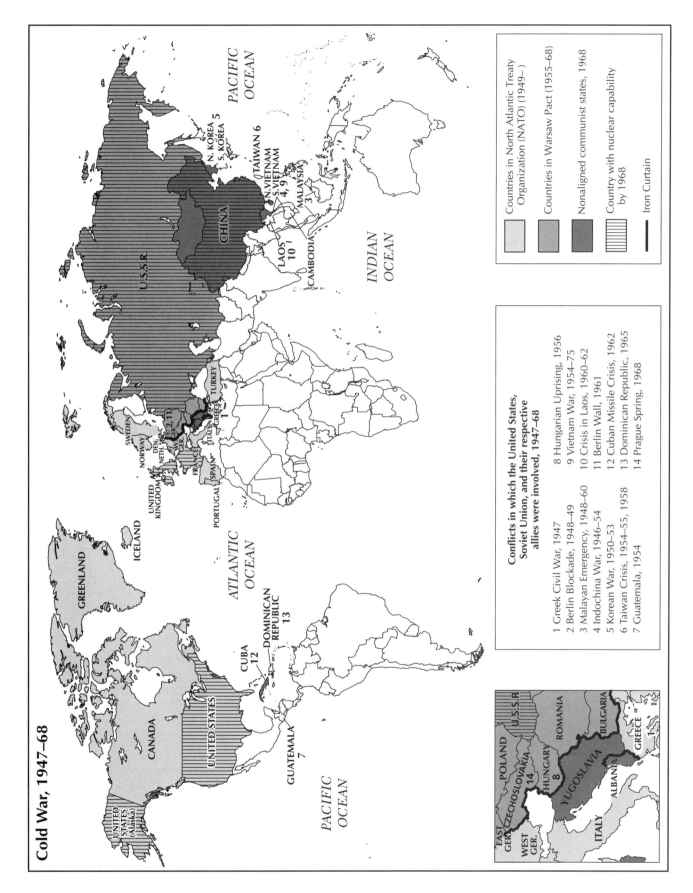

Cold War, 1947–68

PACIFIC OCEAN

PACIFIC OCEAN

ATLANTIC OCEAN

INDIAN OCEAN

UNITED STATES (Alaska)

CANADA

UNITED STATES

GREENLAND

ICELAND

GUATEMALA 7

CUBA 12

DOMINICAN REPUBLIC 13

U.S.S.R.

CHINA

N. KOREA 5

S. KOREA 5

TAIWAN 6

N. VIETNAM

S. VIETNAM 4, 9

MALAYSIA 3

LAOS 10

CAMBODIA

UNITED KINGDOM

NORWAY

SWEDEN

DEN.

NETH.

W. GER.

E. GER. 2, 11

FRANCE

PORTUGAL

SPAIN

ITALY

GREECE 1

TURKEY

Countries in North Atlantic Treaty Organization (NATO) (1949–)

Countries in Warsaw Pact (1955–68)

Nonaligned communist states, 1968

Country with nuclear capability by 1968

Iron Curtain

Conflicts in which the United States, Soviet Union, and their respective allies were involved, 1947–68

1 Greek Civil War, 1947
2 Berlin Blockade, 1948–49
3 Malayan Emergency, 1948–60
4 Indochina War, 1946–54
5 Korean War, 1950–53
6 Taiwan Crisis, 1954–55, 1958
7 Guatemala, 1954
8 Hungarian Uprising, 1956
9 Vietnam War, 1954–75
10 Crisis in Laos, 1960–62
11 Berlin Wall, 1961
12 Cuban Missile Crisis, 1962
13 Dominican Republic, 1965
14 Prague Spring, 1968

U.S.S.R

POLAND

EAST GER.

WEST GER.

CZECHOSLOVAKIA 14

HUNGARY 8

ROMANIA

YUGOSLAVIA

BULGARIA

ALBANIA

ITALY

GREECE 1

exhausted themselves and their possessions became hotly contested areas. In such regions as the MIDDLE EAST, Southeast Asia, AFRICA, and even South America, the United States often sought to stem the revolutionary tide because it feared that these nationalist movements were sponsored by the Soviet Union. In the name of ANTICOMMUNISM, the United States found itself drawn into several civil wars in which the participants were indistinct and the issues exceedingly complex.

Such an example was the KOREAN WAR, which represented the first real military conflict of the cold war. A former colony of Japan, Korea was divided into two occupation zones that eventually became two separate states, the Republic of Korea sponsored by the United States and the Democratic People's Republic of Korea sponsored by the Soviet Union. Both claimed representation of all Korea. After the United States withdrew its forces in 1949, North Korean forces invaded South Korea in June 1950. Believing that this invasion symbolized a test of American resolve, the United States, under the auspices of the United Nations, sent troops to help the South Koreans. The Americans and Chinese fought directly in late 1950 when the United States approached the Chinese border in its own effort to reunify the Korean peninsula. The United States eventually settled for a draw, when the combatants signed an armistice that reestablished the 38th parallel as the dividing line between North and South Korea.

In later efforts, the American government used less overt means to ensure friendly governments. In 1953, the United States sponsored a coup against the nationalist prime minister of Iran, Mohammad Mossadegh. In 1954, the CENTRAL INTELLIGENCE AGENCY (CIA) helped oust the democratically elected government of Guatemala because it feared that the new government was susceptible to communist influence. These successes spurred the growth of the American intelligence community and created unwarranted faith in the efficacy of covert operations.

The decision to stop short of direct warfare on the part of both the United States and the Soviet Union can in large part be attributed to the prevalence of nuclear weapons on both sides. After the United States detonated the first ATOMIC BOMB over Hiroshima in August 1945, the United States maintained a monopoly over the weapon until 1949. Once the Soviet Union exploded its first atomic bomb in 1949, an extensive and expensive arms race began. During the administration of DWIGHT D. EISENHOWER, the U.S. nuclear arsenal grew from 1,000 to almost 18,000 warheads. During the administration of JOHN F. KENNEDY in the early 1960s, fears about a "missile gap" spurred American production of nuclear weapons to new levels. The number of American missiles jumped from 63 in 1961 to 424 in 1963. During the same period, NATO's nuclear missile power increased 60 percent.

In Cuba, cold war confrontation came to a head. After Fidel Castro took power in a successful coup against the American-backed regime of Fulgencio Batista, the United States initiated a number of covert efforts to remove him from power. Although unsuccessful, and sometimes spectacularly so, as in the BAY OF PIGS invasion, these attempts worried the Soviet Union and it took measures to deter any future efforts. In October 1962, the United States discovered that the Soviet Union was installing medium- and intermediate-range ballistic missiles in Cuba. Acutely conscious that these missiles could reach the United States in a matter of minutes, the Kennedy administration pressed for their removal. After a tense period of time, the American and Soviet governments reached a compromise: the Soviets withdrew the missiles in exchange for an American promise that it would not invade Cuba. Secretly, the United States also agreed to withdraw nuclear missiles from Turkey. With the CUBAN MISSILE CRISIS, the United States and Soviet Union realized how close they had come to a hot war and agreed to take measures to reduce tension.

The biggest factor, however, in initiating the end of the cold war was the American involvement in Vietnam. In 1954, the nationalist forces of Ho Chi Minh decisively defeated the French at Dienbienphu. Unwilling to allow the communist Ho to assume control of the country, the United States stepped in and became the primary sponsor for the South Vietnamese regime during the VIETNAM WAR. After a number of years of gradual escalation, the American government began pumping massive amounts of aid in the mid-1960s to support the South Vietnamese government. The futility of this effort made Americans realize the limits of their power, and many began to call for better relations with communist powers. Agreements to limit the arms race eventually led to a reduction of tension with the Soviet Union.

Further reading: John Lewis Gaddis. *We Now Know: Rethinking Cold War History* (Oxford: Oxford University Press, 1997); Walter LaFeber, *America, Russia, and the Cold War, 1945–1996* (New York: McGraw-Hill, 1997); Melvyn Leffler, *Preponderance of Power: National Security, the Truman Administration, and the Cold War* (Stanford, Calif.: Stanford University Press, 1992).

— Brian Etheridge

communism

In the post–World War II years, communism, the system of government in which property and the means of production are owned by a community instead of individuals, created tensions between the United States and the SOVIET UNION, leading to the COLD WAR.

In the early 19th century, the idea of a communist society arose in response to the plight of the poor and the dislocated at the dawn of modern capitalism. Many communist experiments resulted in communal living societies based on utopian ideals of a classless, propertyless citizenry. Later, communism was associated with the philosophy advanced by German writers Karl Marx and Friedrich Engels, who contended that in order for a true communist society to form, a revolution of the proletariat, or working class, had to take place. Marx and Engels predicted in their *Communist Manifesto* (1848) that revolutions would succeed first in industrialized countries such as France, England, and Germany, but the first successful communist revolution occurred in Russia in November 1917.

Soviet leader Vladimir Ilych Lenin's vision of a communist world order, led by workers, conflicted sharply with Woodrow Wilson's dream of an anti-imperialist, free-trade, capitalist world. Wilson sent American troops into Russia in 1919 to attempt to defeat the Bolsheviks—Russian revolutionaries—and create a moderate republic. When he failed to turn the tide of rebellion, Wilson refused to formally recognize the newly formed Soviet Union as a legitimate government. Not until 1933 did Franklin D. Roosevelt acknowledge the communist government. By that time, many Americans, disillusioned with the failing capitalist system during the Great Depression, were attracted to communism as an alternative system of government. Throughout the 1930s, a number of Americans joined the Communist Party, a decision that haunted many later in life.

Since 1917, the term "communism" has informally come to connote a system of government that accepts the Russian Revolution as a model for all Marxists to follow. The communist state in Russia, first established by Vladimir Ilych Lenin, continued after his death under the leadership of Joseph Stalin. Under Stalin, communism moved even further toward totalitarianism. Several million Russians died during the forced collectivization of the Russian peasantry, the elimination of the kulaks (rich peasants), and purges against political enemies. Then the United States joined the Soviet Union and Great Britain in World War II, in what became a difficult but effective alliance to defeat Nazi Germany, at the cost of 20 million Soviet lives. In the aftermath of the war, most Americans associated communism with its Stalinist version and defined it as a totalitarian, godless, imperialist conspiracy directed by Moscow, which led to ANTICOMMUNISM that culminated in the second "Red Scare" in the early 1950s.

The relationship of the Soviet Union with the rest of the world was consistently troubling to the United States. To Americans, a communist government, wherever it existed, always appeared as a threat. Following World War II, the fear of communist infiltration of the U.S. government prompted officials to take measures to ferret out suspected communist infiltrators. The HOUSE UN-AMERICAN ACTIVITIES COMMITTEE (HUAC), a government agency created to investigate individuals suspected of conducting un-American or subversive actions, led the battle against communism in labor, government, and the arts.

No group was excluded from accusations of communist ties. In 1947, HUAC turned its attention to Hollywood, where the committee, in the hope of uncovering communists, interrogated actors, writers, and directors. A select group of writers and directors, known as the HOLLYWOOD TEN, chose to stand up for their rights and refused to answer questions about any affiliation with the Communist Party. The following year, HUAC focused on ALGER HISS, a former State Department employee, who was suspected of being a secret Soviet agent. Hiss was found guilty of perjury and sentenced to prison. By 1950, JULIUS AND ETHEL ROSENBERG were accused of selling secrets regarding the ATOMIC BOMB to the Soviets. They were convicted and executed. Many feared that communists had made their way into the highest branches of the federal government and attempts to reveal those employees with communist ties were stepped up.

In the 1950s, Wisconsin senator JOSEPH R. MCCARTHY, convinced that communists had indeed penetrated U.S. government agencies, used heavy-handed tactics and panic-inducing accusations to pursue government employees suspected of communist affiliation. "McCarthyism" raised the omnipresent fear of communism across the country. Radio and TELEVISION performers, teachers, college professors, and civil-rights activists faced charges of disloyalty. Congress launched its own loyalty probe, enacting the INTERNAL SECURITY ACT (1950) over HARRY S. TRUMAN's veto. The measure declared that it was illegal to conspire to act in a way that would contribute to establishing a totalitarian dictatorship in America and required members of communist organizations to register with the office of the Attorney General. Intent on rooting out subversion, Congress helped contribute to the feeling held by many Americans that communists constituted an unseen threat to the stability of the nation.

The climate of suspicion and ideological conformity pervaded the nation throughout the 1950s and into the 1960s, and it led to the continued opposition to communist advances around the world. When communist forces from North Korea crossed the 38th parallel and invaded South Korea in 1950, Truman sent troops to defend the American-supported government of South Korea as the KOREAN WAR unfolded. Implementing diplomat GEORGE F. KENNAN's proposed policy of containment, Truman strove to stop the spread of communism into new areas. The commitment to stopping the spread of communism led to massive involvement in Vietnam. Led by communist revolutionary Ho Chi Minh, a nationalist movement sought to take control of the American-backed government of South Vietnam headed by Ngo Dinh Diem. The ensuing struggle in the VIETNAM WAR tore the United States apart, wrought enormous damage in Southeast Asia, and forced a reevaluation of America's cold war policies.

Further reading: François Fure, *The Passing of an Illusion: The Idea of Communism in the Twentieth Century* (Chicago: University of Chicago Press, 1995).

— Philippe R. Girard

Community Action Program (CAP)

One of the most controversial features of President LYNDON B. JOHNSON's WAR ON POVERTY, the Community Action Program comprised one component of the ECONOMIC OPPORTUNITY ACT OF 1964. CAP allocated federal funds and resources to local antipoverty programs in various cities throughout the United States, while advocating grass-roots organization and community activism.

Throughout the 1950s, the issue of poverty took a back seat as politicians and the media highlighted the ever-increasing economic prosperity of America's middle class. Beginning in the early 1960s, however, social activists strove to bring the existence of poverty to public attention in the country. MICHAEL HARRINGTON's best-selling book *The Other America* (1962) and President JOHN F. KENNEDY's growing awareness of the poor highlighted the problem. In late 1963, after Kennedy's assassination, the Johnson administration initiated its War on Poverty, a program that proposed various approaches to attack poverty at its roots. This antipoverty package included the Economic Opportunity Act of 1964, which in turn provided the funds necessary to form approximately 1,000 community action organizations in 50 states within the next three years.

On March 16, 1964, Johnson addressed Congress and stated that the Community Action Program would "strike at poverty at its source" by asking American citizens in locally impoverished areas "to prepare long-range plans for the attack on poverty in their own local communities." In this way, antipoverty programs would not be "imposed on hundreds of different situations" by the federal government but would be enacted by "local citizens [who] best understood their own problems and knew best how to deal with those problems." The programs were to involve the "maximum feasible participation" of local community members, particularly those members actually experiencing poverty. In this way, supporters of CAP hoped to stimulate political activism across America and empower the poor to challenge the more politically capable members of society.

While the overall goal of CAP was to initiate antipoverty programs geared toward the specific needs of a particular community, most programs shared characteristics, including nonprofit corporation status and local governing boards. The staffs of these organizations typically included a large proportion of social workers, academics, and employees drawn from the target population of the poor. Providing outreach services and community organization assistance were two major commitments of most community action programs. These organizations all received their funding from a variety of sources, including foundations, local government agencies, and federal agencies. CAP funds were designed for legal, health, and educational services, as well as other valuable causes in impoverished communities.

While the CAP initiative garnered much support for bringing poverty to the public's attention, many people criticized the programs for simply regulating the poor while maintaining them at or near subsistence levels. The CAP budgets, developed by the Office of Economic Opportunity (OEO), were repeatedly attacked for their failure to appropriate funds that matched the goals of the programs, allocating too much money to some organizations and too little to others. Many also complained that the OEO spread federal funds too thinly over too many antipoverty programs, leaving little for CAP.

A great deal of controversy also arose over the phrase "maximum feasible participation," used within the Economic Opportunity Act itself. Originally, this meant that the poorest members of a community took an active role in the discussions and decisions regarding how the organization in their neighborhood operated. In reality, the poor often were relegated to subordinate positions within the program. Middle-class, college-educated political activists held leadership positions and were more interested in destroying the local power structure than providing services for the needy. These advocates used the CAP funds to form tenant and work unions, develop campaigns to overthrow the local officials, and provide bail for protest demonstrators. The misappropriation of leadership roles and funds led to protest demonstrations, class-action lawsuits against state and federal agencies, and demands that poor people be granted representation on all agencies that dealt with problems of poverty.

This brewing class conflict alarmed Democratic and Republican officials alike as they strove to curb CAP at the federal level. In 1967, Congress began a series of revisions, calling for a decrease in the CAP budget. In that same year, an amendment to the Economic Opportunity Act presented legal difficulties for community action programs to be controlled by poor people. With choices to be made at the community level reduced after 1967, community action shifted to social action movements that were independent of federal sponsorship. The Nixon administration further curtailed community action programs by substituting a national program of income maintenance. In the end, although CAP failed as an antipoverty measure, the program encouraged community activism and organization among the poorest sectors of society.

Further reading: Daniel P. Moynihan, *Maximum Feasible Misunderstanding: Community Action in the War on Poverty* (New York: Free Press, 1969).

— Donna J. Siebenthaler

computer

American computing was born in 1945, and, by 1968, computers helped carry men into space, run complex radar systems for national defense, assist students and researchers throughout the country, and organize massive amounts of information that governed Americans' taxes, their airplane reservations, and even their telephone calls.

In little more than two decades, American computers went from innovative scientific tools to fundamental elements of American life—even if the average American had little personal interaction with machines that remained costly and complex throughout the 1960s.

These decades set the pattern for American computing development that continued through the close of the century, as designers and engineers constructed machines capable of increasingly impressive feats of processing power and speed, coupled with equivalent decreases in physical size and expense. Simultaneously, the industry produced a broad-ranging diversification of computer users and consumers, and developed crucial standards for both operating systems and programming languages. By the 1970s, computers were more powerful, more affordable, and more prevalent than ever imagined, setting the stage for their thorough integration into all segments of American life in the decades that followed.

The patterns of the American computing industry were formed at its very inception. The field began during World War II, when scientists and engineers from the University of Pennsylvania developed the ELECTRONIC NUMERICAL INTEGRATOR AND COMPUTER (ENIAC). This was the world's first computer. Like many subsequent developments, ENIAC's creation was funded by the American military, in this case to develop rapid ways of solving complex equations for artillery ballistics tables. The machine was more a powerful calculator than a modern computer, but unlike its predecessors, which relied on movable parts for their computations, ENIAC was wholly electronic. This was its great advance. Without the physical limitations of moving parts, but with more than 18,000 vacuum tubes and miles of wiring (and weighing nearly three tons), this novel machine could perform more than 5,000 additions or subtractions or 360 multiplications of two 10-digit decimal numbers in a single second. Such speeds were without precedent, and prompted the *New York Times* to predict, "a new epoch of human thought" and scientific development.

This first computer was not without its flaws, however, and its service provided its creators with invaluable experience essential for the development of the more complex and more powerful machines that appeared in the 1950s. Though speedy, ENIAC lacked any means of storing its own data. It could neither retain its computational results for use in later procedures nor perform multiple tasks simultaneously, significant handicaps when computing complex equations. Moreover, its original design offered no means for programmers to switch easily from one assignment to another. Each ENIAC computation used a different wiring pattern, and shifting procedures required the physical rewiring and reconfiguration of the entire machine, a task that often took days to complete. Its developers soon realized that "hard-wiring" numerous programs and typical equations into its circuitry would enhance ENIAC's overall productivity, even though some computational speed would be lost as a result. A machine that could store both programming and data would be far superior in use and function to a faster but inflexible computer, they realized, and future computer designers have followed their lead in this respect ever since. As one of ENIAC's primary developers, John W. Mauchly, stated, "calculations can be performed at high speed only if instructions are supplied at high speed."

Recognizing the need for stored data and programming was a major step on the path toward modern computing. Mathematician John von Neumann brilliantly captured the desirability of such enhancements in his 1945 *First Draft of a Report on the EDVAC*, a paper considered by many to be the seminal document of the entire industry. Von Neumann's essay described a machine that would

Man prepares the UNIVAC computer, 1959   *(Library of Congress)*

capture the speed of ENIAC with stored-program capability and a large internal memory cache. Within a few years, his ideas took shape in working models of stored-program computers with effective data storage: the EDSAC, brought on-line in 1949, and the EDVAC, which began operation in 1951. More widely known than these machines was the UNIVAC, a computer developed for commercial use by Mauchly and John P. Eckert, Jr., ENIAC's principal designers. The UNIVAC was one of the first computers to store its data on magnetic tapes rather than on traditional punch cards, but its greater claim to fame came from its appearance on live TELEVISION to help predict the winner of the 1952 presidential election between DWIGHT D. EISENHOWER and ADLAI STEVENSON. For years afterward, the words "UNIVAC" and "computer" would be virtually synonymous throughout the United States.

The basic form of modern computing, where data storage and accessibility rivaled pure speed as desirable traits in hardware design, was well established by the 1950s. The decade saw tremendous strides in the availability of such machines. The first computers were powerful and fast, but they were also physically massive and tremendously expensive. Only the largest organizations in the country could afford and effectively use such complex products, chief among these the federal government. Indeed, without government support (and in particular, without government funding for COLD WAR programs and military defense), America's computer industry would have been hard pressed to make such rapid technological strides throughout the 1950s and 1960s. ENIAC itself was the product of military funding, and its first program equations for the nation's ATOMIC BOMB research. Unlike private companies or consumers, purchasers such as the Pentagon or the NATIONAL AERONAUTICS AND SPACE ADMINISTRATION (NASA) valued performance and speed far more than cost, and willingly paid companies to develop state-of-the-art systems designed with national security in mind. The government thus sponsored innumerable research projects that profit-conscious companies might otherwise have foregone, though the results of this labor typically enhanced civilian products over time. Many important technological developments, such as magnetic tape memory, real-time operation, and the digital transmission of data via phone lines, were all developed in this manner, either for specific military functions or for defense contractors primarily concerned with satisfying government's needs.

Aside from government use, computer ownership in the 1950s was still wholly the domain of large companies and universities. By the close of the decade, however, the ranks of computer users would begin to swell, as numerous military-inspired developments made the machines increasingly smaller and cost effective. There were nearly 6,000 general-purpose electronic computers installed in the United States in 1960, whereas the number at the start of the 1950s could have been counted on one hand. Over 70 percent came from the International Business Machines company (IBM), and most others from seven smaller companies. Though these smaller companies developed many innovative products, the larger IBM consistently led the way in both production runs and development. In 1957, the company marketed a spinning disk for random-access storage of data. This so-called Random Access Memory (RAM) device ensured that data stored at any point on a disk storage unit could be accessed with virtually the same speed as information stored at any other point on the drive, a development that greatly enhanced the operating speed of future machines. One of the first users of IBM's new disk was United Airlines, which stored its entire reservation system on such a machine. IBM also developed the first commercially profitable computer based on transistor technology, the 7090, which replaced vacuum tubes as the machine's basic operating structure. Invented by William Shockley and his research team at Bell Laboratories in 1948, the development of the sold-state transistor was arguably the most important postwar development in the realm of electronics. Vacuum tubes were both notoriously unreliable and expensive, and transistors required less power and operated at a far faster rate. Computers using transistor technology thus required less maintenance, while simultaneously offering greater performance and speed (at a smaller physical size), allowing computer designers to improve both the performance and the accuracy of their machines considerably.

IBM's 7090 was the classic "mainframe" computer, and typified how computers were used throughout the 1960s. A large machine that featured a bulky console filled with blinking lights, buttons, and switches (that supported Hollywood's enduring vision of what a computer should be), the 7090 required its own climate-controlled environment and highly trained operators. Since computer time was such a valuable commodity for these expensive machines, programming was typically conducted in "batches." Users submitted their programs on decks of punched cards to the mainframe's operators, returning to retrieve their data several hours or days later. The concept of direct personal access to the machine, and of users retrieving results within moments of program submission, was simply not possible in this age when few mainframe processors were idle for even a few moments in a typical week. This was a time-consuming process, but still far faster than anything available only a decade before. Of greater hindrance to computer users was the industry's lack of a unified programming standard. Because each mainframe used a different operating system, consumers could not easily transfer their programming from one machine to another. For example, none of

IBM's first six computers developed in the 1950s with semiconductor circuits could run programs written for another. Without a uniform operating system, transfer of data and programming from one machine to the next proved a daunting, if not impossible, task.

Programming and software development lagged behind advances in hardware during the early days of computing. Indeed, the term "software" only developed after 1959. The industry took a major step toward a uniform programming standard in 1964 when IBM introduced its System/360 line of computers. Unlike the individually designed products that came before, these machines were developed as a family of computers, each suited to particular customer needs, and run by the same operating programs, thus allowing consumers to integrate different machines with different functions. The company pledged that future computers in the family would use the same programming code. The 360 series comprised IBM's first attempt at unifying the growing diversity of programming languages then in existence (such as FORTRAN, COBOL, and Pascal), and virtually the entire industry followed the company's lead. Firms throughout the country produced peripheral devices and computer equipment specifically designed for compatibility with the IBM system. Late in 1964, the RCA Corporation even introduced a family of four computers, the Spectra 70 series; its makers promised it would be fully compatible with any 360 (and cost 40 percent less).

Competition made these machines increasingly affordable, and computer prices fell in the late 1960s. Such systems were still designed primarily for business and government, but cracks in that trend appeared in 1968, when Digital Equipment Corporation (DEC) introduced its PDP-8, the first of the "minicomputers," at the reasonable cost of merely $18,000 a machine. Though more expensive than the average American home at the time, the advent of the minicomputer with its integrated circuits foreshadowed the shape of things to come. Armed with such circuits (called chips), first developed in 1957 by engineers working for Texas Instruments and Fairchild Semiconductor (and designed primarily to direct America's ballistic missiles), computer designers were finally freed from the cost and reliability constraints of transistors or tubes. These semiconductor chips contained complex circuits using lines "drawn" with chemicals, and one transistor-sized chip could contain the equivalent of a dozen transistors. Chips allowed computer makers to further miniaturize their machines, and they allowed programmers the space and power they required to make their own products even more potent. Consumers were the primary benefactors of these developments, and the market bloomed. Between 1968 and 1972, around 100 new companies offered microcomputers on the commercial market, introducing an average of one new computer every three weeks. These were driven by a myriad of new programs. IBM's lead in the field diminished in 1968 with its decision (made under threat of antitrust litigation by the federal government) to divorce its programming and hardware divisions. The decades to come saw computers become more powerful, more affordable, and more available.

Further reading: James Cordata, *The Computer in the United States: From Laboratory to Market, 1930 to 1960* (New York: M.E. Sharpe, 1993); H. H. Goldstine, *The Computer from Pascal to Von Neumann* (Princeton, N.J.: Princeton University Press, 1980).

— Jeffrey A. Engel

Congress of Industrial Organizations (CIO)

The CIO was formed in 1938 as part of the UNION MOVEMENT to help organize workers in mass-production industries such as steel, coal, and automobiles.

During World War II, the CIO supported government defense efforts, and in return for following a no-strike policy, the federal government required all workers in defense-related factories to join the union. As a result, membership in the CIO rose from 4 million in 1938 to over 6 million by 1948. At the same time, concerns about wartime inflation led LABOR, BUSINESS, and government to limit wage increases and instead provide workers with ever more lucrative benefit packages. After the war, the CIO unions renewed their struggle for higher wages and benefits by calling hundreds of strikes, sometimes against entire industries. In 1945 alone, unions in both the CIO and AMERICAN FEDERATION OF LABOR (AFL) conducted 4,750 strikes that involved 3.4 million workers, including a major walkout by the United Automobile Workers against GENERAL MOTORS. This strike was particularly important because the union demanded that the company increase wages without increasing prices. Although labor did not get this concession, the demand influenced later collective bargaining in which unions won an automatic COST-OF-LIVING ADJUSTMENT (COLA), as well as annual automatic wage increases arising from savings based on technological advances.

By 1946, the number of strikes reached unprecedented levels, and although labor was generally victorious, there was also increased criticism and condemnation of its growing power. The following year, Congress passed the TAFT-HARTLEY ACT, which tried to curb the power of organized labor. It outlawed the closed shop (where a worker had to join a union before getting a job), the secondary boycott, and the use of union dues for political activities. The law also instituted an 80-day "cooling-off" period for strikes affecting national safety or health, and required all union officials to swear under oath that they were not communists. The law was a stinging defeat for the AFL and CIO, which denounced Taft-Hartley as the "slave labor bill."

The next major wave of CIO union activism began in 1950 and climaxed in 1952 when the number of workdays lost because of strikes exceeded the total of every preceding postwar year except 1946. The most serious work stoppage was the 53-day strike by the United Steelworkers in 1952. President HARRY S. TRUMAN attempted to seize the STEEL INDUSTRY, a move the Supreme Court later ruled unconstitutional. Although the CIO scored several victories in these labor disputes, they impeded defense industries during the KOREAN WAR, attracting antiunion criticism from political commentators and the press.

The growing anticommunist hysteria of the post–World War II years reduced the effectiveness of the CIO. During the 1930s, some key CIO organizers held that industrial unionism would lay the foundations for the ascendancy of COMMUNISM in the United States, even though rank-and-file workers had little interest in communism. For years, some of the CIO's largest unions had procommunist leaders or followed communist-influenced policies, and while this was not a major issue in the early history of the organization, by the late 1940s, some influential CIO leaders strongly criticized the presence of these groups. These tensions increased when America became embroiled in the Second Red Scare with its anticommunist agitation in the late 1940s and early 1950s. Eventually the CIO felt pressure to rid the organization of unpatriotic elements. In 1949, the executive committee formally expelled 11 left-wing unions, an action that resulted in the loss of nearly 1 million members, including many who were black and female.

During the postwar years, the CIO also attempted to expand its membership into the southern United States. Although the vast majority of CIO members were located in the North and Midwest, the CIO leadership wanted to organize the mining, textile, and transport workers of the South who were notoriously underpaid and seemed ideal candidates for unionization. In the process, the CIO faced issues of race, a weak union tradition, and strong pro-business governments. As a result, a major southern organizing campaign conducted in 1946 met with only limited success.

Actions like the Taft-Hartley Act, the seizure of the steel industry, and the events of the Red Scare eventually led to unification of the two major American labor organizations. The process began as early as 1950 when the AFL and the CIO formed a United Labor Policy Committee to deal with government labor policies, and the committee soon became involved in other areas of organizational cooperation. In 1952, the deaths of AFL president William Green and CIO president Philip Murray also removed two of the main antagonists in the bitter rivalry between the two organizations, and brought the AFL and CIO closer to a merger. Early in 1955, a Joint Unity Committee was formed, and a new constitution was drafted. The formal merger of the labor organizations came in December 1955. George Meany, who had succeeded Green as head of the AFL, was elected president of the new AFL-CIO, which now had a membership of 16 million members, equal to about 30 percent of all employed Americans.

Further reading: Robert Zieger, *The CIO, 1935–1955* (Chapel Hill: University of North Carolina Press, 1995).

— Dave Mason

Congress of Racial Equality (CORE)

Multiracial and committed to a nonviolent strategy, CORE took part in many of the 1960s civil rights struggles, including SIT-INS, voter registration drives, and FREEDOM RIDES, before shifting to a more militant stance.

The Congress of Racial Equality was founded in 1942 at the University of Chicago by James Leonard Farmer, a black Methodist minister, George Houser, a white Methodist minister, Bernice Fisher and Homer Jack, two white divinity students at the University of Chicago, James R. Robinson, a white Catholic and pacifist, and Joe Guinn, a black NATIONAL ASSOCIATION FOR THE ADVANCEMENT OF COLORED PEOPLE (NAACP) member. Farmer became the group's leader.

Committed to the principle of nonviolence, CORE's first action was the desegregation of the City Roller Rink in Chicago. Other early efforts included a campaign to desegregate Palisades Amusement Park in New Jersey and a "journey of reconciliation" that set a biracial team of 16 people on a ride through the upper South to test a Supreme Court decision outlawing SEGREGATION in interstate travel. Three of the riders were arrested in North Carolina and sentenced to 30 days on road gangs.

CORE gained national attention in May 1961, following a Supreme Court decision holding that segregation in interstate transportation facilities was unconstitutional. Together with the STUDENT NONVIOLENT COORDINATING COMMITTEE (SNCC), CORE organized freedom rides, which carried biracial teams through the South in an attempt to desegregate bus terminals. The freedom rides, while unsuccessful in the short term, brought the civil rights struggle much attention. As a result, CORE's budget increased to $750,000 in 1961. While most of the money came from northern white liberals, CORE membership quickly moved to include a majority of southern black activists. In the spring and summer of 1962, CORE led less-publicized efforts to desegregate restaurants along Virginia, North Carolina, and Florida highways.

Dr. Martin Luther King, Jr., addressing CORE demonstrators who are protesting the seating of the Mississippi delegation during the Democratic National Conference, Atlantic City, New Jersey, 1964   *(Library of Congress)*

Throughout the mid-1960s, CORE organized nationwide boycotts and sit-ins to force corporations to hire more blacks, targeting Sears and Roebuck, California's Bank of America and Lucky Stores, along with New York and Cleveland construction sites. In 1963, CORE-supported sit-ins and demonstrations reached their apex with the August 28 MARCH ON WASHINGTON. That summer, CORE's national director James Farmer was almost killed by troopers as he organized registration drives and desegregation protests in Plaquemine, Louisiana.

On April 22, 1964, CORE demonstrators disrupted the opening of the New York World's Fair, chanting "Freedom Now!" as President LYNDON B. JOHNSON delivered a speech. Farmer, Bayard Rustin, and MICHAEL HARRINGTON were arrested. The 1964 Summer Project saw SNCC and CORE members organize freedom schools, registration drives, and the MISSISSIPPI FREEDOM DEMOCRATIC PARTY (MFDP), which tried to replace the segregated state DEMOCRATIC PARTY. On June 21, James Chaney, a black CORE member and white CORE workers Michael Schwerner and Andrew Goodman were shot dead near Meridian, Mississippi, while on their way to help register black voters.

The violence CORE activists faced, along with impatience on the part of blacks, pushed CORE to adopt a more militant program of action. In 1964, grass-roots community organization replaced direct action as CORE's weapon of choice. Many CORE workers blamed white members for the lack of responsiveness on the part of local blacks and advocated programs of racial pride and autonomy, organized by blacks, as the main solution. Propositions to bar whites from membership in CORE multiplied and many whites left the organization. CORE's commitment to nonviolence waned, as local activists sought the protection of self-defense groups, such as the Deacons for Defense. Farmer praised the Deacons' work at the 1965 CORE convention in Durham, North Carolina, where Jonesboro Deacons leader Ernest Thomas delivered a speech.

In January 1966 Farmer stepped down as national director. CORE chose Floyd McKissick over the less militant George Wiley as his successor. McKissick supported separatism and moved CORE's headquarters to Harlem in August 1966. That same year, the national CORE convention in Baltimore adopted BLACK POWER as the organization's main slogan, renounced nonviolence in favor of self-defense, and condemned the VIETNAM WAR.

Even though CORE's positions were not quite as radical as those of SNCC, the organization lost most of its white membership and financial support, which translated into rising deficits and acute financial problems starting in 1966. In mid-1968, Roy Innis, the chairman of the Harlem chapter, replaced McKissick as national director. Innis centralized CORE's structure, created the CORE Special Purpose Fund to increase fund-raising, and started reducing the organization's $1 million debt. Innis toned down CORE's objectives, advocating Black Nationalism and community economic development. Even though it never managed to regain the influence it had garnered in the early 1960s, CORE, under the leadership of Innis, survives to this day.

Further reading: Inge Powell Bell, *CORE and the Strategy of Nonviolence* (New York: Random House, 1968); August Meier and Elliott Rudwick, *CORE: A Study in the Civil Rights Movement, 1942–1968* (New York: Oxford University Press, 1973).

— Philippe R. Girard

conservatism

Conservatism sought to resist liberal advances in the years following the establishment of the welfare state.

The period following World War II constituted the low point for American conservatism in national politics. Although liberal hopes of expanding the social service state often met with resistance in the context of postwar prosperity, conservatism could not find a base for any real counterreaction against the LIBERALISM of the NEW DEAL.

Republicans and conservative southern Democrats in Congress managed to frustrate many of President HARRY S. TRUMAN's more liberal legislative reforms. After Republicans took control of Congress in 1946, the failure of moderate Republican THOMAS E. DEWEY to get elected in 1948, along with the Democrats' taking back of Congress, reflected the American people's desire not to scale back the social service state to pre-Depression levels. Even the election of a Republican war hero president in 1952, DWIGHT D. EISENHOWER, did not represent a serious threat to liberalism's ascendancy.

In response to their travails, American conservatives began to attack liberals as being soft on COMMUNISM at home and abroad. This was not limited only to Republicans attacking Democrats, although the most infamous use of the communist issue as a means to power was that of Republican senator JOSEPH R. MCCARTHY of Wisconsin. In 1949 and 1950, a number of events opened the way to attacking liberals for their alleged soft stance against communism: the explosion of the first Soviet atomic bomb, the realization that the Soviets had obtained atomic secrets from American operatives, the communist victory in China, and the conviction of ALGER HISS, a New Deal figure, for perjury in denying he had had communist connections. Although so-called McCarthyism produced some short-term successes for conservative politicians, it led to no real change in political policy. In short, anticommunist foreign policy and the gradual growth of the social service state marked the American political scene in the 1950s, as conservatism remained on the outside looking in. Domestic prosperity helped to mute liberal dreams for expanding the role of the state, but the national mood at the same time offered no opportunity for a conservative reaction against liberalism.

A new conservative movement began in the 1950s, though, and came to dominate American politics. A new generation of conservatives began restructuring their ideology to include a strong anticommunist and interventionist role in foreign policy combined with calls for capitalism to function without state interference. Books like William F. Buckley's *God and Man at Yale* (1951) and *Up from Liberalism* (1959), BARRY GOLDWATER's *The Conscience of a Conservative* (1960), Willmoore Kendall's *The Conservative Affirmation* (1963), and Frank Meyer's *What Is Conservatism* (1964) espoused these ideas and formed the basis of what would become a neo-conservative movement. This burgeoning movement also found a voice in a number of journals, including *Human Events, The Freeman, National Review,* and *Modern Age.*

The new conservatives abandoned the traditional isolationism of their fellows to stay in touch with political reality in the COLD WAR world. Unlike cold war liberals, though, the new conservatives stressed liberation of communist nations over simple containment. On the domestic front, new conservatives continued traditional conservative calls for laissez-faire capitalism, but they couched the calls in new terms. New conservatives argued that unfettered capitalism, with government intervention at a minimum, was an inherent moral good. Thus, they managed to combine the interests of libertarians who wanted little to no government interference in economic matters with the interests of traditionalists who sought to maintain a conservative social order, often based on Christian theology.

Still, neo-conservatism was slow to take root. In 1964, Republican presidential candidate Barry Goldwater sounded the neo-conservative trumpet of virulent ANTICOMMUNISM and maintenance of the American social order, namely racial SEGREGATION, but he was crushed in the November election by liberal Democratic incumbent LYNDON B. JOHNSON. However, the neo-conservative movement continued to grow, and, as the 1960s wore on, it gained more support. Neo-conservatives appealed to working-class Americans, once the bulwarks of the Franklin D. Roosevelt coalition for the Democrats, by concentrating on issues such as the growth of a welfare society and a perceived moral decline in America. Conservative Republicans sought to win support in the South and West from independents and wavering Democrats, and so secure these regions to go along with their strongholds in the Midwest and Great Plains. The strategy relied on southern whites' disenchantment with liberal support for African-American civil rights and a more general perception that "limousine liberals" in Washington, D.C., were out of touch with common Americans.

Richard M. Nixon, a more moderate Republican, gained the REPUBLICAN PARTY nomination for president in 1968 and proceeded to win the White House. Nixon's election marked a victory for a more moderate conservatism, in the tradition of Dewey and Eisenhower, but which also relied on the new base of support being carved out by neo-conservatives. The neo-conservative movement came of age by 1968 and, having found its spokesperson in California governor Ronald Reagan, dominated the American political scene by 1980.

Further reading: Mary C. Brennan, *Turning Right in the Sixties: The Conservative Capture of the GOP* (Chapel Hill: The University of North Carolina Press, 1995); Jerome L.Himmelstein, *To the Right: The Transformation of American Conservatism* (Berkeley: University of California Press, 1990).

— Kevin P. Bower

consumer movement

The consumer movement called for greater federal regulation of consumer products in the early 1960s through the passage of a number of consumer protection laws.

The consumer movement in post–World War II America had its roots in the work of several writers. In the 1950s, VANCE PACKARD's *The Hidden Persuaders* (1957) attacked American advertisers for employing psychological manipulation in ADVERTISING while JOHN KENNETH GALBRAITH's *The Affluent Society* (1958) blamed advertising for creating an America in which the pursuit of private goods won out over the need to provide for the public good by building hospitals, schools, and museums. In the early 1960s, three more authors wrote books that addressed more specific problems in American consumer industries. RACHEL CARSON's *Silent Spring* (1962) exposed the dangers of indiscriminate pesticide use, David Caplovitz's *The Poor Pay More* (1967) focused on the struggles of low-income consumers, and Jessica Mitford's *The American Way of Death* (1963) described abuses in the funeral sales industry.

By the early 1960s, consumer protection had moved beyond the pages of books and into the programs of President JOHN F. KENNEDY. Kennedy delivered a Consumer Bill of Rights to Congress in 1962 in which he called for the rights to safety, information, personal product and service choice at competitive prices, and a fair hearing by government regarding the formulation of consumer policy. Kennedy's message was an important symbolic move, putting consumer issues at the forefront, but real legislative achievements were also underway. The Kefauver-Harris Amendments to the Federal Food, Drug, and Cosmetic Act of 1962 required, among other things, that new drugs be tested for efficacy as well as safety before being released for marketing. The Kefauver-Harris Amendments arose as a reaction to the efforts of Frances Kelsey, a Food and Drug Administration doctor, who narrowly prevented the widespread marketing of thalidomide, a drug that produced birth defects in Great Britain and West Germany, in the United States.

Despite these efforts, the United States still lacked a cohesive consumer movement. The next step came with the publication of Ralph Nader's *Unsafe at Any Speed* in 1965. Nader was trained as a lawyer at Harvard and left his law practice in Hartford, Connecticut, in 1963 to devote himself to consumer protection. *Unsafe at Any Speed* indicted the AUTOMOBILE INDUSTRY for ignoring personal and environmental safety in car design. The book became a hit, selling nearly 500,000 copies and establishing Nader as the driving force of the consumer movement. In the wake of *Unsafe at Any Speed* and the creation of the Center for the Study of Responsive Law, which Nader established as a consumer watchdog group, the federal government passed a number of important consumer protection laws. The NATIONAL TRAFFIC AND MOTOR VEHICLE SAFETY ACT OF 1966 was passed as a result of Nader's book, while Nader and his cohorts lobbied for laws to protect children from dangerous toys, bring about truth in packaging, provide truth in lending, and mandate better inspection of food.

The consumer movement peaked in the early 1970s, when the administration of Richard M. Nixon created the Consumer Product Safety Commission to coordinate federal consumer protection efforts and to further protect consumers. The movement lost steam in the face of increased deregulation in the federal government, but consumer protection retained a prominent role. In 1980, Ralph Nader turned over control of his movement to Public Citizen, an umbrella organization for a number of consumer groups. Nader himself remained an active and recognizable voice for consumer protection.

The consumer movement is especially important because its achievements continue to protect American consumers and set a precedent for federal involvement in regulating new consumer products as they emerge.

Further reading: Robert N. Mayer, *The Consumer Movement: Guardians of the Marketplace* (Boston: Twayne Publishers, 1989).

— Kevin P. Bower

cost-of-living adjustment (COLA)

The cost of living became an economic issue after World War II as workers worried about the impact of inflation, and the inclusion of COLA clauses in labor union contracts became common.

The cost of living is considered to be the amount of money needed to purchase the goods and services required to maintain a certain standard of living. Since World War I, when knowledge of price movements was thought to be helpful in order to maintain a stable national economy, cost-of-living statistics, provided by the Bureau of Labor Statistics (BLS), have become important figures for economic management.

Although cost-of-living wage adjustments were made during World War I when economists identified unstable prices as an economic problem, interest in COLAs fell when prices stabilized in the late 1920s. Interest in COLAs reappeared, however, as World War II destabilized prices and inflation began to affect real earnings. A 1942 survey of manufacturing firms disclosed that 40 percent had agreements which included COLA clauses, whereas only 5 percent of the contracts had included such provisions in 1939. When the War Labor Board applied the Economic Stabilization Act to freeze wages in 1942, approximately 2 million workers were covered by COLA clauses.

The union movement was at its peak in 1948 when GENERAL MOTORS (GM) and the United Auto Workers Union (UAW) attracted national attention with the settlement of a two-year agreement that included a COLA clause adjusting basic wages for the rise in the cost of living since 1940. The COLA clause was based upon the BLS Consumer Price Index (CPI), a monthly report used to determine the cost of living by measuring the change in prices for a mixed market basket of goods and services. The agreement additionally allotted a 2 percent "annual improvement factor" wage increase, intended to share GM's productivity gains with workers.

While other unions and companies were at first reluctant to follow GM and the UAW, by 1956, renewed inflation had fostered the adoption of COLA clauses into most union-management contracts. From 1958 to 1960, 4 million workers, half of all employees under major labor-management agreements were covered by COLA clauses. Just as COLA agreement popularity peaked during the late 1950s, prices fell by half in 1958, and averaged only 1.4 percent annually over the next eight years. As a result, union interest in COLAs sharply fell again. BLS surveys revealed that between 1961 and 1970, the proportion of workers under major agreements who were covered by COLA clauses averaged only 25 percent.

A new period of inflation beginning in 1966 once again fostered an increasing union interest in COLAs. It was a sharp increase in prices from 1973 to 1975, however, that brought a renewed interest in COLAs comparable to that of the late 1950s. By the end of 1975, an estimated 8 million workers were covered by some version of a COLA clause.

Further reading: Daniel Quinn Mills, *Government, Labor, and Inflation* (Chicago: University of Chicago Press, 1975).

— Jason Reed

Council of Economic Advisors (CEA)

The Council of Economic Advisors (CEA) was created as part of the EMPLOYMENT ACT OF 1946, a landmark piece of legislation that made it the policy and responsibility of the federal government to design economic policies to promote maximum employment, production, and consumer purchasing power. The role of the CEA in this process was to provide nonpartisan advice and consultation to the president when formulating these policies.

The CEA's role was to provide information on current and anticipated economic trends and to recommend national economic policies to fulfill the goals under the law. The CEA consists of three members appointed by the president and confirmed by the Senate. It issues a wide array of economic reports and studies during the year, and it is required to submit an annual report on the state of the ECONOMY each December.

The CEA was created as part of a broader effort by the federal government to improve its ability to control the economy and prevent a recurrence of the Great Depression. The adoption of the idea that fiscal policy could influence the domestic economy demonstrated increased acceptance by federal officials of the theories of John Maynard Keynes, who outlined the potential for government involvement in the economy in his landmark 1936 work *The General Theory of Employment, Interest and Money.* Keynes attacked classical economic thought that said that a free-market economy tended to produce full employment and maximum utilization of economic resources, and instead contended that spending, for both consumption and investment, was the critical element in determining the level of employment. He further argued that if private enterprise could not induce people to spend, then there were governmental means to do this. In 1939, Keynes's ideas influenced the creation of the National Resources Planning Board, established to improve the long-range economic planning capabilities of government.

Keynesian theories also affected economic planners during World War II, who feared that when the war ended the country would again fall back into depression. One important way to avoid this was to focus on postwar employment, especially since more than 10 million servicemen would need jobs when they left the military. In 1945, Congress took up consideration of a full employment bill that would make it the responsibility of the government to provide jobs for everyone who was willing to work. This idea, however, was very controversial, and after months of debate, the measure President HARRY S. TRUMAN finally signed into law as the Employment Act of 1946 was significantly different from what was originally proposed. Instead of making it the responsibility of the government to ensure full employment, the law mandated only that the government set domestic policies that would promote economic growth, with the CEA helping officials attain this goal.

The idea of an independent advisory group responsible to the president was a new and controversial initiative. Even though all CEA members had to have a background in economics, legislators feared they would be able to manipulate or even control national economic policy. Despite such concerns, Congress felt that a permanent body was necessary to provide the type of information needed to fulfill the objectives of the law. As hoped, the CEA helped educate and increase the economic literacy of policymakers. Because its reports were based on factual and analytical precision, the CEA has provided an unbiased account of past trends and prospects for the future. Finally, the CEA has become a center for economic research, innovation, and experimentation that improves its ability to focus on long-term objectives.

The Employment Act of 1946 with the creation of the CEA represented a major expansion of government's role in the economy. It institutionalized macroeconomic planning by the federal government and made the executive and legislative branches responsible for enactment of laws that would promote growth. This law was also part of a broader trend to increase government activism and involvement in the national economy.

Further reading: Stephen Kemp Bailey, *Congress Makes a Law: The Story Behind the Employment Act of 1946* (Westport, Conn.: Greenwood Press, 1950).

— Dave Mason

counterculture

The counterculture movement of the 1960s reflected the loss of faith in the American system for many young people and a willingness to experiment with new social and cultural patterns.

Most members of the counterculture tended to be young, white, well educated, and from a comfortable economic background. Many experimented with illicit drugs, free sex, sexual patterns, and different social and marital arrangements. The powerful post–World War II ECONOMY raised the expectations of young Americans, giving room for such radical cultural expressions.

The Beat movement grew out of the jazz culture of the 1940s and 1950s. Beats, or "Beatniks" as their critics sometimes called them, strove to be "cool," appearing detached from "square" society, seeking instead individualism and freedom. A central figure of the Beat movement was JACK KEROUAC. Kerouac coined the term BEAT GENERATION, which first meant weariness with American life, but later came to connote peacefulness and beatitude. Born of French-Canadian parents in Lowell, Massachusetts, Kerouac excelled at sports, earning an athletic scholarship to Columbia University in 1940. In the early 1940s Kerouac met poet ALLEN GINSBERG, and author William Burroughs. In 1946, he met Neal Cassady, whose manic lust for life became an inspiration to the group of writers. The Beats became nationally known in 1956 with the publication of Ginsberg's *Howl and Other Poems* and Kerouac's novel *On the Road* the following year. Because of the frank nature of *Howl*, media reports sensationalized the book and some critics called for its suppression. But the scandal only increased the fame of the Beats. *On the Road* was also a frank testament to the Beat lifestyle, openly celebrating their appetites for drugs, sex, or whatever thrills they could find. The novel quickly became a classic of countercultural LITERATURE, inspiring a generation of young Americans, especially those who found the 1950s a stifling decade in which to come of age. Other preeminent Beats included poets Michael McClure, Lawrence Ferlinghetti, whose City Lights Bookshop in San Francisco was central to Beat culture, and Gary Snyder.

Like the Beats before them, many young people in the 1960s, especially college students, criticized what they perceived to be a culture of conformity on the part of their parents' generation, favoring individualism over "fitting in." Many young Americans were inspired by the Beats. Others learned to question authority through involvement with campus political movements such as the STUDENTS FOR A DEMOCRATIC SOCIETY (SDS) and the FREE SPEECH MOVEMENT at the University of California at Berkeley. Other sources of the counterculture include a resurgent feminist movement, sparked by BETTY FRIEDAN's *Feminine Mystique* in 1963, which inspired many young women to question traditional roles. That same year, Harvard University dismissed TIMOTHY LEARY for

Allen Ginsberg, Timothy Leary, and Ralph Metzner (left to right) standing in front of a 10-foot plaster Buddha, preparing for a "psychedelic celebration" at the Village Theater, New York City   *(Library of Congress)*

experimenting with LSD and other drugs on himself and his students. Leary, who was often flanked at public events by Allen Ginsberg, became a hugely popular figure in the counterculture, urging students to "Tune in, turn on, drop out." Americans began to popularly recognize rebellious youth as "Hippies" by 1965. Two years later, thousands of hippies, "freaks," and others descended upon San Francisco, declaring a "Summer of Love." Many hippies judged mainstream society overly rational and technological, opting for things "natural," such as organic foods, marijuana, and nudism. Rock musicians such as the BEATLES, BOB DYLAN, and Janis Joplin became iconic figures whose recordings and concerts were of central significance in the lives of their fans.

There is no single coherent narrative of the counterculture in the 1960s; the number of movements and fads is too numerous to catalog briefly. As the decade progressed, some countercultural ideas and customs became more pop-ular or acceptable, among them relaxed styles of dress, long hair, vegetarianism, ROCK AND ROLL music, and extramarital sexual activity. Advertisers began to employ catchwords and styles favored by hippies in order to appear "with it" in the eyes of consumers. At the same time, many countercultural groups drifted further from mainstream society. Some fled from the cities for rural communes in remote places such as Taos, New Mexico, or to rural outposts in Northern California. Others such as Abbie Hoffman, Jerry Rubin and their Youth International Party, or "Yippies," embraced political radicalism and revolution. At the Democratic National Convention in Chicago in the summer of 1968, the Yippies gained national attention when they proposed the nomination of a pig for president and became involved in violent riots that convulsed Chicago's streets. Many countercultural figures, including Rubin and Hoffman, were arrested at the convention, and the narrow victory that November of "law and order" candidate Richard M. Nixon may have been influenced, albeit negatively, by the actions of the radical counterculture.

Further reading: Todd Gitlin, *The Sixties: Years of Hope, Days of Rage* (New York: Bantam, 1987); David Horowitz, Michael Lerner, and Craig Pyes, eds., *Counterculture and Revolution* (New York: Random House, 1972); Doug Rossinow, *The Politics of Authenticity: Liberalism, Christianity and the New Left in America* (New York: Columbia University Press, 1998).

— Patrick J. Walsh

credit cards

Credit cards expanded the buying power of postwar consumers, allowing Americans to purchase goods and services with little regard for income restrictions.

Prior to 1950, charge cards were a novelty for the rich, used in lieu of carrying large amounts of money, allowing the holder to sign for merchandise and services. Most Americans could not afford the luxuries of the rich and prosperous, making automobiles, washing machines, and other large-scale purchases beyond the means of the average consumer. The effects of the Great Depression and the onset of World War II further limited the market production of commodities and the buying capabilities of most families.

The postwar boom of the 1950s ended production constraints, and brought an abundance of products and goods to American markets. With it came an increased desire to own the newest appliances, televisions, and automobiles. Americans willingly went into debt to purchase those products that had been beyond their means during the lean years of the 1930s and 1940s. Retailers capitalized on this trend and promoted installment buying, allowing consumers to make large purchases on a monthly payment plan; smaller purchases were still made with cash. In February 1950, Frank McNamara, a New York businessman, discovered that he had forgotten his wallet elsewhere while dining out and the idea for a charge card that favored credit buying on a smaller scale was born. McNamara founded the Diners Club, and he offered the first charge card constructed of cardboard to 200 people. Diners Club allowed its members to charge meals at 27 New York City restaurants. For an annual fee of $3, cardholders were billed monthly with the balance to be paid in full each month.

In 1951, Franklin National Bank of New York introduced the first bank credit card. For a minimum monthly payment, consumers could make purchases at a small number of businesses that recognized the card. In 1958, the American Express card and Bank of America's BankAmericard joined the growing number of bank-issued cards that consumers found easy and convenient to use. Within three months of the issuance of the first American Express card, 500,000 people owned the card, and in less than 10 years, 2 million cardholders used American Express at the checkout counter. The popularity of credit cards increased steadily throughout the 1950s and 1960s, with American Express offering a more durable plastic card in 1959.

The growth of credit cards had an enormous impact on the ECONOMY, changing buying habits and making it easier for consumers to finance purchases. Manufacturers encouraged this spending by introducing new models of various products on a yearly basis, urging consumers to buy the latest models. Businesses turned to ADVERTISING and TELEVISION in an effort to market their products on a larger scale. Middle-class families joined with the very wealthy in buying products that reflected their status and prosperity, and increasing numbers of Americans tried to keep up with their neighbors by buying the latest products that continually flooded the market. Consumer credit increased from $8.4 billion in 1946, to nearly $45 billion in 1958, reflecting the enthusiasm that people had in using credit cards, installment plans, and loans in the postwar period. By 1965, 5 million credit cards were in circulation, with the largest increase in use taking place in the late 1970s with the introduction of Master Card in 1979.

Further reading: David S. Evans, *Paying with Plastic: The Digital Revolution in Buying and Borrowing* (Cambridge, Mass.: MIT Press, 1999); Robert A. Henrickson, *The Cashless Society* (New York: Dodd, Mead, 1972).

— Susan V. Spellman

Cuban missile crisis

The Cuban missile crisis was a standoff between the United States, the SOVIET UNION, and Cuba during October 1962.

The Soviets had deployed nuclear missiles in Cuba that were capable of reaching targets in the United States. For two tense weeks, the world hovered on the brink of nuclear war. Disaster was averted when Soviet leader Nikita Khrushchev agreed to remove the missiles in exchange for an American pledge not to invade Cuba.

After the failure of the BAY OF PIGS invasion, the administration of JOHN F. KENNEDY had Cuba removed from the Organization of American States, tightened the economic blockade, and authorized OPERATION MONGOOSE, an interagency task force devoted to the overthrow of Fidel Castro. In response, Castro moved closer to the Soviet Union, requesting military protection against another American invasion. Khrushchev responded with an offer to deploy Soviet nuclear weapons to Cuba.

The Soviet leader had several reasons to make this offer. He wanted to deter an American attack against Cuba, but he also sought to shore up the nuclear imbalance. By improving the Soviet Union's strategic position, he would be able to cut back conventional military forces, reduce overall defense spending, shift more funds into the civilian economy, and raise the Soviet standard of living. Although Castro had asked for more traditional military aid, he agreed to Khrushchev's proposal. He wanted to stave off a future American invasion, enhance Cuba's geopolitical position, and contribute to strengthening the socialist camp.

The first Soviet missiles arrived in Cuba in the late summer and early autumn of 1962. By early October, the Soviet deployment included medium-range ballistic missiles with 1-megaton warheads and a range of 1,100 nautical miles, nuclear-capable light bombers, and cruise missiles. The increased Soviet activity on the island did not escape the notice of American intelligence and the press, but Kennedy was confident that the weapons were defensive, such as surface-to-air missiles. He warned the Soviets that they should not deploy offensive weapons to a nation only 90 miles from the southern coast of the United States.

On the morning of October 16, Kennedy was informed that American reconnaissance had detected offensive missile sites in Cuba. The president immediately called his closest high-level advisers to the White House. This group of policymakers constituted the Executive Committee of the National Security Council, or ExComm, and together with Kennedy they made most of the policy decisions during the crisis.

For the next week, ExComm met secretly to discuss various diplomatic, political, and military options. They weighed the merits of an air strike, an outright invasion, a naval quarantine to prevent the deployment of additional weapons, and negotiation through the United Nations. Realizing that an air strike would not be able to eliminate all of the weapons, Kennedy opted for the quarantine. A

ERECTOR

HARDSTAND FOR ERECTOR

FIRING TABLE

MRBM LAUNCH SITE 1
SAN CRISTOBAL, CUBA
25 OCTOBER 1962

TRACKED PRIME MOVER

MISSILE SHELTER TENTS

MISSILE TRANSPORTERS

Picture from a spy satellite showing a missile launch site in Cuba　*(John F. Kennedy Library)*

quarantine would keep Soviet ships from reaching Cuba, but it was not called a blockade, for a blockade was an act of war.

On the evening of October 22, Kennedy addressed the nation on TELEVISION. He described the nuclear missile sites in Cuba and announced the quarantine. Several hours before, he had informed the Soviets that their missiles had been detected. The next week marked the most dangerous phase of the crisis. By October 27 all of the medium-range missiles in Cuba were assembled and could be tipped with nuclear warheads in four hours. In the meantime, a Soviet commander shot down an American U-2 reconnaissance plane, heightening the tension. Fortunately, cooler heads

prevailed. After the quarantine went into effect, Khrushchev ordered many of his ships to turn back.

On October 26, Khrushchev offered to remove the weapons if the United States promised not to invade Cuba. The next day, another letter arrived with the additional stipulation of a public trade of the Soviet missiles in Cuba for the American Jupiter missiles in Turkey. Kennedy found this additional condition unacceptable, but several advisers suggested ignoring the second message and responding positively only to the first letter. This tactic proved successful.

On October 28, Khrushchev announced that work on the missile sites would cease and the weapons would be dis-

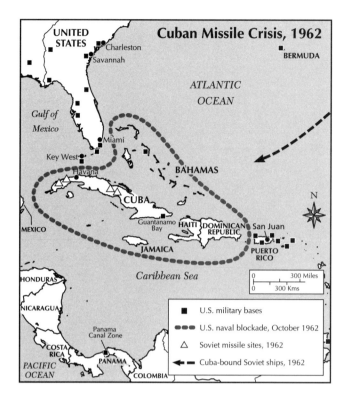

Cuban Missile Crisis, 1962

UNITED STATES

Charleston
Savannah

BERMUDA

ATLANTIC OCEAN

Gulf of Mexico

Miami

Key West

Havana

BAHAMAS

CUBA

N

MEXICO

Guantanamo Bay

HAITI

DOMINICAN REPUBLIC

San Juan

PUERTO RICO

JAMAICA

Caribbean Sea

HONDURAS

NICARAGUA

Panama Canal Zone

COSTA RICA

PANAMA

PACIFIC OCEAN

COLOMBIA

| | 300 Miles |
| | 300 Kms |

■ U.S. military bases

●●● U.S. naval blockade, October 1962

△ Soviet missile sites, 1962

◀─ ─ Cuba-bound Soviet ships, 1962

mantled and returned to the Soviet Union. In return, Kennedy pledged not to invade Cuba, although Operation Mongoose continued unabated until the president's death in 1963. Kennedy also secretly agreed to remove the Jupiter missiles from Turkey.

Despite haggling among all three parties over the details of removal of the weapons, the crisis ended peacefully and all offensive missiles were shipped back to the Soviet Union. Kennedy terminated the quarantine on November 21. The danger of the crisis and the threat of nuclear war led both Khrushchev and Kennedy to try to improve U.S.–Soviet relations, including establishing a hotline to provide for constant communication. Although they achieved only limited success, the post-crisis thaw in relations did contribute to the LIMITED TEST BAN TREATY OF 1963.

Further reading: Aleksandr Fursenko, and Timothy Naftali, *"One Hell of a Gamble": Khrushchev, Castro, and Kennedy, 1958–1964* (New York: W. W. Norton, 1997); Mark J. White, *The Cuban Missile Crisis* (London: Macmillan Press, 1996).

— Jennifer Walton

D

defense budget

Following World War II DEMOBILIZATION, the defense budget at times experienced major cuts, but then rose dramatically to meet the needs of the COLD WAR.

After the sizable defense buildup accompanying World War II, the United States sought to lower defense expenditures to more reasonable levels in peacetime. President HARRY S. TRUMAN wanted to scale back the defense budget, while at the same time raising the military's effectiveness. As Truman's presidency continued, the consistently lower budget allocations gradually began to worry many military leaders, who felt the continued cutbacks would limit the efficiency of any military action. Truman hoped that foreign economic aid, including the MARSHALL PLAN, would also curtail any aggressiveness by the SOVIET UNION, lessening any need for additional expenditures.

Nevertheless, Truman gradually relented, though he still retained a stranglehold over the disbursement of funds. With the 1949 communist takeover of China, the Soviet ATOMIC BOMB test, and countries demanding American assistance, it became imperative that the budget be increased. By fiscal year 1949, though Truman only requested $10.3 billion for defense, the actual expenditures totaled just over $12 billion. The same thing happened during the next fiscal year, though the excess was smaller.

Security issues demanded increased funding. The National Security Council, in an effort to repel security risks, drafted NSC-68, a document calling for larger budget expenditures to strengthen American defenses overseas and combat communist propaganda. Once presented with NSC-68, Truman quickly approved it. NSC-68 was not implemented immediately, but the start of the KOREAN WAR in June 1950 sped up the process. By December, Truman declared a national emergency, calling for additional defense expenditures. The defense budget quadrupled during this time.

The Korean War ended in a stalemate in 1953. By then, DWIGHT D. EISENHOWER had been elected president. Eisenhower knew that defense expenditures needed to be cut. Because he did not fully agree with the reasoning of NSC-68, he was forced to revise the Truman defense budgets. In the first fiscal year alone, Eisenhower cut approximately $10 billion, with about half of that cut coming directly from national security measures.

Eisenhower also altered the defense plans in another way, with his "New Look" or "Massive Retaliation" policy. Focusing more on nuclear deterrents and large-scale retaliation for any threatening action, he reallocated dollars to the air force, often at the expense of the army and navy. This would, his administration claimed, give a "bigger bang for the buck." Throughout his presidency, Eisenhower sought to limit the burden on the American people so as not to lead the country toward financial dire straits, which he felt could occur if the militarization of American society continued. In his farewell address at the end of his second term, Eisenhower warned of the United States becoming a MILITARY-INDUSTRIAL COMPLEX.

By Eisenhower's second term, arguments over defense spending continued. The Gaither Report, a top-secret security document calling for an immediate increase in spending, only exacerbated the president's problem when it was leaked to the press. The Soviet Union's 1957 launching of *Sputnik* also led to calls for additional defense spending, as did the growing crisis over Berlin. As had Truman, Eisenhower ultimately relented somewhat, though not nearly as much as military leaders and others wanted. The battle was not over, though; in the 1960 election year, Eisenhower's submissions were not nearly high enough for legislators hoping to spend more on local projects and to close a supposed missile gap with the Soviets.

When JOHN F. KENNEDY became president in 1961, there was a slight budget deficit left from the Eisenhower administration. Despite this and a slow economy, Kennedy increased military spending, focused mainly in a program called "Flexible Response," on the more conventional weapons rejected by Eisenhower. As the Berlin question continued to cause problems, Kennedy further increased the budget and eventually called for a civil defense program that included fallout shelters.

The VIETNAM WAR issue became more predominant during the Kennedy administration, and after his assassination, LYNDON B. JOHNSON further expanded American presence in Southeast Asia. By 1968, the American troop involvement reached its peak. Substantial amounts of money were required to support the more than 500,000 American troops in Vietnam. On the domestic front, Johnson promoted his GREAT SOCIETY, but there was not nearly as much money as was needed for both of these endeavors. Nevertheless, in the five years Johnson was president, the actual military budget increased from $51 billion to $76 billion; within those numbers, spending for missiles and nuclear-related devices dropped considerably, while, as in the Kennedy administration, expenditures for conventional weapons skyrocketed, almost doubling.

Further reading: Michael Hogan, *A Cross of Iron: Harry S. Truman and the Origins of the National Security State 1945–1954* (Cambridge, U.K.: Cambridge University Press, 1998); Diane Kunz, *Butter and Guns: America's Cold War Economic Diplomacy* (New York: Free Press, 1997); Michael Sherry, *In the Shadow of War: The United States since the 1930s* (New Haven: Conn.: Yale University Press, 1995).

— D. Byron Painter

demobilization, after World War II

America's military and economic demobilization proceeded very rapidly after the end of World War II.

Demobilization started as early as Victory in Europe Day on May 8, 1945, and accelerated after Victory in Japan Day on August 14. The size of the U.S. armed forces plunged from 12 million men and women in June 1945 to 4 million by the middle of 1946 and to 1.5 million in June 1947, by which time the armed forces reached their peacetime level. Economic demobilization proceeded accordingly. The annual rate of spending for military expenses dropped from $90.9 billion in January 1945 to $10.3 billion in the second quarter of 1947.

Troops were dispersed systematically. The army created a point system that was later copied by other services. Under this system, each soldier received one point for each month of army service since September 1940, one point for each month served overseas, five points for each Service Cross, Silver Star, and Purple Heart, and 12 points for each child under 18 up to a limit of three children. In May 1945, the army announced it would send home every man with 85 or more points. The requirements decreased in subsequent months, falling to 60 total points by November.

This rapid demobilization had much to do with strong pressure from Congress. Troops, along with their family and friends, sent millions of letters asking for speedy return, warning their congressional representatives that any delay would cost them votes. Mothers even sent baby shoes accompanied by the words, "Please bring back my daddy."

Popular support for demobilization embodied an American political tradition going as far back as the War of Independence. Americans were concerned that a large peacetime standing army would require the expansion of the federal government and high taxes. Traditional isolationism, the emphasis on domestic pursuit of wealth rather than on international adventurism, and hatred for the extensive government controls required by a wartime economy, all created pressure for quicker demobilization.

Rapid demobilization in 1946–47 created a variety of military and strategic problems. The army lacked sufficient troops to guard its large supply depots against theft and to carry out its occupation duties in Germany, Austria, Japan, and Korea. Withdrawal from Western Europe raised concerns that the SOVIET UNION, which had not demobilized as fast or as thoroughly, could further expand its sphere of influence in Europe. The Soviet army numbered 3 million troops (down from 11 million during the war), with most located in or near Eastern Europe. Dwindling numbers of ground troops made overreliance on a large air force and on the ATOMIC BOMB the only strategic option, and obliged the State Department to use economic tools such as the MARSHALL PLAN rather than military threats to achieve its foreign policy goals.

Many business leaders feared that the economic impact of demobilization would create a recession, or even a return to the Great Depression. Fifty percent of the gross national product, which had grown from $101 billion in 1940 to $214 billion in 1945, was connected with military expenses by war's end. Many feared that unemployment, created with the cancellation of large military contracts, would increase with the return of 12 million demobilized servicemen.

These fears eventually proved unfounded. Civilian consumption, fueled by large wartime savings, quickly replaced military contracts. Many veterans went to college under the provisions of the 1944 G.I. Bill instead of entering the workforce. Overtime work diminished as the necessities of war production ceased to justify its existence. Many workingwomen went back home as their husbands came back from the war. In August 1946, with more than two-thirds of the armed forces demobilized, unemployment remained at 3.3 percent.

Further reading: Jack Stokes Ballard, *Military and Economic Demobilization after World War II* (Colorado Springs: University of Colorado Press, 1983).

— Philippe R. Girard

Democratic Party

In the two decades after World War II, the Democratic Party moved to the left of the political spectrum, alienating its southern, conservative wing while maintaining faith in the power of government to cure the ills of American society and play a dominant role in the world outside.

In the years directly after World War II, many Americans continued to perceive the Democratic Party as the party of the NEW DEAL. To some extent this was true: President HARRY S. TRUMAN oversaw the development of several New Deal–type programs, including the G.I. Bill, the FEDERAL HOUSING ADMINISTRATION, and the Commission on Civil Rights. He also echoed Roosevelt by promising a FAIR DEAL to all Americans. Nevertheless, in 1946 the Democrats lost control of Congress. Even within his own party Truman was compelled to placate conservative southern legislators bent on denying any power to civil rights legislation. In the 1948 presidential election, both its liberal and conservative wings abandoned the party. In 1947, former vice president Henry A. Wallace had formed the PROGRESSIVE PARTY, perceiving an alleged slavish allegiance to big business at the expense of human rights by the Democrats. An even greater threat to the Democrats' power came from the STATES' RIGHTS PARTY, popularly known as the Dixiecrats. In their party platform the Dixiecrats declared their support for "segregation of the races and the racial integrity of each race." In the November presidential election, Governor J. Strom Thurmond of South Carolina, the Dixiecrats' candidate, won four Southern states. Republican candidate THOMAS E. DEWEY won much of the Northeast and Midwest but, although heavily favored to win, was unable to shake the Democrats' hold on the White House.

Four years later, in a wide-open race for president, the Democrats settled on Illinois governor ADLAI STEVENSON. A symbol of the party's liberal wing, Stevenson hoped to extend the New Deal and Fair Deal, but stood little chance against the widely popular General DWIGHT D. EISENHOWER. Stevenson, whose divorce likely cost him support of many Catholic voters, won no state north of West Virginia or west of the Mississippi. The Democrats retook control of Congress at the midterm election, however, criticizing their Republican opponents as weak on defense while stressing the need for a strong United States presence in the United Nations. When Stevenson again faced Eisenhower in the 1956 election, the Democrats were once more unable to unseat the president.

As the election of 1960 approached, Democrats, and their presidential candidate JOHN F. KENNEDY, warned of a supposed "missile gap" separating the United States from the SOVIET UNION. With the help of organized labor, Catholics, and African-American voters, the Democrats retook the White House. On the state level, the party prospered as well, holding 35 governors' chairs. Kennedy's victory represented a generational shift in the party. Narrowly defeating Vice President Richard M. Nixon, Kennedy declared the nation at the edge of a "new frontier." Under Kennedy, the Democrats continued to pursue internationalism, initiating involvement that would develop into the VIETNAM WAR. In the year before his 1963 assassination, Kennedy began to use the power of the federal government to enforce desegregation and proposed a sweeping civil rights bill. After Kennedy's death in November, he was succeeded by LYNDON B. JOHNSON. Johnson's presidency is thought by some to represent the high water mark of American LIBERALISM. He instituted his GREAT SOCIETY, a wide slate of social programs, moving beyond the economic policy of the New Deal to address issues of race and poverty. During the mid-1960s, the Democrats passed the CIVIL RIGHTS ACT OF 1964 and the VOTING RIGHTS ACT OF 1965 and began such social welfare programs as VOLUNTEERS IN SERVICE TO AMERICA (VISTA) and HEAD START. Under Johnson, the Democrats waged a WAR ON POVERTY.

Despite Johnson's reelection in 1964, sectional tension in the party continued to be played out at the national convention. In this case, the state of Mississippi seated an all-white delegation, causing intense dissent among civil rights workers and blacks. In addition, the interventionist and internationalist style of government pursued by the Democrats was beginning to lose its widespread favor. This was largely due to the American struggle to win the conflict in Vietnam. By 1968, spending on the Vietnam War was several times larger than spending for social programs. As the war continued, a growing number of Americans voiced their opposition to its continuance. Johnson, challenged for the 1968 nomination by antiwar candidate EUGENE MCCARTHY, did not seek reelection. The assassinations of MARTIN LUTHER KING, JR., in April and Democratic frontrunner senator ROBERT F. KENNEDY of New York in June further shook the political faith of many Americans. At the Democratic National Convention in Chicago that August, violence burst out both in the hall and on the streets. The party, in disarray, nominated Vice President HUBERT H. HUMPHREY of Minnesota. A New Deal Democrat, Humphrey was defeated by Nixon in November, as many southern Democrats left the party to vote for the rabble-rousing segregationist GEORGE C. WALLACE, former governor of Alabama.

Further reading: John Gerring. *Party Ideologies in America, 1828–1996* (Cambridge, U.K.: Cambridge University Press, 1998); Robert Allen Rutland, *The Democrats: From Jefferson to Clinton* (Columbia: University of Missouri Press, 1995).

— Patrick J. Walsh

Dennis v. United States (1951)

The *Dennis* v. *United States* case was part of the effort to stop the spread of COMMUNISM within the United States.

As the fear of domestic subversion spread throughout the nation after World War II, the administration of President HARRY S. TRUMAN attempted to eliminate the Communist Party of the United States (CPUSA) by enforcing the Smith Act. The Smith Act (1940) made it a federal offense to advocate the violent overthrow of the government. When Eugene Dennis, the general secretary in the CPUSA, was found guilty of violating the Smith Act in 1949, he was sentenced, along with 10 other members, to five years in prison. On appeal in 1949, the Supreme Court reviewed the case and subsequently affirmed the conviction by a 6-2 vote.

Eugene Dennis (originally known as Francis X. Waldron) was a veteran of the Comintern, a Moscow-based agency that worked to promote progressive coalitions against the spread of fascism in South Africa, China, and the Philippines. A graduate of the Lenin Institute in Moscow, he took on the position of general secretary for the CPUSA. Because of his position, he was charged under the Smith Act with advocacy and intent to overthrow the U.S. government by violent means. Despite the fact that the Smith Act had been enforced only once before, it now became more important as the COLD WAR intensified.

The case began with a suspect grand jury indictment. Thomas Clark, attorney general of the United States, wanted to test the feasibility of an indictment under the Smith Act in early 1948. Aided by the Justice Department's prosecutors, however, a grand jury indictment of Dennis and the other co-defendants was obtained without Clark's or President Truman's prior approval. This bureaucratic initiative pleased Truman in the election year of 1948, complementing his platform that outlined a tough policy on communism.

The rancorous trial began in January 1949 in United States District Court. For the government to win a conviction under the Smith Act, it had to establish that the co-defendants "willfully and knowingly conspired to organize a group that taught and advocated the overthrow of the government by sufficiently violent means."

The codefendants were represented by a defense team, all of whom were members of the left-wing National Lawyers Guild, which consisted of Harry Sacher of New York, Abraham Isserman of New Jersey, Richard Gladstein of San Francisco, and George Crockett of Detroit.

International events provided the backdrop for the trial. The SOVIET UNION successfully tested an ATOMIC BOMB while the trial wound on through appeals, and the Chinese were in the midst of a violent revolution that soon ended in a communist triumph. On the home front, the trial of ALGER HISS, a former State Department employee accused of communist ties, unfolded at the same time as *Dennis* and in the same courthouse. As a result, the jury had no difficulty concluding that the CPUSA constituted a threat to national security. At the conclusion of the district court trial, 10 defendants, including Dennis, were sentenced to five years in prison.

Immediately following the verdict, Judge J. H. Medina found the defense counsel in contempt of court for deliberately prolonging the trial in order to increase chances of an acquittal.

The U.S. Second Circuit Court of Appeals, under Chief Judge Learned Hand and Judges Swan and Brigham, however, upheld the lower court's decision. The appeals court asserted that there was demonstrable evidence that exhibited intent to overthrow the government by violent means.

On June 4, 1951, the Supreme Court of the United States, by a 6-2 majority, affirmed the decisions of both the lower court and appellate court of New York. The KOREAN WAR had escalated during this time, and increasing numbers of people felt that the CPUSA posed a "clear and present danger" that required the suppression of First Amendment rights. The majority opinion assumed that the CPUSA was organizing a "violent overthrow" simply because it willfully advocated such a course in its Marxist-Leninist doctrines and literature.

Justices Hugo Black and William Douglas both argued, in separate dissents, that speech was advocacy and should not be punishable because it did not create a "clear and present danger." Moreover, Black wrote that "in calmer times when present pressures, passions, and fears subside, the First Amendment liberties will be restored to the high preferred place where they belong in a free society."

Further reading: Michael Belknap, *Cold War Political Justice* (Westport, Conn.: Greenwood Press, 1997); Stanley Kutler, *The American Inquisition* (New York: Hill & Wang, 1982).

— John E. Bibish IV

Dewey, Thomas E. (1902–1971)

Thomas E. Dewey ran as Republican candidate for the American presidency in 1944 and 1948, after having become nationally famous by prosecuting several notorious New York gangsters in the 1930s. He also won the governorship of New York in 1942, 1946, and 1950.

Dewey was born on March 24, 1902, in Owosso, Michigan, to George Martin Dewey, a staunch Republican newspaper editor, and Annie Louise Thomas. Although Dewey showed an interest in politics from an early age, he also showed great promise as a baritone singer and for a time it appeared that his future might be in music. He studied music and law at the University of Michigan, graduating with a bachelor's degree in 1923. In the same year he moved to New York to study music while also attending Columbia Law School. Columbia sparked Dewey's interest in law and he soon abandoned music, graduating with a law degree in 1925.

After finishing law school, Dewey worked at two Wall Street law firms and became active in reform-minded Republican political clubs. By the end of the decade, Dewey had begun to make a name for himself among New York Republicans. In 1931, he left Wall Street for a job as chief assistant U.S. attorney for the southern district of New York. When his boss resigned in November 1933, Dewey succeeded him as U.S. attorney on an interim basis until Dewey himself was replaced by Franklin D. Roosevelt's new appointee in December. Dewey excelled at prosecuting organized crime and became New York governor Herbert Lehman's choice as special prosecutor when the governor became concerned with the power of criminal rackets in 1935. Dewey, who had returned to private practice, accepted the offer and by 1936 scored a spectacular success prosecuting the notorious mobster Charles "Lucky" Luciano. Dewey became nationally famous for his racket-busting and Hollywood soon began churning out movies like *Smashing the Rackets* and *Racket Buster* based on his exploits. Dewey capitalized on his popularity by running for Manhattan district attorney in 1937 and became the first Republican to win that office in 25 years. His success caught the attention of the REPUBLICAN PARTY and he ran for governor of New York in 1938, narrowly losing to the popular incumbent Lehman. Dewey's reputation was still on the rise, though, and he might even have received the Republican nomination for president in 1940 had not the growing war crisis made the older, more interventionist Wendell Willkie a more attractive candidate.

Dewey did win the governorship of New York in 1942 and continued to establish himself as a progressive-minded Republican. He won the 1944 Republican presidential nomination but could not muster more than 46 percent of the popular vote running against President Roosevelt in the midst of World War II. Still, his percentage of the popular vote was the highest for a Republican in the Roosevelt years.

After being easily reelected as governor of New York in 1946, Dewey again gained the Republican nomination in 1948. Many assumed he would defeat unpopular Democratic president HARRY S. TRUMAN. Truman ran a fierce campaign, though, securing the middle of the political spectrum in the face of opposition from the liberal PROGRESSIVE PARTY of HENRY A. WALLACE and the segregationist STATES' RIGHTS PARTY of Strom Thurmond. In the meantime, Truman worked tirelessly to paint Dewey as little different than the "do-nothing" Republican

Thomas E. Dewey (center) with Thomas J. Curran, Manhattan GOP leader, on return from a campaign tour
(Library of Congress)

Congress in power since 1946. Still, virtually all opinion polls predicted a Dewey victory. In a stunning upset, Truman won the popular vote from Dewey by a 49 percent to 45 percent margin while collecting 303 electoral votes to Dewey's 189. The Democrats also recaptured control of Congress.

The defeat was a crushing one for Dewey and was the defining moment of his career in popular and historical memory. Nonetheless, he continued as an important force in the more moderate, progressive wing of the Republican Party. Dewey won a third term as governor in 1950 and helped DWIGHT D. EISENHOWER secure the party's nomination in 1952 over Dewey's bitter rival, the conservative Ohio senator ROBERT A. TAFT. Dewey also played a role in getting the 1952 vice-presidential nomination for his young protégé, California senator Richard M. Nixon.

Dewey retired from the governorship of New York in 1955 and took up law again in New York City. He remained active in the Republican Party, sometimes advising Eisenhower and, later, Nixon. Nixon offered Dewey the chance to be nominated for chief justice of the Supreme Court in 1968 but Dewey declined, partially so he could care for his ailing wife. He died in Florida in 1971.

Further reading: Richard N. Smith, *Thomas E. Dewey and His Times* (New York. Simon & Schuster, 1982).

— Kevin P. Bower

Dixiecrat Party   See States' Rights Party

domesticity   See marriage and family life

Dow Chemical Corporation

Originally founded to produce bleach, the Dow Chemical Corporation became a global SCIENCE and TECHNOLOGY company producing a wide array of chemicals, plastics, and agricultural products.

Established in 1897 by Herbert Dow, the company initially focused on developing a new way to make bleach. Dow had discovered a process by which bleach could be produced more cheaply and effectively. In January 1898, Dow made its first sales of bleach, but ceased making bleach to explore other ventures in 1913. The direction of the Dow Chemical Corporation took a rapid turn as the United States entered World War I in April 1917. In order to contend with the use of chemical weapons by Germany, Dow plunged into the production of these chemical agents. Herbert Dow abhorred this fact, calling the production of chemical weapons "the worst thing I ever had to do." The company produced tear gas, chlorine gas, and, most deadly of all, mustard gas. By 1918, 90 percent of Dow's production was for war purposes.

Following the conclusion of World War I, Dow diversified into other fields. The company developed Dowmetal pistons, constructed with magnesium, which was a third lighter than aluminum. In 1921, Tommy Milton won the Indianapolis 500 equipped with Dowmetal pistons.

Over the next few decades, Dow Chemical Corporation researchers perfected a method for producing vinyl chloride, the basic element in plastic products. The group produced Saran Wrap and Handi-Wrap, consumer products that became familiar items in the home. Dow also perfected the process of obtaining bromine from seawater, a critical element in an antiknock gasoline compound that kept an automobile engine running smoothly.

Perhaps the biggest challenge the Dow Chemical Corporation faced came with the onset of the VIETNAM WAR. Dow became the leading producer of napalm, a type of jellied gasoline that stuck to people's bodies and burned at an intense heat. It was used to dislodge troops from fortified positions, which proved highly effective in the jungles of Southeast Asia. Due to TELEVISION footage from the field, however, protesters argued that napalm was also being used against innocent civilians, including women and children. Although military officials denied this, the Dow Chemical Corporation took the brunt of the protests. Often protesters carried signs saying "Dow Shall Not Kill," and "Napalm burns babies, Dow makes money." In addition to napalm, the Dow Chemical Corporation, along with other companies, also produced Agent Orange, a chemical defoliant that was used in Vietnam. Although these chemicals came under constant criticism, the Dow Chemical Corporation regained its position as one of the leaders of chemical research and production following the Vietnam War.

By the end of the 20th century, the Dow Chemical Corporation earned annual profits of $20 billion through its wide variety of products.

Further reading: E. N. Brandt, *Growth Company: Dow Chemical's First Century* (East Lansing: Michigan State University Press, 1997).

— Clayton Douglas

Dulles, John Foster (1888–1959)

John Foster Dulles was President DWIGHT D. EISENHOWER's first secretary of state, serving from 1953 to 1959.

Born in Washington, D.C., on February 25, 1888, Dulles was the grandson of John Watson Foster, an ambassador, international lawyer, and Benjamin Harrison's secretary of state, and the nephew of Robert Lansing, Woodrow Wilson's secretary of state. Dulles graduated from Princeton in 1908 and attended the Sorbonne in Paris the following winter before heading to the George Washington University law school in 1909.

Dulles spent the first half of his career as an international lawyer. In 1907, he attended a peace conference in The Hague, the Netherlands. In 1911, he joined the New York law firm of Sullivan and Cromwell, and accompanied the U.S. delegation to the Versailles Peace Conference in 1919, serving as legal counsel and as a member of the war reparations commission. He helped draft the United Nations charter at the Dumberton Oaks conference in 1944, and he attended the conference to set up the organization in San Francisco in 1945, where he served as senior adviser. He single-handedly negotiated the 1951 Japanese Peace Treaty.

When Eisenhower was elected president in November 1952, he chose Dulles as his secretary of state. The nation's chief diplomat brought strong opinions to the office. A devout Presbyterian and the son of a minister, Dulles possessed a strong moralistic streak that led him to view issues in black-and-white terms and prevented him from seeking common ground with the SOVIET UNION.

Along with Eisenhower, Dulles devised a policy described as the New Look, which relied on the threat of massive retaliation with nuclear weapons if the Soviet

John Foster Dulles (right) shakes hands with his brother Allen Welsh Dulles at La Guardia Field, New York City *(Library of Congress)*

Union proved belligerent. This was a way of providing adequate defense while limiting spending. Abandoning containment as an immoral policy that accepted communist control of parts of ASIA and EUROPE, the New Look sought to lessen Soviet influence by preaching the need for liberation of captive nations from the Soviet yoke. Aware of the limited geographic reach of the NORTH ATLANTIC TREATY ORGANIZATION (NATO), Dulles initiated talks to establish the SOUTHEAST ASIA TREATY ORGANIZATION (SEATO) in an effort to unite nations in Southeast Asia in a similar defense pact.

During the 1950s, many Asian and African countries gained their independence. When some of these opted in favor of neutralism, Dulles was intent on making sure the third world chose the American side in the cold war. Neutralism, he declared, was immoral. He was furious when Egyptian leader Gamal Abdel Nasser sought to play the Soviet Union against the United States. When Nasser nationalized the Suez Canal after Dulles abruptly withdrew his offer to fund Nasser's pet project, the Aswan Dam, Dulles was furious, but he still kept allies in the MIDDLE EAST from destroying Egypt.

In other areas of the globe, ANTICOMMUNISM took precedence over third world sympathies. The United States funded France's war to keep Indochina French (1945–54). After the Geneva Accords (July 1954) temporarily divided Vietnam, the United States shored up the South Vietnamese government of Ngo Dinh Diem in the first move toward the VIETNAM WAR. In 1953 and 1954, the CIA helped overthrow the left-leaning nationalist governments of Mohammad Mosaddeq in Iran and Jacobo

Arbenz in Guatemala. Soon after Fidel Castro gained power in January 1959, U.S.–Cuban relations turned sour.

Sick with cancer, Dulles resigned on April 15, 1959, and he died the next month. Though he was often criticized for his harsh, calculated methods, particularly his support for "brinkmanship"—pushing an adversary to the brink—Eisenhower called him "one of the truly great men of our time."

Further reading: Townsend Hoopes, *The Devil and John Foster Dulles* (Boston: Little, Brown, 1973); Ronald W. Pruessen, *John Foster Dulles: The Road to Power* (New York: Free Press, 1982).

— Philippe R. Girard

DuPont Corporation

The DuPont Corporation, one of the oldest industrial companies in the United States, helped develop and produce nuclear weapons during the arms race of the COLD WAR, in addition to providing the public with many consumer goods.

The DuPont Corporation was founded in Delaware in 1802 by Éleuthère Irénée du Pont to produce black powder, and later, other explosives. As blasting powders became more important, the company produced "soda powder," the first industrial explosive, in 1857. When three of du Pont's great-grandsons acquired full ownership of the company in 1902, they introduced the basic hierarchical structure associated with the modern corporation. Having been forced by the U.S. government to divest part of its manufacturing capacity in 1912, because it was considered a monopoly, DuPont diversified, acquiring a 25 percent stake in GENERAL MOTORS.

In the 1920s, following DuPont's invention of nylon, the main focus of production shifted to textiles and chemicals. Some products included plastics, photographic film, and agricultural chemicals. The company developed synthetics like Lucite, Teflon, Orlon, Mylar, Kevlar, and Dacron.

At the onset of the cold war, federally funded nuclear research linked the company to university scientists who could further the development of nuclear weapons. As the cold war unfolded, an ever-tighter relationship among scientists, corporations, and the military developed. After the SOVIET UNION detonated an ATOMIC BOMB in 1949, the United States built a number of nuclear centers, such as Livermore Laboratory near San Francisco, which supplemented a similar facility at Los Alamos, New Mexico.

Meanwhile, in 1950 DuPont assumed responsibility for a new plant in South Carolina intended to produce nuclear materials for HYDROGEN BOMBS. In so doing, it became an important part of the MILITARY-INDUSTRIAL

COMPLEX, which President DWIGHT D. EISENHOWER warned Americans to be wary of in his farewell address in 1961. Nonetheless, DuPont found itself falling behind, as other industries took the lead in cold war research. DuPont, still committed to the chemical field, was unable to hire the researchers it needed.

During the 1960s, DuPont introduced Lycra brand spandex, which was popular as colorful swimwear material. DuPont introduced electronic materials, too, but the company concentrated on consumer items that featured Nomex and Kevlar brand fibers.

In the 1980s, DuPont acquired Conoco Inc., an oil firm later sold in 1999. Concentrating on the biological sciences and their expansion, Dupont purchased the biotechnology company Pioneer Hi-Bred International in 1998 for $7.7 billion.

Further reading: David A.Hounshell, *Science and Corporate Strategy: Dupont R&D, 1902–1980* (Cambridge, U.K.: Cambridge University Press, 1989); Graham D. Taylor and Patricia E. Sudnik, *DuPont and the International Chemical Industry* (Boston: Twayne, 1984).

— John E. Bibish IV

Dylan, Bob (1941–)

Bob Dylan is one of the most influential songwriters in the history of American music. His folk rock music was the voice of the youth in America during the 1960s.

Dylan was born Robert Allen Zimmerman on May 24, 1941, in Duluth, Minnesota. He began writing poetry, which he later set to MUSIC, at the age of 10. He taught himself both electric and acoustic guitar during his early teen years, along with the piano. During high school, he formed many rock bands, playing songs from his earliest influences such as ELVIS PRESLEY, Little Richard, and Jerry Lee Lewis. Upon graduation from high school in 1959, Dylan attended the University of Minnesota in St. Paul.

During his time in St. Paul, Dylan focused mainly on his songwriting and performing at local clubs in a part of the city called Dinkytown. Soon Dylan lost all interest in his studies, and by 1960, he had left St. Paul for life on the East Coast. Dylan had heard of the folk movement in Greenwich Village in New York City, and he moved there to join it.

Upon arriving in New York, Dylan fulfilled a lifelong dream of meeting folk legend Woody Guthrie. Dylan visited the ailing Guthrie on a regular basis and sang Guthrie his songs. At the same time, Dylan was successful on the club circuit in the Village. Soon he was playing in the student center at Columbia University.

In 1961, he officially changed his name from Zimmerman to Dylan, broke out of the folk circle, and began to expand into other types of music. He played

Bob Dylan, 1967 *(Library of Congress)*

harmonica on a Harry Belafonte album, and he even sang solo in Carnegie Hall. Though only 53 people, mostly close friends, showed up, his review in the *New York Times* was outstanding, and it led to a contract with Columbia Records.

The following year, Dylan released his first album, which featured only two original songs. Though the album was not a success, Dylan's distinct singing voice and acoustic guitar work were widely noted by critics. His next album, released in 1963, *The Free Wheelin' Bob Dylan*, was a huge success, with songs such as "Blowin' in the Wind" and "A Hard Rain's A-Gonna Fall."

The Times They Are A-Changin' promoted a new message. Dylan had grown tired of being the poster boy for the FOLK MUSIC REVIVAL and he wanted out. Dylan reaffirmed this growing separation from the movement with the album *Another Side of Bob Dylan* and the song "It Ain't Me Babe," in which he explained he was not the leader young people were searching for. Meanwhile, Dylan had gotten involved with Joan Baez, one of folk music's biggest names. This relationship, though it did not last long, proved beneficial to both Dylan and Baez. He used her previous fame and connections to further his music, and Baez used some of his unreleased songs.

By 1965, the relationship between Baez and Dylan was fading, and it was time for yet another change in Dylan's music. He released the album *Bringing It All Back Home,* a half-acoustic, half-electric collection that was mostly rejected by his folk fans, but it was a success on all other fronts. The acoustic song "Mr. Tambourine Man" was released on the album, and The Byrds soon picked it up and made it a hit in an upbeat, electric version. After this album was released, Dylan played at the Newport Folk Festival using his electric guitar, and he was booed off the stage by his folk fans. Dylan formed a new fan base, outside the folk movement, that came from the youth of the COUNTERCULTURE. His songs conveyed social messages and spoke out against U.S. involvement in Vietnam. Many young people embraced his music and its message of peace.

After breaking with Baez, Dylan released his album *Highway 61,* and he married Sara Lowndes. He and Sara immediately had children, and Dylan continued to work, releasing two more albums, *Highway 61 Revisited* and *Blonde on Blonde.* Not long after, Dylan was injured in a motorcycle accident, and this changed his musical agenda again. After the accident, he recovered in seclusion with his family in Woodstock, New York. Dylan did not tour again for eight years. In 1967, he released *John Wesley Harding,* which had a country sound. In 1968, he played at a Woody Guthrie Memorial Concert. He returned to the privacy of his home and to his family after the concert.

Dylan has gone on to release several more albums, which contain some of his biggest hits. He began to tour again in the early 1970s, and he continues to tour, singing his classics from his early years and new songs that he has recently composed.

Further reading: Clinton Heylin, *Bob Dylan: A Life in Stolen Moments: Day by Day, 1941–1995* (New York: Prentice Hall International, 1996); Bob Spitz, *Dylan: A Biography* (New York: McGraw-Hill, 1989).

— Matthew Escovar

"dynamic conservativism"   See modern Republicanism

E

Economic Opportunity Act of 1964

The Economic Opportunity Act of 1964 comprised the legislation behind President LYNDON B. JOHNSON's War on Poverty, and expanded many existing antipoverty programs while creating several new ones.

The Johnson administration tapped Democratic Congressman Phil Landrum of Georgia to introduce the sweeping antipoverty program that Johnson had called for in his 1964 State of the Union address. The Economic Opportunity Act created several new federal programs, including the JOB CORPS, VOLUNTEERS IN SERVICE TO AMERICA (VISTA), and work study. The Job Corps provided housing, employment, and job training for 16 to 21 year olds. Through work study, disadvantaged students could obtain work through vocational and higher educational institutions to help them meet the costs of furthering their education. VISTA created a nationwide force of volunteers to staff state and local antipoverty programs. Participants received living allowances and small stipends while serving with the program. The measure authorized the Department of Health, Education, and Welfare to establish pilot programs to give job training and placement assistance to heads of households receiving Aid for Dependent Children payments as well.

Federal funding was provided for state and local antipoverty initiatives. Any programs, public or private, that helped people get jobs, job training and educational assistance, or improved the living conditions of the poor were eligible for funding, if they were administered by an organization that was already helping the poor. The federal government paid most costs of these programs initially, but it reduced its involvement over time to 50 percent. The act also offered federally guaranteed loans to small businesses and farmers to stabilize their operations and create jobs.

Perhaps the most controversial aspect of the bill was the creation of the Office of Economic Opportunity, a new federal agency to oversee the War on Poverty. The purpose of this office was to coordinate the nation's antipoverty programs, many of which were at least partially funded by this bill. Critics charged that this was "an unneeded layer of federal authority" and "a dangerous assault on the established system of state-federal relationships." Republicans ultimately introduced an antipoverty bill of their own that eliminated the Office of Economic Opportunity, Job Corps, and VISTA. The administration overcame this challenge by agreeing to amendments that effectively gave governors veto power over government activities in their state that were authorized or funded by the Economic Opportunity Act. This change still allowed privately run programs to receive federal assistance under the bill, regardless of the governor's approval.

Giving governors control over how the measure affected their states was not the only compromise that the Johnson administration had to make to get the act passed. The administration's original bill had been more generous to farmers. For example, the government was to establish a program to sell farmland to poor farmers below the land's market value. Congress deleted this provision and turned grants to farmers into guaranteed loans. Dairy farmers, however, did get relief that they had been seeking. The final bill authorized indemnity payments to dairy farmers who were unable to sell milk because it still contained traces of recently banned pesticides.

Several major organizations voiced their opinions on the measure. Labor groups, led by the AFL-CIO supported it, as did the URBAN LEAGUE and NATIONAL ASSOCIATION FOR THE ADVANCEMENT OF COLORED PEOPLE (NAACP). The Farm Bureau, National Association of Manufacturers, and the U.S. Chamber of Commerce opposed it.

Debate in Congress over the bill was spirited. Republicans claimed that the bill and the entire War on Poverty were merely "election year gimmicks." They seized on the fact that LADY BIRD JOHNSON owned thousands of acres of land in Alabama with desperately poor farm laborers living on it as evidence of the administration's insincerity on the issue. The bill's opponents also interjected race into the debate. They raised the specter of uncontrolled, integrated Job Corps camps in southern states and the NAACP receiving federal aid for its activities under the guise of combating poverty. The administration responded to these attacks by pointing out that 80 percent of Americans in poverty were white.

The measure was portrayed as a way to solve the problem of poverty. Conceived in the spirit of the NEW DEAL, these new programs went beyond providing economic assistance to the poor. The worker training and educational aspects gave some poor the skills to bring themselves out of poverty, and, more important, the training to stay out of poverty. Those who benefited became, as the bill's supporters put it, "taxpayers, not taxeaters." While these programs undoubtedly helped many people improve their lives and escape poverty, they did not end it. Measuring the act by the standards set by the rhetoric of its supporters was not entirely successful.

Further reading: Irwin Unger, *The Best of Intentions* (New York: Doubleday, 1996).

— Dave Price

economy

In the decades immediately following World War II, the United States entered one of the longest sustained economic expansions in the history of the country while contending with COLD WAR anxieties and the persistence of poverty.

The economic optimism that characterized America in the 1920s ended with the stock market crash of 1929. With the onset of the Great Depression in the 1930s, Americans witnessed poverty at its deepest levels. The illu-

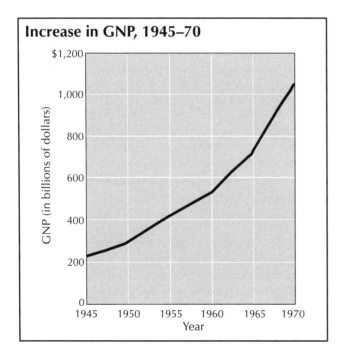

Increase in GNP, 1945–70

sion of permanent prosperity shattered as the unemployment rate and bread lines continued to grow. When President Franklin D. Roosevelt entered office in 1932, a new hope spread across the United States as he implemented his NEW DEAL, a welfare program to work in conjunction with the capitalist system, that sought to help those who could not help themselves. While the New Deal created dozens of relief measures and initiated the slow process to economic recovery, America remained unable to fully escape the Great Depression. The advent of World War II, however, brought the impetus needed to mobilize American industry for wartime production. Men and women not serving overseas went to work in the factories, building and producing everything from airplanes and merchant ships to uniforms and chemical weapons. The unemployment rate fell and the economy boomed as the entire country took part in the war effort.

As Americans returned home after World War II, the thriving economy relieved any lingering doubts of another depression and strengthened the position of the United States as the richest nation in the world. The gross national product (GNP) took a giant leap from just over $200 billion in 1945 to almost $300 billion in 1950. By 1960, the GNP surpassed $500 billion and reached $685 billion in 1965. It jumped to a staggering $970 billion by 1970. In 1945, per capita personal income was $1,223, and by 1970, that figure rose to $3,945. Almost 60 percent of all families in the country could boast of being a part of the middle class by 1970.

Cognizant of the role of spending in promoting economic revival, just as English economist John Maynard Keynes had predicted, legislators attempted to put in place such a program that could prevent a future downturn. The EMPLOYMENT ACT OF 1946 was one way in which economists worked to institutionalize the ideas of Keynes. The initial bill called for the government to monitor the economy and maintain full employment by requisite spending or other fiscal tools if a downturn threatened. Though liberals and labor leaders supported the bill, business leaders denounced it as anticapitalist. In its final form, the act created a COUNCIL OF ECONOMIC ADVISORS to report to the president on the state of the economy. The president would then make an annual address to both Congress and the nation on the report's findings. The act, however, did not commit the government to use fiscal policy to maintain full employment when the economy turned downward.

Although the war energized American industry, factories concentrated on producing goods for the military rather than consumers. During the war, many Americans made more money than they ever had previously, but they could not spend all they earned. By the war's end, Americans had an estimated total savings of $140 billion that they were eager to spend. Furthermore, families had more discretionary income than ever before. Real purchasing power rose by 22 percent between 1946 and 1960, allowing more people to satisfy both their needs and wants. This was a dramatic change from the Great Depression era when less than 25 percent of all families had any discretionary income.

United States production companies after the war quickly realized the increased purchasing power of the working American and began to offer a whole host of new products for the average consumer. Using wartime TECH-NOLOGY, companies developed a wide variety of machines and gadgets to be used in the home. With the use of ADVERTISING, the CONSUMER MOVEMENT of the 1950s created a constant demand for the newest products. By 1956, 81 percent of American families owned TELEVISION sets, 67 percent owned vacuum cleaners, and 89 percent owned washing machines. The expansion of private credit made it possible for a large majority of Americans to bene-fit from the material abundance of the 1950s. Families could purchase the new products with less savings, using a store's installment program or CREDIT CARDS. Throughout the 1950s and 1960s, indebtedness grew fivefold and sur-passed income increases.

The AUTOMOBILE INDUSTRY played an important role in the economic boom as well. The total number of cars made in the United States jumped from 2 million in 1946 to 9 million in 1965. By 1960, 74 million automobiles were in operation throughout the country, while millions of out-dated models piled up in junkyards. Companies offered a wide variety of engines and colors; each year's model fea-tured its own distinguishing options, including grills and tail fins. Owning the latest or fastest model became part of the American dream and symbolized middle-class status. President DWIGHT D. EISENHOWER's administration spent $26 billion on the INTERSTATE HIGHWAY ACT OF 1956, allowing for the construction of over 40,000 miles of fed-eral highway and boosting car sales even more. While it became the largest public works expenditure in American history, the act failed to invest in mass transportation, increasing both pollution and the nation's dependence on a constant supply of cheap oil.

Like the automobile industry, the housing industry also played an important role in the postwar economic expan-sion. As servicemen returned home from the war, they needed affordable and well-located housing. Construction companies began mass-producing houses just outside the cities, resulting in the SUBURBANIZATION of the 1950s and 1960s. The 1944 G.I. Bill offered low-interest home mort-gages to servicemen along with priority for many jobs and educational benefits. With the use of automobiles and the new highway system, millions of veterans were able to pur-chase their own suburban homes and commute to jobs in the cities. With the onset of the BABY BOOM, owning a

home became even more of a necessity for the average American family. In 1940, 43 percent of American families owned their own homes, compared to 63 percent in 1970.

Though the United States produced half of the world's goods, the country continued to move from a goods-pro-ducing economy to a service-providing economy in the years after World War II. In the 1950s and 1960s, the num-ber of people working to sell, distribute, or maintain goods continually increased. By 1956, the majority of American workers held white-collar jobs in the service industries. While clerical workers enjoyed better pay and more leisure time than did factory workers, work in huge corporations was often monotonous and subject to bureaucratization. Many labor leaders worried about worker displacement and alienation, while business leaders argued that the increase in white-collar jobs actually led to more employ-ment opportunities and safer work.

Not all Americans held white-collar jobs. Many peo-ple still worked as factory workers on assembly lines. They, too, were able to take part in the American dream of own-ing a house in the suburbs and having two cars in the garage thanks to substantial union gains made throughout the 1950s and 1960s. By the end of the 1950s, a COST-OF-LIVING ADJUSTMENT (COLA) was a common feature in most union contracts, protecting workers against inflation. With the 1955 merger of the AMERICAN FEDERATION OF LABOR (AFL) and the CONGRESS OF INDUSTRIAL ORGANI-ZATIONS (CIO), both trade and industrial unions unified under a single organization that represented more than 90 percent of the country's 17.5 million union members. Union members largely succeeded in gaining middle-class affluence, but by the end of the 1960s, the union move-ment slowed down as membership stabilized.

Following World War II, government and big BUSI-NESS became more dependent on one another than at any previous time in the history of the United States. During the war, the government relied on American industry to supply the necessary materials for the war effort. It was the government's active economic role in business that finally stimulated the economy and ended the Depression. After the war, government continued to take part in the economy by allowing business to buy almost 80 percent of the factories built by the government during the war. In 1950, public spending accounted for 7 percent of the GNP, and by 1960, that figure rose to 9.4 percent. When cold war tensions escalated, Congress created the Department of Defense in 1947 with a budget of $13 billion, rising to $47 billion by 1953. More than half of the total national budget each year went to the Department of Defense, boosting both the aircraft and electronics industries.

The close ties with big business produced a government policy that favored industrial concentration. Government contracts encouraged the expansion of big corporations, shutting out smaller firms. Few antitrust actions resulted in the rise of oligopolies and conglomerates that dominated American capitalism in the postwar years. Franchise operations such as MCDONALD'S and Kentucky Fried Chicken also expanded. Foreign markets became a viable option for large corporations, as the development of plants overseas increased market size and offered cheap labor costs.

Most Americans accepted the government's active role in the economy as a way to both stimulate and sustain the economic expansion. They recognized that military spending had a positive impact on the economy. At a time when the United States was both peaceful and prosperous, most citizens of middle-class status were content to enjoy the economic boom. They praised the American capitalist system as a way to maintain the freedom of business enterprise and private institutions while redistributing income so that all citizens could partake of the wealth. JOHN KENNETH GALBRAITH, a prominent economist, went so far as to call the entire nation an "affluent society" and argued that poverty was not a "massive affliction" for the country.

Under the Eisenhower administration, this affluent society dominated the nation's consciousness. Before World War II, economic health was commonly measured by the volume of employment and industrial productivity. By the 1950s, however, most economists placed a heavy emphasis on overall economic growth measured in the GNP. Although inflation continued and the unemployment rate remained steady at 6 percent, the GNP and average personal income continued to increase during Eisenhower's presidency. The United States experienced the greatest peacetime prosperity it had ever known, and Eisenhower remained fiscally conservative throughout his time in office, making little effort to manipulate federal fiscal policy to stimulate economic growth.

The realization that the economy was heavily dependent on government spending temporized the economic optimism that characterized the 1950s. After the KOREAN WAR when the defense budget was cut, the economy took a similar dive. Although the economy soon recovered, many experts wondered what would happen when the government again made further cutbacks. In his 1961 farewell address, Eisenhower cautioned against the growing "economic, political, and even spiritual" influence of the MILITARY-INDUSTRIAL COMPLEX.

When President JOHN F. KENNEDY took office in 1961, his administration began to look for ways to stabilize the economy and sustain the expansion of the 1950s. The Kennedy administration made clear its support of the economic theories of John Maynard Keynes, whereby government regulation of the money supply and fiscal policy prevented the regular pattern of booms and busts that characterized the capitalist system. In 1962, Kennedy proposed a tax cut to stimulate the economy based on the advice of Keynesian economists but did not live long enough to see it

through. Once in office, President LYNDON B. JOHNSON pushed the tax cut through, and it worked. The GNP rose 7.1 percent in 1964, 8.1 percent in 1965, and 9.5 percent in 1966. The economic policy of both Kennedy and Johnson met with distrust and hostility from business leaders as they saw government interference in the free market a step closer to socialism. In reality, this economic policy largely favored individual corporations and did little to curtail the existing distribution of wealth and power in America.

Despite the continuing economic expansion of the 1960s, some economists and social critics began to address the issue of poverty in the United States. While economists in the 1950s argued that the poor benefited from the economic boom in ways comparable to the very rich, poverty remained a significant and persistent part of the American landscape. In 1962, MICHAEL HARRINGTON published *The Other America*, a work that emphasized the existence of poverty and the inequality of income distribution throughout the country. The existence of persistent poverty led Kennedy to initiate an expansion of the welfare state that had stagnated under the Eisenhower administration. While Kennedy brought these issues to the forefront of America with his NEW FRONTIER, President Johnson and his GREAT SOCIETY made the greatest strides for America's poor. The Great Society consisted of social programs to help the poor and disadvantaged, as well as middle- and upper-class Americans. Although Johnson's programs failed to eradicate poverty, they did serve to bring the issue of socioeconomic disadvantage to public attention. No longer could Americans claim that all was well in the country due to the economic boom and growing middle class.

Though poverty remained an issue for the United States, the decades immediately following World War II brought unprecedented prosperity and productivity to the country. The economic growth that characterized postwar America continued to affect the nation well into the 20th century.

Further reading: Charles C. Alexander, *Holding the Line: The Eisenhower Era, 1952–1961* (Bloomington: Indiana University Press, 1975); Stephen Kemp Bailey, *Congress Makes a Law: The Story behind the Employment Act of 1946* (New York: Columbia University Press, 1950); Alonzo L. Hamby, *Man of the People: A Life of Harry S. Truman* (Oxford, U.K.: Oxford University Press, 1995); Allen J. Matusow, *The Unraveling of America: A History of Liberalism in the 1960s* (New York: Harper & Row Publishers, 1956).

— Donna J. Siebenthaler

education

After World War II, driven partly by COLD WAR tensions, American education underwent extensive changes.

During the early decades of the 20th century, primary schools provided education for all children up to the age of about 12, but only the wealthy went on to further schooling. High school and college education in the United States was just for the rich and the upper middle class. Secondary education was a fairly new concept, based on the European style of education designed for the small number of students planning to go on to college.

After World War II, education underwent a major change. It became an important issue for many more Americans, as experts offered ideas on how to expand educational opportunities in the United States and make schooling more available to the masses. Education became relevant to the everyday lives of Americans, as schools directed attention to the need for social, civic, and economic competencies. Most Americans believed that, like primary schooling, both secondary and college education should be made easily accessible to all.

The demand for better schools at all levels was further fostered in the 1950s by a growing consumer culture. The American dream of every family owning an automobile and a house with a yard could be achieved only through education. Primary education, which taught basic skills, remained important, while secondary schooling for everyone, not just the rich, became an important next step. Secondary schools, which came to be known as high schools, were now increasingly common in small towns across America. The curriculum of high schools became broader than it had been before the war, offering advanced mathematics, English, sciences, humanities, languages, and a host of other subjects necessary for the pursuit of what Americans came to feel was the good life. A prevailing assumption was that graduating from high school was necessary to secure a good job, defined as the ability to buy the abundant material goods now available.

Other factors also influenced the advancement of education. In 1957, the Soviet Union launched *Sputnik,* the world's first orbiting satellite. When Americans learned that the Russians had beat the United States into space, the country panicked. Americans believed that, if the Soviets already had a more highly developed TECHNOLOGY than the United States, their educational system must be superior. In response, President DWIGHT D. EISENHOWER signed the National Defense Education Act on September 2, 1958. The act authorized grants to improve instruction in science, math, and foreign languages, with total expenditures of around $1 billion. With the National Defense Education Act in place, state and local governments dispersed funds to various educational institutions.

In the 1960s, President JOHN F. KENNEDY began a drive to create programs that ensured that all students would receive a well-rounded education and an opportunity to attend college. He called for aid to education during his administration, but legislation was not passed until 1965 under President LYNDON B. JOHNSON and his GREAT SOCI-

ETY. The ELEMENTARY AND SECONDARY EDUCATION ACT OF 1965 played a major role in furthering the education of the average American. The measure made it more possible for all children, even the impoverished, to receive a quality education, bolstering the number of children able to pass college entrance exams. Congress also passed the Higher Education Act of 1965, a measure that provided a permanent program of financial aid to both public and private colleges as well as to individual students. This program sought to ensure that members of every social class could secure access to a higher education. The act allowed universities to expand and build new libraries, and fostered improvement in the overall quality of universities.

The most dramatic shift in college education came with the return of servicemen from World War II. The Serviceman's Readjustment Act of 1944, or the G.I. Bill as it was commonly called, dispersed funds for veterans to attend college. Following World War I, the National Defense Education Act of 1920 had provided military training in conjunction with higher education. Under this measure, the Reserve Officers Training Corps (ROTC) was established at universities around the country. It established military training programs as part of academic coursework. The aim of this program was to prepare reserve and noncommissioned officers for future military service. The G.I. Bill, however, was a comprehensive act that allowed veterans more than just military training. It included provisions such as: one year of schooling for veterans who had served at least 90 days, with additional schooling equal to the time they spent on active duty; payment for books and supplies, as long as the amount did not exceed $500; and a monthly allowance of $50. Veterans could attend any college desired, as long as it was an accredited school.

The G.I. Bill made a tremendous difference. In 1930, less than 10 percent of all high school graduates had gone on to further education; by 1965, more than one half of all high school graduates did so. While many veterans enrolled in large, four-year universities, almost one half of veterans began their education at community colleges. In 1940, approximately 200,000 students were enrolled in community colleges. By 1968, nearly 2 million students chose to attend junior colleges. Aggregate numbers soared. In 1945, over 900,000 students were enrolled in two- and four-year colleges and universities. By 1947, over 2 million students were enrolled in such institutions. Veterans comprised nearly 50 percent of students in attendance.

Throughout the 1950s and 1960s, the rise in student enrollments extended to graduate schools and professional schools. Increasingly, larger numbers of students chose to pursue education beyond a baccalaureate degree to earn masters or doctoral degrees at graduate schools. Others chose to enter professional schools for specialized training in areas such as law, business, medicine, dentistry, and veterinary science.

Many schools were at first unequipped to deal with such large numbers of students. Prefabricated housing and recycled Quonset huts, which once provided housing for soldiers, became part of the landscape on many college campuses in the early postwar years. Only later did permanent new buildings appear. The profusion of students also created a need for more professors in the classroom. In 1940, the nation's colleges and universities employed approximately 145,000 full-time teaching employees; in 1960, that number had doubled to over 300,000. Large numbers of students chose to extend their education by entering graduate school to become professors. By the end of the 1960s, about 30,000 Ph.D.s annually were awarded to students across the United States.

Meanwhile, student activism became an important part of college life in the 1960s. Students participated in SIT-INS, picket lines, and other demonstrations, petitioning the government, among other issues, against the violation of civil rights of African Americans. College students also participated in the FREEDOM RIDES into the Deep South to desegregate transportation facilities. In 1964, the FREE SPEECH MOVEMENT at Berkeley sought to protect political and civil rights for all Americans. By 1965, students could be found protesting the U.S. government's actions in the VIETNAM WAR.

The post–World War II efforts by the United States to make the nation's educational system competitive with the rest of the world were largely successful. Education at the primary, secondary, and post-secondary levels improved dramatically in the postwar years.

Further reading: John S. Brubacher, *Higher Education in Transition: A History of American Colleges and Universities, 1636–1968* (New York: Harper & Row, 1968); Lawrence Cremin, *Popular Education and Its Discontents* (New York: Harper & Row, 1990); Christopher J. Lucas, *American Higher Education: A History* (New York: St. Martin's Press, 1994).

— Matthew Escovar and Megan D. Wessel

Eisenhower, Dwight D. (1890–1969)

Following a successful military career, Dwight D. Eisenhower entered the political world and served as the 34th president of the United States.

Dwight David Eisenhower was born on October 14, 1890, in Denison, Texas. A year after his birth, the Eisenhower family moved to Abilene, Kansas, where Eisenhower spent the rest of his childhood. Although the family lived in poverty, Eisenhower won a merit appointment to the U.S. Military Academy at West Point, New York. While at West Point, he suffered a serious knee injury that sidelined him from participating in both football and baseball. Following his graduation from West Point in 1915, he held a variety of military posts, including service as an aide to the assistant secretary of war in Washington, D.C., where he met General DOUGLAS MACARTHUR, who was the Army Chief of Staff at the time.

Following the Japanese attack on Pearl Harbor in 1941, Eisenhower rose to become supreme commander in the European Theater during World War II. He devised Operation Torch, which successfully gave the Allies a foothold in North Africa. His finest moment came in planning Operation Overlord, the Allied invasion of Europe on June 6, 1944, in Normandy, on the coast of France. The whole operation depended upon the weather at the time of invasion. Although the weather conditions were not ideal, Eisenhower ordered the invasion to proceed. Unable to predict the outcome of his orders, he kept a message in his wallet accepting personal blame if the Allies suffered a defeat. Operation Overlord, however, was a success, and the Allies went on to victory over the Axis powers.

Returning to the United States a war hero, Eisenhower served as Army Chief of Staff. Leaving the army in 1947, he accepted the post of president of Columbia University. In 1950, Eisenhower left his post at Columbia University, as President HARRY S. TRUMAN called upon him to serve as the supreme commander of the NORTH ATLANTIC TREATY ORGANIZATION (NATO) defense forces.

In 1952, Eisenhower won the Republican nomination for president. His advisers then suggested that Eisenhower choose a young, staunch anticommunist for the position of vice president. Although Eisenhower had never had an extended private conversation with Senator Richard M. Nixon, he chose the Californian as his running mate. On election night, Eisenhower beat his Democratic opponent, ADLAI STEVENSON, with 55.1 percent of the popular vote and 442 electoral votes.

After taking office in 1953, Eisenhower was immediately faced with finding a way out of the KOREAN WAR, which had begun three years before. By moving nuclear warheads to the island of Okinawa, Eisenhower gained the upper hand in dealing with China. Facing possible nuclear intervention, China signed an armistice effectively ending the war. In addition to this foreign affairs crisis, America was also entangled in Vietnam, sending millions of dollars of aid to the French-controlled government. Eisenhower realized the potential quagmire of greater American involvement in Vietnam, and he resisted large-scale expansion of the role of the United States. He did support the formation of the SOUTHEAST ASIA TREATY ORGANIZATION (SEATO) to try to cope with crises in the area.

On the home front, Eisenhower was committed to promoting a less activist government. While accepting the innovations of the NEW DEAL, he nonetheless wanted to scale back government intervention in the ECONOMY. Also given the opportunity to influence the courts, he appointed

Dwight D. Eisenhower talking with Clare Boothe Luce   *(Library of Congress)*

EARL WARREN as chief justice of the Supreme Court in 1953. Later in his career, Eisenhower objected to the extent of Warren's judicial activism.

Eisenhower also faced the unchecked allegations of Senator JOSEPH R. MCCARTHY concerning rampant communist infiltration within the government. Following the ARMY-MCCARTHY HEARINGS, the president took action. Although he never publicly repudiated McCarthy, Eisenhower strongly encouraged Republican senators to vote for the condemnation of the senator in 1954, which effectively ended McCarthy's political career.

Following his reelection in 1956, Eisenhower was faced with yet another crisis at home. After the decision of the WARREN COURT in *BROWN V. BOARD OF EDUCATION* (1954), which declared that segregated schools were unconstitutional, the president was compelled to uphold the ruling. When a number of African-American students were denied entrance to Little Rock's all white Central High School, Eisenhower sent army paratroopers and National Guardsmen into Arkansas to enforce the Supreme Court's mandate.

Eisenhower was active on other fronts as well. He created the NATIONAL AERONAUTICS AND SPACE ADMINISTRATION (NASA) in response to the 1957 Soviet launch of *Sputnik*, the first man-made satellite to circle the earth. He also supported the INTERSTATE HIGHWAY ACT OF 1956, which authorized the construction of over 40,000 miles of access roads, forming the world's most complex highway network.

Eisenhower died on March 28, 1969, nine years after leaving office.

Further reading: Stephen E. Ambrose, *Eisenhower,* Vol. 1, *Soldier, General of the Army, President-Elect 1890–1952* (New York: Simon & Schuster, 1983); Stephen E. Ambrose, *Eisenhower,* Vol. 2, *The President* (New York: Simon & Schuster, 1984); Michael R. Beschloss, *Eisenhower: A Centennial Life* (New York: HarperCollins, 1990); Greenstein, Fred I. *The Hidden Hand Presidency: Eisenhower as Leader* (New York: Basic Books, 1982).

— Clayton Douglas

elections

Presidential and midterm elections constitute an important barometer of social and political trends.

As the country emerged from the Great Depression and World War II, the DEMOCRATIC PARTY held a clear edge in electoral politics. The NEW DEAL coalition that had united rural residents of the West and South with northern, urban ethnics had guaranteed Democratic control of both the White House and Congress since 1932. But the REPUBLICAN PARTY broke this hold by capturing both chambers of Congress in 1946 and the White House in the 1950s. Democrats regained control of Congress in the mid-1950s and held it for the next 15 years, retaking the White House again in 1960.

HARRY S. TRUMAN's transition into the White House did not go smoothly, and the 1946 midterm elections marked the low point of his tenure. The Republican Party gained control of both houses of Congress for the first time since 1930, winning a 245-188 majority in the House and a 51-45 lead in the Senate. Republicans capitalized on the public perception of Truman's ineffective leadership, a Democratic Party fractured into liberal and conservative wings, rampant postwar inflation, and the normal tendency of the out-of-power party to pick up congressional seats in midterm elections. Buoyed by this success, Republicans expected to expand their control and to retake the White House in 1948.

Harry S. Truman, president-elect, holds up edition of *Chicago Daily Tribune* with headline "Dewey Defeats Truman" *(Library of Congress)*

Republican Party leaders had every reason to be confident in the 1948 presidential elections. As the campaign proceeded, the Democratic Party split into three camps. Henry A. Wallace's PROGRESSIVE PARTY promised to siphon off the most liberal voters, and when Truman endorsed a strong civil rights plank at the Democratic convention, conservative southerners left the party as well. South Carolina governor Strom Thurmond headed the STATES' RIGHTS PARTY—known as the Dixiecrat Party—further weakening Truman's position. Meanwhile, the Republicans stood solidly behind New York governor THOMAS E. DEWEY, who had run well against Franklin D. Roosevelt for president in 1944. Popular California governor EARL WARREN joined Dewey on the Republican ticket.

In response to these challenges, Truman and his advisers developed an ingenious strategy for the 1948 campaign: combine appeals to the old New Deal coalition while at the same time casting the Republican Congress as opposed to reform. To implement this plan, Truman sent an array of reform proposals to Congress, including housing reform, education aid, and a civil rights bill. As expected, these bills failed—but Truman successfully portrayed himself as a Roosevelt-style reformer blocked by an insensitive Congress. Truman also campaigned extensively, logging 22,000 miles and 271 speeches during the campaign season. Up until the eve of the election, however, the polls continued to predict a landslide victory for Dewey. These expectations led to the famous "Dewey Defeats Truman" headline run by the *Chicago Tribune* on the night of the election, published before a last-minute swing to Truman. Truman won the election (49.6 percent of the vote and 303 electoral votes to 45.1 percent and 189 for Dewey)—and the Democrats retook both houses of Congress (263-171 in the House and 54-42 in the Senate)—by holding together the New Deal coalition of union members, farmers, and urban ethnic voters. The Democratic splinter parties did not do as well as expected, although Thurmond's popularity in the South served notice of future troubles for the Democratic Party.

The Democratic victory of 1948 carried over to 1950; although the Republicans picked up five Senate and 28 House seats, the Democrats remained in control of both chambers (49-47 and 234-199). ANTICOMMUNISM, both as a domestic concern and as a commentary on the Truman administration's handling of the KOREAN WAR, emerged as the key issue of the 1950 midterm contests and remained a central topic of political debate for the next several elections.

When Truman decided not to run for reelection in 1952, General DWIGHT D. EISENHOWER emerged as the most popular potential candidate—but no one knew which party he would join. Eisenhower chose the Republican Party, with Senator Richard M. Nixon of California as a running mate. They faced Illinois governor ADLAI STEVEN-

SON and Alabama senator John Sparkman, chosen in an effort to make the Democratic ticket more appealing to southerners. The Republicans again used the anticommunism issue effectively, and also contrasted Eisenhower's status as a war hero and political outsider with the Democrats' mishandling of the Korean conflict and the corruption scandals that had plagued the Truman administration. Eisenhower won easily, claiming 55 percent of the popular vote and 442 electoral votes, and the Republicans once more took control of both houses of Congress, albeit by the slimmest of margins (221-211 in the House, 48-47 in the Senate, with one independent vote).

The 1952 presidential election marked the emergence of a new force on the political scene: TELEVISION. Over 15 million households had televisions in 1952, compared to 178,000 in 1948. Eisenhower used the new medium effectively, running the first political commercials during the campaign.

Republican control of Congress proved short-lived. Despite continued emphasis on anticommunism, the 1954 midterms brought the Democrats a one vote lead in the Senate (48-47) and a 29-seat majority in the House (232-203). Rather than anticommunism, the election swung on economic issues, namely, rising unemployment and falling farm prices.

Democrats retained control of Congress (233-200 and 49-47) and Eisenhower remained in the White House in the election of 1956, a rematch of the popular president with Adlai Stevenson. Eisenhower needed little help in the election, and war in the MIDDLE EAST over the SUEZ CRISIS made Americans more likely to return an experienced leader to the White House. Eisenhower captured over 57 percent of the popular vote and easily won the Electoral College, 457 to 73. Television again played an important role, as 36 million homes now boasted TV sets. Both candidates employed prestigious New York ADVERTISING firms to help manage their campaigns.

Despite Eisenhower's personal popularity, the Republican Party faced a difficult situation in the 1958 midterms because the ECONOMY, booming since the end of World War II, had slowed. What started as a mild downturn in 1957 became a full-blown recession in 1958, especially hurting industrial workers and Midwestern farmers. The Democrats accused the administration of being insensitive to rising unemployment and economic suffering. The strategy worked: the Democratic majorities exploded to 64-34 in the Senate and 283-153 in the House. This sweeping victory for the Democrats positioned them well for the 1960 election.

These prospects helped make the 1960 Democratic presidential nomination a hotly contested one. JOHN F. KENNEDY quickly emerged as a frontrunner and received the nomination, with Senator LYNDON B. JOHNSON of

Texas (himself a presidential hopeful) as a running mate. They faced Richard Nixon and Senator Henry Cabot Lodge of Massachusetts. Four issues dominated the campaign: the adequacy of American military defense, the aggressiveness of foreign policy, the future of civil rights, and the need for continued economic growth. Kennedy took the initiative on all four issues, forcing Nixon to defend the policies of the Eisenhower administration. The Democrats focused especially on the "Missile Gap" (the idea that the Russians had outstripped the United States in missile production) and on civil rights. The Democratic convention endorsed the most liberal civil rights agenda in the party's history. Kennedy helped his cause with a well-publicized phone call to Coretta Scott King while her husband MARTIN LUTHER KING, JR., was being held in a Georgia jail on a trumped-up traffic violation. Kennedy prevailed in one of the closest elections in American history, winning by just under 115,000 votes out of 69 million cast. Kennedy earned 49.7 percent of the popular vote and 303 votes in the Electoral College to 49.5 percent and 219 for Nixon. Democrats maintained their majority in Congress, although they lost seats in the House (now 263-174, and 65-35 in the Senate).

Scholars have pointed to several decisive issues in the close election. Kennedy's RELIGION (he was the first Catholic elected president and only the second nominated) cost him votes in the national tally, but probably helped him win key northern, urban states with large ethnic populations. Kennedy also picked up 70 percent of the African-American vote, which also might have decided the election. Television, too, played a role: over 60 million viewers watched each of four televised debates that contrasted the composed Kennedy with a sweating, nervous Nixon. Although Kennedy might not have won the debate in terms of content, he clearly won the image war.

The 1962 midterm elections were important ones for Kennedy. He had accomplished little of his domestic agenda during the first two years of his term. Kennedy went against the recommendations of his advisers and took an active role in the midterm campaign, staking his own prestige on the outcome. Democrats lost only five seats in the House (258-177), and gained seats in the Senate (for a 67-33 majority)—the most successful midterm election by the in-party (other than 1934) since 1866. And the composition of the new Congress proved more sympathetic to Kennedy's goals, since moderates had replaced obstructionist conservatives in several southern Democratic seats. The 1962 midterm contest provided Kennedy with both the mandate and the momentum necessary to implement his reform agenda.

The 1964 presidential elections soundly confirmed this mandate for liberal reform. Lyndon Johnson chose Senator HUBERT H. HUMPHREY of Minnesota, the party's most vocal liberal, as a running mate. They faced Senator BARRY GOLDWATER of Arizona and a Republican Party that had turned sharply to the right. Goldwater's 1960 book, *The Conscience of a Conservative*, had become the manifesto of the Republican right, and he based his campaign on its ideas: aggressive COLD WAR foreign policy, little regulation of BUSINESS, and the dismantling of government welfare programs like social security. Johnson took advantage of the narrow Republican appeal and cast his campaign broadly, appealing to business and labor interests, urban and rural

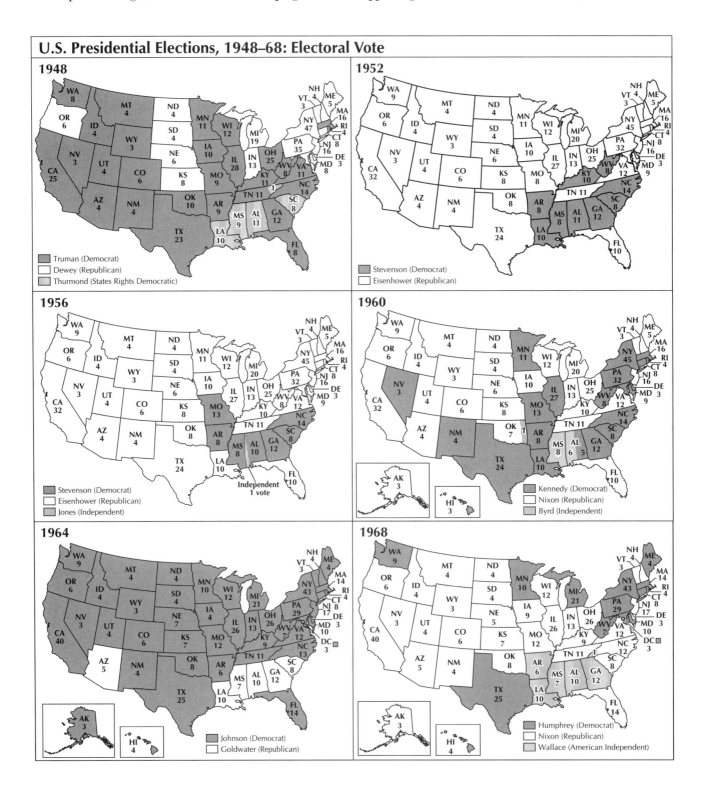

U.S. Presidential Elections, 1948–68: Electoral Vote

1948

Truman (Democrat)
Dewey (Republican)
Thurmond (States Rights Democratic)

1952

Stevenson (Democrat)
Eisenhower (Republican)

1956

Stevenson (Democrat)
Eisenhower (Republican)
Jones (Independent)

1960

Kennedy (Democrat)
Nixon (Republican)
Byrd (Independent)

1964

Johnson (Democrat)
Goldwater (Republican)

1968

Humphrey (Democrat)
Nixon (Republican)
Wallace (American Independent)

regions, and all racial and ethnic groups. Johnson's position as Kennedy's heir, his advocacy of civil rights and liberal domestic reform, and a fear of Goldwater's CONSERVATISM, along with the fear that he might ignite a nuclear war, produced a landslide victory. Johnson garnered 61 percent of the popular vote and 486 electoral votes, more even than Roosevelt in 1936, to 38.5 percent and 52 for Goldwater. Democratic margins widened in both chambers of Congress (295-140 and 68-32). The realignment of southern voters that had begun under Eisenhower continued, however, and Goldwater claimed five states in the Deep South. Perhaps more important, his campaign laid the groundwork for the nation's rightward shift in the coming decades.

This rightward turn became evident two years later, when the Republican Party made significant gains in Congress. Race riots, fears of a white backlash to civil rights legislation, the rise of the COUNTERCULTURE, unease over the VIETNAM WAR, and inflation caused Americans to question Johnson's leadership; his approval ratings plummeted from 66 percent in November 1965 to 44 percent in October 1966. These concerns persisted through the 1966 election. Although the Republicans remained in the minority in Congress (187-247 and 36-64), their successes ended the era of GREAT SOCIETY reform and heralded a new age of Republican political power.

Republican gains and growing domestic unrest guaranteed that Johnson would face a challenge for the Democratic nomination in 1968. Senator EUGENE MCCARTHY of Minnesota and Senator ROBERT F. KENNEDY of New York both announced their bids for the presidency based on antiwar platforms. As Johnson watched his support erode, he decided to withdraw from the election to avoid polarizing the country further, and Vice President Humphrey entered the race with the aim of rebuilding the liberal coalition of farmers, African Americans, union members, and urban ethnics. Kennedy had claimed control of the race with a victory in the California primary when his assassination threw the election into turmoil. Humphrey emerged to head the Democratic ticket, although violence outside the Democratic national convention in Chicago tarnished his nomination. Southern conservative GEORGE A. WALLACE complicated the election by entering the race on a third-party ticket.

Republican nominee Richard Nixon capitalized on this social unrest. The murders of Kennedy and Martin Luther King, Jr., race riots, and antiwar protests fostered the feeling that the nation was coming apart at the seams. Nixon promised a "secret peace plan" for Vietnam and a return to "law and order." This time, it was Nixon who prevailed in a close race, easily winning in the Electoral College (301-91) but securing the popular vote by less than 1 percent (43.4 percent-42.7 percent). Humphrey

managed to win only a single southern state (Texas), ending Democratic control of the region that had endured since Reconstruction. Nixon won because of social unrest, the stalemate in Vietnam, and by tapping into middle-class unrest over Johnson's WAR ON POVERTY. Democratic majorities in Congress slipped further still, to 243-192 in the House and 57-43 in the Senate. The Republicans had laced together a coalition of voters in the West, the South, and the Midwest, a coalition that delivered five of the next six presidential elections to the Republican Party.

Further reading: Paul S. Boyer, *Promises to Keep: The United States since World War II* (Boston: Houghton Mifflin, 1999); Gary W. Reichard, *Politics As Usual: The Age of Truman and Eisenhower* (Arlington Heights, Ill.: Harlan Davidson, 1988).

— Jim Feldman

Electronic Numerical Integrator and Calculator (ENIAC)

ENIAC, the University of Pennsylvania's Electronic Numerical Integrator and Computer, was the world's first wholly electronic digital COMPUTER.

Introduced to an eager public on February 15, 1946, the machine revolutionized computational science and radically advanced the speed by which mathematical equations could be solved. Problems that once would have taken months of simple hand calculations or days with the assistance of a differential analyzer now took only minutes. In the words of the *New York Times'* first report on the machine, ENIAC promised "a new epoch of human thought."

Computing machines were nothing new by the early 1940s. Humans have used one type, the abacus, for nearly 5,000 years, and many still use this elegant tool even today. In the 1930s, engineers at the Massachusetts Institute of Technology developed a "product integraph," which solved simple equations through analog functioning. Later that decade, the International Business Machines corporation (IBM), with the aid of Harvard mathematicians, produced a sequence-controlled calculator capable of computing tables of mathematical functions such as sines and cosines. Unlike these early calculators, however, ENIAC was wholly electronic, functioning by turning vacuum tubes on and off. This was its great advance. It used no moving parts to perform its calculations, and it could thus function at astonishing speeds unhindered by the physical limitations of its predecessors. Its design proved capable of performing over 5,000 additions or subtractions or 360 multiplications of two 10-digit decimal numbers in a single second. No other machine on the planet could even approach these figures.

Such speed made complex problems appear simple, and the machine was designed with one specific problem in mind. In the early 1940s, America was at war against the Axis Powers, engaged in a conflict in which SCIENCE and TECHNOLOGY played a far greater role than ever before. In particular, America's army required hundreds of complex ballistic tables for powerful artillery pieces, tables that listed the expected trajectory of shells through hundreds of trajectories. Each of these tables required thousands of computations and could take a trained mathematician using the most advanced tools of the time nearly a month to complete. Dozens of "human computers," mainly young women with advanced mathematics degrees, were engaged in producing such tables at the University of Pennsylvania's Moore School of Electrical Engineering, home to the world's largest differential analyzer, but a faster method was needed. John W. Mauchly, a young professor, and John P. Eckert, Jr., a graduate student, proposed a machine that would use more than 18,000 vacuum tubes operating at a rate of 100,000 pulses per second to calculate the time-consuming tables. Immersed in a desperate war, the army agreed to fund the project.

The top-secret machine took nearly two years to build. Completed in the war's final year, Mauchly and Eckert's 30-ton creation, housed in a good-sized room, appeared too late to be used for its original purpose of calculating ballistic tables. Instead, ENIAC's first task dealt with calculations required for the construction of the ATOMIC BOMB. Data was fed to ENIAC on punched cards, and the final results were themselves punched onto cards. Electronic circuits involving miles of wire performed the arithmetic computations, with such success that its operators eventually formed a waiting list of more than two years for eager users. Though a technological watershed, the machine was by no means perfect. Each new computation or program used a different wiring pattern, and thus shifting from one type of calculation to another required a manual rewiring of the machine that often took days—time that was in high demand for the world's only functioning computer. This difficulty was overcome in 1948 by hard-wiring over 80 operations into the machine, albeit at a loss of some operating speed. Hard-wired operations were controlled by ENIAC's operator at a main console, and could be shifted—the machine in essence reprogrammed—at the flick of a switch, a technique that foreshadowed future computer designs.

As originally designed, ENIAC was also unable to store its data or results, even in the midst of its own computations. The machines' creators had recognized the significance of this deficiency while in the midst of its construction, and began designing its successors, the EDVAC and the EDSAC, in 1944 even before ENIAC ran its first program. Data storage and stored programming would be the hallmarks of these new machines. Though a marvel of its day, ENIAC's monopoly on electronic computing was, by necessity, short-lived. Its architecture and design were themselves never copied, and though the computer worked for many years at the university and at the U.S. Army's Aberdeen Proving Ground in Maryland, its greatest contribution to the nascent field of computer science lay in its very existence. It proved rapid electronic machines both viable and useful, and it provided a testing ground for a whole generation of computer pioneers.

Further reading: Barkley W. Fritz, "ENIAC—A Problem Solver," *IEEE Annals of the History of Computing* 16, no. 1 (1994): 25–40; Scott McCartney, *ENIAC, the Triumphs and Tragedies of the World's First Computer* (New York: Walker Press, 1999).

— Jeffrey A. Engel

Elementary and Secondary Education Act of 1965

The Elementary and Secondary Education Act of 1965 (ESEA) provided federal financial support to children who needed it, both in public and parochial schools. JOHN F. KENNEDY began the campaign for educational aid during his presidency. Americans at this time thought the educational system needed to be improved because of COLD WAR fears. They were concerned when the SOVIET UNION launched the first satellite into space. The thought that a communist country could launch a satellite first made Americans feel inferior and underschooled. Many felt the need to better educate their children.

Kennedy faced many problems while trying to get the program started. A crucial issue involved the separation of church and state. Kennedy was not opposed to providing aid to parochial schools, but because he was the first Roman Catholic to be elected president, he was advised that he could not risk a program of aid to Catholic schools in his first months in office. A fear that critics might charge that American governmental policy was being made by the pope in Rome led Kennedy to deny aid to parochial schools. The Catholic Church became angry at Kennedy's stance, which proved problematic because Kennedy needed its support to pass the bill. Other complicated issues included whether segregated schools should receive funding, which Kennedy supported, and whether there would be federal control as a result of federal funding. The assassination of Kennedy in 1963 halted progress on the proposed bill.

President LYNDON B. JOHNSON, who succeeded Kennedy, wanted to move beyond the Kennedy legacy by creating a GREAT SOCIETY, which provided something for everyone. In addition to a tax cut, medical care for the elderly, and civil rights legislation, it included better educational opportunities for all. The Elementary and Secondary Education Act, in Johnson's plan for a Great Society, included equal educational opportunities for the disadvantaged, improved libraries, and better programs for gifted and slow learners. The ESEA in Johnson's view constituted an important component of the WAR ON POVERTY. Those who supported the measure thought that it would break the cycle of poverty.

Johnson overcame some of Kennedy's problems with the bill by saying he refused to take it to Congress without support from the National Education Association and the National Catholic Welfare Conference, which represented public and parochial schools, respectively. Johnson did not have to deal with the issue of whether aid would go only to desegregated schools because of the CIVIL RIGHTS ACT OF 1964, which moved the process of integration along. Johnson's last concern was with who received the money, and how the GOVERNMENT issued the funds. He decided that aid would go only to those individuals with educational disadvantages. The schools themselves would not receive aid. This in turn allowed aid to go to students in both public and parochial schools.

Republicans originally opposed the bill because they thought Democrats were trying to rush it through Congress. After much debate, however, the House of Representatives and the Senate both voted in favor of the act by overwhelming margins. Johnson signed it four months after sending it to Congress.

The Elementary and Secondary Education Act has continued to help children who are disadvantaged, with Congress modifying the measure as new educational needs surface.

Further reading: Barbara Jordan and Elspeth Rostow, eds. *The Great Society: A Twenty-Year Critique* (Austin Texas: Lyndon Baines Johnson Library and Lyndon B. Johnson School of Public Affairs, 1968); Tom Wicker, *JFK and LBJ* (New York: William Morrow, 1968).

— Megan D. Wessel

Employment Act of 1946

The Employment Act of 1946 represented the legislative outcome of a hotly contested policy dispute over the federal government's role in providing full employment for Americans.

Based on sections of the "Economic Bill of Rights" enunciated in Franklin D. Roosevelt's 1944 State of the Union message, the bill was first introduced in January 1945 as the "full employment bill" by five prominent NEW DEAL senators, including Democrat James Murray of Montana and Democrat Robert Wagner of New York. It was rewritten almost beyond recognition before becoming law over a year later.

Originally the bill required the president to provide Congress with annual estimates of both the nation's projected workforce and the number of jobs likely to be created by the public and private sectors. If the number of jobs amounted to less than the predicted labor force, the president was to propose action that would stimulate private-sector job creation, such as tax incentives, or cause more public sector employment, such as public works programs. A joint committee of Congress was to have final say over which of the president's suggestions would be adopted. To preempt opposition that suggested the bill paved the way for direct federal government involvement in the economy, limits were placed on what the president could recommend.

Opposition erupted. Influential members of Congress and several powerful organizations, including the National Association of Manufacturers, the U.S. Chamber of Commerce, and the Farm Bureau, opposed the bill. Many arguments against the bill involved practical matters, such as the difficulty of making the type of employment forecasts called for and the potential cost. A few even suggested that unemployment was positive because fear of job loss kept workers from slacking off. The most passionate arguments against the bill linked full employment policies with the fascist and communists governments feared by most Americans. Ohio Republican senator ROBERT A. TAFT warned, "we can provide for full employment in the United States, Russia does it; Germany does it . . . if we are willing to sacrifice freedom, we can secure employment."

The bill supporters, including many labor unions and congressional New Dealers, also used fear of totalitarianism. Republican senator Wayne Morse of Oregon reminded his colleagues that "it was unemployment of the masses in Germany and in Italy . . . that brought about the rise of Mussolini and Hitler." Already sensing the COLD WAR struggle for the world's loyalty, Senator Murray promised, "that through this measure . . . we can prevent unemployment and prove to the world that democracy can work." Supporters emphasized domestic benefits of the bill as well. They claimed that full employment would raise the standard of living for all Americans as well as take away the incentive of big BUSINESS to wipe out its smaller competitors.

The bill generated considerable debate, though it did not divide along partisan lines. *Congressional Quarterly* noted, "party lines practically vanished during the debate." Although the bill passed, the changes made to it indicate that its opponents were largely successful in rendering it ineffective. Phrasing was changed to dilute the government's commitment to full employment, with the word "full" even being dropped from the bill's title. Instead of detailed estimates and policy proposals, the final bill stipulated that the president was merely to provide a yearly economic report to Congress on America's employment situation and how federal policy affected it. The joint congressional committee was given power to review the report, but not to initiate legislation. An important addition to the bill was the creation of a COUNCIL OF ECONOMIC ADVISORS to assist the president in preparing the economic report.

Despite its weakened final form, some believed that, with sympathetic people in the Council of Economic Advisors and the Joint Economic Committee in Congress, the law could affect major policy changes. The Republican victory in 1946 dashed those hopes, as the new majority made Senator Taft chair of the committee.

This ineffectiveness has led to questions about whether it was a failure. Certainly, it did not live up to the hopes expressed in Roosevelt's "Economic Bill of Rights." Nevertheless, the bill did create the Council of Economic Advisors. Although the council might not have gained the trust of Congress, it has been an invaluable aid to presidents in considering a host of economic issues since its creation.

Further reading: Stephen Kemp Bailey, *Congress Makes a Law: The Story behind the Employment Act of 1946* (New York: Columbia University Press, 1950); J. Brodford Delong, *Keynesianism, Pennsylvania Avenue Style: Some Economic Consequences of the Employment Act of 1946* (Cambridge, Mass.: National Bureau of Economic Research, 1996).

— Dave Price

Engel v. Vitale (1962)

Engel v. Vitale (1962) was a highly controversial judicial decision that held unconstitutional the recitation of a prayer composed by a group of clergymen for the New York Board of Regents as part of its program of "moral and spiritual training in the schools."

In this decision, the Supreme Court ruled that the State Board of Regents of New York violated the establishment clause, a section of the First Amendment of the Constitution, by mandating the daily recitation of a prayer composed by the government. The prayer in question read: "Almighty God, we acknowledge our dependence upon Thee, and we beg Thy blessing upon us, our parents, our teachers and our country." This daily invocation was adopted on the recommendation of the Board of Regents, and it was said aloud at the beginning of each school day, in every classroom, in the presence of a teacher.

Five plaintiffs, all parents of children, brought the lawsuit. The plaintiffs, with the backing of the American Civil Liberties Union, included members of the Jewish faith, the Society for Ethical Culture, the Unitarian Church, and one nonbeliever. The defendants represented the Board of Education of Union Free School District Number Nine.

The lawsuit challenged the constitutionality of the practice of school prayer on two separate grounds. First, the plaintiffs argued that the use of the official prayer in public schools was contrary to their religious beliefs and practices and thus infringed on their constitutionally guaranteed free exercise of religious rights. Second, they alleged that both the state law authorizing the use of prayer in the public schools and the school district's regulation ordering the recitation of the prayer violated the establishment clause. The New York State Supreme Court upheld the prayer recitation based on its conclusion that the practice did not amount to religious instruction and was permissible as an "accepted" practice.

On December 4, 1961, the U.S. Supreme Court agreed to hear the case. *Engel* was argued on April 3 and 6, 1962. In a 6-1 decision, with neither Justices Felix Frankfurter nor Byron White participating, the U.S. Supreme Court reversed the state decision, holding the daily recitation of the regent's prayer to be in violation of the establishment clause.

Justice Hugo L. Black, writing for the Court, held that "the Establishment clause . . . is violated by the enactment of laws which established an official religion whether those laws operate directly to coerce nonobserving individuals or not . . ." The Court ruled that neither the nondenominational character of the prayer nor the fact that students could be excused from the ceremony allowed this legislation to circumvent the restrictions of the establishment clause. The Court ignored the fact that the prayer did not promote a belief of any kind. Rather, the justices focused on the state's promotion of religious practices in the public schools, concluding that this promotion alone was constitutionally prohibited. More narrowly, the Court focused on the fact that the prayer was composed by the state, holding that "it is no part of the business of the government to compose official prayers for any group of American people to recite as a part of a religious program carried on by the government."

Justice Potter Stewart wrote the sole dissent in *Engel*. In a scathing opinion, he asserted that the Court had violated the free exercise rights of the other students in the district, and he vigorously asserted the position that the students who wished to say the prayer should be permitted to do so.

After the ruling, many people were outraged, calling for the impeachment of Chief Justice EARL WARREN. Many members of Congress likewise delivered heated responses. Some genuinely believed the Court's decision was incorrect, whereas others expressed general criticisms of the Court, which had earlier handed down desegregation decisions they found objectionable. Representative George Andrews of Alabama said, "They put the Negroes in the schools and now they've driven God out." Congressman John Rooney of New York warned, "that the ruling could put the United States schools on the same basis as Russian schools." At a news conference, President JOHN F. KENNEDY responded: "We have in this case a very easy remedy, and that is to pray ourselves." Despite the ruling, prayer in public schools remains an emotionally charged issue.

Further reading: Robert S. Alley, *School Prayer: The Court, the Congress, and the First Amendment* (Buffalo, N.Y.: Prometheus Books, 1994); Terry Eastland, *Religious Liberty in the Supreme Court: The Cases That Defined the Debate over Church and State* (Washington, D.C.: Ethics and Public Policy Center, 1993); Thayer S. Warshaw, *Religion, Education, and the Supreme Court* (Nashville, Tenn.: Abingdon, 1979).

— Elizabeth A. Henke

environmental movement

After World War II, the center of environmental politics shifted from Progressive-era "conservation," which stressed efficient use and management of natural resources, to a newer "environmentalism," which stressed issues such as pollution, environmental degradation, and the preservation of wilderness.

New groups and leaders came forward, and the role of government in addressing environmental problems greatly expanded. As environmental questions moved into the policy arena, a new rank of environmental professionals emerged, sometimes generating tension with the grassroots movement of concerned citizens that developed during the same period.

Although the conservation movement benefited in the 1930s from a range of NEW DEAL programs, it received low priority during and after World War II. When DWIGHT D. EISENHOWER became president—in the midst of rapid economic expansion, rising affluence, cheap energy, and escalating consumer spending—his administration actively dismantled older New Deal conservation policies. Representative actions of the era included auctioning off federal lands, the defeat of proposals for new public power projects modeled on the Tennessee Valley Authority, and the privatization of publicly owned energy resources.

Nevertheless, the seeds of many important new issues took root in the immediate postwar years. Pennsylvania's Donora-Webster "killer smog" of 1948, for example, killed 20 people and raised unsettling questions about air pollution and public health. Highly publicized nuclear tests created awareness of the dangers of radioactive fallout and generated a successful drive to ban atmospheric nuclear testing. The negative environmental effects of population pressure, too, gained a wide audience in Fairfield Osborn's best-selling *Our Plundered Planet* (1948). Perhaps the most

important work of the period, however, was Aldo Leopold's *A Sand County Almanac*, published posthumously in 1949. Especially popular among environmental activists of a later era, the book eloquently argued that all people, as members of a "biotic community," had ethical responsibilities to maintain the health and diversity of the natural world.

Leopold, whose life work was grounded in the earlier conservation movement, also embodied the ability of conservationist groups founded before World War II to adapt to (and shape) the newer environmental agenda. For example, Howard Zahniser, executive director of the Wilderness Society, drafted the Wilderness Act, a key piece of environmental legislation passed in September 1964. The National Wildlife Federation, originally founded to promote hunters' interests, increasingly advocated environmental concerns that sometimes seemed to contradict its advocacy of hunters' rights. Most important was the Sierra Club, founded by John Muir at the beginning of the 20th century in California to foster an appreciation for the "cathedrals" of American wilderness. Under the leadership of David Brower, the Sierra Club championed the cause of wilderness preservation, spearheading drives against large dams in places like Echo Park (1955), Glen Canyon (1963), and the lower Grand Canyon (1966). The Sierra Club also took the lead in popularizing breathtaking nature photography, and especially landscape photography, to build support for preserving and protecting wild nature.

The publication of RACHEL CARSON's *Silent Spring* in 1962, however, constituted the major catalyst for grassroots environmentalism. The book touched a nerve by dramatizing the dangers that ubiquitous "miracle" pesticides such as DDT posed to the health of plant and animal life. Carson was careful to moderate her position, objecting only to the indiscriminate use of pesticides and to what she saw as the hubris of trying to "control" nature, but her book prompted a firestorm of controversy and fierce resistance to her claims. Despite well-financed opposition, her work raised enough public concern to lead the Environmental Protection Agency (EPA) to ban DDT by 1972.

Through the 1960s, the American public became increasingly concerned with environmental issues, catching the attention of national political leaders. Big business, too, often sought federal regulations to standardize the increasing agglomeration of local and state environmental regulations. As a result, the 1960s and early 1970s saw a wave of significant new federal environmental laws, including the Wilderness Act (1964), the Motor Vehicle Air Pollution Control Act (1965), the Water Quality Act (1965), the Air Quality Act (1967), the Clean Air Act Amendments (1970), the National Environmental Policy Act (1970), and the Federal Water Pollution Control Act (1972).

By the late 1960s, however, a growing number of Americans became disillusioned with regulatory and

Smog obscures view of lower portion of downtown highrises, Los Angeles, California, 1966   *(Library of Congress)*

technical solutions to environmental problems, leading them to call instead for personal solutions to environmental ills. Criticizing the United States as a "society of waste," some members of the era's COUNTERCULTURE called for a movement "back to the land." Pleading for heightened "ecological consciousness" and adopting Native Americans as icons for harmonious coexistence with nature, these new environmentalists read publications like the *Whole Earth Catalog* and *Mother Earth News* and promoted decreased consumption and community-based recycling centers, stressing lifestyle issues over regulating industrial polluters. This different emphasis created an uneasy tension between "new" and "traditional" environmentalists, and set the stage for the changes and debates within environmentalism during the 1970s.

Further reading: Samuel Hays, *Beauty, Health, and Permanence: Environmental Politics in the United States, 1955–1985* (Cambridge, U.K.: Cambridge University Press, 1987).

— Christopher W. Wells

Equal Employment Opportunity Commission (EEOC)

The Equal Employment Opportunity Commission (EEOC) investigated claims of discrimination by employers violating Title VII of the CIVIL RIGHTS ACT OF 1964.

Established on July 2, 1965, the EEOC sought to "ensure equality of opportunity by vigorously enforcing federal legislation prohibiting discrimination in employment." Of greatest concern was preventing discrimination on the basis of religion, race, sex, color, national origin, age, or disability.

An independent regulatory agency, the EEOC informed the public about antidiscrimination laws and worked to ensure basic rights for oppressed groups in American society. In addition to Title VII, the EEOC in time came to enforce the 1963 Equal Pay Act, which prohibited discrimination on the basis of gender for similar work in similar conditions; the 1967 Age Discrimination in Employment Act, which barred discrimination against employees aged 40 and older; and the 1973 Rehabilitation Act, which prohibited discrimination against federal employees with a disability.

As part of LYNDON B. JOHNSON'S GREAT SOCIETY programs, the Civil Rights Act of 1964, and the subsequent development of the EEOC, grew out of the larger Civil Rights movement. Throughout the 1960s, activists fought SEGREGATION and its discriminatory effects on African Americans, challenging the president and Congress to pass comprehensive legislation that recognized their rights as citizens. Other groups joined the fight for equality, as Latinos, Native Americans, and women spoke out against intolerance and discriminatory practices, demanding new laws to address numerous expressions of racism in American life. The passage of the Civil Rights Act of 1964 constituted a major step toward eradicating racism across the country.

Established as a response to inequality in the job place, the EEOC was originally limited to information gathering, mediation, and legal support. It relied on negotiation, persuasion, and voluntary compliance in an effort to coerce private employers to end discriminatory hiring practices. In 1972, Congress passed the Equal Employment Opportunity Act that expanded the power of the EEOC. This measure gave the EEOC the right to file legal suits against employers accused of discrimination, subpoena relevant witnesses and documents, and examine charges of discrimination in the federal government. Soon thereafter, the EEOC won several verdicts against major corporations, thereby increasing the consciousness of employers, and accelerating their willingness to comply with the law.

A number of Supreme Court decisions helped contribute to the EEOC's importance as a regulatory agency. In 1971, the Supreme Court ruled that practices that appeared fair in their form but discriminatory in their function were illegal. This included preemployment tests that were not job-related, especially if they were more likely to exclude blacks and other minorities. The court extended its reasoning to rule out using arrest records as a method of screening job candidates.

In addition to eliminating sources of discrimination, the EEOC worked to prevent its recurrence. Headquartered in Washington, D.C., it was led by five commissioners appointed by the president and confirmed by the Senate. A general counsel assisted the commissioners with litigation recommendations, policy shifts, and definitions of the law. Over 100 offices throughout the country engaged in outreach programs that increased public awareness about employment discrimination. Outreach efforts included regular reports on discrimination, national conferences on the topic, and a commitment to sending representatives to underserved areas to inform members of the public about their rights.

In later years, the EEOC adopted a National Enforcement Plan that articulated its mission as threefold. First, it would work to prevent discrimination through education and outreach programs. Next, it would encourage voluntary resolutions of disputes. Finally, if resolution could not be reached, it would seek to use strong and fair enforcement to maintain the laws.

Further reading: Clinton L. Doggett and Lois T. Doggett. *The Equal Employment Opportunity Commission* (New York: Chelsea House, 1990).

— Kirstin Gardner

Escobedo v. Illinois (1964)

The Supreme Court decision in *Escobedo v. Illinois*, a precursor to MIRANDA V. ARIZONA, marked a significant step in safeguarding the rights of suspects in police investigations. By stretching the constitutional requirement of right to counsel, *Escobedo* restricted the police from interrogating an individual without an attorney present.

On the night of January 19, 1960, Daniel Escobedo was arrested without a warrant and interrogated by police about the fatal shooting of his brother-in-law. Escobedo made no statements to the police and was released the following afternoon on a writ of habeas corpus, drafted by his retained attorney, Warren Wolfson, saying he was being held without charge.

Eleven days later, Benedict DiGerlando, an acquaintance of Escobedo now in police custody, told the police that Escobedo had fired the fatal shots in the murder of his brother-in-law. DiGerlando was later indicted along with Escobedo. The police again arrested Escobedo and brought him to police headquarters to be interrogated. On the way to the police station, Escobedo was told that

DiGerlando had named him as the shooter. The police encouraged him to confess to the crime, but Escobedo declined and asked to speak to his attorney.

Shortly after Escobedo reached police headquarters, Wolfson, Escobedo's attorney, arrived and requested to speak to him. The lawyer was denied access to his client repeatedly for the next three to four hours. Officers in the Homicide Bureau told him on several occasions that he could not speak to Escobedo because the police had not finished questioning him. Wolfson remained at the station from 9:00 P.M. that evening until 1:00 A.M. the following morning; despite quoting passages from the Criminal Code to on-duty officers, Wolfson was never allowed to see his client.

Meanwhile, Escobedo continually requested, unsuccessfully, to speak to his lawyer. He later testified that police told him his lawyer "didn't want to see him." During the interrogation, the police encouraged Escobedo, who had yet to reveal any knowledge of the crime, to pin the shooting on DiGerlando. When police arranged a confrontation between Escobedo and DiGerlando, Escobedo denied firing the fatal shots and claimed that DiGerlando had done so, thereby implicating himself in the plot. Escobedo's statements were then used to convict him of murder. His conviction was affirmed by the Supreme Court of Illinois.

Attorneys for Escobedo decided to appeal his case to the federal level. The U.S. Supreme Court agreed to hear the case on appeal, and it was immediately recognized by legal scholars that the case carried momentous judicial import. The central question before the Court was whether or not the right to counsel extended to the moment of arrest.

Bernard Weisberg, a vocal critic of police interrogatory powers, argued the *Escobedo* case for the American Civil Liberties Union. In his brief, Weisberg examined current police interrogation manuals and highlighted what he considered unfair and inherently coercive police tactics which were considered lawful at the time. Weisberg harshly criticized the "virtually unlimited discretionary power" of police interrogators, which he claimed eroded the basic fairness of a criminal proceeding.

In arguing for the state of Illinois, Northwestern University law professor (and future Illinois governor) James Thompson warned the Court that any decision to extend the right to counsel would eliminate confessions as a tool for the police. Thompson predicted that such a decision would cripple law enforcement officers by requiring them to inform a suspect of his right to counsel.

In a 5-4 decision, the Supreme Court reversed Escobedo's conviction. Justice Arthur Goldberg wrote the majority opinion, holding that because Escobedo was being detained as a suspect, by refusing to honor his request to consult an attorney, the police had denied him his constitutional right to counsel as provided by the Sixth and Fourteenth Amendments.

Legal scholars criticized the *Escobedo* opinion, claiming that at times it appeared to constitute a broad attack on police interrogatory powers and the use of confessions, while the language at other points tended to be confining and specific to the facts of the *Escobedo* case.

Justices John Harlan, Potter Stewart, and Byron White each wrote dissenting opinions, claiming that the majority's decision would unjustifiably shackle legitimate police investigative methods, and that the right to counsel should only attach at the initiation of formal proceedings against a defendant.

The *Escobedo* decision was subject to widespread controversy over the next two years. Narrow interpretations of the Court's decision only recognized a suspect's right to counsel when he or she chose to exercise that right. Broader readings, however, including the interpretation of James Thompson, asserted that *Escobedo* required that a suspect be informed of the right to counsel.

Contention over the scope and meaning of *Escobedo* was erased in 1966 with the landmark decision in *Miranda v. Arizona*. The Supreme Court bolstered *Escobedo* by requiring in the *Miranda* decision that police inform a suspect of his or her right to remain silent and to have legal counsel present. These requirements were to be carried out in what would become the famous "Miranda warnings."

Further reading: Walter V. Schaefer, *The Suspect and Society: Criminal Procedure and Converging Constitutional Doctrines* (Evanston, Ill.: Northwestern University Press, 1967).

— Guy R. Temple

Europe (and foreign policy)

Following World War II, Europe became a dangerous power vacuum that invited intervention from the world's new superpowers, the United States and the SOVIET UNION.

As the uneasy alliance between these two powers disintegrated and both eventually became engaged in the COLD WAR, Europe found itself divided between them. In both the Western and Eastern blocs, European nations were largely denied the ability to make independent decisions, and attempts to break free from their alliances met with marked hostility and, with regard to the Eastern bloc, occasionally outright force.

The military situation in Europe following World War II provided the Soviet Union with control over Eastern Europe. With its armies spread out across the Balkans, the Soviet Union installed friendly governments in several Eastern European countries in order to create a buffer zone against a revived Germany. In Poland, Soviet leader Joseph Stalin, claiming that the nation had served as a "corridor" for German advances, insisted that the new Polish government cohere around a group of communist exiles known as the Lublin Poles. For added protection, the Soviet Union absorbed the states of Estonia, Latvia, and Lithuania. In 1947, the Soviet Union overthrew the democratically elected noncommunist government of Hungary. The following year, it helped communists seize power in Czechoslovakia. With communist states also in Romania, Bulgaria, and Yugoslavia, the Soviets forged a sphere of influence in 1955 that was institutionalized as the Warsaw Pact.

Fearful that the Soviet Union sought to extend its sphere of influence farther west, the United States sought to rebuild Western Europe as a bulwark against COMMUNISM. In February 1946, GEORGE F. KENNAN, an American diplomat in Moscow, wrote a "Long Telegram" that urged American policymakers to realize the severity of the communist threat, arguing that the Soviet Union blended Russia's historic sense of insecurity with an expansive political ideology. To meet this danger, Kennan articulated what became known as the "containment" policy, which stated that the United States should contain the Soviet Union within its present boundaries; such a policy, Kennan believed, would ultimately enable the internal contradictions of communist ideology to unravel the Soviet Union. The next year, the Truman administration, in response to perceived communist aggression in Turkey and Greece, provided economic and military aid and announced that the United States would assist any nation attempting to resist communist subjugation. In 1948, the United States offered the MARSHALL PLAN, which outlined an aid package for reconstructing Western Europe, then in 1949 created the NORTH ATLANTIC TREATY ORGANIZATION (NATO), a permanent alliance with other

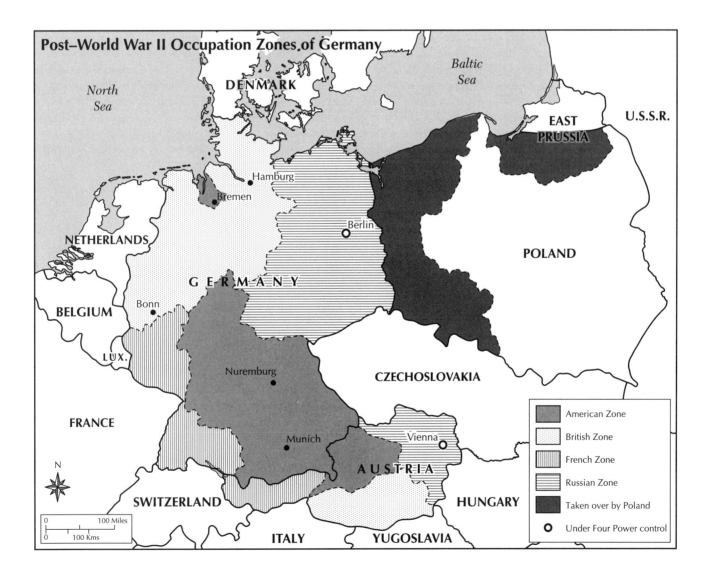

Post–World War II Occupation Zones of Germany

Western European states and Canada designed to deter Soviet aggression, proclaiming that an attack against one member of the alliance would be considered an attack against all.

This division persisted throughout the 1950s and 1960s despite attempts in both blocs to strike a more neutral course. In Western Europe, the administration of French president Charles de Gaulle offered the greatest challenge to American leadership. After taking power in 1959, the former leader of Free French forces during World War II sought to reduce American influence in France and reach some sort of accommodation with the Soviets. De Gaulle pursued a unilateral French nuclear weapons program, closer ties for France with the Soviet Union, and greater French influence in the Third World. He untied French currency from the dollar and pulled French troops out of NATO. Despite all of de Gaulle's efforts, however, France remained wary of the Soviet Union and thus remained firmly embedded in the Western bloc.

The Soviet Union faced even greater threats to its leadership. Three years after Joseph Stalin's death in 1953, the new Russian premier Nikita Khrushchev shocked communist Europe with a scathing denunciation of Stalin's brutal policies. Interpreting his speech as an implicit endorsement of Yugoslavian premier Josip Tito's independent policies, revolutionaries in Poland and Hungary moved for greater independence from Moscow. In Poland, the Soviet Union responded to riots with force. In Hungary, where revolutionaries actually established a new government and announced that Hungary was leaving the Warsaw Pact, the Soviet Union crushed the resistance, killing at least 4,000 Hungarian students and workers. By the late 1960s, the Soviet Union faced another potential threat when Czechoslovakia, under Alexander Dubček, attempted to initiate a major reform of the communist system. Spurred by communist intellectuals, economists, and politicians, the Prague Spring, as the movement came to be known, sought to enable greater popular participation in the political system, foster the growth of free enterprise, and promote greater respect for individual liberties. Under Leonid Brezhnev, the Soviet Union responded to Dubček's reform with an invasion and occupation of Czechoslovakia.

The division of Europe persisted well into the next quarter century. Symbolized by the construction of the Wall in the divided city of Berlin, Europe remained split between two hostile superpowers. Efforts to achieve both autonomy and harmony in Europe reached fruition with the age of détente.

Further reading: A. W. DePorte, *Europe between the Superpowers: The Enduring Balance* (New Haven, Conn.: Yale University Press, 1979); Mark Mazower, *The Dark Continent: Europe's Twentieth Century* (New York: Knopf, 1999).

— Brian Etheridge

F

Fair Deal

The Fair Deal was HARRY S. TRUMAN's domestic policy agenda calling for civil rights legislation, national health insurance, and other programs aimed at improving American society.

In his State of the Union address on January 15, 1949, Truman announced his domestic agenda for the next four years. "Every segment of our population and every individual," Truman proclaimed, "has a right to expect from our government a fair deal." The president outlined an expansion of many of Franklin D. Roosevelt's NEW DEAL policies into a series of programs that came to be known as the Fair Deal. Only a few planks of this ambitious agenda, however, passed through a hostile Congress to become legislation.

Truman proposed the Fair Deal at the height of his presidential career. His victory in the closely contested election of 1948 over THOMAS E. DEWEY signaled Truman's emergence from the shadow cast by his predecessor. Truman had earned his victory by holding together the New Deal coalition of farmers, union members, and urban ethnic voters. On the strength of this election success, the president proposed an ambitious domestic agenda that carried through his 1948 campaign promises and expanded many New Deal programs. The Fair Deal called for broader social security coverage; an increase in the minimum wage; a repeal of the anti-union TAFT-HARTLEY ACT; the development of power programs modeled after the Tennessee Valley Authority (such as the Columbia Valley Administration); an expanded federal housing program; federal aid to education; and a national health insurance program. Truman later added several civil rights measures to his Fair Deal proposals, including a federal antilynching law and the establishment of a permanent FAIR EMPLOYMENT PRACTICES COMMITTEE (FEPC) to regulate racial discrimination in the workplace.

From the start, the Truman administration faced several obstacles in enacting the Fair Deal. Although the DEMOCRATIC PARTY enjoyed a majority in both houses of Congress, a coalition of Republicans and conservative southern Democrats held control of the legislative process and successfully prevented passage of most Fair Deal programs. Truman needed the support of the southern Democrats to achieve his foreign policy objectives in the COLD WAR, and he was unwilling to risk these goals to push his domestic agenda. Perhaps most significantly, Truman proposed the Fair Deal just as the country was becoming more conservative and pulling back from the commitment to reform that had marked the 1930s.

These obstacles scuttled most Fair Deal legislation. For example, Truman had called for a national health insurance system that relied for funding on federal payments in combination with employee and employer contributions. The American Medical Association and the American Hospital Association, worried about a decrease in doctors' income, denounced the plan as "socialized medicine." Truman settled instead for a more conservative bill that funded the construction of new hospitals. Fair Deal plans for federal coordination of hydroelectric power in the Pacific Northwest stalled in Congress, as did Truman's proposals for federal aid to education and his attempt to repeal the Taft-Hartley Act (which limited unions' powers to conduct boycotts and enforce closed shops, where employees had to join unions before getting jobs).

Truman's civil rights initiatives had little chance of succeeding in a Congress controlled by conservative southern Democrats who opposed any action that threatened SEGREGATION. Although a weak FEPC bill did pass the House, the president agreed to hold off on a Senate vote on the bill in return for congressional support for his foreign aid policies. Stalled in Congress, Truman used executive orders to advance his civil rights initiatives, such as the appointment of African Americans to mid-level government posts and judiciary positions and the denial of federal contracts to firms that practiced racial discrimination.

Despite these setbacks, Truman did succeed in passing some parts of the Fair Deal agenda. Most of these successes, however, came in packages scaled down from the original proposals. The Social Security Act of 1950 increased the level of benefits in the social security program, and extended coverage to more than 10 million people, including agricultural workers (Truman had asked for an extension to 25 million workers). The National Housing Act of 1949 authorized the construction of 810,000 federal housing units (down from Truman's request for over 1 million). The administration also secured a raise in the minimum wage from 40 to 75 cents an hour.

The failure of most Fair Deal legislation is not surprising. Despite its lack of success, however, the Fair Deal remains important. Truman's vision of a "fair deal"—especially in housing, education, and civil rights—set the stage for debates over domestic reform for the next several decades.

Further reading: Robert J. Donovan, *The Tumultuous Years: The Presidency of Harry S. Truman, 1949–1953* (New York: W. W. Norton, 1982); Gary W. Reichard, *Politics As Usual: The Age of Truman and Eisenhower* (Arlington Heights, Ill.: Harlan Davidson, 1988).

— Jim Feldman

Fair Employment Practices Committee (FEPC)   See Volume VIII

family life   See marriage and family life

Faubus, Orval (1910–1994)

Orval Faubus served six consecutive terms as governor of Arkansas (1955–67), and gained the national spotlight for his controversial role in the 1957 standoff at Little Rock's Central High School, in which he called on the Arkansas National Guard to prevent the school's desegregation.

Orval Eugene Faubus was born January 7, 1910, the son of a poor farmer, in Greasy Creek, Arkansas, a small Ozark Mountain community. He worked at a variety of jobs as a young man, including two terms as Madison County Circuit Clerk. Faubus enlisted in the U.S. Army in 1942, and he was commissioned as an officer in Europe, where he served from 1942 to 1946.

Following his return from his World War II service, Faubus worked as Huntsville, Arkansas, postmaster, and in 1949, was appointed to the Arkansas State Highway Commission. He became state director of highways in 1952, and he served for two years. In 1954, Faubus made a bid for governor.

Faubus defeated incumbent Francis Cherry in the 1954 Arkansas Democratic primary. Faubus later defeated Republican Pratt Remmel in the November 1954 election.

The politics of race and integration played a prominent role in the campaign, for in May of that same year, the Supreme Court handed down the landmark BROWN v. BOARD OF EDUCATION decision, ruling public school racial SEGREGATION unconstitutional. Governor Cherry had made it clear that Arkansas would comply with the Supreme Court ruling. Likewise, in his campaign as challenger, Faubus had pledged that "the rights of all will be protected but that the problem of desegregation will be solved on the local level, with state authorities standing ready to assist in every way possible." A southern populist and New Deal Democrat, Faubus began his first term as governor with a liberal gesture, appointing six black men to the state Democratic Committee. He soon found that he could not afford such goodwill. Political opponents forced him to alter his liberal course, accusing him during the 1956 reelection campaign of being "soft" on racial issues.

Beginning with the city of Charleston, a few public schools across the state of Arkansas gradually began to comply with the Supreme Court's ruling to end segregation "with all deliberate speed." Opposition to integration, however, grew increasingly fierce. Faubus, campaigning for reelection in 1956, became vocal in his resistance to desegregation. In January 1956, he reported to the press that "85 percent of all the people" of Arkansas opposed desegregation, according to a statewide poll he had commissioned. Nonetheless, segregationist leaders rallied around former state senator James Johnson as a Democratic candidate for governor, accusing Faubus of taking a "do-nothing" stand on desegregation. In a July 1956 campaign speech, Faubus responded to the criticism, stating, "No school district will be forced to mix the races as long as I am governor of Arkansas."

Faubus defeated Johnson for the Democratic nomination, and he was reelected governor in 1956. In the same election, voters approved three segregation measures on the ballot, including an act authorizing school districts to assign students to schools in ways that reflected opposition to integration, and the Act of Interposition, putting the state on record as being in opposition to "racial mixing" in schools. In March 1956, all eight members of the Arkansas congressional delegation signed the SOUTHERN MANIFESTO, pledging, along with other congressmen, to use "all lawful means" to resist and overturn the *Brown* decision.

Faubus actively resisted integration in his second term. Even as the Little Rock School Board prepared plans to integrate Central High School the following fall, he signed anti-integration legislation in February 1957 that included provisions allowing parents to refuse to send their children to desegregated schools and authorizing the use of state and local funds to pay for legal fees incurred in the anti-integration battle. Faubus antagonized the NATIONAL ASSOCIATION FOR THE ADVANCEMENT OF COLORED PEOPLE

(NAACP) by signing into law a requirement for organizations such as the NAACP to disclose membership and financial information, which put members at risk of violent attacks from anti-integration whites.

The desegregation effort officially began on September 4, 1957, when nine black students attempted to enter Central High School. The students were turned away by members of the Arkansas National Guard, called in by Faubus on orders to stand guard in front of the school to avert violence. Two weeks later, Federal District Judge Ronald Davies ruled that Faubus had used the National Guard not to maintain law and order but to prevent integration. The governor removed the guardsmen, but when the nine black students again attempted to attend school on September 23, a mob of 1,000 anti-integration whites became so unruly that the police feared a loss of control and escorted the students out a back exit. Prompted by pleas from Little Rock mayor Woodrow Mann, President DWIGHT D. EISENHOWER dispatched 1,000 members of the 101st Airborne Division to Central High, and he federalized the National Guard. Under the escort of army troops, the nine black students attended school, ending the standoff.

For the next several years, Faubus utilized everything in his power as governor to resist the integration process, going so far as to close all Little Rock public high schools in 1958. His efforts to slow the progress of desegregation won him reelection for four more terms. He ran for governor three more times during the 1970s and 1980s, but he was unsuccessful. Faubus continued to defend his anti-integration efforts until his death in 1994, at the age of 84.

Further reading: Irving J. Spitzberg, *Racial Politics in Little Rock, 1954–1964* (New York: Garland Publishing, 1987).

— Guy R. Temple

Federal-Aid Highway Act of 1956 See Interstate Highway Act of 1956

Federal Employee Loyalty Program

HARRY S. TRUMAN initiated the Federal Employee Loyalty Program on March 25, 1947, with the aim of rooting out all communist sympathizers within the federal government.

The program comprised part of the anticommunist crusade that unfolded in the first decade of the COLD WAR. Fear of internal communist subversion accompanied Soviet advances in Eastern Europe, and led to the belief in the United States that national security was at stake. With the Federal Employee Loyalty Program, Truman hoped to squelch the possible charges that he was "soft on communism."

The program began with fingerprinting over 2 million federal employees. Along with fingerprinting, loyalty questionnaires sought to determine any questionable background. Agencies sent names to a "national-agency name check" in the files of the Federal Bureau of Investigation, the Civil Service Commission, the armed forces and the HOUSE UN-AMERICAN ACTIVITIES COMMITTEE (HUAC). The name search sought to uncover any information that might lead to "reasonable doubt" as to an employee's loyalty to the United States.

In 1950, Congress passed Public Law 733 that permitted the termination of any employee, without due process of law, for reasons of "national security." A security risk constituted not only someone whose loyalty was in question, but also someone whose character made him or her vulnerable to disclosing classified information under pressure or blackmail. By 1952, more than 40,000 federal employees had undergone investigations, with interviews of neighbors, friends, schoolmates, fellow employees, and former teachers. After 1953, President DWIGHT D. EISENHOWER demanded that a full investigation for every "sensitive position" in government be conducted. This was soon expanded to include every position in government.

When employees were suspected of being disloyal, they were sent before one of over 200 agency loyalty boards located across the country established by the Truman administration. Employees were given the opportunity to appeal to one of 14 regional boards and also to the 25-member Loyalty Review Board.

The program, however, did not ensure that, once cleared of disloyalty charges, an employee was free from harassment. Many employees found themselves charged and cleared seven or eight times as criteria became increasingly stringent. Eventually, many of those who had undergone investigation numerous times were suspended without pay or simply dismissed.

Many employees reacted to the investigations with fear and suspicion. Some referred to the practices the government was using as "Gestapo methods," alluding to the Nazi secret service interrogations. The goal of all employees was to avoid an investigation. Many practiced extreme caution, unwilling to discuss any political opinions inside or outside of the office. Employees of the federal government avoided conversational topics such as admitting China to the United Nations, developing atomic energy, supporting civil rights, and debating religion. Since involvement in any organization concerned with any kind of social reform immediately put a federal employee under suspicion, many felt that it was better not to join at all. No one could be sure which group would appear on the attorney general's list of suspicious or subversive organizations. For a time, even the Consumers Union was on the list.

By the late 1950s, the Supreme Court began to reassert the rights of due process, including the right to cross-examine hostile witnesses. Rulings of the Supreme Court had the effect of restoring more than 100 employees to their jobs and led to dropping proceedings against more than 75 others. Over the course of the Federal Employee Loyalty Program, about 8,000 employees were forced to resign, three went to prison, at least seven were driven to suicide, and one died of a heart attack.

Further reading: David Caute, *The Great Fear: The Anti-Communist Purge under Truman and Eisenhower* (New York: Simon & Schuster, 1978); Griffin Fariello, *Red Scare* (New York: W. W. Norton, 1995); Athan Theoharis, *Harry S. Truman and the Origins of McCarthyism* (New York: Quadrangle Books, 1971).

— Sarah Brenner

Federal Housing Administration

The New Deal's National Housing Act of 1934 established the Federal Housing Administration (FHA), which was the dominant force in federal housing until the 1960s.

The FHA's long-term mortgages required small down payments to purchase a home in the 1930s, and insured mortgages by providing guarantees against families losing their homes. The widespread loss of jobs and income, as a result of the Great Depression, led to a higher number of foreclosures and tenant evictions with creditors and borrowers both hit hard. This in turn hurt the building industry. The FHA made it possible for an average middle-class family to be able to afford a home within its financial means and bolstered the building industry at the same time.

Returning World War II veterans needed housing, and the FHA expanded aid to the housing industry to meet the high demand. With a growing clientele during the housing shortage crisis, it became politically difficult to attack the program. Congress was reluctant to touch the program because it facilitated the profitable business transactions of a key group of private market participants.

From the start of the program, the FHA turned away from the cities and minorities to support a growing suburbia and an expanding white middle class. FHA programs supported racially segregated neighborhoods; the FHA believed this was the way to safeguard its financial investment. The agency also ignored the problems of rehabilitating and repairing older, still sound housing stock in inner-urban areas. This practice was encouraged by the businesses and attitudes of the time.

The administration of DWIGHT D. EISENHOWER succeeded in slowing federal involvement in social welfare. The role of the FHA, Republicans believed, was to aid the private bankers in serving the middle class. Not until the return of liberals to the White House in the 1960s did pressure increase toward more governmental action to aid the disadvantaged and minorities. In 1962, an executive order of JOHN F. KENNEDY prohibiting racial SEGREGATION in FHA programs changed the agency's mandate. Instead of guaranteeing market-rate loans to qualified families, the FHA became a source of below-market interest loans, and it began to focus on inner-city development. Various programs supported by the FHA helped nonprofit organizations assist moderate-income families. More sensitive management of the programs, better administration, better understanding of the community, more tenant involvement, and expanded social services led to many successful endeavors in which better environments and housing for families were created. In other cases, though, the nonprofit organizations were just fronts for developers. The programs led to enormous profits for some of these builders, who did shoddy work to make a larger profit. There were also cases of mismanagement of funds and housing, which led to the units falling into disrepair.

Under FHA subsidy programs, builders, banks, and real estate firms were guaranteed a profit. But the quality of the housing was called into question, as many units were substandard. Poor construction or rehabilitation of buildings led to the abandonment of these structures. The low-income families who lived in these units could not afford the upkeep of these buildings. The same agency that helped create suburbia in the 1940s, 1950s, and 1960s, helped destroy inner-city communities at the same time.

Further reading: John Egan, et al. *Housing and Public Policy: A Role for Mediating Structures* (Cambridge, Mass.: Ballinger Publishing Company, 1981); R. Allen Hays, *The Federal Government and Urban Housing: Ideology and Change in Public Policy* (Albany: State University of New York Press, 1985).

— Robert A. Deahl

folk music revival

The folk MUSIC revival flourished throughout the decade of the 1960s and into the 1970s. Songs with a clear political message led to the development of an urban folk music revival that intertwined with the political upheaval of the 1960s.

In the 1930s and 1940s, the NEW DEAL's Works Progress Administration brought traditional African-American folk songs to the attention of urban middle-class audiences at the same time that singers with left-wing political sympathies promoted folk songs that they felt reflected the voice of the people. Singers such as Woody Guthrie and Sarah Ogan Gunning were among those who encouraged the spread of folk songs. In the 1950s Pete Seeger and the

Weavers carried on the tradition of Woody Guthrie by bringing their music and political message to a wider audience as they began to develop their music on college campuses. With such hit songs as "Good Night Irene," and "The Midnight Special," the group paved the way for the folk singers of the 1960s to bring the revival to mainstream culture. Seeger was one of the leading influences in developing folk music as a new form of popular music in the United States. Along with many other members of the entertainment industry, Seeger and the Weavers were targeted in the anticommunist hysteria of the 1950s and blacklisted, making it difficult for them to work.

There were four kinds of folk music singers who emerged during the 1960s. Traditional performers learned their folk music through the culture in which they were raised. Many of these performers stayed away from the mainstream and instead sang at folk festivals, on college campuses, and in coffeehouses. This first type of folk music included singers such as Sarah Ogan Gunning, Mississippi John Hurt, and Glenn Ohrlin. Other performers, many of them white middle-class suburban or urban young people, immersed themselves in both the culture and music of traditional singers and began to popularize it. Among those who could be called "emulators" were the New Lost City Ramblers, Dave Van Ronk, and the Jim Kweskin Jug Band.

Still other performers took traditional text and music and rewrote songs to appeal to mainstream urban audiences. They included such groups as the Kingston Trio. Finally, there were singers who attempted to blend traditional and urban aesthetics in their performance without losing the political messages they were conveying. The music of this group blended folk, classical, jazz, and pop styles. The fourth group created the mainstream sound of the urban folk song revival in the 1960s. Singers in this category remain popular and include Joan Baez, Peter, Paul and Mary, and BOB DYLAN.

Folk music became intertwined with the Civil Rights Movement. Singer Guy Carawon revived the old spiritual "We Shall Overcome," taught it to civil rights volunteers, and helped it become the marching song of the movement. Baez and Dylan sang songs to protest the VIETNAM WAR and racism, and also sang in support of the movement for WOMEN'S STATUS AND RIGHTS. Dylan's song "Blowin' in the Wind," sung by Peter, Paul and Mary as well as Dylan himself, became a standard protest song.

The folk music revival contributed to the anti-war protests of the late 1960s and continued through the turbulence of the 1970s. Many folk singers found the greatest forum for their political messages with the COUNTERCULTURE of the "hippie" generation. The folk music revival truly reached a high point with the participation of many folk singers in the most historically significant concert of the era, Woodstock. Woodstock brought together such folk and rock greats as Baez, Jimi Hendrix, The Who, and Jefferson Airplane, who sang the war protest song "Volunteers." Woodstock, which was intended to be only a small gathering, caught the attention of the nation as it became the largest gathering of entertainers and fans up to that time to protest peacefully the war in Vietnam and the injustices of the era.

Folk music captured the attention of the population in the 1950s through the 1970s with its political messages criticizing the problems of the era.

Further reading: R. Serge Denisoff, *Great Day Coming: Folk Music and the American Left* (Urbana: University of Illinois Press, 1971); Robert Shelton, *No Direction Home: The Life and Music of Bob Dylan* (New York: Beech Tree Books, 1986).

— Sarah Brenner

Pete Seeger performing on stage at Yorktown Heights High School, Yorktown, N.Y., 1967   *(Library of Congress)*

Ford Motor Corporation

The Ford Motor Corporation constituted one of the major automobile manufacturing companies in the 20th-century United States.

Craftsman Henry Ford founded the Ford Motor Company in his small Detroit, Michigan, workshop in 1903. By 1921, the company employed over 32,000 people and produced over 930,000 cars per year. In the 1920s, Ford was a national and international hero, hailed, in the phrase of historian William E. Leuchtenburg, as the "high priest of mass civilization." The Ford Motor Company's Model T stimulated American's demand for automobiles, for unlike previous cars, it was both inexpensive and tough. The use of standardized parts kept the price low, as did the production of cars in just one color—black.

During World War II, Ford stopped making automobiles and produced airplanes in his new mile-long plant at Willow Run, near Detroit. It contained 1,600 pieces of heavy machinery along with 75,000 jigs and other fixtures. At full tilt, it employed over 42,000 people, and was, according to aviator Charles Lindbergh, "a sort of Grand Canyon of the mechanized world."

Passenger car production resumed in the summer of 1945. Henry Ford's grandson became president of the company that same year, and Ford himself died in 1947 at the age of 83. The Ford Motor Company became a publicly held company with the public sale of common stock in 1956, a major change from the days when Ford kept everything in his own hands.

The company found itself involved in a public relations disaster with the introduction of the brand-new Edsel in 1957, which became available at just about the time the SOVIET UNION launched Sputnik, the world's first artificial satellite. The new car, with a front grille that looked like a toilet seat, seemed to be a symbol of flabby, materialistic American culture in the 1950s that could not compete with Russian technological expertise.

In the 1960s, the company received favorable exposure when the company's president, Robert McNamara, who had helped revive Ford's fortunes, became secretary of defense in the administration of JOHN F. KENNEDY.

Further reading: Robert L. Shook, *Turnaround: The New Ford Motor Company* (New York: Prentice Hall, 1990).

— Theresa Ann Case

foreign policy   See Africa, Asia, Latin America, etc.

Free Speech Movement

The Free Speech Movement at the University of California at Berkeley sought to protect political and civil rights in the 1960s. It was the first major action in the nationwide student revolution.

The University of California had long been a place marked by student activism. In 1936, the students reacted vigorously to the university's policy requiring the approval of its president for off-campus speakers and the use of campus facilities by nonapproved groups. The students protested by using flatbed trucks at the university's entrances in order to speak. In 1956, when Democratic presidential candidate ADLAI STEVENSON was not allowed to speak on campus, he ended up addressing students atop a car parked in a corner of campus.

Further conflict at Berkeley started in September 1964 when the dean of students sent a letter to all student organizations to inform them that the sidewalk area in front of the campus would no longer be available for setting up tables, raising funds, recruiting members, and giving speeches for off-campus political and social action. Later that month, five students were cited for violating the newly formed regulations against manning tables, and they were asked to appear before the dean of the university. Over 400 students signed statements saying that they were equally responsible for performing such activity, and they appeared in Sproul Hall, the university's main administration building, requesting that they also be subject to disciplinary hearings. All of the students were refused access to the dean, except for the original five students and three leaders of the protest group. The university's chancellor finally announced the indefinite suspension of the eight students. Other students protested the ruling, and they remained at Sproul Hall until the following morning. Later that month these students formed the United Front, which brought together students from all the various political organizations on campus.

On October 1, a major uprising occurred when Jack Weinberg, a former student, set up a civil rights information table on the campus. He was confronted by two deans and the police and was arrested for trespassing. Before the police could drive him to jail, a mob of 4,000 students surrounded the police car holding him. MARIO SAVIO, the main speaker of what came to be called the Free Speech Movement, then jumped on top of the police car and launched into a speech about how students were going to hold a rally until the university administration gave them back their civil right to organize politically. Savio led the protestors in negotiations with the administration. He also led the protestors in the first of many SIT-INS in Sproul Hall. The sit-in at this demonstration lasted 36 hours. Eventually, the police dragged away and arrested 773 of the protestors, including Savio. In response, students called a strike, and only 17 to 18 percent of the student body attended classes. The strike led Clark Kerr, the university's chancellor, to back down and grant the students the right to unrestricted political protest on campus. For his role in the uprising, Savio, along with several other students, was suspended from school.

Soon the university's graduate students and teacher's assistants agreed to strike unless the suspended students were allowed back into the school. In December, Kerr invited students to the Greek Theatre to declare amnesty for all actions before December 3. This in turn allowed the students who were suspended to come back to the university without any consequences. In April 1965, Savio stepped down as leader of the Free Speech Movement. It soon faded, and it was eventually renamed the Free Student Union.

The Free Speech Movement created a backlash that resulted in the election of Ronald Reagan as governor of California in 1966. He supported traditional values and promised to bring student disruptions under control.

Further reading: Susan Gilmore and Michael V. Miller, eds., *Revolution at Berkeley: The Crisis in American Edu-* *cation* (New York: Dial Press, 1965); David L. Goines, *The Free Speech Movement: Coming of Age in the 1960s.* (Berkeley, Calif.: Ten Speed Press, 1993).

— Megan D. Wessel

freedom rides

In May 1961, a biracial coalition from the STUDENT NONVI-OLENT COORDINATING COMMITTEE (SNCC) and the CONGRESS OF RACIAL EQUALITY (CORE) traveled throughout the South in an attempt to desegregate bus terminals.

The decision to organize the rides built on decades of attempts to end SEGREGATION in road transportation. In 1947, the Supreme Court banned discrimination in interstate travel. Later that year, CORE organized a freedom ride in the upper South, labeled the "journey of reconciliation." On December 1, 1955, ROSA PARKS refused to cede her seat to a white passenger on a Montgomery, Alabama, bus, triggering a year-long confrontation that ended with a December 13, 1956, Supreme Court ruling that banned

Freedom riders, sponsored by the Congress of Racial Equality, gather outside a burning bus in Anniston, Alabama, 1961   *(Library of Congress)*

segregation on buses and desegregated the city buses. In 1961, the Supreme Court also decided that segregated terminal facilities were unconstitutional, prompting the freedom rides.

On May 4, 1961, 13 passengers, including six whites, several journalists, and SNCC's JOHN LEWIS and Henry Thomas, chartered Greyhound and Trailways buses and left Washington, D.C., for New Orleans. They made their way through Virginia and North Carolina without encountering any violent opposition. The first incident occurred on May 9 in Rock Hill, South Carolina, where 20 people attacked the freedom riders, Lewis most prominently, as they tried to enter the white waiting room. Freedom riders made it out of the room unharmed after the police intervened. In Winnsboro, South Carolina, CORE's white member Jim Peck and SNCC's Thomas were arrested as they entered a white lunchroom. The buses continued their way through Georgia without further incident.

As it entered Anniston, Alabama, a mob attacked the Greyhound bus, slashed its tires, and broke its windows. When the bus left town, white demonstrators burned it and beat its occupants. They continued their trip on another bus. Another mob entered the Trailways bus, forcing its black occupants to move to the back section of the vehicle. The bus was once again attacked in Birmingham, Alabama, where many riders, including Peck, were severely beaten. The ride ended there when no bus agreed to take the riders any farther. The riders flew to New Orleans where they attended a May 17 rally celebrating the seventh anniversary of the 1954 BROWN v. BOARD OF EDUCATION decision.

On May 17, 1961, a second Freedom Ride organized by Diane Nash, coordinator of student activities for the Nashville Christian Leadership Council, SNCC, and Nashville student movements, left Nashville for Alabama, Mississippi, and New Orleans. On May 19, at the request of Alabama governor John Patterson, Alabama state circuit judge Walter B. Jones enjoined freedom riders from entering the state. When they ignored the order, the 10 riders, including two whites, were arrested in Birmingham, kept in jail for the night, and sent back to Tennessee by Police Chief Eugene "Bull" Connor the following day. They returned by car to Birmingham, where Patterson, at President JOHN F. KENNEDY and Attorney General ROBERT F. KENNEDY's request, provided them with an escort as they moved to Montgomery on May 20. There, the escort disappeared and a mob attacked the riders, severely injuring several of them, including Lewis and the Department of Justice's special envoy, John Seigenthaler, before the police broke up the crowd. MARTIN LUTHER KING, JR., who acted as chairman of the coordinating committee for the rides, went to Montgomery where he delivered a sermon at Ralph Abernathy's First Baptist Church.

When a mob threatened his listeners, Robert Kennedy sent federal marshals at King's request to protect them. Patterson declared martial law in Montgomery and sent 800 national guardsmen to the scene. On May 23, the riders boarded two buses to Jackson, Mississippi, where 27 of them were arrested for attempting to use segregated facilities.

Over the next months, several hundred protesters were arrested as they tried to desegregate facilities in Jackson. So many activists were imprisoned and refused to pay bail that nearby jails had to be used. STOKELY CARMICHAEL, who became SNCC's chairman in May 1966, and Ruby Doris Smith, who became SNCC's executive secretary the same year, were two of the many demonstrators sent to jail. Carmichael spent 50 days there. The Interstate Commerce Commission finally issued a September 22 ruling, effective November 1, banning segregation in bus and train terminals. While the ruling was not immediately implemented in small towns, integration gradually became the rule in southern transportation facilities. In the spring and summer of 1962, CORE led a less-publicized effort to desegregate restaurant facilities along Virginia, North Carolina, and Florida highways.

The freedom rides triggered increased militancy on the part of both SNCC and black leaders. The dangers protesters faced made nonviolence less appealing to many. The realization that the federal government was carefully weighing political expediency with its official sympathy toward the protesters also disturbed many activists. The Kennedy administration, concerned about the risks of violent confrontations that freedom rides entailed, urged the Civil Rights movement to support voter registration drives in the following months.

Further reading: James Peck, *Freedom Ride* (New York: Simon & Schuster, 1962).

— Philippe R. Girard

Friedan, Betty (1921–)

Betty Friedan was one of the prominent leaders of the American feminist movement that swept the United States during the 1960s.

In her book *The Feminine Mystique* (1961), Friedan raised questions regarding middle-class women's place in American society. Millions of women related to Friedan's frustration at the lack of opportunity, and, as a result, many were drawn into the feminist movement.

Born Bettye Naomi Goldstein on February 4, 1921, in Peoria, Illinois, Friedan grew up in a middle-class Jewish household. Despite the family's financial success, the Goldsteins were not allowed to join the Peoria Country Club because they were Jews. Friedan was also excluded from a sorority while in high school because she was Jewish. Her experiences with anti-Semitism contributed to her recognition of inequality and her desire to improve society. She studied psychology at Smith College, where she graduated summa cum laude in 1942. She planned to continue her education in psychology and enrolled as a graduate student at the University of California at Berkeley in the fall of 1942. She spent one year at Berkeley, and then moved to Manhattan, where she worked as a journalist until 1952. She continued to work as a free-lance writer from 1952 to 1963. She married Carl Friedan in 1947.

As a suburban middle-class housewife and mother of three children in the 1950s, Friedan, like many women, experienced what she later termed "the problem that has no name." She felt that a purely domestic life was inhibiting for many women, who focused exclusively on their husbands and children, without any time to realize their own full potential or develop their own identity. In 1957, she devised a questionnaire for her 15th college reunion. Friedan discovered that many of her Smith classmates felt the same way she did. They were dissatisfied with their domestic lives, and they felt that something was missing. Friedan used her classmates' responses as a basis for *The Feminine Mystique,* which applied primarily to white, middle-class women.

In *The Feminine Mystique,* Friedan criticized the popular theory that women could only find fulfillment through their roles as wives and mothers. She argued that the suburban environment could be oppressive to many women, and that they needed to develop their own identity in order to be happy. This meant that they needed to be more than just homemakers; they needed to be educated and have their own careers. The success of her book launched Friedan to national prominence.

As one of the leaders of the newly revived feminist movement, Friedan was a founding member of the NATIONAL ORGANIZATION FOR WOMEN (NOW) in 1966. Friedan and the other members of this organization were dedicated to the realization of full equality for women in all areas of American life. As the first president of NOW, Friedan tackled everything from job discrimination to fair marriage and divorce laws. She served as president until 1970 and was involved in every aspect of the organization, including the decision in 1967 to support the Equal Rights Amendment (ERA).

Friedan continued to maintain a position of national prominence. In August 1970, she helped to organize the Women's Strike for Equality, which commemorated the 50th anniversary of the Nineteenth Amendment, granting women the right to vote. An extremely successful national protest, the march served to broaden the visibility of the feminist movement. She also played a key role in the development of the National Women's Political Caucus in 1971,

Betty Friedan, 1960 *(Library of Congress)*

an organization that was dedicated to increasing the number of women in politics.

In contrast to radical feminists such as Gloria Steinem, Friedan represented a more moderate alternative. Friedan appealed primarily to white, middle-class women, while Steinem and various others wanted to broaden the movement to include working-class, minority, and lesbian women. In several articles in the 1970s that *McCall's* magazine published, Friedan criticized Steinem and feminist politician Bella Abzug for taking the movement too far to the left. She claimed that they promoted an environment that encouraged women to blame men for everything, instead of working together to change America for the better. She argued that these radical feminists would ultimately undermine the quest for WOMEN'S RIGHTS AND STATUS. Friedan expanded on these ideas in *The Second Stage* (1981). She advocated a moderate stance and criticized both liberals and conservatives for contributing to the backlash against the movement. She argued that it was imperative for the movement to recognize that heterosexual relationships and families played important parts in women's lives.

Friedan continued to write and lecture throughout the 1980s and 1990s. *The Fountain of Age* (1993) focused on the process of aging. The book appealed to the white, middle-class elderly of America, and presented aging as a positive aspect of life, with numerous opportunities for the elderly. In 1996, at a labor conference, she affirmed her support for strong unions.

Further reading: Daniel Horowitz, *Betty Friedan and the Making of* The Feminine Mystique (Amherst: University of Massachusetts Press, 1998).

— Lori Nates

G

Galbraith, John Kenneth (1908–)

John Kenneth Galbraith was one of the leading economists of the 20th century.

Galbraith was born on October 15, 1908, in Ontario, Canada, and educated at the University of Toronto, the University of California at Berkeley, and Cambridge University in Great Britain. He began his career teaching economics in 1934 at Harvard University and later taught at Princeton University. During World War II, he served in several U.S. government agencies, including the National Defense Advisory Committee and the Office of Price Administration. From 1943 to 1948 he served on the editorial board of *Fortune* magazine, and in 1949, he returned to Harvard as the Warburg Professor of Economics. From 1961 to 1963, on leave from Harvard, he served as U.S. ambassador to India. He acted as an adviser for presidents JOHN F. KENNEDY and LYNDON B. JOHNSON, as well as for presidential candidates EUGENE MCCARTHY and George McGovern.

Galbraith is considered by many to be the "Last American Institutionalist," a reference to the American Institutionalist School of economic thought commonly associated with economists Thorstein Veblen, John Commons, and Wesley Mitchell. The Institutionalists stressed the importance of historical, social, and institutional factors in shaping economic laws, and they dominated American economics from the early 1900s until the 1930s, when the Keynesian Revolution transformed economics. Galbraith, a student of Veblen, revived Institutionalist ideas after World War II with works that brought increased attention to an economic structure that focused on the great corporation as the characteristic organization in American business.

Galbraith's first major work was *American Capitalism* (1952) in which he contended that American society suffered from a sickness that had its roots in the competitive ideal in industrial organization. Galbraith introduced the concept of countervailing power as an antidote to that sickness. He argued that the existence of concentrations of power, such as in unions, was not detrimental if they formed a counterbalance to another concentration of power.

Galbraith achieved widespread recognition and success with his book *The Affluent Society* (1958). In this work, aimed at the general public, he attacked the myth of "consumer sovereignty" and argued that America had reached a stage in its economic development that should enable it to direct its resources toward the provision of better public services rather than the production of consumer goods. Galbraith criticized America's "economics of abundance" and called for less emphasis on production and more attention to public services. This widely discussed and debated book helped to shape the WAR ON POVERTY initiated by the Kennedy and Johnson administrations.

Galbraith's *The New Industrial State* (1967) focused on intellectual and political innovations. He asserted that large, capital-intensive firms tried to create environments that minimized the risks to capital. Such ideal conditions included high degrees of certainty in terms of product demand, labor supply, market competition, and regulatory and tax policies. To achieve this, large corporations attempted to enhance the demand for their products by advertising heavily and lobbying government to maintain a stable public policy. In labor matters, large corporations found it convenient to deal with large, predictable labor unions. The result was a symbiotic relationship between big business, big government, and big labor, which Galbraith called the New Industrial State.

One of Galbraith's salient characteristics remained his critical attitude toward conventional economics. He challenged the assumptions that firms were profit maximizing and that demand and supply determined the allocation of resources. Galbraith believed that free enterprise tended toward monopoly, that economic growth did not imply growth in the quality of life, and that resource allocation decisions lay primarily in the hands of the managers and professionals in big corporations and government departments.

Galbraith's theories also exerted a profound influence on public policy. In particular, his efforts to show that structural reasons, as opposed to unfair practices, underlay the growth of giant corporations contributed to the Justice Department's backing away from antitrust prosecutions in the 1960s. Although Galbraith's ideas and theories fell outside mainstream economics and often attracted criticism from academics, he remained one of the best-known economists in postwar America.

Further reading: Charles H. Hession, *John Kenneth Galbraith and His Critics* (New York: New American Library, 1972); J. Ron Stanfield, *John Kenneth Galbraith* (New York: St. Martin's Press, 1996).

— Dave Mason

Gallup Poll

The Gallup Poll, founded in 1935, has served as a resource for the American people to gain a better understanding of public opinion through random sampling.

George Horace Gallup, a public opinion statistician from Jefferson, Iowa, established a method of public opinion sample surveys, later named Gallup Polls. After teaching journalism at Drake University from 1929 to 1931, and then at Northwestern University from 1931 to 1932, Gallup founded the American Institution of Public Opinion in 1935. The organization conducted nationwide surveys of opinion on political, economic, and social issues in the United States. Combined with a more scientific method of polling called probability sampling, the Gallup Poll randomly selected a small sample of people who, if selected correctly, represented the opinions of a larger group of people. National Gallup Polls aimed to "present the opinions of a sample of people which are exactly the same opinions that would have been obtained had it been possible to interview all adult Americans in the country." To reach this goal, Gallup developed the principle of the equal probability of selection. This assumed that if each member of a population had an equal likelihood of being selected, the resulting sample would represent the whole population.

The Gallup Poll, while performing a variety of surveys, was most famous for pre-election surveys. The 1936 presidential election brought public attention to Gallup's organization when Gallup accurately predicted the victory of Franklin D. Roosevelt over Alfred M. Landon for U.S. president. Despite wrongly predicting the victory of THOMAS E. DEWEY over HARRY S. TRUMAN in the 1948 presidential election, the Gallup Polls continued to survey voters in subsequent presidential elections and developed a reputation for accuracy.

Gallup employed a specific process to ensure every American equal opportunity of "falling into the sample."

Beginning in 1935, Gallup representatives conducted the earliest polls in person, scattering across the nation to interview people door-to-door. For nearly 50 years, this was the standard interviewing method until telephones became common in households and phone interviews replaced the in-person approach.

Generally, the target audience focused on those persons 18 years of age and older, labeled "national adults," who lived in noninstitutional environments. With the audience established, Gallup decided on the number of interviews to be conducted. Next, Gallup went to far-reaching lengths to make contact with the specific, randomly chosen adults living in American households. If the randomly selected adult was not at home, the interviewer returned at a later date to question that individual.

Wording questions utilized in polling proved the most difficult aspect of conducting the surveys. Compiling clear, unbiased questions required attention and sensitivity, as well as a thorough understanding of current issues and public opinion. Specific wording of a question could very easily affect the manner in which an individual answered a question. To Gallup's credit, however, he consistently posed a question exactly as it was written. He contended that, "if the exact wording of a question is held constant from year to year, then substantial changes in how the American public responds to that question usually represent an underlying change in attitude." Gallup intended always to present the polls objectively and accurately.

Gallup conducted public opinion polls on presidential approval, public policy, and various key issues. He asked the public for opinions on many issues, including presidential proposals such as social security, questions on family life, civil defense, foreign aid, the federal budget, American prestige, armed forces, and the role religion and church played in the household. On January 17, 1949, for example, Gallup asked the public, "Have you heard about the civil rights program suggested by Truman?" Of those queried, 64 percent had heard about the program while 36 percent had not. Of those who had heard of the program, Gallup followed up with, "Do you think Congress should or should not pass the program as a whole?" To this question 27 percent responded positively, while 22 percent said no, and 15 percent had no opinion. Gallup asked other questions concerning public opinion on the TAFT-HARTLEY ACT, noncommunist oaths, whether or not all members of the Communist Party should be removed from jobs in the United States, and whether or not people felt Senator JOSEPH R. MCCARTHY should be censured for his anticommunist actions and accusations.

The Gallup Poll intended to "amplify the voice of the public," not distort it. People throughout the United States still rely on the polls to gain an understanding of public opinion and to forecast patterns of voting.

Further reading: George Horace Gallup, *The Pulse of American Democracy: The Public Opinion Poll and How It Works* (New York: Simon & Schuster, 1940).

— Susan F. Yates

gays and lesbians

Faced with intense scrutiny by law enforcement during the 1950s, gays and lesbians nonetheless began an unprecedented level of political and social organization, laying the groundwork for important gains in the future.

Prior to World War II, religious, medical, and legal condemnations of homosexuality permeated society so fully that they prevented any tangible social or political interaction. By 1940, however, the massive mobilization for the war—especially the sex segregation of millions of young, single women and men both at home and abroad—profoundly affected how homosexuals viewed themselves and their sense of community. The military's psychiatric screenings for homosexuality were so perfunctory, and the need for personnel so great, that careful relations among homosexual servicemen and women often went unchecked. Gay women working industrial jobs on the home front also experienced new opportunities to interact. By the end of the war, a solid, though still small, gay subculture began to emerge in America's larger cities, centered especially in gay bars.

Homosexual acts, however, were still against the law in every state, and the vast majority of gay men and women were frightened of public exposure. The increasing paranoia over domestic COMMUNISM, fueled in large part by Senator JOSEPH R. MCCARTHY's anticommunist crusade, did not help matters either. Reports of several gay State Department employees receiving discharges on the grounds of "moral turpitude" led the U.S. Senate to launch a full inquiry into government employment of homosexuals in June 1950. Testimony by psychiatric experts presented homosexuality as a sign of pathology and mental disease. In 1953, ALFRED C. KINSEY's groundbreaking reports on America's sexuality—which indicated surprisingly high incidences of homosexual experiences "in every age group, in every social level [and] in every conceivable occupation"—helped to fuel anti-gay paranoia as much as it helped to shatter long-held attitudes about homosexual tendencies. Discharges for homosexuality in both government agencies and the military increased substantially. Law enforcement, bolstered by the support of J. EDGAR HOOVER's Federal Bureau of Investigation, began a broad campaign of increased surveillance and harassment of homosexuals and gay establishments.

With the unparalleled increase in homosexual oppression came an equally unparalleled increase in homosexual, or "homophile," organizations. In November 1950, Harry Hay and four gay male colleagues started the most prominent of these groups, formally naming it the Mattachine Society in April 1951. Their founding principle was the recognition of homosexuals as an oppressed minority group distinctive from the heterosexual majority, a concept unfathomable before World War II. After the group successfully defeated the arrest of one of its founders for allegedly propositioning a plainclothes police officer in June 1952, membership rolls swelled in various "guilds" along the California coast, though at its peak the society was never much larger than 2,000 people.

By 1953, the group's biggest strength—the founders' past involvement in the Communist Party imbued them with a strong sense of group organization and a knack for political activism—also proved to be its greatest liability. With anticommunist pressures mounting, more conservative members of the group staged a successful takeover at Mattachine conventions in April and May 1953. They shifted the group's focus away from establishing a homosexual minority through public activism, instead adopting an accommodating view directed at presenting homosexuals as virtually no different from members of middle-class heterosexual society. Almost immediately, membership plunged, and by the early 1960s, the national organization splintered off into more activist-minded East-Coast groups and the more conservative San Francisco contingent.

Though it did include lesbian members, the Mattachine Society dealt almost exclusively with the concerns of gay men, so, in 1955, a San Francisco–based lesbian couple, Del Martin and Phyllis Lyon, formed the Daughters of Bilitis (DOB) with six other women. Many lesbians had children from heterosexual marriages in the past, and the prospects for now-single women earning an adequate wage were slim in the 1950s. The DOB viewed its role as offering lesbians "help, friendship, acceptance and support."

With all homophile organizations suffering from chronically low membership, their journals, including the *Mattachine Review,* the DOB's *Ladder,* and the independent *ONE,* served as vital instruments for reaching out to lesbians and gay men who did not reside in major cities. They also helped give the homophile movement its biggest victory. In January 1958, the U.S. Supreme Court, headed by Chief Justice EARL WARREN, unanimously overturned lower court decisions permitting the Los Angeles postmaster's seizure of *ONE* on the grounds that it was "obscene." Indeed, court decisions allowing the dissemination of literature previously deemed indecent—particularly the work of the BEAT GENERATION, led by openly gay poet ALLEN GINSBERG—became a turning point for the homophile movement, as more and more material about lesbians and gay men made its way into mainstream American society.

By the late 1960s, the homophile movement, greatly overshadowed by the Civil Rights movement and the movement for WOMEN'S STATUS AND RIGHTS, had made some gains, but still had only limited accomplishments to show for its efforts. It was not until June 27, 1969, that the full-fledged national gay rights movement began, when a routine police raid of Stonewall, a gay bar in New York City's Greenwich Village, erupted into several days of rioting by gay men and lesbians and created a greater sense of public consciousness than ever before.

Further reading: John D'Emilio, *Sexual Politics, Sexual Communities: The Making of a Homosexual Minority in the United States 1940–1970* (Chicago: University of Chicago Press, 1983); John Loughery, *The Other Side of Silence: Men's Lives and Gay Identities: A Twentieth-Century History* (New York: Henry Hold and Company, 1998).

— Adam B. Vary

General Electric

The General Electric Company, established in 1892 by Thomas Edison, changed the way people lived in the United States with its many different inventions.

Thomas Edison invented the electric light bulb in 1879. The stock of his company, Edison Electric Light Company, skyrocketed, and, in 1892, the company merged with Thomson-Houston to form the General Electric Company (GE). The invention of the light bulb popularized the use of electricity, and by the turn of the 20th century, the industry was growing at an extremely rapid rate. GE immediately capitalized on this growing market by inventing household appliances, including the first portable fans, electric washing machines, and radios. Through the first part of the 20th century, GE moved into plastics and locomotives, and began the first TELEVISION network, which later became NBC. GE quickly became one of the largest companies in the United States.

By the 1940s, GE's importance was evident. The company developed the first jet engines for the U.S. military. Radar, first developed in 1935, was now used effectively in World War II, providing assistance in both bombing and antiaircraft efforts. Radar also detected the enemy from long distances away. These advancements put the United States far ahead of any other country in military and conventional TECHNOLOGY.

GE's contributions continued through the 1950s. In 1951, the company developed the J79, its most famous jet engine. This model became the first commercial jet engine, which powered the world's fastest jet transports. The J79 formed the basis for the J93 engine, released in 1959, which was capable of traveling at three times the speed of sound. GE won an Air Force contract to produce the J93. It also continued work on the electric light, introducing an all-weather headlight that was mass-produced, and sold to car and locomotive companies. This one invention aided travel for millions of Americans, and it improved automobile safety.

The 1960s brought more inventions and innovations from General Electric. On the home appliance front, the company produced refrigerators, blenders, and many other kitchen aids. It sold the first self-cleaning oven to the public in 1963. GE also helped the fast-food industry take off, by inventing an oven that could reheat frozen food to table temperature in under a minute. General Electric was a household name and it continued to remain in the spotlight. In 1962, Bob Hall, a GE engineer, invented the first solid-state laser, later used in compact disc players and laser printers. By the close of the 1960s, General Electric owned several companies in such fields as appliances, aircraft, railways, plastics, electricity, and medical equipment, and it constituted one of the major corporations in the United States.

Further reading: James Cox, *A Century of Light* (New York: A Benjamin Company/Rutledge Book, 1979).

— Matthew Escovar

General Motors

In 1955, automobile manufacturer General Motors (GM), capitalizing on post–World War II prosperity and consumer demand, became the first U.S. corporation to post a profit of $1 billion.

GM was founded in 1908 in Flint, Michigan, by William C. Durant, a keen businessman who had become a millionaire in the horse-drawn carriage business. In 1904, Durant bought the financially troubled Buick Motor Car Company. Seeking a strategic advantage to ensure longevity and success in the auto industry, Durant embarked on a massive campaign, acquiring within two years more than two dozen automobile companies, including the Olds Motor Vehicle Company and the Cadillac Automobile Company. Durant's aggressive and expansionistic attempts to outstrip the Ford Motor Company and control the auto industry overextended GM financially. Investors took control of GM from Durant, who then embarked on yet another auto industry venture, creating the Chevrolet Motor Company. Chevrolet adopted the Ford Motor Company's strategy of mass-producing cheap automobiles for the working class. Chevrolet was a success, putting Durant in a financial position to acquire enough GM stock to take control of the company again, and, in 1918, Durant merged Chevrolet with GM.

Upon the entry of the United States into World War II in 1941, GM switched from civilian automobile production to manufacturing tanks, airplanes, weapons, and other war supplies to support the Allied forces' war effort. Following the war, GM returned to producing cars and trucks, introducing new innovative features such as automatic gearboxes, power-assisted steering and brakes, air conditioning systems, and safety belts.

Alfred Sloan completely redesigned GM in the 1950s and made it into the world's biggest and most profitable company. The passage of the INTERSTATE HIGHWAY ACT OF 1956, aided by the general prosperity and economic growth of the postwar era, created a wave of auto consumerism that was responsible for the huge success of GM in the 1950s. Sloan's great skill in mass-production management made use of the American consumer's eye for style and fashion to keep engineering costs down. GM introduced car models that, year after year, exhibited little more than cosmetic changes.

GM also took advantage of the surge in mass media ADVERTISING and marketing. American TELEVISION viewers were aroused by shiny Chevrolet BelAirs and Pontiac Bonnevilles that sat on rotating stages as elegantly dressed commercial actresses pointed out their impressive features.

By the end of the 1950s, GM faced problems with expensive union contracts, antitrust pressures from the government, and finally, competition from the Volkswagen Beetle, introduced in 1958. A final blow came in 1965 when Ralph Nader published *Unsafe at Any Speed.* Nader attacked the American auto industry's safety standard in general, but specifically targeted Chevrolet's Corvair as a dangerous car.

Postwar consumerism had put no pressure on the auto industry for improvements in fuel efficiency, durability, serviceability, environmental protection, TECHNOLOGY, or safety. The lack of concern for these factors left the industry unprepared for the foreign competition and fuel crisis challenges of the 1970s.

Further reading: Timothy Jacobs, *A History of General Motors* (New York: Smithmark, 1992).

— Jason Reed

G.I. Bill   See Volume VIII

Gideon v. Wainwright (1963)

The case of *Gideon v. Wainwright* led to a decision by the U.S. Supreme Court that required states to provide legal counsel for indigent defendants regardless of the degree of crime they are accused of.

The Sixth Amendment to the U.S. Constitution provides individuals the right to legal counsel in the event that they are accused of a crime. Prior to 1963, however, this provision remained vague and did not provide for whom and to what extent this right was to be offered.

In June 1961, Clarence Gideon, an indigent electrician, was arrested and charged with breaking into a pool hall in Panama City, Florida. Although police accused Gideon of attempting to steal beer, Coke, and money from a cigarette machine, he declared his innocence. In August, as the case went to trial, Gideon informed the judge that he was not prepared for his trial because he had failed to obtain legal defense. Gideon then requested the court to provide him with counsel. The judge responded, "Mr. Gideon, I am sorry, but I cannot appoint counsel to represent you in this case. Under the laws of the State of Florida, the only time the Court can appoint Counsel to represent a defendant is when that person is charged with a capital offense. I am sorry, but I will have to deny your request to appoint Counsel to defend you in this case."

With the denial of counsel, the trial continued. Gideon, ill-prepared and unable to adequately represent himself in court, was convicted by the jury and sentenced to five years in prison. At the time of Gideon's trial, the Sixth Amendment right to counsel was applicable only at the federal level and states had the discretion to determine the use of this amendment. Many, including Florida, elected not to apply the privilege of counsel to the impoverished at the state level.

In an attempt to appeal his sentence, Gideon filed a petition to invalidate his conviction on the grounds that the state of Florida's refusal to provide him with counsel violated his constitutional rights. The Florida Supreme Court denied the petition. After this defeat, Gideon filed an appeal with the U.S. Supreme Court. In 1962, after his second appeal, the Supreme Court decided to hear Gideon's case. In January 1963, Abe Fortas, Gideon's court-appointed counsel, asserted that it was unconstitutional for states to create independent legislation determining the appointment of legal counsel to a defendant, and, by so doing, they violated Gideon's Sixth Amendment rights. The Gideon team further argued that by allowing states to implement only certain elements of the Bill of Rights, the Fourteenth Amendment was also being violated. This amendment states that "No state shall make or enforce any law which shall abridge the privileges or immunities of citizens of the United States." The court issued its decision in March 1963. The justices reversed Gideon's conviction on the grounds that he was denied due process provided by the Sixth Amendment when Florida courts denied him legal counsel. Justice Hugo Black, delivering the court's opinion stated, "The individual, and especially the indigent, is in greatest need of his constitutional rights when he finds himself in trouble with the law." The decision of the U.S. Supreme Court led to a new trial for Gideon.

Represented by competent legal counsel, Gideon was acquitted. The decision in *Gideon v. Wainwright* provided for the protection of those accused of crimes, however minor or serious. The Court concluded that states were constitutionally required to provide legal counsel for criminal defendants too needy to afford their own attorney. The case also served to illustrate the power of the federal government over state government. Previously, states had the choice of implementing certain parts of the U.S. Bill of Rights. The *Gideon* case illustrated that the ultimate power to determine acceptable boundaries of civil liberties rested with the federal government.

Further reading: Maureen Harrison and Steve Gilbert. *Landmark Decisions of the United States Supreme Court* (New York: Excellent Books, 1991); Philip B. Kurland *The Supreme Court and the Judicial Function* (Chicago: University of Chicago Press, 1975).

— Erin Craig

Ginsberg, Allen (1926–1997)

As one of the most influential voices of the BEAT GENERATION, Allen Ginsberg's poetry and writing questioned the very essence of American life.

Ginsberg grew up in Paterson, New Jersey, the son of Louis and Naomi Ginsberg. As a child, Allen was exposed to a variety of factors that had a profound effect upon his later life as well as his poetry. Louis, Allen's father, was himself a published poet. Naomi Ginsberg, however, may have left a more powerful impression upon her son. Haunted by episodes of schizophrenia, Naomi found it difficult to fulfill her role as mother to Allen. It was also during this time that Allen recognized his budding homosexuality, which played a pivotal role in both his professional and his private lives.

In 1943, Ginsberg headed off to Columbia University in New York. Originally, he studied to be a labor lawyer, though he soon changed his major to literature. During this period he met future authors William S. Burroughs and JACK KEROUAC, who became prominent members of the Beat Generation. This talented group all shared a common realization, namely, that although America experienced a new era of profound opportunity following World War II, there was a dark side to this success. Ginsberg and his compatriots focused upon the controversial elements in American life, such as racial issues and an emerging new drug scene. This world fascinated these men, and along their journey of exploration they developed what they termed a "New Vision" for looking at life. Ginsberg and his peers believed that life could be understood only by expanding one's own experiences, that truths could be found in different realities as well as in the lower levels of life. In addition to these thoughts, perhaps the most important aspect of this "New Vision" was the idea that all aspects of life should be explored as freely and openly as possible.

Poet Allen Ginsberg leads a group of demonstrators outside the Women's House of Detention on Greenwich Avenue in Greenwich Village, demanding the release of prisoners arrested for use or possession of marijuana, 1965 *(Library of Congress)*

In the early 1950s, Ginsberg headed to San Francisco to join the burgeoning poetry movement. In 1955, he changed the face of poetry with the publication of *Howl*, a poem that gave voice to the outcasts of American society. Ginsberg accomplished this in the poem's opening lines: "I saw the best minds of my generation destroyed by madness, starving hysterical naked dragging themselves through the Negro streets at dawn looking for an angry fix, angelheaded hipsters burning for the ancient heavenly connection to the starry dynamo in the machinery of night." The poem challenged the status quo of America by addressing such taboo topics as homosexuality and recreational drug use. *Howl,* however, was not a hit with everyone. In fact, the publisher of the first few editions of *Howl* faced charges for knowingly selling obscenity. Fortunately, the judge took a different view and recognized *Howl* as a poem of social importance.

Following the success of *Howl,* Ginsberg continued to develop as a poet and writer. In another controversial poem entitled *America* (1956), he yet again challenged American social and political views. Ginsberg then went on to write *Kaddish* (1959), a stirring tribute to his mother. Filled with compassion, the poem integrated all of the best memories as well as the worst concerning his mother's illness.

During the 1960s, Ginsberg remained active in the political and cultural movements of the time. He became involved with TIMOTHY LEARY, the leader of the psychedelic drug movement. Ginsberg believed that psychedelic drugs were a perfect way to empower individuals to search their own minds, especially the young. The friendship between Ginsberg and Leary lasted until Leary's death 35 years later. In addition to his friendship with Leary, Ginsberg befriended the BEATLES as well as BOB DYLAN. The work of Ginsberg and those within the Beat Generation had a profound effect upon these artists' works. Ginsberg was also present at the disastrous 1968 Democratic Convention in Chicago. Ginsberg, however, was outraged at the violent protests that erupted, and he instead supported nonviolent demonstrations.

Allen Ginsberg remained active in politics and culture for the rest of his life. On April 5, 1997, Allen Ginsberg succumbed to cancer of the liver at the age of 70.

Further reading: Graham Caveney, *Screaming with Joy: The Life of Allen Ginsberg* (New York: Broadway Books, 1999); Allen Ginsberg, *Selected Poems: 1947–1995* (New York: HarperCollins, 1996); Michael Schumacher, *Dharma Lion: A Critical Biography of Allen Ginsberg* (New York: St. Martin's Press, 1992).

— Clayton Douglas

Goldwater, Barry (1908–1998)

Barry Goldwater, an Arizona senator and the 1964 Republican presidential candidate against incumbent LYNDON B. JOHNSON, was one of the postwar architects of CONSERVATISM, a program stressing individual liberty and free enterprise rather than government welfare programs in the United States.

Goldwater was born on January 1, 1908, into a prominent Phoenix, Arizona, family that owned a chain of general stores throughout the state. A mediocre student at first, Goldwater enrolled at the Staunton Military Academy in Virginia, where he graduated first in his class. He spent only one year at college, however, returning home to work in the family business when his father died in 1929. Goldwater was a successful manager, desegregating all the stores and establishing a five-day workweek. During World War II, Goldwater, a passionate aviator, flew supply planes from the United States to ASIA. Upon returning home, he left the family business, choosing instead to run for the Phoenix

city council in 1949. In 1952, unhappy with his country's participation in the KOREAN WAR, he campaigned for the U.S. Senate as a Republican.

After narrowly defeating incumbent Ernest W. McFarland—a powerful Arizona politician and the Senate majority leader—Goldwater established himself as an influential spokesperson for the conservative wing of the REPUBLICAN PARTY. He criticized what he saw as an encroaching welfare state, opposed foreign arms sales, and attacked any rapprochement with COMMUNISM in EUROPE and ASIA. Goldwater believed that his party's positions embodied too soft a response to the policies of former presidents Franklin D. Roosevelt and HARRY S. TRUMAN, calling President DWIGHT D. EISENHOWER's general acceptance of their welfare programs "a dime store NEW DEAL." His comments earned the senator the respect of conservative Republicans in the West and the resentment of liberal Republicans in the East.

An increasingly prominent conservative leader with a reputation for always speaking his mind, Goldwater became a popular speaker at Republican fundraisers and was easily reelected to the Senate in 1958. In 1960, he published *The Conscience of a Conservative*, which outlined Goldwater's ideals: belief in the free enterprise system, a robust and well-maintained military, custom and tradition over what Goldwater called change for the sake of change, a limited government, the constitutional process, and the advancement of spirituality rather than material wealth. At the 1960 Republican convention, Goldwater received 10 votes on the first ballot for the presidential nomination, but withdrew himself from consideration in favor of Vice President Richard M. Nixon. In his speech at the convention, however, Goldwater urged his fellow conservatives to "take this party back."

In 1962, Goldwater began the groundwork for a 1964 presidential campaign, eager to run against President JOHN F. KENNEDY; the president's assassination in 1963, however, caused Goldwater to consider strongly dropping out of the race. His concern about continuing the eastern liberal wing's dominance over his party led Goldwater to run, nonetheless, what he knew would be a difficult campaign. Goldwater's casual statements about the use of nuclear weapons—he once joked about "lobbing one into the men's room of the Kremlin"—elicited strong criticism from his own party. Critics attacked the senator as an extremist who would pull the country into a third world war, and while he helped end SEGREGATION in his own state, the senator's vote against the CIVIL RIGHTS ACT OF 1964 (on the grounds that it was unconstitutional) lost him any substantial support from the African-American community. Goldwater lost the New Hampshire primary to write-in candidate Henry Cabot Lodge, but he upset his main competition, Governor Nelson Rockefeller of New York, in the California primary. Goldwater went to the Republican convention in San Francisco with enough delegates to win the nomination.

At the convention, Goldwater again courted controversy in his acceptance speech when he said "extremism in the defense of liberty is no vice and moderation in the pursuit of justice is no virtue." He had a strained relationship with the press; his aides frequently asked journalists to note what the senator meant and not what he said. Johnson's presidential campaign further attacked Goldwater as "a raving, ranting demagogue who wants to tear down society," running an infamous TELEVISION campaign advertisement showing a young girl picking petals off a flower while a man's voice counted down to a nuclear explosion. Goldwater countered that the Johnson administration was "corrupt [and] power-mad, fail[ing] to provide moral leadership or control crime and disorder." Regardless, Goldwater won only six states and received just 36 percent of the vote.

Goldwater remained out of politics for four years, running for Arizona senator again in 1968, and he was reelected to the position until his retirement in 1987. His efforts to promote conservatism led to the election of Richard Nixon and later Ronald Reagan and contributed to the rebirth of conservatism in the United States. He died on May 29, 1998, of complications from a stroke.

Further reading: Bart Barnes, "Barry Goldwater, GOP Hero, Dies." *Washington Post,* May 30, 1998; Barry Goldwater with Jack Casserly, *Goldwater* (New York: Doubleday, 1988); Rick Perlstein, *Before the Storm: Barry Goldwater and the Unmaking of the American Consensus* (New York: Hill & Wang, 2001).

—Adam B. Vary

Gonzáles, Rodolfo "Corky" (1929–   )

Rodolfo "Corky" Gonzáles was one of the most important Chicano civil rights advocates of the 1960s; in addition to his activities as a civic leader, political reformer, and Chicano nationalist, he became widely known for his 1967 epic poem *Yo Soy Joaquín* (I am Joaquin), which inspired thousands of youthful Chicanos to demand their full civil rights.

Gonzáles was born in the Mexican barrio of Denver, Colorado, to seasonal farm workers. He was forced to move many times during his childhood while his parents sought work. He attended four grade schools, three junior high schools, and two high schools. He later said that his many teachers tried to teach him "how to forget Spanish, to forget my heritage, to forget who I was." Despite these hardships he graduated from high school at the age of 16. By the age of 10, he was already working alongside his parents in the sugar beet fields. He became interested in boxing as a

way to escape poverty. At the age of 20 he entered competitive boxing. In his career he won 65 of his 75 fights. By the end of his ring experience, he was the third ranked contender for the World Featherweight title.

In 1953, Gonzáles left the ring to operate a neighborhood bar and to work as a bail bondsman. He was active in Democratic politics in his hometown of Denver, and he advanced to district captain in 1959. The following year he became coordinator of the Colorado Viva Kennedy campaign that supported JOHN F. KENNEDY for the presidency, and chairman of the local WAR ON POVERTY program. Soon after, he was appointed to the Steering Committee of the Anti-Poverty Program for the Southwest, the national board for Jobs For Progress, and the community board of the Job Opportunity Center, and he became president of the National Citizens Committee for Community Relations. Many Mexican Americans criticized him and called him a puppet in the political system. In early 1966, the *Rocky Mountain News,* a local newspaper, published reports charging that Gonzáles allegedly discriminated against whites and blacks in his antipoverty programs. The mayor of Denver asked Gonzáles to resign or told him he would be fired. Gonzáles resigned all of his political jobs and ended his Democratic affiliation. Because of this experience, Gonzáles lost faith in existing political institutions. The target of his anger and bitterness became the Anglo system.

Soon after his resignation, he developed the Crusade for Justice, a program promoting Chicano self-definition and self-determination. In 1968, he bought an old school and church buildings in a condemned section of the barrio in downtown Denver. He converted the buildings into a school, theater, gym, nursery, and cultural center. During that same year, he and REIES LÓPEZ TIJERINA led a Chicano contingent in the Poor People's March on Washington, D.C. There he issued his "Plan of the Barrio," calling for improved EDUCATION, with bilingual classes and teachers, and with provisions for teaching the history and culture of Mexican Americans. He also called for better housing, more barrio-owned businesses, and restitution of Spanish and Mexican pueblo land grants.

Throughout the 1960s and 1970s, Gonzáles was active in organizing and supporting school walkouts, demonstrations against police brutality, and legal cases on behalf of arrested Chicanos. He called for militant demonstrations among Mexican Americans all over the country to draw attention to their problems. He demanded that the federal government take immediate steps to provide Mexican Americans with equal education and employment opportunities. He also organized mass demonstrations against the increasingly unpopular VIETNAM WAR. He advised Chicano students to refuse to fight in Vietnam because Chicanos were used as "cannon fodder against a beautiful people with whom Chicanos have no quarrel. The fight for freedom, land, culture, and language isn't in Vietnam. It is here in the Southwest."

Gonzáles made one of the most important contributions to the Chicano Movement in instituting Chicano Youth Liberation conferences that focused and defined goals of Chicano youths. In further developing his ideas of Chicano self-determination and nationalism, he launched the Colorado Raza Party.

In addition to his accomplishments as a civic leader, he achieved a unique position as the foremost poet of the CHICANO MOVEMENT through his poem *Yo Soy Joaquín* (1967). This epic poem played a central role in the development of Chicano self-identity, especially among youths. Its verses state in part:

> I am Joaquin,
> lost in a world of confusion,
> caught up in the whirl of a gringo society,
> confused by the rules,
> scorned by attitudes,
> suppressed by manipulation,
> and destroyed by modern society.

Although he suffered a debilitating automobile accident in October 1987, Gonzáles continued, in a more subdued manner, his activities in support of civil rights for Chicanos and Native Americans.

Further reading: Christine Marin, *A Spokesman of the Mexican American Movement: Rodolfo "Corky" Gonzáles and the Fight for Chicano Liberation, 1966–1972* (San Francisco: R & E Research Associates, 1977).

— Elizabeth A. Henke

government (state and local)

In the post–World War II years, state and local governments took on new roles as responsibilities changed in response to the growing role of the federal government.

The growth of the federal government provided the framework for changes at other levels. The NEW DEAL of President Franklin D. Roosevelt established the principle that the federal government would help those who could not help themselves. HARRY S. TRUMAN's program, the FAIR DEAL, followed the same patterns that the New Deal had defined. When Republican DWIGHT D. EISENHOWER won the presidency in 1952, he wanted to scale back the role of the federal government, but refused to eliminate reforms, such as Social Security, that were now part of American life, and his acceptance of the broad outlines of the New Deal underscored its role in the country once and for all. In the 1960s, JOHN F. KENNEDY's NEW FRONTIER and LYNDON B. JOHNSON's GREAT SOCIETY further extended the reach of federal power. More and more,

national government took responsibility for functions it had not handled before.

Meanwhile, local and state governments were necessarily defining a new role for themselves. With the huge SUBURBANIZATION movement, school districts proliferated. State governments began to realize that some small school districts simply were not viable, and mandated that they be consolidated. The growth of the national highway program, mandated by the INTERSTATE HIGHWAY ACT OF 1956, made transportation easier, and the act encouraged the consolidation process. Districts understood that if minimum standards were not met, consolidation had to occur.

At the same time, many urban regions began to establish special sewer and water districts, with fee authority to charge customers for services. Prior to the huge expansion of public works in the New Deal era, consumers paid for services, such as water, on the basis of a property tax. Now they began to pay fees based on their actual consumption. These new districts were autonomous. They had their own governing boards. They could issue bonds for construction. They set the clean water standards they intended to follow. The states maintained audit responsibility and engaged in some oversight, but most decisions were still taken at the district level.

Still another development involved the creation of gated communities. These residential areas were governed on the basis of covenants within a larger community. They were like community associations, which provided services and which had the power of coercion even though they were not, strictly speaking, real governments. The creation of these gated communities began in the 1920s, but they accelerated in the 1950s.

Municipal governments became increasingly professionalized in the postwar years. Federal expansion encouraged the trend toward professionalism in the delivery of services to constituents.

Further reading: Nancy Burns, *The Formation of American Local Governments: Private Values in Public Institutions* (New York: Oxford University Press, 1994); Evan McKenzie, *Privatopia: Homeowner Associations and the Rise of Residential Private Government* (New Haven, Conn.: Yale University Press, 1994).

— Clayton Douglas

Graham, Billy (1918–)

William Franklin Graham, Jr., better known simply as Billy Graham, was a Presbyterian clergyman who became a world-renowned Christian evangelist in the 1950s and the decades that followed.

Born on November 7, 1918, in Charlotte, North Carolina, and raised in the reformed Presbyterian Church, Graham became a "born again" Christian (repenting of sins and receiving Christ as his savior) at a revival meeting in North Carolina when he was a teenager. Instilled with a passion for ministry, he began his career in 1943 as pastor of a Baptist church and shortly thereafter became involved with Youth for Christ (YFC), a religious organization, whose mission was to bring the gospel of Jesus Christ to young people everywhere. Eventually, Graham developed his own dreams of a nationwide religious revival. In September 1949, Graham saw his dream become a reality as he and a team of fellow visionaries led a three-week tent revival in Los Angeles.

The mid-1940s and the early 1950s were receptive years for a new voice in evangelical Protestantism. Two major world wars surrounding a period of severe economic depression left the American people with little sense of material or national security. In this time of transition, people searched for something stable. Graham offered a sense of meaning and purpose obtained through a life rooted in RELIGION. Across the nation, people flocked to churches searching for the spiritual fulfillment that Graham's teachings offered.

By the 1950s, it was apparent that the United States was in a state of religious revival. Across the country, Graham led three-day to eight-week-long revivals. Often taking place in concert halls, amphitheaters, and football stadiums, these revival meetings opened with testimony from widely known "born again" Christians, followed by MUSIC, and concluded with Graham's powerful message calling people to come into a new relationship with Jesus Christ. He represented the fundamental Protestant beliefs that Jesus was Lord, God was the sovereign power, and people's lives could be changed through religious conversion.

Those previously uninvolved in church activities sought a stable set of beliefs during times of difficulty. Confusion caused by dislocation induced by war and unemployment, together with the longing for a consistency in life that resisted the continual changes of society, brought the nation to church. Critical voices became muted and religion gained both popularity and respectability.

Graham felt it important to present his message in the context of modern-day political and social circumstances. "Geared to the times, anchored to the Rock," became the motto of Graham's movement as he saw the importance of being knowledgeable in current events. At the same time, he was a meticulous strategic planner. With each crusade, Graham and his team, the Billy Graham Evangelical Association (BGEA), exerted an enormous amount of effort to prepare a city for an upcoming event.

The period of the COLD WAR had a profound impact on people throughout the nation. Graham passionately despised this "Godless COMMUNISM," and he felt that it was not only a threat to America but also a battle between Christ and the anti-Christ. Graham spoke to this issue at revivals as well as on the radio and TELEVISION, calling the American people to "be born again by the Holy Spirit, by repenting of their sins, and receiving Christ as Savior. The greatest and most effective weapon against Communism today is to be born again Christian."

In the 1960s, Graham was an advocate for the Civil Rights movement. Speaking in favor of the CIVIL RIGHTS ACT OF 1964, he rejected claims that the Christian Bible supported SEGREGATION or barred intermarriage. In an article that appeared in *Life* magazine, Graham set forth his clear belief that racial prejudice was a sin, and he repeated this consistently in interviews and press conferences.

Graham was the only religious leader to maintain personal relationships with every U.S. president since DWIGHT D. EISENHOWER. With no political affiliations, Graham served as a type of spiritual adviser and political strategist for the president, and he established particularly close relations with presidents Eisenhower, JOHN F. KENNEDY, LYNDON B. JOHNSON, and Richard M. Nixon.

Further reading: Joe E. Barnhart *The Billy Graham Religion* (Philadelphia: United Church Press, 1972); Billy Graham, *Just As I Am: The Autobiography of Billy Graham* (London: HarperCollins Publishers, 1997); William Martin, *A Prophet with Honor: The Billy Graham Story* (New York: William Morrow, 1991).

— Susan F. Yates

Great Society

Following JOHN F. KENNEDY's death in Dallas on November 22, 1963, LYNDON B. JOHNSON launched an ambitious set of programs, known as the Great Society, whose main goals were racial equality and the eradication of poverty.

Presenting his ECONOMIC OPPORTUNITY ACT OF 1964 to Congress, Johnson articulated the goals of the WAR ON POVERTY he launched to achieve his dream of a Great Society. In a speech he gave at a 1964 Democratic fund-raising dinner, Johnson told the audience: "We have been called upon—are you listening?—to build a great society of the highest order, a society not just for today or tomorrow, but for three or four generations to come."

The Great Society programs were designed to improve American life for everyone. As most Americans experienced unprecedented prosperity, the persistence of pockets of poverty in the United States, revealed in MICHAEL HARRINGTON's *The Other America* (1962), became unacceptable. Liberals, inspired by economist John Maynard Keynes's *General Theory of Employment, Interest and Money* (1936), held that welfare spending would pay for itself through increased economic growth and government income. The tragic death of Kennedy created a popular desire to see the few timid social measures he had advocated expanded and adopted as a tribute to the deceased hero. Johnson's landslide victory over Republican presidential candidate BARRY GOLDWATER in November 1964 gave Johnson a popular mandate and vast majorities in both houses of Congress to carry out whatever reforms he presented. The dire poverty Johnson had experienced when he was young pushed antipoverty measures high on his personal agenda. Johnson's oversized ego, mixed with deep-seated insecurity, compelled him to outdo Franklin D. Roosevelt's NEW DEAL and prove that he was more than simply the executor of Kennedy's political estate. Johnson's experience in Congress gave him the political know-how to push controversial bills through Congress.

A 1964 tax cut was the first of several legislative initiatives. At the same time, Johnson turned his attention to civil rights. His good relations with Illinois Republican and Senate minority leader Everett McKinley Dirksen allowed him to defeat a southern Democratic filibuster and to sign the CIVIL RIGHTS ACT OF 1964, banning discrimination in public facilities, schools, unions, and the workplace. The VOTING RIGHTS ACT OF 1965 forbade state laws aimed at disenfranchising black voters.

Other measures dealt with the poor. The Economic Opportunity Act of 1964 created a wide variety of educational, training, loan, and assistance programs for the needy. Among these programs, the JOB CORPS provided 100,000 young, unemployed men and women with training and job experience; COMMUNITY ACTION PROGRAMS (CAP) aimed at solving urban poverty through grass-roots community efforts; HEAD START sought to foster the healthy development of low-income families. Johnson, who considered EDUCATION the key to his own upward social mobility, signed the ELEMENTARY AND SECONDARY EDUCATION ACT OF 1965, which gave better educational opportunities to the poor through federal subsidies. Created in 1965, MEDICAID and MEDICARE paid for part of the old and the poor's health care costs. Social security benefits were also increased. The 1968 Housing Act proposed to build 600,000 federally subsidized housing units over the following 10 years. Under the provisions of the act, the federal government gave poor people a lower mortgage rate when they bought a house and partially subsidized the operations of real estate developers willing to build or to renovate low-cost housing.

Other programs targeted immigration, the arts, and the environment. The IMMIGRATION ACT OF 1965 abolished the quota system established in 1924. With the 1965 measure, immigrants were accepted on a first-come, first-served basis, regardless of their racial or national origins. The National Foundation of the Arts and Humanities Act of 1965 created the NATIONAL ENDOWMENT FOR THE ARTS and the NATIONAL ENDOWMENT FOR THE HUMANITIES. The Federal Water Quality Administration was formed in 1965, while the National Air Pollution Control Administration, created in 1955, gained some regulatory powers under Johnson's program.

Great Society programs met with only partial success. The Community Action Programs ended in failure, as did other programs marred by incompetence, hasty planning, and corruption. Medicaid and Medicare endured, but they proved costly over the long run. Johnson's landmark civil rights legislation failed to improve race relations permanently as black militancy, increased by rising expectations, met white backlash. The WATTS RIOT (1965) and BLACK POWER marked the radicalization of the black Civil Rights movement. The November 1966 midterm election, in which Democrats lost 47 seats in the House of Representatives, and the popular 1968 third-party candidacy of Alabama governor GEORGE C. WALLACE showed that the white middle class questioned Johnson's objectives as they grew concerned about street violence, government expansion, and political divisions. As the Great Society moved from providing opportunities to giving away entitlements, traditional economic CONSERVATISM prevailed. The VIETNAM WAR, whose costs, combined with those of the Great Society, increased inflation and budget deficits, helped to destroy the Democratic coalition. Overall, the Great Society programs' goals—achieving racial harmony and eradicating poverty—were so ambitious that complete success was difficult at best.

Further reading: Gareth Davies, *From Opportunity to Entitlement: The Transformation and Decline of Great Society Liberalism* (Lawrence: University Press of Kansas, 1996); Allen J. Matusow, *The Unraveling of America: A History of Liberalism in the 1960s* (New York: Harper & Row, 1984).

— Philippe R. Girard

H

Hamer, Fannie Lou (1917–1977)

An energetic, dedicated, and spiritual civil rights leader, Fannie Lou Hamer led voter registration drives, marched for civil rights, and employed the United States judicial system to demand fair treatment for African Americans, especially those seeking equality in Mississippi.

One of 20 children born into a family of sharecroppers in the Mississippi Delta, on October 6, 1917, Fannie Lou Townsend spent much of her youth in the cotton fields. She was a solid student but her formal education ended after the sixth grade, when she started to work full time in the fields. In 1944, she married Perry Hamer, a sharecropper. After bearing two daughters, Fannie Lou Hamer was sterilized in 1961 without her permission or knowledge.

Hamer was 44 years old when the STUDENT NONVIOLENT COORDINATING COMMITTEE (SNCC) visited her hometown of Ruleville, Mississippi, in 1962 to register voters. Influenced by SNCC, Hamer attempted to register. She was denied her right to vote on the pretense that she could not explain the 16th section of the Mississippi constitution. That evening, she was evicted from the plantation where her family lived because of her refusal to abandon civil rights activities. By December of that year, she assumed the role of a fieldworker for SNCC, earning a reputation as a powerful singer who could inspire protesters, and she became a local leader for the Civil Rights movement in Sunflower County, Mississippi.

In June 1963, Hamer attended a Charleston voter registration training session. By then, Hamer had successfully registered to vote but she continued to work for justice for all African Americans. On her way home from the training session, she and her colleagues were harassed, arrested, and severely beaten by police in Winona, Mississippi. Hamer publicized this incident to direct public attention to the racism and violence prevalent in the South. Moreover, she incorporated this episode of violence into her personal narrative. In public speeches, she told people around the country the story of her life and the violence and cruelty she faced while engaging in civil rights work. She testified before a federal jury about the occurrence, but the Winona police were never convicted.

An active participant of the Mississippi Freedom Summer project in 1964, Hamer led volunteer orientation sessions and continued to testify about the role of racism in Mississippi and America. She was a core member of the MISSISSIPPI FREEDOM DEMOCRATIC PARTY (MFDP), a predominantly black political organization that challenged the power of the all-white DEMOCRATIC PARTY of Mississippi. Because of the widespread disenfranchisement of African Americans in Mississippi, the MFDP demanded that the Democratic Party recognize MFDP delegates at the national convention in Atlantic City. Protesters attracted media attention and the Democratic Party responded by establishing a credentials committee to listen to its complaints. Hamer testified before the committee and gained national recognition for her compelling narrative and personal conviction. Ultimately, the Democratic Party and the MFDP reached a compromise and MFDP delegates gained a few seats at the convention.

Hamer earned a reputation as a civil rights leader who encouraged others through her personal stories, dramatic voice, and powerful singing abilities. She also ran for several political positions, including both House and Senate seats. She continued to use the justice system to publicize civil rights abuses in America. In 1965, Hamer filed a lawsuit that challenged the legitimacy of elections in Sunflower County where African Americans were denied the right to register. One year later, new elections were ordered in several of the towns in the county.

Hamer led and participated in civil rights protests throughout the United States. She challenged distorted notions of equality and worked to end SEGREGATION, expand voting rights, relieve poverty, stop violence, and ensure better health care within the African-American community. By 1969, she participated in new initiatives, including a Pig Bank and Freedom Farm, to help alleviate hunger and poverty. In 1971, she helped found the National Women's Political Caucus. Although she suffered from health problems throughout much of the 1970s, she continued her pursuit of justice and equality until her death in 1977.

Further reading: Chana Kai Lee, *For Freedom's Sake: The Life of Fannie Lou Hamer* (Urbana: University of Illinois Press, 1999); Kay Mills, *This Little Light of Mine: The Life of Fannie Lou Hamer* (New York: Dutton, 1993).

— Kirstin Gardner

Harrington, Michael (1928–1989)

Michael Harrington, author and lecturer, devoted his career to raising awareness about the persistence of poverty in the United States.

His most famous work, *The Other America: Poverty in the United States* (1962), made the startling assertion that, despite the general prosperity of the 1950s, between one-fourth and one-fifth of Americans still lived in poverty. Harrington's revelations about the extent of poverty in the United States shocked many Americans and prompted President JOHN F. KENNEDY to call for federal action to reduce poverty in the United States. After Kennedy's assassination, President LYNDON B. JOHNSON launched a series of antipoverty initiatives known as the WAR ON POVERTY.

Edward Michael Harrington was born in St. Louis, Missouri, on February 24, 1928, and raised in an Irish Catholic family. He attended the College of the Holy Cross in Worcester, Massachusetts, studied law for one year at Yale University, and earned a master's degree in English literature from the University of Chicago. During the 1950s, Harrington worked as a social worker in St. Louis, as an associate editor of the *Catholic Worker,* and as a staff member of a settlement house in New York City. His experiences working with America's poor convinced him that social justice could be achieved only through a transformation of American capitalism into a system of democratic socialism. An outspoken social critic, he devoted the rest of his career to political activism and the study of poverty and other social problems in America.

Harrington first achieved national prominence with the publication of *The Other America.* In this book, he appealed to the conscience of the nation by pointing out the shameful fact that, in the most prosperous nation in the world, between 40 million and 50 million Americans lived in poverty. This "other America"—the America that had not benefited from the strong economic growth of the postwar decades—consisted largely of three groups: the rural poor of Appalachia, African Americans in the Deep South and urban ghettoes, and the aged. Much of this poverty remained invisible to most Americans. The rural poor had become invisible as more and more Americans concentrated in metropolitan areas. Harrington noted that travelers through the Appalachian region noticed the beautiful landscapes but failed to see the profound impoverishment that riddled the economically troubled region. The rise of suburbia similarly made the urban poor invisible by distancing white middle-class Americans from the depressing conditions of segregated inner-city slums. The growing population of Americans over the age of 65—at least half of whom could not afford decent housing, adequate nutrition, or medical care—remained close to home where they went unnoticed by society. Harrington's revelations in *The Other America* became widely influential in the antipoverty initiatives of the 1960s, for which Harrington became one of Johnson's consultants. Programs established under the ECONOMIC OPPORTUNITY ACT OF 1964, the APPALACHIAN REGIONAL DEVELOPMENT ACT OF 1965, and the MEDICARE Act of 1965 sought to attack some of the causes of poverty in the United States.

In later writings, Harrington returned to the issue of poverty and the need for greater government action to alleviate the inequities caused by the American capitalist system. In *Toward a Democratic Left: A Radical Program for a New Majority* (1968), he proposed a new leftist political alignment among the poor, minorities, and labor organizations along with the "new class" of public-sector workers, which included professionals and educators. This alliance, Harrington believed, would carry the potential to expand upon the groundwork of the War on Poverty and promote a program of greater government planning in the ECONOMY. In *The New American Poverty* (1984), Harrington presented an updated analysis of poverty in the United States (emphasizing the increasing influence of global economic factors) and outlined proposals for government remedies for the persistent social ills arising from economic inequalities. Harrington wrote numerous other books and articles on poverty and socialism, including *The Accidental Century* (1965), *Fragments of the Century* (1973), *The Twilight of Capitalism* (1976), *The Vast Majority: A Journey to the World's Poor* (1977), and *Socialism: Past and Future* (1989).

In addition to his scholarly writings, Harrington worked as a political activist for a variety of democratic socialist organizations. He was a spokesman for the Democratic Socialists of America; a member of the national executive board of the Socialist Party of America, 1960–68; chairman of the board of the League for Industrial Democracy, 1964–89; chairman of the Democratic Socialists Organizing Committee, 1973–82; and co-chair of the Democratic Socialists of America, 1982–89. From 1972 until his death in 1989, Harrington held the position of professor of political science at Queens College of the City University of New York.

Further reading: Michael Harrington, *The Long-Distance Runner: An Autobiography* (New York: Holt, 1988); Loren J. Okroi, *Galbraith, Harrington, Heilbroner: Economics as Dissent in an Age of Optimism* (Princeton, N.J.: Princeton University Press, 1988).

— Susan Allyn Johnson

Hayden, Tom (1939–)

Thomas Emmett Hayden was one of the central figures of the NEW LEFT and student movements of the 1960s.

Born in Royal Oak, Michigan, on December 11, 1939, Hayden attended the University of Michigan where he served as editor of the *Michigan Daily* student newspaper. On a trip in 1960 to Berkeley, California, Hayden was inspired by the political atmosphere there, and during his senior year he immersed himself in student activism.

After graduating in 1961, Hayden fully devoted himself to the burgeoning student movement. He moved to Atlanta, Georgia, where he worked as field secretary for the newly formed STUDENTS FOR A DEMOCRATIC SOCIETY (SDS), reporting on the southern Civil Rights movement. Not content merely to write about the movement, Hayden took part in activities organized by the STUDENT NONVIOLENT COORDINATING COMMITTEE (SNCC). Because of his participation, Hayden was beaten by whites in McComb, Mississippi.

In 1962 Hayden wrote *The Port Huron Statement*, intended as SDS's mission statement but adopted generally as the New Left's manifesto. Influenced by sociologist C. WRIGHT MILLS, Hayden, in *The Port Huron Statement* espoused participatory democracy, questioned the morality of the COLD WAR, and advocated activism among students. After its ratification, Hayden was elected president of SDS. SDS and *The Port Huron Statement* spread across college campuses, motivating a generation of students raised in the affluence of the 1950s to work for economic and racial equality and against apathy in America.

In 1963, Hayden helped form the Economic Research and Action Project (ERAP) as part of SDS, with the aim of improving the economic lives of urban, working-class Americans on a grass-roots level. Hayden moved to Newark, New Jersey, where he organized poor blacks against poverty, crime, and an unresponsive city government. Hayden left Newark after the city's riots in July 1967.

Hayden's next cause became the VIETNAM WAR. After its escalation in 1965, Hayden became increasingly devoted to ending the war. During December 1965, he visited North Vietnam, which increased government suspicion of him and the New Left in general as communist sympathizers. Indeed, Hayden openly admired the North Vietnamese and championed their cause. In 1967, Hayden returned from a second trip to North Vietnam having secured the release of three American prisoners of war.

By 1968, the seemingly endless war had frustrated the New Left. While pondering more confrontational tactics to end the war, Hayden participated in the Columbia University student strike of April 1968. Later that year, Hayden went to Chicago, Illinois, to organize the National Mobilization Committee's demonstrations at the Democratic National Convention (DNC). The demonstrations were intended to challenge the government's insistence on continuing the Vietnam War in the face of widespread public disapproval. Specific plans were vague, but the demonstrators intended to increase antagonism toward the government, reflecting the movement's growing disillusionment with nonviolent tactics.

Violence erupted outside the DNC as Chicago police and national guardsmen, under orders of Mayor Richard Daley, indiscriminately beat demonstrators, reporters, and bystanders. Antiwar activists were initially blamed for what was later acknowledged to be a police riot. As one of the main organizers, Hayden was charged with conspiracy to create a public disturbance and tried as one of the Chicago Seven in 1969. After a sensational trial, Hayden was found guilty of inciting violence and sentenced to jail for contempt of court. In 1972, these verdicts were overturned on appeal.

After the havoc of Chicago, the New Left disintegrated. Some activists became more extreme and violent while others, including Hayden, withdrew from the movement. Hayden relocated to Oakland, California, in 1969 where, after participating in the People's Park demonstrations in Berkeley, he joined a commune. Members later voted to expel Hayden because of his dominant personality and he moved to Venice, California.

By 1972, Hayden had returned to the cause of ending the Vietnam War. With Jane Fonda, an actress who opposed the war and had angered many with her own trip to North Vietnam, Hayden organized the Indochina Peace Campaign (IPC), which successfully lobbied Congress to cut funding for the war.

Inspired by the IPC's success, Hayden entered California politics in an attempt to move 1960s values into mainstream politics. After losing his bid for election to the Senate in 1976, Hayden formed the Campaign for an Economic Democracy, which mirrored his goals for the ERAP in Newark. In 1982, supported by the funding of Fonda, who was now his wife, and her Hollywood connections, Hayden won election to the California State Assembly from Santa Monica, and he served there until he won election to the State Senate in 1992. Hayden continues to confront attacks on his radical past while, in his political work, he focuses on ecological concerns and the threat of large corporations to the lower classes.

Further reading: Tom Hayden, *Reunion: A Memoir* (New York: Random House, 1988); James Miller, *Democracy Is in the Streets: From Port Huron to the Siege of Chicago* (New York: Simon & Schuster, 1987).
— Paul Rubinson

Head Start

Head Start began in 1965 as a part of President LYNDON B. JOHNSON's WAR ON POVERTY and represented a critical component of his GREAT SOCIETY legislation, which sought to equalize educational, economic, and political opportunities among Americans.

Sargent Shriver, director of the Office of Economic Opportunity, played a leading role in launching Head Start. Upon discovering that about half of America's 30 million poor in 1964 were children, he committed leftover funds from the failed COMMUNITY ACTION PROGRAM to a summer program that would offer economically disadvantaged preschoolers a "running head start" in school. Shriver's hope was that early intervention by federally funded local institutions might provide poor children with a solid educational and psychological foundation for academic and personal success. This goal enjoyed widespread appeal because it targeted children, who could not be faulted for their economic and social status.

Conservatives viewed Head Start as a means to rescue the "deserving poor" from "culturally deprived" surroundings, while liberals admired its community-based approach, which they expected would empower poor neighborhoods to organize politically. Head Start's instant popularity also signaled a broader shift in American culture away from viewing poverty as a moral problem to seeing it and other social problems as the product of a negative environment. In addition to educational instruction, Head Start provided its students with basic medical and dental care as well as two nutritious meals per day. By the fall of 1965, Congress approved plans to expand Head Start to a 10-month program.

Like many other Great Society projects, Head Start was hastily conceived and implemented. Johnson promised it would substantially raise the IQ levels of hundreds of thousands of America's children, despite the paucity of evidence to support this claim. Its administrators enacted Head Start only 12 weeks after its announcement and on a nationwide basis rather than as a pilot project. While promoters' appeal for immediate and massive action to end poverty struck a chord with the public, inspiring thousands to volunteer at Head Start centers, the program paid a high price in quality. Edward Zigler, one of Head Start's original planning committee members, remembered watching a grant review force rubber stamping piles of applications, with little regard for the merits of individual proposals. Even Head Start's strongest supporters admitted that many of its programs ran the gamut from mediocre to poor in quality. Moreover, Head Start suffered from a lack of trained teachers. Many of those initially hired had little to no previous teaching experience or training in early childhood education. Due to poor pay, turnover among teachers has hovered at around 60 percent.

Despite budget setbacks in the 1970s and 1980s, Head Start continued. Defenders, while acknowledging the program's rather fleeting effects on educational achievement, sought to reform and expand it rather than to dismantle it. They pointed out that its policy of "maximum feasible parental participation" attracted the firm support and active involvement of parents, a significant number of whom returned to school and entered the workforce as a result of their experiences with Head Start. Increases in funding in the 1990s ensured the program's survival, though critics continued to argue that Head Start had a negligible long-term effect on graduates. Some claimed that gains in grades and self-esteem disappeared by the time students entered high school. Others asserted that genetic factors were more important than early intervention in children's academic success.

Head Start continues as a federal program with over 2,000 local affiliates helping disadvantaged children gain an edge in school performance and achievement.

Further reading: Kay Mills, *Something Better for My Children: How Head Start Has Changed the Lives of Millions of Children* (New York: Plume, 1999); Edward Zigler and Sally J. Styfco, eds. *Head Start and Beyond: A National Plan for Extended Childhood Intervention* (New Haven, Conn.: Yale University Press, 1993).
— Theresa Ann Case

Heart of Atlanta Motel, Inc. v. United States (1964)

In *Heart of Atlanta v. United States,* the Supreme Court ruled unconstitutional discrimination in services to anyone based on race.

In its ruling on December 14, 1964, the U.S. Supreme Court decided that the CIVIL RIGHTS ACT OF 1964 had been violated in Georgia because the Heart of Atlanta Motel had denied lodging to an African-American couple. The Court upheld a federal district court decision that prohibited the Heart of Atlanta Motel from discriminating against African Americans. It also reversed another federal district court decision that held the public accommodations section unconstitutional in a case involving a Birmingham, Alabama, restaurant.

The *Heart of Atlanta* case stemmed directly from the recent Civil Rights Act of 1964. The law contained numerous titles and sections. Title II and its seven sections dealt exclusively with goods, services, facilities, and places of accommodation. Each of these declared that it was illegal to discriminate on the basis of race, creed, religion, or national origin. In dealing with businesses, the act specified different places of public accommodation affected by the commerce of temporary visitors seeking lodging. These establishments included inns, motels, hotels, restaurants, and motion picture houses. The Heart of Atlanta Motel in Atlanta, Georgia, came under the jurisdiction of this section of Title II.

The Heart of Atlanta Motel argued that Congress, by passing the Civil Rights Act of 1964, had not only exceeded its power under the Commerce Clause, giving it the ability to regulate, prohibit, and protect trade among states, but also had violated Fifth Amendment rights by not allowing the motel to pick its own customers. Attorneys for the motel claimed that according to the Fifth Amendment, their client lost potential property, taken away without just compensation. The final argument declared that this also violated the Thirteenth Amendment, because Congress required the motel to rent motel rooms to African Americans, which, they affirmed according to the language of the Thirteenth Amendment, was "involuntary servitude."

The government, on the other hand, countered by stating that African Americans were unable to acquire suitable accommodations because the motel was interfering with interstate commerce in such a way that only Congress could rectify the situation by using its commerce clause power as specified by the U.S. Constitution. The government also argued that the Fifth Amendment did not forbid the type of regulation found within the Civil Rights Act, nor did the damage involve taking away private property. Finally, the government argued that the assertion of a Thirteenth Amendment violation lay outside the scope of its initial purpose, because in this case there existed nothing pertaining to genuine slavery or disabilities associated with human bondage.

The main question before the WARREN COURT in *Heart of Atlanta* was whether Congress, by passing the Civil Rights Act of 1964, had exceeded its Commerce Clause powers by depriving motels, like the Heart of Atlanta, the right to choose their own customers. Justice Thomas Clark, a member of the Warren Court from 1949 to 1967, delivered the majority opinion for a unanimous court without dissent. This majority opinion declared that the Commerce Clause, found within the first article of the U.S. Constitution, allowed Congress to regulate forms of commerce. The Civil Rights Act of 1964 was not illegal in this case because the applicability of Title II was "carefully limited to enterprises having a direct relation to the interstate flow of goods and people." The Court continued by saying that obstructions in commerce might be removed according to the discretion of Congress, not the courts. The Heart of Atlanta, however, because it practiced racial discrimination, something not permitted by the U.S. Constitution, could not have legally obstructed the commerce power.

The Court concluded, in a unanimous decision, that places of public accommodation had no right to discriminate against certain guests without governmental regulation. Indeed, at this time, 32 states had already passed legislation banning such discrimination, and the decision underscored the acceptability of the measures passed.

At the same time, on December 14, 1964, the U.S. Supreme Court also barred a state from prosecuting demonstrators who had used peaceful means to bring about desegregation in places of public accommodation. Almost 3,000 SIT-IN demonstration prosecutions were brought before the Court, some dating back to 1960. Justice Hugo Black, in a dissenting opinion, expressed opposition to the concept that the law could aid those who took it into their own hands.

Further reading: Mary L. Dudziak, *Cold War Civil Rights: Race and the Image of American Democracy* (Princeton, N.J.: Princeton University Press, 2000); *Heart of Atlanta Motel, Inc. v. United States*, 379 U.S. 241 (1964).
— John E. Bibish IV

Hispanic-American movement See Latino movement

Hiss, Alger (1904–1996)

In 1948, Alger Hiss, a former State Department employee, became a target of the HOUSE UN-AMERICAN ACTIVITIES COMMITTEE (HUAC), a congressional committee that sought to ferret out communist subversion in the United States.

The accusation that he was a communist agent, and his subsequent conviction for perjury, made him a salient figure in an America that, at the end of the 1940s, already was deeply involved in the COLD WAR.

Born on November 11, 1904, in Baltimore, Maryland, Hiss had a distinguished educational background, graduating from Johns Hopkins University and Harvard Law School, and then embarking upon a career of public service. He first served as a clerk for Supreme Court justice Oliver Wendell Holmes. After the election of Franklin D. Roosevelt to the presidency in 1933, Hiss joined the Department of Agriculture. Later, during World War II, he worked for the State Department as an aide to the assistant secretary of state for the Far East. Near war's end, he appeared at Yalta as a presidential adviser.

Following a brilliant career with the State Department, Hiss served as president of the Carnegie Endowment for International Peace, a private foundation dedicated to averting future wars. During this period, Hiss faced perjury charges for allegedly lying about his past connections with the Communist Party and passing classified documents to a communist spy located in the United States. WHITTAKER CHAMBERS was Hiss's primary accuser. Chambers, a confessed communist agent in the 1930s, later an editor at *Time* magazine in the 1940s, testified before HUAC that Hiss had been a member of the Communist Party. Chambers asserted that he had collected party dues from both Hiss and his wife. Hiss denied that he knew Chambers and likewise denied that he had any past affiliation with the party. Under relentless questioning from HUAC member Richard M. Nixon, however, Hiss was forced to admit that he had known Chambers, even acknowledging that he had let him use his car and live in his apartment, although Hiss maintained that Chambers had used the name of George Crosley at that time. Still, Hiss denied ever being a communist and challenged Chambers to repeat his accusations outside of Congress where congressional immunity would not apply and Hiss could sue Chambers for libel.

In response, Chambers went on the radio program *Meet the Press* and labeled Hiss a communist. Hiss sued. Chambers then revealed that Hiss had passed him secret State Department documents to be turned over to the SOVIET UNION. Chambers dramatically produced microfilms of the documents he claimed to have received from Hiss, documents that were typed copies of State Department records reproduced on a Woodstock model typewriter

Alger Hiss and wife leaving a New York Federal court, 1950 (*Library of Congress*)

once owned by Hiss. These were the famous "pumpkin papers," so-called by the press because Chambers had kept them hidden in a pumpkin in his vegetable garden.

Hiss denied the charges of espionage and received unequivocal backing from the administration of HARRY S. TRUMAN. Secretary of State DEAN ACHESON was quoted as saying, "I do not intend to turn my back on Alger Hiss." Such an endorsement carried with it much political weight, and Republican detractors of the administration soon labeled Acheson a communist sympathizer. Nonetheless, Acheson stuck by his statement, this despite being good friends with Hiss's brother Donald, and not Alger. Truman added that the charges against Hiss were a "red herring" designed to deflect criticism from Republican failures at the polls in 1948.

The first Hiss trial ended in a hung jury in July 1949. But on January 21, 1950, at the conclusion of a second trial, Hiss was convicted of two counts of perjury for having lied about his communist connections in the 1930s. He spent nearly four years in prison.

This confrontation between NEW DEAL LIBERALISM and resurgent CONSERVATISM carried with it far-ranging ramifications. Hiss's past service in the State Department cast further suspicion upon a body already suspected of harboring communists. His backing by Truman and Acheson further compromised an administration struggling against partisan opposition to defend its record regarding supposed communist infiltration of the federal government. The Hiss case allowed Nixon, a newcomer to the House, to gain exposure as a staunch anticommunist. And, the Hiss trial prepared the way for Senator JOSEPH R. MCCARTHY and his anticommunist crusade.

After serving his prison term, Hiss attempted to rehabilitate both his career and his reputation. He became a frequent lecturer on college campuses. Claims by his defenders that Nixon had framed him gained more credence after that president's Watergate debacle. Though evidence of his guilt seems inescapable today, the issue is still hotly debated among scholars, reflecting the continuing polarization between cold war conservatives and liberals.

Further reading: Allen Weinstein, *Perjury: The Hiss-Chambers Case* (New York: Knopf, 1978).

— Matthew Flynn

Hollywood Ten

The Hollywood Ten were members of the motion picture industry accused of association with communist organizations in 1947.

The Hollywood Ten consisted of screenwriters Alvah Bessie, Lester Cole, Ring Lardner, Jr., John Howard

Lawson, Albert Maltz, Samuel Ornitz, and Dalton Trumbo, directors Herbert Biberman and Edward Dmytryk, and producer Adrian Scott. The HOUSE UN-AMERICAN ACTIVITIES COMMITTEE (HUAC) cited these men for contempt of Congress for refusing to answer questions during investigations into communist activities in the motion picture industry.

Congressional conservatives used HUAC to accuse liberals and radicals in government, the diplomatic corps, academia, and Hollywood of harboring communist sympathizers. In particular, HUAC tried to prove that communists sought to infuse movie scripts with propaganda. Referring to the movie industry, conservative congressman John Rankin claimed, "Unless the people in control of the industry are willing to clean house of Communists, Congress will have to do it for them."

Many Hollywood studio executives, artists, and union representatives bristled at HUAC's proposed actions. They argued that very few "fellow travelers" worked in Hollywood, many having been disillusioned with Marxism-Leninism years earlier. Furthermore, they claimed that a motion picture was the product of collaboration, impenetrable to the political whims of writers and directors. Several actors, including Humphrey Bogart and Katharine Hepburn, organized the Committee for the First Amendment to protest the impending "witch hunt." Although they were not communists themselves, these artists wanted the witnesses to declare their political affiliations proudly and to denounce further government interference. The Hollywood community appeared united against HUAC with only a vocal minority of anticommunists encouraging the investigation.

Undeterred, in September 1947, HUAC issued subpoenas to 43 studio executives, labor leaders, and filmmakers, evenly divided between "friendly" and "unfriendly" witnesses. Together, the accused hired their own counsel and debated their legal strategy. Although a few wanted to proclaim their political beliefs, others believed this was foolhardy given the COLD WAR's charged atmosphere. Trumbo and Lardner argued that witnesses could challenge HUAC's inquiry into an individual's personal politics by asserting their Fifth Amendment right to prevent self-incrimination. They reasoned that the First Amendment prevented Congress from investigating or legislating political party affiliation. Eventually, 10 of the witnesses considered unfriendly to HUAC believed they could effectively resist the committee by answering questions in their own way.

On October 20, Representative J. Parnell Thomas, chairman of the committee, convened the hearings by calling "friendly" witnesses to testify. Among them, Louis B. Mayer, Walt Disney, and Gary Cooper asserted that although Hollywood's "red" minority existed and caused trouble, members of this group did not control film content. When asked, they offered up the names of suspected communists.

HUAC called the first 10 unfriendly witnesses and asked each in turn about past and current affiliations. After invoking their First Amendment right guaranteeing free speech, some responded to the interrogation with sarcasm, some lectured the committee, and all appeared antagonistic. In one dramatic instance, Thomas ordered police to restrain and remove Lawson as he charged HUAC with "Hitler tactics!" Members of the Committee for the First Amendment were especially upset with the Ten's daring refusal to answer questions. Rather than being martyrs, the Hollywood Ten appeared like rowdy radicals even to their defenders. "It was a sorry performance," director John Huston later wrote, "I disapproved of what was being done to [them], but I also disapproved of their response." Hollywood's united front dissolved.

Feeling emboldened, HUAC sought contempt citations against the Ten on November 24. The next day, 50 top Hollywood executives issued their own condemnation and foreshadowed the blacklisting to come. A communist would find no employment until he declared under oath that he was not a communist. The executives promised "to eliminate any subversives."

For the next six months, the Hollywood Ten embarked on a legal struggle to keep their jobs and stay out of prison. By May 1948, all 10 had been tried, convicted, fined, and sentenced to prison. In June, an appeals court ruled that because of the "chaotic times" and the fact that Hollywood "plays a critically important role in the molding of public opinion" as "a potent medium of propaganda dissemination," Congress had a right to investigate "whether or not they are or ever have been communists." Likewise, the Ten's breach of contract cases against the studios failed. In April 1950, the Supreme Court refused to hear their appeals. In June, the Hollywood Ten prepared for prison sentences ranging from six months to one year.

Prison life, the blacklist, and protracted lawsuits placed an overwhelming financial burden and social stigma on the Hollywood Ten. Only Dmytryk renounced his past activities. He published an open letter and appeared before Hollywood's Rehabilitation Committee, a group formed to show publicly Hollywood's commitment to ANTICOMMUNISM. Headed at one time by Ronald Reagan, this panel cleansed the repentant communists. After appearing once again before HUAC to "name names," Dmytryk won a studio contract. The others sporadically worked by employing pseudonyms and ghost writing. Trumbo, using the name Robert Rich, even won an Academy Award for the best screenplay of 1956. The blacklist effectively endured for the Hollywood Ten and hundreds of other victims until 1960, when a new generation of producers and directors insisted on changing the practice.

Further reading: Larry Ceplair and Steven Englund, *The Inquisition in Hollywood* (Berkeley: University of California Press, 1979).

— Andrew J. Falk

Hoover, J. Edgar (1895–1972)

A staunch anticommunist crusader, J. Edgar Hoover headed the Federal Bureau of Investigation (FBI), building it into a highly effective arm of federal law enforcement.

Hoover was born in Washington, D.C., on January 1, 1895. He studied law at George Washington University, where he earned his Masters of Law in 1917, the same year he joined the Department of Justice as a file reviewer. In 1919, he became special assistant to Attorney General A. Mitchell Palmer, overseeing the mass roundup and deportation of suspected communists following World War I. With the formation of the American Communist Party in 1919, Hoover found his lifelong calling: a self-styled crusade to destroy COMMUNISM in the United States. He began labeling anyone who disagreed with his rigid views—labor leaders, civil rights workers, and antiwar protesters—as communists. To root them out, he compiled files on radicals or anyone who dared to criticize him and developed a network of anonymous informants.

Hoover was named director of the FBI in 1924. Although the FBI was officially subordinate to the attorney general, Hoover successfully gained and ferociously maintained control of the operation. He built a reputation for efficiency by reorganizing the agency. He recruited agents and instituted rigorous methods of selecting and training personnel. He also established a fingerprint file, a

J. Edgar Hoover   *(Library of Congress)*

scientific crime lab, and the FBI National Academy, which provided special training for selected individuals.

He also organized well-publicized captures of famous bandits such as John Dillinger, "Pretty Boy" Floyd, and "Baby Face" Nelson to earn his reputation as the ultimate G-man, the nation's indefatigable crime fighter. Although Hoover was never actively involved in the arrests, he arrived just before the news photographers. Thus, he could argue that his successful pursuit of the "10 Most Dangerous Public Enemies" required ever-greater budgets. The arrest of Dillinger as well as the capture of Bruno Hauptmann, convicted kidnapper of aviator Charles Lindbergh's baby, brought much prestige to the organization, and enhanced Hoover's reputation, making the FBI virtually untouchable. Ironically, Hoover failed to seriously take on organized crime and went so far as to deny the existence of a Mafia. His hands-off policy allowed the Mafia to conduct illegal operations free of FBI surveillance.

Beginning in the 1940s, Hoover resurrected the specter of the early days as he pursued his life-long crusade against communists. The FBI brought JULIUS AND ETHEL ROSENBERG to trial for passing atomic secrets to the SOVIET UNION. Not only did he bask in the favorable publicity that accompanied the Rosenberg case but he also built alliances with red-baiters in Congress, such as Richard M. Nixon, who, with the FBI's assistance, pursued ALGER HISS, accusing him of being a communist. Hoover provided JOSEPH R. MCCARTHY with information and witnesses, helping McCarthy continue his witch hunt of suspected communists in government. FBI agents even wrote speeches for the Wisconsin senator. In return, McCarthy attacked Hoover's enemies.

Hoover's hatred toward radicals of every kind led him to openly attempt to discredit the Civil Rights movement. He portrayed movement leaders as communists, calling MARTIN LUTHER KING, JR., "the most dangerous and effective Negro leader in the country." Hoover collected and maintained a damaging file on King's private life, which he used to thwart the movement.

Hoover ruled the FBI through fear. He had files full of embarrassing if not incriminating evidence of all presidents other than HARRY S. TRUMAN, who admired Hoover. In 1971, Richard M. Nixon, a former collaborator with the director, asked Hoover to put the bureau at the president's disposal to investigate his own personal enemies and got a flat refusal. As a result, Nixon tried unsuccessfully to fire Hoover.

Hoover refused to be challenged; anyone who dared to do so was placed on the enemies list and hounded. While Hoover's ostensible intent was to build an efficient crime-fighting agency, 96 percent of the bureau's efforts were directed at investigating communists and left-wing radicals as defined by Hoover. He retained his post, however, until his death at age 77.

Further reading: Curt Gentry, *J. Edgar Hoover: The Man and the Secrets* (New York. W. W. Norton, 1990).

— Gisela Abels

House Un-American Activities Committee (HUAC)

Formed by Martin Dies in 1938, the House Un-American Activities Committee (HUAC) emerged as one of the main institutions of ANTICOMMUNISM during America's Red Scare of the late 1940s and early 1950s.

Inspired by memories of the 1920s when the Communist Party was a significant power in America, the committee spent much of its time hunting communists. Fundamentally conservative, the committee also tried to tie advocates of Franklin D. Roosevelt's NEW DEAL to COMMUNISM.

In 1945, Democratic representative John Rankin of Mississippi made HUAC a permanent committee by forcing an immediate vote during the first session of Congress. While not its chair, the racist and anti-Semitic Rankin became the committee's true leader. As COLD WAR tensions escalated, HUAC investigated leftist groups including labor unions, political organizations, and the media. In the tradition of the Dies committee, Rankin also attempted to defame the New Deal as a communist conspiracy.

In 1947, suspecting that communists had infiltrated the film industry, Republican representative J. Parnell Thomas of New Jersey (later convicted of fraud) led an investigation that brought HUAC into the public spotlight. During the Hollywood hearings, the committee heard from "friendly witnesses," conservative Hollywood figures who confirmed rumors of rampant communism. HUAC questioned 10 "unfriendly witnesses," asking "Are you or have you ever been a member of the Communist Party?" The witnesses, labeled the HOLLYWOOD TEN, refused to answer by invoking the First Amendment. The witnesses instead challenged the constitutionality of inquiring about a citizen's political beliefs.

As the committee had no power to prosecute, HUAC cited the Ten for contempt of Congress, sentencing them to jail for six to 12 months plus a $1,000 fine. Hollywood executives feared a public backlash and worked with HUAC to remove communists from the industry. Promising to make anticommunist films, executives also blacklisted the Ten to ensure they would not work in Hollywood again. The blacklist only grew longer as the anticommunism scare spread.

Despite the successful Hollywood hearings, HUAC had yet to find any communist plot that threatened national security, although it claimed one existed. The ALGER HISS case provided HUAC with its first (and only) evidence of communist corruption in the Democratic administration. In 1948, journalist and editor WHITTAKER CHAMBERS identi-

fied Hiss, a former State Department official and New Dealer, as a communist agent. Chambers alleged that Hiss had given him government documents while the two were communists in the 1930s. While Hiss's eloquent self-defense absolved him in the eyes of the public and most HUAC members, committee member Richard M. Nixon was neither impressed nor convinced by Hiss's testimony. Aided by the Federal Bureau of Investigation (FBI), Nixon pursued Hiss relentlessly but professionally. At a second hearing, Hiss was much more vague and unconvincing. When Hiss sued Chambers for libel, Chambers revealed documents Hiss had given him in the 1930s, which he had hidden in a pumpkin. Indicted on two counts of perjury, Hiss was sentenced in 1950 to five years in prison. Republicans relished the disgrace to the New Deal. Nixon's work propelled him to the Senate and vice presidency; in 1953, 185 of 221 Republican representatives requested an appointment on HUAC.

After reaching the heights of its power and influence during the Hiss trial, HUAC experienced an irreversible decline. Senator JOSEPH R. McCARTHY stole much of the committee's anticommunist thunder, and by the mid-1950s, with the Red Scare over, HUAC served little purpose.

HUAC nevertheless continued investigating unions, colleges, churches, organizations of nuclear scientists, feminist groups, civil rights groups, and even art shows. Hearings played out similarly to the Hollywood hearings but with different results. Friendly witnesses would give HUAC the names of communists; the accused would plead the Fifth Amendment's protection against self-incrimination—unlike the Hollywood Ten, who used the First Amendment's protection of free speech. HUAC would cite the accused for contempt but the Supreme Court consistently overruled these convictions. Despite being overturned, HUAC's accusations carried much weight. To the public, pleading the Fifth Amendment was equivalent to an admission of being a communist; many who did so lost their jobs.

HUAC's success at exposing communists was largely due to the support it received from the FBI, an ostensibly nonpartisan government agency. When the FBI was unable to prosecute its leftist enemies for lack of evidence or wished to preserve its nonpartisan reputation, the bureau fed its information to HUAC. A contempt of Congress citation, or the mere stigma of pleading the Fifth Amendment, served as punishment for the FBI's enemies. Thus throughout the 1940s, 1950s, and 1960s, HUAC acted as an unofficial FBI enforcer.

In 1960, during hearings in San Francisco, local students started a small riot against HUAC. Americans tired of HUAC's abusive questioning and dubious constitutionality. By the late 1960s, the committee had become an obsolete relic of a bygone era. In 1969 HUAC was renamed the

House Internal Security Committee; in 1975, the House abolished it altogether.

Further reading: Richard M. Fried, *Nightmare in Red: The McCarthy Era in Perspective* (New York: Oxford University Press, 1990); Walter Goodman, *The Committee: The Extraordinary Career of the House Committee on Un-American Activities* (New York: Farrar, Straus, & Giroux, 1968).

— Paul Rubinson

Huerta, Dolores   See United Farm Workers

Humphrey, Hubert H. (1911–1978)

As both a United States senator and the 38th vice president of the United States, Hubert Horatio Humphrey was a leading champion of civil rights and other liberal causes.

Born in Wallace, South Dakota, on May 27, 1911, Humphrey grew up in nearby Doland, the son of a local drugstore owner. Humphrey began his college career at the University of Minnesota, but dropped out before finishing because of the Great Depression. He continued his schooling, earning a degree from the Denver College of Pharmacy in 1933. He later returned to the University of Minnesota where he graduated magna cum laude with a major in political science in 1939. Humphrey completed his education in 1940 at Louisiana State University, graduating with a master's degree.

After practicing pharmacy for several years, Humphrey taught political science and became involved in state politics. An ardent supporter of the NEW DEAL, Humphrey was elected mayor of Minneapolis in 1945, and he was reelected in 1947 by a record 50,000-vote margin. In 1948, Humphrey gained wide exposure at the Democratic National Convention when he argued successfully that the platform should include a firm civil rights plank, whatever the objections of southerners in the party. It was time to "walk forthrightly into the bright sunshine of human rights," he declared. That same year, Humphrey won election to the U.S. Senate. At the forefront of the fight for MEDICARE programs, Humphrey cosponsored a health insurance bill in 1949 that would have broadened the Social Security program. A similar measure eventually became law in 1965 during Humphrey's term as vice president.

Humphrey built personal ties with other politicians and was a very popular senator. "Let's not have one enemy," he proclaimed. Reelected to the Senate in 1954, he campaigned for the presidency in 1960. Following his defeat to JOHN F. KENNEDY in the West Virginia primary, Humphrey withdrew from the presidential race, and after reelection to the Senate in 1961, he became assistant majority leader. During this term, Humphrey helped win Senate approval of the LIMITED TEST BAN TREATY OF 1963, which banned atmospheric nuclear explosions. Humphrey also played a pivotal role in the passage of the CIVIL RIGHTS ACT OF 1964, mandating desegregation of public accommodations. President LYNDON B. JOHNSON assigned Humphrey to push the bill through the Senate, and, after passage, Humphrey declared that the victory was "my greatest achievement."

In 1964, Johnson chose Humphrey as his running mate. As vice president, Humphrey served as chairman of the NATIONAL AERONAUTICS AND SPACE ADMINISTRATION (NASA), and he played a key role in the administration's efforts to reduce poverty, secure civil rights for minorities, and push legislation aimed at helping the working class.

Humphrey went on numerous foreign visits to explain the U.S. position on the VIETNAM WAR. Disagreeing with Johnson, Humphrey felt that the United States should limit its part in Vietnam to military assistance, supplies, and training. In an effort to convince Johnson to delay bombing, Humphrey argued behind the scenes, "To escalate, to bomb in Vietnam, was to court it, or at least to invite another entanglement with the Chinese of the unpleasant kind that had snarled us up in Korea." Overruled, Humphrey supported Johnson's policy in Vietnam.

In 1968, Johnson's decision not to run for reelection made Humphrey a leading candidate for the Democratic nomination with Maine senator Edmund Muskie as his running mate. Critics of Vietnam, however, opposed Humphrey for his support of the Johnson administration during the escalation of the Vietnam War. In the final count, Humphrey lost by 1 percent of the popular vote to Republican Richard M. Nixon.

Humphrey taught at Macalaster College from 1969 to 1970, before returning to the Senate in 1970. In 1972, he unsuccessfully sought the Democratic presidential nomination, and, following this defeat, he decided not to challenge front-runner Jimmy Carter for the nomination in 1976. Despite an operation for cancer in late 1976, Humphrey was reelected to the Senate. He was elected to his last political office as deputy president pro tem of the Senate in 1977. In 1978, he died of cancer in Waverly, Minnesota, leaving his wife to finish out his term in the Senate.

Further reading: Hubert H. Humphrey, *The Education of a Public Man: My Life and Politics* (New York: Doubleday, 1976); Carl Solberg, *Hubert Humphrey: A Biography* (London: W. W. Norton, 1984).

— Susan F. Yates

hydrogen bomb

The hydrogen bomb was a weapon designed to release nuclear energy with much greater magnitude than its precursor, the atomic bomb.

The mushroom cloud from the hydrogen blast at Eniwetok in the Pacific in 1952   *(National Archives)*

The United States developed the first such device in 1952 to deter Soviet aggression. While its proponents claimed it provided national security, opponents argued that the bomb created fear and uneasiness in America and around the world.

In 1942, while working on the Manhattan Project to create an atomic bomb, nuclear physicists Edward Teller and Enrico Fermi discovered the possibility of using atomic TECHNOLOGY to ignite a thermonuclear reaction, like that on the surface of the sun. A fission reaction like the one used at Hiroshima resulted from split atoms creating energy and releasing heat. The heat generated from fission, surpassing the temperature of the earth's core, sparked a chain reaction using heavy water, leading to a hydrogen explosion. After the successful use of atomic weapons in Japan in 1945, Teller tenaciously lobbied the government to develop such a hydrogen bomb. Unlike his colleagues, particularly Albert Einstein and J. ROBERT OPPENHEIMER, Teller expressed few reservations about exploring America's nuclear frontiers.

In 1949–50, COLD WAR events intervened as civilian and military leaders debated the nuclear program's future. Within a span of six months, the SOVIET UNION detonated an atomic device, communists overtook China, and American inspectors uncovered security lapses at Los Alamos and in the State Department. America's atomic monopoly and postwar pride in unlocking atomic secrets vanished. President HARRY S. TRUMAN promptly ordered the ATOMIC ENERGY COMMISSION (AEC) to initiate a hydrogen bomb program. Despite a stockpile of over 200 atomic bombs, American officials believed "the Super" would best deter Soviet expansion.

With the help of crude computers, Teller and mathematician Stanislaw Ulam led a successful effort to manufacture a hydrogen bomb at California's Lawrence Livermore Laboratory. The first thermonuclear test took place on the Pacific atoll Eniwetok on November 1, 1952. Code-named "Mike," the device weighed 65 tons and yielded 10.4 megatons of TNT, the unimaginable equivalent of 1,000 atomic bombs. It was enough to incinerate

New York City. In seconds, the three-mile-wide mushroom cloud vaporized the island, leaving a crater one-half mile deep and two miles wide. Observation crews felt the intense heat 30 miles away.

As with the atomic bomb, the world situation changed. American physicist Herbert York wrote that the explosion marked "a moment when the course of the world suddenly shifted, from the path it had been on to a more dangerous one. Fission bombs, destructive as they might have been, were thought of [as] being limited in power. Now, it seemed, we had learned how to brush even these limits aside and to build bombs whose power was boundless." Just as in 1945, Americans experienced both relief and anxiety. The United States enjoyed the security in advancing beyond Soviet capabilities, but worried about the potential apocalypse the hydrogen bomb promised. Also, as in the case of atomic technology, the Soviets developed their own device earlier than expected, in 1953.

This shocking development fueled the domestic hunt for spies and communist sympathizers, particularly, in the atomic program. The "red scare" revealed atomic spies, such as German scientist Klaus Fuchs, and American accomplices, such as JULIUS AND ETHEL ROSENBERG. But the investigation also persecuted those merely guilty by association. Red hysteria even ensnared Oppenheimer, who, in 1954, was denied his security clearance at the AEC after Teller's damaging testimony against him. Oppenheimer's reservations about the martial uses of nuclear power cost him his reputation and any influence in the nuclear program.

America's hydrogen bomb, so quickly matched by the Soviets, also marked an acceleration of the ARMS RACE. Throughout the 1950s, the superpowers continued to seek nuclear advantage through the deployment of powerful delivery systems. Other countries also created atomic and hydrogen bombs, some using them for leverage against old regional enemies. The success and promise of the hydrogen bomb program prompted DWIGHT D. EISENHOWER to favor a nuclear arsenal over conventional forces. His "New Look" strategy provided what his administration called "more bang for the buck." But "brinkmanship" with the Soviets also held obvious risks.

While few Americans could adequately comprehend the complex technology behind the bomb, many appreciated its potential for swift devastation. Most complied with civil defense drills, some constructed fallout shelters, and a few promoted disarmament. A vocal minority of pacifists, such as SANE (National Committee For a Sane Nuclear Policy), organized a campaign to prevent further construction, testing, and deployment. After the CUBAN MISSILE CRISIS brought the superpowers dangerously close to nuclear war, Americans, Soviets, and nearly 100 other nations signed the LIMITED TEST BAN TREATY OF 1963 designed to curtail atmospheric testing. Five years later, over 60 countries signed the Nuclear Nonproliferation Treaty. By the end of the century, however, over two dozen countries possessed nuclear weapons.

Further reading: Richard Rhodes, *Dark Sun* (New York: Simon & Schuster, 1995).

— Andrew J. Falk

I

immigration

Immigration to the United States changed significantly in the 1960s with the landmark IMMIGRATION ACT OF 1965 that dramatically altered the ethnic, religious, and cultural composition of the American people.

With the National Origins Act of 1924, the United States closed its doors to the population of eastern and southern EUROPE. The measure established quotas based on the presumed desirability of various nationalities, in particular, immigrants from northern and western Europe. Preference for visas was accorded annually on the basis of 2 percent of the foreign-born population of each nationality as determined by the 1890 U.S. census. In 1890, there were comparatively more immigrants from western and northern European countries, and this limited the opportunity for citizens of southern and eastern European countries to enter the United States.

The MCCARRAN-WALTER ACT of 1952, passed over President HARRY S. TRUMAN's veto, reaffirmed the national origins quota system established in the 1924 measure. The 1952 law removed the ban on immigration from ASIA and Pacific areas. At the same time it gave immigration officials more authority to exclude and deport "undesirable" aliens. With the COLD WAR in full swing, many Americans were suspicious of those coming from southern and eastern European countries that were either sympathetic to or controlled by the SOVIET UNION. Giving more authority to immigration officials to deport or exclude undesirables from the United States caused immigration from southern and eastern Europe to effectively stop as a result of the communist threat.

In the 1960s, with support from both political parties, new policies created a more favorable climate for immigrants and refugees. The Immigration Act of 1965 revised the McCarran-Walter Act and altered the national quota system. It established annual immigration limits that included 170,000 aliens from outside the Western Hemisphere, and 120,000 from the Western Hemisphere for a total admission of 290,000 immigrants per year, although exceptions to the

IMMIGRATION TO THE UNITED STATES	
1945	38,119
1950	249,187
1955	237,790
1960	265,398
1965	296,697
1970	373,326

Source: Statistical Yearbook of the Immigration and Naturalization Service, 1997.

limits meant that the number of immigrants who entered the country far exceeded the annual quota. The new quotas significantly increased the number of immigrants allowed into the United States, compared to previous decades. During the 1960s, nearly 350,000 immigrants entered the country each year. By the 1970s, the number had risen to 400,000. Family members of U.S. citizens were exempted from the quotas, along with political refugees, who were now defined as victims of natural calamities and religious or political persecution. This allowed many new groups into the country, including Indochinese refugees who fled to the United States in response to unsettled conditions in Southeast Asia created by the VIETNAM WAR.

The 1965 measure did prevent some from entering the United States by establishing three categories of individuals who were excluded from the country: people with mental diseases and drug or alcohol addictions; criminals, prostitutes, and those with contagious diseases; and those considered subversive. Even with these exclusions, the Immigration Act of 1965 benefited many groups, including Asians and Latin Americans, although the measure was initially intended to promote the unification of eastern European family members previously denied admission to the United States.

Despite strict monitoring of the immigration system, large numbers of people entered the country illegally.

The largest number of individuals coming to the United States illegally arrived from Mexico. Many undocumented persons found work in agriculture, harvesting crops or planting nursery stock. While it is difficult to determine how many illegal immigrants came to the United States, some estimate that anywhere between 1 million and 5 million crossed the border annually beginning in the 1950s, with even larger numbers in more recent years. In the early 1950s, the Immigration and Naturalization Service reported that it had deported nearly 3.8 million Mexicans from the United States. Many of those who crossed the border came in search of a higher standard of living and relief from hunger, poor medical care, and impoverished conditions.

Like many immigrants before, those who came to the United States in the 1950s and 1960s formed communities in large towns and cities across the nation. Beginning in 1959, large numbers of Cubans—in search of political asylum from the new communist government under Fidel Castro—settled in Miami, Florida, and in urban areas in New York and New Jersey. Asian and Filipino immigrants established communities in cities in Hawaii and California while Chinese immigrants often settled in the Chinatowns of New York, San Francisco, and Los Angeles. Many immigrants favored living in ethnic boroughs in major cities upon arrival in the United States, but many later moved to small, outlying towns as they adapted to their new home.

Further reading: Roger Daniels, *Coming to America: A History of Immigration and Ethnicity in American Life* (New York: HarperCollins, 1990).

— Sarah Brenner

Immigration Act of 1965

The Immigration Act of 1965 consisted of a series of amendments to the Immigration Act of 1924, making it easier for people from other countries to immigrate into the United States.

Known as the "melting pot," America had welcomed new immigrants since the late 1700s. At the beginning of the 20th century, however, the United States tried to slow the large and steady stream of immigrants from around the world. Americans felt that the country possessed a thriving, level population. In fact, there were so many people in the country that even with industrialization, some felt that there were not enough jobs to keep the population employed. Given these factors, the U.S. government passed the National Origins Act of 1924. This legislation imposed a "quota system" on the number of people allowed to immigrate from each country. The measure mainly affected southern and eastern Europe, which provided the

largest numbers of new arrivals at the end of the 19th century and in the first two and a half decades of the 20th.

When JOHN F. KENNEDY became president in 1960, the issue of immigration surfaced again in Washington. For the first time since the restrictions of 1924, the United States was willing to begin loosening its restraints on immigration. Though Kennedy supported easing restriction, the measure did not become law until LYNDON B. JOHNSON's presidency.

Amendments to the Immigration Act of 1924 made it easier for people to come to America. The Immigration Act of 1965 sought to eliminate the quota system, allowing for more people to immigrate from southern and eastern Europe, India, and China. The quota system was not entirely abolished until 1968; it took the government three years to phase it out. The Immigration Act of 1965 gave preference to certain groups of people for the first time. Members of the immediate family of a U.S. citizen, including parents, husbands, wives, brothers, and sisters, were now able to immigrate more swiftly. The new act also allowed political refugees to enter the country at a faster rate. Finally, people who excelled in certain professions or skills were given priority over others.

This caused major changes in the patterns of immigration. After the 1924 act was passed, immigration into the United States tapered off. No longer was there the massive immigration that the United States had experienced before the act. In 1965, in a slow period in immigration, the Immigration Act of 1965 led to a dramatic increase in numbers. Several hundred thousand a year could now come. Some arrived from LATIN AMERICA in the aftermath of Fidel Castro's seizure of power in Cuba. Others came from Southeast ASIA in the aftermath of the VIETNAM WAR. After years of closed doors, the United States again provided a window of opportunity to people from abroad.

Further reading: David Jacobson, *The Immigration Reader* (Malden, Mass.: Blackwell Publishers, 1998).

— Jennifer Howell

Indian Claims Commission

The Indian Claims Commission, established in June 1946, worked as a quasi-judicial branch of Congress, hearing and resolving all claims against the Untied States on behalf of any Indian tribe, band, or other identifiable group of Native Americans.

Such claims included those arising under the Constitution, laws, or treaties of the United States and executive orders of the president, those resulting if the treaties, contracts, or agreements between tribes and the United States were revised on the grounds of fraud, duress, unconscionable consideration, mutual or unilateral mistake, or those arising from the taking by the United States, whether as a result of a treaty of cession or otherwise, of lands owned or occupied by Native American tribes without payment or compensation agreed to by tribes.

Historically, government policy toward Indian tribes has vacillated. Prior to World War II, the U.S. government supported tribal efforts at autonomy for more than a decade. In the 1950s, however, the government no longer encouraged self-government, choosing instead to enact a TERMINATION POLICY. The administration of DWIGHT D. EISENHOWER pushed for a settling of all outstanding claims and advocated the elimination of reservations as legitimate political entities. To facilitate termination by way of assimilation, the government instituted an urban relocation program to encourage Native Americans to leave their reservations and move to the cities. As a result of this policy, many Native Americans faced poor housing facilities, including overcrowding, high rents, and widespread discrimination. These conditions led to increased Indian activism in the late 1960s. Many tribes used the Indian Claims Commission to obtain monetary compensation for lost lands and to force the government to acknowledge their presence. As more tribes exercised their power as a legal entity within the Indian Claims Commission court system, the termination policy became a less viable option. By the end of the 1950s, Eisenhower modified the policy, rendering his termination policy ineffective in anything but a legal sense.

The Indian Claims Commission constituted both a product of past moral wrongdoing and an effort to relieve some of the burden on the U.S. Court of Claims, previously the only legal venue for tribal issues. Ninety percent of the claims handled by the commission concerned issues of land, with remaining cases regarded as accounting cases. Land cases were heard in three complex stages: title, value-liability, and offsets. Initially, attorneys defined those lands historically occupied by Native Americans. Next, they established the value of land at the time it was appropriated by the United States; and finally, assuming liability, they offset any proper payment against that value before the case was closed. Accounting cases involved assessing the management of tribal monies by the U.S. government as the appointed legal guardian for the tribes. As with land cases, records revealed overwhelming evidence of mishandling and malfeasance.

Congress originally established a period of 10 years for Native American tribes to file claims against the United States. This period was later extended. By 1951, Native Americans filed a total of 852 claims for more total acreage than existed in the entire United States. Overlapping claims accounted for the confusion. As of June 30, 1967, awards totaling $208 million were made in 101 cases, with 133 cases dismissed for various reasons. By 1978, when the Indian Claims Commission ceased operation, it had awarded over $800 million on nearly 300 claims. The decisions provided not only legal proof but also a cognizance that many past treaties and other agreements between the United States and Native Americans were immoral and unjust.

Further reading: U.S. Indian Claims Commission. *Indian Claims Commission Decisions* (Boulder, Colo.: Native American Rights Fund, 1973); Wunder, John R. *"Retained by the People": A History of American Indians and the Bill of Rights* (New York: Oxford University Press, 1994).
— Nichole Suzanne Prescott

Indian movement   See Native American movement

Internal Security Act (1950)

In the wake of COLD WAR anticommunist fears, Congress passed the Internal Security Act in an effort to protect the United States from communist infiltration.

As anticommunist fears developed after World War II and came to a peak after the outbreak of the KOREAN WAR on June 24, 1950, Congress began to debate the best manner in which to protect the United States from internal communist subversion. The internal threat of COMMUNISM clearly concerned both Democrats and Republicans in Congress, who could point to the ALGER HISS case and the government's successful prosecution of 11 Communist Party officials as recent examples of the need for legislation to defend the United States from within. Congressmen agreed that loyal Americans should support any anticommunist legislation that was drafted, placing opponents, even those who viewed such legislation as unconstitutional, in the position of being un-American.

In this context, Democrats and Republicans raced to outdo one another in writing and passing the strongest anticommunist legislation. President HARRY S. TRUMAN initiated the final stage of this race by submitting to Congress a proposed bill designed to deal more harshly with espionage and aliens. Democratic senator Patrick J. McCarran from Nevada responded by crafting an even more repressive proposal, combining his bill, which dealt with alien communists, with another bill that required the registration of communists. Six liberal Democratic senators responded to McCarran's bill with what they viewed as an even more potent proposal that authorized the detention of those likely to engage in espionage and sabotage during a time of internal emergency as declared by the president. Based on the precedent, upheld by the Supreme Court, established by the exile and incarceration of Japanese Americans during World War II, this concentration camp bill, as it came to be known, was proposed to avoid the perceived evils of McCarran's bill. The bills were eventually combined into a single bill and passed over Truman's veto.

The McCarran Internal Security Act as enacted on September 23, 1950, consisted of two sections. Title I, or the Subversive Activities Control Act, proclaimed that a communist organization posed a clear and present danger to the United States. While the statute declared that Communist Party membership was not a crime, it ordered communist organizations and their members to register with the attorney general. The organizations were also required to file periodic financial statements with the attorney general and to identify any LITERATURE they wrote or TELEVISION or radio program they produced. The act established a bipartisan Subversive Activities Control Board to decide which groups the law covered. Although the registration requirements of Title I resulted in considerable litigation, no communist group ever registered under its mandate.

Title I also tightened espionage and immigration laws to protect the United States from internal communist subversion. The act sought to prosecute individuals involved in efforts to establish a totalitarian regime in the United States under the direction of a foreign government. It also strengthened espionage laws by sharpening provisions of the law dealing with obtaining, possessing, or transmitting defense secrets. The act made it illegal for people seeking nonelective office or U.S. government employment or work in any defense facility to conceal membership in a communist group. Officers or employees of the U.S. government or defense facilities were also barred from contributing funds or services to communist organizations. Members of communist organizations were not allowed to use U.S. passports. Aliens belonging to communist organizations were now ruled excludable and deportable. Naturalization was denied to members of communist organizations, and the act allowed for the denaturalization of immigrants who joined a communist organization within five years of becoming American citizens unless such persons could prove they had been "innocent dupes."

Title II, or the Emergency Detention Act, based on the model of Executive Order 9066, incarcerating the Japanese, mandated detention of persons likely to engage in espionage and sabotage during a time of national emergency. It called for the attorney general to issue warrants for detention against those believed likely to conspire to engage in sabotage or espionage against the United States. It also included a right to appeal for those detained, but the attorney general could withhold evidence or sources deemed potentially dangerous to national security. Detainees denied release could appeal their case to a bipartisan Detention Review Board, which was required to hear the case within 45 days. The board, however, had no time limit imposed on its decision. Although Title II was never invoked, Congress made

appropriations between 1952 and 1957 to fund construction of six detention sites.

The McCarran Internal Security Act ultimately accomplished little. In 1967, a lower court found the registration provision unconstitutional and the government did not appeal. Title II was repealed, with Japanese Americans leading the movement to do so, in 1971. The Subversive Activities Control Board was abolished in 1973.

Further reading: Richard M. Fried, *Nightmare in Red: The McCarthy Era in Perspective* (New York: Oxford University Press, 1990); Ellen Schrecker, *Many Are the Crimes: McCarthyism in America* (Boston: Little, Brown, 1998).

— Allan Wesley Austin

Interstate Highway Act of 1956

The Interstate Highway Act of 1956, known officially as the Federal Aid Highway Act of 1956, created over 40,000 miles of expressways, providing a comprehensive system of roads that mobilized Americans in an increasingly fast-paced society.

By the beginning of the 1950s, congested traffic plagued urban areas, while roads in poor repair cost drivers time, money, and occasionally their lives. Support for an interstate highway system, which would connect America's major cities to facilitate commerce and travel, had been growing since the early 20th century. Until the end of World War II, however, America's railroads constituted the primary method of transporting goods and people. In 1944, Congress authorized a national system of interstate highways, although no source of funding was designated for this purpose. Plans for an interstate system stalled again during the KOREAN WAR, which diverted supplies from the construction industry.

When DWIGHT D. EISENHOWER was elected president in 1952, America's highways were in dire shape. The post–World War II economic boom jumpstarted car sales, and, whereas America's traffic volume in 1950 had already surpassed levels predicted for 1958, Americans were still driving on roads built mostly before 1930. Eisenhower felt that construction of an interstate system would create numerous jobs and make travel more efficient and pleasant. The threat of nuclear warfare, always present during the COLD WAR, made the efficient evacuation of American cities a priority as well. In the event of nuclear attack, the existing roads of most American cities would be hopelessly clogged with traffic. A president anxious to cure America's highway ills, combined with an added defensive impetus, lent increased weight to the great wave of popular and political support for a revamped highway system.

Although most Americans agreed on the need for a new highway system, no one could agree on its primary

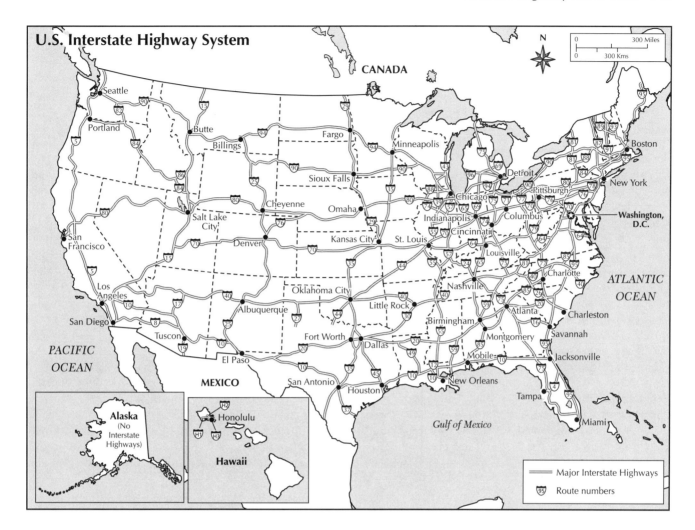

U.S. Interstate Highway System

purpose or on how to fund its construction. Engineers sought to alleviate traffic problems while city officials wanted to build the highway system as a way of revitalizing decaying downtown areas. Few auto users, truckers especially, were willing to pay extra taxes to fund construction, especially because auto taxes had been diverted in the past from highway funding to nonrelated areas.

In 1954, Eisenhower appointed Lucius Clay to head the President's Advisory Committee on a National Highway Program in order to formulate a working proposal to build and fund the interstate highway system. According to Clay's plan, the federal government would pay as much as 90 percent of the costs of building the highways using bonds and taxes, while the states would pay the remainder. Like all previous highway bills, Clay's proposal fell victim to a gridlocked Congress, while politicians and the so-called highway lobby—a fragmented group of transportation, construction, and motorist associations—argued over the method of funding. When Congress adjourned in August

1955 without passing a highway bill, it seemed there might never be a national highway system.

By 1956, many states were preparing to build their own highways using their own means. In April, however, the House approved a highway bill written by Hale Boggs of Louisiana and George Fallon of Maryland. The Boggs-Fallon bill managed to provide for 90 percent federal funding without imposing high taxes on truckers. Taxes on fuel, tires, and new vehicles would pay for construction, and the Highway Trust Fund was created to ensure that those taxes were not diverted to other areas. Refusing to contest the bill on partisan grounds, and under pressure to pass significant domestic legislation, the Eisenhower administration supported the bill. On June 26, the Senate passed the bill 89-1, and on the same day, the House approved it so overwhelmingly that votes were not even counted.

On June 29, Eisenhower signed the Interstate Highway Act, bringing the National System of Interstate and Defense Highways into being. More than 40,000 miles of roads were planned at a cost of $25 billion, making it the largest public works program in history. The new interstate highway system, when finished, would connect most cities of 50,000 residents or more and all continental states with controlled-access, multilane expressways.

The Interstate Highway Act had a far-reaching impact on most Americans and much of America itself. In the end, those concerned with traffic patterns and commerce won out over those hoping to revitalize America's inner cities. The act proved a mighty boost to the automobile, trucking, and construction industries. It cemented Americans' well-known love affair with their cars, as the number of registered cars rose above 73 million by 1960, compared to just under 40 million in 1950. The new interstate system opened countless markets for motel and fast food restaurant chains. Yet not everyone was to thrive in the new age of highways. While 28,800 miles of highway opened between 1956 and 1969, the same period of time saw the closing of 59,400 miles of railroads to passenger service. Air quality in urban areas suffered, mass transportation fell into disuse, and expressways encouraged suburban growth, furthering the plight of inner cities.

Further reading: Mark Reutter, "The Lost Promise of the American Railroad," *Wilson Quarterly* (Winter 1994): 10–35; Mark H. Rose, *Interstate: Express Highway Politics, 1941–1956* (Lawrence: The Regents Press of Kansas, 1979).

— Paul Rubinson

inventions See technology

Israel (and foreign policy)

With the destruction of European Jewry in the Holocaust, many Western leaders responded to Zionist calls for the establishment of a Jewish homeland in Palestine, creating the state of Israel.

Among those who responded was President HARRY S. TRUMAN, who argued that the European refugees had the right to settle in Palestine. In November 1947, the United Nations approved a plan to partition Palestine into Arab and Jewish states. In May 1948, the existence of the state of Israel was officially declared, and the United States immediately recognized the new nation. The two countries have shared a close relationship ever since.

The Arab countries surrounding Israel refused to recognize the new nation. They argued that Palestine was Arab territory and proclaimed their support for the Palestinian Arabs. Hostilities soon erupted in the MIDDLE EAST, leading to a series of wars in the region.

On May 15, 1948, one day after the establishment of Israel, armies from Syria, Lebanon, Jordan, Iraq, and Egypt invaded Israel. The Israelis successfully defended the new nation, and they proceeded to conquer various Palestinian towns. Thousands of Palestinians fled from their homes. This was the beginning of the refugee crisis that still exists today, with both sides blaming the other for creating this situation.

The United Nations immediately became involved in trying to bring about a peaceful end to the conflict. There were two cease-fires in June and July, but there was no true end to the fighting until January 1949. Several armistice agreements were signed between February and July 1949. The United States played an important role in the eventual settlement. At first, Truman demanded that Israel return to its original borders; however, Israel had no intention of doing this. Eventually, however, Truman yielded to political pressure, and he did not insist that Israel relinquish its newly conquered territory.

The map of the Middle East had been dramatically transformed by the war. Israel now possessed large amounts of new territory, including all of Galilee and the Negev as well as the entire Palestinian coast, with the exception of the Gaza Strip. Israel was now one-quarter larger than it had been under the original partition. In addition, the Palestinian state no longer existed.

The United States soon discovered that it was difficult to maintain peace in the Middle East. In 1956, Egypt nationalized the Suez Canal. Israel, with the support of France and Great Britain, proceeded to attack Egypt and capture the Sinai Peninsula.

In response, the United Nations issued a resolution commanding Israel to withdraw its troops immediately from the region. President DWIGHT D. EISENHOWER demanded that Israel return the Sinai to Egypt, and he condemned British and French involvement in the conflict. The SOVIET UNION strongly criticized the three countries for threatening Egypt and jeopardizing the stability of the region.

In the U.S. Jewish community, there was strong pressure for Eisenhower to support Israel. This tense situation continued until February 1957, when Eisenhower warned Israeli prime minister David Ben Gurion of serious repercussions if Israel did not withdraw from the Sinai. These repercussions included possible sanctions and the withholding of private assistance to Israel. One week later, Israel agreed to U.S. demands. In March, Israel departed from the Sinai.

The foreign policy of the United States was profoundly affected by this war. Fearing growing Soviet influence in the Middle East, in January 1957, the Eisenhower Doctrine stated that, if necessary, the United States would use armed forces to prevent COMMUNISM from securing a base in the Middle East. The Arab nations, however, did not trust the United States, and the Eisenhower Doctrine only served to further alienate them.

War broke out once again in the region in 1967. In the Six-Day War, Israel successfully defeated the combined forces of Egypt, Syria, and Jordan. The conflict began in May 1967, when Syria claimed that Israel was sending troops to its border. Egypt then became involved, with President Gamal Abdel Nasser sending numerous troops to the Sinai and closing the Strait of Tiran to Israeli shipping. King Hussein of Jordan joined in the growing conflict, and he signed a mutual defense pact with Egypt. This greatly worried the Israelis, who feared that their country was about to be attacked. In June, the Israelis launched both air and ground attacks against the Egyptians, and also defeated the Jordanian and Syrian armies. As a result of their victory, the Israelis gained even more Arab territory, including the West Bank, Gaza Strip, and Golan Heights.

Once again, the United States was involved in trying to bring about a peace agreement in the region. American interests still revolved around reducing Soviet influence, maintaining access to oil, and guaranteeing Israel's safety. In addition, President LYNDON B. JOHNSON strongly believed that maintaining good relations with Israel was in the best interests of U.S. policy; some critics argued that this belief came at the expense of American relationships with Arab countries. Indeed, after the war, Arab relations with the United States worsened, Soviet influence in the region continued to increase, and the United States discovered in the years to come that a lasting peace would be extremely difficult to maintain in the Middle East.

Further reading: Donald Neff, *Fallen Pillars: U.S. Policy towards Palestine and Israel since 1945* (Washington, D.C.: Institute for Palestine Studies, 1995); Cheryl A. Rubenberg, *Israel and the American National Interest: A Critical Examination* (Urbana: University of Illinois Press, 1986).

— Lori Nates

J

Job Corps

Created under the ECONOMIC OPPORTUNITY ACT OF 1964 as part of the WAR ON POVERTY launched by President LYNDON B. JOHNSON, the goal of the Job Corps was to provide education, vocational training, and work experience that would enhance the career opportunities of disadvantaged youths.

As one of several job training programs launched during the 1960s, the Job Corps targeted teenagers and young adults in response to rising rates of youth unemployment and alarming revelations by the military that one out of every three American young men failed to meet their minimum mental and physical requirements.

Job Corps training centers were located at rural and urban residential installations. The purpose of establishing residential centers was to remove trainees from impoverished neighborhoods where, it was believed, debilitating influences such as high crime rates, widespread unemployment, and pervasive feelings of hopelessness destined many youths to dismal futures. The vast majority of Job Corps enrollees were high school dropouts between the ages of 16 and 21 years, two-thirds of whom entered the program with reading and mathematical skills below the sixth-grade level. Job Corps centers offered vocational and remedial educational instruction to all enrollees. An integral goal of the educational program was to prepare enrollees to pass the General Educational Development (GED) test for high school equivalency. Along with providing educational and vocational training, Job Corps centers offered health care and counseling services to trainees.

Vocational training varied according to the type of center. The Job Corps established three kinds of centers. The large (1,000–3,000 trainees) centers for male participants offered vocational training in fields such as automobile and machine repair, construction trades, appliance repair, and service occupations. The smaller (100–250 trainees) centers for men targeted enrollees most lacking in basic reading and math skills. These centers were located in rural areas and provided work experience on conservation projects, vocational training in fields such as construction, as well as a strong focus on remedial education. In addition, medium-sized (300–1,000 trainees) centers for women offered training for careers in business and clerical work, food service, health care, and childcare. In its first year of operation, 300,000 youths applied for admission to the Job Corps, although the program held spaces for only 10,000. By 1968, Job Corps enrollment had reached 65,000 trainees. Crucial to these vocational training programs was the involvement of BUSINESS corporations (notably IBM, RCA, and Litton Industries) and union training programs.

The Job Corps, however, was plagued by problems, including persistently low rates of completion among its participants. Since targets of the program were young high school dropouts, problems were likely from the outset. In its first decade, only 26 percent of participants completed Job Corps training programs. One factor that contributed to the high dropout rate was the residential nature of the program, which proved to be a difficult adjustment for many participants. In the program's early years, participants were deliberately relocated far from their homes on the theory that removal from "unhealthy" environments was a crucial aspect of transforming these youths into self-disciplined, productive members of the labor force. Thus, participants often found themselves in dormitories at training centers located thousands of miles from home. Feelings of homesickness and isolation contributed to high dropout rates; over 40 percent of enrollees left within the first 40 days of the program. The low rates of completion provoked sharp criticisms of the program; defenders of the Job Corps, however, argued that a high dropout rate was inevitable considering that enrollees had already quit high school and many were already among the hard-core unemployed.

The Job Corps quickly became one of the most controversial programs of the War on Poverty. In addition to questions raised by the high dropout rate, the program's high cost per enrollee provoked criticism. Residential training was expensive—averaging $9,000 per enrollee-year, or $4,600 per enrollee—during the first decade of the program. President Johnson defended the cost of the program, stating: "One thousand dollars invested in salvaging an unemployed youth today can return forty thousand in his lifetime." Critics, however, complained that the cost per participant was on par with the cost of sending a student to an elite university. Supporters of the program maintained that if the program could turn unemployed youths—who seemed destined to futures marked by frequent periods of unemployment and dependency on public assistance—into individuals with marketable skills who could secure and retain profitable employment, then investing in their futures was worth the expenditure. The most fundamental criticism of the Job Corps, though, centered on just how effective the program was in producing long-term benefits for participants. Early follow-up studies of Job Corps participants yielded unimpressive results. Enrollees improved their educational levels only slightly and—although they had higher rates of employment and improved earnings in the first six months after leaving the program—studies showed that participants were no better off than other disadvantaged youths in the long term.

During the presidency of Richard M. Nixon, administration of the Job Corps was transferred to the Department of Labor, where it struggled to survive in the face of budgetary cutbacks. The program, although somewhat modified in form, continues to offer vocational training to low-income youths.

Further reading: Michael Bernick, *The Dream of Jobs: The Job Training and Anti-poverty Programs of the Past Two Decades—and Their Results* (Salt Lake City: Olympus Publishing, 1984); Christopher Weeks, *Job Corps: Dollars and Dropouts* (Boston: Little Brown, 1967).

— Susan Allyn Johnson

Johnson, Lady Bird (1912–   )

Lady Bird Johnson earned a reputation as an environmentally conscious first lady during LYNDON B. JOHNSON's administration and pursued her interest in beautifying America long after his presidency.

Claudia Alta Taylor was born on December 22, 1912, in the 600-person town of Karnack, Texas. The only daughter of a wealthy merchant, her mother died when she was six; her Aunt Effie played a significant role in her upbringing. Claudia assumed her lifelong nickname "Lady Bird" in childhood. Isolated and frustrated with small town life, she moved to Dallas for a college education in 1928 and attended St. Mary's Episcopal School for Girls. In 1930, she transferred to University of Texas Austin where she pursued a dual degree in journalism and history, graduating with honors in 1933.

After a short courtship in 1934, she married Lyndon Baines Johnson, then a congressional aide with political promise. In 1937, she facilitated his victory for the 10th district congressional seat in Texas by contributing her time, energy, and money. Later, she ran his congressional office while her husband served in World War II. Lady Bird supported Johnson and his political career throughout his life and their marriage of over 40 years.

In 1943, she invested inheritance money in KTBC, a small radio station in Austin. She also purchased a home in Washington, D.C., that year and started commuting between Austin and Washington, D.C. Lady Bird's business interests prospered as the radio station won a license from the Federal Communications Center and grew in size. In 1952, she purchased a TELEVISION station in Austin and continued to invest in real estate. By the mid-1960s her business ventures were estimated to be worth between $7 million and $10 million.

Lady Bird bore two daughters, Lynda Bird in 1944 and Lucy Baines in 1947. While she juggled the role of mother, business owner, and political wife, Johnson moved up the political ladder. He was elected to the U.S. Senate in 1948 and won the vice presidency in 1960. Lady Bird quickly adapted to the public attention that surrounded these positions. During the 1960 presidential campaign, she assumed a key role in organizing and recruiting female voters. Acting as the most visible woman in the DEMOCRATIC PARTY she campaigned throughout the country. After Johnson was elected vice president, Lady Bird attended dozens of official meetings and parties as a representative of the White House and started to promote some of her political concerns, including environmental conservation and civil rights.

After the assassination of JOHN F. KENNEDY, Lady Bird assumed the position of first lady with reluctance and courage. Within a year, she used her political presence to push for the adoption of the CIVIL RIGHTS ACT OF 1964. She also campaigned vigorously for Johnson's reelection in 1964, traveling across much of the country to secure votes for him.

As first lady, Lady Bird envisioned a broad-based group of projects to beautify America. Defining her concern as "conservation," she believed that efforts to clean up America would lead to better standards of living. Some mocked her concerns as trivial, but her efforts reflected a tradition of female activism focused on preserving the environment that dated back at least 50 years. She launched antilitter campaigns and recruited big businesses to join in this effort. Moreover, she initiated programs to clean up the interstate highways, by removing junkyards and regulating outdoor advertisements with billboards. Her involvement with this cause was instrumental in the passage of the 1965 Highway Beautification Act.

In 1965, she created the Society for a More Beautiful National Capital that concentrated on maintaining and improving the appearance of monuments, parks, and public vistas in Washington, D.C. She effectively used the media to publicize these efforts and recognized the potential of increasing tourism to the capital through this effort. The organization also worked, less successfully, to improve the inner core of Washington, D.C. Lady Bird's concern for the environment, along with the president's support of this agenda, added legitimacy to conservation causes and helped set the climate for the ENVIRONMENTAL MOVEMENT of the 1970s.

Throughout the 1970s, Lady Bird continued her conservation efforts. She launched a Town Lake Beautification program near Austin and honored Texas highway departments for impressive beautification programs. After Johnson's death in 1973, she represented him at many official gatherings and constantly reminded the public of his legacy in enactment of environmental and civil rights legislation. In 1982, she opened a Wildflower Research Center near Austin.

Further reading: Lewis L. Gould, *Lady Bird Johnson: Our Environmental First Lady* (Lawrence: University Press of Kansas, 1999).

— Kirstin Gardner

Johnson, Lyndon B. (1908–1973)

The 36th president of the United States, Lyndon Johnson pursued the largest agenda of domestic reform since Franklin D. Roosevelt's NEW DEAL.

Johnson's vision of a GREAT SOCIETY included successful attempts to expand civil rights, education aid, and access to health care. Throughout the 1960s, however, Johnson played a decisive role in escalating a destructive and divisive war in Vietnam that ultimately tarnished his accomplishments.

Born in Stonewall, Texas, on August 27, 1908, Johnson was raised in a middle-class family, the son of a state representative. After graduating from a state teacher's college, Johnson spent time as an instructor at a poor, largely Hispanic high school. In 1931, he accepted a position as clerk to a Texas congressman and less than four years after arriving in Washington, he became head of the National Youth Administration (NYA) for Texas. In 1937, campaigning as a vocal supporter of Roosevelt's New Deal, Johnson won a special election to Congress as a Democrat. Johnson quickly earned a reputation as a skilled politician and legislator. Elected to the Senate in 1948, he became the youngest majority leader in history in 1955. Frustrated in

his own attempt at the presidential nomination in 1960, Johnson was elected vice president on a ticket with JOHN F. KENNEDY. Johnson found the office politically weak and frustrating. Then, in November 1963, Kennedy was assassinated during a visit to Dallas, Texas.

Johnson moved quickly to calm a shattered nation. Citing the need to honor Kennedy's legacy, Johnson pushed for the domestic reforms that his predecessor had endorsed but had been unable to attain. In July 1964, despite a 75-day filibuster and the opposition of conservatives from both parties, Johnson signed the CIVIL RIGHTS ACT OF 1964. The bill prohibited racial discrimination in all public accommodations and expanded access to education and employment for minorities. In August of that same year, Johnson gained congressional passage of the ECONOMIC OPPORTUNITY ACT OF 1964, which established the JOB CORPS and HEAD START.

Later that year, Johnson was elected president in his own right with a landslide victory over Republican BARRY GOLDWATER. Johnson's own political skills and desire to build a lasting legacy, combined with economic prosperity, a large Democratic congressional majority, and a burgeoning Civil Rights movement, created an opportunity for major reforms. In another landmark civil rights bill, Johnson won passage of the VOTING RIGHTS ACT OF 1965, which expanded federal oversight of elections and outlawed devices used to inhibit minority voting in the South. The MEDICARE bill of that same year insured that all Americans over 65 would have health coverage, while the establishment of MEDICAID made the same guarantee to the indigent. Other Great Society reforms focused on slum clearance, affordable housing, and environmental protection.

Johnson's attempts to implement foreign policy were less successful. While his administration inherited an American presence in the VIETNAM WAR, it was Johnson's decision to embark on the massive escalation of American involvement in the Saigon regime's struggle against the communists of both South and North Vietnam. Following a perceived attack by torpedo boats on U.S. destroyers in August 1964, Congress passed the Gulf of Tonkin Resolution, which Johnson later used to fight an undeclared war in Indochina. When, by 1965, military success for the Saigon regime failed to materialize, Johnson introduced more American ground troops and began a sustained bombing campaign of North Vietnam.

Privately skeptical of the chances for American success in Vietnam, Johnson acted out of fear that the loss of Vietnam to the communists would threaten his domestic achievements. With the near universal support of his advisers and many American citizens, Johnson based his decisions on a COLD WAR foreign policy consensus—articulated in the TRUMAN DOCTRINE—that communist aggression anywhere in the world had to be stopped by the United States. Though troop escalations were gradual, by 1967

Lyndon B. Johnson being sworn in as president by federal district judge Sarah T. Hughes aboard *Air Force One,* as wife Lady Bird, former first lady Jacqueline Kennedy, and others look on, 1963 *(LBJ Library Collection)*

there were 485,000 Americans in Vietnam. In addition to frustrations over American casualties and military setbacks, critics attacked Johnson for not clearly articulating the objectives of the war.

By 1967, college students and antiwar activists organized massive demonstrations around the country against American involvement in Vietnam. In January 1968, the surprise Tet Offensive by the North Vietnamese completely destroyed the administration's arguments that America was winning the war and that it would soon end. Later that same year, Johnson surveyed a country ravaged by massive social

and political upheaval. By 1968, the American presence in Vietnam peaked at 550,000 troops, and antiwar sentiment continued to spread throughout American society. These factors, along with his own low poll numbers, led Johnson to announce to a stunned nation that he would not seek reelection. In the final months of his presidency, Johnson secluded himself in the White House as urban riots raged around the country and the war in Vietnam continued.

Johnson retired to his Texas ranch in 1969. He suffered a fatal heart attack there in January 1973 and died one day after the United States agreed to a cease-fire in Vietnam.

Further reading: Robert Dallek, *Flawed Giant: Lyndon Johnson and His Times, 1961–1973.* New York: Oxford University Press, 1998; Doris Kearns, *Lyndon Johnson and the American Dream* (New York: Harper & Row, 1976).

— Douglas G. Weaver

journalism

Journalism both reflected and influenced many of the changes that rippled through American society in the years following World War II.

During the period prior to World War II, newspapers and radio comprised the most important parts of the world of journalism. Between 1914 and 1927, the use of newsprint doubled in the United States, as Americans read about major events. The rise of radio in the 1920s brought the news to even larger numbers of people across the nation. Millions more Americans were now linked together by a common focus—and by a collective access to the news—than ever before.

The rapid rise in popularity and influence of TELEVISION during the early 1950s influenced journalistic standards and traditional news outlets in a number of ways. The number of television sets in the country rose from 6 million in 1950 to 84 million in 1970. From 1952 to 1960, the percentage of homes with televisions grew from 34 percent to 86 percent. The 1952 presidential election between DWIGHT D. EISENHOWER and Illinois governor ADLAI STEVENSON was the first in which television news coverage had a major role in defining the candidates and the issues. As political candidates and their advisers saw the power of television to shape public opinion, national political campaigns and enterprising journalists began to focus resources on the new medium.

One of the other effects of the rise of television was the reallocation of ADVERTISING dollars from print-based media to television. By 1957, companies were spending almost $1.5 billion annually in television ads. While some of this resulted from an increase in overall advertising expenditures, the portion represented by the shift from print-based advertising, especially magazine advertising, into television advertising hurt the revenue base for print-based media. It also signaled a decline in the proportion of newspapers Americans read, changing the way they received their daily news updates.

The nightly news show on one of the three broadcast networks became the way many Americans learned the news of the world. Edward R. Murrow was the first preeminent television journalist. In 1951 he began his *See It Now* daily news series on CBS. He was the first major national journalist with the courage to confront Senator JOSEPH R. MCCARTHY in the reckless search for communists. CBS cancelled *See It Now* in 1958, but Murrow continued to work on the CBS documentary series, *CBS Reports.* It was in that series that Murrow narrated "Harvest of Shame," a groundbreaking 1960 report on the status of migrant farm workers. Other shows paired teams of journalists to report the news. The most famous anchor team of the late 1950s and 1960s was NBC's pairing of Chet Huntley and David Brinkley. *The Huntley/Brinkley Report* was on the air from 1956 until 1970.

Most newspapers, especially in the smaller markets, obtained their national and international news from one of the two major press bureaus. United Press and the International Press Service merged in 1958 to create United Press International (UPI). UPI and the Associated Press were the two dominant news bureaus for the next 20 years.

The 1960s brought a series of challenges for journalists. The increasing violence associated with the Civil Rights movement and the growing involvement of the United States in the VIETNAM WAR, often called the first "televised war," presented unique challenges to journalists. Many civil rights leaders consciously used the news media as a vehicle to advance their social and political agendas.

Edward R. Murrow broadcasting the 1956 election returns *(Library of Congress)*

They knew that as news and images of racial violence spread to the North, many would see for the first time the effects of racism. Millions of people saw the ghastly images of Eugene "Bull" Connor turning vicious police dogs and high-pressure hoses on peaceful demonstrators in Birmingham, Alabama, in 1963.

Television brought similarly horrifying images into American homes during the Vietnam War. Meanwhile, journalists covering the war found themselves targets of criticism from those at home who supported the conflict. Everyone involved knew that documentaries and the nightly news had a tremendous impact on public opinion about the war. In one famous incident, reporter Morley Safer's 1965 television report on "The Burning of the Village of Cam Ne" drew heavy criticism because it cast U.S. Marines in a negative light for actions that led to the killing of Vietnamese civilians. David Halberstam of the *New York Times* won the Pulitzer Prize in 1964 for his reports from Vietnam. Others felt they were overlooked because of the nature of their coverage.

The 1970s ushered in a new mistrust of the government and a concern over the power of journalists to shape events. The publication of the Pentagon Papers documenting the history of the Vietnam War, and the press exposure of President Richard M. Nixon's involvement in the Watergate affair simultaneously showed the American people the need for a strong press to counter a secretive government, yet raised doubts in many about the increasing power of journalists to shape and control major events. In spite of the rise of television news, it was newspaper journalists who were at the forefront of new investigative journalism techniques. Because much of this reporting questioned government policies, these journalists were also often seen as being antiestablishment and often faced criticism for their efforts.

Further reading: Edwin Emery and Michael Emery, *The Press and America: An Interpretive History of the Mass Media,* 8th ed. (Boston: Allyn & Bacon, 1996).

— John Day Tully

K

Kennan, George F. (1904–)

George F. Kennan enjoyed an illustrious career as a diplomat and as a scholar, making his most famous contributions to American foreign policy as the first articulate exponent of the doctrine of containment and as a forceful realist thinker.

Born in Milwaukee, Wisconsin, on February 16, 1904, Kennan attended St. John's Military Academy in Delafield, Wisconsin, before obtaining a B.A. from Princeton University and then studying at the Foreign Service School in Washington, D.C. He served as vice consul in Geneva, Hamburg, Berlin, Tallinn, and Riga and studied Russian history and language at the Oriental Seminary at the University of Berlin. In 1931, he returned to Riga as a third secretary, where he stayed until 1933.

Aside from a short stint as consul in Vienna, Kennan spent the next four years in various posts at the U.S. embassy in Moscow where he witnessed firsthand the great Stalinist purges. He then moved to Prague and Berlin. He was temporarily held captive in Germany and spent the rest of the war in the State Department, Lisbon, London, and Moscow.

Kennan next taught at the National War College and became director of the State Department's Policy Planning Staff where he was, along with Charles Bohlen, the department's foremost specialist on the SOVIET UNION. Aside from a few years serving as ambassador to the Soviet Union and to Yugoslavia, he spent the rest of his life at the Institute for Advanced Study at Princeton University as a member, professor, and professor emeritus.

Kennan's most important contribution as a diplomat was his formulation of the doctrine of containment, which he most famously presented in a "Long Telegram" he sent from Moscow on February 22, 1946, in lectures at the National War College and in an article entitled "The Sources of Soviet Conduct," published in *Foreign Affairs* in July 1947. The article was published anonymously under the pseudonym "X." It was necessary to stop the Soviet Union from encroaching on other territory anywhere in the world, he affirmed.

In direct contrast to the views of Americans such as 1948 presidential candidate HENRY A. WALLACE, Kennan argued that the Soviet Union was inherently expansionist and insecure, for ideological as well as historical reasons, and that no policy of peaceful coexistence was possible. This expansion would be achieved most likely by political means, given Russia's low resources in the short term. The United States should follow a highly realistic policy that would reject idealistic interventionism and focus on the most important areas, namely, EUROPE and Japan. The overarching goal was to maintain a balance of power in ASIA and Europe by helping U.S. allies to rebuild and by making sure they would not fall within the Soviet orbit. Economic aid, rather than military intervention, was the preferred means of action. Economic growth would prevent social unrest, thus preempting communist expansion through political means. Effective political and military counterpressure would also be used to prevent further communist penetration.

In works such as *American Diplomacy* (1951), Kennan lamented the influence public opinion and idealism exerted on American foreign policy. He constantly advocated that a policy of realism be implemented by a diplomatic elite. In the late 1950s he started distancing himself from COLD WAR policies. Kennan was an early opponent of America's involvement in the VIETNAM WAR, and he called for nuclear arms control and a policy of détente with the Soviet Union. He opposed economic aid to Third World countries, arguing that the money would be better spent in the United States, and he refused to advocate sanctions against the apartheid regime in South Africa.

Kennan developed his ideas in a vast body of literature, winning the Pulitzer Prize and National Book Award for *Russia Leaves the War* (1956) and *Memoirs, 1925–1950* (1967).

Further reading: John L. Gaddis, *Strategies of Containment: A Critical Appraisal of Postwar American National*

Security Policy (Oxford, U.K.: Oxford University Press, 1982); George F. Kennan, *Memoirs* (Boston: Little, Brown, 1967–1972); David A. Mayers, *George Kennan and the Dilemmas of U.S. Foreign Policy* (New York: Oxford University Press, 1988).

— Philippe R. Girard

Kennedy, Jacqueline (Jacqueline Onassis)
(1929–1994)

Jacqueline Lee Bouvier Kennedy, wife of President JOHN F. KENNEDY, brought to the role of first lady a youth, beauty, and attention to culture that contributed to the notion that the Kennedy administration was modeled after the mythological Camelot of King Arthur's day.

Jackie, as she was affectionately called, was born July 28, 1929, to John Vernon Bouvier III and Janet Lee. Jackie's early years were divided between New York City and East Hampton, Long Island. In 1942, Janet Lee divorced John Bouvier and married Hugh D. Auchincloss. Jackie and her younger sister, Caroline Lee, were brought to Auchincloss's home near Washington, D.C., and spent the summers at his estate in Newport, Rhode Island.

Jacqueline received an education that reflected her upper-class background. After preschool, Jackie entered into Miss Chapin's School, a New York private school for daughters of well-to-do families. Her formal education continued at Miss Porter's School in Farmington, Connecticut, where the girls were allowed and encouraged to keep horses.

In 1947, Jackie was officially presented to the world of the social elite at her "coming-out" dance. She was a success, and the New York press proclaimed her "Debutante of the Year" for the 1947–48 social season.

After her social triumph, Jackie studied at Vassar, where she began to explore her interest in traveling. She spent her junior year at the Sorbonne in France, before graduating from George Washington University. In 1952, she became an inquiring camera girl at the Washington *Times-Herald*. While at the *Times-Herald*, Jackie was asked to write a column about new members of Congress, whose numbers included a young senator from Massachusetts named John Fitzgerald Kennedy.

Charlie Bartlett, a Washington correspondent for the *New York Times* and friend of both John and Jackie, decided that they were made for each other and, in June 1951, succeeded in arranging an intimate meeting between the two. The courtship between John and Jackie was private and often they spent quiet evenings with Bartlett and his wife or went to a movie with John's brother, ROBERT F. KENNEDY, and his wife Ethel. In the summer of 1953, the formal announcement appeared of Senator John F. Kennedy's engagement to Jacqueline Bouvier. The two were married September 12, 1953, at St. Mary's Church in Newport, Rhode Island.

Caroline Bouvier Kennedy, the first of the couples' children, was born in November 1957. John F. Kennedy, Jr., their second child, was born the morning after Thanksgiving, 1960. Two months later, the family moved to the White House after Kennedy's successful election campaign. Just three years after the birth of John, Jr., tragedy struck Jackie when Patrick Bouvier Kennedy was born prematurely on August 7, 1963, and died two days later.

As first lady, Jackie strove to make the White House a museum of American history and decorative arts as well as a family residence of elegance and charm. She worked hard to bring the arts to the White House and succeed in having some of the most famous musicians of the era, such as cellist Pablo Casals, play at the White House. Her interest in the arts inspired an attention to culture never before evident at a national level. Jackie set the tone for women's fashion in the early 1960s with her bouffant hairstyle, low-heeled pumps, and sleeveless sheath dresses along with her pillbox hats. Jackie also agreed to accompany a television crew around the White House so that the average American could view the national monument. The program was broadcast on January 14, 1962.

Jackie's ability to speak three languages proved to be a valuable asset in entertaining foreign guests at the White House. The press popularized the resurgence of youth, beauty, and art within the White House, which it characterized as the American Camelot, as Jackie set the social tone for the Kennedy administration. On November 22, 1963, the dream of Camelot was cut short with the assassination of John Fitzgerald Kennedy.

After moving out of the White House, Jackie craved privacy for herself and her children, but the public would never allow Jackie to have such privacy. She moved to New York City, and, in 1968, she married a wealthy Greek businessman, Aristotle Onassis, and lived abroad for a time. After Onassis's death in March 1975, Jackie moved back to New York were she lived and worked as an editor at Doubleday until her own death in 1994.

Further reading: Wayne Koestenbaum, *Jackie under My Skin: Interpreting an Icon* (New York: Farrar, Straus, & Giroux, 1995); Mary Thayer, *Jacqueline Bouvier Kennedy* (New York: Doubleday, 1961).

— Sarah Brenner

Kennedy, John F. (1917–1963)

John F. Kennedy was the youngest man elected president of the United States, and served from 1961 until his assassination in 1963.

John Fitzgerald Kennedy was born on May 29, 1917, one of eight children, to an Irish Catholic political family. His father, Joseph Kennedy, a self-made millionaire, headed the Securities and Exchange Commission under president Franklin D. Roosevelt and later served as ambassador to Great Britain.

After preparatory school, Kennedy enrolled at Harvard University, from which he graduated in 1940. In September 1941, JFK enlisted in the U.S. Navy, and eventually he became the skipper of a patrol torpedo (PT) boat in the Pacific. He made a name for himself in the navy after his boat, PT 109, was split in half by a Japanese destroyer and he led his crew to safety. He received the navy and marine medal for heroism while he was in the hospital for back surgery.

In 1945 Kennedy decided to run for congressional office in Massachusetts. At the age of 29, he had an impressive war record, his father's financial backing, youth, and a popular name; he won a seat in the House of Representatives the next year. In 1952, after three terms in the House, Kennedy decided to run for the Senate, and he won the election. While serving as a senator, Kennedy had a limited legislative record, but he won the Pulitzer Prize for his book *Profiles in Courage.*

In 1960, Kennedy won the Democratic nomination for president. As a running mate, he chose LYNDON B. JOHNSON, whose southern ties could help carry the South. During the campaign, Kennedy went on TELEVISION against Republican nominee RICHARD M. NIXON in the first televised debates. Kennedy's handsome appearance and cool rationality made him appealing to the public. He won the election in one of the tightest races on record.

At the age of 43, Kennedy was the youngest president ever to take office, and was also the first president born in the 20th century. Despite his charismatic appeal, he enjoyed but modest legislative success. He was outspoken, though, and he flooded Congress with requests, one of which was to put a man on the moon. He became the first

President John F. Kennedy greets Peace Corps volunteers, 1962   *(John F. Kennedy Library)*

president to allow press conferences to be televised live for he wanted direct communication with the public. In March 1961, Kennedy created the PEACE CORPS, which sent many young Americans to poor countries as teachers, heath care providers, and technicians.

Kennedy appointed an unprecedented number of African Americans to office, including NATIONAL ASSOCIATION FOR THE ADVANCEMENT OF COLORED PEOPLE (NAACP) attorney THURGOOD MARSHALL. Kennedy also took steps against racial discrimination in federal employment. Under Attorney General ROBERT F. KENNEDY, the Justice Department stepped up enforcement of existing voting rights laws. With Kennedy making an effort in race relations, many blacks felt they had an ally in the White House, even though he was unable to secure passage of a civil rights bill aimed at providing equal accommodations for blacks and whites.

Kennedy believed he played an even more important role in foreign affairs. On April 17, 1961, he supported a CENTRAL INTELLIGENCE AGENCY (CIA) plan to invade Cuba in an attempt to liberate the island from Fidel Castro, the communist ruler. The BAY OF PIGS invasion turned out to be an embarrassment to the nation. Kennedy took total responsibility for the failure. Later Kennedy recouped lost prestige in the CUBAN MISSILE CRISIS, in which he stood up to the SOVIET UNION and leader Nikita Khrushchev, and he forged the removal of mid-range missiles from Cuba

Kennedy increased aid to South Vietnam in the VIETNAM WAR. He eventually sent 16,000 military advisers, some of whom saw combat. With the United States clearly opposing COMMUNISM in Vietnam, Kennedy left a legacy to his successor, Lyndon B. Johnson.

On November 22, 1963, the nation and the world were stunned as Kennedy was shot to death as he rode in a motorcade in Dallas, Texas. Within hours of the shooting, the Dallas police arrested LEE HARVEY OSWALD, Kennedy's alleged assassin. With the aid of television, Kennedy's assassination became a dramatic public event.

Further reading: Ralph G. Martin, *A Hero for Our Time: An Intimate Story of the Kennedy Years* (New York: Macmillan, 1983); Herbert Parmet, *JFK, The Presidency of John F. Kennedy* (New York: Dial Press, 1983); Richard Reeves, *President Kennedy: Profile of Power* (New York: Simon & Schuster, 1993); Vito N. Silvestri, *Becoming JFK: A Profile in Communication* (Westport, Conn.: Praeger, 2000).

— Robert A. Deahl

Kennedy, Robert F. (1925–1968)

Robert "Bobby" F. Kennedy, brother of President JOHN F. KENNEDY, played an important role in American government from the early 1950s until he was assassinated in 1968.

Kennedy, born in Brookline, Massachusetts, on November 20, 1925, enjoyed the affluent lifestyle of the legendary Kennedy family. Many strong values were instilled in him during his youth. He enrolled at Harvard University and then left in 1944 to join the U.S. Navy near the end of World War II. After his discharge, Kennedy returned to Harvard where he played intercollegiate football and received his undergraduate degree in 1948. After graduation, he attended the University of Virginia Law School, from which he graduated in 1951. Soon after, Kennedy was admitted to the Massachusetts Bar.

With strong family political connections in Washington, D.C., Kennedy began his career as a congressional investigator working under JOSEPH R. MCCARTHY. Kennedy did not stay in this position for long. Seven months later, he walked out on McCarthy in protest against the methods he used to expose people as communists. He later returned as a congressional investigator and helped lead the Senate Select Committee on Improper Activities. He resigned from his position in 1960 to help manage the presidential campaign of his brother John.

During his brother's presidency, Robert became attorney general. He received some criticism for obtaining such a powerful position so early in his career. When his brother was questioned about appointing Robert, John Kennedy stated, "I see nothing wrong with giving Robert some legal experience before he goes out to practice law." During his time in this office, Robert supported the Civil Rights movement. Through his work he encouraged the desegregation of schools across the South. He was also a strong supporter of the CIVIL RIGHTS ACT OF 1964, which extended equal rights to minorities.

In 1964, Kennedy ran for, and won, the senatorial election in New York. The win came easily due to the popularity of the Kennedy family and Robert's strong support of civil rights.

Kennedy found Senate work slow-paced compared to prior political activities. Even so, he accomplished several things for the state of New York. He secured funding to build parks in poor neighborhoods, sponsored parties for underprivileged children, and aided the disadvantaged around the state. Kennedy also waged a revolutionary campaign against cigarette companies. Realizing the potential health hazard associated with smoking, Kennedy pressured the cigarette companies, TELEVISION, and magazines alike to discontinue cigarette advertisements. Kennedy received little support on this issue, but he continued to fight against these powerful conglomerates. While in office, Kennedy also led the opposition to the escalation of the VIETNAM WAR. He was against the violence, and felt the matter could be solved through peaceful negotiations.

U.S. attorney general Robert Kennedy reporting to President Johnson in Washington, D.C., 1964   *(Library of Congress)*

In March 1968, after much thought, Robert F. Kennedy announced his bid for the presidency. Kennedy again received massive support in his campaign, especially from minorities across the United States. He won 5 of the 6 presidential primaries that he entered, winning his last in California. On June 6, 1968, after delivering his victory speech to his supporters in Los Angeles, Kennedy was fatally shot by an Arab immigrant, Sirhan Bishara Sirhan, and he died shortly after at the Good Samaritan Hospital. Sirhan was quickly convicted of first-degree murder.

In a variety of offices, Kennedy helped fight the battle for equality in America.

Further reading: William J. Vanden Heuvel and Milton S. Gwirtzman, *On His Own: Robert F. Kennedy, 1964–1968* (Garden City, N.Y.: Doubleday, 1970); George Plimpton, ed. *American Journey: The Times of Robert Kennedy* (New York: Harcourt Brace Jovanovich, 1970); Arthur M. Schlessinger, Jr., *Robert Kennedy and His Times.* 2 vols. (Boston: Houghton Mifflin, 1978).

— Jennifer Howell

Kerouac, Jack (1922–1969)

Jack Kerouac, author of the meandering novel *On the Road,* was one of the most influential writers of the BEAT GENERATION, which stressed spontaneity and spirituality in writing and in life.

Kerouac was born in Lowell, Massachusetts, on March 12, 1922, to Leo and Gabrielle Kerouac. His parents were of French-Canadian descent and spoke French at home; Kerouac did not learn English until he entered school at the age of six. In high school, Kerouac excelled at football, earning a scholarship to Columbia University in 1940. In his first year of college, he was injured and sat out the rest of the football season. By his sophomore year, Kerouac had lost interest in football and college and dropped out to join the U.S. Navy. In boot camp, he hated the discipline and left the military with an honorable discharge.

After leaving the navy, Kerouac moved to New York to join his girlfriend, Edie Parker. Through Parker, Kerouac met William Burroughs, a morphine addict who became a mentor, and ALLEN GINSBERG, a young poet. Kerouac also came into contact with Neal Cassady, who had moved to

New York from Denver. Life to Cassady was "pleasure and kicks," and Ginsberg fell in love with him. Together, this group of men formed the leadership of the Beat Generation and embodied the angst and energy of the group.

Kerouac worked at odd jobs and occasionally shipped out as a merchant seaman. In 1946, he began writing his novel *The Town and the City*. The novel fictionalized Kerouac's boyhood in Lowell and the new world he discovered in New York, especially the Greenwich Village area. Kerouac described the disillusioned intellectuals, referring to them as "beat," a term that came to epitomize Kerouac, Ginsberg, Burroughs, Cassady, and the postwar generation. After *The Town and the City* failed to bring Kerouac fame, he hitchhiked to Denver to see Cassady. In 1951, Kerouac began to write *On the Road*, a story about his adventures traveling with Cassady. The novel was turned down by two publishers, including Kerouac's own publisher who found the book too "new and unusual" to appeal to the public. Following this failure, Kerouac moved to Mexico to see Burroughs. While there, he began to experiment with drugs and wrote poetry. In 1954, author and editor Malcolm Cowley agreed to publish *On the Road*, as long as Kerouac agreed to edit the manuscript, which was simply a 250-foot roll of paper with a lack of standard punctuation and structure. *On the Road* finally appeared in 1957, and it was an immediate success, prompting others to use Kerouac's unstructured and chaotic style of writing in their work.

Following the success of *On the Road*, Kerouac wrote a series of other books about adventures with Cassady and his other friends. *The Dharma Bums* (1958) dealt with West Coast Beats, while *Visions of Cassady* (1960) centered on conversations with Neal Cassady in which Cassady gave his thoughts on travels, girls, and cars. Kerouac's books found a large audience on college campuses, where groups of "beatniks" gathered in coffeehouses to read the words of their heroes, and celebrate their unconventional, anti-materialistic lives.

In his last years, Kerouac went into semi-retirement and seclusion in Florida to take care of his invalid mother. He spent much of his time drinking and listening to jazz MUSIC. Kerouac made one more appearance in the 1960s and shocked his audience of readers when he came out in support of the VIETNAM WAR. In 1969, after a night of heavy drinking, Kerouac began to hemorrhage and was rushed to the hospital where he died at age 46.

Further reading: Ann Charters, *Kerouac: A Biography* (San Francisco: Straight Arrow Books, 1973); Dennis McNally, *Desolate Angel* (New York: Random House, 1979).

— Sarah Brenner

King, Martin Luther, Jr. (1929–1968)

Martin Luther King, Jr., was one of the most influential black leaders of the 20th century and a key figure in the Civil Rights movement.

Born on January 15, 1929, in Atlanta, Georgia, King was the son of the pastor of the Ebenezer Baptist Church. He entered Morehouse College at the age of 15, and he later studied at the Crozer Theological Seminary and Boston University, where he received a doctorate from the School of Theology.

In 1954 King became the pastor of the Dexter Avenue Baptist Church in Montgomery, Alabama. The next year, on December 1, 1955, ROSA PARKS, an African-American seamstress and civil rights activist, refused, while riding a Montgomery city bus, to give up her seat to a white male passenger. In the resulting bus boycott by the black citizens of Montgomery, King became a spokesperson. With the support of other civil rights leaders, King inspired 50,000 African Americans to walk with pride as part of a campaign based on nonviolence such as that of the Indian leader Mohandas Gandhi, whom King had studied. King was also elected president of the Montgomery Improvement Association. The Montgomery bus boycott lasted 381 days, ending on December 20, 1956, when a court order ended the bus company's policy of racial SEGREGATION in transportation.

Near the end of the bus boycott, 52-year-old civil rights activist ELLA BAKER approached King with the idea of forming a permanent organization of black ministers to coordinate civil rights activities in the South. King established the SOUTHERN CHRISTIAN LEADERSHIP CONFERENCE (SCLC) in 1957 and served as the organization's president. He traveled throughout the United States, supporting nonviolent civil rights struggles. In 1960, King went to Atlanta, Georgia, to support a student-led civil rights campaign. He participated in SIT-INS over racially segregated lunch counters, and, along with 36 students, he was arrested. He was sentenced to four months of hard labor.

King's incarceration came to the attention of Democratic presidential candidate JOHN F. KENNEDY, who enlisted his brother ROBERT F. KENNEDY to pressure the sentencing judge to terminate King's sentence, and King was released. Kennedy's decision to aid King was believed to play a crucial part in securing the support of African Americans in his narrow presidential victory over Richard M. Nixon.

In 1963, King and the SCLC, directed their attention to Birmingham, Alabama. King labeled Birmingham "probably the most thoroughly segregated city in the United States." The SCLC decided to boycott downtown department stores, hold marches and demonstrations, and present a petition to desegregate stores and lunch counters and to provide employment opportunities. King and SCLC vice president Ralph Abernathy led a march to City Hall, where they and their fellow marchers were halted by police and arrested. In jail, King wrote the famous "Letter from Birmingham Jail," which attracted national attention and became an important statement in the struggle.

In the summer of 1963, King helped organize the MARCH ON WASHINGTON, in which 250,000 people descended upon the nation's capital in the largest protest yet held. At the march, King gave his famous "I Have a Dream" speech from the steps of the Lincoln Memorial. To listeners, and audiences worldwide, he proclaimed: "I say to you today, my friends, that in spite of the difficulties and frustrations of the moment, I still have a dream. It is a dream deeply rooted in the American dream. I have a dream that one day this nation will rise up and live out the true meaning of its creed: 'We hold these truths to be self-evident: that all men are created equal.'"

After passage of the CIVIL RIGHTS ACT OF 1964, which outlawed discrimination in public accommodations, King turned to the issue of voting. He organized a march in Selma, Alabama, where more than 2,000 people tried unsuccessfully to register to vote. When they refused to leave, over 1,500 people were arrested. King said, "This is Selma, Alabama. There are more Negroes in jail with me than there are on the voting rolls."

The SCLC next planned a 54-mile march from Selma to Montgomery, where the marchers planned to present a list of grievances to the governor. After being halted three times, the marchers were finally allowed to proceed to Montgomery in March 1965. At the beginning, only 3,200 people marched in protest, but by the time King was ready to speak from the steps of the state capitol, nearly 50,000 people were in attendance. President LYNDON B. JOHNSON, in response to turbulence in Selma, introduced a voting rights bill in Congress, which became the VOTING RIGHTS ACT OF 1965 after its passage in August.

By the mid-1960s, King's message of nonviolence and integration failed to address the growing anger of a black underclass trapped in poverty. As new, more radical leaders such as MALCOLM X and STOKELY CARMICHAEL began to advocate militant action, King answered by campaigning for more advanced reforms. In January 1966, the SCLC launched a crusade to address slum conditions in Chicago. King, however, was disappointed that his following in the North was not nearly as strong as in the South, and the campaign was a failure. As a result, King shifted his focus from civil rights—an issue closely associated with middle-class African Americans—to fighting for economic equality among the poor.

King faced resistance when he publicly declared his opposition to the VIETNAM WAR. While he voiced his opin-

Rev. Dr. Martin Luther King, Jr., at a New York press conference, 1961   *(Library of Congress)*

ion as early as 1965, King became embroiled in the protest in 1967, denouncing the actions of the government and angering many Americans who continued to support Lyndon Johnson. King emphasized the disproportionate number of African Americans who fought and died in the war and the war's effect on civil rights reform. As more funds were directed toward the conflict in Vietnam, less money was available for social programs that benefited African Americans. Once having praised Johnson for his civil rights stand, King now criticized him for his continued involvement in Vietnam.

Meanwhile, King became even more committed to class issues and the plight of the urban poor. He called for a redistribution of wealth from the rich to the poor, and, in the fall of 1967, he began organizing the Poor People's March on Washington. His focus on economic rights led him in 1968 to Memphis, Tennessee, where he supported striking sanitation workers. Black workers had been sent home when it began to rain, while white workers were allowed to stay, earning a whole day's pay. When black workers were compensated with only two hours pay, they banded together against the city of Memphis, demanding equal treatment and pay. King joined the strike, hoping that a nonviolent walkout would help further his message of economic equality. In April, he gave a moving speech to encourage the strikers and reaffirm his commitment to racial equality, stating, "I may not get there with you. But we as a people will get to the promised land." The following day, on April 4, King was assassinated as he stood on the balcony of the Lorraine Hotel in Memphis. At his funeral, he was carried to his resting place near the Ebenezer Baptist Church in Atlanta on a mule-drawn cart. Eighteen years later, Martin Luther King, Jr. Day became a nationally recognized holiday.

Further reading: Taylor Branch, *Parting the Waters: America in the King Years, 1954–1963* (New York: Simon & Schuster, 1998); Taylor Branch, *Pillar of Fire: America in the King Years, 1963–65* (New York: Simon & Schuster, 1998); William R. Miller, *Martin Luther King: His Life, Martyrdom, and Meaning for the World* (New York: Weybright & Talley, 1968).

— Robert A. Deahl

Kinsey, Alfred C. (1894–1956)

A pioneer sex researcher, Alfred C. Kinsey and his research team collected over 18,000 sex histories between 1939 and 1956. His widely publicized and informative studies introduced sex as a topic for public discussion, recognized sexual diversity, and paved the way for modern sex research and therapy.

Born to strict Methodist parents on June 23, 1894, in Hoboken, New Jersey, Kinsey was frail and ill throughout much of his youth. He expressed interest in botany in high school, started college at Stevens Institute (the school where his father taught) in 1912, and transferred to Bowdoin College in 1914. Kinsey excelled at Bowdoin, graduating magna cum laude with a B.S. in biology and psychology and securing a scholarship to the Busse Institute at Harvard for studies in applied biology.

Kinsey studied gall wasps (tiny insects) in graduate school, earning his Ph.D. in 1919. In 1920, Indiana University hired Kinsey as an assistant professor of zoology. Kinsey merited a reputation as a world-renowned expert on gall wasps by 1930 with the publication of his authoritative 577-page study *The Gall Wasp Genus Cynips— A Study in the Origin of the Species.* Kinsey identified new species of gall wasps and advanced theories of evolution and taxonomy.

Kinsey expressed interest in sex as a subject for scientific research throughout the 1930s. In 1938, he taught the first marriage course at Indiana University and noted the vast amount of ignorance surrounding sex. In his marriage course, which became one of the most popular courses at the university, Kinsey offered an open and frank discussion of sex. He also invited students to share their sexual histo-

ries with him and conducted extensive one-on-one interviews with volunteers. Collecting these sex histories foreshadowed the more systematic study that he would launch a year later.

Similar to his gall wasp studies, Kinsey decided to collect huge samples of sex histories. He soon began interviewing people throughout the country, especially studying communities in Chicago and New York. In particular, he interviewed male homosexuals and theorized about the continuum of human sexuality. He devised a now famous graded scale that ranged from 0-6 and reflected sexual identity. A score of zero indicated exclusive heterosexuality, while a score of six showed exclusive homosexuality.

In 1939, Kinsey launched his statistical study of sex that defined the physiological facts of sex and documented what people did during sexual activity, a subject virtually untouched by science up to that point. His substantial

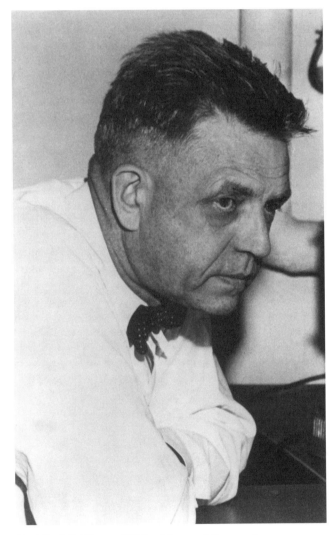

Dr. Alfred C. Kinsey, 1954 *(Library of Congress)*

interviews recorded individual sex histories. Public criticism of his subject matter mounted and in 1940 Indiana University president Herman Wells asked Kinsey to choose to pursue either full-time sex studies or the continuation of his marriage course. Kinsey opted to pursue his research on sex. In that year he also offered his first formal paper on his sex research at the American Association for the Advancement of Science.

Over the next several years, Kinsey pursued his sex studies and collected tens of thousands of interviews. He was intrigued with documenting all sexual behavior, especially sexual behavior that was frequently labeled "unusual" or "perverted." He collected statistics on masturbation, erotica, homosexuality, bisexuality, and sadomasochism—topics shrouded by public ignorance. He continued teaching and lecturing, although most of his attention was directed toward his sex research. In 1941, Kinsey won a research grant from the National Research Council. With the first of many grants from this organization, Kinsey was able to hire additional researchers and expand the scope of his study. By 1947 he had amassed enough data to warrant the creation of the Institute for Sex Research. In addition to holding his interview material, the institute would house Kinsey's vast library on subjects and artifacts related to sexuality.

In 1948, Kinsey published the first report from his research, *Sexual Behavior in the Human Male.* It garnered unprecedented popular acclaim, and the publisher quickly sold thousands of copies. Moreover, academic journals and popular magazines devoted space to discuss sex and Kinsey's research. In one frequently cited report, Kinsey concluded that 37 percent of the male population had at least one homosexual experience over the course of a lifetime and that 4 percent were exclusively homosexual. In 1953, he published *Sexual Behavior in the Human Female,* again to wide acclaim. Some of the most notable findings in this volume included the biological impossibility of the vaginal orgasm, the frequency of female masturbation, and the physiological similarities of sexual response in men and women. Although he envisioned a nine-volume series based on his research, health problems prevented him from attaining this goal. He continued to amass sex histories, conducting his last interview in 1956. He died later that year at the age of 62.

Further reading: Jonathan Gathorne-Hardy. *Sex: The Measure of All Things, A Life of Alfred C. Kinsey* (Bloomington: Indiana University Press, 1998).

— Kirstin Gardner

Korean War

The Korean War was the first major American military engagement after World War II.

At its core a civil war, the Korean War pitted South Korea (Republic of Korea) against North Korea (Democratic People's Republic of Korea) in a struggle to reunite a nation divided in the aftermath of World War II. Fighting alongside the Republic of Korea Army were American and other forces mobilized under the banner of the United Nations (UN). The (North) Korean People's Army was joined by Chinese army forces and supported by the SOVIET UNION.

The underlying cause of the Korean War was the nature of the post–World War II occupation of Korea. Since 1910 Korea had been controlled by Japan and then Allied troops occupied the former Axis possession following World War II. In an arrangement necessitated by the rapid end of the war, American forces held the southern half of the country below the 38th parallel while Soviet forces occupied the northern half. Since the Koreans were not believed to be fit for immediate self-government, the Americans in the South and the Soviets in the North worked to develop favorable political elites and groom them for self-governance. The result led to the creation of the separate states of South Korea, under the leadership of Syngman Rhee, and North Korea, under the leadership of Kim-Il Sung. Both men and their respective governments saw themselves as the rightful leaders of all of Korea and were supported as such by the respective occupying powers.

Prior to 1950, pressure mounted on the administration of President HARRY S. TRUMAN to deal with the perceived international threat of COMMUNISM at home and abroad. The 1947 TRUMAN DOCTRINE underscored the theory of containment, whereby the United States would attempt to prevent the spread of communism beyond where it already existed. In 1949, however, communist forces under the leadership of Mao Zedong emerged victorious in China, and the Soviet Union successfully detonated an ATOMIC BOMB. The Truman administration was blamed for "losing" China, and an ARMS RACE developed between the United States and the Soviet Union. As a result, American fears of communism escalated. When war broke out in Korea, the Truman administration was politically compelled to intervene.

The conflict began on June 25, 1950, when North Korean forces crossed the 38th parallel and invaded South Korea. Kim Il-Sung masterminded the invasion after securing approval from both Soviet leader Joseph Stalin and Mao Zedong. North Korean forces advanced swiftly through the South, capturing the capital city of Seoul on June 28. South Korean forces were in disarray, severely outgunned by the Soviet- and Chinese-backed army of the North.

American secretary of state DEAN ACHESON insisted that the United States respond swiftly to defend South Korea. In order to rally public and international support, the American government asked the UN Security Council to condemn the North Korean aggression and repel the invasion. The Soviet delegate to the Security Council held the power to veto this decision, but he was currently boycotting the council, and so action proceeded. American forces therefore fought the Korean War under the banner of the United Nations (UN), joined by British, Canadian, Australian, and other troops. Due in part to UN involvement, the United States never officially declared war against North Korea or China. The Korean War was instead referred to as a "United Nations police action."

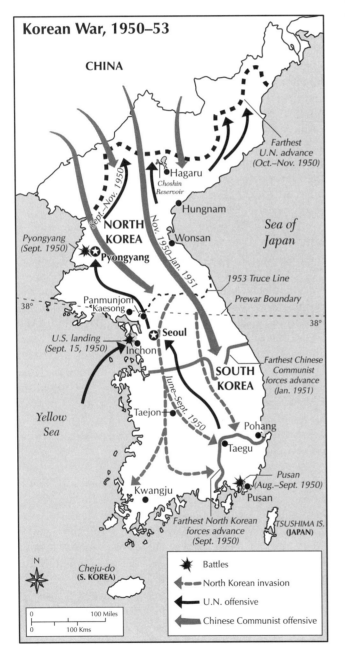

The first American troops arrived in South Korea in early July and were put under the overall command of General DOUGLAS MACARTHUR. South Korean and UN forces were forced to retreat to the southeastern tip of the peninsula around the city of Pusan until sufficient American military strength was present in Korea. After a North Korean assault on Pusan was repelled, MacArthur's troops staged an amphibious assault behind the front lines on the city of Inchon, catching the North Koreans by surprise and forcing them to retreat in disarray. By October, South Korean troops were chasing the North Korean army back across the 38th parallel, and under authority from the UN General Assembly, UN forces joined South Korea in invading the North in an attempt to unify the country.

Shortly after the advancement of UN forces across the 38th parallel, Mao Zedong ordered Chinese troops to cross the Yalu River and join the fighting on the side of the North Koreans. Although UN forces swiftly advanced up the peninsula, capturing the North Korean capital of Pyongyang and driving as far as the Yalu River in some areas, the entry of China into the war balanced the playing field. In December 1950, Chinese and North Korean troops successfully drove South Korean and UN forces back beyond the 38th parallel. By June 1951, a series of offensives and counteroffensives left the war a stalemate. Although fighting continued well into 1953, most major territorial penetrations were over by mid-1951.

Meanwhile, tension between Truman and General MacArthur escalated, boiling over in April 1951, when Truman relieved MacArthur of his command. MacArthur strongly advocated the use of atomic weapons against North Korean and Chinese targets, but Truman was unwilling to risk having a "police action" turn into a nuclear war. General Matthew Ridgway replaced MacArthur as commander in Korea, and MacArthur returned to a hero's welcome in the United States. Truman's conflict with the popular MacArthur and the stalemate in Korea helped undermine the president's credibility at home. Although eligible to seek another term, Truman declined to run for reelection in 1952. Instead, World War II hero DWIGHT D. EISENHOWER won the presidential election, having campaigned in part on a pledge to go to Korea in order to end the war.

A state of stalemate persisted from mid-1951 through 1953 largely because the two sides were unable to work out a compromise on the issue of prisoners of war (POWs). North Korea mistreated many American and allied POWs, and many captured North Korean soldiers wanted to remain in South Korea. In addition, Syngman Rhee and the South Korean government stymied progress in securing an end to hostilities by insisting that any peace plan should reunify Korea.

Finally, on July 27, 1953, a cease-fire agreement was signed, ending the Korean War. American casualties during

Pvt. Seiju Nakandakarc and Pvt. Ralph Saul operate a new 3.5 bazooka on the front lines somewhere in Korea, 1950 *(Library of Congress)*

the conflict totaled approximately 34,000 dead and many more wounded, with other UN nations suffering modest casualties. An estimated 4 million Koreans died during the war, with two-thirds of that number civilians. The physical destruction to the peninsula, and especially to North Korea's economic infrastructure, was incalculable. Tension between the two halves of Korea persisted, with North Korea going so far as to boycott the 1988 Summer Olympics in Seoul.

The long-term effects on the United States also ran deep. The United States and the People's Republic of China did not normalize relations until 1973. Additionally, although Eisenhower sought to curtail military expenditures, the Korean War played a key role in the expansion of what Eisenhower called the MILITARY-INDUSTRIAL COMPLEX. The budget for U.S. defense spending was increased by billions of dollars during the war, while the conflict established a precedent for American military intervention against communism in remote parts of the globe, leading in part to eventual American intervention in the VIETNAM WAR.

Further reading: Bruce Cumings, *Origins of the Korean War* (Princeton, N.J.: Princeton University Press, 1981); Peter Lowe, *The Korean War* (New York: St. Martin's Press, 2000).

— Phil Huckelberry

Korematsu, Fred   See Volume VIII

Kroc, Ray See McDonald's

Ku Klux Klan (KKK)

The Ku Klux Klan, a white supremacy organization originally founded in Tennessee in 1865, experienced a resurgence in membership during the Civil Rights movement that took place in America during the middle of the 20th century.

After fading at the end of Reconstruction, the KKK was revived at Stone Mountain, Georgia, in 1915. The KKK was active in the 1920s, with its membership reaching millions of people. By the 1930s, however, Klan membership declined due to the Great Depression, feuding among leaders, and the exposure of terrorist activities undertaken by members. The racial turmoil ignited by the Civil Rights

Robert Shelton, imperial wizard of the Ku Klux Klan, stands before a burning cross in Hemingway, South Carolina, 1965 *(Library of Congress)*

movement gave the KKK a window of opportunity to revive. While the Klan took aim at Jewish, Catholic, and black Americans in the 1920s, its focus by the middle of the 1900s was largely against blacks.

The "Invisible Empire," another name for the KKK, was (and is) led by the "Imperial Wizard," followed by leaders such as the "Grand Dragon," "Titan," and "Cyclops." Over the years, the Ku Klux Klan has relied heavily upon the secrecy maintained by its members. Most of the acts that the organization engaged in were illegal terrorist actions, requiring the utmost loyalty from members in maintaining secrecy. To aid in masking members' identity, KKK members donned what became trademark white robes and hoods during demonstrations and raids.

The Civil Rights movement troubled many whites in the South. Reconstruction failed to integrate blacks into American life and end racism, and the white community became accustomed to the practice of SEGREGATION in the South. Because the Civil Rights movement sought to put an end to the traditional practices of Southern society, many white Southerners became outraged at such efforts and interest in the KKK grew.

The Ku Klux Klan relied heavily upon scare tactics to intimidate blacks and whites alike who attempted to seek equal rights for all. Many of these methods were extremely violent, sometimes leading to murder. The KKK was known for burning crosses, schools, and churches. Members also bombed buildings, beat and maimed people, committed murders, and lynched African Americans who pushed too hard for equality. Indeed, the KKK was responsible for most of the transgressions against civil rights activists at this time.

In 1965, the HOUSE UN-AMERICAN ACTIVITIES COMMITTEE (HUAC) opened a public investigation of members of the KKK. The committee first questioned Robert M. Shelton, Jr., the imperial wizard, then other Klan leaders. Many of these members utilized their constitutional rights to remain silent to avoid self-incrimination. Most of the members did not testify out of fear for their own personal safety. Klansman Ralph Pryor stated, "The government can't protect me. . . . If I testify, some day they are going to find me in Selma, Alabama, with 30 bullet holes in me, and that killer is going to get off scot free." An article in the *New York Times* during the trial of Klansman Daniel Burros, a leader in New York, exposed the fact that he was born and raised Jewish. Upon the publication of this article, Burrows committed suicide out of fear of his fellow Klansmen's reaction to the news.

These committee hearings produced extensive knowledge of the workings of the KKK. They revealed over 15,000 active Klansmen during this time in states all over America. Imperial Wizard Shelton was convicted of contempt of Congress for not producing subpoenaed records and received a sentence of one year of jail time.

The Ku Klux Klan began to lose its following again toward the end of the 1960s. Just as the reputation for committing heinous crimes weakened the organization at the end of the 1920s, the Klan's identification with such acts caused its demise yet again decades later. People exposed as members of the Klan were now the ones who experienced public ridicule.

Even so, the KKK is still alive and active in America today, its presence usually made visible in marches and demonstrations. While it does not enjoy the large numbers and support that it once did, it still attracts a following.

Further reading: Keesing's Research Report, *Race Relations in the USA 1954–1968* (New York: Charles Scribner's Sons, 1970); Nancy MacLean, *Behind the Mask of Chivalry: The Making of the Second Ku Klux Klan* (New York: Oxford University Press, 1994); Jack Nelson, *Terror in the Night: The Klan's Campaign against the Jews* (New York: Simon & Schuster, 1993).

— Jennifer Howell

L

labor

Changes in labor during the postwar years reflected the country's efforts to cope first with DEMOBILIZATION and with an economic boom.

From the end of World War II through the 1960s, the percentage of the country's population that engaged in paid labor rose slightly, but steadily, from what it had been before the fluctuations of the Great Depression and World War II. By the late 1960s, more than 60 percent of the non-institutionalized adult population engaged in some form of compensated labor. The tasks and occupations that these people performed differed in many ways from those done by previous generations.

Aside from ever-increasing mechanization of most production processes, there were important structural changes taking place in the ECONOMY that affected the type of labor Americans did. AGRICULTURE declined drastically as an occupation throughout the period, falling from over 15 percent of the nation's workforce to around 3 percent by the late 1960s. Manual labor and manufacturing also lost ground, although not nearly as dramatically. Until the early 1950s, these traditional blue-collar occupations comprised a little more than 40 percent of jobs in America. By the late 1960s this had declined to around 36 percent. Professional and managerial positions grew steadily, from less than 15 percent of the workforce before the war to more than 20 percent by the late 1960s. Jobs in sales and clerical fields grew even more impressively. Accounting for a little more than 16 percent of all jobs before World War II, they constituted almost 25 percent at the end of the 1960s. Other SERVICE SECTOR professions saw a slight rise as well. It is also important to note the great reduction in the importance of paid domestic household service. Before World War II, it accounted for 4 in 10 jobs in the service sector. By the end of the 1960s, it was less than 1 in 8.

Shifts in America's occupational makeup influenced labor trends that had started during the Depression and war years. The war effort left America's workforce with more female employees and a stronger union structure. These trends were not consistently maintained in the years immediately after the war. During the war, many women entered the workplace to replace men who left to serve in the military. Although there was a noticeable drop in the percentage of American women working outside the home in the years immediately after World War II, the percentage of women in America's labor force remained higher than it had been in previous decades. By the late 1950s, the percentage of female workers had again reached the level it had in wartime, and it continued to climb. By 1968, more than 40 percent of the female population worked, up from a wartime high of 35 percent.

War work also gave women the opportunity to enter fields from which they had previously been excluded, especially in heavy industry. Although more women did work in these industries than before, women gained substantially in other sectors of the economy as well. Prior to World War II, women had constituted the majority of workers in the service industry (around 60 percent), and a preponderant majority in the domestic household sector of that industry, comprising around 95 percent of employees in that category. Even as that sector declined in economic importance, women still dominated the service industry in about the same proportion as before. The biggest gains for women, however, occurred in the clerical and sales sectors of the economy. Although they played a major role before the war, making up well over 40 percent of that part of the workforce, it was in the first decades after World War II that they began to dominate the clerical and sales sector. By the late 1960s, women comprised more than 60 percent of employees in that field. Over 40 percent of all women workers were employed in clerical and sales positions, double the number that worked in the next largest category, the domestic service industry. Women also significantly increased their presence in the managerial and professional

Occupational Distribution, 1940–70

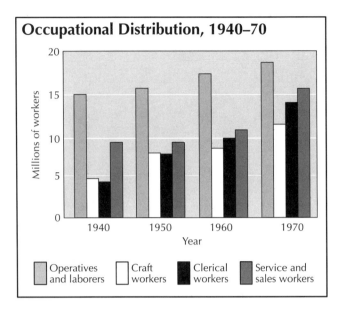

The percentage of workers represented by the UNION MOVEMENT continued to rise in the first decade after the war, leveling off at slightly more than 25 percent of all laborers by the mid-1950s. These years also appeared promising for organized labor because of the 1955 merger of the AMERICAN FEDERATION OF LABOR (AFL) and the CONGRESS OF INDUSTRIAL ORGANIZATIONS (CIO). This proved, however, to be the high-water mark for the American union movement in the 20th century. Although union membership continued to rise numerically, the percentage of the workforce that was unionized steadily declined starting in the late 1950s. Scholars have attributed this drop to several long-term economic changes that occurred during this period. Some of the decline was caused by a decrease in the share of America's workforce that was employed in sectors that were traditionally heavily unionized, such as manufacturing and mining, and the spreading of those sectors to areas that were historically hostile to unions. Labor leaders did try to compensate for this decline by branching into sectors of the economy that they previously ignored, such as agriculture with the UNITED FARM WORKERS and public sector employees through the American Federation of State, County, and Municipal Employees. Corruption scandals and unfriendly federal legislation such as the TAFT-HARTLEY ACT and Landrum-Griffin Act also hurt the effectiveness of unions, as did the increasingly aloof attitude of many union leaders to their rank and file, dubbed "Tuxedo Unionism" by critical union members.

Despite the waning influence of organized labor, American workers saw some important improvements in their position during the first decades after World War II. Employment contracts began to include many provisions favorable to workers; such as medical coverage, paid vacations, guaranteed annual wages, and automatic COST-OF-LIVING ADJUSTMENTS (COLA). The minimum wage was increased by every administration in this period, quadrupling from $.40 cents an hour in 1945 to $1.60 in 1968.

The administration of LYNDON B. JOHNSON was most friendly to the American laborer. With his ECONOMIC OPPORTUNITY ACT OF 1964, the federal government took a sustained, active role in helping even the most disadvantaged citizens acquire the skills needed to be productive members of the workforce through programs such as the JOB CORPS and encouragement of college work-study. The CIVIL RIGHTS ACT OF 1964 empowered the federal government to respond to worker complaints of racial and gender discrimination.

The character and conditions of American labor changed significantly from 1945 to 1968. Jobs shifted from the traditional mainstays of the economy, such as agriculture and manufacturing, to the more white-collar service sector, and office work positions. Although organized labor experienced some difficult times at the end of the period,

sector, from 1 in 8 to 1 in 4 during the war. This trend continued a steady, but slower, increase through the late 1960s, by which time almost 32 percent of white-collar workers in America were female. Women even gained some ground in the declining sectors of agriculture and manufacturing.

The type of woman working also changed during this period. Prior to World War II, most women who worked had never been married. The war reversed this situation. Married women outnumbered all others in the workforce. They maintained and expanded their preeminent position from 1945 to 1968. After the war, about 38 percent of working women had never been married, while 46 percent of female workers were currently married. By 1968, married women accounted for 63 percent of the female workforce and only 22 percent of working women had never been married. The percentage of women in the workforce who were widowed or divorced declined slightly in the postwar years from 17 percent to 14.6 percent.

Despite the gains made by women, the American workforce was still primarily male. Men held more than 75 percent of the better paying, more influential professional and managerial positions. Male dominance was even greater in blue-collar work, embodying the majority of the workforce. Over 80 percent of America's blue-collar laborers were male. Although the percentage of men in the workforce did drop slightly following World War II, by the late 1960s, over 80 percent of white men worked and over 75 percent of African-American males were employed. This discrepancy between the percentage of African-American and white males in the workforce comprised a new trend that started in the 1960s. In previous years, the percentage of men in each group that worked was roughly the same.

workers not only secured concrete gains from their employers, but also, by the 1960s, saw the federal government using its power to help the most vulnerable workers acquire and keep jobs.

Further reading: Robert H. Zieger, *American Workers, American Unions, 1920–1985* (Baltimore: The Johns Hopkins University Press, 1986).

— Dave Price

La Raza Unida

A Mexican-American political party established by José Angel Gutiérrez and other students in south Texas in 1970, La Raza Unida, or The United People, grew out of the Mexican-American Youth Organization formed in 1967 by Gutiérrez and several other students, which aimed at solving problems and developing leaders in the Chicano community.

From its birth in Texas, La Raza Unida spread throughout the Southwest. Under the guidance of RODOLFO "CORKY" GONZÁLES, leader of the Crusade for Justice, an active 1960s militant nationalist group based in Denver, Colorado, La Roza Unida gained support in Colorado. Meanwhile, in California, La Raza Unida expanded from the Northern California Bay Area to San Diego within six months. Other La Raza Unida affiliations soon followed in Arizona, New Mexico, and the Midwest.

The members, goals, and philosophies of La Raza Unida varied depending on the individual state and local communities. For instance, in Northern California, the party included Central and South Americans and Cubans as well as other Spanish-speaking people. The constituency in Southern California consisted mainly of Mexican Americans. The aspirations of La Raza Unida in Texas included rallying for Chicano representation, exposing and confronting Anglos as exploiters of Mexican Americans, and acquiring economic power for Chicano communities. California branches sought reforms in education, labor, and the prison system, as well as control of land and equality for women. The Colorado organization envisioned building the Aztlan nation, the mythic Aztec Indian homeland in the American Southwest, to serve Chicano people.

The main ideological differences within La Raza Unida stemmed from differences between Gutiérrez and Gonzáles. While both deemphasized national politics, Gonzáles called for a nationalist and socialist sociocultural revolution that would unite Chicanos and other oppressed groups. Gutiérrez sought to balance power through local action, using the party's national structure to garner attention and support for community efforts.

From its inception, La Raza Unida achieved numerous political gains, particularly in Texas and California. In 1970, La Raza Unida candidates won a total of 11 school board and city council elections in three south Texas cities. By 1971, party members successfully secured the offices of mayor and two city commissioner positions in San Antonio. In the same year in Oakland, California, La Raza Unida challengers made a strong showing, capturing 25 to 35 percent of the vote in school board elections.

Socially, the party provided leadership roles for women and it became a strong tool to unify Chicano communities throughout the Southwest. Mexican-American women participated as candidates and in the day-to-day affairs of the party. Their efforts provided the stimulus for the development of La Raza Unida's two feminist organizations: the Mujeres Pro-Raza Unida (Texas) and the Federación de Mujeres de la Raza Unida (California). The membership of La Raza Unida brought together poor Chicanos and Latinos, the young and the old, students, welfare recipients, ex-convicts, conservatives, radicals, and people who had never been involved in politics. The political victories of the early 1970s demonstrated that Chicanos could successfully unite to achieve positive change against a discriminatory system.

The political impetus of La Raza Unida spurred a cultural awakening in Chicano music, history, and literature. Chicano scholars challenged perceptions of Mexican Americans as passive victims and helped establish Chicano studies program at numerous universities. Although, at times, La Raza Unida invoked violence, it raised the political consciousness of a generation of Mexican Americans, particularly the youth, on an unprecedented scale.

Despite the successes in the elections of the early 1970s, La Raza Unida's influence had all but faded by 1978. From the outside, the party had been weakened by repeated sabotage from local courts that removed candidates and rejected or reversed vote counts. From within, La Raza Unida suffered from diverging ideologies, lack of young, trained organizers, few financial resources, and a general loss of appeal. Gutiérrez's 1982 resignation of his seat on the increasingly Democratic Party–controlled county commissioner's court in Crystal City, Texas, ended La Raza Unida's activities and influence.

Further reading: Ignacio M. García, *United We Win: The Rise and Fall of La Raza Unida Party* (Tucson: University of Arizona Press, 1989); Fernando Piñon, *Of Myths and Realities: Dynamics of Ethnic Politics* (New York: Vantage Press, 1978).

— Michelle Reid

Latin America (and foreign policy)

Latin America has long been an immediate and important sphere of influence for the United States, but during the COLD WAR, tensions between countries grew increasingly hostile as the influence of Soviet COMMUNISM made its way into the Southern Hemisphere.

During the post–World War II era, Latin America suffered from economic and social problems, including stagnant economic growth, poverty, illiteracy, inadequate health care, and a population boom. The United States hoped to see gradual, peaceful modernization led by a moderate political center, but the sharp divide between the rich and the poor left little room for moderation. Nationalist movements gained support and took on an anti-American character. The U.S. government feared that revolutionary nationalism would invite Soviet influence into this critical region. It sought to protect American investments, the market for U.S. exports, the strategic value of the Panama Canal, Caribbean naval bases, and reserves of oil and copper. In the process, Latin America became a cold war battleground.

The administration of HARRY S. TRUMAN launched two programs designed to transform the Monroe Doctrine into a more collective, multilateral effort. The 1947 Rio Pact was a defensive military alliance that promised reciprocal assistance if Soviet intervention threatened any country in the Western Hemisphere. The Organization of American States (OAS) was formed in 1948 to settle inter-American disputes. Article 15 of the OAS charter, inserted against American wishes, stated that member states did not have the right to intervene in the affairs of other member states.

Throughout the 1950s and 1960s, Latin America witnessed political instability that included a series of military coups, which were sometimes supported or organized by the CENTRAL INTELLIGENCE AGENCY (CIA). For example, the administration of DWIGHT D. EISENHOWER spearheaded a coup against the elected leader of Guatemala, Jacobo Arbenz Guzmán, in 1954. Foreigners, led by the United Fruit Company (UFCO), owned most of the big plantations that produced bananas and coffee for export in Guatemala. Arbenz sympathized with workers' strikes and expropriated and redistributed large amounts of UFCO land that lay fallow. In compensation he paid the company the low value it had set on the land for taxation purposes. The Eisenhower administration did not want this land redistribution to set a bad precedent throughout Latin America, and the administration became convinced that Guatemala had come under communist influence. Alarmed, Arbenz signed an arms deal with the Soviet Union. In response, the CIA planned a coup, selecting General Carlos Castillo Armas to lead an invasion of 150 troops and a few minor air raids from Honduras. The CIA-run radio station broadcast threats of a huge invasion force, and Arbenz, who commanded a disloyal army, panicked and fled Guatemala. Castillo took power, executing hundreds of Arbenz supporters in the process, and though he was assassinated in 1957, a long line of military dictators followed him.

The late 1950s marked a low point in inter-American relations. When Vice President Richard M. Nixon toured South America in 1958, he was met everywhere by angry anti-American demonstrations protesting U.S. support of armed strongmen in Venezuela and Cuba and interventions such as the Guatemala incident. An angry mob almost killed Nixon in Caracas, Venezuela. During the following year, Panamanians rioted in protest of continued American control of the Canal Zone, and Fidel Castro's rebels seized power in Cuba. The Castro government launched an ambitious reform program and expropriated U.S.–owned oil companies and other privately owned firms. Many attributed these developments to an international communist conspiracy.

Worried about its global image and Soviet encroachment, the American government sought to improve relations with Latin America and to bring about rapid social and political improvements in the late 1950s and early 1960s. Initiatives such as the Inter-American Development Bank and the ALLIANCE FOR PROGRESS that sought to promote economic and social development, however, were largely unsuccessful at combating the poverty and inequity of many Latin American societies. Furthermore, ANTI-COMMUNISM and the desire for stability continued to trump any intentions of altruism.

This pattern held during the presidency of LYNDON B. JOHNSON. The United States tacitly supported a military takeover in Brazil in 1964 after João Goulart, facing serious economic trouble, began to seize U.S. properties. The Brazilian military took power and began a 20-year dictatorship, while Johnson ordered an American naval fleet to stand off the coast of Brazil in case it was needed. In 1965, Johnson sent 20,000 American troops to the Dominican Republic to intervene in a civil war between the military regime and forces supporting Juan Bosch, an elected radical reformer. This intervention lasted for one year and helped put in power Joaquin Balaguer, a pro-American military man. Order was eventually restored and elections were held in 1966. The crisis in the Dominican Republic produced the Johnson Doctrine, which stated that an American president could use military force whenever he felt COMMUNISM threatened the Western Hemisphere.

Further reading: Walter LaFeber, *Inevitable Revolutions: The United States in Central America.* 2d ed. (New York: W. W. Norton, 1993); Stephen G. Rabe, *Eisenhower and Latin America: The Foreign Policy of Anticommunism* (Chapel Hill: University of North Carolina Press, 1988); ———, *The Most Dangerous Area in the World: John F. Kennedy Confronts Communist Revolution in Latin America* (Chapel Hill: University of North Carolina Press, 1999).

— Jennifer Walton

Latino movement

In the years following World War II, Latinos joined together in a united effort to bring about better political, economic, and educational opportunities for Spanish-speaking Americans across the nation.

Throughout the 20th century, increasing numbers of Mexican Americans and other Latin Americans immigrated to the United States. In the postwar period, many Mexican Americans, called Chicanos, entered the United States as BRACEROS, providing much-needed field-hand support to western AGRICULTURE. Under an agreement with the Mexican government, nearly 220,000 Mexicans entered the United States between 1942 and 1947, working in California truck farms, Texas cotton fields, and Northwest sugar-beet fields. The wartime employment boom also contributed to the rise of Latino populations in West Coast cities and other urban areas, as families and individuals came to America in search of greater opportunities and work. The largest numbers of Latinos came to the United States from the Caribbean, South America, Puerto Rico, and Mexico, settling primarily in the southwestern states, New York, and regions of Florida.

Once in the United States, however, opportunities were not often forthcoming. Large numbers of PUERTO RICANS, like many Mexicans under the BRACERO program, were brought to the United States through Operation Bootstrap in the 1940s and thereafter to work in fields and factories. Both groups, however, experienced racial hostility and were pushed out when economic pressures disfavored their presence. While they remained effectively disenfranchised at this time, it was this kind of treatment that primed both groups for a civil rights struggle.

During the 1950s political participation was curtailed in the Puerto Rican community, in New York specifically, by use of English literacy tests and later, sixth-grade educational equivalency tests that most first-generation emigrants could not pass. Community organizations formed in response to these injustices to provide social and economic assistance for Puerto Ricans.

Puerto Rico's commonwealth status, imposed after the 1898 Spanish-American War when Puerto Rico became a U.S. protectorate, led to nationalist sentiments for political autonomy. A group of Puerto Rican nationalists, including Lolita Lebrón, opened fire on the floor of the U.S. House of Representatives after displaying a Puerto Rican flag and proclaiming a desire for independence. While five congressmen were wounded, and the activists were sentenced to life in prison, they later received a presidential pardon, at which time Lebrón returned to Puerto Rico and became president of the Nationalist Party.

By the 1960s, Puerto Ricans questioned the progress being made in mainstream politics and became politically discontented with their local representatives, including the few elected Puerto Ricans, who some felt to be too focused on accommodation and personal political advancement. Riots erupted in Puerto Rican ghettoes with many identifying their struggle with that of African-American and Chicano activists. Groups such as the Young Lords were formed with the notion of community self-defense, much like the BLACK PANTHERS and the Brown Berets. Initiated in Chicago in 1967, the Young Lords later affiliated with other young militants in New York City as the party's ideas spread.

Meanwhile, among Mexican Americans the civil rights struggle was referred to as *El Movimiento* or the Chicano Movement. While it did not fully manifest itself until after 1968, the development of the movement can be observed in the decades leading up to that watershed year. The movement was multidimensional in character and included a student movement, an antiwar movement, demands for social justice and land rights, labor unionization efforts, a political party, and an arts movement, all expressive of regional experiences and concerns. Later, the movement also included issues raised by the concerns of Chicana feminists for WOMEN'S RIGHTS AND STATUS.

Elements of the movement extended back to when Mexican Americans organized mutual aid societies and League of United Latin American Citizens (LULAC) chapters earlier in the 20th century to support their communities, but some felt that these organizations should not take strong political stances. Responding to earlier pressures to Americanize, Mexican Americans returned home from World War II with a renewed sense of expectation that the United States would live up to its promises of equality. Despite their anticipation, Mexican Americans continued to suffer from injustices. In 1948 the G.I. Forum was created following the refusal to allow the burial of a Mexican-American war veteran in a "whites only" cemetery in Corpus Christi, Texas. Mexican Americans continued to organize, after successfully pressuring politicians to acknowledge and respect those who had supported the war effort, regarding other issues.

The movement also focused on another issue that had long been of concern to Mexican-American communities, namely, the inferior conditions of their schools. Community groups had been struggling for decent schools, and they demanded that the situation be remedied. The 1948 *Mendez* v. *Westminster School District* decision prohibited SEGREGATION of Mexican-American students and helped to set the stage for the 1954 *BROWN V. BOARD OF EDUCATION* ruling. Though the structure of formal segregation eventually began to give way, the predominant school experience of Mexican Americans remained characterized by informal segregation and so the struggle for educational improvements continued beyond the legal realm.

By the 1960s many Chicanos became critical of working within the system and suspicious of political accommodation, and, consequently, they wanted to change the terms of the debate. Confrontation became the preferred political strategy, though some organizations and leaders, committed to the earlier mainstream approach, continued to work within the DEMOCRATIC PARTY to try to achieve reforms. The Latino movement as a whole, however, sought to challenge the values of the dominant society, offering a critique of capitalism and calling for a renewed sense of culture and identity. An important element of this effort—like that of other social movements by people of color at this time—was a strong sense of the need for people to recover their histories and, with that knowledge, spark consciousness and politicization. Movement newspapers such as *El Grito del Norte,* established by activist Elizabeth "Betita" Martinez, spread information about political meetings and conferences and the ideas espoused at them.

The Latino movement and the migrant farm worker's struggle became intertwined in California with the formation of El Teatro Campesino by Luis Valdez in 1965. Valdez, who had been a student activist and traveled with a delegation of the Progressive Labor Party to Cuba, was an early critic of the accommodation and assimilation of earlier Mexican-American organizations. A radical organization, the Teatro was an effective consciousness-raising tool.

The desires and activities of the farm workers in California launched César Chávez and Dolores Huerta to status as national figures within the movement. As trained Community Services Organization (CSO) organizers committed to social justice, they helped to build the National Farm Workers Association (NFWA), which later merged with a union of Filipino farm workers into the UNITED FARM WORKERS in 1966. Activities in California helped encourage farm workers in Texas to hold marches and strike as well. When their demands were not received sympathetically, student activists in the Mexican America Youth Organization (MAYO) took note and helped organize Raza Unida conferences that in 1970 resulted in the formation of LA RAZA UNIDA to exert further pressure on the political process.

At about the same time in New Mexico, the long-held resentments of Latino farmers, and a tradition of protest, led to the enthusiastic response to the charismatic leadership of REIES LÓPEZ TIJERINA. The group Tijerina founded, La Alianza Federal de las Mercedes (The Federal Land-Grant Alliance), asserted land claims dating back to the 1848 Treaty of Guadalupe-Hidalgo. While not effective in regaining lands, Tijerina did become a notable symbol for participants in the movement. The activities of the Alianza inspired Chicanos to struggle for their civil rights and also brought attention to the poverty in the region.

Women provided another crucial element to the struggle. Though Chicana feminism did not flower until 1970, the seeds of the feminist critique lay in the experiences of women in the 1960s and in their analysis of the limitations of cultural nationalism. Feminists believed racism was a source of oppression for Chicanos, but they also felt that issues of sexism were being overlooked. The concerns of gay and lesbian Chicanos, who organized in opposition to the homophobia present in this (as well as other social movements of the time), later became more visible, especially as the Chicano movement made gains in institutions of higher education.

Further reading: Alma M. García, ed. *Chicana Feminist Thought: The Basic Historical Writings* (New York: Routledge, 1997); Juan Gómez-Quiñones, *Chicano Politics: Reality and Promise, 1940–1990* (Albuquerque: University of New Mexico Press, 1990); F. Arturo.Rosales, *Chicano! The History of the Mexican American Civil Rights Movement* (Houston: Arte Público Press, 1996); Rodolfo D. Torres, and George Katsiaficas, eds. *Latino Social Movements: Historical and Theoretical Perspectives* (New York: Routledge, 1999).

— Toni Nelson Herrara

League of Women Voters

Throughout its existence, the League of Women Voters (LWV) has functioned as a political mobilizer, increasing awareness of WOMEN'S STATUS AND RIGHTS, encouraging women to work through traditional channels to achieve political goals, and forming part of the women's rights wing of the feminist movement.

The LWV, a nonpartisan organization, emerged from the suffragist era to become one of the leading forces critically analyzing governmental problems and educating the public about these problems. In the post–World War II period, the LWV switched from defending the special interests of women to a broader program that encouraged women to become political activists. The league in these years worked to inform citizens about such issues as internationalism and economic development.

An offspring of the National American Woman Suffrage Association, the LWV formed in 1920 after the Nineteenth Amendment to the U.S. Constitution granting women the vote had been approved. With its sole purpose fulfilled, the older group disbanded and left the work of educating women about politics to the LWV. From its earliest years, the league defined as its mission the removal of legal and administrative discrimination against women. Reorganized in 1946, the league became activist and political though still determinedly nonpartisan. The changes enabled the LWV to take action on governmental measures and policies in the public interest by providing information, building public opinion, and supporting legislative measures. The LWV defined its role as influencing all parties by influencing the public. It neither supported nor opposed any political party, but it did encourage members as individuals to participate actively in the party or campaign of their choice.

With the number of people involved hovering around 100,000 in the 1940s, the LWV never managed to attract mass membership. It remained essentially a volunteer organization with unpaid national officers. Most members were in their 30s and 40s, married, college-educated, middle class, and white. Branches existed in all the states, as well as 1,050 localities, with nonpartisan community service contributing to a membership jump in the 1950s. Members preferred to participate in study groups, provide voter service, and concentrate on local political issues, while only a very small portion of the members encouraged the league to support legislation.

The LWV achieved its greatest success in creating public roles for women denied access to the usual sources of power. Its members became seasoned civic activists, and the issues that they focused upon included economic development, water pollution, U.S. security, individual freedom, and voter service. Equitable electoral apportionment also became a league concern, and several state branches pursued legal remedies to stop the disenfranchisement of urban dwellers by rural-dominated legislatures.

As internationalism expanded after the end of World War II, the LWV became an energetic supporter of the new United Nations (UN). When the San Francisco Conference convened to formally draft the UN Charter in 1945, Anne Hartwell Johnstone served as the league representative. Invited by the State Department to consult, she promoted league ideas for regional peace machinery and UN control over the development of atomic energy. When she was asked by the U.S. delegation to assume leadership in helping resolve the question of creating a Commission on the Status of Women as a specialized UN agency, Johnstone agreed. Although the LWV took no official position in support of such a body, its representative did work to establish the commission.

League internationalism also found expression in its consistent support for foreign economic assistance. The LWV backed the MARSHALL PLAN in 1948. It insisted that the key to expanding world trade lay through reciprocal trade agreements and the encouragement of imports. To educate citizens about the importance of world trade, the organization conducted a nationwide grass-roots survey in 1954 to help local communities better understand the actual impact of foreign trade on their own communities.

The League had long sought to avoid conflict by using educational tactics and it continued this strategy when faced with the question of civil rights for African Americans. All of the southern branches of the LWV had attempted to avoid internal disruption by staying neutral on the question of school desegregation. The national organization maintained an indirect approach to civil rights until the mid-1960s. In 1964, the LWV stated that it believed every citizen's right to vote should be protected, that everyone should have access to free public EDUCATION, and that no group should suffer legal or administrative disability. In 1966, a league consensus emerged for support of government programs promoting equal opportunity for all in education and employment. In 1968, the LWV agreed to support equal housing. The organization's social agenda also expanded to include the WAR ON POVERTY and the urban crisis. Having dropped its opposition to the Equal Rights Amendment in 1954, the league slowly became more active on behalf of women's interests in the late 1960s.

Further reading: Naomi Black, *Social Feminism* (Ithaca, N.Y.: Cornell University Press, 1989); Louise Young, *In the Public Interest* (New York: Greenwood, 1989).

— Carynn Neumann

Leary, Timothy (1920–1996)

Timothy Leary was a Harvard psychologist who, during the 1960s, promoted spiritual discovery through the use of drugs such as LSD (lysergic acid diethylamide). As a leader of the COUNTERCULTURE of the 1960s, Leary's slogan "Tune in, turn on, drop out" combined the pharmaceutical and sexual revolutions of the time.

Timothy Francis Leary was born in Springfield, Massachusetts, on October 22, 1920, the son of devout Irish Catholics. His father was an alcoholic, which caused strain in the household. Leary attended West Point and served in the U.S. Army during World War II. He earned a Ph.D. in psychology at the University of California at Berkeley. While at Berkeley, Leary traveled to Europe on a research grant and was visited by Frank Barron, a colleague. Barron told of the mushrooms he had eaten in Mexico, and the two discussed the possibility that these mushrooms could be the key to psychological metamorphosis. Upon returning to the United States, Leary taught at Harvard University. There he met colleague Richard Alpert. The two experimented with hallucinogenic mushrooms, and then later tried LSD themselves. They conducted experiments at Harvard on the effects of drugs on psychological and religious experiences. Against the wishes of the university, Leary and Alpert used students in their research, which led to the dismissal of both men in 1963.

Leary moved to New York, and was visited by members of the BEAT GENERATION such as ALLEN GINSBERG, JACK KEROUAC, and William Burroughs. In 1969, Leary was arrested and sentenced to 10 years imprisonment for marijuana possession. Richard M. Nixon referred to him as "the most dangerous man in America." In September 1970, helped by the Weather Underground, a radical revolutionary group, Leary escaped from the California State Men's Colony. He traveled to Algeria, was later captured in Afghanistan in 1973, and returned to a California prison. He was paroled in 1976 because of his cooperation in the investigation of others involved in the drug scene. Due to the investigation, Leary was denounced by his own son, Jack, and Ginsberg and Alpert, now known as Baba Ram Dass.

Leary proved to be an influential member of his generation. Like so many others, he tried to break conventional norms and challenge the repressive beliefs about sexuality that had been handed down to him through his parents. He served as the director of psychological research for the Kaiser Foundation, was a stand-up comedian and actor, and author. He even ran for governor in California in 1970.

Leary strongly believed in the positive effects of drugs on the human mind and on their promotion of spiritual discovery. Leary used his psychological expertise to convince younger generations of the benefits of drugs. His slogan "Tune in, turn on, drop out" still serves as a symbol of the counterculture and upheaval of the 1960s. "Tune in" encouraged interaction with the world, while "turn on" referred to the activation of neurons and genetics within one's body, usually with drugs. "Drop out" simply meant detaching oneself from the mundane patterns of everyday life. The public and the press regarded this as an invitation to forget all responsibility and productivity.

When interviewed and questioned about his beliefs, Leary often responded, "Don't ask me anything. Think for yourself and question authority." This mentality was very much alive during his reign as a high priest of the LSD culture.

After Leary faded from the public scene, he continued preaching about the powerful effects of drugs on the human mind and spirit. He published books, such as *Flashbacks: An Autobiography,* in 1983, in which he described his experiences in the 1960s and the countercultural revolution. During the 1980s, Leary toured college campuses, making speeches about his beliefs. He began a software company called Futique and believed that the Internet would become the LSD of the 1990s. He was active in producing his own website, including a virtual tour of his home and recent writings.

In 1996, Leary died at his home of prostate cancer at the age of 76.

Further reading: Timothy Leary, *Flashbacks: An Autobiography* (Los Angeles: J. P. Tarener, 1983). Timothy Leary, *Changing My Mind, Among Others* (Englewood Cliffs, N.J.: Prentice Hall, 1982); Martin A. Lee, *Acid Dreams:* *The CIA, LSD, and the Sixties Rebellion* (New York: Grove Press, 1985).

— Jennifer Parson

lesbians   See gays and lesbians

Levitt, William J. (1907–1994)

William Levitt applied assembly-line techniques to the construction of houses, and with his fast and cheap methods, he helped build the suburbs of the 1950s.

Levitt was born on February 11, 1907, in Brooklyn, New York. After high school, he attended New York University, then set out on his own, later reflecting, "I got itchy. I wanted to make a lot of money. I wanted a big car and a lot of clothes." In the late 1920s, Levitt's father took control of a number of partially finished homes after a real estate slump, and gave William and his brother, Alfred, the chance to finish the job. The pair completed the houses quickly and successfully, and soon they formed the company Levitt & Sons to tackle other projects. William served as the company's president and handled the sales, advertising, and financing, while Alfred designed the first new Levitt house, which was finished and sold in 1929, just a few months before the onset of the Great Depression.

By 1933, despite the Depression, the Levitts continued developing the area along Long Island's North Shore. The number of houses reached 200 and sold for $9,100 to $18,500 each. In 1941, the number of houses reached 1,200. In 1942, the federal government contracted with the Levitts to mass-produce housing for the navy in Norfolk, Virginia. Levitt was then shipped out to Oahu, Hawaii, in 1944, with a U.S. Navy construction unit known as the Seabees. Unburdened by union restrictions on building, Levitt, like others in his unit, began to brainstorm ideas on faster and more efficient building methods.

Before World War II, Levitt had bought a thousand acres of farmland on Long Island, and, in 1946, when he returned home, he began building the largest housing project in American history. He named it Island Trees, but it became known simply as Levittown. The houses were simple: two bedrooms, one bathroom, a kitchen, and a living room. They were designed with the young family in mind. The first Levittown included 17,000 houses and approximately 82,000 people. The Levitts furnished land for churches, schools, and swimming pools, creating full-fledged communities from scratch.

Levitt combined the assembly-line techniques used by Henry Ford to mass produce houses and create the large suburban neighborhoods of the 1950s. One construction team poured foundation after foundation. Another team framed one house after another, and an additional

Aerial view of Levittown, 1954   *(Library of Congress)*

team installed windows and doors. This process was far quicker and cheaper than completing one house and then moving on to the next. Levitt cut the cost of his homes to about $13,500, significantly less than what other builders charged for a house of comparable size.

One problem with Levitt's plan was that virtually all of the homes looked the same. The inhabitants often appeared to look the same as well. Author John Keats described Levittown: "For virtually nothing down, you too can find a box of your own in one of the fresh-air slums we're building around the edges of American cities . . . inhabited by people whose age, income, number of children, problems, habits, conversations, dress, possessions, perhaps even blood types are almost precisely like yours."

Another more serious problem, largely unnoticed in the 1950s, was the discrimination practiced in the sale of homes in Levittown. African Americans found that they were not welcome in these communities. William Levitt claimed his business would not be able to compete if he did not follow these discriminatory practices.

Despite his critics, Levitt grew increasingly popular. In 1950, he was on the cover of *Time* magazine, and he quickly became a celebrity. The publicity began to pull the company, and the two Levitt brothers, apart. In 1952, the Levitts moved their building operation to Pennsylvania, where they built another 17,000 houses, then, in 1954, William Levitt and his brother Alfred decided to split the company. In 1958, William Levitt again moved his company, this time to New Jersey, where he constructed a 12,000-home Levittown. By 1960, land surrounding the cities grew scarce and the demand for housing began to fall. Levitt tried to branch out to other areas and built smaller communities, but his profits continued to drop. In 1967, he sold his company to the International Telephone & Telegraph Corporation (ITT) and agreed not to build in the United States for 10 years. In the early 1970s, Levitt again suffered financially when the price of his stock in ITT crashed. He tried to bounce back with a new real estate corporation, but he failed. Levitt died at age 86 having never recovered from his losses.

Further reading: David Halberstam, *The Fifties* (New York: Villard Books, 1993).

— Jennifer Parson

Lewis, John (1940–   )

John Lewis, a prominent African-American civil rights activist, was a relentless organizer and participant in numerous SIT-INS, FREEDOM RIDES, and protest marches throughout the South in the 1960s.

Lewis was born February 21, 1940, in Troy, Alabama, the son of parents who operated a cotton and peanut farm in rural Pike County. As a boy, he lived in a world of his own, refusing to participate in farm work because he told his parents it was like gambling with nature. Instead, Lewis spent his time preaching to and baptizing chickens, which he considered to be the only farm animals worthy of adoption as the world's innocent creatures. His religious intensity later characterized his unswerving dedication to civil rights. By the time he was a teenager, despite a stammering voice and shyness, he was a regular Baptist preacher throughout the area. His inspiration came from the weekly radio sermons of MARTIN LUTHER KING, JR., in the mid-1950s. Lewis was the first person from his family to graduate from high school, doing so in 1957, and after that he hoped to follow his hero King to Morehouse College. Real-

izing that the college's tuition was beyond his family's means, he instead enrolled in the only school he could find that charged no tuition, Nashville's American Baptist Theological Seminary.

His first opportunity to meet King came in the late 1950s when Lewis enlisted the help of the civil rights leader with his plans to gain admittance to all-white, segregated Troy State College in Alabama. When those plans failed to materialize, Lewis returned to Nashville and enrolled at Fisk University to pursue a degree in philosophy. There, influenced by theories of nonviolent forms of social protest, as well as the growing efforts of blacks to protest SEGREGATION laws throughout the South, he became a civil rights activist. In 1960, Lewis and several other Nashville blacks conducted their first sit-ins in the city's "white only" lunch counters. Despite being repeatedly arrested by police and harassed by the community, Lewis and the others continued their protests. Eventually, they joined forces with leaders of similar student groups across the South to form the STUDENT NONVIOLENT COORDINATING COMMITTEE (SNCC).

With an unwavering belief in civil rights and nonviolent protest, as well as a willingness to risk his own life, Lewis emerged as the foremost young leader of the CIVIL RIGHTS MOVEMENT. He was a frequent participant in the more dangerous forms of protest, including the freedom rides in the summer of 1961, which challenged racial discrimination in bus facilities throughout the South. Lewis, like other freedom riders, endured vicious physical beatings, and numerous arrests during the rides. Lewis also led much-publicized marches against segregated movie theaters in Nashville.

Lewis's commitment to continue such protests, despite physical dangers, distinguished him as a role model of the early nonviolent protests. He was unanimously elected chairman of SNCC in 1963, the same year in which he made his noteworthy speech at the march for civil rights in Washington, D.C., criticizing the administration of President JOHN F. KENNEDY for not proceeding quickly enough with legislation calling for civil rights. As chairman of SNCC, Lewis maintained a course of nonviolence. Eventually more militant elements of the organization, those espousing principles of "BLACK POWER," grew restless with Lewis's leadership. In 1966, he was ousted as SNCC chairman by STOKELY CARMICHAEL, and he resigned from the organization.

Lewis went on to work for the Field Foundation, first as a director of community organization projects in the Nashville area, eventually becoming director of the foundation's Voter Education Project (VEP) based in Atlanta. As VEP director from 1970 until 1977, Lewis led grassroots efforts to organize southern black voters and to provide political education to young people. In 1977, he was appointed by President Jimmy Carter to be director of U.S. operations for Action, a federal agency that oversaw various economic recovery programs on the community level. That same year, Lewis ran for political office, finishing second in the Democratic primary for Georgia's fifth congressional district.

In 1982, he was elected to the Atlanta City Council, a position in which he became known for his close attention to the needs of the poor and elderly. Lewis's popularity and respect from the people earned him the Democratic nomination for Congress, defeating former SNCC ally Julian Bond in 1986. In his role as congressman, Lewis remained a prominent and respected figure in the struggle for civil rights.

Further reading: Taylor Branch, *Parting the Waters: America in the King Years 1954–63* (New York: Simon & Schuster. 1988); John Lewis with Michael D'Orso, *Walking with the Wind: A Memoir of the Movement* (New York: Simon & Schuster, 1998).

— Elizabeth A. Henke

liberalism

The fundamentals of liberalism lay in the proposition that the government had responsibility for the welfare of all its citizens and accepted the need for a more active government role to help those who were unable to help themselves.

The period between the end of World War II and the election of Richard M. Nixon to the presidency in 1968 arguably contains both the high-water mark and the demise of the age of American liberalism. As a political philosophy, liberalism has had many definitions, but in the postwar United States it has come to represent the belief in governmental intervention in the market, the social reform arena, and the realm of international affairs. The proliferation of liberal institutions and policies of the Franklin D. Roosevelt administrations after 1933 revolutionized the role of the federal government in America, even if they did not bring about the end of the Great Depression. Thus, after the war, President HARRY S. TRUMAN found himself equipped with new tools for domestic and international action, as well as an overall resolve on the part of the American people that the government had a right to exercise its power.

Although the liberal wings of both the DEMOCRATIC PARTY and the REPUBLICAN PARTY were largely ascendant after 1945, each party's conservative wing actively opposed the expansion of the federal government. During the 1950s and 1960s, the Republican Party's liberal eastern wing sought to continue the policies of the NEW DEAL and to extend the reach of American social, business, and governmental institutions abroad. The only Republican

president between 1933 and 1969, General DWIGHT D. EISENHOWER, was sympathetic to many of the New Deal programs he inherited, and he was elected twice. Significantly, the more conservative, midwestern wing of the party, led by Ohio senator Robert A. Taft, failed to capture the White House. When conservative Arizona senator BARRY GOLDWATER captured the Republican nomination in 1964, for example, he lost overwhelmingly to LYNDON B. JOHNSON. This is largely due to the fact that during this period the many beneficiaries of liberalism, among them ethnic Northeasterners, members of labor unions, and African Americans, moved into the Democratic Party in dramatic numbers. There was likewise a regional struggle in the Democratic Party, in which liberal western and eastern Democrats clashed openly with conservative southerners angered by the party's integrationist policies. This first occurred in 1948, when J. Strom Thurmond, the governor of South Carolina, abandoned the Democrats to run for president as the candidate of the antiliberal STATES' RIGHTS PARTY, and again in the 1960s, when southern politicians directly interfered with the federally mandated (and enforced) integration of public schools. Perhaps the most dramatic episode came when Governor GEORGE C. WALLACE of Alabama literally blocked the entry of African Americans into the University of Alabama until confronted by federalized members of the National Guard.

In the 1960s, the liberalism of Democratic administrations both at home and abroad helped redefine voting patterns as many white southerners, previously reliable voters for Democrats regardless of the party's candidate, began to drift into the arms of the Republican Party. On the other hand, many southern blacks, who until the VOTING RIGHTS ACT OF 1965 found political participation a difficult enterprise, all but deserted the Republican Party for that which had passed legislation supporting civil rights and aid to the impoverished. These changes occurred largely on the national level: many southern candidates for state and local offices remained Democratic, long after these changes in national election voting appeared.

It is possible that American liberalism contained the seeds of its own demise. As the 1960s wore on, the continuation of social problems, in spite of Johnson's WAR ON POVERTY, suggested that governmental action was not a simple cure-all. Some white voters were put off by their belief that, despite expanded government programs for the poor and federal protection for civil rights, African-American leaders appeared to become more outspoken in their quest for social justice. Others, on both the political left and right, were put off by the continuing intervention of the United States in the VIETNAM WAR in Southeast ASIA, where increased military spending did not yield a favorable outcome. Thus, in the election of 1968, both liberals and conservatives deserted the Democratic Party, ensuring the election of Republican Richard M. Nixon. While cautious to correct what he felt were the excesses of Johnson's liberalism, and prepared to oppose such policies as school busing to win the votes of southern whites, Nixon was no laissez-faire isolationist. He sought to improve relations with communist China and to use the power of the presidency to regulate the economy. Yet the lessons that Americans of all political stripes appeared to draw from the ongoing Vietnam War, and the ambiguous results of Johnson's GREAT SOCIETY, pointed to a lapse in the belief in government's ability to improve their lives.

Further reading: Alan Brinkley, *Liberalism and Its Discontents* (Cambridge, Mass.: Harvard University Press, 1998); Alonzo Hamby, *Liberalism and Its Challengers: From F. D. R. to Bush* (New York: Oxford University Press, 1992).

— Patrick J. Walsh

Limited Test Ban Treaty of 1963

The Limited Test Ban Treaty prohibited atmospheric, underwater, and high-altitude nuclear testing. The treaty was signed by the United States, Great Britain, and the SOVIET UNION in August 1963 and entered into effect later that year following ratification.

During the 1950s, the major powers engaged in an ARMS RACE that became increasingly lethal as a result of radioactive fallout in the atmosphere. After the Soviet Union implemented a unilateral testing moratorium in 1958, the United States did the same, and that voluntary initiative lasted for several years. Even so, talks about a more permanent solution failed when the Soviets shot down an American U-2 reconnaissance plane. Angered by DWIGHT D. EISENHOWER's initial claims that the U-2 was merely a weather plane gone awry, Soviet premier Nikita Khrushchev walked out of a superpower summit in Paris, and ended the test ban negotiations.

Test ban talks resumed in March 1961, but they were initially unsuccessful. President JOHN F. KENNEDY made several modifications to the American position, offering a ban on high-altitude tests. On-site inspections proved to be the key sticking point. In time, the Soviets demanded only two or three; the United States wanted eight or 10. Even though that latter number was scaled down from what Kennedy and his military advisers had initially sought, there was still tremendous difference between the two positions.

Outside events affected the arms control negotiations. After the BAY OF PIGS fiasco and the meeting in Vienna between Khrushchev and Kennedy in June 1961, superpower relations deteriorated, and so did the test ban negotiations. In the fall of 1961, the Soviets broke the voluntary ban on nuclear testing that had been in place since 1958 and detonated a 50-megaton device, equivalent to more than 3,000 bombs of the type dropped on Hiroshima in 1945. Kennedy responded in kind by resuming both underground and atmospheric nuclear testing. By late autumn, the talks in Geneva had ended.

After the 1962 CUBAN MISSILE CRISIS, both Kennedy and Khrushchev realized just how quickly an international dispute could escalate to nuclear war. Both leaders wanted to take steps to prevent worldwide destruction. Khrushchev's apparent defeat in the missile crisis worsened Sino-Soviet relations, and he now had to face two powerful enemies, the United States and China. He therefore softened his stance on several issues, including arms control. When Kennedy wrote to Khrushchev in April 1963 to suggest that high-level talks to discuss a test ban treaty resume, the Soviet premier accepted immediately and offered to host the talks in Moscow.

Kennedy delivered a speech at American University in June 1963 that called for peace and restraint, sending a signal to the Soviets that he was ready to negotiate on arms control. The speech was also part of a public relations effort to secure congressional support for a test ban treaty. Kennedy argued that the treaty would improve American security by curbing the arms race, reducing radioactive pollution, and allowing continued antiballistic missile research.

Intensive talks lasted for 10 days in Moscow in July 1963. It soon became clear that the Soviets would not accept on-site inspections, which the United States required for a comprehensive test ban. The priority then shifted to securing a limited test ban agreement. Representatives from the United States, the Soviet Union, and Great Britain signed the treaty in August. American public opinion supported the treaty and it passed the Senate by a vote of 80 to 19 on September 24, 1963.

The Limited Test Ban Treaty never fulfilled the hopes of Kennedy or Khrushchev. While it reduced the amount of radioactive pollution in the atmosphere, it did not halt the proliferation of nuclear weapons. Efforts to include France and China as signatories to the treaty failed, and it did not stop all forms of testing. After the treaty was signed, underground testing actually accelerated. Still, it amounted to an important first step in arms control.

Further reading: George Bunn, *Arms Control by Committee: Managing Negotiations with the Russians* (Stanford, Calif.: Stanford University Press, 1992).

— Jennifer Walton

literature

Literature after World War II underwent a shift in both style and focus, as it reflected changing attitudes toward race, gender, family, sexuality, youth, and war.

Prior to World War II, American literature experienced a period of rebirth, as a group of authors both home and abroad—including Ernest Hemingway, John Steinbeck, Gertrude Stein, Langston Hughes, and F. Scott Fitzgerald—reacted to the demoralizing violence of World War I, the decadence of the 1920s, and the poverty of the Great Depression in the 1930s. While many of them continued to write after World War II, only Hemingway, with *The Old Man and the Sea* (1952), for which he won the Pulitzer Prize for literature the same year, matched his work before the war.

Instead, a new group of authors, most of them born in the 20th century, began to examine the effects of World War II and its aftermath on the United States. *The Naked and the Dead* (1948), about an infantry platoon fighting on a small Japanese island, was immediately heralded as the first great World War II novel, and its 25-year-old author, Norman Mailer, became an instant celebrity. While he never equaled the success earned by his first novel, Mailer remained a prominent literary figure for the rest of the century. James Jones's *From Here to Eternity* (1951), set in Pearl Harbor in the weeks before the December 1941 attack that pulled the United States into the war, was immortalized by the 1953 movie version starring Burt Lancaster and Frank Sinatra. Jones followed the book up in 1962 with *The Thin Red Line*, depicting the Battle of Guadalcanal, the second in his trilogy about the war (the third of which was published in 1978).

Joseph Heller's *Catch-22* (1961), with its emphasis on satire and its use of surrealism, represented a departure from the common World War II novel. Heller flew 60 combat missions in EUROPE during the war, and while working in the publishing industry in the late 1950s, he wrote *Catch-22*, about a U.S. Army Air Corps captain struggling to stay alive while stationed in the Mediterranean during World War II. The title refers to an army regulation that discharges pilots for insanity after flying too many combat missions; to request not to fly, however, means that the pilot is sane and therefore must fly the missions. Heller's novel became synonymous for no-win situations, and while it was not a rousing critical success, it became considerably popular as a cult novel.

Drama, too, reflected issues of social concern, but only some themes were war-related. With *All My Sons* (1947), about a son returning home from the war only to discover his father's role in war profiteering, playwright Arthur Miller examined the effects of the war on the home front rather than the battlefield. Much of American theater, though, dealt with issues that rent apart the fabric of American society. Miller's most famous play, *Death of a Salesman* (1949), told the story of Willy Loman, an aging member of the workforce who deludes himself into believing he is a man of true importance. Winning the Pulitzer

Arthur Miller   *(Library of Congress)*

Prize for drama, *Salesman* was celebrated as a modern tragedy, proof that the American dream could be just as damaging as it was inspiring. Lorraine Hansbury's *A Raisin in the Sun* (1959)—the first play by an African-American woman to be staged on Broadway—told a similar story, as a black father must decide whether to move his family into an all-white neighborhood. The plays of Tennessee Williams, most notably the Pulitzer Prize–winning *A Streetcar Named Desire* (1947) and *Cat on a Hot Tin Roof* (1955), examined the underlying sexual frustrations of southern white women in a rough and violent society. Other notable plays included Edward Albee's *Who's Afraid of Virginia Woolf?* (1962), about a married couple's night of angry confrontation; Miller's *The Crucible* (1953), an allegory set during the 1692 Salem witch trials about the anticommunist paranoia of Senator JOSEPH R. MCCARTHY; and the posthumous debut in 1956 of *A Long Day's Journey into Night*, Eugene O'Neill's masterpiece about the American family.

Southern literature received considerable attention during the postwar years. While his best material was written well before World War II, it was only during and after the war that William Faulkner's work became recognized as one of the most groundbreaking bodies of literature of the 20th century. Known primarily for his series of novels set in the fictitious southern county of Yoknapatawpha, of which

The Sound and the Fury (1929) constituted the most prominent, Faulkner examined issues of race, class, family, and gender in the South, earning him the Nobel Prize for literature in 1950. Robert Penn Warren, a prominent southern writer, won the Pulitzer Prize for *All the King's Men* (1947), which told the story of the rise and fall of a fictitious southern governor based on Louisiana politician Huey P. Long.

The best-recognized and successful southern novel of the period, however, was Harper Lee's *To Kill a Mockingbird* (1960). Lee's father, a respected lawyer in her home town of Monroeville, Alabama, served as the inspiration for Atticus Finch, the father of Scout, *Mockingbird's* narrator as an adult looking back on her childhood. The novel's two parallel storylines follow Atticus as he defends a black man accused of raping a white woman, and Scout, as she and her friends investigate the mysterious recluse Boo Radley, who lives across the street. The novel earned Lee the Pulitzer Prize and praise from the Alabama legislature. It became a staple of high school English curriculums, and was made into a classic film in 1962 staring Gregory Peck, who won an Academy Award for his performance as Atticus.

Other authors attacked the materialism and shallowness of post–World War II American life. *The Catcher in the Rye* (1951), J. D. Salinger's only published novel, was a popular coming-of-age story that earned its author wide praise. The story follows Holden Caulfield, a self-conscious 16-year-old searching for innocence and honesty in a world filled with "phonies." Salinger's use of slang and reliance on dark humor emphasized the sensibilities of the era's youth, winning him a devoted following of readers both young and old.

While Richard Wright's *Native Son* (1940) explored the treatment of African Americans by white society through the sensational storytelling of the protest novel, several other black authors chose to take different approaches to presenting black culture in America. Ralph Ellison's *Invisible Man* (1952), his first and only novel, follows an inexperienced southern black youth who travels to Harlem to fight in the Civil Rights movement, only to be ignored by both the black and the white communities. Ellison's book, a passionately written story about discovering the "black" identity within American society, was considered by critics as one of the most powerful novels of the postwar period, helping to spark the consciousness of the AFRICAN-AMERICAN MOVEMENT. Ellison's nonfictional counterpart was JAMES BALDWIN, whose two autobiographical essays *Notes of a Native Son* (1955) and *The Fire Next Time* (1963) match Ellison's passion in their lucid assessment and ultimate critique of black America, including Wright's use of the protest novel. Baldwin was also a novelist; his first book, *Go Tell It On the Mountain* (1953), dealt with African-American issues; his second, *Giovanni's Room* (1959), was noteworthy in its frank portrayal of a homosexual man's journey in Europe.

Issues of sexuality were prominent during this period, no better reflected than in Vladimir Nabokov's highly controversial novel *Lolita* (1958), about a middle-aged man's affair with a 12-year-old girl. Nabokov was born in St. Petersburg in 1899, but left Russia in 1919, lived in Europe until 1940, and became a U.S. citizen in 1945. Though he began writing while still living in Russia, Nabokov was unsuccessful until he published *Lolita*. When no American publisher accepted the book, it was first published in France in 1955. Once published in the United States, it made its way to number one on *The New York Times* bestseller list, and it was heralded as a brilliant dark comedy.

No stranger to controversy themselves, the writers of the BEAT GENERATION also tackled heretofore taboo subjects like drug use and homosexuality. Through such works as ALLEN GINSBERG's long-form poem *Howl* (1956), JACK KEROUAC's stream of consciousness novel *On the Road* (1957), and William S. Burroughs's highly experimental novel *Naked Lunch* (1961), the Beats (as they were christened by Kerouac) rejected mainstream society and mainstream writing in favor of finding an alternative for both. Precursors to the COUNTERCULTURE of the 1960s, the Beats preferred a lively, exuberant style that underscored their critique of American culture.

Norman Mailer, who became known more for a style of journalism called the "nonfiction novel" than for fiction writing, examined followers of the Beats in his essay *The White Negro (1957)*. He noted that this segment of white youth co-opted both African American slang and sensibility. Mailer wrote several other nonfiction books, including *The Armies of the Night* (1968) about his arrest at a demonstration in October 1967 as part of the antiwar movement. Truman Capote, known earlier for his novels *Other Voices, Other Rooms* (1948) and *Breakfast at Tiffany's* (1958), is best known for his nonfiction work, *In Cold Blood* (1966), about a 1959 multiple murder in Kansas. Tom Wolfe won wide praise with his book about author Ken Kesey and the countercultural hippies in *The Electric Kool-Aid Acid Test* (1968), in which he described the impact of getting stoned on the drug LSD.

Nonfiction works critiquing cultural attitudes and the CONSUMER MOVEMENT of the 1950s and 1960s were popular during this period. VANCE PACKARD exposed the tricks of the ADVERTISING trade in *The Hidden Persuaders* (1957), and he went on to write several other books analyzing various aspects of U.S. society. Biologist RACHEL CARSON, in *Silent Spring* (1962), examined the damaging effects of pesticide use, raising public awareness about the dangers of pollution in general. Consumer advocate RALPH NADER's *Unsafe at Any Speed* (1965) criticized the American automobile industry, and the GENERAL MOTORS Corporation's Corvair in particular, for their lack of safety precautions, leading directly to the passage of the NATIONAL TRAFFIC AND MOTOR VEHICLE SAFETY ACT OF 1966. BETTY FRIEDAN'S *The Feminine Mystique* (1963) depicted women's dissatisfaction with their traditional role within the family, and the book is seen as one of the central works of the movement for WOMEN'S STATUS AND RIGHTS in the middle to late 1960s.

Popular genre novels, mass-produced in paperback, also became more prevalent during the postwar period. Science-fiction writer Ray Bradbury's *The Martian Chronicles* (1950) served as a cautionary tale about materialistic humans from Earth devastating an idyllic society on Mars. Bradbury's novels and short stories continued to be popular well into the final years of the century. Pulp novelist Mickey Spillane's *I, the Jury* (1947) constituted his first hit in his series of books, known for their violent content and sexual innuendo, featuring detective Mike Hammer. Selling for 25 to 50 cents a copy, the books became among the best-selling works of fiction up to that point in publishing history. Children's mystery novel series featuring the Hardy Boys and Nancy Drew, created by syndication publisher Edward Stratemeyer in the 1920s and 1930s, were widely popular among young readers after World War II, and the characters quickly became part of POPULAR CULTURE. Grace Metalious's *Peyton Place* (1956) exposed the dark, unseemly underbelly of what on the surface appeared to be a quaint New England town. The book sold 10 million copies in paperback by 1966; its progressive treatment of women contributed to both its success and its reputation as a harbinger of the feminist movement in the 1960s.

Poetry after World War II went through a transition period, moving from the influences of the rigid form of T. S. Eliot into a more open, emotional style reminiscent of poets like Walt Whitman and D. H. Lawrence but unique onto themselves. The 1940s saw poetry collections like Robert Lowell's *Lord Weary's Castle* (1946) and Theodore Roethke's *The Lost Son and Other Poems* (1948) adhere to Eliot's use of formal structuring and lyricism. By the 1950s, however, many poets turned to an open, unfolding style using direct and prosaic language. Lowell's *Life Studies* (1959) and *For the Union Dead* (1964) typified this style, and Lowell himself influenced poets like Anne Sexton, known for her confessional poems *To Bedlam and Part Way Back* (1960) and *All My Pretty Ones* (1962). Beat poets like Ginsberg, Lawrence Ferlinghetti, and Gregory Corso also popularized the new style.

Further reading: Marcus Cunliffe, ed., *American Literature since 1900,* vol. 9 (New York: P. Bedrick Books, 1987); David Halberstam, *The Fifties.* New York: Villard Books, 1993; Robert F. Kiernan, *American Writing since 1945: A Critical Survey* (New York: Frederick Ungar Publishing, 1983).

— Adam B. Vary

LSD

A hallucinogenic drug discovered by Swiss chemist Albert Hoffmann, LSD helped define the COUNTERCULTURE of the 1960s.

Lysergic acid diethylamide (LSD) was discovered in 1943 and made available to select researchers by Sandoz Pharmaceuticals in 1947. One of the earliest American groups to show an interest in the powerful new hallucinogen, the CENTRAL INTELLIGENCE AGENCY (CIA), authorized a secret LSD research program ("MK-ULTRA") in 1953 as part of its long-standing search for a truth serum. The program attracted an unorthodox crew to begin with, and, as agents tested the drug on themselves, their experimental designs became increasingly bizarre. Perhaps the most disturbing was the 1955 Operation Midnight Climax, in which unwitting men were lured from bars to an agency-funded bordello where they were dosed with LSD and observed through one-way mirrors. Despite such efforts, researchers never found LSD to be of any value as a mind control drug, and in the early 1960s the program closed up shop.

In addition to its own ill-fated operation, the CIA had also channeled funds to legitimate psychological researchers intrigued by the prospect of a psychosis-inducing drug. As the decade wore on, attention turned from "model psychoses" to LSD's therapeutic potential. Two main strategies emerged. In "psycholytic" therapy small doses of the drug were administered as an adjunct to psychoanalysis. In "psychedelic" ("mind manifesting") therapy, introduced by Canadian LSD pioneer Henry Osmond in 1957, a large dose was used to telescope years of therapy into a single session. Such techniques briefly became fashionable, especially in Los Angeles's art-and-film colony.

Attached to the growing numbers of clinical researchers, a loose network of lay partisans saw hallucinogens as sacramental portals to a more profound metaphysical realm. Aldous Huxley, the famed English novelist, was one of the earliest of these LSD proselytizers. His series of rhapsodic, yet highly literate, books on the subject, including *The Doors of Perception* (1954), *Heaven and Hell* (1956), and the psychedelic utopian novel *Island* (1962), advertised the existence of hallucinogens to a widening circle of followers. By the late 1950s, Huxley's circle had merged with the LSD therapy circuit, bringing together psychiatrists with notable intellectuals and artists. On the East Coast, a similar network was springing up around a young Harvard psychologist named TIMOTHY LEARY, whose hallucinogen research seminar had evolved (with some help from poet ALLEN

GINSBERG) into a never-ending series of what could best be described as drug parties.

The surreal genteel atmosphere of these early psychedelic explorations did not last for long. Researchers were experimenting on themselves, and, as with the CIA, the results were unpredictable. Some became messianic about the drug's transformative potential, and their research programs later tended to evolve into plans for a chemically engineered cultural revolution. By the mid-1960s, this radical mind-set had taken hold of a highly visible vanguard of evangelists, some of whom had become youth culture heroes. Leary became one of the best known of these drug gurus, famously exhorting Americans to "turn on, tune in, and drop out" as he continued his research in the stately New York mansion that served as his headquarters after his expulsion from Harvard in 1963 for allowing undergraduates to participate in experiments after promising not to involve them. Even stranger than Leary's actions were the inspired antics of novelist Ken Kesey, who had begun his LSD career as a volunteer research subject. Later immortalized in Tom Wolfe's *The Electric Kool-Aid Acid Test* (1968), Kesey and his band of "Merry Pranksters" sponsored LSD festivals known as "Acid Tests" that helped California become the center of a rapidly expanding psychedelic movement.

Egged on by enthusiasts like Leary, Kesey, and an ever-widening pantheon of cultural icons like the BEATLES, a growing number of young people experimented with LSD. San Francisco's Haight-Ashbury neighborhood, already the unofficial capital of the "hippie" world, became the mecca of the new distinctly antipolitical movement. In 1967, the huge "Human Be-In" capped a series of LSD festivals. But the Haight, ecstatic as it seemed in its best moments, was far removed from the carefully structured setting called for by LSD researchers in their earlier, more sober days. Already in 1965 observers had begun to note an alarming rise in the frequency of "bad trips," many of which ended up in emergency rooms. As negative publicity mounted, the government took steps to combat America's "LSD epidemic." By the end of 1966 the drug was illegal in all 50 states, and the Food and Drug Administration had effectively halted further medical research. Within a few years, the psychedelic movement's most visible leaders, Kesey and Leary, were either in prison or in hiding. Many, like Kesey himself, claimed to have moved beyond drugs in their search for transcendence; Leary's former colleague Richard Alpert, for example, returned from India as the (more or less) clean-living guru Baba Ram Dass. Americans continued to take LSD recreationally, but the momentous sense of doing so as part of a revolutionary movement had permanently faded.

Further reading: Martin A. Lee and Bruce Shlain. *Acid Dreams: The Complete Social History of LSD: The CIA, the Sixties, and Beyond* (New York: Grove Press, 1992).

— David Herzberg

Luce, Henry   See Volume VIII

M

MacArthur, Douglas (1880–1964)

Douglas MacArthur served as a commander in the Philippines during World War II, as occupation commander of post–World War II Japan, and as head of the United Nations (UN) forces during the KOREAN WAR.

MacArthur was born on January 26, 1880, in Little Rock, Arkansas, the third and youngest child of Arthur MacArthur, Jr., and Mary "Pinkie" Pinckney. He graduated from West Point in 1903 with the rank of second lieutenant. His first assignment sent him to the Philippines where he contracted malaria and was forced to transfer back to the United States. He held stints as a military aide to President Theodore Roosevelt and as a company commander at Fort Leavenworth, an army training center. MacArthur went on to serve on the U.S. Army General Staff, followed by an assignment to Veracruz, Mexico, in 1914, during the Mexican Revolution.

MacArthur quickly rose through the army ranks. As a major, he assisted Franklin D. Roosevelt, then assistant secretary of the navy, in implementing the expansion of the army for service in World War I. His idea to incorporate National Guard units into the army resulted in his promotion to colonel and chief of the newly established 42nd "Rainbow" Division. In Europe, between 1917 and 1919, MacArthur fought in numerous battles and received several commendations for his skill and bravery, including a promotion to brigadier general. He returned to the United States in the spring of 1919 and for the next two years served as the superintendent of West Point. Then new orders sent MacArthur to the Philippines, where, in 1925, he received a promotion to major general. In 1928, he was reassigned as army commander of the Philippines Department.

From 1930 to 1935, MacArthur served as head of the army. During this time, he directed his efforts toward preserving the army's strength in the midst of Great Depression–era budget constraints. In 1935, he went on to serve as military adviser and field marshal in the Philippines.

After an admirable career, MacArthur retired from the army in 1937.

In 1941, at the age of 61, MacArthur was recalled into active duty to shore up military forces in defense of U.S. interests in the Pacific against an impending Japanese invasion. MacArthur's troops valiantly attempted to delay Japanese seizure of the Philippines, despite being cut off from supplies and weakened by disease and hunger. With the landing of Japanese troops in the Philippines, Roosevelt ordered MacArthur and his staff to Australia in 1942. MacArthur was named supreme commander of the Southwest Pacific area, with orders to defend the territory. His forces established defensive posts in New Guinea and successfully expelled the Japanese from the island in 1943. Bolstered by Allied military reinforcements, MacArthur launched a series of offensive maneuvers designed to seize strategic areas of New Guinea and the Solomon Islands.

General Douglas MacArthur   *(Library of Congress)*

Ultimately, his soldiers succeeded in neutralizing Rabaul, formerly a Japanese stronghold. Maintaining his momentum, MacArthur's forces advanced toward the Philippines, attacking the islands of Morotai, Leyte, and Mindoro in 1944. Finally, despite fierce opposition from Japanese military units, American troops entered the Philippine capital of Manila. Within a month, MacArthur established U.S. control of Manila. Six months later, he secured the remaining islands.

For his leadership in the war effort, MacArthur was given the rank of five-star general, and an appointment as commander of army forces in the Pacific. As commander of the Pacific troops, MacArthur planned to direct an invasion of Japan. After the United States dropped the first ATOMIC BOMB on Hiroshima on August 6, 1945, and another bomb on Nagasaki, the Japanese opened negotiations for surrender. MacArthur's subsequent appointment as supreme commander of the Allied Powers and Far East commander included directing the U.S. occupation of Japan. Between 1945 and 1951, MacArthur single-handedly administered a series of orders that demobilized the Japanese military and restored the economy. In addition, he initiated a series of reforms in the areas of education, public health, labor, and land redistribution.

President HARRY S. TRUMAN's administration gradually decreased MacArthur's authority. With the start of the KOREAN WAR in 1950, MacArthur, now at age 70, became involved in implementing strategies for defending American interests in Korea. The United Nations Security Council named him commander of the operation, and with few combat-ready troops available, he was ordered to defend South Korea. In September, his military assaults quelled the North Korean advance toward Pusan, as his naval forces landed at Inchon. This action resulted, initially, in the retreat of North Korean troops, and the UN control of Seoul, South Korea's capital. Seeing a quick end to the war, MacArthur ordered his troops beyond the 38th parallel and into North Korean territory in November. He launched a simultaneous naval assault near Wonsan, on the east coast. Meanwhile, MacArthur assured Truman that there was no threat from Chinese forces in Manchuria. Yet, in November, massive Chinese forces launched a counterattack, which yielded 11,000 casualties for the troops under MacArthur's command, and forced MacArthur to retreat. MacArthur went back on the offensive, and two months later he stabilized the front line just south of Seoul.

For his public disagreement with U.S. and UN policy in Korea, along with insubordination and an unwillingness to contain the war, Truman relieved MacArthur of his command on April 11, 1951. MacArthur received a groundswell of popular support, until negative publicity from a Senate investigation of his dismissal quelled public opinion. The delegates to the 1952 Republican convention considered MacArthur a possible presidential nominee. During that same year, he became board chairman of the Remington Rand Corporation. In 1959, with the death of General GEORGE C. MARSHALL, MacArthur became senior officer in the U.S. Army.

MacArthur lived the remainder of his life in New York City. He died at the age of 84 on April 5, 1964, in Washington, D.C., after complications following gallbladder surgery.

Further reading: D. Clayton James, *The Years of MacArthur*, 3 vols. (Boston: Houghton-Mifflin, 1970–1985); William Manchester, *American Caesar: Douglas MacArthur, 1880–1964* (Boston: Little, Brown, 1978); Geoffrey Perret, *Old Soldiers Never Die: The Life of Douglas MacArthur* (New York: Random House, 1996).

— Michelle Reid

Malcolm X (1925–1965)

Malcolm X fought for civil rights for African Americans during the 1950s and 1960s. He preached equality for blacks in America by any means possible and through the teachings of the Nation of Islam.

Malcolm was born on May 19, 1925, in Omaha, Nebraska, to Earl and Louise Little. Earl Little was a minister and active organizer in the Universal Negro Improvement Association (UNIA), an institution that actively sought to create separate institutions for blacks to be able to prosper. After the KU KLUX KLAN made several threats to Earl for his activity in the UNIA, he moved his family to Lansing, Michigan, in 1930. Only one year later Earl was found dead, near the family's home, on a trolley car track. Malcolm's mother Louise was admitted into a mental health hospital in 1939, after she suffered a complete breakdown. Malcolm had already been put into foster care. He received education only up to the eighth grade, when his older sister Ella asked him to join her and her husband in Boston.

Malcolm worked in Boston for a short time. By 1942, he had moved out of Boston into the Harlem area of New York City, where he worked in a dining car on a railroad. Not satisfied with his pay, he turned to crime, forming a gang that robbed rich households in the neighborhood. In February 1946, he was caught during a robbery and sent to a Charlestown, Massachusetts, prison for seven years. In prison, Malcolm came to know the teachings of the Nation of Islam led by ELIJAH MUHAMMAD. He converted to Islam in prison, dropped his "slave" name Little, and adopted only the X.

In 1952, Malcolm was paroled and he immediately went to work for the Nation of Islam as an administrator and a minister. Malcolm was a charismatic speaker, and

Malcolm X   *(Library of Congress)*

African Americans flocked to him to hear him preach. The black youth of America were looking for a more militant leader than MARTIN LUTHER KING, JR. Malcolm preached that African Americans should fight for equality and freedom from white oppression by any means necessary; if violence was the only way to achieve this freedom, then that was the answer. The Nation of Islam spread quickly among the black community in urban areas, and Malcolm established new mosques in Boston, Philadelphia, and Hartford. In only a few short years, the Nation had exceeded 30,000 members. Malcolm's message went to mainstream America after a TELEVISION interview with Mike Wallace, on a show called *The Hate That Hate Produced.* During the program, Malcolm explained that the black population of America would no longer stand for the oppression and violence that was being carried out against them by whites. He encouraged African Americans everywhere to join the Nation of Islam, and to break the chains of more than 300 years of oppression.

In 1963, Malcolm and Elijah Muhammad found themselves pitted against one another in charting the future of the Nation of Islam. Malcolm had become the voice of the Nation of Islam, and his popularity had far exceeded that of Elijah Muhammad, which created tensions within the organization. Malcolm left the Nation of Islam and founded Muslim Mosque Inc., where he began to take a less militant stance, and he started to preach for a more secular black community in America. For many years, Malcolm and King had been at odds with the Civil Rights movement and its approach to gaining equality. Malcolm now promoted a less aggressive form of change, as King had been doing for years. Malcolm wanted black communities to take control of their own neighborhoods, not by violence or force, but through the ballot box. In 1964, he made a pilgrimage to Mecca, and there his views changed most significantly. He found himself sitting, eating, and praying next to white Muslims. He thought that if this could be achieved in Mecca, then surely it could occur in other places as well. Malcolm changed his position on SEG-REGATION from the white race to integration; he also officially changed his name from Malcolm X to El-Hajj Malik El-Shabazz. When he returned from Mecca, his first step toward integration was the acceptance of contributions from white supporters.

Malcolm X was stopped before he could ever bring his plan of integration and equality to mainstream America. On February 21, 1965, while giving a speech in the Audubon Ballroom in New York City, he was assassinated by several black gunmen from another part of the Muslim movement.

Further reading: George Breitman, ed. *Malcolm X Speaks: Selected Speeches and Statements* (New York: Pathfinder Press, 1965); Malcolm X with Alex Haley, *The Autobiography of Malcolm X* (New York: Grove Press, 1966).

— Matt Escovar

McCarran Act   See Internal Security Act (1950)

McCarran-Walter Act

The McCarran-Walter Act of 1952 was designed to reform IMMIGRATION law and naturalization procedures, solidifying them under a single section of federal code.

The act, sponsored by Democratic representative Francis Walter of Pennsylvania and Democratic senator Pat McCarran of Nevada, made important changes to the U.S. immigration policy. Although the heart of the quota system put in place by the 1924 National Origins Act was retained, the new law made some modifications to it. Asian countries, which had previously been denied the right to send immigrants, were each assigned the minimum quota of 100 immigrants annually. Even this meager amount could be cut because of the most blatantly racist feature of the bill, which required that any immigrant with at least one-half Asian ancestry be counted in the quota. No such feature applied to other people of mixed ethnicity. The same minimal quota was also granted to immigrants from European colonies. This reduced the number of people who could immigrate from these areas because previously they were listed under the much larger quota of the country that ruled over them. All quotas were restructured by requiring that half of the quota be reserved for people with special skills. Children and spouses of American citizens were allowed to come to the United States outside the quota framework.

Naturalization and deportation procedures were also changed. The existing prohibition against people of certain ethnic backgrounds (most notably Asians) from becoming American citizens was removed. Executive branch officials, however, were given more power and latitude in deporting resident aliens. The president was given the power to halt all immigration.

The bill's supporters praised it as a way to help families and end racial and gender discrimination in immigration and naturalization. They also argued that the procedural changes made by the bill would enhance government efforts "to weed out subversives and other undesirables from citizenship." The bill's supporters believed that it would have "a favorable effect on our international relations, particularly in the Far East."

While praising some features of the bill, especially those that expanded citizenship and allowed easier immigration for family members, the bill's critics maintained that in many cases it did the opposite of what its supporters claimed. They pointed out that the national origins formula on which the quota system was based was discriminatory. This led the *New York Times* to describe the bill as "racist, restrictionist, and reactionary." President HARRY S. TRUMAN went even further when he vetoed the bill, pointing out that several members of the NORTH ATLANTIC TREATY ORGANIZATION (NATO) had extremely low quotas and that this was a source of tension within the alliance. Truman went on to say that the retention of quotas was counterproductive because "we do not need to be protected against immigrants from those countries—on the contrary we want to stretch out a helping hand." He saw the United States as a haven for those who fled COMMUNISM.

Other major objections to the bill involved the expanded power it gave the executive branch. Aside from the unprecedented power of the president to close off all immigration, critics charged that the parts of the bill touted as protecting the United States from dangerous immigrants went too far, in assuming that every alien had a suspicious character that needed to be monitored. The ease with which the act gave government officials the right to deport aliens had great potential for abuse, especially since little distinction was made between serious crimes and petty offensives. This power and discretion left immigrants at the mercy of government bureaucrats and therefore in a more vulnerable position than they had previously occupied.

Despite these objections, there was overwhelming support for the measure and Congress overrode Truman's veto. While the McCarran-Walter Act had serious shortcomings, it encompassed steps toward the goal of equal treatment under the law for all ethnic groups in America.

Further reading: Reed Veda. *Postwar Immigrant America: A Social History* (Boston: Bedford Books, 1994).

— Dave Price

McCarthy, Eugene (1916–)

Eugene McCarthy, a U.S. senator from Minnesota, nearly captured the 1968 Democratic presidential nomination running as a staunch opponent of the VIETNAM WAR, and; as a result, President LYNDON B. JOHNSON dropped his bid for reelection.

Eugene Joseph McCarthy was born March 29, 1916, in the rural farming village of Watkins, Minnesota. McCarthy's family was strongly rooted in the local Catholic church, and he spent his first 11 years of schooling at St. Anthony's School in Watkins. At the age of 15, McCarthy left home and enrolled at St. John's Preparatory School in Collegeville, Minnesota. The institution, run by the Benedictine monks of the St. John's Abbey, shaped McCarthy's intellectual and spiritual life both as a prep school student and as an undergraduate at the adjacent St. John's University. While excelling academically at the university, McCarthy was also an outstanding athlete, playing both baseball and hockey.

Following his graduation from St. John's University in 1935, McCarthy found little work in the Depression-era job market for a 19-year-old with a bachelor's degree in English, regardless of his academic record. He took up work as a public schoolteacher, and briefly as a school principal, while working on his master's degree from the University of Minnesota. He returned to St. John's as a faculty member from 1940 to 1943 before leaving to serve in the War Department's military intelligence division until the end of World War II.

In 1948, McCarthy made his first successful bid for public office, running on Minnesota's Democratic-Farmer-Labor Party ticket for the U.S. House of Representatives. During his stint in the House, McCarthy became known for his decidedly liberal voting record. Elected to the Senate in 1958, McCarthy served with relatively little national attention until the fall of 1967, when he announced his plans to challenge President Johnson for the Democratic presidential nomination. The centerpiece of McCarthy's surprise candidacy was his determined opposition to the war in Vietnam.

As a senator in 1964, McCarthy supported the Gulf of Tonkin Resolution, which gave the president broad discretionary powers over U.S. involvement in Vietnam following an apparently unprovoked attack on American vessels in international waters. By 1967, however, McCarthy had become a vocal critic of the war and the president's handling of the conflict. The Johnson administration initially disregarded his single-issue candidacy, but McCarthy collected a loyal following of Democrats who opposed continued involvement in the war. McCarthy had not, in fact, been the first choice of ANTIWAR MOVEMENT leaders to challenge Johnson. After several leading Democrats refused to run against the president, activists turned to the little-known senator from Minnesota, and McCarthy responded favorably. His campaign began to gain steam during the winter of 1968, and in the March 1968 New Hampshire primary, McCarthy captured 20 of 24 delegates, prompting Johnson's shocking withdrawal from the presidential race.

McCarthy went on to sweep the next three primaries, but ROBERT F. KENNEDY, the younger brother of assassinated President JOHN F. KENNEDY, defeated the Minnesota senator in four of the following five primaries. Kennedy had initially rejected the plea from antiwar leaders to enter the nomination race against Johnson, which had opened the door for McCarthy to accept the antiwar mantle. Kennedy's entrance into the campaign brought an end to McCarthy's momentum in the primaries, and after Kennedy was assassinated following his victory in the California primary, Vice President HUBERT H. HUMPHREY declared himself a candidate for the nomination despite not being entered in a single state primary.

At the 1968 Democratic Convention in Chicago, which was characterized by violent clashes between Chicago police and antiwar and civil rights protestors in the city's parks and streets, McCarthy lost the nomination to Humphrey. The turmoil outside the convention hall greatly disturbed McCarthy, who addressed a crowd of over 2,000 protestors in Grant Park on the final night of the convention, hoping to calm the volatile situation. TELEVISION cameras captured the disruption at the convention and broadcast it to viewers across the country. The images of police violence and tear gas assaults on the demonstrators seriously impaired the chance of success for Humphrey in the general election, which he lost to Republican Richard M. Nixon.

In 1970, McCarthy decided not to run for reelection in the Senate, and Humphrey won his seat. McCarthy made two more campaigns for the presidency in 1972 and 1976, but then he retired to a career of writing and lecturing.

Further reading: Albert Eisele, *Almost to the Presidency* (Blue Earth, Minn.: The Piper Company, 1972).

— Guy R. Temple

McCarthy, Joseph R. (1908–1957)

Capitalizing on American fears of COMMUNISM during the COLD WAR, Senator Joseph R. McCarthy dominated the political landscape of the early 1950s with his accusations of communist infiltration within the U.S. government. His use of broad allegations with little or no evidence to support them induced a paranoia within American culture that came to be known as McCarthyism.

Born on November 14, 1908, in a small town in northeastern Wisconsin, McCarthy was the son of Irish Catholic farmers. He was a boisterous child who worked both on the farm and in his own businesses until 1929, when he graduated high school in only one year. He entered Marquette University the following year, where he studied law, graduating in 1935, and he then worked for a prominent Wisconsin attorney. Unsatisfied with his job, McCarthy ran a series of aggressive campaigns for district attorney (which he lost in 1936) and circuit judge (which he won in 1938) that were characterized by thorough, resourceful, and ruthless inflammatory rhetoric and distortions of the truth.

McCarthy enlisted in the U.S. Marine Corps in 1942. While on leave in 1944, he unsuccessfully sought the Republican nomination for the Senate, even though he was considered a NEW DEAL Democrat and a staunch supporter of President Franklin D. Roosevelt. McCarthy returned to military service until the end of World War II, and, in 1946, he defeated incumbent senator Robert La Follette, Jr. for the Republican nomination and Democrat John M. Murphy in the general election. During the campaign, McCarthy used communism as an issue to attack his opponents. He was not the first to do so; Republicans, anxious to reclaim the majority after over 10 years of Democratic rule in the White House and Congress, knew that the issue of "domestic subversion" within the DEMOCRATIC PARTY was too simple and too effective to ignore.

On February 9, 1950, in a speech to the Ohio County Women's Republican Club of Wheeling, West Virginia, McCarthy claimed he had "a list of 205 that were known to the Secretary of State as being members of the Communist Party and who nevertheless are still working and shaping the policy of the State Department." McCarthy never intended the speech to be the start of a nationwide crusade against communism, but by the next day his claims were picked up by the Associated Press and wired to newspapers across the country. Two days later in Nevada, McCarthy charged that there were 57 "card-carrying Communists" in the State Department. In testimony before the Senate on February 20, he presented 81 "cases" of treason, most of which came from an old list of past, present, and prospective State Department employees, who had been largely cleared of any meaningful wrongdoing. The Senate resolved to open bipartisan formal hearings on the matter, concluding in June that McCarthy had proved nothing.

McCarthy's impact and influence, however, only grew. He became synonymous with the issue of communist subversion in government, traveling across the country making accusation after accusation with scant hard evidence to back up his claims. He matched any attack made on his own credibility with an equally harsh attack on his accusers' loyalty to the United States, a tactic of instant suspicion and paranoia that his critics termed "McCarthyism."

As a political force, McCarthy quickly grew indispensable. He attacked the administration of President HARRY S. TRUMAN for its failure to stop the communist takeover of mainland China in 1949, specifically singling out Secretary of Defense GEORGE C. MARSHALL, insinuating that Marshall let the takeover go unchecked. One measure of McCarthy's power came in 1952 when presidential candidate DWIGHT D. EISENHOWER neglected to defend Marshall, who was his commanding officer during World War II. When the Republicans regained control of the Senate that same year, a reelected McCarthy became the chair of the Committee on Government Operations of the Senate and its permanent subcommittee on investigations.

By the end of 1953, McCarthy failed to produce any substantive discovery of treason or domestic subversion within the U.S. government. His charges against the U.S. military provoked a feud that led to the ARMY-MCCARTHY HEARINGS. Nationally televised for the first time, the hearings allowed the majority of Americans to see McCarthy's sensational style of interrogation at work rather than just read his statements in the newspaper. The hearings eroded McCarthy's support. The Republicans lost control of the Senate in the 1954 elections, and in December, the Senate, including 22 Republicans, voted to condemn McCarthy and his behavior. Afterward, he became an outcast in Washington, and he was often the only senator to cast a dissenting vote. His thinly veiled alcoholism grew worse while his shaky health deteriorated, and on May 2, 1957, he died of severe liver disease while still in office.

Further reading: Robert Griffith, *The Politics of Fear: Joseph R. McCarthy and the Senate* (Lexington: University Press of Kentucky, 1970); David M. Oshinsky, *A Conspiracy So Immense: The World of Joe McCarthy* (New York: Free Press, 1983); Thomas C. Reeves, *The Life and Times of Joe McCarthy: A Biography* (New York: Stein & Day, 1982).

— Adam B. Vary

McDonald's

The first nationwide fast food restaurant, McDonald's took the concept of the assembly line and adapted it to food production, capitalizing on the growth in SUBURBANIZATION during the 1950s.

Before founding McDonald's, brothers Richard and Maurice McDonald failed at practically every BUSINESS venture they attempted. They moved to California from their home in New Hampshire in hopes of working in the movie business. Odd jobs for studios did not suit them, however, and their movie theater quickly folded in the midst of the Great Depression. In 1937, the brothers opened a hot-dog stand near the Santa Anita racetrack, but it was only successful during racing season. In 1940, with a $5,000 loan from the Bank of America, they opened a larger drive-in restaurant in the growing city of San Bernardino; it was an immediate success, making an annual profit of $40,000.

The brothers, however, were not satisfied. It took approximately 20 minutes for their customers to get their food, and with more and more families living farther away from their jobs, they had less and less time to spend waiting for a meal. The McDonald brothers realized that in order to speed production, they needed to streamline the restaurant, which meant smaller menus and higher volume. In 1948, they closed their business and invented what became the blueprint for the fast food restaurant. They focused their menu on the hamburger, by far their most popular item; rather than have a messy condiment stand, all burgers had ketchup, mustard, onions, and two pickles. Paper wrappers and cups replaced silverware and dishes; two custom-made stainless steel grills replaced a single cast-iron grill, and a machine that made peppermint patties was adapted to make hamburger patties instead. Finally, the work was specialized: two workers each just made the hamburgers, milkshakes and french fries, two more just wrapped the burgers, and three others just took orders at the counter. Much like WILLIAM J. LEVITT's mass-production system of building suburban houses, the McDonald brothers turned food production into an assembly-line process.

When the newly renovated McDonald's restaurant opened in early 1949, business dropped off at first; teenage boys, who used the old drive-in as a hangout spot, were not welcome at the new family friendly location. By 1950, though, the brothers' hard work paid off. The cheap prices (hamburgers were 15 cents and an entire family could eat for only $2.50), quick service, and clean facilities appealed to the small family, and, by 1951, McDonald's gross profit was 40 percent higher than before the change. The restaurant quickly became legendary in the restaurant world, and the McDonald brothers were inundated with requests for information about their operation

One such interested person was RAY KROC, a 52-year-old self-made businessman who in the early 1950s was selling a milkshake mixer that could handle up to five shakes at a time. While his business was actually declining elsewhere in the country—small town drugstores and soda shops were closing as people moved to the suburbs—McDonald's was using 10 of his machines by 1954, and Kroc went to San Bernardino to investigate why. Thoroughly impressed with what he found, Kroc approached the brothers about running their franchise operation. The brothers had sold their system to a few people in the region for a share of the profits, but their interest remained in their own store; they did not have the time or the patience for running a national operation. They hired Kroc to run it for them.

While the McDonald brothers invented the fast food restaurant, Kroc made McDonald's a national institution. He was a rabidly persistent businessman who recognized that in order for McDonald's to succeed as a national chain it had to be the same wherever a customer went. He imposed strict controls on menu options, pricing, quality control, cleanliness, and presentation, demanding franchisees to conform to every single specification. He moved the national headquarters to Chicago and opened his own franchise in the suburb of Des Plaines, stopping by every day before work to open the store and on his way home to clean up and close. In 1956, he awarded 12 franchises; by 1960, the total number reached 228, and it continued to rise, increasing by about 100 per year. While Kroc demanded strict conformity, he treated franchisees fairly, passing breaks in produce prices on to them and taking 1.9 percent of their receipts rather than charging high franchise fees up front.

In 1961, Kroc, who by this time saw the McDonald brothers as freeloaders letting him do all the work, bought them out for $2.7 million. In 1963, McDonald's introduced the Ronald McDonald character that quickly became part of American POPULAR CULTURE, and it was the first restaurant in the country to buy ADVERTISING on TELEVISION. In 1965, with 710 McDonald's restaurants in 44 states, the company went public on the New York Stock Exchange. In 1976, McDonald's made over $2 billion in business, and reached over 20,000 locations across the globe by the end of the century.

Further reading: Marshall William Fishwick, ed., *Ronald Revisited: The World of Ronald McDonald* (Bowling Green, Ohio: Bowling Green University Popular Press, 1983); David Halberstam, *The Fifties* (New York: Villard Books, 1993); Ray Kroc with Robert Anderson, *Grinding It Out: The Making of McDonald's* (New York: St. Martin's Press, 1977, 1987).

— Adam B. Vary

March on Washington (1963)

On August 28, 1963, approximately 250,000 supporters of the Civil Rights movement gathered in Washington, D.C., to call upon the White House to ban racist laws and give black Americans equal opportunity in employment and education.

The march demonstrated to the world and Congress that the time had come for true equality for all men and women regardless of race. One of the largest demonstrations of the Civil Rights movement, the March on Washington proved that positive changes could occur through peaceful means.

Conditions throughout the United States in the 1960s reflected a staunch coalition of mostly southern Americans committed to a system of SEGREGATION. Protestors met in April, called together by MARTIN LUTHER KING, JR., a young black Baptist minister and president of the SOUTHERN CHRISTIAN LEADERSHIP CONFERENCE (SCLC), and Reverend Fred Shuttlesworth to denounce segregated conditions across the South. Gathering in Birmingham, Alabama, the demonstrators were broken up by local police who used brutal methods such as fire hoses and dogs to disband the protestors. The BIRMINGHAM CONFRONTATION forced President JOHN F. KENNEDY to increase the efforts of the government to pass comprehensive federal antidiscrimination legislation.

To lobby for passage of such a measure, civil rights leaders, pressed by black activists, arranged a massive March on Washington in August. Demonstrators assembled for the event included Protestant, Catholic, and Jewish leaders, and celebrities such as diplomat RALPH BUNCHE, writer JAMES BALDWIN, entertainers Sammy Davis, Jr., Harry Belafonte, and Lena Horne, and former baseball player JACKIE ROBINSON. Folk music artists of the early 1960s were there as well. Joan Baez, BOB DYLAN, and Peter, Paul, and Mary led the crowd in songs associated with the movement, such as "Blowin' in the Wind" and "We Shall Overcome."

On this occasion King made his moving "I Have a Dream" speech. "I have a dream," King declared, "that one day this nation will rise up and live out the true meaning of its creed: 'We hold these truths to be self-evident, that all men are created equal.' I have a dream that one day on the red hills of Georgia, the sons of former slaves and the sons of former slave-owners will be able to sit together at the table of brotherhood." King concluded by quoting from an old hymn: "Free at last! Free at last! Thank God almighty, we are free at last!"

Other activists spoke to the assembled crowd with the intention of persuading both black and white Americans to step up their civil rights activities in a peaceful manner. JOHN LEWIS, chairman of the STUDENT NONVIOLENT COORDINATING COMMITTEE (SNCC), stated, "For the first time in 100 years this nation is being awakened to the fact that segregation is evil and it must be destroyed in all forms. Our presence today proves that we have been aroused to the point of action."

Protester demands included the passage of civil rights legislation in Congress, immediate elimination of all racial segregation in schools, protection for civil rights demonstrators from police brutality, a large program of public works to remedy unemployment, a law preventing discrimination in the workplace, an increase in the minimum wage, and self-government for the District of Columbia. These concerns reflected issues that many African Americans faced: a lack of fair and equal employment and education.

At the conclusion of the rally, the crowd dispersed with a speed and order that emphasized the nonviolent nature of the demonstration. In the months following the march, Kennedy was assassinated and LYNDON B. JOHNSON took up the fight for the passage of comprehensive civil rights legislation. While Kennedy introduced such legislation to Congress in June 1963, it was over one year before Johnson signed the CIVIL RIGHTS ACT OF 1964, barring discrimination on the basis of race in all public accommodations, with an equal opportunity clause making it illegal for employers to discriminate in hiring on the grounds of race, religion, sex, or national origin.

Further reading: Herbert Garfinkle, *When Negroes March: The March on Washington Movement in the Organizational Politics for FEPC* (New York: Atheneum, 1969); David J. Garrow, *Bearing the Cross: Martin Luther King, Jr. and the Southern Christian Leadership Conference* (New York: William Morrow, 1986).

— Kim Richardson

marriage and family life

Despite unprecedented economic prosperity, America suffered from instability and uncertainty after World War II. While hailing the middle-class myth of prosperity and abundance for all, post–World War II Americans took refuge from the dangers of the outside world by withdrawing into the security of the family home.

Following World War II, the average age of men and women who married began to drop and the birthrate began to rise. The rising birthrate was perhaps the most significant indication of the monumental change that had taken place in middle-class America's perception of domestic stability and family values. After nearly a hundred years of steady decline, postwar American married couples not only reversed the birthrate trend but also caused it to skyrocket to a 20th-century high, creating the BABY BOOM. As men and women of the late 1940s and 1950s married in ever-increasing numbers, they also reversed the divorce rate, which had been on a steady rise since World War I and peaked at the close of World War II. The reversal of these long-term demographic trends came as Americans embraced family life more aggressively and with more confidence than ever before.

Although they put a high premium on family life, postwar Americans regarded gender roles in a rigid and traditional way. The husband and father resumed the identity of "breadwinner" while the wife and mother resumed the identity of "homemaker," as reflected in situational comedies like *Ozzie and Harriet* and *Father Knows Best.* The return of the woman's role as homemaker was perhaps most significant, as it effectively stripped women of the unprecedented level of independence that they had experienced during World War II.

There was, however, an underside to economic prosperity. While peace, low divorce rates, and a booming economy all defined the American dream to middle-class Americans who had lived through an economic depression and a world war, the euphoria associated with the transition from the adversity of the 1930s and early 1940s to the peace and prosperity of the late 1940s helped to hide a less pleasant side of American society. As women's lives became predetermined by the new postwar family ideology, an all white middle-class migration to the suburbs further institutionalized racism and inner-city poverty. The suburban phenomenon excluded non-whites, for as middle-class whites fled the city for the suburbs, the largely black minority population was left behind. While working-class blacks did not enjoy the postwar prosperity that most middle-class whites enjoyed, they did experience similar rises in birth and marriage rates.

At the same time, the post–World War II years were marked by threats to the American way of life that even the walls of the family home could not keep out. COMMUNISM, atomic weapons, and the COLD WAR induced an overwhelming anxiety. The fear of atomic annihilation and radioactive fallout reached epic proportions by the late 1950s. Magazines often contained images that fused the atomic age and domesticity, showing families in their neatly organized fallout shelters. *Consumer Reports* in March 1959 warned consumers about radioactivity in "The Milk We Drink." The fear of communism was maintained by effective political propaganda suggesting that, without vigilance, communism would spread from country to country until it threatened the very existence of the United States.

By the late 1950s, the illusion of stability began to reveal the effects of these disturbing undercurrents. Breaching class lines, the BEAT GENERATION, MUSIC, and a new political ideology based on activism rather than adaptation began to expose American poverty and question the rigid institutionalized boundaries established and embraced by the post–World War II generation. The baby boomers who came of age in the 1960s and 1970s created a COUNTERCULTURE and a new focus on WOMEN'S STATUS AND RIGHTS resulting in the weakening of the nuclear family as the central building block in American society.

The Great Depression of the 1930s, World War II, and the politics of the cold war all played major parts in creating and shaping the revival of the family. The hardship and fear associated with all these events led Americans to cling to rigid gender roles for the freedom from adversity that they offered. The baby boomers, however, were disenchanted with the society that their parents had created. They grew up in the affluence of the postwar years and they saw the consequences of the stability that their parents had so desperately sought in uneven distribution of wealth, sexual frustration, and institutionalized gender and racial inequality. As a result, the upheaval of baby boomers produced an unprecedented divorce rate and a corresponding decline in the rate of marriages and births.

Further reading: Elaine Tyler May, *Homeward Bound: American Families in the Cold War Era* (New York: Basic Books, 1988).

— Jason Reed

Marshall, George C.   See Volume VIII

Marshall, Thurgood (1908–1993)

Thurgood Marshall was the first black justice to serve on the U.S. Supreme Court.

Born on July 2, 1908, in Baltimore, Maryland, Marshall attended an all-black public school, and then went on to the integrated Lincoln University in Pennsylvania where he received his undergraduate degree with honors in 1930. After being turned down by the Maryland School of Law because he was black, Marshall applied to and was accepted by the Howard University School of Law, a predominately black institution in Washington, D.C. In 1933, Marshall graduated, and in the same year he was admitted to the Maryland Bar.

Marshall's first venture into law came when he opened his own practice in Baltimore. Taking primarily the civil rights cases of those who could not afford a lawyer, he did not make much money in his early years of practice. He later had the opportunity to defend a black student attempting to gain admission to the University of Maryland School of Law, the same school that had earlier rejected Marshall. He won the case.

The NATIONAL ASSOCIATION FOR THE ADVANCEMENT OF COLORED PEOPLE (NAACP) noticed Marshall's activities. In 1936, Marshall accepted the position as NAACP lawyer and assistant counsel, and later he became chief counsel. He and his staff began a lengthy effort to overturn the 1896 judicial ruling of *Plessy v. Ferguson*, which mandated separate facilities for blacks and whites, as long as they were equal. To that end, he set up the NAACP Legal Defense and Education Fund, which aimed at working though the courts to have SEGREGATION, particularly in schools, declared illegal.

During his time with the NAACP, Marshall argued many cases. In 1950, he won two Supreme Court cases involving graduate schools. In *Sweatt v. Painter,* the Court ruled that a black law school could not be inferior to a segregated white law school in the same area and still meet the test of constitutionality. The second case, *McLaurin v. Oklahoma State Regents,* ruled that a school could not accept a student, and then confine him or her to certain areas on the basis of race. Marshall defended minorities throughout the United States, preparing cases in Missouri and the University of Texas where blacks were excluded from juries. Meanwhile, he challenged discrimination in other areas as well. During and after World War II, he was an outspoken opponent of the government detention of Japanese Americans, and in 1951, he traveled to Japan and South Korea to investigate the mistreatment of blacks by white southern officers and the unfair practices of military courts trying blacks.

In 1954, Marshall and his staff took on their most important and influential case in BROWN V. BOARD OF EDUCATION. The Supreme Court headed by EARL WARREN ruled unanimously that "separate educational facilities [were] inherently unequal," overturning the "separate but equal" doctrine of the 1896 decision in *Plessy v. Ferguson.* This victory gave children the right to attend desegregated public schools. This victory made Marshall a national figure. With the Democrats in the control of the White House, Marshall made it known he wanted a judgeship.

On September 23, 1961, after eight months in office, President JOHN F. KENNEDY appointed Marshall to the U.S. Court of Appeals for the Second Circuit, serving New York. There was a one year delay before he could take up the position for numerous southern white sena-

Thurgood Marshall, NAACP chief counsel, before the Supreme Court, 1958   *(Library of Congress)*

tors did all they could to block the appointment. During his tenure as a federal appellate judge, Marshall wrote 150 opinions and presided over many cases in which the Supreme Court reversed none of his 98 majority decisions. Some of his more important decisions included finding loyalty oaths required of New York teachers unconstitutional, limiting the authority of immigration officials to summarily deport aliens, and enforcing the Fourth and Fifth Amendments in cases of illegal search and seizure and double jeopardy.

In 1965, President LYNDON B. JOHNSON appointed Marshall to the post of solicitor general of the United States. This entailed representing the government in cases before the Supreme Court. Marshall won 14 out of 19 cases. His most important achievement came in the MIRANDA V. ARIZONA decision, which required police to inform suspects of their rights.

In 1967, Johnson nominated Marshall to the Supreme Court. Even with stiff opposition from the president's own DEMOCRATIC PARTY, he was confirmed by a Senate vote of 69 to 11. On October 2, 1967, Marshall was sworn in and took his seat. He became the first black to sit on the bench, and the first justice from Maryland since Chief Justice Roger B. Taney. Marshall served for 24 years on the bench before his retirement in 1991. On January 24, 1993, he died in Bethesda, Maryland.

Further reading: Randall Walton Bland, *Private Pressure on Public Law: The Legal Career of Justice Thurgood Marshall, 1934–1991* (Lanham, Md.: University Press of America, 1993); Michael D. Davis and Hunter R. Clark. *Thurgood Marshall: Warrior at the Bar, Rebel on the Bench* (Secaucus, N.J.: Carol Publishing Group, 1992); Mark V. Tushnet, *Making Civil Rights Law: Thurgood Marshall and the Supreme Court, 1936–1961* (New York: Oxford University Press, 1994).

— Robert A. Deahl

Marshall Plan

The Marshall Plan, or the European Recovery Program, was an American assistance package designed to rebuild the devastated countries of Western Europe following World War II.

Although initiated in part by humanitarian concerns, the Marshall Plan constituted an indispensable element of American strategy in the political, economic, and ideological struggle known as the COLD WAR. In particular, American policymakers feared that economic instability on the European continent would invite both economic depression and communist subversion. They also worried that stagnant European demand would threaten the economic boom in the United States that had begun with American

entry in the war and had been sustained by continued international demand.

At the end of World War II, EUROPE lay in shambles. The major powers had exhausted themselves: Great Britain and France were still reeling, Italy, Greece, and Turkey bordered on chaos, and Germany lay in ruins. Europe also faced a severe manpower shortage: over 35 million people had died during the war. Hordes of displaced persons, buffeted by the ravages of war, wandered about the continent. Fearful that such economic dislocation invited communist influence, the administration of HARRY S. TRUMAN sought to rebuild Western Europe.

Secretary of State George C. Marshall first publicly enunciated the European Recovery Program on June 5, 1947, in a speech at Harvard University. Marshall called upon the nations of Europe to unite and tackle European reconstruction in a comprehensive and collective fashion. Initially included in this call were the nations of both Western and Eastern Europe. Marshall told the nations of Europe that if they could devise a comprehensive plan of reconstruction, the United States would fund it.

At a summer meeting in Paris, representatives from Great Britain, France, and the SOVIET UNION met to hammer out details of the proposal. Wary of capitalist penetration into Eastern Europe, the Soviet foreign minister Vyacheslav Molotov argued against any collective action, preferring instead a flexible plan able to address the needs of specific countries. Knowing that the United States desired collective action, the British and French foreign ministers squashed Molotov's initiatives, prompting his departure. Although the United States had offered aid to the Soviet Union, American policymakers believed that the Russians would never accept it on American terms, knowing that American assistance would undermine Soviet control in Eastern Europe. Moscow's rejection helped the Economic Cooperation Act pass Congress easily in March 1948—69 to 17 in the Senate and 329 to 74 in the House.

From April 1948 to December 1951, almost 13 billion American dollars flowed into Western Europe under the direction of the Economic Cooperation Administration. In all, 16 countries participated in the program: Austria, Belgium, Denmark, France, Greece, Iceland, Ireland, Italy, Luxembourg, the Netherlands, Norway, Portugal, Sweden, Switzerland, Turkey, the United Kingdom, and western Germany. The greatest funding went to Great Britain, France, Italy, and West Germany. Direct grants accounted for the bulk of this aid. The money was used to restore industrial and agricultural production, establish financial stability, and expand trade. Seventy percent of the aid was spent on goods from the United States, thereby ensuring the continued international demand for American products. While some Europeans feared that the Marshall Plan served as an instrument for perpetual American domi-

Nations in the Marshall Plan, 1948

nance, most Europeans recognized that the assistance helped revive Western Europe.

Americans, for the most part, viewed the Marshall Plan as a runaway success. The European Recovery Program became a model for other U.S. initiatives designed to bolster countries and regions against communist influence. Truman declared as much with his POINT FOUR speech in 1949, in which he exhorted Americans to embark on a bold new program to provide technical assistance to third world countries.

Further reading: Michael J. Hogan, *The Marshall Plan: America, Britain, and the Reconstruction of Western Europe, 1947–1952* (Cambridge: Cambridge University Press, 1987).

— Brian Etheridge

massive resistance   See White Citizens' Councils

media   See journalism

Medicaid

Established in 1965 as an amendment to the Social Security Act of 1935, Medicaid offered financial assistance for medical bills for the poor of America.

In the late 1950s, the American government began to grapple with the problems facing the poor in securing medical insurance. Large numbers of the poor population of the United States had no insurance coverage, which contributed to the declining health of the lower class. Congress first addressed this issue with the Kerr-Mills Act of 1960, which provided government financial assistance to low-income families and the elderly.

The GREAT SOCIETY of President LYNDON B. JOHNSON in the 1960s sought to do something for everyone. Continuing the commitment of the NEW DEAL for government to help those who could not help themselves, it provided medical care to the poor for the first time. Amendments to the Social Security Act of 1935 became law in 1965. The two main components of this reform were Medicaid and MEDICARE, financial medical assistance for the elderly, both of which were to be administered through the U.S. Department of Health, Education, and Welfare. These programs were intended to extend health care insurance to the poor and elderly who, for the most part, did not possess any form of health insurance.

Under the Medicaid program, the federal government would match state funds for certain required programs such as "hospital and physicians' services, care in a skilled nursing facility, home health service, family planning, and early diagnosis and treatment of illnesses." Some optional forms of coverage included prescription drugs, eyeglasses, and care in intermediate-care facilities, which states could provide at their own discretion. Those eligible for these programs were categorized as "low-income people that are aged, blind, disabled, pregnant, or members of families with dependent children, and certain other children."

Medicaid did not enjoy strong support after its implementation. Criticism immediately focused on the way individual states ran their programs. Since each state determined what constituted the income level necessary to receive Medicaid, discrepancies among the individual states occurred. Some states established poverty lines that included a larger number of the poor than other states. Also, each state was able to determine what extra services it would apply to qualifiers of Medicaid. Some states offered many of the extra options while other states offered none.

Medicaid also received criticism due to the sizable cost of the funding for the program. Analysts estimated that the annual cost would amount to a little over $1.3 billion in 1965. By 1968, however, the yearly government funding for Medicaid had more than doubled, and the funds needed to support the program grew in each succeeding year. The government had not anticipated correctly the number of people who would be eligible for this program and the benefits that it provided.

Since the implementation of Medicaid in 1965, there have been numerous amendments to the original legislation. Medicaid has become a hot political topic, due to the amount of funding it now requires. Many physicians do not agree with the way that Medicaid covers their patients, and some have tried to avoid patients who use this form of coverage.

By initiating Medicaid, the federal government, for the first time, began to take a serious look at the availability of health care and insurance for the underprivileged of American society. The program resulted in an increase in the quality and amount of care that low-income people received, making it a revolutionary piece of legislation.

Further reading: John Holahan, *Financing Health Care for the Poor* (Lexington, Mass.: Lexington Books, 1975).
— Jennifer Howell

Medicare

Medicare constitutes a federally sponsored program that provides health insurance to the elderly and the poor in an effort to protect them from the financial ruin of health care bills.

President HARRY S. TRUMAN first promoted a national comprehensive health insurance program during his tenure. Truman gave his presidential endorsement in 1945, but the proposal was continually rejected until LYNDON B. JOHNSON took office in 1964.

For many years, Congress was simply not interested in a health care program for the elderly. Even so, in 1952, some congressmen began to introduce measures they knew had no chance of passage as a way of keeping the idea alive. They found continued resistance from members of Congress and the public, who believed that health insurance should be dealt with at the state, and not the federal, level. They also faced the opposition of the American Medical Association, which claimed that any such program amounted to socialized medicine.

A 1963 survey by the government paved the way for support for a medical aid program. It showed that nearly half of the elderly in the United States had no type of health insurance at all.

There were two issues that needed to be resolved in order for a health insurance bill to be passed: eligibility and coverage. Congressman Wilbur Mills, a Democrat from Arkansas, found the way to solve both these problems in order for Congress to pass Medicare. He decided that Medicare would allow those elderly 65 and over who were eligible to receive Social Security or Railroad Retirement benefits to obtain health insurance under Title XVIII of the Social Security Act. He also decided that Medicare would be divided into two main parts. The first part provided hospital insurance, covering hospital and nursing care. The second part dealt with supplemental medical insurance, covering physician, outpatient, and ambulatory services. Such services as preventive services, dental care, eye care, and prescription drugs were not covered under Medicare. These could be covered under a companion MEDICAID program that catered to the needs of the poor. Congress agreed on these terms, and the House of Representatives passed the bill by a 307 to 116 vote, while the Senate passed it the next day with a vote of 70 to 24. The program became law as part of the amendments to the Social Security Act of 1935 when Johnson, as part of his GREAT SOCIETY programs, signed the legislation on July 30, 1965.

Physicians, like patients, were uncertain about just how the Medicare program would work. They were worried about the amount that they charged their patients, because the Medicare program was going to codify and freeze their definitions of reasonable charges. As a result, physician fees more than doubled in the year preceding the enactment of Medicare. The overall service charge of hospitals also increased by 21.9 percent in the first year of Medicare's operation.

Medicare covered all expenses during a patient's first 60 days of hospitalization, and a portion of the cost for an additional 30 days. The insurance covered a room accommodating two to four beds, drugs while a patient was hospitalized, and other supplies and services. Once released from the hospital, the patient was not charged the first 20 days of an extended-care facility. The patient was allowed unlimited free visits from nurses for up to one year after discharge from the hospital or extended-care facility.

Medicare continued to develop with the passage of an amendment in 1972 that allowed people who were disabled also to receive assistance.

Further reading: Theodore R. Marmor, *The Politics of Medicare* (Chicago: Aldine, 1973); Monte M. Poen, *Harry S. Truman versus the Medical Lobby: The Genesis of Medicare* (Columbia: University of Missouri Press, 1979).

— Megan D. Wessel

medicine

The period following World War II witnessed great advancement in medicine. Congress generously funded numerous research projects as the idea that health was a God-given right of every citizen evolved. Enormous strides were taken against viruses, cardiovascular disease, and mental illness. New drugs improved the general quality of many people's lives.

In November 1945, seven months after taking office and three months after the end of World War II, President HARRY S. TRUMAN delivered a message to Congress in which he set forth what he considered to be the deficiencies in the field of medicine. He proposed that "Congress adopt a comprehensive and modern health program for the nation, consisting of five major parts each of which contributes to all the others." He called for the construction of hospitals and related facilities through federal grants-in-aid to the states, the expansion of public health services, also through grants-in-aid to the states, federal support of medical education and medical research, a system of prepayment for medical care, financed through an expansion of "our compulsory social insurance system," and protection against loss of wages from disability or sickness, again by expansion of the social insurance system.

The concept of an organized national attack on major disease problems through the establishment of institutes in a large research center gained momentum in the late 1940s. The Mental Health Institute was established in 1946, and both the National Heart Institute and the National Institute for Dental Disease were authorized in 1948. The Omnibus Act passed by Congress in 1950 gave the Surgeon General of the United States in conjunction with the Public Health Service (USPHS) the power to establish institutes to deal with major disease problems. The National Institute of Neurological Disease and Blindness, the National Institute of Arthritis and Metabolic Diseases, and the National Institute of Allergy and Infectious Diseases were founded in accordance with this legislation. Congress provided funds for the NATIONAL INSTITUTES OF HEALTH (NIH) and the National Science Foundation (NSF), and it allocated $5 million in 1950 to the ATOMIC ENERGY COMMISSION for the specific purpose of atomic research in the treatment of cancer. The KOREAN WAR occasioned a brief pause in the steady rise in the medical research budget, but, in 1952, the upward trend resumed. During the administration of DWIGHT D. EISENHOWER, Congress regularly added $8 million to $15 million to the amount proposed by the administration for the NIH budget. By 1956, the annual NIH budget had risen to almost $100 million.

The NIH contributed by developing a vaccination for rubella, new advances in the treatment of hypertension, rheumatic heart disease, and stroke. Antihypertensive drugs were first used in 1950; by 1968, the death rate from hypertensive heart disease declined 59 percent. The NIH also contributed to the development of new techniques for heart and vascular surgery.

The government also supported building hospitals. In 1946, Congress enacted the Hospital Survey and Construction Act, known as the Hill-Burton Act, to provide funds to the states for orderly planning and construction of hospitals. The act also forbade government interference in the operation of the hospitals. In 1964, amendments to the original Hill-Burton Act provided support for construction of nursing homes, diagnostic treatment centers, chronic-disease hospitals, and rehabilitation facilities. By 1965, the federal government had provided almost $2 billion to match about $4 billion provided by sponsors for the construction of 6,700 projects involving 285,000 hospital beds and 1,880 health units of various types.

The MEDICARE program was signed into law by President LYNDON B. JOHNSON in 1965, along with the MEDICAID program. They were designed to provide medical care for the elderly and the "medically needy." Under Medicare and Medicaid, hospital care was less costly to the patient than care in the home, and the increase in hospitalization measures resulted in the rise of medical costs. Despite problems, the measures provided health care for those who previously could not afford it.

The nation made progress in fighting disease. In July 1946, the Centers for Disease Control (CDC), headquartered in Atlanta, Georgia, was established under the name Communicable Disease Center. The CDC grew out of the Office of Malaria Control in War Areas (MCWA), an emergency World War II organization designed to reduce potential malaria transmission in the proximity of military establishments. Atlanta was selected as the MCWA's home base because it was the central point of endemic malaria. The CDC was the first federal health organization ever set up to coordinate a national control program against a whole category of diseases. In 1947, plague control activities were transferred to CDC. The Epidemic Intelligence Service, whose members were popularly known as "the disease detectives," was established in 1951.

In 1962, Congress passed the Vaccination Assistance Act to help states and communities carry out intensive immunization programs against polio, diphtheria, whooping cough, tetanus, and other diseases, as new vaccines became licensed. By the end of the year, approximately 47 percent of the population was covered. A measles vaccine was added to the program in 1965 and a rubella vaccine in 1969. On June 24, 1970, the CDC became the Center for Disease Control, and later still the Centers for Disease Control.

The period after World War II constituted a time of great discovery in the field of medicine, from new drugs and vaccines to new surgical procedures. Streptomycin was developed and became a popular cure for tuberculosis and other infections. As its popularity grew, the bulk price dropped from $24 per gram in 1946 to 25 cents by the mid-1950s. Broad-spectrum antibiotics ended various diseases, while anticoagulants prevented hemorrhaging. In the 1940s, the first modern drug to treat leprosy was introduced, along with medicines to control epilepsy, and Benadryl, one of the first antihistamine drugs. In 1949, Dramamine was introduced as a motion sickness medication. In 1950, Banthine inaugurated a whole new approach to the treatment of ulcers.

There were many advances in treatment for cardiovascular diseases in the 1950s. In 1952, researchers discovered that electric shock could restart a heart. In 1954, external cardiac massage was combined with mouth-to-mouth breathing to maintain life for more than an hour after heart failure. The year 1952 brought the invention of the first cardiac pacemaker. They were later improved in the 1960s by the use of batteries, and finally a self-contained pacemaker was devised that could be implanted under the skin. In the years following the KOREAN WAR, techniques were improved for the insertion of cardiac catheters. With a catheter in the heart chambers or in the aorta or pulmonary artery, it became possible to record pressure curves, withdraw blood for measurement of oxygen content, detect an abnormal passage, inject indicator substances for the detection of malfunctioning valves, or introduce material for visualization of a select portion of the heart. Angiocardiography allowed doctors to form clear pictures of the different parts of the heart by injecting a radiopaque substance into a vein and taking X-ray pictures. All of this resulted in more precise cardiac diagnosis and greatly improved methods of treatment.

Heart surgery was improved during the war, due to the necessity of removing bullets from the heart. Blood vessel clamps lead to an increase in open-heart surgery. When the body's temperature was lowered to around 86 degrees, the oxygen requirement of the brain and other tissues was reduced so that the circulation could be shut off without harm for 15 to 20 minutes, allowing the surgeon to have a clear, dry field to work with. A few such operations were performed using this technique in the early 1950s, but by the mid-1950s, the whole field of cardiac surgery underwent a tremendous change as the result of a new technical development—the heart-lung machine. The heart-lung machine oxygenated blood, allowing blood to bypass the heart and lungs during surgery and permitted a surgeon ample time for work on the heart. In 1967, the first successful heart transplant was performed in South Africa. There were also liver and kidney transplants at about the same time.

The invention of the birth-control pill was launched by Margaret Sanger, a supporter of women's control over reproduction since the 1920s. By the 1950s, she campaigned aggressively for oral contraception to make birth control easier than before. Sanger persuaded Katherine Dexter McCormick, a wealthy heiress, to fund the necessary research. With financial backing, a team of scientists and doctors figured out how the female menstrual cycle worked, and then determined how to treat it hormonally so that ovulation would not take place. Testing took place in the mid-1950s in Puerto Rico, Haiti, and Mexico City. The failure rate was 1.7 percent, far better than for diaphragms or condoms. In 1960, the Food and Drug Administration approved the first oral contraceptive. In 1961, 14 percent of new patients at Planned Parenthood clinics chose oral contraception, and by 1964, that number had grown to 62 percent.

"THE PILL" became available during the rebellious 1960s, and it promoted more open sexuality. Most important, the pill allowed women to more easily control their own reproduction, enabling them to work outside the home. "Modern woman is at last free as man is free," said Clare Boothe Luce, a playwright and former member of Congress.

The COLD WAR era was a time of remarkable learning. Vaccines helped eradicate diseases that had killed millions in the past. Up until this point, polio had been a crippling disease, and the means of transmission were unknown. Many lived in fear of the disease that left its victims deformed, or dependent on "iron lung" machines to stay alive. In 1952, Jonas E. Salk, professor of research bacteriology at the University of Pittsburgh, developed and tested an inactivated vaccine made of dead virus. The vaccine was given in the form of a shot, and within months of its successful testing, over 5,000 schoolchildren had been vaccinated.

Within a few years, Albert B. Sabin, professor of research pediatrics at the University of Cincinnati College of Medicine, had developed an attenuated vaccine, one made of weakened live virus, that could be administered orally. This vaccine prevented the virus from multiplying in the intestinal tract, something Salk's vaccine did not do. Sabin's vaccine cost one-tenth what Salk's cost, and by 1961, 5 million people had been vaccinated with the live-virus vaccine, and it was 80 to 95 percent effective.

The CDC participated in the field trials that were conducted in 1954 for the Salk polio vaccine. In April 1955, two weeks after the Salk vaccine was released, six cases of polio in children who had received the vaccine were reported. Two days later the CDC's Poliomyelitis Surveillance Unit was established. It concluded that the cases were the result of a single manufacturer, and that manufacturer was shut down. The role of the CDC in a national health emergency was clearly established during this incident, setting a precedent for the immediate development of similar surveillance programs. In 1962, the CDC helped administer the first Sabin oral polio vaccine. Polio cases fell from 13,850 in 1955 to 5 in 1975. The CDC also worked with the World Health Organization (WHO) to eradicate smallpox. WHO established a global program to eradicate

smallpox within 10 years in 1966. CDC gave direction to the program in 19 west and central African countries. By the fall of 1975, smallpox was endemic only in Ethiopia.

After nine years of development, a vaccine was developed for the measles in 1954. With widespread use, the number of cases of measles reported in 1968 had fallen to 220,000 from the prevaccine level of 4 million annually. In 1964, scientists discovered that rubella, or German measles, a relatively mild disease, was connected to congenital deformities in children of mothers who contracted rubella early during pregnancy. A successful large-scale production of rubella vaccine was finally achieved in 1968, and distribution began in the United States.

Psychiatry was another field that enjoyed many scientific advances in the years following the war. During World War II, physicians realized that mental disease was a real problem. Some 1,100,000 men were rejected for military duty because of mental or neurological disorders. When these were added to the rejectees for mental and educational deficiencies, the total came to 1,767,000 out of 4,800,000. By 1946, psychiatric disorders accounted for 60 percent of all hospitalization under the Veterans' Administration. Before this time, many mentally ill were sent to asylums where there was no attempt to make them well. New research discovered many drugs, which helped treat psychotic illnesses, and as a result the number of patients confined to mental hospitals declined rapidly after peaking in 1955. Antipsychotic drugs, such as chlorpromazine and haloperidol, revolutionized the treatment of schizophrenia. Lithium was found to help alleviate periods of mania, and monoamine oxidase inhibitors could relieve depression. Shock therapy and frontal lobotomies to treat schizophrenia and anxiety gave way to drug therapy.

Child looks on as syringe with polio vaccine is made ready, 1962   *(Library of Congress)*

Further reading: James Bordley, M.D., *Two Centuries of American Medicine* (Philadelphia: W. B. Saunders, 1976).
— Elizabeth A. Henke

Meredith, James (1933–)

A civil rights activist, James Meredith served as the central figure in the desegregation of the University of Mississippi in 1962, and later he worked to increase African-American voter registration.

Meredith was born on June 25, 1933, in Kosciusko, Mississippi, to Cap and Roxie Meredith. He divided his childhood between working on his parents' farm and attending a training school for blacks, where he was known as the smartest and strongest boy in his class. In order to receive a better high school EDUCATION, Meredith moved with his uncle to St. Petersburg, Florida, when he was 17 years old. After graduating from high school, he joined the U.S. Air Force and served for nine years. Meredith then enrolled at the all-black Jackson State University in Jackson, Mississippi. Although he completed his degree requirements, he did not graduate because he refused to pay the diploma fee.

In September 1962, Meredith became the first African American to enroll at the University of Mississippi. While a court order confirmed his right to enter the school, Mississippi governor Ross Barnett led the opposition and refused to allow Meredith to enter the registrar's office. In response, President JOHN F. KENNEDY ordered federal marshals to escort Meredith to his classes. As school officials led Meredith to his dormitory, riots erupted outside, leaving two men dead, 175 people injured, and 212 people arrested. At Kennedy's request, national guardsmen and 22,000 army troops moved in to restore order. U.S. police troops remained on campus until Meredith graduated in 1963 with a bachelor's degree.

Following graduation, Meredith moved to Nigeria and studied at Ibadan University. When he returned to the United States one year later, he worked toward a law degree at Columbia University. In the summer of 1966, he embarked on a solitary, 16-day "walk against fear," which took him from Memphis, Tennessee, to Jackson, Mississippi, to encourage African-American voter registration for the upcoming primary. Meredith believed that if he could walk unarmed through Mississippi during primary-election week, he might induce black people to overcome their fears of white violence and get them to the polls. On the second day of the walk, an assailant shot Meredith two times. Although his injuries were not serious, the incident sparked outrage from civil rights organizations across the country. Civil rights activists, including MARTIN LUTHER KING, JR., carried the walk on to Jackson where STOKELY CARMICHAEL, leader of the STUDENT NONVIOLENT COOR-DINATING COMMITTEE (SNCC), called for BLACK POWER, resulting in a rift between moderate and militant wings of the Civil Rights movement.

Later in 1966, Meredith published *Three Years in Mississippi* about the racial injustice existing in his home state. He then returned to law school and received his degree from Columbia University in 1968. That same year, he ran for a seat from Harlem, in New York City, in the U.S. House of Representatives but lost to ADAM CLAYTON POWELL. Returning to Mississippi, Meredith distanced himself from public life and became involved in several business ventures. In 1984 and 1985, he taught a course on blacks and the law at the University of Mississippi. September 1989 marked his return to public life as he joined the staff of North Carolina senator Jesse Helms, an archconservative. After working as a domestic policy adviser for several years, Meredith and Helms eventually parted company. Meredith then threw his support behind conservative David Duke's unsuccessful bid for the REPUBLICAN PARTY's 1992 presidential nomination.

Further reading: Taylor Branch, *Pillar of Fire: America in the King Years, 1963–1965* (New York: Simon & Schuster, 1998); Henry Hampton and Steve Fayer, *Voices of Freedom: An Oral History of the Civil Rights Movement from the 1950s through the 1980s* (New York: Bantam Books, 1990).
— Donna J. Siebenthaler

Metropolitan Redevelopment Act See Model Cities program

Mexican-American movement See Latino movement

Middle East (and foreign policy)

Although the Middle East was peripheral to official American interests before World War II, the United States became deeply involved in Middle Eastern affairs in the postwar period, and the nation began to play a highly visible role that persisted throughout the COLD WAR.

Although the U.S. government had very little official interest in the region before 1941, American citizens had long been involved in Middle Eastern affairs. American private involvement during this time period was either humanitarian or economic. Missionaries had been active in the Ottoman and Persian empires since the early 19th century. American missionaries, predominantly Presbyterian, had organized numerous mission schools and even some universities, such as Roberts College in Turkey, the Syrian Protestant College (later to become the American

University of Beirut), and the Alburz College of Tehran. After World War I, the vast oil reserves of the Middle East attracted the attention of American oilmen, who tried on numerous occasions to procure oil concessions in the region. The U.S. government often acted to protect American citizens and informally to support American business interests in the Middle East.

World War II and the rise of the cold war drastically increased the official American role in the region. Soon after its entry into World War II, the United States invaded North Africa with a view toward eliminating the Nazi threat to the Middle East from the west and participated in the Anglo-Russian joint occupation of Iran in the east. After the war, Great Britain, formerly the dominant Western power in the region, saw its presence gradually decline before an increased American role in the Middle East. As Allied wartime cooperation gave way to Soviet-American confrontation in the cold war, the United States became deeply enmeshed in regional politics. The first sign of official American interest was the U.S. role in expelling the Soviets from northern Iran in 1946, one of the scenes of the first cold war conflicts between the SOVIET UNION and the United States. This was followed by the promulgation of the TRUMAN DOCTRINE, which provided massive amounts of aid to Greece and Turkey (and also Iran) in order to contain the spread of COMMUNISM.

As the cold war took shape, American involvement in the Middle East followed two basic principles: preventing the Soviets from gaining influence in the region and maintaining Western access to inexpensive Middle Eastern oil. Middle Eastern oil was deemed vitally important to European recovery, which was in turn considered crucial to prevent communist revolutions in Western Europe. Although cold war concerns motivated American policymakers, the complexity of regional politics combined with the prior imperial claims of allies such as Great Britain and France had an important influence on the way American foreign policy was actually carried out in the region.

One theme that confronted American policymakers in the Middle East during the cold war was the rise of indigenous nationalist movements that questioned and threatened American hegemony. For example, various Arab nationalists, most notably Egyptian president Gamal Abdel Nasser, tried to play the Soviet Union and the United States against one another in order to procure large amounts of aid. Iranian politicians tried to do the same thing, although with mixed results. After Iranian prime minister Mohammad Mossadegh nationalized the British-owned Anglo-Iranian Oil Company in 1953, the United States turned a deaf ear to British pleas to restore their oil concession; after Mossadegh threatened to turn to the Soviets for aid, however, the United States helped to overthrow the nationalist government and reestablish monarchical rule.

The Arab-Israeli conflict constituted one of the central concerns confronting the United States. After the formation of the state of Israel in 1948, there was continuing conflict between the Israelis, the Palestinians, and neighboring Arab states. Although the Arab-Israeli conflict was not intrinsically a cold war problem, American policymakers recognized that the instability caused by the conflict hurt American interests. As a result, the United States tried to maintain regional stability and support various rounds of peace talks between Israel and its neighbors.

The end of the cold war brought with it great change with regard to American foreign policy but there has been more continuity than change with regard to the Middle East. Although containing the Soviets was no longer an issue, the objective of maintaining access to the region's oil reserves remained as important as ever. The key issue at the heart of the Persian Gulf War of 1991 was preventing Iraqi president Saddam Hussein from gaining permanent control over the oil reserves of both Kuwait and Saudi Arabia. In addition, the threat of so-called Islamic fundamentalism has replaced communism, especially in the wake of the Islamic revolution of 1979 in Iran. All the while, the United States has continued to play a highly visible role in the Middle East peace process.

Further reading: James Goode, *The United States and Iran: In the Shadow of Musaddiq* (New York: St. Martin's Press, 1997); Burton I. Kaufman, *The Arab Middle East and the United States: Inter-Arab Rivalry and Superpower Diplomacy* (New York: Twayne Publishers, 1996).

— Matthew M. Davis

migration trends

The post–World War II economic and population boom resulted in a series of demographic changes. Movement westward increased dramatically. Meanwhile, millions of white Americans left the cities for the suburbs, while southern African Americans and other minorities moved north to take their places.

Many returning African-American veterans decided not to wait for the end of SEGREGATION and discrimination in the South, and instead they headed north when they returned from the war. Nearly one out of five southerners left the region for northern cities and industrial jobs during the 1940s in a migration pattern that had begun during World War I. Because of this departure, southern farm population declined 60 percent between 1940 and 1960, forcing those farmers who could afford it to mechanize or switch to easier crops to grow and harvest, such as soybeans, and causing those who could not to lose their farms. Tens of thousands of farmers lost their livelihoods.

At the same time, the South, after the war, began to market itself to the big businesses of the North by establishing recruiting offices to tout its nonunion labor, low taxes, cheap land, and the absence of government interference. Combined with the widespread use of air conditioning, these factors served to attract many to Florida, Texas, and other southern states in what came to be called the Sun Belt. Federally funded military bases and weapons production spurred the economies in many states.

Many war workers and their families had streamed into western cities with large numbers choosing to live in California, and the trend continued after the war. Western cities grew phenomenally, and, by 1963, California passed New York as the nation's most populous state.

The KOREAN WAR sparked increased military expenditures, and aircraft production in California accounted for more than 40 percent of the total increases in manufacturing employment between 1949 and 1953. By 1962, the Pacific Coast as a whole held almost half of all Defense Department research and development contracts.

As the population shifted westward after World War II, another form of movement was taking place. Millions of white Americans fled the inner city for the suburbs. Fourteen of the nation's largest cities lost population in the 1950s. As central cities became places where poor nonwhites clustered, new urban and racial problems emerged. Many businesses pulled out of the areas, and buildings fell into disrepair. Due to low income and discriminatory real estate policies, many blacks and Latinos were forced into the run-down sections of the inner city. This exacerbated the nation's racial and ethnic stratification and laid the groundwork for future problems. Eventually, such unfair practices led to rioting and political unrest among minority communities.

For many white middle-class people, cities were places to work but leave at five o'clock. In Manhattan, south of City Hall, the noontime population of 1.5 million dropped to 2,000 overnight. "It became a part-time city," as one observer wrote, "tidally swamped with bustling humanity every weekday morning when the cars and commuter

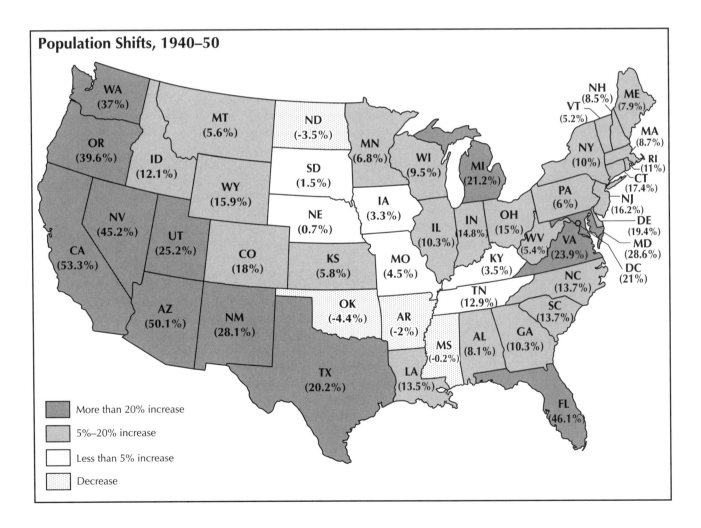

Population Shifts, 1940–50

WA (37%)
OR (39.6%)
MT (5.6%)
ND (-3.5%)
MN (6.8%)
WI (9.5%)
MI (21.2%)
NH (8.5%)
VT (5.2%)
ME (7.9%)
MA (8.7%)
NY (10%)
RI (11%)
CT (17.4%)
ID (12.1%)
SD (1.5%)
PA (6%)
NJ (16.2%)
NV (45.2%)
UT (25.2%)
WY (15.9%)
NE (0.7%)
IA (3.3%)
IL (10.3%)
IN (14.8%)
OH (15%)
WV (5.4%)
VA (23.9%)
DE (19.4%)
MD (28.6%)
DC (21%)
CA (53.3%)
CO (18%)
KS (5.8%)
MO (4.5%)
KY (3.5%)
NC (13.7%)
AZ (50.1%)
NM (28.1%)
OK (-4.4%)
AR (-2%)
TN (12.9%)
SC (13.7%)
MS (-0.2%)
AL (8.1%)
GA (10.3%)
TX (20.2%)
LA (13.5%)
FL (46.1%)

- More than 20% increase
- 5%–20% increase
- Less than 5% increase
- Decrease

trains arrived, and abandoned again at nightfall when the wave sucked back—left pretty much to thieves, policemen, and rats." By the end of the 1950s, a third of all Americans resided in suburbs; in 1970, 38 percent did.

Suburbs provided a piece of the American dream for many people, a place of their own. When veterans returned from World War II and married in record numbers, many shared living quarters with their extended families because the construction of new housing had slowed during the Depression, and practically stopped during World War II. Government-issued mortgages, especially for veterans, and low interest rates fueled the building boom after the war. The pioneer of postwar SUB-URBANIZATION was WILLIAM J. LEVITT, a builder who recognized the advantages of mass production during World War II, when his firm constructed housing for war workers. Levitt's team worked as an assembly line, with tasks broken down into individual steps. Groups of workers each performed a single job on each tract. The construction costs at Levittown, New York, a community of 17,000 homes built in the late 1940s, were only $10 per square foot, compared with the $12 to $15 common elsewhere.

Migration trends affected the environment in negative ways. The scarcity of water in the West required massive water projects to support the growing population. Suburbs replaced huge tracts of fields and forests that were divided into standard squares, each with a house, a two-car garage, and a manicured lawn. It was cheaper to cut trees down than to work around them. The move to the suburbs and to the Sun Belt states stretching from Florida to California continued in subsequent decades, as did the decline and decay of historic inner-city communities.

Further reading: Alferdteen Harrison, *Black Exodus: The Great Migration from the American South* (Jackson: University Press of Mississippi, 1991); Bernard L Weinstein,. *Regional Growth and Decline in the United States: The Rise of the Sunbelt and the Decline of the Northeast* (New York: Praeger Publishers, 1978).

— Elizabeth A. Henke

military-industrial complex

The military-industrial complex—the vast network of government, commercial and military resources and personnel maintaining the U.S. armed forces—grew exponentially during the COLD WAR, becoming so powerful that in 1961, President DWIGHT D. EISENHOWER warned against it during his farewell address.

At the turn of the 19th century, advances in military TECHNOLOGY brought officials in the United States military and government together with those in the scientific and BUSINESS communities in an effort to modernize the

armed forces. When the country entered World War I, the ECONOMY went through a profound shift in order to supply the complex needs of the military, including the formation of the War Industries Board (WIB), an official agency overseeing the economic changes. For the first time in the country's history, the private economy worked with the military in a close and complex partnership.

During World War II, the demands of military production promoted even closer military-industrial cooperation, which was aided greatly by government-sponsored wartime economic planning during the interwar years. The collaboration proved to be one of the decisive factors in both winning the war and helping to pull the country out of the Great Depression.

When World War II ended and the cold war began, the economic influence of the military continued. The European economy was decimated by the war, leaving a vacuum of both economic and political power that the United States and the SOVIET UNION rushed to fill before the other could do so. Brought together to defeat a common enemy during the war, both countries harbored a strong sense that the other was its ideological enemy and would stop at nothing to destroy the other in order to reign supreme in the world. In the MARSHALL PLAN (named after Secretary of State George C. Marshall), the United States distributed a total of $13 billion in aid from April 1947 to December 1951 to almost every noncommunist European country in an effort to prevent any economic instability that could lead to communist infiltration. American production provided the goods Europeans needed to maintain stability in the cold war, and the policy of "containment," directed at minimizing any communist expansion, perpetuated the need for a large and well-funded military.

The threat of nuclear war was the largest factor in encouraging this policy. The monopoly over the ATOMIC BOMB enjoyed by the United States ended in September 1949, when the Soviets successfully tested an atomic device. Seven months later, the State Department, led by Secretary of State DEAN ACHESON, drafted NSC-68 (National Security Council Document 68), arguing that a drastic increase in the defense budget—from approximately $13 billion to a minimum of $35 billion—was necessary to maintain the "eternal vigilance" needed to contain COMMUNISM. Two months later, the United States entered the KOREAN WAR, and defense expenditures increased to an average of $50.4 billion throughout the conflict. Both Marshall and General Omar Bradley disputed the need for such a drastic increase, arguing that such disproportionate military spending—the federal budget rose twentyfold from 1932 to 1952, with over half the increase going to the military—could greatly damage the U.S. economy, but the expansion continued.

The lines between industry and the military continued to blur into the 1950s. During Eisenhower's administration, Charles E. Wilson, the former president of GENERAL MOTORS, became secretary of defense. During his confirmation hearings, Wilson famously declared "I thought what was good for our country was good for General Motors, and vice versa." Covert operations overseen by the CENTRAL INTELLIGENCE AGENCY (CIA), designed to overthrow leftist governments at risk of converting to communism while protecting Western business interests, went unchecked by Congress, and they remained hidden from the general public in an effort to protect national security. While the CIA executed successful operations in Iran in 1953 and Guatemala in 1954, the failed BAY OF PIGS invasion of Cuba in 1962 illuminated the limitations of unsupervised military expansion.

While Eisenhower was fully aware of all of the CIA's actions during his administration, he became increasingly wary of the growth of the military and its growing ties to industry. In his farewell address in 1961, he first coined the phrase "military-industrial complex," warning the country that it "must guard against the acquisition of unwarranted influence, whether sought or unsought by the military-industrial complex." Only "an alert and knowledgeable citizenry," he maintained, could "compel the proper meshing of the huge industrial and military machinery of defense with our peaceful methods and goals." While Eisenhower's comments drew considerable attention, military expenditures remained a large part of the country's budget well into the 1990s, facilitated by the VIETNAM WAR as well as large increases in defense spending by President Ronald Reagan in the 1980s.

Further reading: David Halberstam, *The Fifties* (New York: Villard Books, 1993); Paul A. C. Koistinen, *The Military Industrial Complex: A Historical Perspective* (New York: Praeger Publishers, 1980).

— Adam B. Vary

Mills, C. Wright (1916–1962)

A liberal social critic and controversial sociologist, C. Wright Mills criticized the economic and political framework of 1950s America through his influential writings, including the 1956 book, *The Power Elite.*

Born in Waco, Texas, on August 28, 1916, to Charles Grover Mills, an insurance agent, and Frances Ursula Wright, a devout Catholic housewife, Mills spent a lonely and alienated childhood attending Catholic parochial schools and public high schools in various cities throughout west Texas. After graduating from high school, Mills enrolled as an engineering student at the University of Texas, Agricultural and Mechanical. Finding the social

sciences more to his liking, he transferred to the University of Texas in Austin and graduated in 1938 with a B.A. in philosophy and sociology. Mills then enrolled at the University of Wisconsin, where he obtained a Ph.D. in 1942 for his research on pragmatism and the rise of professionalism in America. That same year, Mills took his first teaching job at the University of Maryland, where he stayed until 1944, when he received a part-time job at Columbia University in New York. He eventually earned a permanent position and remained at Columbia for the rest of his career.

Mills always saw himself as an outsider within the field of sociology. He highlighted his role of maverick scholar by riding a motorcycle and wearing flannel shirts and combat boots to class. Often Mills was uncomfortable with his colleagues, and he distanced himself from the traditional paradigms of his profession. He attacked American sociologists for failing to understand the complexity of the social and political stratification engulfing 1950s America. He argued that mainstream sociologists were more interested in defending the status quo than in addressing social problems.

Throughout his career, Mills's work centered on themes of power and powerlessness. He argued that the growth in modern societies of massive, bureaucratic structures made most human beings powerless. He claimed that the power actually rested in the hands of the elite bureaucrats, subordinating the independent intellectuals within the economic and political structure.

Mills espoused his controversial theories in a series of books beginning with *The New Men of Power* (1948), a work about labor and its leaders. In *White Collar* (1951), he argued that the rise of the American middle class would change the very nature of American society. The increasing varieties of professional labor, including managers, bureaucrats, and salaried employees, signaled new hope and prosperity for most Americans. Mills envisioned a darker version of America as "a great salesroom, an enormous file, an incorporated brain, a new universe of management and manipulation." He argued that the repetitive paperwork of the professional world would increase the discontent of millions of Americans who had no voice in the bureaucratic decisions that influenced their lives. In his most popular book, *The Power Elite* (1956), Mills focused on the corporate, political, and military elite. He investigated the social structures used by elites to perpetuate themselves, and he explained how the electoral process was perverted to maintain power in the hands of the bureaucrats. Mills argued that the concentration of power under the control of a minority, such as bureaucrats, endangered American democracy.

In the last years of his life, Mills changed the focus of his work to concentrate on a number of different issues. He became increasingly concerned with the nuclear ARMS RACE and addressed the problem in *The Causes of World War Three* (1958). In 1959, Mills published *The Sociological Imagination,* a book outlining a new sociological paradigm incorporating a multidisciplinary approach and a more global perspective. The following year, Mills published *Listen Yankee! The Revolution in Cuba* in which he offered support to the Castro revolution. Widely read and severely criticized by his colleagues, this work cost Mills much of his creditability in his field. In his final work, *The Marxists* (1962), he linked the Marxist tradition with the democratic tradition and argued that the two systems were in certain instances compatible.

Although his books received much criticism at the time of publication, social critics later rediscovered his theories. By the early 1960s, Mills's influence increased both within the field of sociology and with the lay public. In 1961, President DWIGHT D. EISENHOWER warned about the MILITARY-INDUSTRIAL COMPLEX, and its increasing power over American society, in terms that suggested Mills's power elite. Radical organizations such as STUDENTS FOR A DEMOCRATIC SOCIETY (SDS) adopted his theories and incorporated them into the ideology of the NEW LEFT. This resurgence of his theories came posthumously; Mills died in 1962 of a heart attack at the age of 45.

Further reading: Irving Louis. C. Horowitz, *Wright Mills: An American Utopian* (New York: Free Press, 1983); Rick Tilman, *C. Wright Mills: A Native Radical and His American Intellectual Roots* (University Park: Pennsylvania State University Press, 1984).

— Donna J.Siebenthaler

miracle drugs

The term miracle drug is used to describe the class of pharmaceuticals known as antibiotics, introduced for widespread use in the 1940s and 1950s.

The period after World War II was one of MEDICINE's golden ages. It is hard to imagine another comparable span of time that witnessed the introduction of so many new and genuinely important drugs. Innovations such as cortisone (1952), a steroid used to treat arthritis, Jonas Salk's polio vaccine (1955), the birth control pill (1960), and minor tranquilizers gave physicians vastly expanded powers to treat a host of physical and mental illnesses, many of them for the first time. But antibiotics comprised the true miracle drugs of the period, and it is these drugs that brought about the most significant changes in the fight against disease.

"Antibiotic," a term coined by soil microbiologist Selman Waksman in 1942, literally means "life against life" and refers to "a chemical substance produced by a microorganism which destroys or inhibits the growth of other microorganisms."

Although the antibacterial properties of the penicillium mold had been known since the 1870s, and Alexander Fleming had published his famous paper on the subject in 1929, not until 1940 did researchers conceive of administering penicillin internally instead of as a topical antiseptic. When used in this way the drug precipitated striking recoveries even in severely infected patients, but the drug was difficult to make—several early recipients recovered only to worsen and die after the supply ran out. War-pressed governments quickly funneled money into developing the drug on a larger scale. The most successful such effort took place in America, where in 1941 the War Production Board coordinated a penicillin production program to supply the army. Production techniques advanced rapidly, and, by the end of the war, all restrictions on the drug's availability to civilians were waived.

Three new important antibiotic discoveries followed closely upon penicillin's heels: streptomycin (1943), the broad-spectrum antibiotics chloramphenicol (1947), and the first tetracyclines (1948–50). This powerful crop of new drugs gave the physician potent weapons against a wide range of infectious diseases, including bacterial pneumonias and meningitis, tuberculosis, dysentery, and sexually transmitted diseases such as syphilis and gonorrhea. While most infectious diseases had already declined drastically since the 19th century as the result of better hygiene, nutrition, and sanitation, antibiotics proved remarkably effective in combating those that remained. Mortality from the eight most important diseases treatable by antibiotics decreased 56.4 percent between 1945 and 1955, while the corresponding decline for all other causes of death was only 8.1 percent. Mortality from tuberculosis alone dropped 75.2 percent. The impact was perhaps even greater in surgery, especially in areas such as cardiac surgery, organ transplantation, and the management of severe burns. One statistician estimated in 1958 that 1.5 million American lives had already been saved by antibiotics and their weaker predecessors the sulfanilamides. Before antibacterials, four out of five children's deaths were microbially related; 20 years after their introduction, four out of five were nonmicrobial. Across the board, the chronic illnesses of aging and lifestyle-related health problems—those associated with smoking, drinking, and poor nutrition—replaced infectious diseases as the primary health scourges.

The impact of antibiotics was not limited to mortality statistics. The systematic screening of soil samples that had produced the second round of antibiotics served as a model for later pharmaceutical research. The wealth of new drugs discovered over the next decades owed much to this inspiration. Physicians basked in an unprecedented degree of prestige and public confidence. And, not least, the pharmaceutical industry was transformed. In the name of efficiency, the wartime penicillin program had encouraged the growth of large firms that could produce and ship finished products. This raised the value of brand names just as valuable new drugs were being developed. Suddenly, pharmaceuticals became one of the nation's most profitable industries, and high-pressure ADVERTISING and fierce competition between firms soon followed. The stakes were high: antibiotics were the best-selling class of drugs on the market and provided from one-sixth to one-third of the profits of such major producers as Lilly, Parke Davis, and Pfizer. Inevitably, excesses occurred. Critics charged that dangerous side effects were deliberately downplayed or even ignored in drug advertisements. A series of price-fixing and corruption scandals erupted, culminating in Senator Estes Kefauver's drug industry hearings in 1959. And many physicians worried that the drugs were being used against viral illnesses like the common cold over which they held no sway. Resistant strains of bacteria would certainly result from such overexposure, they warned—a chilling possibility given that all major classes of antibiotics had been discovered by 1959. But even such concerns over profiteering and overuse were, in a sense, only testimonies to just how wondrous the postwar miracle drugs really were.

Further reading: Helmuth Maximilian Bottcher, *Wonder Drugs: A History of Antibiotics*, trans. by Einhart Kawerau (Philadelphia: Lippincott, 1964); Mark S. Gold, *Wonder Drugs* (New York: Pocket Books, 1987).

— David Herzberg

Miranda v. Arizona (1966)

In the case of *Miranda v. Arizona*, the principles of the Fifth Amendment were challenged in the Supreme Court, and rules were established before a suspect needed to talk to the police.

The Fifth Amendment to the U.S. Constitution provides individuals the right to be free from self-incrimination. More accurately, this amendment allows those accused of a crime the "right to remain silent." Law enforcement authorities, however, did not always honor that right.

On March 10, 1963, in Phoenix, Arizona, Ernesto Miranda, a mentally retarded 23-year-old, was arrested on charges of rape and kidnapping. The allegations arose after a movie theater employee had been abducted from her job one week earlier and raped. She described her attacker as a man of Mexican descent. Miranda's car, matching the description of the assailant's, was stopped one week after the incident occurred and Miranda was taken to police headquarters. He was placed in a line-up with three other men of Mexican descent and tentatively identified by the victim as her attacker. Miranda was interviewed by police and told that he had been positively identified as the suspect. After two hours of interrogation, he signed a written confession that included a section stating that he had been advised of and understood his constitutional rights as provided by the Fifth Amendment.

On June 7, 1963, Miranda appeared in court with Alvin Moore, his appointed attorney. In his cross-examination, Moore highlighted the essence of the Miranda case. He asked one of the arresting officers if he had advised Miranda of his right to remain silent and refrain from self-incrimination. The officer responded in the affirmative. Moore then asked the officer if he had advised Miranda of his right to legal counsel prior to making a statement. To this question the officer answered, "No." Arguing this point, Moore stated that the policeman's actions violated Miranda's Fifth Amendment rights. Although the officers had advised Miranda of his right to refrain from self-incrimination, they had not advised him of his right to have an attorney present while making a statement. Yale McFate, the judge in Miranda's first trial, disagreed with Moore's argument and stated, " The constitutional right to silence did not extend to the jailhouse." The judge's determination to stand by his decision led to Miranda's conviction and he was subsequently sentenced to two consecutive terms of 20 to 30 years in prison. The debate over Miranda's and other suspects' privilege to be advised of their rights against self-incrimination led all the way to the U.S. Supreme Court.

Chief Justice EARL WARREN issued the Supreme Court's decision on June 3, 1966. Speaking on behalf of the 5-4 majority, Warren stated, "Prior to any questioning the person must be warned that he has the right to remain silent, that any statement he does make may be used as evidence against him, and that he has the right to the presence of an attorney, either retained or appointed." This decision led to Miranda's conviction being overturned by the court.

The ideas at issue in *Miranda* have served as a source of controversy from the time it was decided. Opponents of the decision claim that the ruling gave "a green light to criminals," allowing them more rights than the victims of crime. Subsequent cases have broadened the *Miranda* ruling by holding that an attorney, if requested by the suspect, must be present during any police interrogation. Originally intended to protect the indigent and ignorant, the practice of reading "Miranda Rights" to a suspect has become a part of standard operating procedure for police departments across the United States.

Further reading: John Hogrogain, *Miranda v. Arizona: The Rights of the Accused* (New York: Lucent Books, 1999).

— Erin Craig

Mississippi Freedom Democratic Party

The Mississippi Freedom Democratic Party (MFDP) was founded in April 1964 to challenge the right of the all-white Mississippi Democratic Party to represent the state at the national convention in August 1964 in Atlantic City, New Jersey.

The political party formed one segment of the larger Mississippi Summer Freedom project, which sent black and white volunteers to the state to work on voter registration and education initiatives. Under the direction of Staughton Lynd, a white professor at Spelman College in Atlanta, Georgia, hundreds of black and white northern students took part in freedom schools, whose goal was to provide an alternative to Mississippi's public school system for blacks. Northern volunteers also participated in registration drives, gathering at Miami University in Oxford, Ohio, for training. On Freedom Days, held every two or three weeks, volunteers from the STUDENT NONVIOLENT COORDINATING COMMITTEE (SNCC) urged blacks to try to register to vote collectively. On June 21, James Chaney, a black member of the CONGRESS OF RACIAL EQUALITY (CORE) and white CORE workers Michael Schwerner and Andrew Goodman were shot dead near Meridian, Mississippi. All three were associated with the MFDP and the Mississippi Summer Freedom project.

Activists Bob Moses and William Higgs first developed the idea to create a desegregated DEMOCRATIC PARTY in Mississippi. Moses presented the project to the Council of Federated Organizations on February 9, 1964. The party was officially founded on April 26,1964, in Jackson. Aaron Henry, a member of the NATIONAL ASSOCIATION FOR THE ADVANCEMENT OF COLORED PEOPLE (NAACP) became its first chairman. Lawrence Guyot replaced him in the fall of 1964. Other important members included Annie Devine, Victoria Gray, and FANNIE LOU HAMER, a member of the Student Nonviolent Coordinating Committee and the daughter of Mississippi sharecroppers. While the MFDP was open to all races, most of its members were black. The MFDP fielded four candidates in the democratic primaries held on June 2, 1968. Most notable were Gray, who opposed Senator John Stennis, and Hamer, who ran for Congress.

The MFDP held its first convention in Jackson in early August 1964. The convention selected 68 delegates including four whites and SNCC's Charles McLaurin, Guyot, Hamer, E. W. Steptoe, Devine, and Hartman Turnbow. When they arrived in Atlantic City, MFDP delegates petitioned the Credentials Committee to recognize them as the only delegates from Mississippi, or, at the very least, to have a minority report read on the convention floor.

On August 19, President LYNDON B. JOHNSON, wary of losing Southern states to Republican presidential candidate BARRY GOLDWATER, informed civil rights activists in a meeting at the White House that he opposed their efforts to unseat the regular Mississippi Democratic delegation. Johnson asked J. EDGAR HOOVER, director of the Federal Bureau of Investigation (FBI) to tap MFDP supporters'

phones and to keep him informed of their efforts at the convention. On August 22, when Hamer, testifying in front of the Credentials Committee, delivered an emotional description of the way she had been beaten in jail in June 1963, Johnson called an impromptu press conference to direct TELEVISION coverage away from the hearings.

In front of the Credentials Committee, MFDP counsel Joseph Rauh argued the party's case. The MFDP was the only party open to both blacks and whites, thus truly representing the state's voters. The official Democratic Party was not loyal to Johnson either, as many members supported Goldwater's bid for the presidency.

Oregon congresswoman Edith Green's compromise solution, under which all the members of both delegations who pledged loyalty to the Democratic Party would be allowed to vote as part of an enlarged Mississippi delegation, was rejected. On August 23, the MFDP refused a proposal to attend the convention and speak but not vote. Johnson then suggested that two of the MFDP's delegates, Aaron Henry and Ed King, be accepted as delegates-at-large, while other delegates would be admitted as nonvoting participants in the convention. Several people, including MARTIN LUTHER KING, JR., advised the MFDP to accept this compromise, but they refused. MFDP delegates still managed to attend the convention, prompting the Mississippi Democratic delegation to leave in protest. In November 1964, the MFDP nonetheless endorsed Johnson for president, but Goldwater carried Mississippi. In September 1965, the MFDP lost an attempt to challenge the right of Mississippi's congressmen to represent the state in Washington, D.C. The 1968 national Democratic Convention in Chicago refused any segregated state delegation.

After their failure to unseat the national Democratic delegation, MFDP members grew disenchanted by conciliatory attempts to change the political system through legal methods. They had played by the rules, they argued, and not even northern liberals had been willing to accept their moral right to represent Mississippi.

Further reading: Jennifer McDowell, *Black Politics: A Study and Annotated Bibliography of the Mississippi Freedom Democratic Party* (San Jose, Calif.: Bibliographic Information Center for the Study of Political Science, 1971).

— Philippe R. Girard

Model Cities program

The Model Cities program, passed by Congress in November 1966, encouraged participating cities to confront actively social and economic problems as well as physical decay in poor, urban areas throughout the United States.

By the mid-1960s, issues of race and poverty had reached a crisis point in cities across the nation. The WATTS UPRISING of 1965 demonstrated that the crisis in inner-city America needed attention. The existing solutions—urban renewal, public housing, the WAR ON POVERTY, and federal urban aid—could not solve the continued problems of crime and poverty. The need for a new approach set the stage for the emergence of the Model Cities program. President LYNDON B. JOHNSON, in his desire to conquer poverty and build a GREAT SOCIETY, felt the need to create an agency that would "stop erosion of life in urban centers among the lower and middle income population," and in turn "offer qualifying cities of all sizes the promise of a new life for their people."

The Model Cities program established community-based Model Demonstration Agencies (MDAs) to coordinate urban development efforts in poverty areas. Working side by side with the COMMUNITY ACTION PROGRAM (CAP), the Model Cities program ushered in community-based service institutions, including those dealing with antipoverty, welfare, housing, manpower, and neighborhood health and community development. Together, CAP and the Model Cities program constituted forerunners for later movements for greater governmental responsiveness, bringing more direct forms of citizen involvement in local public affairs.

Government officials chose the Department of Housing and Urban Development (HUD) as the administering agency for this program. The Model Cities program, a cooperative effort of federal, state, and local resources, required community involvement in the planning and development process. To qualify for the program, cities needed to demonstrate their readiness to stop decay in their neighborhoods as well as make a substantial impact in the development of the city over a period of six years. Upon acceptance into the program, the city received federal backing to pursue every available social program for urban improvement.

Before action took place, cities underwent a three-phase planning process. First, each city analyzed the major problems of the community, their causes, and the interrelationship between them. Within this framework, cities were responsible for developing long-range goals, approaches to achieve these goals, and priorities in carrying through these goals. In the second and third stages of planning, the cities broke down the cost analysis for their five-year objectives and then translated goals into specific program proposals. At the end of the planning process, cities submitted the completed proposal for final approval. In late 1967 and early 1968, HUD selected 75 cities out of the 200 submitted for the first round of planning grants.

Across the nation, these Model Cities worked to implement different kinds of social programs. EDUCATION was a major component of most programs, using 20 percent of the allotted funds. Urban renewal and housing, citizen participation, health, manpower and job development, economic and business development, crime, relocation, evaluation, and program administration made up other program branches.

While Johnson felt that the Model Cities program was "the most important domestic measure before the Congress," and spoke of its impact on "the future of the American cities," many members of Congress remained doubtful. Many felt the funding would spread the program so far and thin that it would fail to do any city much good. Senator ROBERT F. KENNEDY complained that model cities were "a drop in the bucket" and that "a domestic Marshall Plan" was essential to deal with the nationwide crisis.

Twenty-two years later, in 1988, critics pronounced the program a failure. According to the *New York Times*, the program never had a fair chance: "As envisioned, the program would have concentrated billions in huge demonstration grants to a handful of cities. Such grants would have tested whether comprehensive aid could create a realistic chance of eradicating blight. It didn't, because such aid never materialized. Eventually the money was shoveled around only a half-inch deep anywhere. The program was destined to fail."

Further reading: Robert Dallek, *Flawed Giant: Lyndon Johnson and His Times, 1961–1973* (Oxford, U.K.: Oxford University Press, 1998); Marshall Kaplan, *The Model Cities Program: The Planning Process in Atlanta, Seattle, and Dayton* (New York: Praeger Publishers, 1970).

— Susan F. Yates

modern Republicanism

Modern Republicanism was the phrase used to describe President DWIGHT D. EISENHOWER's approach to governing during his two terms in office in the 1950s.

Also referred to as "dynamic conservatism" or "new Republicanism," the phrase originated in the desire of Eisenhower and other moderate conservatives in the 1950s to pursue pragmatic, rather than overtly ideological, goals, such as "holding the line" on government spending and expansion. More of a slogan than a clearly defined political philosophy, the phrase represented an amalgam of traditional Republican beliefs—individualism, private initiative, and private enterprise—together with acceptance of some governmental responsibility for the welfare of its citizens. The overarching feature of modern Republicanism was its accommodation to the NEW DEAL. Maintaining the status quo, rather than attempting to dismantle New Deal programs, reflected the general tenor of the 1950s in its moderation and cultivation of consensus politics.

Specifically with regard to domestic policy, accommodation meant that Eisenhower, with the prodding of a Democratic majority in Congress, agreed to a slight boost in the minimum wage, creation of the interstate highway system, and an expansion in the number of people who were eligible for Social Security. His aversion to large-scale federal involvement was evident, however, in his refusal to support proposals for universal or even broader health coverage. In foreign policy, Eisenhower and his secretary of state, JOHN FOSTER DULLES, pursued the strategy of "containing" the SOVIET UNION. Notwithstanding the rhetoric of "rollback" and "massive retaliation" that Dulles often used, the Eisenhower administration for the most part practiced a foreign policy consistent with the internationalist outlook established by its predecessors. Containment was of a piece with modern Republicanism in its attention to means and ends. Eisenhower was especially attuned to the relationship between national security goals and the budgetary means with which the United States could pursue them.

Less consistent, however, was Eisenhower's response to the burgeoning Civil Rights movement. While most adherents of modern Republicanism, such as New York governor Nelson Rockefeller, fully supported the Civil Rights movement, Eisenhower was at best a most reluctant and uncertain ally. A firm believer in states' rights, the president refused to use his office to support what constituted the most salient domestic issue of his two terms in office—school desegregation. Only when faced with an insubordinate governor in Arkansas, the demagogic ORVAL FAUBUS, did Eisenhower act decisively by sending federal troops in 1957 to Little Rock to enforce a school desegregation order.

Despite the president's enormous success in the presidential elections of 1952 and 1956, by the end of his tenure Republicans discovered that the leader of their party had few coattails with which to ride into public office. Republicans saw Democrats gain sizable majorities in both houses of Congress following the 1958 midterm elections. Conservative Republicans were therefore eager to gain control of the party's platform and secure for themselves a place in a party that had been dominated by the liberal wing during Eisenhower's presidency.

Inextricably tied to the personal influence of Eisenhower, modern Republicanism as an outlook within the Republican Party that accepted responsibility for social welfare at the national level seemed to fade soon after Eisenhower left office. The task of maintaining modern Republicanism was left to Nelson Rockefeller, who represented the liberal wing of the party. Rockefeller faced fierce opposition from members of the New Right, a loose coalition of Republican Party members and conservative intellectuals who regarded Rockefeller and like-minded Republicans with contempt. The spokesman of this group was BARRY GOLDWATER, a conservative senator from Arizona, who received his party's nomination for president in 1964 by promising to end the practice of what he called "dime-store New Dealism." LYNDON B. JOHNSON's landslide victory in that election made it clear that modern Republicanism as it was conceived in the 1950s was not the basis for a new moderate electoral majority.

Further reading: Mary C. Brennan, *Turning Right in the Sixties: The Conservative Capture of the GOP* (Chapel Hill: University of North Carolina Press, 1995); Chester J. Pach and Elmo Richardson, *The Presidency of Dwight D. Eisenhower* (Lawrence: University Press of Kansas, 1991).

— Kirk Tyvela

Monroe, Marilyn (1926–1962)

Marilyn Monroe was an American motion-picture actress who became the most famous international sex symbol of the 20th century.

Born Norma Jean Mortensen on June 1, 1926, in Los Angeles, California, to an emotionally unstable mother and a father she never knew, Norma Jean spent her youth in

Marilyn Monroe, in a scene from the motion picture *The Seven Year Itch,* 1955   *(Library of Congress)*

foster homes and orphanages. In 1942, she married Jim Dougherty and dropped out of high school to work in an aircraft production plant. At the defense plant she was discovered by a U.S. Army photographer who used her as a model for posters for the troops. In short time, she signed with a well-known modeling agency, bleached her hair platinum blonde, and changed her name to Marilyn Monroe. Her image appeared regularly in national publications, where she was recognized as one of the most popular pin-up girls of the period. This early work led to an audition with 20th Century-Fox film studio, where she made a brief appearance in two small-budget MOVIES.

Her early acting efforts went relatively unnoticed and she was subsequently cut by the studio. In 1950, 20th Century-Fox reconsidered and signed Monroe to another contract and her career blossomed, beginning with bit parts in *The Asphalt Jungle* (1950) and *All about Eve* (1950). These earliest works reflect movie directors' inability to recognize her talents for anything beyond the role of the typical "dumb blonde." At Fox she languished, playing bit parts, most often the role of a mistress or an overtly sexual temptress. Yet Monroe took acting seriously, opting to study at the Actors' Lab in Hollywood and under famous acting coach Lee Strasberg in New York City in an attempt to overcome the dumb blonde stereotype.

While minor roles in dramas gained her attention in the movie industry, Monroe's gift for comedy led to her greatest success. Her comedic roles in movies such as *Gentlemen Prefer Blondes* (1953), *How to Marry a Millionaire* (1953), and *The Seven Year Itch* (1955), which included one of the most recognized images of Monroe where she stood over a subway grating causing her dress to billow all around her, earned her more respect. Her humor derived in part from the fact that, in her roles, her gorgeous, blonde characters did not seem to understand why people thought she was beautiful or funny. Meanwhile, her growing body of work brought her increased recognition as a sex symbol. Her physical voluptuousness combined with her natural sex appeal made Monroe an international star, and many imitated her look. During the KOREAN WAR, she toured with the United Service Organization (USO)—a volunteer agency that helps meet the needs of armed service personnel—entertaining American troops.

Monroe returned to Hollywood and married baseball star Joe DiMaggio in 1954. But her marriage to DiMaggio was short-lived, and the couple divorced a year later. In 1956, Monroe married playwright Arthur Miller, whom she had met while in New York. Following her marriage to Miller, Monroe starred in more complex film roles, including *Bus Stop* (1956), *The Prince and the Showgirl* (1957), *Some Like It Hot* (1959), and *The Misfits* (1961). Her performance in *Bus Stop* was considered by critics to be her most accomplished, while her appearance in *Some Like It Hot* proved to be her most popular with fans.

During this period, Monroe was being treated for depression and illness. Prescribed heavy doses of prescription drugs, she became increasing unreliable on the movie set, often forgetting her lines or failing to appear for work. The last movie Monroe completed was *The Misfits* (1961), written for her by Miller. One week after the movie opened, she and Miller divorced. While working on her next movie, she was fired from the set of *Something's Got to Give*—costarring Clark Gable and Montgomery Clift—for her erratic behavior. Two months later, Monroe's career was cut short on August 5, 1962, when she was found dead in her home in Los Angeles from an overdose of sleeping pills.

Further reading: Fred Lawrence Guiles, *Norma Jean: The Life of Marilyn Monroe* (New York: McGraw-Hill, 1969); Graham McCann, *Marilyn Monroe* (New Brunswick, N.J.: Rutgers University Press, 1987).

— Susan V. Spellman

Montgomery bus boycott See Rosa Parks

movies

Following World War II, movies reflected larger social and cultural issues, including the frustrations of the youth movement and the problems of ANTICOMMUNISM, and they faced challenges in attempting to deal with these explosive questions.

In the decade and a half after the war, the once unified vision of Hollywood film production fragmented as studios produced films targeting specific audiences and reflecting contemporary issues. Economic pressures in the 1940s forced the movie industry to rely more on overseas distribution and cost-cutting measures in order to keep films profitable. A government antitrust ruling against Paramount and other major studios further spurred changes in the process of making movies. By the 1960s, Hollywood lost its monopolistic hold on the filmmaking industry as producers looked overseas or shot on location to keep costs lower and make sure the industry remained competitive with TELEVISION.

Financial concerns, however, did not hinder the technical progress of the film industry. During the 1950s, color films became the standard rather than the exception. The switch to color film was expensive due to the higher cost of film and processing. Further progress was made as directors and cinematographers improved techniques for shooting film and editing outdoor shots to match color correctly. Lightweight cameras allowed for greater mobility and realism in filming.

In the late 1950s, the film industry began incorporating *cinéma vérité* by using lightweight cameras to capture both image and sound. The artistic "Direct Cinema" movement took *cinema vérité* (a hands-off approach to filmmaking) to its extreme by treating the camera as a silent observer of real life. Another innovation, Cinerama, used multiple cameras to produce a single image, which was projected on an oversized screen. Most films in Cinerama tended to be travelogues, though director John Ford's 1962 film *How the West Was Won* showed the medium worked for narrative films, too.

The HOUSE UN-AMERICAN ACTIVITIES COMMITTEE (HUAC) disrupted the careers of people working in all aspects of the film industry. The government, suspicious of Hollywood's liberal tendencies, called writers, actors, and other film workers before the committee to ask the accused if they had been members of the Communist Party or if they could name people who were. The HUAC committee ruined the career of PAUL ROBESON, the leading African-American actor of the 1930s and 1940s. The HOLLYWOOD TEN, a group of influential producers, directors, and screenwriters, including several eastern European immigrants, refused to name names or reveal information about their past to the committee in 1947. The American film industry blacklisted them, but after serving jail terms for contempt of Congress, the Hollywood Ten continued to work using pseudonyms or by filming overseas. Although Dalton

Hollywood screenwriters and directors (left to right) Samuel Ornitz; Ring Lardner, Jr.; Albert Maltz; Alvah Bessie; Lester Cole; Herbert Biberman; and Edward Dmytryk walk up steps of federal courthouse to face trial on charges of contempt of Congress for their defiance of the House Un-American Activities Committee, 1950   *(Library of Congress)*

Motion picture actress Natalie Wood displays new drive-in movie speakers, Hollywood, California, 1957   *(Library of Congress)*

Trumbo won the 1956 screenwriting Academy Award for *The Brave One,* he was unable to claim it since he had written the screenplay under a pseudonym. The emotional pressure to denounce coworkers as communists left deep scars in Hollywood and lasting bitterness between those who yielded to HUAC and those who remained silent. The pall of anticommunism changed the types of films made in Hollywood. In reaction to HUAC, American filmmakers became vocal anticommunists, reluctant to experiment with anything that might be considered threatening.

In the mid-1940s to 1950s, genre films like film noir movies and westerns reached their peak of popularity. These films followed certain conventions. Film noir, a name earned for the darkly lit scenes and preponderance of nighttime shots filmed in black and white, brought together rugged detectives and dangerous women on the trail of a mystery. Dripping with cynicism, these films reflected post–World War II doubt that the world was inherently good and COLD WAR fears of TECHNOLOGY. The diversity

and flexibility of the genre attracted top talent. Howard Hawks directed Humphrey Bogart and Lauren Bacall in *The Big Sleep* (1946), in which the plot was secondary to style and the on-screen chemistry. Alfred Hitchcock directed several film noir movies, including *Notorious* (1946), staring Cary Grant and Ingrid Bergman in a tale of love and fear of Nazi conspirators; The *Wrong Man* (1956), about the failure of justice to acquit a wrongfully accused man; and *Vertigo* (1958), which pictured Jimmy Stewart's obsessive love for Kim Novak and fear of heights. Actor Orson Welles and writer Graham Greene worked together on *The Third Man* (1949). Set in postwar Vienna, the plot revolved around the danger of trusting a former ally, and reflected the uncertainty of U.S.–Soviet relations. With the rise of color films, this genre rapidly declined in the late 1950s, but it never fully disappeared.

Westerns also reflected a cold war sensibility. The Old West frequently served as an allegory for American and Soviet relations. The good guys wore white and stayed true to American ideals of liberty and justice, whereas the enemies wore black and represented Soviet corruption and land hunger. The movie-going public enjoyed westerns throughout the 1940s and 1950s before they lost their appeal and degenerated during the 1960s. John Ford, the leading director of westerns, blended together a popular mix of sentimentality, nostalgia, and stunning composition that showed power, strength, and an idealized masculinity. Some of Ford's most successful westerns, such as *She Wore a Yellow Ribbon* (1949), *The Searchers* (1956), and *The Man Who Shot Liberty Valance* (1962), starred actor John Wayne. *The Searchers* was atypical for the genre because it showed the harshness of American treatment of Native Americans, and John Wayne's hero had complicated systems of morality, which differed from contemporary ideals. Wayne's reputation for playing strong, stoic heroes solidified his patriotic image, but his off-screen political activism in conservative groups and support of the VIET-NAM WAR made him a target of the COUNTERCULTURE and other liberal movements.

Horror films maintained their popularity and science fiction movies proliferated, in part through low-budget productions commonly called B-movies. B-movies featured no-name talent (although some future stars began their careers in them), second-rate special effects, and poor production quality. Aliens and space-age developments were common in both horror and sci-fi films. Mysterious aliens reflected American views toward the Soviets and other communist states. Although average Americans had little contact or knowledge of either, they believed that Soviets and communists wanted to destroy the American way of life. The cheap productions tended to be profitable and were mainstays of the drive-in movies popular with the youth market. The results could sometimes be laughable, as in director Ed Wood's 1956 film *Plan 9 from Outer Space,* often cited as the worst film of all time. But the genre also produced thought-provoking works like *The Day the Earth Stood Still* (1951) in which mankind's violence doomed the species to become dinner for alien invaders. In the 1956 film *Invasion of the Body Snatchers,* alien pod people who replicated the human form but lacked human reason and soul represented American's collective fear of a communist invasion. Stanley Kubrick's 1968 film *2001: A Space Odyssey* was a masterpiece both of visual style and social commentary about man's relationship to outer space and technology. In this film, mankind's reliance on technology made it fall victim to machinery.

Although the film industry promoted youthful stars from its inception, the 1950s brought a new type of star to Hollywood. These men and women used sex appeal and angst together with a naturalistic acting style to create multidimensional characters. Marlon Brando, with his mumbling delivery and rebellious image, made a successful transition from stage to film. He received Academy Award nominations four years in a row for the sexually charged *A Streetcar Named Desire* (1951), *Viva Zapata!* (1952), about a Latin-American revolution, the period piece *Julius Caesar* (1953), and *On the Waterfront* (1954). Brando's Oscar-winning performance in *On the Waterfront* showed the gritty underside of American culture through the eyes of a down-and-out boxer. Even so, Brando failed to achieve the same attention as James Dean. Dean epitomized 1950s teenage angst and restlessness in *Rebel without a Cause* (1955), with his portrayal of a juvenile delinquent trying to go straight after moving to a new city. Born in 1931, Dean appeared in three major films, as a rebellious son in *East of Eden* (1955), *Rebel without a Cause,* and the posthumous *Giant* (1956), about infidelity on a cattle ranch. James Dean died in 1955 in a car crash while driving his Porsche Spyder to a racing competition. Fans of his acclaimed film performances have used this early death to immortalize Dean and the rebellious, yet sensitive young man he portrayed in his films.

Women, too, enjoyed notable success. MARILYN MONROE was the major female sex symbol of the 1950s, and her reputation persisted following her death. Unlike the foreign-born beauties Brigitte Bardot, Sophia Loren, and Gina Lollobrigida, Monroe embodied the American ideal of the girl-next-door. Frequently cast as "the dumb blonde," Monroe exuded sexuality, innocence, and wholesomeness at the same time. Despite her image, she was savvy about the film industry and even formed her own production company. Monroe brought comedic skills and feminine charm to such films as *Gentlemen Prefer Blondes* (1952), about showgirls on vacation, and *Some Like It Hot* (1959), in which she played a member of an all-female band that is joined by two men hiding from the mob. Her performance in the romantic comedy *Bus Stop* (1956) earned her critical praise and commercial success. Like James Dean, Marilyn Monroe suffered an untimely death in 1962, leaving behind many memorable films and an enduring image.

During the 1950s and 1960s, the blend of MUSIC and movies changed to reflect additional elements of POPULAR CULTURE. The early 1950s marked the end of the grand-scale musicals with *An American in Paris* (1951) and *Singin' in the Rain* (1952). During the 1960s revival of the musical genre, filmmakers reinterpreted popular Broadway musicals such as *West Side Story* (1961) and *The Sound of Music* (1965). Musicians ventured into film in an updated form of the musical that targeted the youth market. ELVIS PRESLEY made a string of movies in the 1950s, including *Jailhouse Rock* (1957) and *Viva Las Vegas* (1964), that brought his swiveling hips to theaters across America. The plots in both films served as a way to connect musical numbers. Elvis strayed little from the traditional musical format but used ROCK AND ROLL instead of show tunes. In spite of poor critical reviews, Presley's films proved successful with the public who found his personality and image attractive. In the 1960s, the BEATLES developed a precursor to modern music videos with upbeat films like *A Hard Day's Night* (1964), *Help* (1965), and the animated film *Yellow Submarine* (1968) that promoted a fun-filled lifestyle as well as their music.

In spite of Hollywood's dominance, some significant work came from outside of mainstream production. Established actors like Peter Fonda, who starred as a motorcycle-riding hippie in *The Wild Angels* (1966), and Dennis Hopper lent their skills to the growing counterculture market. These films continued the focus on the youth culture that was important to earlier films like *Rebel without a Cause.* Also working outside of the established film industry, Russ Meyer made soft-core pornography and B-movies beginning with *The Immortal Mr. Teas* in 1959, which earned nearly $1 million dollars in profit. His *Faster Pussycat! Kill! Kill!* (1965), considered a classic B-movie, featured three women killers, who violently attacked only when men made sexist comments.

Within the film industry, the director's style gained prominence over the studio's style by the early 1960s. Innovative directors broke from traditional genres and, perhaps more important, moral constraints. Mike Nichols's 1967 film *The Graduate* broke taboos by featuring a relationship between an older married woman and her daughter's boyfriend. The controversial subject matter and excellent acting of Dustin Hoffman and Anne Bancroft ensured the film's critical and commercial success. Director Arthur Penn achieved similar success with the historical drama *Bonnie and Clyde* (1967). Featuring Faye Dunaway and Warren Beatty as the titular antiheroes, the film's graphic violence served as a model to later directors.

Further reading: David N. Meyer, *A Girl and a Gun* (New York: Avon Books, 1998); Robert Sklar, *Movie-Made America: A Cultural History of American Movies* (New York: Vintage Books, 1994).

— Lyra Totten-Naylor

Muhammad, Elijah (1897–1975)

Under the leadership of Elijah Muhammad, the Nation of Islam became a significant factor in the development of American Islam and African-American racial consciousness.

Born Elijah Poole in Sandersville, Georgia, on October 7, 1897, he was the seventh of 13 children. Living in the segregated South, Elijah and his family bore the brunt of racial slurs and discrimination. Even Elijah's father, a Baptist minister, failed to protect his son from this racist environment. During the winter of 1907, while taking some firewood into town to sell, Elijah encountered a large group of whites in the African-American section of town. Elijah recognized one of his friends hung from a tree, the victim of a lynching. He questioned how this could happen "in the midst of his own people." The subdued reaction of the African-American community along with the brutality of the whites disgusted Elijah, and from that point on he openly advocated African-American separatist doctrines.

In 1919, Elijah married Clara Belle Evans, and between 1921 and 1939 they had eight children. In 1923, Elijah and his family moved to Detroit, Michigan, leaving the turmoil of the South behind. Introduced to a variety of African-American organizations, Elijah explored groups such as the United Negro Improvement Association (UNIA) and the Black Shriners; each intrigued Elijah, but none kept his interest. In 1931, he met Wallace D. Fard and his group the Allah Temple of Islam (ATI). The ATI adopted Islamic beliefs and symbols, such as a crescent-and-star motif, the adoption of Arabic names, the prohibition of pork, and the separation of the sexes. Furthermore, Fard introduced new elements to the ATI, such as the belief that whites were devils, and a paramilitary unit called the Fruit of Islam. Elijah became Fard's most ardent supporter, and he took on the role of Supreme Master of the ATI. Following this change, Fard bestowed the name Muhammad upon Elijah. From this point on, Elijah Poole became Elijah Muhammad, the messenger of the ATI.

Due to their connection with a ritualistic murder, the ATI horrified the Detroit police, who attempted to shut down the organization. In the hopes of escaping punishment, Fard agreed to disband the ATI, but he simply changed its name to the Nation of Islam. Forced to leave Detroit, Fard handed leadership of the Nation of Islam to Muhammad. Faced with major opposition, Muhammad fled Detroit to avoid assassination. He settled in Washington, D.C., where he took advantage of the Library of Congress to further educate himself.

The Nation of Islam went through trying times from 1943 to 1946, when Muhammad was jailed for draft evasion. While in prison, he recognized various factors he could use to strengthen the organization, employing radio to broadcast the message of the Nation to other African Americans. In so doing, he effectively reached many potential members. In addition to this idea, he saw that prison served as the perfect model for resource collectivization, a system in which the people controlled ownership and the means of production together. Muhammad believed he could use this approach in the African-American community to unite the population.

Following his release from prison in August 1946, Muhammad approached the Nation of Islam with renewed vigor. Pooling their resources, Muhammad and the members opened a number of small African-American Muslim-owned businesses in Chicago. The money poured in, and the Nation bought a large amount of real estate. The Nation of Islam became the most prosperous African-American organization in the United States.

Perhaps the most significant event to occur to both Elijah Muhammad and the Nation of Islam during this period was the recruitment of MALCOLM X in 1948. Charismatic and energetic, Malcolm X was one of the most successful organizers and recruiters for the Nation. New temples and schools opened around the country, as the organization surged with new members, including Louis Farrakhan, recruited in 1955. As a collective organization, the Nation advocated a more militant stance in the Civil Rights movement, which opposed the viewpoint of leaders such as MARTIN LUTHER KING, JR.

The birth of Muhammad's first illegitimate child called his leadership into question. In all, he fathered 13 unrecognized children with seven different women. Muhammad's actions violated the same moral codes that he preached to the Nation. He also used the funds of the Nation of Islam for personal gain. He traveled in a Lockheed executive jet and wore a lavish fez said to be worth $150,000. In addition to these problems, Muhammad was accused of ordering the assassination of Malcolm X in 1965. Muhammad continued to lead the Nation of Islam until his death from heart failure on February 25, 1975, at the age of 77.

Further reading: Claude Andrew Clegg III, *An Original Man: The Life and Times of Elijah Muhammad* (New York: St. Martin's Press, 1997); Karl Evanzz, *The Messenger: The Rise and Fall of Elijah Muhammad* (New York: Pantheon Books, 1999).

— Clayton Douglas

Murray, Pauli (1910–1985)

In the course of achieving noteworthy stature in the fields of LITERATURE, law, and RELIGION, Pauli Murray became a distinguished African-American educator, an ardent leader in the Civil Rights movement, and vocal proponent of WOMEN'S STATUS AND RIGHTS.

Murray was born in Baltimore, Maryland, on November 20, 1910. Her father was a graduate of Howard University and a teacher and principal in the Baltimore public schools. In 1914, her mother died of a cerebral hemorrhage and she went to live with her aunt and maternal grandparents in Durham, North Carolina. Her father, who suffered from typhoid fever, had to be hospitalized, and he was unable to care for Pauli and her five siblings.

Murray graduated first in her high school class in Durham, and traveled to New York City to gain the necessary academic qualifications in a local high school to be able to attend Hunter College. In her sophomore year at Hunter, she had to leave school temporarily after the stock market crash of 1929. She went on to graduate in 1933 with a major in English and a minor in history. She was employed by the New Deal's Works Progress Administration (WPA) as a teacher in the New York City public schools.

As a young adult, Murray stood ahead of her time in her resistance to the Jim Crow SEGREGATION practices of the South. Whenever possible, she walked, rather than rode the segregated buses. In the fall of 1938, she took a more unorthodox step toward fighting racial discrimination. She applied for admission to the graduate school at the University of North Carolina, an all-white institution. The dean rejected her application on the grounds that "members of your race are not admitted to the University." Her quest for admission became public news because the Supreme Court had recently ruled in *Gains* v. *Canada* that it was the duty of a state to furnish graduate and professional training to all the residents of the state based on an equality of right. Only the second black person ever to apply to the university, Murray received widespread publicity, which resulted in black students filing applications at other southern universities. Murray began to see the importance of her role as a pioneer in the struggle for equality and opportunity in higher EDUCATION.

Murray's career in law began in 1940 when she was arrested and charged with disorderly conduct and creating a public disturbance. She and a friend refused to move to a broken seat in the back of a Greyhound bus in Petersburg, Virginia, and they were jailed for three days, then found guilty and ordered to pay a fine. As a result of that episode, Murray enrolled at the Howard University Law School in 1941 with the intent of becoming a civil rights lawyer. During her senior year of law school, she was elected president of her class and chief justice for the university's Court of Peers. Her senior thesis, with its argument that the "separate but equal" doctrine did violence to the personality of the minority individual, was so eloquent that it was used by Oliver Brown's lawyers in the landmark *BROWN* v. *BOARD OF EDUCATION* (1954) case. Previously, students with achievements similar to Murray's were offered fellowships to study at Harvard University, but when she applied, she was rejected from the school on the basis of her gender.

She entered Boalt Hall School of Law at the University of California, Berkeley, for further study, and passed the California Bar examination. In January 1946, she became the first black deputy attorney general of California.

In 1951, Murray published her first book, *States' Laws on Race and Color*. THURGOOD MARSHALL called the book the Bible for civil rights lawyers fighting segregation laws. Murray worked as an associate attorney in New York City from 1956 to 1960. From there she went to Ghana to teach at Ghana School of Law. She returned to the United States in 1961 and began graduate study at the Yale University Law School, where she became the first African American to receive the degree of Doctor of Juridical Science.

In 1962, Murray, whose stature as a legal scholar, educator, and activist in a number of civil rights groups had become well known, was selected as a member of the Committee on Civil and Political Rights, one of seven study committees set up as part of the PRESIDENT'S COMMISSION ON THE STATUS OF WOMEN, created by JOHN F. KENNEDY in 1961. There she met BETTY FRIEDAN, and in October 1966, Murray, and 31 other women who met in Washington, founded the NATIONAL ORGANIZATION FOR WOMEN (NOW).

In 1972, Murray was named professor of law and politics at Brandeis University, where she taught for five years. In the last decade of her life, she felt drawn to the religious life, and, in 1973, she enrolled in the General Theological Seminary, subsequently becoming the first black woman to serve as an Episcopal minister. She spent the remainder of her life writing and traveling the country speaking. In 1985, she died of cancer.

Further reading: Pauli Murray, *Pauli Murray: The Autobiography of a Black Activist, Feminist, Lawyer, Priest and Poet* (Knoxville: University of Tennessee Press, 1989).
— Elizabeth A. Henke

music

Music has always reflected the changes in society, both socially and culturally. The newly evolving music of the 1950s and 1960s clearly mirrored the cultural changes of the time.

In the post–World War II years, most Americans longed for stability. After surviving two world wars and a massive depression, the nation needed a secure environment. The music of the late 1940s and early 1950s reflected this mood. Soft, noncontroversial music—like that of Frank Sinatra ("Young at Heart")—accompanied these trends. This music was slow, melodic, and easy to listen to.

The American musical providing music with a story line, also remained popular at this time. Famous musicals such as *Oklahoma!, South Pacific,* and *Westside Story* were received enthusiastically in New York and then around the country. These musicals also began to cross over into MOVIES, giving musicals a new and larger market. The music heard in these musicals, also played on the radio, was happy and light, reflecting the atmosphere of many of the shows.

Throughout the 1950s and 1960s, concert music audiences continued to enjoy classical music written and performed by American composers and artists. Many

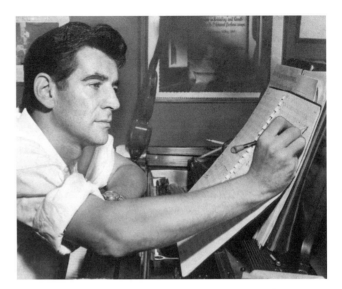

Leonard Bernstein, making annotations to a musical score, 1955   *(Library of Congress)*

composers earned an international reputation for their work. Aaron Copland, a well-known American composer, produced many compositions, including operas, ballets, chamber music, concertos, and symphonies. Many of his best works—such as *Appalachian Spring, Billy the Kid,* and *Rodeo*—incorporated American folk melodies. Leonard Bernstein, best known as the conductor of the New York Philharmonic, wrote several symphonies and ballets, but his musicals brought him the greatest attention. His *Wonderful Town* (1953), *Candide* (1956), and *West Side Story* (1957) were produced on Broadway and elsewhere around the country, reaching millions of people. Meanwhile, more innovative works began to emerge, as composers experimented with sounds and melodies, making more complex and innovative music. John Cage and Earle Brown were two American composers who composed these more progressive forms of concert music, using everyday objects such as pots and pans to create sounds in modern compositions.

Symphony orchestras and opera companies benefited from the support of the NATIONAL ENDOWMENT FOR THE ARTS (NEA), established in 1965. The NEA provided funds to individuals and institutions for the promotion of the arts. Grants to institutions, however, required matching funds from private donors. This need encouraged private and state support of all kinds, including large donations from corporations such as the DUPONT COMPANY and International Business Machine Corporation (IBM). The increase in financial support allowed symphonies and opera companies to reach larger audiences and helped schools of music expand in their size and scope. In the post–World War II era, the number of symphony orchestras nearly doubled by the 1970s. While opera had difficulty at first in finding a large audience in the United States, some opera companies successfully worked to promote the works of American composers. The Metropolitan Opera Company in New York, the first opera company to produce an American work, continued to perform American-composed operas, including Aaron Copland's *The Tender Land* (1954) and Samuel Barber's *Vanessa* (1958) and *Antony and Cleopatra* (1966). As the popularity of opera grew, cities across the nation, such as Seattle, Houston, and Santa Fe, supported their own opera companies.

Throughout the United States, conservatories and universities became training centers for young musicians and singers, and increasing numbers of students focused their attention on a career in the performing arts. Schools such as the Juilliard School of Music in New York, the Boston Conservatory in Massachusetts, and the Eastman School of Music in Rochester, New York, provided training in the careers of orchestration, singing, and conducting.

The influence of classical music and opera in America was challenged by the burgeoning popularity of new forms of music. During the 1950s, rhythm and blues moved into mainstream culture. A traditionally African-American form of music, rhythm and blues became popular through the support of teens. Strong beats sometimes coupled with the music of brass instruments characterized this kind of music. Prevailing American prejudices opened the door for white interpretations of rhythm and blues songs, tapping into the growing youth market.

These new interpretations of rhythm and blues quickly turned into the beginnings of an entirely new form of music. The term "ROCK AND ROLL," coined by Cleveland disc jockey Alan Freed, gave a name to this new music. With bands like Bill Haley and the Comets, who sang "Rock around the Clock," rock and roll became a great success with the profitable teen market. Singer ELVIS PRESLEY, known as the "King of Rock and Roll," became a cultural icon and the symbol of rock music. His popular songs "Hound Dog" and "Don't Be Cruel" were played on every radio station around the country. Elvis came to symbolize the coming of a new era of American music.

At the same time, the BEAT GENERATION, headed by ALLEN GINSBERG and others, performed a kind of music of its own. Beats were known for reading or even composing poems with jazz music playing in the background. Beats opened the door for people tired of a safe and bland society to express themselves. Their use of drugs opened the way for greater drug use by musicians in the next decade.

A powerful African-American recording label arose in the 1960s. Motown Records became one of the largest black-owned businesses in America. The artists of Motown formed a new type of rhythm and blues. Some famous artists like Stevie Wonder and the Temptations rose from this label. Diana Ross and the Supremes, probably

Motown's most popular group of the decade, embodied the beginnings of rhythm and blues.

During the 1960s, yet another form of expressive music was emerging. Slow melodic songs characterized the FOLK MUSIC REVIVAL, promoting peace and happiness. Introduced to songs in past decades by guitar-playing Woodie Guthrie, and later by banjo player Peter Seeger, mainstream America began to listen to folk music. The Weavers, for example, were popular into the late 1940s, with songs like Leadbelly's "Good Night Irene." Folk music artists included Joan Baez, who sang, accompanied by her guitar, about a number of causes. She and others sang "We Shall Overcome," the anthem of the CIVIL RIGHTS MOVEMENT, after it had been revived and popularized by Guy Carawan, another folk singer. Probably the most famous artist of this movement was BOB DYLAN, who sang songs such as "Blowin' in the Wind" protesting civil rights abuses

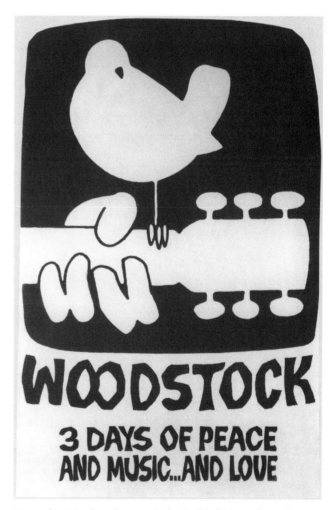

Poster for Woodstock, a music festival held over three days on Max Yasgur's farm in Bethel, New York, 1969 *(Library of Congress)*

and songs reflecting political upheaval such as "The Times They Are A-Changin'."

Other musical changes developed out of the COUNTERCULTURE of the 1960s. Hippies, first congregating in the Haight Ashbury section of San Francisco, stressed the bohemian lifestyle, long hair, homemade clothes, and a desire to engage in free love. Drugs also composed a large part of this culture. From LSD to marijuana, these people took a variety of drugs to "free their minds." Many famous artists arose from this culture.

American musicians were not the only ones to participate in the musical revolution taking place. The BEATLES, a rock group from Liverpool, England, became an instant success in America with songs like "Love Me Do" and "I Want to Hold Your Hand." They later created innovative music with each new album and gained in popularity, along with other groups such as Mick Jagger and the Rolling Stones. They symbolized all that parents feared in this new culture, namely, sex, drugs, and rock and roll.

Jimi Hendrix was another popular player on the rock scene. With his electric guitar, he embodied the new age of rock with songs like "Purple Haze" and "All Along the Watch Tower." The loud soul-filled chords caught the attention of many young Americans. He showcased his musical talents at Woodstock, with many other artists, and he played the rock music festival's grand finale with his own electric guitar version of the "Star Spangled Banner." Hendrix's guitar music was extremely popular and influential in rock music, even after his death from a drug overdose in 1970. Janis Joplin was another popular rock artist who likewise died from a drug overdose.

The music of Joplin and Hendrix exemplified and accompanied a new wave of music called "psychedelic rock." This music was associated with the hallucinogenic drugs of the time. One of the most famous of these groups was Jefferson Airplane. A folk rock band, it released an album called *Surrealistic Pillow,* which included the famous song "White Rabbit." The song carried so many drug references that many radio stations would not play it. This song also invited people to follow TIMOTHY LEARY's advice, "Tune in, turn on, drop out."

During this time, radical new ideas that rebelled against all of society's norms were expressed through various forms of music. Music emerged as a medium to convey thoughts and feelings of social discontent, and, for the first time, in a significant way targeted the youth of America as a musical market.

Further reading: David R. Pichaske, *Popular Music and Culture in the Sixties* (Granite Falls, Minn.: Ellis Press, 1989).

— Jennifer Howell

N

Nader, Ralph   See Volume X

National Aeronautics and Space Administration (NASA)

NASA, an independent federal agency, was created in 1958 to foster research on flight and SPACE EXPLORATION.

NASA grew initially as an successor to the National Advisory Committee for Aeronautics, which, since its creation in 1915, had researched flight, rocketry, missile TECHNOLOGY, and space exploration. The push for a new agency arose out of the tension associated with the COLD WAR between the United States and the SOVIET UNION. The 1957 launching of two Soviet satellites, *Sputnik I* and *II,* energized the American government to meet the challenge and regain the lead in SCIENCE and space technology. In response, the Senate created the Special Committee on Space and Aeronautics to frame legislation for a permanent federal agency, while President DWIGHT D. EISENHOWER created the President's Science Advisory Committee to do the same thing. One year later, Congress passed the National Aeronautics and Space Act of 1958. Eisenhower signed the law on July 29 and NASA began operation in October.

A major concern raised during NASA's creation involved the tension over proposed military and civilian purposes for the new agency. Many military leaders and their congressional allies wanted NASA to form part of the defense establishment. Others, including Eisenhower, opposed such close ties and argued successfully for the creation of a civilian agency. Though a civilian organization, NASA still retained close ties to the military with many of its developments used for military purposes.

Soon after its creation, NASA devoted most of its resources to placing a human in space. To this end, NASA created Project Mercury and introduced the first seven astronauts to the public in April 1959. The project moved at a deliberate pace until Soviet accomplishments acceler-ated NASA's plans. On April 12, 1961, Soviet cosmonaut Yuri Gagarin became the first human in space, orbiting the Earth once before returning. The Americans followed with Alan Shepard's trip aboard *Freedom 7* on May 6, 1961. Concerned with American prestige and the possibility of losing ground in the cold war, two weeks later President JOHN F. KENNEDY publicly supported a NASA project to land a human on the moon by the end of the 1960s. Out of this came the Apollo program, which cost nearly $20 billion and strengthened connections between NASA, universities, and private companies devoted to flight and space exploration. The program succeeded in July 1969 when astronaut Neil Armstrong became the first person to walk on the Moon.

Although public and political support for the Apollo program had been strong, NASA's funding levels had begun to drop even before its success. While NASA's budget increased from $500 million in 1960 to $5.3 billion in 1965, it dropped to $3 billion by the early 1970s. Interest in space exploration diminished for three reasons. First, the social movements of the 1960s, especially the Civil Rights movement, led Americans and their political leaders to focus on domestic issues. Funding was channeled into LYNDON B. JOHNSON's GREAT SOCIETY programs, specifically, the WAR ON POVERTY, which began in 1964 and served as the central part of Johnson's domestic agenda. Second, the government devoted resources to its growing involvement in the VIETNAM WAR. Finally, the economic stagnation of the 1970s eroded further hopes of increasing NASA's budget.

Although largely successful and beneficial, there have been problems and tragedy in NASA's history. Three astronauts—Virgil Grissom, Edward White, and Roger Chaffee—died in a fire aboard an Apollo capsule as it sat on the launch pad in January 1967. Three others nearly died aboard *Apollo 13* in April 1970, when an exploding oxygen tank brought the craft close to destruction. These losses contributed to questions about NASA's goals, competence, and use of resources.

As funding dropped, NASA focused on three major areas: launching unmanned probes to explore the solar system, developing a space station, and creating a reusable launch vehicle. Several unmanned programs, including Viking, Mariner, Voyager, and Galileo, provided a rich set of data on the solar system. In May 1973, NASA launched *Skylab,* an experimental space station. Finally, NASA launched the first space shuttle in 1981, which today serves as the agency's main vehicle for transporting humans into space.

Further reading: Roger D. Launius, *NASA: A History of the U.S. Civil Space Program* (Malabar, Fla.: Krieger Publishing, 1994).

— Gregory S. Wilson

National Association for the Advancement of Colored People (NAACP)

The foremost civil rights organization in the United States, the National Association for the Advancement of Colored People (NAACP) was the forerunner to the modern Civil Rights movement for racial equality.

Composed of white and black intellectuals committed to ending SEGREGATION and ameliorating the plight of black Americans, the organization was founded in 1910. The NAACP in its early inception set as its overarching goal the achievement of equal rights through gradualist, legalist means.

A multiracial organization, the NAACP differed in its outlook from the self-improvement and accomodationist message of Booker T. Washington, an educator and former slave who stressed the importance of economic self-determination for blacks, conceding that segregation was a fact of life. Growing opposition to the pernicious Jim Crow laws, providing for segregated facilities throughout the South, coupled with Washington's refusal to challenge the existing structure of race relations, led to a new approach articulated by W. E. B. Du Bois, a Harvard trained sociologist and political philosopher. The tactics the NAACP used to gain equality for blacks were persuasion and legal action. These included attempting to educate mostly northern whites through publication of *The Crisis,* a journal edited by Du Bois.

The NAACP grew quickly; by 1918, the organization had started local branches in every southern state, with membership in the South exceeding that of the North by 1919. This was largely due to the efforts of James Weldon Johnson, the national field secretary and organizer and later the first black executive secretary of the organization. In the main, however, the NAACP emphasized direct legal action as the primary means through which to effect change. In the 1920s, these actions included an antilynching campaign and, in 1930, a successful effort to block the confirmation of Judge John J. Parker to the Supreme Court.

The zenith of the NAACP's success came during what historians frequently refer to as the "Second Reconstruction" in the 1950s and 1960s. The legalist approach of the NAACP proved enormously successful in removing the judicial linchpin of segregation, the doctrine of "separate but equal" established by the Supreme Court in the case of *Plessy* v. *Ferguson* (1896). In a series of five cases that were grouped together, NAACP counsel—headed by THURGOOD MARSHALL, later a Supreme Court justice—argued that separate educational facilities for white and black children were by their very existence unequal. In 1952, the case of BROWN V. BOARD OF EDUCATION (1954) came before the Supreme Court. Two years later, on May 17, 1954, Chief Justice EARL WARREN—an appointee of DWIGHT D. EISENHOWER—returned a unanimous decision in favor of the plaintiffs, thereby rendering the *Plessy* doctrine, and school segregation, unconstitutional. A year later the Court ordered that desegregation should proceed "with all deliberate speed." But as the hopes of many were raised by the legal successes of the NAACP in the 1950s, opposition grew to the *Brown* case in particular, and to the Civil Rights movement in general. Local southern NAACP chapters faced constant harassment and legal battles with attorneys general intent on crippling the ability of the organization to function. In 1956, a series of injunctions against the NAACP in eight southern states forced the organization temporarily to suspend operations. The state of Alabama, meanwhile, outlawed the organization for nine years. And by 1956, 101 members of Congress had attached their names to a SOUTHERN MANIFESTO, a document that argued that the Warren court had abused its judicial power.

As the Civil Rights movement experienced rising expectations due to the legal success of the NAACP, other civil rights groups, such as the CONGRESS OF RACIAL EQUALITY (CORE) and the STUDENT NONVIOLENT COORDINATING COMMITTEE (SNCC), began to attract younger adherents, many of whom were committed to direct action and nonviolent confrontation. Together with the NAACP's own youth councils, these organizations spearheaded such efforts as the Montgomery bus boycotts, SIT-INS, FREEDOM RIDES, and the MARCH ON WASHINGTON. Many of the leadership and organizing skills that student leaders of these organizations demonstrated in the 1960s resulted directly from the efforts of the NAACP.

Further reading: Aldon D. Morris, *The Origins of the Civil Rights Movement: Black Communities Organizing for Change* (New York: Free Press, 1984); Robert Weisbrot, *Freedom Bound: A History of America's Civil Rights Movement* (New York: W. W. Norton, 1990).

— Kirk Tyvela

National Endowment for the Arts (NEA)

The National Endowment for the Arts (NEA) is an independent government agency that provides funding for the creation, dissemination, and performance of the arts.

Congress created the agency in 1965 along with the NATIONAL ENDOWMENT FOR THE HUMANITIES. Both were part of President LYNDON B. JOHNSON's domestic agenda called the GREAT SOCIETY.

The birth of the NEA owes much to the particular historical context of post–World War II America. Economic growth, greater leisure time, and an increase in educational levels of Americans all contributed to a growing demand for the arts. The COLD WAR between the United States and SOVIET UNION played an important part as well. Excellence in the arts became a key component in convincing the world's people of American superiority. Without a national endowment, however, funding at the state and local levels remained low. As president, JOHN F. KENNEDY tried unsuccessfully to use his influence to create a national arts program. Johnson, as he did with other legislation, framed the need for national arts and humanities organizations as part of Kennedy's unfulfilled legacy. An alliance of both arts and humanities served a political purpose. Pairing arts with the less controversial humanities gave the act greater support, and Johnson signed the National Foundation on the Arts and the Humanities Act on September 29, 1965.

Art forms funded by the NEA include crafts, dance, film, fine arts, LITERATURE, MUSIC, sculpture, and theater. Most grants go to nonprofit organizations such as orchestras, theaters, museums, and schools, or to support arts festivals. Some grants go to individual artists and these have been among the most controversial. Through the encouragement and financial support of the NEA, symphony orchestras, theaters, and dance companies experienced a tremendous growth and resurgence in popularity in the late 1960s.

The chair of each organization is a presidential appointee who serves a four-year term upon confirmation by the Senate. Advising the NEA chair is a 26-member National Council on the Arts, composed of private citizens also appointed by the president. The NEA has fostered the growth of local, state, and regional arts agencies that usually match NEA funds for a project. Originally, only five state arts agencies existed; in later years, other states, too, developed their own agencies.

While public demand for federal support of the arts was high, a weak congressional consensus on federal support kept funding for the NEA relatively low during the agency's early years. With a budget of only $2.5 million in 1966, the NEA was able to offer little assistance to many nonprofit dance, opera, and theater companies, and symphony orchestras. In later years, the NEA's budget grew to over $123 million, although controversy over issues of funding and contention between supporters and opponents within the government threatened the existence of the agency.

Further reading: Joseph Wesley Zeigler, *Arts in Crisis: The National Endowment for the Arts versus America* (Chicago: A Cappella Books, 1994).

— Gregory S. Wilson

National Endowment for the Humanities (NEH)

The National Endowment for the Humanities (NEH) is an independent government agency that supports the study of human history, thought, and culture through the preservation of cultural resources, education, research, and public programs.

Congress created the NEH in the National Foundation on the Arts and the Humanities Act of 1965, which also created the NATIONAL ENDOWMENT FOR THE ARTS (NEA). According to the legislation, the term "humanities" includes the study of language, linguistics, LITERATURE, history, jurisprudence, philosophy, archaeology, comparative RELIGION, ethics, and the history, criticism, and theory of the arts.

Like the NEA, the president appoints the NEH chair to a four-year term, pending confirmation by the Senate. Advising the chair is the National Council on the Humanities, which consists of 26 private citizens whom the president appoints and the Senate confirms. Between 1965 and 1999, the NEH awarded more than $3.1 billion for 56,000 fellowships and grants. These went to institutions such as museums, libraries, and archives for preserving, storing, and providing public access to collections. The NEH also funds museum exhibitions, TELEVISION programs, and historic sites. Individuals receive support for teaching and research in the humanities. Two prestigious awards in this category include the Jefferson Lecture and the National Humanities Medals. Recently, the NEH has begun to fund projects that make use of the Internet to increase public awareness of the humanities.

The creation of the NEH grew from the particular historical context of post–World War II America. Economic growth and the support for veteran EDUCATION through the G.I. Bill led to an increase in college enrollments. The BABY BOOM between 1945 and 1964 added further pressure for an expansion of education. With that expansion came rising expectations for increased government support among academics, humanists included. In addition, the COLD WAR led to wider support for education as a means of showcasing American superiority in world affairs. While the sciences received the most attention, in 1962 the American Council of Learned Societies recommended the creation of a national endowment for art and humanities and JOHN F. KENNEDY gave his approval. After Kennedy's assassination, LYNDON B. JOHNSON called for the creation of these endowments as a legacy to the slain president. Johnson also considered federal support for arts and humanities as constituting an important part of his domestic agenda, the GREAT SOCIETY. An alliance of both arts and humanities helped the bill through Congress, since the humanities generated less controversy. Johnson signed the National Foundation on the Arts and the Humanities Act on September 29, 1965.

Although the principle of granting support to the humanities had been established, differences remained within Congress and between Congress and the academic community over the nature of that support. During its early years, academics on the National Council on the Humanities believed in subsidizing their profession, while Congress expected a more equitable distribution among the states. With a budget in 1966 of $2.5 million, the NEH had limited funds with which to work.

In subsequent years, an increase in the NEH's budget, combined with supportive leadership, helped the agency make substantial strides in supporting the humanities through the funding of television programs, research, and public libraries and museum exhibits.

Further reading: Ronald Berman, *Culture and Politics* (Lanham, Md.: University Press of America, 1984).

— Gregory S. Wilson

National Institutes of Health (NIH) (including NIMH)

The National Institutes of Health (NIH), which comprise 25 separate institutes and centers organized under the U.S. Department of Health and Human Services, is the preeminent federal agency responsible for conducting medical research. It received its current name in 1948.

One of eight health agencies within the Public Health Services, the NIH conducts basic and applied research, including clinical trials and experimental procedures for treating chronic and infectious diseases. It works to improve the prevention, diagnosis, and treatment of a wide variety of medical conditions, and the agency encourages the dissemination of biomedical information to the larger medical community.

The origins of the NIH date to 1887, when a young doctor named Joseph J. Kinyoun set up a laboratory in the Marine Hospital on Staten Island, New York, in order to treat merchant seamen. In 1902, the Hygienic Laboratory, as Kinyoun's office was known, moved to Washington, D.C., and took on the authority of testing and regulating biological products mandated by the Biologics Control Act (1902). In 1912, the Marine Health Service was given a new name—Public Health Service (PHS)—and additional responsibili-

ties. The PHS was charged with conducting research on chronic and infectious diseases. Taking shape in its more recognizable form, the service was reorganized under the Ransdell Act (1930) and renamed the National Institutes of Health in 1948. The creation of the National Cancer Institute came one year before the NIH moved, in 1938, to a large, privately donated estate in Bethesda, Maryland.

The post–World War II decades saw substantial support for federal medical research in the United States. An expanded role for SCIENCE and MEDICINE soon became recognized as serving the national interest. Prior to the 1940s, popular and congressional sentiment was disinclined to support an extensive role for the federal government in support of medical research. Now medical professionals and scientific researchers found the postwar climate highly conducive to expanding both the size and the scope of their work.

The period between 1955 and 1968 was the golden age of expansion for the NIH under the directorship of James A. Shannon. During this time, the level of research and training conducted by the facility (and its budgets) grew at a tremendous pace. So, too, did advances in tests used to screen patients for certain kinds of cancer, as well as the treatment of diabetes. By 1960, the NIH comprised 10 distinct institutes, expanding to 15 by 1970.

Created as a specialized institute within the NIH, the National Institute of Mental Health (NIMH) was formally established in 1949, three years after President HARRY S. TRUMAN signed the National Mental Health Act. One of the original four research institutes housed within the National Institutes of Health, the NIMH is dedicated to the diagnosis, treatment, and prevention of mental illness. Under the rubric of mental health, the NIMH was later responsible for conducting research on child development, alcoholism, and suicide prevention.

Prior to World War II, the consensus among medical professionals held that those who suffered from severe and chronic mental illness required institutionalized care; hospitals, which catered exclusively to those patients and which received public funds, were deemed the most appropriate facilities for such care. Until the 1940s, most professional psychiatrists practiced in these public institutions. As with much else in American society, World War II changed this consensus. A younger generation of psychiatrists, many of whom worked in federal agencies during the war, and sympathetic lay groups, lobbied for changes in the treatment of the mentally ill. In 1955, a report issued by the Joint Commission on Mental Illness, *Action for Mental Health*, laid the basis for new efforts through the NIMH directed at setting up community-based mental health centers. Beginning in the 1960s, a shift toward community-based outpatient therapy supplanted the earlier emphasis on institutionalized treatment and care for the mentally ill.

By the late 1990s, the NIH supported over 35,000 researchers at 1,700 universities, medical schools, hospitals, and research centers throughout the United States and in other countries. The organization further advances medical knowledge by administering the National Library of Medicine, the most comprehensive collection of medical information in the world.

Further reading: Gerald N. Grob, *From Asylum to Community: Mental Health Policy in Modern America* (Princeton, N.J.: Princeton University Press. 1991); Victoria A. Harden, *Inventing the NIH: Federal Biomedical Research Policy, 1887–1937* (Baltimore: Johns Hopkins University Press, 1986).

— Kirk Tyvela

National Organization for Women (NOW)

The National Organization for Women, founded in 1966, brought together feminist activists demanding equal rights for women.

In the immediate post–World War II years, the momentum for WOMEN'S STATUS AND RIGHTS, evident in the early 20th century, waned. Many of the feminist organizations that sprouted in prior decades continued their work in subtle fashion, as the media celebrated the contented suburban housewife and declared feminism dead. The monumental importance of women's labor contributions during the war effort in the 1940s was put aside as the traditional domestic role of women reemerged.

Prompted by numerous studies on the position of women in society and the workplace, President JOHN F. KENNEDY established the PRESIDENT'S COMMISSION ON THE STATUS OF WOMEN in 1961. Unfortunately, many regarded the commission as merely a means for Kennedy to pay off his political debts to those women who supported his campaign. The commission was hardly a force for reform. Led by Esther Peterson, assistant secretary of labor and director of the Women's Bureau, it worked to block the passage of the Equal Rights Amendment (ERA) in Congress in 1963. Women did achieve a landmark success, however, with the inclusion of a clause banning discrimination based on gender as well as race in Title VII of the CIVIL RIGHTS ACT OF 1964.

The EQUAL EMPLOYMENT OPPORTUNITY COMMISSION, established to enforce Title VII, came under fire from feminist activists for its handling of sex discrimination cases. This growing dissatisfaction peaked at the third annual conference of the Commission on the Status of Women in Washington, D.C., in June 1966, with a call for a national civil rights organization to actively protect the interests of women. It was during the conference that a group of women, including Dorothy Haener of the United

Auto Workers, Yale law professor PAULI MURRAY, and Mary Eastwood of the U.S. Department of Justice, gathered in the Washington Hilton hotel room of BETTY FRIEDAN, outspoken feminist and author of *The Feminine Mystique,* a landmark book exploring the frustration of the modern woman forced to seek fulfillment in traditional female roles. After much debate, the group agreed on the need for an organization, defined what its purpose would be, and, at the final session of the conference, established the National Organization for Women (NOW).

By October 1966, when the first NOW conference convened, over 300 women and men had joined the membership, naming Kay Clarenbach of the Wisconsin Governor's Commission on the Status of Women the organization's chair. The members in attendance worked to hammer out a statement of purpose, in which they pledged that the organization would work to ensure the equal rights of women, and to "give active support to the common cause of equal rights for all those who suffer discrimination and deprivation."

The formation of NOW, and its development into the largest women's activist organization in the country, with over 250,000 members, strengthened the spirit of feminism and sparked a national movement to secure equal rights for women. Throughout the remainder of the 1960s and 1970s, the National Organization for Women added more causes to its initial platform of ending employment discrimination against women. NOW campaigned heavily, and successfully, for women's abortion rights and pregnancy employment leave options. Through lobbying and litigation, NOW achieved great success in securing more child care options for working women, and ensured the passage of state-level equal rights amendments and comparable worth legislation, guaranteeing equal pay for equal work for women.

NOW continues to campaign for the rights of women in the workplace and in other parts of American society, often taking its movement outside of the United States to focus attention on the discrimination faced by women in less-developed areas of the world.

Further reading: Sara M. Evans, *Born for Liberty: A History of the Women's Movement in America* (New York: Free Press, 1989); Betty Friedan, *The Feminine Mystique* (New York: Dell Publishing, 1963).

— Guy R. Temple

National Outdoor Recreation Review Commission

In 1958, Congress established the National Outdoor Recreation Review Commission to study the outdoor recreation resources found in land and water areas of the United States.

The SUBURBANIZATION of the late 1940s and 1950s carried environmental consequences that few Americans understood in the early post–World War II years. This rapid development often was poorly planned, and it impinged on some of the nation's most beautiful countryside. Highways encircled every American city while neon signs and billboards filled any open spaces left undeveloped. Despite the encroaching ugliness, Americans were not highly conscious of environmental issues.

As economic prosperity created more complex highway strips and taller skyscrapers, more Americans began to appreciate natural environments as important parts of their own standard of living. By the 1950s, most Americans enjoyed more free time due to the shorter workweek, and many Americans took longer vacations. They began to spend their time away from the developed cities. As they explored the natural environments of the country, Americans also considered how to protect them.

Due to the growing concern about the environment, Congress established the National Outdoor Recreation Review Commission in 1958. The commission was created to study and take inventory of the outdoor recreation resources and opportunities found in land and water areas of the United States. A committee of 15 members reported its findings and recommendations to both the president and Congress. Following this report, the commission was authorized to grant funds to federal and state organizations to use toward the preservation and development of recreational areas. According to the commission, it hoped to provide "for the American people of present and future generations such quality and quantity of outdoor recreation resources as [was] necessary and desirable for individual enjoyment and to assure the spiritual, cultural and physical benefits that such outdoor recreation [provided]." The committee surveyed national forests, national parks, reservations, wildlife beaches, and coastal lines in order to determine where to develop recreational facilities. These facilities provided opportunities for various outdoor activities, including hunting, fishing, camping, skiing, and boating.

The National Outdoor Recreation Review Commission marked only the first step toward the development of environmental legislation in the 1960s. The commission led to passage of the NATIONAL WILDERNESS PRESERVATION ACT OF 1964. Following this measure, the NATIONAL TRAILS ACT OF 1968 and the WILD AND SCENIC RIVERS ACT OF 1968 were passed as well.

Further reading: Senate Committee on Governmental Affairs, *National Outdoor Recreation Resource Review Commission: Hearing*, 98th Cong., 1st sess., June 28, 1983 (Washington, D.C.: U.S. Government Printing Office, 1984); Senate Committee on Interior and Insular Affairs, *Outdoor Recreation Resource Commission: Hearing*, 85th Cong., 1st sess., May 15, 1957 (Washington, D.C.: U.S. Government Printing Office, 1957).

— Donna J. Siebenthaler

National Science Foundation   See science

National Security Act of 1947

The National Security Act, passed by Congress in July 1947, coordinated and unified the U.S. armed forces and reorganized the overall military effort.

The command structure of the military services previously had been coordinated only through informal arrangements. After World War II ended, a more permanent and secure arrangement was necessary. The National Security Act of 1947 emerged out of debates over the possible unification of the armed services in the face of concerns about the ability of foreign policymakers and the military to cope with the problems of the COLD WAR. Proponents of the measure claimed it was necessary to protect the country from its enemies. Critics of the proposal, such as Republican senator Edward V. Robertson of Wyoming, feared it would lead to military domination of all foreign policy, and all natural and human resources. "We must not let out fear of Communism blind us to the danger of military domination," warned Robertson.

The National Security Act, passed by Congress, created several new agencies to coordinate the efforts of existing military bodies. They included the National Security Council (NSC), which was created to improve interdepartmental coordination of defense and foreign policy matters, and the National Security Resources Board, which was commissioned to develop plans for economic mobilization in the event of war. The National Security Act also created the CENTRAL INTELLIGENCE AGENCY (CIA). The CIA was designed to replace the existing Central Intelligence Group that was informally organized immediately following World War II. The CIA was to serve as the principal civilian source of foreign intelligence for the president of the United States and other decisionmakers in the executive branch.

One of the most important aspects of the National Security Act was the reorganization of military departments carried out under the act in an effort to provide for greater coordination between the departments. The measure merged the War Department and the Navy Department into a new National Military Establishment (NME). The NME was to be headed by a secretary of defense appointed by the president. The NME included the Department of the Army and the Department of the Navy as well as the new Department of the Air Force, which had been recently designated as an independent military service. A number of other defense-related agencies created during World War II, such as the Research and Development Board and the Munitions Board, were also placed under the authority of the secretary of defense. The NME was a failure because the secretary of defense had no real power or authority over the secretaries of the army, navy, and air force and the

NME could do little more than encourage them to cooperate. Following the release of the Hoover Commission report in 1949, which proved that the NME was unwieldy and inefficient, Congress passed the National Security Act of 1949. It amended the 1947 act by eliminating the National Military Establishment and creating in its place the Department of Defense (DOD) as an executive department that had the separate service departments squarely under its authority. This reorganization diminished the power of the separate service secretaries and gave the defense establishment a united voice.

The National Security Council (NSC) also coordinated the activities of all executive branch departments concerned with national security. According to the measure, the NSC comprised the president, the vice president, the secretary of state, and the secretary of defense. Other major foreign policy officials, such as the CIA director and the chair of the Joint Chiefs of Staff, were not statutory members but frequently participated in NSC meetings.

Further reading: Demetrios Caraley, *The Politics of Military Unification: A Study of Conflict and the Policy Process* (New York: Columbia University Press, 1966); Michael J. Hogan, *A Cross of Iron: Harry S. Truman and the Origins of the National Security State, 1945–1954* (Cambridge, U.K.: Cambridge University Press, 1998); Melvyn P. Leffler, *A Preponderance of Power: National Security, the Truman Administration, and the Cold War* (Stanford, Calif.: Stanford University Press, 1992).

— Elizabeth A. Henke

National Traffic and Motor Vehicle Safety Act of 1966

The National Traffic and Motor Vehicle Safety Act of 1966, which created the National Highway Traffic Safety Administration (NHTSA), represented a full-scale effort at establishing safety standards for all motor vehicles.

The need for some kind of regulatory agency responsible for establishing and enforcing safety standards on the nation's roadways reflected the growing importance of the AUTOMOBILE INDUSTRY, both because of its economic function and because Americans were increasingly reliant on private transportation. Public awareness of the issue of transportation safety had been raised in 1965 through a combination of governmental and private efforts. A Senate investigation led by Senator Abraham Ribicoff of Connecticut discovered that since 1960 nearly one out of every five cars manufactured in the United States had been recalled, many of them for safety defects. Attempts at improving transportation safety were further bolstered by RALPH NADER, a Harvard Law School graduate and consumer advocate, with the publication of his book *Unsafe at Any*

Speed (1965). Attacking the poor safety record of the automobile industry, Nader argued that cars such as the Corvair were designed with styling, rather than safety, in mind.

Nader's efforts paved the way for the National Traffic and Motor Safety Act of 1966, which set safety standards for vehicles on public highways, provided for inspection to ensure compliance, and created the National Motor Vehicle Safety Advisory Council.

At the same time, LYNDON B. JOHNSON, eager to consolidate the more than 30 government agencies responsible for regulating all types of transportation, pushed for the creation of a catchall agency designed to streamline and modernize the nation's transit systems. The goal was to put the responsibility for regulating air, water, and road transit all under one roof. To this end, the Department of Transportation (DOT) was created in 1966. At a White House signing ceremony, the president proclaimed that the task of the newly created department was "to untangle, to coordinate, and to build the national transportation system for America that America is deserving of."

One goal of the National Traffic and Motor Vehicle Safety Act of 1966 was to create an agency responsible for setting safety standards for new cars. This agency, housed within the Department of Transportation, was the National Highway Traffic Safety Administration (NHTSA). Beginning with 1968 model-year cars, the NHTSA issued a series of safety standards designed to reduce the number of traffic fatalities and accidents, responsible for some 50,000 deaths per year. These standards included uniform bumper heights, seat belts, and improved braking systems.

There have long been more vehicles on the road in the United States than any other country, yet the United States enjoys one of the best safety records in the world. The National Traffic and Motor Vehicle Safety Act is at least partially responsible for this record.

Further reading: James J. Flink, *The Automobile Age* (Cambridge, Mass.: MIT Press, 1988).

— Kirk Tyvela

National Trails Act of 1968

The National Trails Act of 1968 established the National Trails System as part of an extended effort to preserve the landscape.

Facing threats to the viability of the Appalachian Trail, created in the 1920s, the Appalachian Trail Conference appealed to Congress for protection for both environmental and recreational reasons. President LYNDON B. JOHNSON was interested in environmental issues and regarded preservation of wilderness sites as part of his GREAT SOCIETY. Designed to meet public demands for more areas of outdoor recreational activity, the National Trails Act provided a mechanism to establish and maintain a nationwide hiking network. As cities continued to grow, many areas became polluted with little vegetation or areas of aesthetic quality remaining. As Johnson stated, "Once our national splendor is destroyed, it can never be recaptured."

In 1965, Johnson advanced the idea of a nationwide system of trails run by volunteers, based on a 1962 government study that highlighted the importance of national trails and noted the abilities of volunteers to manage them. Later, the Department of the Interior published a report on "Trails for America," further providing support for national trails. The combination of these two publications advanced the idea of creating a national trails system, and led to the passage of the National Trails Act in 1968.

The National Trails Act, also known as the National Trails System Act, set up the system of pathways. The act promoted public enjoyment, accessibility, and appreciation of outdoor areas and the nation's historic resources. The trails could be established either near urban centers or in more remote scenic and historical areas. Located near varying terrains, the scenic trails encompassed deserts, marshes, grasslands, mountains, canyons, rivers, forests, or any landforms that exhibited significant characteristics of the physiographic region. Historic trails followed previous routes of historical significance to the nation.

The measure initially supported two trails, the Appalachian Trail and the Pacific Crest Trail, because they represented ideal examples of scenic and historic trails. The Appalachian Trail began in Maine and extended to Springer Mountain in Georgia, a total distance of about 2,160 miles. The Pacific Crest Trail ran for 2,350 miles from the Mexican-Californian border northward along the mountain ranges of the west coast to the U.S.–Canada border near Lake Ross in Washington state.

Each individual trail fell under control of either the secretary of the interior or the secretary of agriculture, and each was to be run by either the Forest Service or Bureau of Land Management. The secretary in control of each trail could issue regulations regarding its management, development, protection, and administration. Most trails allowed bicycling, cross-country skiing, day hiking, equestrian activities, jogging, overnight and long-distance backpacking, snowmobiling, and surface water and underwater activities. Some trails even permitted motorcycles or four and two-wheel vehicles, though this was rare.

Related legislation such as the NATIONAL WILDERNESS ACT OF 1964 and the WILD AND SCENIC RIVERS ACT OF 1968, demonstrated the drive to beautify and protect these natural areas, allowing for areas of recreation and enjoyment.

Further reading: Bill Bryson, *A Walk in the Woods: Rediscovering American on the Appalachian Trail* (New York: Broadway Books, 1998); William Gray, *The Pacific Crest Trail* (Washington, D.C.: National Geographic Society, 1975).

— Katherine R. Yarosh

National Wilderness Preservation Act of 1964

The National Wilderness Preservation Act of 1964, often known simply as the Wilderness Act, sought to "secure for the American people of present and future generations the benefits of an enduring resource of wilderness."

The act had its origins years before in the efforts of the U.S. Forest Service to set aside federally owned lands that could not then be developed. Facing pressure from developers who wanted to transform wilderness areas into mass recreation sites, people who wanted to keep the wilderness unchanged recognized the need to act. In 1924, the Forest Service began to set aside remote areas of national forests that would remain in their natural state. Aldo Leopold, a Forest Service employee in the 1920s and a staunch environmentalist, was one of those who wanted to promote an awareness of undeveloped areas as part of an effort to protect them.

In those early years, roads were permitted in the national parks, but logging, grazing, and mining were prohibited. Administrative regulations rather than laws served as the framework for managing these areas.

There was continuing competition between wilderness enthusiasts and mining, lumbering, and livestock entrepreneurs, and, over the next several decades, members of the Wilderness Society and the Sierra Club began to argue that legislation, rather than administrative discretion, which could shift under pressure, was necessary to manage and maintain wilderness areas.

The legislative history of the Wilderness Act began in 1955. A draft bill soon faced serious criticism from commercial interests, who feared they would be excluded from wilderness areas or restricted from developing them as they chose. The opponents included the American Mining Congress, the American Pulpwood Association, and the American National Cattlemen's Association. Initially, the Forest Service, too, was opposed to the bill, arguing, as one official noted, that "It hurt our pride, to suggest we had to have our hands tied by law." New versions of the bill appeared in 1958 and 1959, though President DWIGHT D. EISENHOWER appeared uninterested in the legislation.

In the 1960s, President JOHN F. KENNEDY's support for wilderness legislation made a difference. The Agriculture and Interior Departments now became enthusiastic supporters of such a measure. Eventually, legislators in both houses of Congress proved sympathetic, and agreement on a compromise was reached just before Kennedy's assassination.

The Wilderness Act, signed into law on September 3, 1964, by President LYNDON B. JOHNSON as part of his

GREAT SOCIETY, defined wilderness as an area where the earth and its community of life were untrammeled by man, where man himself was a visitor who did not remain, and as an area of undeveloped federal land retaining its primeval character and influence, without permanent improvements or human habitation. To be so designated, a wilderness area required at least 5,000 acres that contained features of scientific, educational, ecological, scenic, or historical value. Lands also had to possess opportunities for solitude or a primitive and unconfined type of recreation, and to appear to be affected primarily by nature with man's influence unnoticeable. All four of these requirements had to be met for an area to receive federal protection. The National Wilderness Preservation system initially included 54 national forests containing 9.1 million acres.

The act mandated the secretary of agriculture and the secretary of the interior to submit joint recommendations to the president about the suitability of any area for preservation as a wilderness. After reviewing roadless areas within the National Park System and the National Wildlife Refuge System, the secretaries were to report on the state of the wilderness system, offering new regulations and recommendations.

This was "a great forward step," said Senator HUBERT H. HUMPHREY, one of the early supporters of the legislation. "The wilderness bill preserves for our posterity, for all time to come, 9 million acres of this vast continent in their original and unchanging beauty and wonder," President Johnson declared. Another 50 million acres were earmarked for consideration of possible inclusion in the next ten years.

Further reading: Dennis M. Roth, *The Wilderness Movement and the National Forests* (College Station, Tex.: Intaglio Press, 1990); Douglas Strong, *Dreamers and Defenders: American Conservationists* (Lincoln: University of Nebraska Press, 1988).

— Katherine R. Yarosh

Native American movement

The movement to establish and safeguard the rights of Native Americans came of age in the 1960s, as Indians learned important lessons from the examples of the Civil Rights movement.

Indians had long faced problems with the policies of the federal government. In 1887, the Dawes Act, also called the General Allotment Act, authorized the breaking up of tribal lands into individual land allotments comprised of approximately 40–160 acres. Although this action aimed at persuading the Indians to become farmers, it led instead to the widespread sale of tribal lands to whites. By 1934, when the Wheeler-Howard Indian Reorganization Act

overturned the General Allotment Act, the land owned by Indians had dropped to one-third of what it was in 1887. The first serious legislative effort to deal with the Indian's problems of landlessness, poverty, lack of education, and demoralization came in 1934 in the form of the Indian Reorganization Act (IRA). Specifically, the act prohibited any further allocating of tribal land, restored tribal ownership of reservation lands, authorized the recovery of any unclaimed surplus lands, and set up a fund for the acquisition of new land. The IRA also encouraged tribes to adopt written constitutions for self-government and granted these governments limited powers, providing the legislative basis for modern tribal government. Tribes were also authorized to organize tribal business corporations to pursue economic development activities.

One outcome of the initiatives supported by the IRA included the establishment of the INDIAN CLAIMS COMMISSION (ICC) in 1946. The ICC was established to settle claims of those Indian groups that could prove a loss of lands due to past government malfeasance and to expedite handling of tribal claims against the United States. The existence of the ICC stimulated many tribes to pursue claims. By 1978, when the ICC ceased operation, over $800 million had been awarded to various tribes providing legal and moral proof of unjust treatment of Indians by the government.

In 1944, representatives of more than 50 IRA tribal governments, together with American Indian employees of the Bureau of Indian Affairs (BIA) office, organized the National Congress of American Indians. Also referred to as "the United Nations of the tribes," the National Congress of American Indians became a leading Indian advocacy organization during the postwar years. The intertribal organization was dedicated to the protection, conservation, and development of Indian natural and human resources.

Faced with a conservative backlash in politics, federal policy regarding Native American tribes shifted during the 1950s. After World War II, the government returned to a goal of rapidly assimilating Indians, as set forth in its TERMINATION POLICY. Congress called for the termination of special federal programs and trust relationships with Native Americans, in the hope that this policy would hasten the assimilation of Indians into mainstream society. On many reservations, resources were inadequate to support the resident Indian population. Affirming the policy of termination, the federal government, rather than supporting initiatives to aid the Indians, decided to encourage Indian migration to urban areas. This effort was known as the Relocation Program. Misleading slogans, such as "Free the Indians from the Reservations," gave the impression that the government was liberating the Indians, but, in reality, it was trying to disband and dissolve Indian tribes. Under the administration of President DWIGHT D. EISENHOWER, the government sought to abandon the federal government's historic relationship with the Indians, to stop dealing with tribes as sovereign entities, to deny Indian treaty rights, and to turn Indian affairs over to the states. In 1953 Congress approved the termination policy, declaring it national policy by repealing legislation prohibiting the sale of alcoholic beverages to Indians, and transferring civil and criminal jurisdiction over local Indian reservations to five states. The legislation also provided that other states could assume civil and criminal jurisdiction over reservations without consultation with other tribes. Many states, however, did not exercise this newfound right because of the immense expense involved and the insignificant financial returns that were projected on taxing Indian land.

There were many reasons for the increasing national support of termination. World War II generated a spirit of nationalism that made Indian culture and sovereignty seem to be contradictory to the increasingly narrowly defined notion of Americanism. In the atmosphere of the COLD WAR, Indian communal traditions appeared to conservatives to be too similar to COMMUNISM, a perceived threat to democracy and to the United States. Many individual Native Americans, especially those who had served in the armed forces during the war, became embroiled in the era's nationalism as well. They began to identify more as Americans and less as members of sovereign tribes. Some liberals in Congress supported termination as an extension of the Civil Rights movement, relating its assimilationist goals to the racial integration sought by African Americans. For many Native Americans, termination stirred major internal disputes. Off-reservation tribal members, attracted to the per capita distribution that would follow reservation liquidation, generally supported termination. Reservation Indians usually opposed the policy.

By the early 1960s, the policy of termination quickly became controversial and was largely discredited and rejected. It was not, however, officially repudiated until the 1970s when widespread Indian and non-Indian protest brought it to an end. Yet before the demise of the policy, it profoundly affected a number of tribes. For example, in Oregon the Klamath tribe's assets were distributed to individual members, and the tribe simply ceased to exist. The Wisconsin Menominee were also seriously affected, but they managed to avoid total dissolution. Their tribal status was later restored and some tribal property salvaged, including valuable timberland. Some of the groups terminated by Congress under the policy later launched efforts, known as restoration, to regain federal recognition of tribal status.

By the late 1950s, termination came under heavy criticism and support waned. Tribes led by the National Congress of American Indians mounted an increasingly effective opposition and many church groups protested what they saw as a social injustice. Affected tribes sank deeper into poverty. Some were unable to pay their taxes and lost their land. As the dismal results of termination legislation unfolded, anger and opposition grew. This anger led to action. The Red Power movement emerged in the late 1960s, emphasizing pride in Indian culture, tribal sovereignty, and Indian self-determination. Members of this pan-Indian movement demanded that the policy be changed.

Reaction to the termination policy grew among Indians, and many took their fight to the polls. Citizenship had been conferred upon all U.S.–born Indians in 1924, but few Indians ever voted until after World War II. In the 1960s, however, Indian leaders encouraged their followers to vote, and in some state and national elections this Indian vote was decisive. The reaction to termination, however, was mixed. In the years after World War II, some Indians began agitation for civil rights based on United States citizenship, thereby supporting termination. They sought an end to aspects of Indian special status, such as trust restrictions on allotted reservation lands and prohibitions on the purchase of alcohol.

In the 1960s, following other examples of activism that were then heating the social landscape, Native Americans took action. The Civil Rights movement and the ensuing riots of the 1960s had a powerful affect on the Native American movement. The black movement stimulated Indians' awareness of themselves as a separate ethnic group. As a result, Indian activist groups concerned with specifically Indian grievances sprang up, employing at times militant protest tactics. The occupation of Alcatraz Island in San Francisco Bay by members of the AMERICAN INDIAN MOVEMENT (AIM) in 1969 was one of the first of these protests. AIM was founded in 1968 in Minneapolis, Minnesota, to deal with the effects of the urban relocation program of the 1950s, chiefly police harassment and discrimination. AIM was instrumental in giving expression to the anger building up in Native Americans, although it was not the only group that took action.

In the early 1970s, the tribes of the Puget Sound, Washington, area openly disobeyed laws limiting fishing, insisting that they violated century-old treaties. In November 1972, Indian protesters from all over the country occupied the headquarters of the BIA in Washington, D.C. In February 1973, Indians, whose leadership comprised mostly members of AIM, occupied the Pine Ridge Reservation town of Wounded Knee, South Dakota, symbolic as the scene of a massacre of unarmed Sioux by U. S. cavalrymen in 1890. Federal and local police besieged the Indians until May.

These militant actions called attention to Indian grievances. Older, more traditional Indians often strongly opposed such tactics, although decades of peaceful protest had not protected Indian land or civil rights. This created a division between the old and the young, with the younger segment accusing the older of being sell-outs to the white establishment.

The Native American movement of the 1960s emerged as a direct response to implementation of federal termination and relocation policies during the 1950s. It was also a reaction to the broader socioeconomic context, which found Native Americans the poorest, most disempowered, least educated, and most malnourished ethnic group within the United States. For much too long had the United States been allowed to solely determine the fate of Native Americans. Many Indians believed it was time to take action. The slogan "Red Power," plainly borrowed from the most militant wing of the African American Civil Rights movement, reflected the belief that in this time of desperate circumstances, a strong stance in defense of Indian rights was not only necessary but also vital.

If there was a founding moment for the movement, it came in the American Indian Chicago Conference during the summer of 1961, when a group of students, including Clyde Warrior, Herbert Blatchford, Shirley Mill Witt, Vivian One Feather, and Mel Thom, openly revolted against the authority of Native American elders. The group formed itself into an autonomous youth caucus during the conference, writing and publishing a manifesto called *A Statement of Indian Purpose*. In August 1961, the members founded the National Indian Youth Council (NIYC), an organization that served as the cutting edge of Red Power ideology throughout the remainder of the decade.

The events occurring in the political arena following World War II and continuing throughout the 1960s were reflected, critiqued, and satirized in the world of art and entertainment. In the MOVIES, a welcome trend showed Indian characters evolving from the ignorant and savage to complex characters dealing with complicated issues. Storylines involving Native Americans in contemporary times emerged. No longer would Native Americans be relegated to the past in ever-popular westerns. Following the success of Delmar Daves's *Broken Arrow* (1950) many pro-Indian movies appeared. These movies often dealt with the difficulties of assimilation into white society, a direct reaction to the urban relocation programs instituted at this time. Movies provided a venue for social critique of white society and very much appealed to COUNTERCULTURE audiences. For example, *Tell Them Willie Boy Is Here* (1968) created an Indian antihero who confronted authorities trying to control his actions, mirroring the struggles and ideals of not just Indians but also an entire generation of youths.

Red Power and Indian rights also found a voice in LITERATURE and academia. In 1968, N. Scott Momaday won the Pulitzer Prize for his book *House Made of Dawn*. Vine Deloria, Jr., a philosopher and writer, is best known for his 1969 study, *Custer Died for Your Sins: An Indian Manifesto*. In his book, Deloria brought Native American issues to the forefront of discussion by recounting past injustices, reviewing the present situation of Indians, and outlining proposed government policies. Native American studies programs also began to form in academic departments around the country.

Further reading: Vine Deloria, Jr., *Custer Died for Your Sins: An Indian Manifesto* (New York: Macmillan, 1969); Joane Nagel, Troy Johnson, and Alvin M. Josephy, Jr., eds., *Red Power: The American Indian's Fight for Freedom* (New York: American Heritage Press, 1971); Frances Paul Prucha, *American Indian Treaties: The History of a Political Anomaly* (Berkeley: University of California Press, 1994).

— Nichole Suzanne Prescott

New Deal (influence)

President Franklin D. Roosevelt's New Deal was a program designed to deal with the ravages of the Great Depression, and to help those Americans who could not help themselves. It provided a framework for public policy for the next several decades.

The New Deal, beginning with Roosevelt's inauguration in 1933, extended GOVERNMENT aid into many facets of society that had not seen government assistance or control before. It included measures to help farmers and workers, relief and recovery programs, and legislation to reform American society. The Social Security program, for example, provided unemployment insurance and pensions. New Deal legislation was extremely controversial, as it expanded the government's role in society, and it caused controversy within the government. Republicans and southern Democrats, who favored small government and wanted to leave the main centers of power at the state level and within the private sector, avidly opposed the legislation.

The New Deal legacy continued after Roosevelt's death in 1945. The FAIR DEAL, under President HARRY S. TRUMAN, constituted a legislative extension of Roosevelt's New Deal. Truman introduced measures such as a national health care program, civil rights legislation against lynching, and measures to establish fair employment practices. Under the Fair Deal, Truman raised the minimum wage, endorsed the Housing Act of 1949 promoting public housing, expanded Social Security coverage, and supported a permanent Fair Employment Practices Committee (FEPC).

When the REPUBLICAN PARTY gained executive power under DWIGHT D. EISENHOWER, the president did not attempt to roll back growth in the powers of the national government. Eisenhower upheld both the New Deal and the Fair Deal legislation. When President JOHN F.

KENNEDY came into office, he patterned his presidency after Roosevelt's, establishing his NEW FRONTIER programs.

President LYNDON B. JOHNSON's idea of a GREAT SOCIETY, created during his presidency, was yet another extension of the New Deal and Fair Deal. Johnson, like Roosevelt and Truman, wanted to better conditions of life for the underprivileged part of American society. With his Great Society, Johnson was able to build upon the legislation of the New and Fair Deals. MEDICARE was enacted under Social Security, providing financial medical assistance to the elderly, and MEDICAID was established to help the poor. The WAR ON POVERTY extended economic reform initiatives of the New Deal and continued the commitment of the government to help those who could not help themselves.

The New Deal and its successors promoted aggressive approaches to federal public policy. Programs extended the powers of the federal government into many different parts of American society that had never witnessed federal legislation before, leaving a legacy still visible today.

Further reading: William Leuchtenberg, *In the Shadow of F.D.R.: From Harry Truman to Ronald Reagan* (Ithaca, N.Y.: Cornell University Press, 1985).

— Jennifer Howell

New Frontier

The New Frontier was the administrative program of President JOHN F. KENNEDY that called for new initiatives in both domestic policy and foreign affairs.

Following Franklin D. Roosevelt's NEW DEAL and HARRY S. TRUMAN's FAIR DEAL, Kennedy called his program the New Frontier. In his inaugural address in 1961, he challenged Americans to "defend freedom in its hour of maximum danger," referring to the COLD WAR struggle with the SOVIET UNION. He also declared that this New Frontier would demand "invention, innovation, imagination, and decision to improve both the United States and the rest of the world."

The New Frontier consisted of two separate agendas, domestic policy and foreign affairs. The domestic agenda in time included a comprehensive civil rights act to guarantee equal access to public accommodations without discrimination, a reduction of taxes to guarantee full employment, and an increase in the minimum wage. It also sought aid for primary, secondary, and even college education. Finally, it proposed dealing with chronic pockets of poverty.

Kennedy's domestic program received little support in Congress. The civil rights bill was bottled up in congressional committees, and the tax cut went nowhere. Aid to EDUCATION failed over the issue of whether support should go to parochial schools.

Congress did pass a measure increasing the minimum wage to $1.25 an hour, and a bill providing federal aid to economically depressed areas to develop new industries. The government also pledged to train and retrain people to equip them with the necessary skills for jobs that were available.

At the same time, the New Frontier included maintaining a firm stance in the cold war. In his inaugural address, Kennedy had asked Americans to "bear any burden, meet any hardship, support any friend, oppose any foe to assure the survival and the success of liberty." He demanded that the United States stop the encroachments of the Soviet Union. To that end, he authorized the ill-fated invasion of Cuba at the BAY OF PIGS, stood up to the Russians in the CUBAN MISSILE CRISIS, and demanded increased military spending as the United States clashed with the Soviet Union over Berlin.

At the same time, Kennedy jump-started the space program and authorized an effort to place a man on the moon before the end of the decade. He created the PEACE CORPS, an agency that trained American volunteers to perform social and humanitarian services overseas. Volunteers were sent mainly to Asia, Africa, and Latin America, where they lived and worked with local inhabitants on projects in AGRICULTURE, EDUCATION, and public health. The overall goal was to promote world peace and friendship with the world's developing nations.

Kennedy's New Frontier often seemed more rhetoric than substance. On the domestic front, in particular, slim congressional majorities made it difficult to get much significant legislation passed. Still, New Frontier innovations provided the framework for LYNDON B. JOHNSON's GREAT SOCIETY.

Further reading: Herbert S. Parmet, *JFK: The Presidency of John F. Kennedy* (New York: The Dial Press, 1983); Richard Reeves, *President Kennedy: Profile of Power* (New York: Simon & Schuster, 1993).

— Katherine R. Yarosh

New Left

The New Left was the name attached to the radical student groups in the 1960s that sought to change the political culture and create a more participatory democratic system.

In 1960, students at the University of Michigan formed STUDENTS FOR A DEMOCRATIC SOCIETY (SDS), an organization intended to encourage and support student political involvement. Two years later, TOM HAYDEN, an early organizer, issued the *Port Huron Statement,* a manifesto for SDS members and a program for action. In the statement, Hayden deplored the contradictions present in American society. Although the United States was a wealthy nation, he argued, many of its citizens lived in poverty. The nation gave lip service to equality, yet angry, violent racism was rampant throughout the country, and despite official protestations that the United States yearned for peace, its leaders advocated ever-deeper involvement in a distant conflict in Vietnam. To counter these contradictions, SDS called for equal opportunity, civil rights, and individual human rights. They called themselves members of a New Left, student-based and more vigorous than the old Left of the 1930s that had fragmented in the 1950s. They believed that students could make a difference, that idealistic, activist youth could change the system and bring about participatory democracy. SDS not only saw itself as a vanguard for a better society, it was also convinced that the general public, once aware of what changes could be accomplished through the democratic process, would follow its lead to a more egalitarian and just society.

The New Left's adherents were usually young students who came from families with affluent white parents. Their members were centered in the universities and often focused their attention on problems close to home. Criticizing the impersonal quality of education, the restriction on political activity, outdated requirements, and the absence of relevant courses, the New Left denounced the association of universities and the government in the development of weapons systems and counterinsurgency plans. In its view, existing scholarship was committed to maintaining the status quo, and followers of the New Left, sometimes drawing on the critique of radical sociologist C. WRIGHT MILLS, called for scholarship directed at changing things for the better.

In order to accomplish their goal, New Left activists urged students on the nation's campuses to put aside their apathy and become involved in making the world a better place in which to live. Despite radical students' zeal at pursuing their objectives, the New Left did make a difference but only on a minority of college and university campuses, and it failed to motivate the nation as a whole. At best, members of the traditional political establishment turned a deaf ear to the students' manifesto; at worst, they condemned the movement's agenda and its followers for failing to conform. Frustrated, many of the original leaders of the New Left became increasingly radicalized. As the United States became openly involved in the VIETNAM WAR and radicals realized that the administration of LYNDON B. JOHNSON was escalating, rather than ending, the war, the New Left became a strident voice of the ANTIWAR MOVEMENT.

By 1969, the movement sought new ways to fight the establishment. The WEATHERMEN, a radical offshoot of SDS, resorted to violence in attacking the police and the public in Chicago as a way to disrupt American society. Members of the Weathermen descended on Chicago to, in their words, "tear pig city apart." Dressed in protective clothing and chanting, "pick up, pick up, pick up the gun,"

they ran through the city smashing shop windows. Later, the group adopted terrorist tactics and used bombs to gain attention to its cause. When three Weathermen building a bomb in a Greenwich Village building blew themselves up, the New Left's radicalism became associated with social disorder. Middle-class Americans, never sympathetic to violent protest, insisted that order be brought back to the streets.

The violent activities of the New Left became intertwined with the COUNTERCULTURE. Some activists found themselves drawn to the freedom of "flower children," garbed in tie-dyed costumes, "hippie communes" that mocked the traditional American family, and rebels who grew long hair and celebrated a drug culture. Some hippies ended up supporting political causes as they became more widespread. Both the New Left and the counterculture counseled: "Never trust anyone over 30!"

Following riots at the Democratic National Convention in 1968, the New Left was anathema to mainstream America. In 1969, newly inaugurated President Richard M. Nixon felt he had a mandate to turn the force of the federal government against student protesters and criminalized activists. Nixon courted what he called the "Silent Majority" to support both "law and order" and his Vietnam War policy.

Further reading: Maurice Isserman, *If I Had a Hammer: The Death of the Old Left and the Birth of the New Left* (New York: Basic Books, 1987); James Miller, *"Democracy Is in the Streets": From Port Huron to the Siege of Chicago* (New York: Simon & Schuster, 1987).

— Gisela Ables

Nixon, Richard M.   See Volume X

North Atlantic Treaty Organization (NATO)

The North Atlantic Treaty Organization (NATO) is a military alliance among the United States, Canada, and the countries of Western Europe.

Signed on April 4, 1949, by founding members Belgium, Canada, Denmark, France, Luxembourg, Iceland, Italy, the Netherlands, Norway, Portugal, the United Kingdom, and the United States, with Greece and Turkey joining in 1952, followed by West Germany in 1955, the North Atlantic Treaty declared that an armed attack against one or more of the treaty members was considered an attack against all.

While the preamble to the 1949 treaty established an interest in maintaining "peaceful and friendly relations throughout the North Atlantic area," NATO's main interest was battling the spread of COMMUNISM. This became the focal point of the organization's policy during the COLD WAR years. In the immediate aftermath of World War II, the fight against communist influence led to the BERLIN BLOCKADE, where the SOVIET UNION barricaded the city of Berlin from receiving supplies by land and sought to cut the city off from Western contact. Combined with a continued presence of a large Soviet military contingent in Eastern Europe, this action raised fears of Soviet expansion in Western Europe.

President HARRY S. TRUMAN sought a redefinition of American foreign policy. Truman's MARSHALL PLAN, an economic attempt to resurrect the war torn countries of Europe, was rejected by the Eastern European nations within the Soviet orbit. As part of a continuing effort to gain an economic and political advantage in EUROPE, Truman, with the help of Congress, created a military accord between the United States and Western European countries, and he pledged to maintain its members' security

NATO and Warsaw Pact Countries, 1955

through a collective effort. In its first decade, NATO became a military organization dependent on U.S. power for security and protection from Soviet bloc invaders.

Critics of NATO argued that the organization carried with it the obligation to assist in war, and, with it, the expense of such a struggle. They also suggested that instead of promoting peace, the alliance invited armed battle with the Soviet Union by creating a ring of NATO forces around the country, possibly prompting Soviet retaliation. Secretary of State DEAN ACHESON defended the pact, claiming "the United States is now the only democratic nation with the resources and productive capacity to help the free nations of Europe to recover their military strength."

One important issue confronting NATO in the 1950s was that of negotiating West Germany's participation in the alliance. The prospect of a rearmed Germany was understandably greeted with widespread unease and hesitancy in Western Europe, but West Germany's military strength was necessary to balance a Soviet threat. Arrangements for West Germany's addition to the alliance were worked out as part of the Paris Agreements of October 1954, which ended the occupation of West Germany by the Western Allies and provided for the restriction of their production of nuclear, biological, and chemical weapons. West Germany entered NATO in 1955.

Tensions within the organization come about when France's participation in NATO became somewhat strained. France's president Charles de Gaulle called American domination of NATO into question, claiming that his country was subjected to automatic war at the decision of strangers. In July 1966, France formally withdrew from NATO's military component, forcing the organization to relocate its headquarters from Paris to Brussels. Though he decried NATO's operational structure, de Gaulle nonetheless continued French adherence to the North Atlantic Treaty should any unprovoked aggression take place.

In case of Soviet-inspired communist aggression, NATO, in the early 1950s, relied partly on the prospect of American nuclear retaliation. With financial help from American investors, NATO's military expenses increased greatly after communist North Korea attacked South Korea in June 1950, triggering the KOREAN WAR. The organization supplemented its protection policy by deploying nuclear weapons at Western European bases beginning in 1957. Throughout the late 1950s and 1960s, NATO's forces were systematically improved with superior weaponry and training that rendered them roughly equal in strength to those of potential adversaries.

NATO continues to support peacekeeping operations throughout the world. On January 10, 1994, the organization approved a "partnership for peace," allowing former East European communist nations limited association with NATO without the full security guarantee of its member countries.

Further reading: Lawrence S. Kaplan, *The Long Entanglement: NATO's First Fifty Years* (Westport, Conn.: Praeger, 1999); Geir Lundestad, *America, Scandinavia, and the Cold War, 1945–1959* (New York: Columbia University Press, 1980).

— Philippe R. Girard

NSC-68

NSC-68, a policy paper drafted and adopted by the National Security Council in the first half of 1950, established American COLD WAR policy for the next 20 years.

Concluding that the SOVIET UNION possessed extensive military capabilities that could be used for aggressive purposes in the near future, NSC-68 called for massive rearmament and a policy of worldwide containment. Within months of the creation of the NORTH ATLANTIC TREATY ORGANIZATION (NATO), the high point of American postwar policy, the Soviet Union exploded an ATOMIC BOMB and China fell to the communist forces of Mao Zedong. Fearful that the United States lacked the capabilities to fend off further communist expansion, officials called for a major FOREIGN POLICY reassessment.

On January 31, 1950, U.S. president HARRY S. TRUMAN asked the State and Defense Departments "to undertake a reexamination of our objectives in peace and war and of the effect of these objectives on our strategic plans." The Defense Department with representatives from the State Department and the National Security Council formed a committee under the chairmanship of Paul H. Nitze, director of the Policy Planning Staff. The committee worked from mid-February to the end of March 1950 drafting a document that addressed Truman's concerns. On April 7, Secretary of State DEAN ACHESON and Secretary of Defense Louis Johnson approved NSC-68, despite the latter's concerns about the cost of its proposals. After North Korean troops crossed the 38th parallel on June 25, Truman gave full support to the new policy.

NSC-68 marked a major shift in the doctrine of containment that Nitze's predecessor, GEORGE F. KENNAN, advocated. Vehement in tone, NSC-68 accused the Kremlin of planning "the complete subversion or forcible destruction of the machinery of government and structure of society in the countries of the non-Soviet world" and estimated that the Soviet Union would be able to launch a massive atomic attack within four or five years. This sense of urgency, reinforced by the explosion of the first Soviet bomb, contrasted sharply with earlier assessments that the Soviet Union represented a long-term threat.

Arguing that a policy aimed at maintaining a global balance of power was inadequate, NSC-68 proposed that the United States should stand ready to oppose communist expansion everywhere in the world, not only in EUROPE. In a cold war in which psychology played a central role, credibility concerns were paramount. "The assault on free institutions," the document read, "is world-wide now, and in the context of the present polarization of power a defeat of free institutions anywhere is a defeat everywhere."

While it hoped "to change the world situation by means short of war," NSC-68 saw military means as the most efficient way to counter the Soviet threat. It ended with four alternative policies. The fourth option, "a rapid build-up of political, economic, and military strength in the free world," was deemed the most appropriate response to the strategic situation. In direct opposition to the economic and political help that had constituted the backbone of American containment policy up to that point, the document's authors concluded that "it is imperative that this trend be reversed by a much more rapid and concerted build-up of the actual strength of both the United States and the other nations of the free world," no matter what the cost might be.

The document did not mention a specific figure, but it pointed out that the U.S. economy was not producing at full capacity and that additional sacrifices could be made. Pentagon officials estimated that a $5 billion increase in the Defense Department budget (to $18 billion) was necessary while policy planning staff were circulating estimates as high as $35 billion to $50 billion. With the outbreak of the KOREAN WAR in June 1950, U.S. military expenses jumped from $13 billion to $50 billion.

Further reading: John L. Gaddis, *Strategies of Containment: A Critical Appraisal of Postwar American National Security Policy* (Oxford, U.K.: Oxford University Press, 1982); Warner R. Schilling, Paul Y. Hammond, and Glenn H. Snyder, *Strategy, Politics and Defense Budgets* (New York: Columbia University Press, 1962); State Department, *Foreign Relation of the United States: 1950, Volume I* (Washington, D.C.: U.S. Government Printing Office, 1977).

— Philippe R. Girard

O

Operation Dixie

Operation Dixie, as the southern labor organizing drive came to be known, was an attempt by the CONGRESS OF INDUSTRIAL ORGANIZATIONS (CIO) to unionize southern industrial workers.

Launched in 1946, the labor-organizing drive experienced some successes, but it was largely a failure because of the CIO's indecision on how to best approach the campaign—as a militant and heroic march into the South or as a less spectacular and more methodical mission.

Since the early days of the CIO, the South appeared to be a natural arena for mass labor organization. The southern labor force numbered over 1.5 million in a diverse array of industries, from mining to manufacturing to textile mills. The South did present unique problems in unionization, for racial lines divided the labor force. While the CIO found strong enthusiasm for organization among black workers, the desire to appeal to whites, who wanted no part in biracial unions, tested the CIO's commitment to egalitarianism. There was also very little tradition of union activism to build upon in the South, which, unlike northern industrial regions, lacked dedicated union sympathizers within the nonlabor community.

The South was too critical a labor battleground to ignore, however, and CIO leaders in the 1940s became increasingly focused on its conquest. A 1939 CIO prospectus read, "As long as the South remains unorganized, it constitutes the nation's number one economic problem and is also a menace to our organized movement in the North and likewise to northern industries." The region's low wages, potential for industrial growth, and influence in congressional politics and on federal legislation made it a prime target for CIO organizing efforts.

From the beginning of the southern drive in the winter of 1946, conflicting perspectives divided the nature of the undertaking. While cautious-minded organizers avoided heroic rhetoric, knowing that it would only alarm fearful southern workers and alert antiunion forces, more radical and spirited CIO leaders trumpeted the movement as a conquest of interests. One headline in the organization newsletter, *The CIO News,* announced the mission as the "Holy Crusade." Experienced southern organizers, such as Textile Workers Union of America vice president George Baldanzi, who had successfully organized some 13,000 cotton workers in Virginia, warned against too militant an approach. "We must clear up . . . the erroneous impression that this is an "Operation Dixie," said Baldanzi in 1946. Cautious minds within the CIO feared that southern workers would associate the unionizing effort with strikes, violence, and community turmoil.

Resistance to organization in the South was strong, and recruiters deployed to rally union support soon faced the harsh reality of an unresponsive labor force. Antiunion sentiment permeated all facets of southern communities. Local religious leaders mockingly declared that CIO stood for *Christ Is Out,* perpetuating the belief held by many southerners that northern union organizers were godless leftists. Local politicians, in connection with the Southern States Industrial Council, warned that the CIO would give blacks social and economic equality and southern democratic institutions would crumble.

In fact, the southern drive did little to challenge SEGREGATION in the South. CIO leaders advocated avoiding the civil rights question entirely. Van Bittner, director of the CIO's Southern Organizing Committee, declared, "We are not mentioning the color of people." While recognizing the importance of black workers in southern industry, Bittner saw that any connection with a larger social agenda would only hurt the union drive.

Though there were minor successes, union organizers often found the membership drive an impossible task. The CIO realized that their teams were unable to establish in-plant committees in order to gain a foothold within the labor force. Organizers accepted as a minor victory the fact that workers took their leaflets or bothered to take a copy of union newspapers. Though the movement fell short of the CIO's expectations by the end of 1946, the organization drive sputtered on throughout the South, almost as an afterthought, until 1953. Critics argued that the operation focused too heavily on the nearly unbreakable textile industry, rather than building upon successes in other areas. Political content had been absent from the campaign, much to the frustration of more left-leaning CIO functionaries, but the political climate of the late 1940s clearly veered to the conservative right. By the end of "Operation Dixie," CIO leaders came to understand that the mass organization glory days of the 1930s had passed, and the heroic street tactics of labor unionizing had to be replaced by a more responsible, progressive, and altogether respectable agenda.

Further reading: Robert Zieger, *The CIO: 1935–1955* (Chapel Hill: University of North Carolina Press, 1995).

— Guy R. Temple

Operation Mongoose

Operation Mongoose was the title given to a series of covert actions the administration of JOHN F. KENNEDY developed as a way to undermine Fidel Castro's government in Cuba in the early 1960s.

When U.S.–Cuban relations fell apart after Fidel Castro seized power on New Year's Day 1959, the administration of DWIGHT D. EISENHOWER started to fund bombing runs against Cuban sugar refineries and train a Cuban exile force for an invasion of the island. As Kennedy took office in 1961, he knew that Republicans would be quick to accuse him of being soft on COMMUNISM, as they had criticized HARRY S. TRUMAN after the loss of China to the communists in 1949. When a U.S.–supported invasion of Cuba ended in complete failure at the BAY OF PIGS in April 1961, the Pentagon and the CENTRAL INTELLIGENCE AGENCY (CIA) examined various ways to rid themselves of Castro. Brigadier General Edward G. Lansdale supervised the operation, codenamed Mongoose, with the strong support of Attorney General ROBERT F. KENNEDY.

Operation Mongoose continued the attacks against Cuba's sugar industry that had originated under Eisenhower, but it also included a whole range of covert operations. Operation Good Times aimed at creating popular resentment against Castro by disseminating doctored photographs picturing him sitting with two gorgeous women enjoying a plentiful meal, over a caption that read "my ration is different." Hoping to kill the Cuban leader, the CIA hired assassins recommended by Mafia boss Johnny Rosselli, offered Castro a poisoned scuba suit, and prepared cigars impregnated with botulism. A plan to sprinkle Castro's shoes with thallium salts, in the hope of destroying his beard (and hence his popularity as a macho male) also failed.

Under Operation Dirty Trick, the United States would have blamed the Castro government had John Glenn's 1962 Project Mercury space flight ended in failure. Operation Bingo was a plan to organize a fake attack against the American base at Guantanamo Bay in Cuba, which would have provided an excuse to launch a retaliatory campaign against Cuba. Other fabricated incidents that were considered included blowing up an American warship (like the *Maine* on the eve of the Spanish-American War of 1898) and sinking a boat filled with Cuban exiles.

Further reading: James G. Blight and Peter Kornbluh, *Politics of Illusion: The Bay of Pigs Invasion Reexamined* (Boulder, Colo.: Lynne Rienner, 1998).

— Philippe R. Girard

Oppenheimer, J. Robert (1904–1967)

Julius Robert Oppenheimer was a nuclear physicist best known for directing the Los Alamos laboratory that designed the United States's first ATOMIC BOMB and for unsuccessfully attempting to curtail further atomic research during the COLD WAR.

Oppenheimer was born on April 22, 1904, in New York City. His father was a German immigrant who had become rich by trading textiles. Oppenheimer studied at the Ethical Culture School in New York before graduating from Harvard in 1925. He excelled in a variety of fields ranging from poetry to Oriental philosophy. While he maintained an interest in these subjects throughout his life, he specialized in the rapidly developing field of nuclear physics and conducted research at Cambridge University's Cavendish Laboratory in England before moving to the University of Göttingen in Germany where he earned his doctorate in 1927. During his years in Europe he was able to study with such notable scientists as Max Born, Niels Bohr, Paul Dirac, and Lord Ernest Rutherford.

In 1929, he took a position at the California Institute of Technology and at the University of California at Berkeley, working on applications of the quantum and relativity theories in his spare time. His research predicted the existence of particles, such as the neutron, positron, and meson, and of celestial bodies such as the neutron star.

On August 2, 1939, Leo Szilard wrote a letter that Albert Einstein signed and delivered to President Franklin D. Roosevelt, warning him of the feasibility and potential destructive power of an atomic bomb. The Advisory Committee on Uranium met with Roosevelt soon after, but little progress was made in the following months. Under the leadership of Arthur H. Compton, the project to design nuclear weapons was launched on December 18, 1941. The name was changed to "Manhattan Engineer District" (now known as Manhattan Project) in August 1942 with Colonel Leslie Richard Groves as the new director.

The project was launched on a massive scale with Oppenheimer serving as the head of the laboratory for weapons research. Oppenheimer selected Los Alamos, New Mexico, as the site and the laboratory went into operation in March 1943. He headed a team of researchers that included over 3,000 people. Work also continued in Chicago, where the first atomic reactor, designed by Enrico Fermi, began functioning on December 2, 1942, and at Oak Ridge, Tennessee, where the plutonium production facilities were located, as well as in more than 30 other facilities in the United States and Canada. The first atomic bomb was successfully tested on July 16, 1945, in the Jornada del Muerto valley at the Alamogordo Bombing Range. The next month, the United States dropped the bomb on Hiroshima and Nagasaki, forcing Japan to surrender. As he tried to comprehend the results of the bombing, Oppenheimer quoted from Hindu scripture saying, "Now I am become Death, the destroyer of worlds."

Following the war, Oppenheimer became chair of the General Advisory Committee of the ATOMIC ENERGY COMMISSION. In 1949, he opposed the construction of the HYDROGEN BOMB. Nevertheless, President HARRY S. TRUMAN ordered the development of the hydrogen bomb in 1950, and it was successfully tested in 1952.

Oppenheimer's political ties brought his ideological beliefs into question. During the Spanish Civil War, Oppenheimer had associated himself with communists as part of an effort to send funds to support the struggle against fascism. While he never joined the Communist Party himself, his wife, his wife's former husband, his brother, his sister-in-law, and several of his friends were communists. With the onset of World War II, he distanced himself from the Communist Party, but he failed to cut his ties to communist friends and hired several communist sympathizers for the Manhattan Project. In an era during which Wisconsin senator JOSEPH R. MCCARTHY made accusations that communists infiltrated the federal government, Oppenheimer's past communist sympathies were deemed sufficient to put his loyalty into question.

On December 23, 1953, the Personnel Security Board withdrew Oppenheimer's security clearance pending further investigation. Following hearings in April–May 1954, the decision to permanently revoke his security clearance was confirmed on June 29, 1954, and was justified by Oppenheimer's failure to cut his ties to former communist friends following his appointment as the head of the Los Alamos laboratory during the war. He came to symbolize the scientist whose attempt to marry moral conscience and work for the military had ended in failure.

In 1947, Oppenheimer was named director of the Institute of Advanced Study at Princeton. Meanwhile, supporters worked for his rehabilitation. President LYNDON B. JOHNSON reinstated his security clearance in 1963. He also received the Enrico Fermi award from the Atomic Energy Commission. He died of throat cancer on February 18, 1967.

Further reading: Peter Goodchild, *J. Robert Oppenheimer: Shatterer of Worlds* (Boston: Houghton Mifflin, 1981); Herbert F. York, *The Advisors: Oppenheimer, Teller, and the Superbomb* (Stanford, Calif.: Stanford University Press, 1989).

— Philippe R. Girard

Oswald, Lee Harvey (1939–1963)

Lee Harvey Oswald was the accused assassin of U.S. President JOHN F. KENNEDY.

Oswald was born in New Orleans, Louisiana, on October 18, 1939. His father, Robert Edward Lee, died two months before he was born. His mother, Marguerite Oswald, often living in poverty, raised Oswald and his two brothers. As a baby, Oswald spent several periods in orphanage care while his mother worked long hours. Growing up, he was often in trouble, and, according to a psychiatrist, was emotionally disturbed. Oswald was considered a "loner," and though he was said to be very interested in books, his grades seldom reflected this interest. Oswald became disenchanted with formal education, and at the age of 17, he dropped out of school to join the U.S. Marine Corps.

Oswald was trained as an aviation electronics technician and his military records indicated that his performance and conduct as a marine were below average. He was never promoted higher than private first class, and was convicted twice in summary courts martial, once for failing to register a weapon and once for disrespect to a noncommissioned officer. Oswald was discharged from the Marine Corps in 1959 at his request, stating that he needed to be home in order to help support his mother. Oswald, however, defected to the Union of Soviet Socialist Republics (USSR) a month later. Once in Moscow, he appeared at the U.S. Embassy to renounce his American citizenship and, as a result, his military discharge was changed to an undesirable discharge.

Though Oswald was denied citizenship in the USSR, he lived and worked in Minsk for approximately two and a half years, where he met and married Marina Prusakova. Oswald, by now an embittered man, became disillusioned with the USSR and turned to the United States for help. He informed a congressman that he wanted to leave the USSR with his Soviet wife, but Soviet authorities refused his request. His plea for U.S. intervention was answered in May 1962, when the State Department became involved and Soviet authorities agreed to let Oswald depart the USSR with his Soviet wife and their new daughter, June.

Returning to the United States in June 1962, Oswald moved to Fort Worth, Texas, with his family. Oswald, still interested in left-wing causes, joined the Fair Play for Cuba Committee, a pro-Castro group. In July 1962, Oswald attempted to join the anti-Castro Cuban Student Directorate in New Orleans. Seeking to infiltrate the organization, he was arrested shortly thereafter in a street fight that erupted when the group encountered him distributing pro-Castro literature to the public.

In October 1963, Oswald took up residence alone in Dallas, Texas. Marina and June went to live with Oswald's relatives in Irving, Texas, where Marina gave birth to their second daughter shortly thereafter. Weeks later, Oswald started a job at the Texas School Book Depository. On November 22, 1963, Oswald went to work at the depository, and at 12:30 P.M. a gunman from the sixth floor of the building fired three shots into President Kennedy's motorcade, killing Kennedy and injuring Texas governor John B. Connally. Police arrested Oswald at a movie theater just over an hour later. Authorities accused Oswald of killing police officer J. D. Tippit, shot shortly after the president's assassination. Oswald emphatically denied shooting either Kennedy or Tippit, insisting that he was a "patsy" for a larger conspiracy. On November 24, as police moved Oswald from the city jail to the county jail before a national television audience, Jack Ruby, a Dallas nightclub owner, fatally shot Oswald while standing in a crowd of police officers and reporters. Lee Harvey Oswald was 24 years old.

A special presidential commission, headed by Chief Justice EARL WARREN, investigated the Kennedy assassination. Despite numerous conspiracy theories, the commission concluded in 1964, in the Warren Report, that Oswald acted alone.

Several pieces of evidence supported the notion that Oswald had not acted alone. Most notable were the nearly impossible shots that Oswald was accused of making. According to the Warren Commission, Oswald rapidly fired three shots from a bolt-action rifle at a moving target, two of the shots hitting the president. Critics called this action

Jack Ruby shoots Lee Harvey Oswald (center) in a Dallas police station, 1963   *(Library of Congress)*

unlikely, especially from a man whose military records indicated that he was only a mediocre shot, scoring average and less than average during his two rifle qualifications in the Marine Corps.

In 1979, a committee from the U.S. House of Representatives acknowledged the likelihood of a conspiracy and reported that a second assassin might have been involved.

Further reading: Norman Mailer, *Oswald's Tale: An American Mystery* (New York: Random House, 1995).

— Jason Reed

P

Packard, Vance (1914–1996)

Vance Packard was one of the most influential social critics of the mid-20th century, known best for his books exposing a variety of unseen threats to the American public.

Vance Packard was born on May 22, 1914, in Granville Summit, Pennsylvania. Born into a strong Methodist family, Packard's exposure to the teachings of the Bible provided the moral framework by which he later judged American society. Life on the family farm also showed him the value of productive work.

As a student at Pennsylvania State University in the mid-1930s, Packard focused on journalism and became assistant editor of the *Penn State Collegian.* It was an exciting time for Packard, as events around campus as well as around the world opened his eyes to politics and political dialogue. He also became interested in LITERATURE, particularly the works of the muckraking journalists of the Progressive period. In his own critiques of college customs, such as fraternity rush, he saw his place in society as the "ironic observer," quick to point out the faults in existing social institutions.

Following his graduation from Penn State, Packard moved on to graduate school at Columbia University, where he earned a master's degree in JOURNALISM in 1937. Upon leaving Columbia University, he began work at the *Boston Daily Record* where his first story as a cub reporter earned him a daily column in the newspaper. Tired of his position on the *Boston Daily Record,* he went to New York, where he got a job with the Associated Press Feature Service. While moving up professionally, Packard resisted conforming to society's expectations and norms for success.

Following a 15-year period with *American Magazine,* Packard decided to try his hand at freelance writing. From 1957 to 1960, Packard met with nothing but success. His critiques of society, *The Hidden Persuaders* (1957), *The Status Seekers* (1959), and *The Waste Makers* (1960), all reached number one on the *New York Times* nonfiction best sellers list within a period of four years. Not only were these works best sellers, but they also exposed the American citizen to what Packard called "systematic optimism-generation." Created by big BUSINESS, mass media, and some intellectuals, these factions proclaimed that America had entered a new era of profound opportunity, a period of narrowing social differences as well as vanishing poverty. In addition to these claims, many people believed that the existence of great material wealth was not important to the average citizen. Packard proceeded to tear apart this naive construct.

In *The Hidden Persuaders,* he argued that new trends in ADVERTISING used fears of psychological obsolescence, sexual inadequacy, and concern over social status to undermine individuality and sell products. Packard was the first to expose the trade secrets of advertisers. His book caused such an uproar that the business community launched an all-out public relations campaign to counter any damage Packard's work might have caused. Following *The Hidden Persuaders, The Status Seekers* raised pointed questions about the supposed nature of increasing social mobility in America and decreasing class divisions. Packard argued the contrary, namely, that America's immense wealth and search for increased status further delineated social divisions. The source of this problem, he declared, was found in a consumer culture enhanced by capitalists. Finally, in *The Waste Makers,* he challenged the use of planned obsolescence by big business to make consumers buy items they wanted but did not necessarily need. These three books opened the eyes of Americans to the awesome power of big business as well as to serious social concerns.

Packard published 12 books over the course of his career. Some of his best-known other works included *The Naked Society* (1964), *A Nation of Strangers* (1972), and *The People Shapers* (1977). His topics ranged from the loss of privacy in American society to human engineering and behavior modification. All of his works raised important questions about the very nature of the social experience. Vance Packard died in 1996 at the age of 82.

Further reading: Daniel Horowitz, *Vance Packard & American Social Criticism* (Chapel Hill: University of North Carolina Press, 1994); Vance Packard, *The Hidden Persuaders* (New York: David McKay, 1957); Vance Packard, *The Status Seekers* (New York: David McKay, 1959).

— Clayton Douglas

Parks, Rosa (1913–   )

Rosa Parks became a symbol of the nonviolent protest advocated by the Civil Rights movement when she refused to give up her seat to a white passenger on a city bus in Montgomery, Alabama.

This act of CIVIL DISOBEDIENCE sparked the Montgomery bus boycott, which began the modern Civil Rights movement by forcing the racial integration of southern city buses. African Americans had long contested SEGREGATION on public transportation. But often their protests were hasty and solitary, militant and profane. Parks was respectable, quiet, and firm in her refusal. Community and religious leaders joined activists in supporting her actions, and together they destroyed longstanding racist practices.

Parks was born Rosa Louise McCauley in Tuskegee, Alabama, on February 4, 1913. Her father James was a carpenter, and her mother Leona taught school. They managed to send Rosa to the private Montgomery Industrial School for Girls from the age of 11. She later took courses at the Alabama State College for Negroes before marrying Raymond Parks, a barber, in 1932. Over the next 23 years, she worked as a clerk and a department store seamstress, and she and her husband were active in the local NATIONAL ASSOCIATION FOR THE ADVANCEMENT OF COLORED PEOPLE (NAACP).

Returning home, tired from work on December 1, 1955, Parks took a seat near the front of the bus. When the bus began to get crowded, the driver stopped the bus and told four African Americans to move to the back so white passengers could ride in front. This was legal in Montgomery and common practice throughout the South. The others moved, but Parks told the driver no. She was arrested. The president of the state NAACP bailed her out of jail that same day, and local activists quickly laid the groundwork to support her and to organize for integration. The episode was not unexpected, and civil rights activists had been waiting for such an event to galvanize them into action. Now they responded as they had planned.

Four days after Parks's arrest, at a meeting at the Holt Street Baptist Church, the Montgomery Improvement Association (MIA) was founded. MARTIN LUTHER KING, JR., the young pastor of Montgomery's Dexter Avenue Church, became its president. The MIA organized a boycott of the Montgomery city bus system, in which passengers refused to ride the buses until they were integrated. MIA leaders organized carpools, printed handbills, and spread word of the protest throughout the community.

The boycott ran for more than a year, 382 days, from December 5, 1955, to December 21, 1956. While a number of whites also boycotted the buses to support their black neighbors, the bus company relied on African American passengers, who comprised 70 percent of the bus system's customers. The boycott severely damaged the bus company's business. The company's owners soon offered to provide black drivers on routes used mostly by blacks, and it promised that drivers would stop making offensive remarks, but the MIA refused to end the boycott until all its demands were met.

Meanwhile, the white mayor of Montgomery called for a "get tough" response to the boycott. A violent backlash developed, led by the WHITE CITIZENS' COUNCIL of Montgomery. In January 1956, a bomb exploded outside King's house. Though no one was hurt, the savagery focused national attention on the struggle. Petty and serious arrests continually threatened the boycott's leaders.

On November 13, 1956, the U.S. Supreme Court upheld an order from a lower court that found Montgomery's segregated bus system illegal. It ordered the integration of Montgomery buses. The MIA organized the push for integration, and later the organization became part of the SOUTHERN CHRISTIAN LEADERSHIP CONFERENCE (SCLC), which planned many other actions in the African American movement for civil rights. King became one of the most celebrated civil rights leaders of the era. Parks continued to work for racial justice in the NAACP and SCLC. She joined the staff of Michigan congressman John Conyers, Jr., where she worked until her retirement in 1988. In 1987, after the death of her husband, she founded the Rosa and Raymond Parks Institute for Self-Development, a career-counseling center for young African Americans.

Parks has received numerous awards and medals for her 1955 action and her later activism. A street in Montgomery was renamed Rosa Parks Boulevard in 1965. She accepted the Spingarn Medal, the NAACP's highest honor, in 1970, and the prestigious Martin Luther King, Jr., Award in 1980. The SCLC established an annual Rosa Parks Freedom Award in her honor. In 1996, President Bill Clinton awarded her the Presidential Medal of Freedom, and she received a Congressional Gold Medal in 1999, the highest honor awarded by the U.S. government to civilians. She continues to travel and speak on civil rights issues and remains a powerful activist.

Further reading: Douglas Brinkley, *Rosa Parks* (New York: Viking Press, 2000); Rosa Parks, *Rosa Parks: My Story* (New York: Dial Books, 1992); Jo Ann Gibson Robinson, *The Montgomery Bus Boycott and the Women Who Started It* (Knoxville: University of Tennessee Press, 1987).

— Barbara M. Hahn

Peace Corps

The Peace Corps was created to send American volunteers abroad to promote good foreign relations and "world peace" by bringing urgently needed social and technical services to developing countries.

The concept of a Peace Corps was first introduced during JOHN F. KENNEDY's 1960 presidential campaign. The idea was quickly realized with establishment of the corps by executive order on March 1, 1961, and the appointment of its first director, Sargent Shriver, Kennedy's brother-in-law. Seven months after its inception, Congress approved legislation formally authorizing the volunteer-based agency.

An element in the foreign affairs component of Kennedy's NEW FRONTIER, the Peace Corps became the most celebrated tangible response to the president's inaugural challenge for commitment to public service. His stirring appeal, "Ask not what your country can do for you, ask what you can do for your country," galvanized thousands of young Americans, inspired to create a better world, by devoting a minimum of two years of their lives as volunteers for the Peace Corps. The only stipulated requirements were that the volunteer be a U.S. citizen, at least 18 years of age, and have no more than two dependents under 18. Volunteers' duties ranged from teaching and developing community projects to establishing vital agricultural and health programs in rural and urban areas of AFRICA, the Near East, LATIN AMERICA, the Caribbean, and ASIA.

While many flocked to serve in the Peace Corps, others volunteered for VOLUNTEERS IN SERVICE TO AMERICA (VISTA), the domestic version of the Corps, or invested their efforts in the growing Civil Rights movement. All of these activists were motivated by Kennedy's call to action, by his promise that they could indeed make a lasting difference, and by their own conviction that their selfless efforts on behalf of humanity would eventually bring about equality, freedom, inclusion, and opportunity for all. The possibilities for effecting concrete change, one volunteer recalled, seemed limitless.

The Peace Corps's strong idealistic bent appealed to those who believed in the positive influence of government and an actively participatory citizenry. There was, however, another motive for the establishment of the Peace Corps other than the sole humanitarian version offered by the government. The volunteer agency was but one of several programs included in Kennedy's policy of nation building. This policy, an integral component of his foreign affairs agenda, was crafted within the framework of the COLD WAR. The policy of nation building advocated technical assistance and financial aid to help developing nations achieve economic and political stability. The policy's overriding objective, however, was to win "the hearts and minds" of those caught in the cold war power struggle between the United States and the SOVIET UNION, and to draw them into America's sphere of influence.

Whether it was Kennedy's ALLIANCE FOR PROGRESS in Latin America, the Agency for International Development that distributed aid in developing nations, or the Peace Corps, these and other similar programs were specifically designed as valuable, noncombative tools in America's efforts to stall the spread of COMMUNISM worldwide. The Peace Corps, therefore, was not only a program used to export America's most positive attributes—youthful idealism, compassion for those less fortunate, perceived moral superiority—but to help initiate the requisite developments needed to insure better futures for developing nations. The Peace Corps was one of America's potent nonmilitary weapons in its cold war arsenal. By mid-1966, the agency announced it had 15,000 volunteers living and working in more than 50 countries, the largest number of volunteers in its history. It was deemed a great success.

The achievements of the Peace Corps, in terms of good public relations and valuable humanistic efforts, spawned the establishment of comparable organizations by other industrialized nations, including Great Britain, Canada, and Sweden, as well as by the United Nations. Yet, in America, numerous potential volunteers became disillusioned with the Corps's principles of hope and idealistically driven activism, both of which began crumbling in the face of continued civil rights abuses at home and the nation's increasingly unpopular involvement in the VIETNAM WAR. And, despite having received full autonomy under President Jimmy Carter and status as an independent federal agency on its 20th anniversary, budget cuts in the 1970s and 1980s also took their toll on the organization. As a result, volunteer rates markedly dropped. In the 1990s, the Peace Corps began receiving greatly expanded federal support, increasing the agency's budget by 50 percent in order to reach a goal of 10,000 volunteers by the year 2003. The cataclysmic political developments that occurred in EUROPE and in Asia during the 1990s also boosted the Peace Corps's viability and visibility. For the first time in the agency's history, volunteers were sent to the SOVIET UNION, China, and Eastern Europe. The Peace Corps had outlasted its cold war objective. Today, it continues to promote its humanistic aims of friendship, understanding, and opportunity worldwide.

Further reading: Roy Hoopes, ed. *The Peace Corps Experience* (New York: Clarkson N. Potter, 1968); Gerald Rice, *The Bold Experiment: JFK's Peace Corps* (South

Bend, Ind.: University of Notre Dame Press, 1985); Karen Schwarz, *What You Can Do for Your Country: An Oral History of the Peace Corps* (New York: Morrow/Avon, 1991); David Searles, *The Peace Corps Experience: Challenge & Change, 1969–1976* (Lexington: University of Kentucky Press, 1997).

— Irene Guenther

"The Pill"

Within two years of its commercial introduction in 1960, the oral contraceptive, commonly called simply "The Pill," helped contribute to an American sexual revolution.

In the 1950s, birth control reformer Margaret Sanger campaigned aggressively for an oral contraceptive that would make birth control easier than current methods. Sanger had been a tireless proponent of women's control over reproduction since the second decade of the 20th century. Now she launched what became a huge, heavily capitalized effort. She persuaded Katherine Dexter McCormick, a wealthy heiress who had been the second woman to graduate from MIT, to fund the necessary research. McCormick enlisted the support of scientists and doctors to determine how the female menstrual cycle worked and then to decide how to treat it hormonally so that ovulation—or implantation if ovulation and fertilization accidentally occurred—would not take place.

In the mid-1950s, the researchers ran two sets of tests on the pill they thought would prevent pregnancy when taken daily. The first, smaller test, conducted in Massachusetts, was a success—not one of the 50 volunteers ovulated. The second, longer-term clinical trial, done in Puerto Rico, Haiti, and Mexico City, was also a success, with a failure rate of only 1.7 percent, much lower than that of diaphragms or condoms. In 1960, the Food and Drug Administration approved Enovid, the first oral contraceptive available on the market.

Within three years of its introduction, more than 2 million women were on the pill, and as the cost dropped, millions more began to use it. In 1961, 14 percent of new patients at Planned Parenthood clinics chose oral contraception. In 1963, the figure had jumped to 42 percent, and in 1964, it soared to 62 percent. By 1990, 80 percent of all women born since 1945 had taken the pill sometime during their lives.

Available just as the rebellious generation of the 1960s was coming of age, the pill removed the fear of pregnancy from sexual experimentation, and it helped lower the age of sexual activity. It led people to speak about sex more frequently and frankly than before. The pill also aided men and women in controlling family size, and it made it easier for women, who were now able to control reproductive patterns, to work outside the home. "Modern woman is at

last free as man is free," said Clare Boothe Luce, a playwright and former member of Congress. In 1993, the *Economist* magazine called it one of the seven wonders of the modern world.

Further reading: Elizabeth Siegel Watkins, *On the Pill: A Social History of Oral Contraceptives* (Baltimore: Johns Hopkins University Press, 1998).

— Heather L. Tompkins

Point Four Program

The Point Four Program sought to give American technological advice and economic aid to developing countries around the world in an effort to bolster U.S. foreign relations with these areas.

In his January 20, 1949, inaugural address, President HARRY S. TRUMAN outlined a new foreign aid program that consisted of four major points of action. The fourth element, called the Point Four Program, provided technical assistance and economic aid to underdeveloped countries. It underwent several phases before ultimately becoming part of the federal Agency for International Development. Point Four served as one of many programs designed to solidify America's position in the COLD WAR and help prevent the spread of COMMUNISM.

Following World War II, the global economy was in a precarious state. Although the United States stood as a financial leader and major lender of international aid, most industrialized economies around the world faced massive rebuilding. Countries that exported raw materials as their primary source of income faced the loss of markets for their goods. Leading economists and politicians cited the global financial crisis following World War I as a contributing cause of World War II. The United States adopted a series of financial aid programs after 1945 in hopes of bringing greater economic stability and preventing a future war.

In 1950, Congress approved the allocation of $35 million dollars for the Point Four Program. Although this was less money than the Truman administration hoped for, it laid the foundation for future aid programs. The program provided foreign aid to less-developed countries, especially in LATIN AMERICA, AFRICA, and ASIA. Initially, the Technical Cooperation Administration division of the Department of State administered all aspects of the program, but later the administration of DWIGHT D. EISENHOWER brought Point Four under general foreign aid program administration.

Point Four shared not just investment capital with its recipient nations but also technical assistance in the form of American expertise and equipment. The program helped countries plan for, receive, and implement advancements in agriculture, health care, education, and transportation. To achieve these goals, Americans traveled to the recipient countries and spent considerable time and money teaching local people how best to use new technologies to benefit their country. U.S. shipments of industrial equipment and machinery caused some controversy in the receiving countries. Critics in countries that had just received independence from colonial governments often decried the machinery as symbols of "neocolonialism," in which the country was economically dependent yet governmentally independent.

Most countries happily received the medical and agricultural technology and advice. They wanted to improve their standard of living and decrease economic dependence on a few cash crops. American advancement in the production of penicillin improved health care around the world. In one of the most important components of the Point Four Program, Americans shared their knowledge of food production. Recipients of this form of aid hoped it would help them decrease their reliance on foreign food imports and increase their self-sufficiency. Americans also shared the use of hybrid seeds, fertilizers, and pesticides. Although use of these technological advances increased agricultural yields, they also created some long-term environmental and health concerns in the regions, which prompted criticism of this and other programs funded by the United States.

The Point Four Program did not represent American altruism alone. The United States hoped to benefit both economically and politically from the generous grants of money, technology and advice. Truman and Eisenhower saw foreign aid as a way to fight communism. Both men believed that people and governments in the receiving countries would look to the United States for political guidance. By seeing the benefits of a capitalist, democratic society, U.S. policymakers thought the countries would become reliable allies against the threat of communism. Congress approved the Point Four measures as part of government spending efforts to counteract domestic and foreign subversive threats. The United States benefited economically by finding new markets for its goods and increasing trade opportunities with resource-rich countries in the developing world.

In many ways, the Point Four Program proved successful for the United States. During its first 10 years, Point Four sent approximately 6,000 technicians to 58 countries around the world. Although other agencies eventually absorbed the program, the United States continued to provide financial and technical assistance through its own channels and through international relief agencies and the United Nations.

Further reading: Jonathan B. Bingham, *Shirt-Sleeve Diplomacy: Point 4 in Action* (New York: J. Day, 1954).

— Lyra Totten-Naylor

popular culture

In the 1950s and 1960s, popular culture—those trends in art and entertainment that society found most appealing—reflected Americans' desire to enjoy their newfound prosperity and national power.

The United States flourished after World War II. Spurred by a postwar economic boom, the gross national product jumped from over $200 billion in 1945 to over $500 billion in 1960. As Americans enjoyed the benefits of prosperity, they experienced substantial changes in cultural tastes. Free of wartime transportation and spending restrictions, the American people, eager to enjoy their leisure time, began to expand their cultural tastes and explore new options in the arts and entertainment.

In the postwar years, American theater featured a broader choice of styles that represented many different groups in society. During World War II, many American theaters featured plays that were little more than propaganda or escapist fare. In subsequent years, dramas such as Arthur Miller's *The Crucible* (1953), about a 17th-century witch hunt that paralleled the communist witch hunts of the 1950s, and Tennessee Williams's *Cat on a Hot Tin Roof* (1955), which focused on the destructiveness of pretense in an American family, drew large audiences to the theater. Lighthearted musicals such as *Guys and Dolls* (1950) and *My Fair Lady* (1956) coupled brilliant lyrics with sophisticated choreography to produce stories that left audiences with a positive feeling about American society. African American plays earned new prominence in the 1950s with works such as Lorraine Hansberry's *A Raisin in the Sun* (1959), the story of an African-American family coping with a financial windfall. Adrienne Kennedy's autobiographical *Funnyhouse of a Negro* (1962) depicted her struggle as an American of mixed racial heritage. Americans increasingly enjoyed the complex storylines and superior performances that theater offered.

While theater offered a diversion from society's larger problems, young writers explored the problems and confusion of American culture. Norman Mailer's novel *The Naked and the Dead* (1948) countered cheery images of the war with a darker view of men engaged in combat. The play *Death of a Salesman* (1949), by Arthur Miller, captured the life of a man lost in illusions of success and out of touch with the realities of life. J. D. Salinger's novel *The Catcher in the Rye* (1951) looked at middle-class life through the eyes of rebellious 17-year-old Holden Caulfield. Other authors addressed the inequalities in American society. Ralph Ellison's *Invisible Man* (1952) explored the indifference of American society toward African Americans in the postwar years.

Meanwhile, new forms of entertainment captured the imagination of the public. The prosperity of the 1950s allowed almost every family to have a TELEVISION in its home. The situation comedies that began appearing on television reflected the conservative ideals of the era. On Monday, October 15, 1951, CBS aired the pioneering situation comedy *I Love Lucy*. The show played on the American stereotype of the dependent housewife and the domineering, breadwinning husband. By 1954, about 50 million people were tuning into the *I Love Lucy* show, making it the most popular television show of the time. The *I Love Lucy* show opened the door for other family-themed comedies such as *Father Knows Best* and *The Ozzie and Harriet Show*. Variety shows began appearing on television as well. *The Ed Sullivan Show* brought popular acts such as the BEATLES and ELVIS PRESLEY to American viewers. *The Mickey Mouse Club* was a variety show for children to watch after school.

As with television, MOVIES became increasingly popular during the 1950s and 1960s. Film stars like Doris Day played to the ideal of the girl next door, and sexy stars like MARILYN MONROE played to the sensual side of American women, while stimulating the fantasies of American men. New genres of film appealed to a broad audience of young viewers. Movies such as *Rebel without a Cause* (1955) captured the imagination and angst of a generation of teenagers who rejected the values of their parents. The movie's star, James Dean, became a teen idol and a film legend. Other types of movies broke away from the feel-good movies popular during the war. *West Side Story* (1961), the tale of star-crossed lovers from different cultures, sought to show a broader slice of American society with its portrayal of the tension between a Puerto Rican girl in love with an Anglo-American boy. *The Graduate* (1967) told the story of a young man disillusioned with the shallow material world of his parents and their friends. The film attracted attention from young baby boomers who had grown restless with a materialistic society.

During World War II, MUSIC centered on the easy sounds of big band orchestras and crooners such as Frank Sinatra. In later years, ROCK AND ROLL music—a blend of black rhythm-and-blues and country and western sounds—gained popularity. Stars such as Elvis Presley shot to the top of the music charts and inspired a generation of teenagers who wanted to become rock and roll stars. In the 1960s, groups like the BEATLES experimented with rock and roll music and earned a new audience of listeners who craved a break from the traditional sounds of the past. The Beatles came from working-class origins, but they sang with American accents and dressed neatly. The result of this mixture was a classless image with broad appeal. The popularity of the Beatles helped pave the way for bands like The Rolling Stones and The Doors.

Other styles of music had a profound impact on American society. The FOLK MUSIC REVIVAL brought political and social messages to the youth of America. In 1958, the Kingston Trio recorded the song "Tom Dooley," which popularized folk music and opened the way for less commercialized performers such as Joan Baez. Songs such as Pete Seeger's "Where Have All the Flowers Gone?" sent a powerful antiwar message to pacifists, antinuclear activists, and soldiers in Vietnam. BOB DYLAN, well-known for his protest songs, initiated a mix of folk and rock music for the first time at the Newport Jazz festival in 1965, opening the way for other rock bands to hit mainstream America.

The culmination of popular musical expression came in the form of a rock festival called Woodstock, held in Bethel, New York, in the summer of 1969. Many of the popular folk and rock groups of the day participated in the peaceful expression of antimaterialistic, antiwar sentiment that the festival represented. The most notable acts included The Who, Jefferson Airplane, and Jimi Hendrix with his unforgettable psychedelic rendition of "The Star Spangled Banner." The festival organizers were expecting a large crowd, but they were overwhelmed when 300,000 to 400,000 people showed up. As a result of the large crowds, roads were blocked and food and water supplies ran short. There was, however, no shortage of free love and drugs. Many spectators camped outside in sleeping bags while they watched, under rainy skies, their musical idols play songs with political messages.

In contrast to the peaceful celebration of popular music at Woodstock, turmoil erupted later in 1969 at Altamont, California, during the last concert of a Rolling Stones tour. The group hired a band of Hell's Angels, a tough motorcycle gang, to enforce crowd control at the concert, with payment in beer. The Angels beat one black man to death and injured others. Accidents took several lives and inadequate medical support hurt many drug-overdosed audience members. Altamont offered a violent contrast to the peaceful, free love feeling of Woodstock, and it showed the darker side of popular culture in the 1960s.

Further reading: David Halberstam, *The Fifties* (New York: Villard Books, 1993); William O'Neill, *Coming Apart* (Chicago: Quadrangle Books, 1971).

— Sarah Brenner

population trends

After World War II, the population of the United States grew rapidly as a result of the BABY BOOM and new drugs that increased life expectancy.

Between 1940 and 1950, the population of the United States increased by 19 million, double the number in the decade before. Then in the period between 1950 and 1960 it increased by almost 29 million, before increasing another 24 million between 1960 and 1970. The largest percentage increase came in the 1950s, when population rose by an extraordinary 19 percent. In the period from 1940 to 1970, as the aggregate population rose from approximately 132 million to 203 million, the overall percentage rise was 54 percent.

The birthrate played an important part in the population rise. Young people in the 1930s had delayed marriage because of the Great Depression. When World War II ended and servicemen returned, many of them rushed to the altar, and had children in record numbers, giving rise to the phenomenon that would be known as the baby boom. The birthrate of more than 25 births per 1,000 was far higher than the Great Depression rate of 19 births per 1,000. In 1957, the peak of the baby boom, 4.3 million babies were born. The rise in the number of children had a dramatic impact on the nation's booming ECONOMY.

Even though the birthrate was the main cause for the rise in population, the falling death rate was also a leading factor. The development of MIRACLE DRUGS meant that people were living longer, free from many diseases that plagued the lives of both young and old. The new drugs included antibiotics, penicillin, and streptomycin, which helped cure bacterial infections. A decade after the war, a polio vaccine was introduced, virtually eliminating the dreaded disease. These new drugs invented during World War II helped raise the average life expectancy. In the 1950s, the average lifespan for whites was 70 years, and for blacks it was 64 years, far higher than the 1920 average of 55 for whites and 45 for blacks.

IMMIGRATION also had an impact on the increase in population. After World War II, immigration totals passed the 100,000 mark for the first time since 1930. Many GIs coming home from EUROPE brought back brides. There was also an increase in Eastern Europeans immigrating to the United States to escape Soviet controlled homelands. Throughout the 1960s, record numbers of immigrants from LATIN AMERICA and Cuba entered the United States, fleeing the dictatorial power of communist leader Fidel Castro. Many immigrants from Mexico arrived illegally, crossing the Rio Grande in unguarded areas whereas others came by legal means. By the mid-1970s, an estimated 12 million illegal immigrants had entered the United States from Mexico. The IMMIGRATION ACT OF 1965 increased the number of immigrants allowed into the United States by eliminating national quotas. This measure opened the way for an increase in the number of Vietnamese and Asians who came to the United States in the aftermath of the VIETNAM WAR.

Further reading: Ira S. Steinberg, *The New Lost Generation: The Population Boom and Public Policy* (New York: St. Martin's Press, 1981). U.S. Bureau of the Census 1940–1970.

— Robert A. Deahl

Powell, Adam Clayton (1908–1972)

A capable but controversial politician and clergyman, Adam Clayton Powell was the first African American elected to Congress from New York.

Born in New Haven, Connecticut, on November 23, 1908, Powell was raised in Harlem, New York, in a middle-class family. While attending Colgate University, the light-skinned Powell suppressed his racial background and attempted unsuccessfully to pass as white. After completing his bachelor's degree at Colgate, he attended Columbia University, receiving a master's degree in religious studies in 1932.

Powell later embraced his racial heritage and began to aid his father in ministering at the Abyssinian Baptist Church, taking over in 1937 following his father's retirement. While in the pulpit, he engaged in political action. Protesting discrimination by promoting the "Don't Buy Where You Can't Work" campaign, he succeeded in breaking hiring barriers in local stores.

Powell's growing interest in politics led him to run for city council as an independent in 1941. Victorious, he became the first black man on the New York City Council. Four years later, Powell secured the support of Democrats and Republicans in winning a seat in Congress. Although not a prominent legislator, Powell demanded that racial epithets not be used on the House floor and that black journalists be admitted to congressional press galleries.

In 1956, Powell supported the Republican DWIGHT D. EISENHOWER, following ADLAI STEVENSON's refusal to meet with him about a civil rights measure that would have ended federal support to segregated schools. During the election of 1960, he returned to support his party and campaigned vigorously for JOHN F. KENNEDY, bringing with him the votes of many blacks. His enthusiasm led to his appointment as chairman of the House Committee on Education and Labor, another first in history for an African American. Powell used his influence to help push through Congress progressive legislation such as MEDICARE, MEDICAID, HEAD START, an increase in the minimum wage, more protection of civil rights, and the CIVIL RIGHTS ACT OF 1964.

At the same time, however, he became embroiled in scandals and accusations. Beginning in the 1950s, several of Powell's aides faced charges of income tax evasion, leading to his own indictment for tax evasion in 1958. The trial resulted in a hung jury and the Department of Justice chose not to penalize him. In another incident, Powell accused a woman of transporting payoffs to police from illegal gambling groups. She sued for libel and won a large settlement. Later, critics attacked Powell for placing his wife on his payroll and billing personal vacations as committee expenses. In the face of such charges, he became a less effective legislator, holding up passage of the ELEMENTARY AND SECONDARY EDUCATION ACT OF 1965 by using his committee position to delay its presentation to Congress for four months while fishing. He further angered both politicians and citizens with his poor attendance at congressional sessions.

In 1967, all of his moves culminated in action by the House, which disregarded a committee's recommendation of censure but excluded Powell from Congress. The House determined that Powell had "wrongfully and willfully appropriated" public funds and "improperly maintained his wife" by placing her on his payroll while she lived in Puerto Rico. Although a special election was held that year and Powell was reelected, the House refused to allow him to take his seat and it lay empty for two years. In January 1967, Powell paid a $25,000 fine, and he was permitted to return to his position but was stripped of seniority. The Supreme Court determined in June of that year that Powell's expulsion was unconstitutional.

Stricken with cancer, Powell lost his reelection bid in 1970 to Charles B. Rangel, and he chose to retire from politics. Withdrawing to the Bahamas for his final days, Powell died in 1972 while visiting Florida.

Further reading: Curtis E. Alexander, *Adam Clayton Powell and the Harlem Renaissance* (New York: Dial Press, 1987); James S. Haskins, *Adam Clayton Powell: Portrait of a Marching Black* (New York: Dial Press, 1974); Adam Clayton Powell, *Adam by Adam: The Autobiography of Adam Clayton Powell, Jr.* (New York: Dial Press, 1994).

— Katherine R. Yarosh

Poverty, War on   See War on Poverty

President's Commission on the Status of Women (1961)

Chaired by Eleanor Roosevelt, the President's Commission on the Status of Women (PCSW) brought visibility and legitimacy to concerns of WOMEN'S STATUS AND RIGHTS as well as raising the consciousness of women.

The PCSW began as a way for President JOHN F. KENNEDY to demonstrate his concern for women's problems and to dampen the persistent demands for an Equal Rights Amendment (ERA). Esther Peterson, a labor lobbyist whom Kennedy had named director of the Women's Bureau, used her clout with the president to commit him to establish a federal commission on the status of women. Peterson was interested in promoting policy initiatives for working women and had long opposed an ERA. At her behest, a small committee composed of women with sympathies to organized labor drafted a proposal for a commission on the status of women. Worried about the economic ramifications of women remaining an underutilized resource, Kennedy established the PCSW by executive order on December 14, 1961. The commission was composed of 11 men and 15 women, including cabinet officers, members of Congress, and leaders in LABOR, RELIGION, EDUCATION, and other professions. It did not reflect geographical diversity nor did it contain a representative from a Spanish-speaking group. The PCSW contained seven subcommittees with more than 100 people, mostly women, involved in its work. The subcommittees drew people from interest groups and think tanks largely representing urban-industrial coalitions.

The PCSW sought to design proposals that would combat sex discrimination in government and private employment and to recommend services that would enable women to contribute economically to society. It was directed to review progress and make recommendations in six areas: employment policies and practices; federal social insurance and tax laws; federal and state labor laws, differences in legal treatment of men and women; new and expanded services that might be required for women as wives, mothers, and workers; and the employment policies and practices of the U.S. government. To explore these areas in depth, the PCSW established committees on civil and political rights, education, federal employment, private employment, home and community, protective labor legislation, and social insurance and taxes.

On October 11, 1963, the PCSW issued its report, *American Women*, to Kennedy. The authors noted that many mothers, particularly African-American ones, had to work and that most women who worked were married. The report pointed out that women's earnings were less than men's and that women in federal service occupied the lower grades. Seeing women primarily as wives and mothers rather than wage earners, the PCSW declared that the adoption of its proposals would directly benefit men as well as women.

American Women avoided an analysis of the ideological roots of women's oppression, focusing instead on specific policy recommendations designed to create opportunities for working women. Although the PCSW ignored the contradiction between greater opportunities for women in the public sphere and their primary responsibilities for the home and family, it did recommend significant changes in government policies and employment and educational practices. In many instances, the commission disagreed with the proposals of a committee. One of the major clashes within the PCSW occurred over regulations dealing with the hours that women could work, with the commission refusing to endorse maximum-hours legislation.

Opponents of the Equal Rights Amendment far outnumbered supporters on the commission but they agreed on a compromise that left open the possibility for future consideration of an amendment. The commission supported an alternative route to equality for women, a proposal developed by Yale Law School professor PAULI MURRAY, who had a long history of civil rights activism. Murray concluded that the Supreme Court would interpret the Fourteenth Amendment as prohibiting unreasonable discrimination based on sex as well as race. The PCSW urged the filing of suits against discriminatory laws in an effort to obtain a Supreme Court ruling that would establish women's right to equal treatment

The PCSW achieved a number of successes. When the Civil Service Commission accepted its recommendation to end the practice of stipulating the sex of applicants, the placement of larger numbers of women became a possibility overnight. State affiliates of the President's Commission on the Status of Women also formed within a few years in 49 states, with Texas as the lone holdout. Composed primarily of women, these commissions extended the documentation of women's unequal status begun by the PCSW. In 1964, members of state commissions began to meet at annual conferences, thereby forming a national network of individuals with information about and heightened awareness of sex discrimination.

The PCSW publicized women's second-class status and tried to position the government behind securing gender equality. By increasing awareness of sex discrimination and establishing mechanisms for action, the PCSW contributed directly to the rise of the women's movement.

Further reading: William H. Chafe, *The Paradox of Change: American Women in the 20th Century* (New York: Oxford University Press, 1991); Margaret Mead and Frances Balgley Kaplan, eds., *American Women* (New York: Charles Scribner's Sons, 1965).

— Caryn Neumann

Presley, Elvis (1935–1977)

Combining elements of African-American rhythm and blues, gospel, and country MUSIC, Elvis Presley was one of the greatest pioneers of ROCK AND ROLL, earning him the nickname "The King."

Elvis Aaron Presley was born in Tupelo, Mississippi, on January 8, 1935. The son of Vernon and Gladys Presley, Elvis grew up in poverty. Vernon Presley was a common laborer, who held jobs ranging from sharecropping to driving trucks. While Vernon appeared shiftless, Gladys Presley was the cornerstone of the family. She wished for a better life for Elvis, instilling a strong work ethic in him, in the hopes that one day he would take a better-paying skilled job.

Elvis's first exposure to music came from the church. A member of the Pentecostal Church in Tupelo, Elvis enjoyed gospel music from an early age. The music had a profound effect on Elvis, who recalled, "When I was four or five, all I looked forward to was Sundays, when we would

Elvis Presley, 1957   *(Library of Congress)*

all go to church. This was the only singing training I ever had." At the age of 11, Elvis received a guitar for his birthday, and he began to learn a few chords. During this period, he listened to black gospel and rhythm and blues at gospel shows and on the radio.

While working as a truck driver in Memphis, Tennessee, in 1954, Presley visited Sam Phillips's Memphis Recording Service. Claiming that he wanted to make a record for his mother's birthday, Presley met Sam Phillips himself. Phillips enjoyed the combination of musical styles that Elvis brought forth in his music, and after hearing him sing a rendition of "That's Allright Mama," Phillips signed Presley to a contract with Sun Records. Presley's stay with Sun was a short one, but the two years with the company were considered some of his most creative. With tracks such as "Blue Moon" (1954), "Baby, Let's Play House" (1955), and "Mystery Train" (1955), Elvis expanded creatively by mixing different elements of music. In 1956, he signed with RCA Victor Records. Some of Presley's most memorable works appeared during his first year with RCA and include hits like "Blue Suede Shoes," "Hound Dog," and "Heartbreak Hotel."

During a 1956 performance of "Hound Dog" on *The Milton Berle Show*, Elvis challenged America's views on sexuality. Gyrating and thrusting his hips, Presley symbolized raw sexuality never before seen on national TELEVISION. An outcry erupted from around the nation, as many people saw Presley's escapades as a blatant result of the sexual undertones of rock and roll. This performance earned him the nickname "Elvis the Pelvis."

In March 1956, Elvis signed with Paramount studios for a three-picture deal. Presley's first screen appearance in *Love Me Tender* (1956), however, was anything but memorable. Although his first screen performance was ineffective, he continued to improve as an actor in MOVIES such as *Loving You* (1957), *Jailhouse Rock* (1957), and *King Creole* (1958). His success allowed him to purchase all the things he did not have as a child. In March 1957, Elvis bought Graceland, a 23-room Memphis mansion.

In December 1957, Presley was drafted into the U.S. Army, serving in an armored division in Bad Nauheim, West Germany. His military service appeared to highlight his patriotism and enhance his appeal.

Following Presley's return to the United States in 1960, he focused mainly upon films, starring in 28 pictures. In addition to his work on screen, Elvis remained active in the studio and on the road. From 1960 through 1976, he recorded such hits as "Are You Lonesome Tonight?" (1960), "Viva Las Vegas" (1963), "Can't Help Falling in Love" (1968), and "Promised Land" (1973).

Elvis married Priscilla Beaulieu on May 1, 1967. One year later, their daughter Lisa Marie Presley was born. The marriage was short-lived, and in 1973 it ended in divorce. Following the divorce, Elvis gained a good deal of weight and became dependent upon prescription drugs. On August 16, 1977, Presley died of heart failure at the age of 42.

Today, the legacy of Elvis Presley remains strong among his fans. Due to his courage in taking risks, rock and roll shifted from the sidelines to the mainstream of American music.

Further reading: Susan M. Doll, *Understanding Elvis: Southern Roots vs. Star Image* (New York: Garland Publishing, 1998); Dave Marsh, *Elvis* (New York: Rolling Stone Press, 1982).

— Clayton Douglas

Progressive Party

One of two groups to split from the DEMOCRATIC PARTY, the Progressive Party represented an ideological faction of liberal Democrats who opposed the hard-line tactics of President HARRY S. TRUMAN toward the SOVIET UNION in the early stages of the COLD WAR.

On July 23, 1948, a group of delegates who wanted to take a more flexible approach to the Soviet Union met in Philadelphia for the founding convention of the Progressive Party. Over the course of three days, the Progressive delegates established a party platform and nominated both a presidential and vice presidential candidate for the national election. The following day, Henry A. Wallace and progressive Democratic senator Glen Taylor from Idaho, accepted the nominations for president and vice president, respectively.

Wallace was an idealistic liberal who had served as secretary of agriculture, vice president, and secretary of commerce under President Franklin D. Roosevelt. Due to fundamental conflicts over foreign policy decisions, Truman removed Wallace from his position as secretary of commerce. As leader of the Progressive Party, Wallace believed Truman's "get tough" policy toward the Soviet Union would only lead to disaster and a possible third world war. Instead, Wallace advocated negotiating with the Soviet Union in order to forge common ground and avoid unnecessary aggression.

The organization's platform as drafted by the delegates focused primarily on criticizing American foreign policy under the Truman administration. The party denounced the anti-Soviet hysteria that was sweeping the United States as a ploy by those in power to mask big BUSINESS monopolies and overextended militarism. To prevent escalating tensions between the two superpowers, supporters of the party called for negotiations and discussions between the United States and the Soviet Union. The Progressives also opposed the MARSHALL PLAN, which was seen by the organization as a tool for American businesses to reap economic rewards at the expense of European countries trying to rebuild after the devastating aftermath of World War II. The organization instead believed that the European Recovery Program should be administered through the United Nations rather than the United States. As with the Marshall Plan, the party denounced the TRUMAN DOCTRINE for its effort to finance and arm what Progressives considered to be the corrupt, fascist governments of Greece and Turkey, and for attempts to support similar governments elsewhere. The organization's platform also advocated world disarmament and an end to universal military training. The platform attacked the development of United States military installations throughout various parts of the world. The party believed such expansion of American military bases could only be seen by other nations as a sign of imperialist intentions. The Progressives insisted on the repeal of the provisions of the NATIONAL SECURITY ACT, which was seen by the party as mobilizing the nation for war rather than working toward peace.

While FOREIGN POLICY played a key role in the party's platform, Progressives were also concerned with domestic issues. According to party members, the biggest challenge to American democracy was big business and the increasing control monopolies wielded over the U.S. ECONOMY. In order to combat this economic inequality, Progressives advocated public ownership of key areas of the economy, including the largest banks, railroad companies, the merchant marine, and the electric and gas industries. The organization also condemned all forms of SEGREGATION and discrimination and demanded equal rights for every American citizen regardless of race, religion, or gender. The party pushed for the creation of a minimum wage and minimum old-age pension as well as the repeal of the 1947 TAFT-HARTLEY ACT, which members felt circumscribed organized labor. The platform called for the planned development of all resources to avoid the economic pattern of boom and bust, the strengthening of rent control, better housing, and social security for all Americans.

Although the Progressive Party established a thorough and well-articulated platform, gaining a fair amount of support among minority groups, it was also highly vulnerable from its inception. Many Americans were reluctant to vote Truman out of office during a time of prosperity, especially after he took steps to initiate his own domestic program. Perhaps most important, the Progressive platform was far too liberal at a time when Americans felt there was indeed something to fear from COMMUNISM and the Soviet Union. The party's conciliatory stand toward the Soviet Union and its eventual endorsement by the Communist Party of the United States caused the demise of the organization. Although Wallace appeared on the 1948 presidential election ballot in 45 states, the party was only able to capture 1,157,057 votes. Shortly after the election, the remaining members of the party grew even more left-wing, opposing the KOREAN WAR, and alienating some of its more moderate members. In the 1952 presidential election, the party supported Vincent Hallinan and Charlotte Boss but netted only 140,023 votes. The Progressive Party dissolved soon after the election.

Further reading: Curtis D. MacDougall, *Gideon's Army* (New York: Masani & Munsell, 1965); Allen Yarnell, *Democrats and Progressives: The 1948 Election as a Test of Postwar Liberalism* (Berkeley: University of California Press, 1974).

— Donna J. Siebenthaler

public health

Americans experienced significant improvements and changes in public health in the years following World War II.

The practice of MEDICINE became more effective, which enhanced the quality and length of life. Much of this improvement resulted from more direct government support of health care. Although statistically the United States remained behind many other industrial countries in measures of public health, Americans were noticeably healthier by the late 1960s than ever before.

America's birthrate skyrocketed in the postwar years, hovering around 24.5 births per 1,000. From there, it began a steady decline until a massive single year slide of more than 7.6 percent in 1965, which signaled the end of the BABY BOOM. By 1968, the birthrate was around 17 births per 1,000. Infant mortality rates also declined significantly, falling from over 35 deaths per 1,000 immediately after World War II to around 20 deaths per 1,000 in the late 1960s.

Health after birth also improved, as witnessed in the increase in life expectancy by 3.5 years from 1946 to 1968. Despite this noticeable rise in life expectancy, the death rate per 1,000 dropped only slightly, remaining around 9.5 per 1,000 for most of the period, compared with a high of 10.1 per 1,000. More concrete evidence of how public health improved can be seen in reductions in deaths from certain diseases. Deaths from tuberculosis, influenza, and pneumonia fell dramatically, accelerating a trend that began earlier in the century. The already low death rates from traditional childhood diseases, which were the targets of aggressive government-sponsored immunization campaigns, fell to virtually imperceptible levels. The development of several MIRACLE DRUGS, antibiotics that fought a host of diseases, was responsible for many of these improvements.

Government involvement in health care became much more pronounced in the postwar era. Much of this activity fell under the purview of the NATIONAL INSTITUTES OF HEALTH (NIH). Congress authorized the NIH not only to help fund and oversee private sector and educational medical research, but to undertake such endeavors itself, laying the groundwork for permanent and direct government involvement in helping to solve health care problems. By 1968, there were over a dozen divisions within the NIH working on specific health issues, such as mental health, heart disease, and infectious diseases.

The surgeon general of the United States led the fight for better public health. One of the most famous federal government initiatives in public health in this era came from Surgeon General Luther Terry. He commissioned the 1964 report that laid the basis for the antismoking movement in America when it concluded that "cigarette smoking is a health hazard of sufficient importance in the United States to warrant appropriate remedial action." Requiring warning labels for cigarettes was just the beginning of a sustained governmental effort to reduce smoking.

The Centers for Disease Control (CDC) constituted another tool the government created to improve public health. The CDC took on increasing responsibilities in the 1950s and 1960s. By the late 1960s, it was in charge of keeping track of the spread of diseases and coordinating vaccination programs against them. It had several noteworthy successes, the most important being the virtual eradication of malaria, polio, and smallpox in the United States.

The development of two vaccines against polio and the ensuing nationwide vaccination program was perhaps the most famous of these medical victories.

There were attempts to give the federal government an even greater role in health care beyond that of coordinating research and carrying out vaccination. President HARRY S. TRUMAN pushed for a National Health Insurance Act, but he was defeated by the efforts of the powerful physicians' lobby, the American Medical Association, which labeled the plan "socialized medicine." Later, LYNDON B. JOHNSON was successful in pursuing a more limited program to provide government-sponsored health insurance. In his MEDICARE and MEDICAID programs, Johnson obtained government coverage for the most medically vulnerable citizens, the elderly and poor. These programs resulted in a major increase in the share of the nation's health care expenditures paid for by the federal government. Until the mid-1960s, the federal government spent around 25 percent of the funds expended on health care. By the late 1960s, the federal government's share approached 40 percent. Overall spending on health care accounted for an increasing share of the nation's gross national product during the period, rising from around 4 percent to 6.5 percent, with the federal government paying more of this increasing cost.

America's public health improved in significant ways between 1946 and 1968. Government became more active by supporting research and vaccination and helping the most medically disadvantaged people obtain health care. Diseases that had plagued Americans for generations were now being stopped in their tracks. Americans were living longer and more disease-free lives by 1968 than ever before.

Further reading: Judith Walzer Leavitt and Ronald L. Numbers, eds., *Sickness and Health in America: Readings in the History of Medicine and Public Health* (Madison: University of Wisconsin Press, 1997).

— Dave Price

public relations   See advertising

Puerto Ricans

Population growth and expansion of commercial AGRICULTURE at the end of the 19th century and the start of the 20th century led many inhabitants to leave the island of Puerto Rico. While many went to Cuba and the Dominican Republic and to other parts of LATIN AMERICA, especially large groups immigrated to the United States, and they continued to come in the post–World War II years.

The earliest migration of Puerto Ricans to the United States began shortly after an unsuccessful rebellion by Creole Puerto Ricans against the Spanish colonial government in 1868. Some of the leaders of the rebellion moved to the United States as political exiles.

Puerto Ricans arrived in the United States in large numbers shortly after the Spanish-American War in 1898, when Spain ceded the island to the United States. It remained a colony until 1917 when the Jones Act made Puerto Ricans citizens of the United States with the right to travel freely between the two countries. This encouraged even more immigration, with New York City being the focal point. Citizenship also made it much easier for Puerto Ricans to regularly travel back and forth between the two countries. Under the Jones Act, it was possible for the island to maintain its own government while the United States established a military base there and controlled all international affairs dealing with the island.

Economic hardship also drove migration after the Spanish-American War. Although many Puerto Ricans were glad to be rid of the Spanish government, under the direction of the United States the economy was increasingly based on the export of coffee. An import tax in the United States caused many Puerto Rican farmers to lose their farms and leave the island. Many of these migrants came to work as seasonal farm workers along the eastern seaboard. Others came to work in factories in urban centers. There, they settled and created their own neighborhoods called barrios.

At the beginning of the 1950s, Puerto Rico was faced with another agricultural crisis that spurred the largest migration of Puerto Ricans to the United States. Operation Bootstrap, a plan to industrialize the island that was sponsored by the U.S. government, was successful in its aims, but it carried the added effect of diminishing agricultural jobs and driving farmers away. Between 1950 and 1970, 600,000 people moved from the island to the United States. The Puerto Rican government actively promoted migration to the United States as an "escape valve" to avoid more poverty and overpopulation on the island. Cheaper air transportation made it even easier to migrate to the United States and return to Puerto Rico. Once in the United States, many Puerto Rican immigrants struggled to survive in the face of low wages, poor health, tenement living, and the harshly different climate of the northeastern United States. In such situations many women were forced to find work outside the home to supplement the family income.

Influenced by the changes brought by the Civil Rights movement and other movements of the 1960s, Puerto Ricans began to work through grass-roots groups to create better living conditions in their communities. The Puerto Rican Legal Defense and Education Fund was created in part to help create counseling and educational guidance for

Puerto Rican youth in the cities. The implementation of bilingual education in the public school system counted among their successes. People in many barrios encouraged the creation of social clubs, religious associations, and athletic teams as ways of creating positive values and creating a viable community. Also in the 1960s and 1970s, radical Puerto Rican political groups such as the Young Lords challenged many of the standard notions held about their community and advocated a radical socialist alternative. They were able to create free breakfast, day care, and health care programs for the poor as well.

In the 1980s and 1990s, many significant changes took place in the Puerto Rican community. Many of the factory jobs in urban areas moved to countries where the wages were lower. Service sector jobs in communications, ADVERTISING, financial services, EDUCATION, and government required high levels of education, which new migrants did not always possess. The media has also persisted in portraying Puerto Ricans in negative images, highlighting drug use, unemployment, and gang membership. Despite these difficulties, there has been an increase in the number of Puerto Ricans who are gaining college degrees and working in the white-collar sector.

Further reading: Juan Flores, *Divided Borders: Essays on Puerto Rican Identity* (Houston: Arte Público Press, 1993); History Task Force, Centro de Estudios Puertorriqueños, *Labor Migration under Capitalism: The Puerto Rican Experience* (New York: Monthly Review Press, 1979); Clara E. Rodríguez, *Puerto Ricans: Born in the U.S.A.* (Boston: Unwin Hyman, 1989).

— Kerry Webb

R

race and racial conflict

During the 1960s, the Civil Rights movement found itself embroiled in racial conflict that was spawned by the tensions created by poverty and SEGREGATION.

As the Civil Rights movement sought to achieve equal rights for African Americans, white resistance often led to trouble. When the Supreme Court, in *BROWN v. BOARD OF EDUCATION* (1954), ruled that school segregation was unconstitutional, the process of desegregation brought massive white resistance in the South. The SOUTHERN MANIFESTO, signed by members of Congress, vowed to fight to preserve segregation and the southern way of life.

Angry southerners were furious at what they felt to be the increasing assertiveness of African Americans. One horrifying episode occurred in 1955 when Emmett Till, a 14-year-old black child, was lynched in Money, Mississippi, when he said "Bye, baby" to Carolyn Bryant, a white woman working in her husband's store. Because he had ignored the racial etiquette of the South, Till was kidnapped at gunpoint by Bryant's husband and his brother-in-law a few days after the incident. Till's body was found in the Tallahatchie River with a bullet lodged in his head and evidence of torture. Despite overwhelming evidence against the two white men who lynched Till, they were acquitted of all charges by an all-white jury. They then sold their confession to *Look* magazine, and gloated over their escape from justice, while Emmett's mother, unable to allow America to turn away from this horrible crime, had her son's mangled body displayed in an open casket in Chicago. The lynching of Emmett Till shaped the consciousness of young African American activists.

When African American college students pioneered SIT-INS during the 1960s as a form of protest, which paved the way for the FREEDOM RIDES of 1961, the pace of social change was accelerated by such nonviolent demonstrations. Blacks sitting-in at Woolworth's in Greensboro, North Carolina, had burning cigarettes pressed into their skin. Freedom riders often found the buses they rode overturned or burned. In the 1963 Birmingham, Alabama, campaign, which demanded the integration of public facilities, guarantees of employment opportunities for black workers, desegregation of schools, and improvement of services in black neighborhoods, demonstrators faced serious violence. The reaction of Eugene "Bull" Connor, the public safety commissioner, to the sit-ins and marches occurring in Birmingham was to arrest all who had participated. Yet the BIRMINGHAM CONFRONTATION was losing momentum until the "children's crusade" rallied schoolchildren to march. This tactic infuriated Connor and his officers, who not only arrested the children but also beat them with nightsticks, and set vicious dogs upon them. Firefighters, acting on Connor's orders, aimed powerful hoses at them, ripping their shirts, cutting their flesh, and lifting them off the ground.

Many of the white business owners were concerned about the escalation of violence. When President JOHN F. KENNEDY sent Burke Marshall, the assistant attorney general for civil rights, to negotiate a settlement, white business owners agreed to integrate and hire African American employees. The following day, KU KLUX KLAN members bombed the A.G. Gatson hotel where the SOUTHERN CHRISTIAN LEADERSHIP CONFERENCE (SCLC) had its headquarters. African American protesters burned cars and buildings and attacked police.

In the summer of 1963, there was a major upsurge in protests across the South with nearly 800 marches, demonstrations, and sit-ins. Ten civil rights protesters were killed and 20,000 arrested, as the white South resisted change. At this point Medgar Evers, the executive secretary for the NATIONAL ASSOCIATION FOR THE ADVANCEMENT OF COLORED PEOPLE (NAACP) in Mississippi, was gunned down in the driveway of his home by a white extremist on June 12, 1963. Evers's death exhibited the anger and hatred that still existed among some white southerners and the lengths to which they would go to prevent change.

In the summer of 1964, the CONGRESS OF RACIAL EQUALITY (CORE) and the STUDENT NONVIOLENT

Nashville police officer wielding nightstick holds African-American youth at bay during a civil rights march in Nashville, Tennessee, 1964   *(Library of Congress)*

COORDINATING COMMITTEE (SNCC) organized the Mississippi Freedom Summer Project. The project, which recruited over 1,000 northern college students, teachers, artists, and clergy to work in Mississippi, was developed to help African Americans to register to vote in order to break the white monopoly over the ballot box in racist states. Some volunteers encountered harassment, firebombs, arrests, beatings, and even murder. Such was the case when three volunteers—two white New Yorkers, twenty-four-year old Michael Schwerner and twenty-one-year-old Andrew Goodman, and a black Mississippian, twenty-one-year-old James Chaney—disappeared. Arrested on trumped up speeding charges, the three volunteers were driven to a deserted road where three carloads of Klansmen waited. Schwerner and Goodman were shot to death, while Chaney was beaten with chains and then shot. This vicious event focused America's eyes on white terrorism, which was now plainly evident, while mobilizing and organizing African Americans throughout Mississippi.

Although the CIVIL RIGHTS ACT OF 1964 contained provisions for helping African American voters to register,

white resistance in the Deep South had rendered such efforts ineffective. Hoping to push passage of the VOTING RIGHTS ACT OF 1965, which did subsequently end the systematic exclusion of African Americans from southern politics, the SCLC announced plans for a mass march from Selma to Montgomery to begin on Sunday, March 7, 1965. Led by MARTIN LUTHER KING, JR., JOHN LEWIS, chairman of SNCC, and Hosea Williams, 600 protesters were brutalized by police officers while trying to cross the Edmund Pettus Bridge.

In August 1965, frustrations with high unemployment and poverty led to riots in the Watts section of Los Angeles, a primarily black neighborhood. For six days, rioters looted, firebombed, and sniped at police and National Guard troops. When the riots ended, 34 people were dead and hundreds were injured. In the summers of 1966 and 1967, urban riots occurred in the poorer neighborhoods of several northern cities, including Newark and Detroit.

After King was assassinated in April 1968, race riots broke out in over 100 cities. In the wake of the riots, President LYNDON B. JOHNSON appointed a National Commission on Civil Disorders, headed by Otto Kerner, the former governor of Illinois. The Kerner Commission blamed white racism for the outbreaks of violence. In its report, the commission warned, "Our nation is moving toward two societies, one black, one white—separate and unequal." Inspired by the blunt assertiveness of MALCOLM X, many African Americans admired his advocacy of self-sufficiency and black separatism. The BLACK PANTHERS preached self-defense against white violence in the form of BLACK POWER, a term coined by SNCC leader STOKELY CARMICHAEL.

Further reading: Harvard Sitkoff, *The Struggle for Black Equality, 1954–1992* (New York: Hill & Wang, 1993).
— John E. Bibish IV

Raza Unida   See La Raza Unida

recreation

After World War II, the rising standard of living enjoyed by most Americans opened up more opportunities to enjoy leisure time.

In the 1950s, Americans found themselves in the midst of a booming entertainment industry. TELEVISION, drive-in movie theaters, and movie houses popped up across the nation. Drive-ins, generally located on the outskirts of towns and cities, provided family entertainment and served as a haven for teenagers. The drive-ins were not concerned with the artistic excellence of the MOVIES; popcorn, candy bars, and hot dogs were very much a part of the evening's entertainment. By the 1960s, drive-in movie theaters made up one-third of the nation's theaters.

With the development of a national highway system across the nation, more people took to the open road, traveling farther and faster. The whole travel industry enjoyed a spectacular boom. In 1962, there were nearly three times as many cars on the road as there had been a quarter century earlier. Nearly two-thirds of those cars were for recreational use only. With more Americans traveling, a need for hotels, national parks, and campgrounds grew. Vacationers crowded the roads; sun worshipers drove to Florida, Arizona, and California while others traveled to ski slopes farther north.

With more Americans traveling to the national parks, a number of these visitors became concerned about the urgent need to save these sites. They sought to protect places for future travelers to experience, explore, and enjoy high mountains, deserts, pine barrens, ocean shores, swamplands, and wild and scenic rivers. Acts were passed in response to the growing concern about the environment engendered by increasing numbers of people wanting to spend time in natural areas for recreational proposes. With the population's growing interest in the wilderness, President LYNDON B. JOHNSON's administration pushed for the Land and Water Conservation Fund of 1964. This led to a continuous source of revenue for acquisition of state and federal outdoor recreation lands, and the act spawned additional legislation, including the WILD AND SCENIC RIVERS ACT OF 1968 and the NATIONAL TRAILS ACT OF 1968.

SPORTS became a popular pastime in the postwar period, as more Americans enjoyed golf, tennis, baseball, basketball, swimming, and football. These sports were not only played by the amateurs but also by college students and professionals. Television brought spectator sports to people's homes, and it made college football the country's most popular Saturday afternoon indoor activity. Larger crowds crammed into stadiums to see their favorite teams play. Professional baseball was also popular at this time, as more people went to the games, and an even larger audience watched at home. Many sports developed into spectator sports, and golf, tennis, and boxing became popular in the 1960s.

No matter what type of recreation they preferred, more Americans were participating in leisure activities during the post–World War II years. Watching television, or taking part in some form of more active entertainment, Americans worked to play. Incentives were given to those who worked harder and better, and, in return, they secured more vacation time. Recreation was no longer solely for the upper class but for all classes, and commercial entertainment became a major industry.

Further reading: Foster R. Dulles, *A History of Recreation: America Learns to Play* (New York: Appleton-Century-Crofts, 1965).
— Robert A. Deahl

religion

Religion became an increasingly visible part of American life in the 1950s and 1960s.

The 1950s were years of American religiosity marked by revivalism and widespread evangelism. BILLY GRAHAM, a southern Baptist minister, became one of the most respected figures in the evangelical movement after World War II. Best known for his citywide revival crusades, speaking about personal salvation and good citizenship, Graham produced influential TELEVISION and radio programs throughout the country. During the COLD WAR years, Graham openly characterized COMMUNISM as the avowed enemy of the United States. Cold war anticommunism energized evangelical religion, as parishioners and congregations were encouraged to do their part in fighting godless communism by embracing Christianity and accepting Christ.

Liberation theology emerged in the post–World War II world in certain left-liberal churches as a mixture of Catholic and Protestant thinking, sprinkled with Marxism.

A leading liberation theologian, Protestant Jurgen Moltmann, attempted to demonstrate that German philosopher Max Weber wrongly linked Calvinism to capitalism. He argued, when examining the common eschatological aspect in each, that Calvinism was more closely related to socialism. Liberation theologians argued that social problems were derived from social conditions, specifically the nature of power relationships in society. They felt the Bible taught a form of consciousness-raising that made people aware of their oppressed state and helped them recognize that revolution against their oppressors was a divine mandate and necessity. This convergence of Christianity and socialism was transplanted to LATIN AMERICA, where Liberation Theology took hold.

After World War II, most fundamentalists remained outside the political realm, although leaders such as Carl McIntire, Billy James Hargis, and Fred C. Schwartz actively opposed the formation of the United Nations and the World Council of Churches, seeing both as communist threats to the sovereignty of the United States. Other Fundamentalists, such as Carl F. H. Henry and Harold Ockenga, rejected this fundamentalist militancy and cultural isolationism. Taking a different approach, fundamentalists felt it best to engage the culture arduously, transforming it with the gospel. Fundamentalism maintained an aggressive posture toward dominant culture, and actively adopted many of American society's values and practices. Much more a state of mind and cultural configuration, fundamentalism did not espouse a set of theological propositions. fundamentalism was closely linked with Evangelicalism, and some fundamentalists may have preferred to describe themselves as evangelicals. The fundamentalist spirit dominated several institutions during this time, such as the Moody Bible Institute, the Southern Baptist Convention, and the Campus Crusade for Christ.

The church, specifically black churches and related religious organizations, played a significant role in the CIVIL RIGHTS MOVEMENT. MARTIN LUTHER KING, JR., a newly active Baptist minister in Montgomery, Alabama, brought attention to the brutality of southern SEGREGATION across the nation. Founder of the SOUTHERN CHRISTIAN LEADERSHIP CONFERENCE (SCLC), King and 60 other black ministers voted to create this southern organization to further the cause of nonviolent opposition to segregation. King and other civil rights leaders wanted to create what they called a "beloved community," in which blacks and whites could live together in cooperation and love. King headed the angry black population in a peaceful boycott of city buses in Montgomery, which led to the 1956 Supreme Court decision nullifying the Alabama law upholding segregated public transportation.

In the 1950s, Buddhism continued to adapt itself eagerly to American culture. Leaders of the BEAT GENERATION, JACK KEROUAC, and ALLEN GINSBERG began to champion Zen in bohemian circles in New York and San Francisco. Of all the Beats, the most serious student of Buddhism was poet Gary Snyder. The Beats contributed considerably to the Buddhist vogue that emerged in the 1950s and 1960s, with Zen centers opening in Los Angeles in 1956, San Francisco in 1959, and New York in 1966. Zen Buddhism constituted a branch of Mahayana Buddhism that contained Buddha's emphasis on meditation, which led to his enlightenment, or satori. Central to Zen practice was *zazen*, a method of sitting in Zen meditation. An individual practicing Zen was not required to be responsible for evaluating anything in the world or even in his or her own thoughts. One lost the capacity to think logically and critically in such a state. The COUNTERCULTURE of the next decade gave rise to alternative religions, some related to Buddhism.

In 1953, President DWIGHT D. EISENHOWER began the tradition of opening the inaugural ceremony with a prayer. This prayer was not considered to be in violation of the Constitution's prohibition against the establishment of religion because the oath of office had traditionally been taken by swearing on the Bible, and legislative sessions at both the state and federal levels were opened in prayer.

In 1955, all U.S. currency bore the inscription, "no nation can be strong except in the strength of God, or safe except in his defense." In July 1956, Eisenhower approved a joint resolution of Congress declaring "In God We Trust" the national motto of the United States. Meanwhile, the phrase "under God," was added to the Pledge of Allegiance.

The 1960s were also marked by charismatic activity. Charismatics traced their origins back to the biblical day of Pentecost, when spiritual gifts, such as speaking in tongues, were bestowed by the Holy Spirit on the early Christians. Charismatics placed emphasis on praising God, rather than the Eucharist or preaching, but they shared the fundamental beliefs of traditional Protestants. This movement formed part of the broader tradition of Pentecostalism, and it represented a shift from the storefront churches of working people and minorities into the sanctuaries of white, middle-class Roman Catholic and Protestant mainstream denominations. Beginning in California, this movement spread across the Midwest into the eastern United States and north into New England. In 1966, the Charismatic movement emerged among Roman Catholics, spreading through networks of Catholic college students in the Midwest. In the South, Southern Baptists and other members of conservative denominations openly opposed the Charismatic movement, feeling it was excessively emotional.

Catholicism received a boost in the election of 1960. JOHN F. KENNEDY, the first Roman Catholic to be elected president, faced opposition from some conservative Christian groups and fundamentalists who feared he would be dominated by his religion's commitments to Rome and the pope. Kennedy, however, placed his Catholic ideology in the private realm. Nonetheless, through television, Roman Catholics gained a greater presence in American society. Fulton J. Sheen's *Catholic Hour* attracted large audiences, bringing Catholicism into living rooms across America. From 1962 to 1965, a council of Roman Catholic clerics sought to reunite Christians throughout the world. Pope John XXIII called the Second Vatican Council (Vatican II), arguing that the language used to convey religious truths must be relevant to contemporary culture. Vatican II resulted in the production of 16 documents that proposed a modernization of the relationship between the Catholic Church and the world, other religions, and the laity. The council opened the doorway for new movements throughout the world, such as liberation theology, that preached the need for freedom.

Jews assimilated into mainstream American society in the postwar years, and by the 1960s they were more integrated than ever before. The anti-Semitism that had been prevalent before the war began to fade, and by the 1960s quotas specifying the number of Jews permitted in some universities and other institutions had begun to diminish. After the shocking experience of the Holocaust, American Jews were supportive of ISRAEL, after it was established as a new state in 1948. Jews took advantage of the G.I. Bill to move to the suburbs, buy their own homes, and then build their own synagogues. As they moved into the middle class, they left their left-wing working-class values behind. One major concern of Jewish leaders was the growth in intermarriage. Barely 3 percent of all Jews intermarried prior to World War II. That figure rose to 6 percent in the 1950s, 17 percent between 1961 and 1965, and 32 percent between 1966 and 1972.

In 1968, a growing feminist movement began to criticize the churches for suppressing women's rights. This wave of American feminism brought pressure on most denominations to ordain women, as well as greater demands for gender equality in church and society. Two books were published that criticized the patriarchal structure of religious denominations and a religious heritage of sexist teachings: *The Church and the Second Sex* by Mary Daly and *Subordination and Equivalence: The Nature and Role of Women in Augustine and Thomas Aquinas* by Kari Borresen. Both attempted to expose this antifeminist hierarchy. Devoted Roman Catholics, Daly and Borresen argued that traditional Christian theology wrongly taught that women were the lesser sex and necessarily submissive to men. They further spoke out against the disapproval of women as teachers and leaders within the Catholic Church.

A movement that drew on expressions of black nationalism was led by ELIJAH MUHAMMAD and built upon the Nation of Islam, drawing in such prominent leaders as MALCOLM X. Also known as the "Black Muslim" tradition, this movement became one of the most controversial of all black religious movements. Appealing to alienated and unemployed urban blacks, this movement pushed for the development among blacks of pride in themselves. Begun in the 1930s by W. D. Fard, the Nation of Islam repudiated the teachings of Christianity and encouraged instead an exotic mythology and a rigorous set of behavioral practices. For Muslims, economic activity was collective rather than individualistic, and the movement substituted revealed for experiential knowledge. An important factor in this movement was its extensive list of dietary prohibitions as well as a parallel list of "clean foods" that provided the staples for a well-balanced, middle-class diet. The Muslims represented a rationalized and militant strategy for achieving their ends, and they advocated violent destruction of their oppressors to achieve resocialization and organization.

Religion became a controversial issue in the American education system, focusing specifically on the issue of separation of church and state. In a 1962 court case, *ENGEL v. VITALE*, the Supreme Court ruled that a 22-word nondenominational prayer written for students in public schools violated the establishment clause of the First Amendment. In 1963, reading the Lord's Prayer and reciting Bible verses in public schools was prohibited in *Abington Township v. Schempp*. In 1968, the clash between religious beliefs and scientific theories came to a head when the Court overturned in *Epperson v. Arkansas* an Arkansas statute that forbade the teaching of evolutionary theory.

Further reading: Peter W. Williams, *Popular Religion in America* (Chicago: University of Illinois Press, 1989).
— Susan F. Yates

Republican Party

The varied successes of the Republican Party since World War II reflect its ability to simultaneously retain its moderate eastern and more conservative midwestern and western membership while attracting new populations of voters, especially southern whites.

A party long in the minority because of its association with the stock market crash of the Great Depression, the Republicans held a congressional majority in both houses for only four years between 1945 and 1968. War hero DWIGHT D. EISENHOWER was elected to the presidency by a broad consensus in 1952 and 1956, perhaps representing the waning bipartisan spirit of an earlier era. Later party successes, including the election of President Richard M. Nixon in 1968, depended on a new electoral coalition of white southerners, blue-collar workers, and fiscal conservatives. This shift reflected the rising ascendancy of the party's conservative wing.

In 1946, the Republicans captured a majority in the House and Senate. In the elections of 1948, however, they failed to capitalize on white southern resentment of integrationist policies pursued by the administration of HARRY S. TRUMAN. Rather than casting their votes for the favored Republican candidate THOMAS E. DEWEY, a majority of voters in four southern states chose J. Strom Thurmond of the STATES' RIGHTS PARTY. Americans reelected Truman and the Republicans lost control of Congress.

Popular disquiet about international events, including the fall of China to COMMUNISM, the Soviet explosion of an ATOMIC BOMB, and the American military involvement in Korea, was beneficial to Republican candidates in the late 1940s and early 1950s. Shrewdly, the party drafted General Dwight D. Eisenhower as its presidential candidate in 1952. Eisenhower was largely indifferent to party politics; few Americans knew his party affiliation until January of the election year. Nevertheless, his appeal was broad and nonpartisan: two in four Democrats polled in the summer of 1952 hoped their party would nominate Eisenhower if Republicans failed to do so. With such widespread backing, Eisenhower easily defeated the intellectual, and divorced, Democratic candidate, ADLAI STEVENSON of Illinois. Eisenhower, or "Ike," as he was popularly known, was overwhelmingly favored by voters in every region of the country including the Deep South, where he made modest inroads on once solidly Democratic territory.

The revitalized party also took both houses of Congress in 1952, although it would hold them for only two years. Led by Ohio senator ROBERT A. TAFT, the Republicans expressed skepticism about the U.S. role in international affairs, especially the United Nations. Many Republicans also voiced criticism of the "Socialist" NEW DEAL programs, accusing Democrats in their 1952 platform of "seizing powers never granted." During the Eisenhower presidency, however, many New Deal programs were protected or even enlarged. The federal government expanded social security and unemployment benefits, and, in 1953, created the Department of Health, Education, and Welfare.

In 1960, Senator JOHN F. KENNEDY of Massachusetts narrowly defeated Vice President Richard Nixon for the presidency. Nixon, a vehement anticommunist as a U.S. congressman and senator, was accused by some of losing because of his acquiescence to the party's more liberal, eastern wing. Yet his defeat may have hinged on public sentiment that the United States was losing the ARMS RACE, as well as on Nixon's inability to master the new political medium of TELEVISION. The two wings of the Republican Party subsequently fought bitterly for control of the party. In 1964, the party turned to Senator BARRY GOLDWATER of Arizona. The conservative Goldwater announced that "extremism in the defense of liberty is no vice," a sentiment his Democratic opponents were able to turn against him. Goldwater was victorious only in the Deep South and in his home state of Arizona. As resounding as this defeat was, it signaled a dramatic regional realignment of American voters, a trend Nixon exploited four years later.

In the tumultuous year of 1968, Nixon won the White House by portraying himself as a critic of the VIETNAM WAR, and a defender of such "traditional" American ideals as patriotism and law and order. Nixon appealed to blue-collar workers and southern whites, two groups increasingly drawn to the Republican Party, and to opponents of integrationist policies such as school busing. During the primaries, Nixon headed off attacks from the right by rival Ronald Reagan, then the governor of California. At the same time, he claimed to have a "secret plan" to end the costly and now unpopular Vietnam War, drawing support away from moderate Republicans such as Nelson Rockefeller of New York. In November, Nixon narrowly defeated Vice President HUBERT H. HUMPHREY, whose campaign was hampered by segregationist GEORGE C. WALLACE, former governor of Alabama, who ran as a third party candidate, capturing five southern states. In victory, Nixon had apparently tapped into the "silent majority" he often mentioned during the campaign. These Americans, a mix of blue-collar workers, middle-class suburbanites, and white southerners, represented the new coalition of American voters, one which would propel the GOP into the White House in four out of the five elections held after 1968.

Further reading: John Gerring, *Party Ideologies in America, 1828–1996* (Cambridge, U.K.: Cambridge University Press, 1998); Robert Allen Rutland, *The Republicans: From Lincoln to Bush* (Columbia: University of Missouri Press, 1996).

— Patrick J. Walsh

Reuther, Walter (1907–1970)

Walter Reuther was an active union leader and president of the United Auto Workers (UAW) for 24 years who fought throughout his entire career for workers' rights and stability in the union.

Reuther was born in Wheeling, West Virginia, on September 1, 1907. His father, Valentine Reuther, was a German immigrant who had come to the United States during the late 19th century. Valentine was an active union member in Wheeling, where he helped to establish the International Union of Brewery Workers, and he was also a member of the American socialist movement. Reuther only attended school through the eighth grade, before going to work in a Wheeling steel mill by the age of 16. At the age of 19, he grew discontented with his life in

West Virginia and left for Detroit to enter the budding AUTOMOBILE INDUSTRY. There he worked for the FORD MOTOR COMPANY, and in his spare time finished high school. He then went on to complete three years at Wayne State University.

While working at Ford, Reuther began to take part in trade union activity, and, as a result, he was laid off in 1932, in the midst of the Great Depression. He then left the country for three years with his brother Victor and traveled to EUROPE, eventually ending up in the SOVIET UNION. The brothers worked for nearly two years in an automobile factory in Gorky. During his time in the Soviet Union, Reuther saw the lack of rights and freedom that the people had under the communist government, and he vowed to fight socialist influence in unions when he returned to the United States.

On his return to Detroit in 1935, Reuther joined Local 174 of the UAW, and he soon became president. He put Local 174 in the spotlight by organizing sit-down strikes against GENERAL MOTORS (GM) in 1937, in which workers sat down at their posts and refused to leave the factory until settlement of the strike. GM finally recognized the UAW as the main bargaining body for the strike, and, in 1939, the UAW became a part of the CONGRESS OF INDUSTRIAL ORGANIZATIONS (CIO), a new organization challenging the older craft-oriented AMERICAN FEDERATION OF LABOR (AFL).

Reuther continued to move up the ladder in the UAW. He was elected vice president in 1942 and president in 1946. By 1952, he was also the president of the CIO, and he played a pivotal role in the merger of the CIO with the AFL. As president of the CIO, Reuther was second only to George Meany, the president of the amalgamated AFL-CIO.

Under Reuther, the UAW continued to grow to over 1 million workers. Throughout his career, Reuther fought for the rights of the workingman in the automobile industry. He wanted to make sure that the members of the UAW benefited from the large-scale consumerism going on in the postwar United States. The car companies were selling automobiles at a rapid rate, making massive profits. Reuther insisted that unskilled autoworkers receive increased pay from the increased profits. He no longer wanted just small wage gains, but, rather, guaranteed annual wages, profit sharing, pension plans, and more holidays for the autoworkers. Reuther was successful in his efforts.

Meanwhile, Reuther's relationship with George Meany deteriorated. Reuther criticized AFL-CIO president George Meany for running the AFL-CIO dictatorially, and he opposed Meany's conservatism and inaction. Reuther felt that Meany did nothing to benefit the working class that he represented. His opposition to Meany eventually ended when Reuther led the UAW out of the AFL-CIO in 1968. The following year, Reuther joined the UAW in an alliance with the TEAMSTERS UNION, expelled from the AFL-CIO earlier because of corruption.

In 1970, Reuther and his wife May were flying in a chartered plane over Michigan when it crashed and killed them both. In his lifetime, he made a lasting impression on labor unions and the UAW, gaining for his constituents many of the rights and benefits they still enjoy.

Further reading: Nelson Lichtenstein, *The Most Dangerous Man in Detroit* (New York: Basic Books, 1995).

— Matthew Escovar

Reynolds v. Simms (1966)

Reynolds v. Simms helped to establish the principle of "one man, one vote" by holding that legislative districts be apportioned on the basis of population.

In the 1960s, the U.S. Supreme Court heard many cases to determine the composition and size of state legislative districts. Prior to the 1960s, the Supreme Court had ruled that the reapportionment of various voting districts did not constitute an issue within its purview but one that, because it involved delineation of districts, should be determined by state legislatures. In 1962, however, the Court reversed its position and concluded that federal courts within individual states could rule on the constitutionality of the size and composition of legislative districts.

In 1961, M. O. Simms, a Jackson County, Alabama, resident, filed suit against a probate judge in federal district court alleging that, as a result of urban growth and outdated census information, individuals within the Jackson County district were being deprived of equal representation in the state legislature. The U.S. Constitution provides for a census every 10 years with both federal and state representation based upon this count. Simms and others within Jackson County charged that representation within their county was based on an outdated census count from 1900. The complainants further maintained that at the time of the 1900 census many of the residents of the county lived in rural areas. Since 1900, Jackson County, like many regions across the United States, had become largely urban. Outdated census figures, therefore, ensured greater representation in the House for decreasing numbers of rural residents while not providing adequate representation for increasing numbers of urban residents.

Responding to pressure provided from related cases heard in the Supreme Court, the Alabama legislature advanced two redistricting plans, both to be put into place prior to the 1966 elections, in an effort to insure equality in representation. The legislature's plans were not successful. In 1962, a district court in Alabama declared that the plans still violated the Fourteenth Amendment's equal protection clause. This clause states, "No State shall make or enforce any law which abridges the privileges and immunities of citizens of the United States; nor shall any State deprive any person within its jurisdiction of the equal protection of the laws." The equal protection clause was violated, stated an Alabama district court, when the legislature stipulated that an election could only be conducted by the standards it had set forth. To hold elections in such a manner would impinge upon the voting privileges of individuals, jurists claimed. Additionally, due to a failure by the state legislature to address the equal distribution of voters within a district, some residents of that area would fail to receive adequate or equal protection through a deprivation of voting equality and representation. In an effort to resolve the issue, the case was appealed to the U.S. Supreme Court.

Three years after Simms initiated his lawsuit against the state of Alabama, the U.S. Supreme Court handed down its decision. The Court held that because there was no reapportionment remedy provided by the state of Alabama, the federal court was obligated to rule on the redistricting of political boundaries to insure the application of the Fourteenth Amendment's equal protection clause. Guaranteeing that the right to vote by individuals within various districts carried the same weight as others within the state, the Supreme Court assisted in enforcing this interest. Speaking on behalf of the Supreme Court, Chief Justice EARL WARREN stated, "Legislators represent people, not trees, not acres. Legislators are elected by voters, not farms, cities or economic interests. As long as ours is a representative government and our legislators are those instruments of government, elected directly by and directly representative of the people, the right to elect legislators in a free and unimpaired fashion is the bedrock of our political system." With this decision, the Supreme Court put into place the principle of "one man, one vote." Further, the Supreme Court required states across the nation to make "an honest and good faith effort to construct districts, in both houses of its legislature, as nearly of equal population as is practicable."

The ramifications of *Reynolds v. Simms* were sweeping. In addition to the "one man, one vote" formula made applicable to state legislatures, the principle also applied to all elected bodies performing government functions. This had a profound effect on schools, highway systems, and public service programs as it provided for equal and representative voting within these systems.

Further reading: John W. Johnson, ed., *Historic U.S. Court Cases, 1690–1990: An Encyclopedia* (New York: Garland Publishing, 1992); Donald Rogers, *Voting and the Spirit of American Democracy: Essays on the History of Voting and Voting Rights in America* (Chicago: University of Chicago Press, 1992).

— Erin Craig

Rickey, Branch (1881–1965)

Branch Rickey is best known for signing JACKIE ROBINSON to play baseball for the Brooklyn Dodgers.

Branch Rickey was born on December 20, 1881, in Stockdale, Ohio. His strict Methodist upbringing helped to shape his character. From an early age he developed an interest in baseball, particularly the intellectual side of the game. He attended Ohio Wesleyan College where he played baseball and managed other sports.

Following his graduation from the University of Michigan Law School, Rickey turned his attention to baseball. He became manager of the St. Louis Cardinals in 1919. By 1925, he had moved to the front office, where he served as general manager for 17 years. At this time there was no official structure for acquiring players; the highest bidder could sign any player. Rickey grew tired of investing time and money in scouting players, only to have them sign with a different team that offered a more lucrative deal. Rickey convinced the Cardinals to purchase minor league teams to develop their own players, creating the minor league farm system that is still used today to cultivate young players.

In 1942, after a switch in Cardinal management, Rickey moved to Brooklyn to become both president and general manger of the Brooklyn Dodgers. After joining the Dodgers, Rickey became interested in moving African American players, who had been confined to the Negro leagues, into the major leagues. In October 1945, he signed two African American players to the Dodger organization. Infielder Jackie Robinson joined the team and became the first black baseball player in major league baseball. In 1947, his first season, Robinson won rookie-of-the-year honors. Although Rickey faced opposition from other owners who said that America was not ready, Rickey continued to sign other African American players, including Roy Campanella and Don Newcombe.

Some critics argued that Rickey was motivated more by the desire for financial gain than by moral concern against SEGREGATION. While the Dodgers did reap considerable rewards in gate receipts, Rickey's action, in ending discrimination in a major American institution, also played a key role in helping to end segregation. In 1950, Rickey moved from Brooklyn to become the vice president and general manager of the Pittsburgh Pirates. He was inducted into the Baseball Hall of Fame in 1967, two years after his death.

Further reading: John C. Chalberg, *Rickey and Robinson: The Preacher, the Player, and America's Game* (Wheeling, Ill.: Harlan Davidson, 2000); Murray Polner, *Branch Rickey: A Biography* (New York: Atheneum. 1982).

— Aaron M. Sharpe

Robeson, Paul (1898–1976)

Paul Robeson was a world-renowned African American singer and dramatic actor, whose commanding voice and magnificent stage presence pushed the roles of black actors beyond the realm of demeaning racial stereotypes. He was an ardent critic of racial inequality and a controversial champion of labor organization and socialist thought, which subjected him to intense federal investigation during the early COLD WAR years and earned him a place on Hollywood's blacklist.

Paul Robeson was born on April 9, 1898, in Princeton, New Jersey, the son of William Drew Robeson, a minister and former runaway slave, and Maria Louisa Bustill, a member of one of Philadelphia's most prominent African-American families. His father was a strong proponent of EDUCATION, and he set high expectations for his five children, sending them to the neighboring Somerville school district because the segregated schools of Princeton did not offer secondary education for blacks.

Robeson was an exceptional student and won a scholarship to Rutgers University. He excelled academically and athletically, earning membership in Phi Beta Kappa, an honorary society that recognizes academic superiority, and he lettered in baseball, basketball, and track. In addition, Robeson was twice named an All-American in football. After graduating in 1919, he entered law school at Columbia University, taking up residence in the Harlem neighborhood of New York at the onset of the Harlem Renaissance, a black arts and cultural movement. During his years at Columbia, Robeson supported himself by playing professional football in a fledgling association that later became the National Football League.

Robeson found his true calling not as an athlete or lawyer but as a performance artist. After several appearances in amateur productions, Robeson's first major professional opportunity came when he was invited to join the Provincetown Players, a Greenwich Village theater company that included, most notably, the playwright Eugene O'Neill. Robeson went on to star in a 1930 London production of *Othello* and the 1932 Broadway production of *Showboat,* which featured his famous rendition of "Ol' Man River."

At the same time that his stage-acting career was thriving, Robeson found growing success with his musical endeavors. In 1925, he became the first black soloist to perform an entire set of spirituals in a recital at the Greenwich Village Theater, helping to revive the traditional African American art form.

Robeson's career in film peaked between the years 1933 and 1942, during which he reprised earlier stage roles in the Hollywood versions of *The Emperor Jones* (1933) and *Showboat* (1936). While his roles in *Song of Freedom* (1936) and *The Proud Valley* (1940) proved exceptions to the rule, Robeson became increasingly dissatisfied with the racially stereotyped characters he was asked to play.

His dissatisfaction with Hollywood mirrored his developing political perspective. While living in London during the 1930s, Robeson studied African languages and took part in the activities of the West African Students Union. He admired the community spirit of African culture, and he became closely acquainted with future nationalist African leaders such as Jomo Kenyatta of Kenya and Nnamdi Azikiwe of Nigeria. But even as he called for black Americans to rediscover their African roots and reject assimilation into white culture, Robeson was opposed to separatism and dreamed of an integrated society.

Robeson's first encounters with socialism came in the 1930s through political discussions with radical activists and scholars, and, in 1934, he made the first of several visits to the SOVIET UNION. He came away impressed with the level of racial equality the communist state presented. Back in England, he became active in labor and peace rallies, and he continued his political efforts when he returned to the United States in 1939, speaking out in support of labor organization and joining black radical W. E. B. Du Bois in calling for antilynching legislation in Washington.

As America became entrenched in the cold war, however, Robeson's socialist sympathies and vocal admiration of Soviet society left him isolated even from other civil rights activists. Though he was not a member of the Communist Party, he held close ties to members of the party's leadership, and, by 1941, the Federal Bureau of Investigation (FBI) had placed him under surveillance. He outraged many Americans in 1949 when the Associated Press quoted him as saying, "It is unthinkable that American Negroes would go to war on behalf of those who have oppressed us for generations against a country [the Soviet Union], which in one generation has raised our people to the full dignity of mankind."

His comments were denounced even by close friends, including Walter White, executive director of the NATIONAL ASSOCIATION FOR THE ADVANCEMENT OF COLORED PEOPLE (NAACP). The HOUSE UN-AMERICAN ACTIVITIES COMMITTEE (HUAC) called hearings to investigate Robeson and assess the patriotic loyalties of other black radicals. Robeson gave a scathing critique of American racial injustice during his testimony before HUAC, and he refused to answer questions regarding his party membership or provide the names of other American Communists. In 1950, the State Department rescinded Robeson's passport and he was effectively silenced by a collective effort of the government, entertainment industry, civil rights leaders, and white liberals. He was blacklisted by both Broadway and Hollywood.

Robeson's battle to defend his political convictions took a personal toll. By 1955, he began to show symptoms of bipolar disorder, and he experienced crippling depression. A 1958 Supreme Court decision allowed Robeson the freedom to travel, and he returned to performing, but three years later he suffered a nervous breakdown and attempted suicide, putting an end to his public appearances.

Despite Robeson's outspoken commitment to racial equality long before it was fashionable, leaders of the CIVIL RIGHTS MOVEMENT largely ignored Robeson and his contributions. He died in 1976 at the age of 78.

Further reading: Martin B. Duberman, *Paul Robeson* (New York: Knopf, 1988); Jeffrey C. Stewart, *Paul Robeson: Artist and Citizen* (New Brunswick, N.J.: Rutgers University Press, 1998).

— Guy R. Temple

Robinson, Jackie (1919–1972)

As major league baseball's first African American player, Jackie Robinson broke the color barrier and became an outspoken supporter of the Civil Rights movement.

Jackie Robinson was born on January 31, 1919, in Cairo, Georgia. His family later moved to Pasadena, California,

Jackie Robinson, 1954   *(Library of Congress)*

where he distinguished himself as an athlete at an early age. In 1937, he enrolled at Pasadena Junior College where, as a sophomore, he led the football team to an undefeated season. He also broke his brother's long jump record and led his team to the league baseball championship in the same day. In 1939, as a student at the University of California at Los Angeles, he became a four-sport letterman. Financial needs forced him to leave after his junior year. He played semi-professional football before enlisting in the army in 1942. After challenging unwritten racial barriers, he was accepted to officer candidate school. While there he was court-martialed for insubordination when he refused to move to the back of an army bus, but he was exonerated because the order was racially motivated. He received a medical discharge in 1945.

After his discharge from the army, Robinson played baseball for one year with the Kansas City Monarchs of the Negro American League. In September 1945, he met BRANC RICKEY of the Brooklyn Dodgers after several scouts had selected Robinson as the best candidate to become the first African American to play major league baseball in the modern era. He was selected as much for his education, temperament, and integrity as his baseball skills. Rickey signed Robinson to play on a Dodger farm team, the Montreal Royals of the International League. Rickey subjected Robinson to a string of racial slurs to test his resolve under several potential scenarios, until he was satisfied that Robinson understood that he had to maintain composure at all times. After playing in Montreal, Robinson was promoted to the Brooklyn Dodgers on April 10, 1947, and he made his debut on April 15, 1947.

Robinson's signing elicited several responses throughout baseball. Many critics argued that African Americans lacked the skill to play in the major leagues. Others worried about the social ramifications. Four players attempted unsuccessfully to block his addition to the team. Some southern players were worried about the reaction they would receive when they returned home. One important exception was Pee Wee Reese, the Dodger's captain from Kentucky, who befriended Robinson. Two incidents early in his career solidified Robinson's place on the team. While playing the Philadelphia Phillies, he was subjected to constant baiting from the Phillie team. After witnessing the racist attack, his teammates rallied around Robinson. Fans in Cincinnati likewise showered Robinson with verbal abuse. Reese walked over and put his arm around Robinson as a sign of support. The initial reservations expressed by teammates and fans were replaced by respect for his baseball abilities and his character. By playing good baseball and showing character strength in spite of verbal abuse from opposing fans and ballplayers, Robinson helped to open the major leagues to all races.

In 10 years as a Brooklyn Dodger, Robinson hit .311 while playing second base. He dominated on the base paths, where his speed confounded the opposition. He was selected to six all-star teams, and, in 1955, he helped the Brooklyn Dodgers win their only World Series title. He refused a trade in 1956 and retired from major league baseball, but he did not retire from the spotlight.

When Robinson signed in 1947, he had agreed to suppress his strong opinions regarding civil rights abuses, but, by 1949, he became outspoken on the issue. Robinson believed that he had a responsibility to use his popularity to expand opportunities for his people. He supported Richard M. Nixon for the presidency in 1960, believing that African Americans should have representation in both parties. He became an active member of the NATIONAL ASSOCIATION FOR THE ADVANCEMENT OF COLORED PEOPLE (NAACP) and was one of its best speakers. After some initial differences, he came to support MARTIN LUTHER KING, JR., and he also exchanged views with MALCOLM X, with whom he found common ground. Robinson's popularity was sometimes adversely affected by his outspokenness, but he continued to fight for equality.

Slowed by diabetes, and nearly blinded by the disease, Robinson made one last public appearance at the 1972 World Series. He used this forum to demand equality in managerial hiring. On October 24, 1972, Jackie Robinson died.

Further reading: Maury Allen, *Jackie Robinson: A Life Remembered* (New York: F. Watts, 1987); Arnold Ramperad, *Jackie Robinson: A Biography.* New York: Knopf, 1997; Jules Tygiel, *Baseball's Great Experiment: Jackie Robinson and His Legacy,* expanded edition (New York: Oxford University Press, 1997).

— Aaron M. Sharpe

rock and roll

The 1950s gave birth to a new era of MUSIC that eroded racial and social barriers in the United States. This music was known as rock and roll.

African American music profoundly affected the evolution of rock and roll. The slave hymns that were sung by fieldhands before the Civil War became the base for the blues, which emerged during the early part of the 20th century. This music was popular among black communities in the South, along with jazz and a form of music known as rhythm and blues. During the 1930s and 1940s, the South was strictly segregated, and no self-respecting white southerner listened to "black music." At this time, blacks began to migrate to the North in search of new opportunities opening up in the manufacturing industry. These African Americans not only brought with them their personal belongings but also their music.

Teenagers of the early 1950s searching for something to define their generation turned to rock and roll. They did not share the hardships of their parents, who had struggled through the Great Depression and World War II. They looked for an exciting outlet, and they turned to the music of rock and roll performers. In 1954, Bill Haley and the Comets released the first big rock and roll hit, "Rock Around the Clock." This song, with its hard driving beat, drew on the rhythms of black music and catapulted rock and roll into the mainstream of white America. Suddenly, every teen in America wanted to hear more of this music.

Radio stations during this time catered to either black music listeners or white music interests. White teens only listened to those stations that played white singers covering the rock and roll songs of their black contemporaries. Singers like Pat Boone sang black rock hits like Little Richard's "Tuttie Fruttie." Black artists, outraged at the attempts of white artists to sing their songs, claimed that the music sung by whites failed to deliver the mood and message intended. Still, the recordings worked to the advantage of African American artists because they gave the music exposure to a previously untouched white market.

One man, Alan Freed, a disc jockey from Cleveland, crossed the race barrier, and played both white and black rock music. It was Freed who first named this new music, coining the term "rock and roll," which referred to descriptions of sex in black music. His show received much attention, and, by 1954, he traveled to New York City and expanded his show to include live acts.

In 1954, ELVIS PRESLEY changed rock and roll history. Elvis, a white artist from the Deep South, captured the essence of rock. Influenced by the black bluesmen of the South, his style developed around their music. Elvis popularized rock and roll in white suburbia with hits such as "Heartbreak Hotel" and "Hound Dog." His voice, typical of black singers, combined with his gyrating moves, made it possible for black music to cross white lines. He also made it possible for other white artists, such as Buddy Holly and the Big Bopper, to break onto the rock scene.

Not every home in America welcomed rock and roll. Many parents of those teens who listened to rock music did not approve of the content of the songs. Many of the songs carried sexual overtones and suggested to teens that drinking and smoking were socially acceptable. This led to a number of religious and social groups openly opposing rock and roll. They attempted to stop radio stations from playing rock music by picketing in front of stations or contacting government representatives.

By the 1960s, rock and roll was entrenched in American culture. Its message changed from the importance of having a good time to serving as an outlet for social concerns. Artists like James Brown hit the music scene in the early 1960s, and he attacked racial and social issues in America through his music. British musicians, such as the BEATLES and the Rolling Stones, came to the United States at this time; their recordings have influenced rock music ever since.

Music also became the voice of the COUNTERCULTURE. U.S. involvement in the VIETNAM WAR prompted artists like BOB DYLAN use rock music to speak out against the U.S. presence in the war. Other artists, such as Jimi Hendrix and the Grateful Dead, experimented with rock and drugs, giving birth to a new form of music, psychedelic rock, that the youth of the late 1960s embraced. Rock and roll changed not only the sound of music but its content as well.

Further reading: Charles Brown, *The Art of Rock 'n' Roll* (Englewood Cliffs, N.J.: Prentice Hall, 1987).

— Matthew Escovar

Roosevelt, Eleanor   See Volume VIII

Roosevelt, Franklin D.   See Volume VIII

Rosenberg, Julius (1915–1953) and Ethel (1918–1953)

The Rosenbergs were the first two American civilians to be executed for espionage and also the first to be executed for that crime during peacetime, despite doubts about their guilt and a worldwide campaign to spare them.

Since his teenage years, Julius Rosenberg, born on May 12, 1918, in New York City, was a radical, who eventually enrolled in the City College of New York, at the time a haven of American radicalism. With the United States in the midst of the Great Depression, COMMUNISM gained numerous converts. Julius met his future wife Ethel Greenglass in 1936. Born on September 28, 1915, in New York City, Ethel had already graduated from high school at age 15 and wanted to be an actress. She became politically active instead, leading a strike when she worked for a shipping company. In 1939, Julius graduated with an electrical engineering degree and the couple married. Eventually, both joined the Communist Party.

During World War II, Julius took a job as a civilian engineer with the U.S. Army Signal Corps. His new position earned him access to American industrial facilities, which made it easier for him to steal secrets and give them to the communists. One of the Americans he recruited into the Soviet intelligence network was David Greenglass, Ethel's brother and a machinist for the Manhattan Project—the secret American effort to construct an ATOMIC

BOMB. Greenglass gave the Rosenbergs information on nuclear weapons, which they turned over to their Soviet connections.

World War II ended in 1945, but Julius Rosenberg continued to spy against the United States. Four years later, the world received a shock: the Soviets had exploded their own nuclear device, much earlier than Americans expected. As fears of the communists grew more intense, the U.S. government took immediate action to ferret out any and all communists in the country.

In 1950, American officials arrested both Julius and Ethel Rosenberg for espionage after scientist Klaus Fuchs, arrested earlier in 1950, confessed to sharing secrets of the Manhattan Project with the Soviets. In time, Fuchs led government agents to Harry Gold, another Soviet spy. Gold, who had served as a courier for the Soviets, led authorities to David Greenglass. Finally, Greenglass implicated both Julius and Ethel Rosenberg. Greenglass's wife, Ruth, was also involved. David Greenglass received a 15-year sentence, whereas his wife was not charged. The Rosenbergs, however, were not so lucky.

David Greenglass was the star government witness against his sister and brother-in-law. Due in large part to Greenglass's testimony, the Rosenbergs were convicted and sentenced to death in March 1951. Judge Irving R. Kaufman delivered a death penalty verdict because he believed that they were responsible for the scientific advances that led to the SOVIET UNION's successful 1949 atomic test. He even blamed the Rosenbergs for the KOREAN WAR and the loss of American lives in that struggle. Kaufman's comments confirmed what Americans believed—that the Rosenberg's had provided vital scientific information, which likely proved useful to the Soviet cause.

The Rosenbergs refused to admit their guilt, choosing instead to appeal the verdict. Following the decision handed down by Kaufman, questions arose about the constitutionality of the Espionage Act of 1917, the law under which the Rosenbergs were convicted. Seven different appeals reached the Supreme Court but all were denied.

As the Rosenberg's execution date neared, world opinion appeared to swing in their favor. Even those who were convinced of their guilt found the sentence unusually harsh. Pro-Rosenberg sympathizers held protest meetings and staged anti-American demonstrations. Appeals for clemency to both Presidents HARRY S. TRUMAN and DWIGHT D. EISENHOWER proved unsuccessful. Finally, on June 19, 1953, the Rosenbergs were electrocuted. Though the guilt of Julius Rosenberg was not questioned, his wife's role was more suspect, and her execution appalled many people, including Federal Bureau of Investigation director J. EDGAR HOOVER. Their execution sparked riots across the country.

Debate about whether or not the Rosenbergs were guilty has continued in the decades after their death. Documents opened after the end of the COLD WAR confirm that Julius was indeed guilty of spying but that Ethel was not. She was nonetheless implicated as part of a government effort to get Julius to confess and identify others involved in espionage.

Further reading: Robert Meeropol and Michael Meeropol, *We Are Your Sons: The Legacy of Ethel and Julius Rosenberg* (Boston: Houghton Mifflin, 1975); Ronald Radosh and Joyce Milton, *The Rosenberg File: A Search for the Truth* (New York: Holt, Rinehart, & Winston, 1983).

— D. Byron Painter

S

SANE (National Committee for a Sane Nuclear Policy)

Officially formed in 1957, SANE served at the forefront of the liberal antinuclear establishment, which grew in stature during the atomic age.

Led by Norman Cousins of the *Saturday Review*, SANE included Eleanor Roosevelt, scientist Linus Pauling, and wealthy poet Lenore Marshall among its members as it was launched on a somewhat informal basis, seeking to inform the American public on the dangers of nuclear weapons and nuclear testing. The organization was founded upon the premise that American governmental mistakes could be rectified, in part by using dialogue, public education, and, especially, direct political action. Within this context, SANE refused to use CIVIL DISOBEDIENCE and noncooperation as possible solutions; instead, persuasion and protest were the methods of choice.

In the first decade after the United States dropped the ATOMIC BOMB on Japan in 1945, a growing revulsion around the world, and especially in the United States, began to form. Opposition formed chiefly among those on the political left and among those who wished to form a type of "world government." Scientists especially lamented any possible health hazards that fallout might have caused. SANE sought as a main goal a nuclear test ban treaty; however, during the administration of DWIGHT D. EISENHOWER the organization proved unsuccessful, as the president preferred to maintain a nuclear threat because it was cheaper to build nuclear devices than to beef up more conventional forces. When the SOVIET UNION, in 1959, announced that it would adhere to a unilateral ban on nuclear testing, the Eisenhower administration eventually followed suit, though both sides subsequently resumed testing.

SANE ran its first full-page ad in November 1957 in the *New York Times*. The advertisement increased the organization's name recognition and encouraged contributions. Though critics panned the ad as biased and one-sided, within a few days of publication, the ad's $4,700 cost had been recouped in donations. Though the group did not favor a grass-roots organization early on, it changed its focus quickly following the ad's positive response. Within six months, over 25,000 Americans had joined the group, in 130 separate chapters. Civil rights leaders such as MARTIN LUTHER KING, JR., and Hollywood stars like Steve Allen and Harry Belafonte also joined the group, as did the famed pediatrician BENJAMIN SPOCK a few years later.

SANE next held a rally at New York's Madison Square Garden in May 1960. Over 20,000 people attended, calling for an end to the ARMS RACE. Just before the meeting, however, the organization faced allegations that its membership included communists, a charge leveled by Connecticut senator Thomas Dodd. Though Dodd admitted that many of the higher-ranking SANE leaders were not communists, he focused on the chapter levels, where evidence existed of communist infiltration. SANE leaders took the charge seriously and ultimately took steps to root out any communist influence.

In time, SANE won a major victory with passage of the LIMITED TEST BAN TREATY OF 1963 signed in Moscow in July. President JOHN F. KENNEDY sent his personal thanks to the organization for its work. The rest of the decade did not prove as productive for SANE as the VIETNAM WAR dragged on and other more militant organizations came to the fore, including the STUDENTS FOR A DEMOCRATIC SOCIETY (SDS). Along with its refusal to engage in the violence more favored by SDS and others, SANE's clout waned. The burgeoning NEW LEFT gradually distanced itself from SANE, as the latter preferred to use "common sense and goodwill," according to executive director Donald Keys. The New Left and SANE were fundamentally different, Keys said, with no common ground on which to work.

SANE spent much of its time discussing Vietnam, especially after 1965. As American intervention continued, SANE became increasingly frustrated with President LYNDON B. JOHNSON. By 1967, it became the first national organization to advocate Johnson's removal from office; the next year, it supported anti-war candidate EUGENE MCCARTHY for president. During the campaign, SANE produced TELEVISION ads attacking antiballistic missiles. These ads, directed at the American people, declared they come "from the people who brought you Vietnam."

By the end of the decade, Vietnam became so important (and nuclear issues less important) to SANE that the word "nuclear" was removed from its name. SANE's influence had lessened just over a decade after it burst on the scene.

Further reading: Paul Boyer, *Fallout: A Historian Reflects on America's Half-Century Encounter with Nuclear Weapons* (Columbus: Ohio State University Press, 1998); Milton S. Katz, *Ban the Bomb: A History of SANE, the Committee for a Sane Nuclear Policy, 1957–1985* (New York: Greenwood Press, 1986).

— D. Byron Painter

Savio, Mario (1942–1996)

Mario Savio was the leader of the FREE SPEECH MOVEMENT at the University of California at Berkeley in the 1960s.

Savio was born December 8, 1942, in New York City to a devout Italian Catholic family. He graduated as the valedictorian of his class of 1,200 at Martin Van Buren High School in Queens. Savio attended first Manhattan College, then Queens College, before going to the University of California at Berkeley, where he enrolled in 1963 as a philosophy major.

Savio became involved with the Civil Rights movement. Like many students of his generation, he went to Mississippi to help register and organize black voters for civil rights causes in the Mississippi Freedom Summer program of 1964.

After returning from Mississippi, Savio and others brought the Civil Rights movement to Berkeley by demonstrating against major San Francisco Bay–area businesses that discriminated against their black employees. His first arrest came at a SIT-IN at San Francisco's Palace Hotel, for demanding that African Americans be hired for positions other than maids.

Savio became known around campus for his leadership skills and activist approach. He believed that civil, expressive, precisely worded, emotional speeches could bring about significant change. A change in university policy that limited the activities of civil rights and political groups on the campus angered Savio, spurring him to action. The change in policy came about because local businesses and their allies on the University of California Board of Regents opposed demonstrations by political groups at the university. These businesses pressured Berkeley's administration

to change its policy on political activity. Savio joined the executive committee of the Free Speech Movement, an organization representing many civil rights and political groups at Berkeley, in an effort to counter the administration's decision.

An uprising at Berkeley in the fall of 1965 produced one of Savio's most recognizable speeches. He used the example given by university president Clark Kerr's description of the modern "multiversity" as a vast machine, stating: "There is a time when the operation of the machine becomes so odious . . . you've got to put your bodies upon the gears . . . you've got to make it stop." This particular demonstration marked a turning point in the Free Speech Movement; it resulted in the arrest of Savio along with an additional 773 protestors.

After his arrest, Savio continued to work with the Free Speech Movement and engaged in more sit-ins. His sit-ins and speeches inspired many protesters, including Joan Baez, one of the best-known folk singers of the 1960s, to continue protesting at Berkeley even after he left the movement in 1965 because of ideological differences.

Further reading: David L. Goines, *The Free Speech Movement: Coming of Age in the 1960s* (Berkeley: Ten Speed Press, 1993).

— Megan D. Wessel

Schlafly, Phyllis   See Volume X

science

In the decades immediately following World War II, science played an increasingly important role in American society, influencing everything from military defense and SPACE EXPLORATION programs to environmental and medical technology.

Prior to World War II, American scientists worked alone or in small, isolated groups, using minimal equipment and funding to conduct their research. With the massive military projects of the war, however, the field of science seemed to change overnight. Suddenly, large groups of scientists began working together toward specific research goals. The U.S. government provided large research budgets to pay for expensive equipment, often cutting in half the time between the scientific idea and its practical application. In order to obtain funding, scientists learned to state their goals in advance and to conduct specific experiments to reach those goals, changing the very structure of the scientific discipline into a more efficient set of procedures. In the process, the reputations of scientists rose significantly, and the public held them in greater esteem than ever before.

Military defense constituted one of the most important areas to benefit from new scientific procedures. During World War II, scientists successfully completed the development of the ATOMIC BOMB, which the United States dropped on Nagasaki and Hiroshima, Japan, to end the war. The development of the HYDROGEN BOMB, or H-bomb, began shortly thereafter. While the atomic bomb used nuclear fission to produce a reaction that released enormous amounts of energy, the H-bomb, also called a thermonuclear bomb, used nuclear fusion, releasing even more energy than the atomic bomb and causing an even greater level of destruction. Although scientists and diplomats argued over whether such nuclear power should be used for destructive purposes, fear that another country might develop and use nuclear weapons against the United States prompted President HARRY S. TRUMAN to order scientists to continue work on the H-bomb. In November 1952, American scientists successfully exploded a thermonuclear device, and in March 1954 the United States exploded the first H-bomb capable of being dropped by an airplane.

With the development of the H-bomb, scientists needed a way to carry nuclear weapons to distant targets across the globe. Although warheads could be placed on bombers, the planes had to be kept on constant alert and were vulnerable to antiaircraft defense systems. A more efficient delivery system arrived with the development of the intercontinental ballistic missile, or ICBM. The ICBM was a long-range missile, which used the science of rocketry to propel nuclear warheads across long distances, thus eliminating the need for bombers.

Although American pilots never flew jets during World War II, the U.S. government accelerated the research and development of jet aircraft beginning in the early 1940s. By the 1950s, jet aircraft replaced slower, propeller-driven planes, and the U.S. Air Force and Navy used large numbers of jets during the KOREAN WAR. In 1951 and 1952, two large strategic jet bombers, the Boeing B-47 and B-52, provided research information for the design of American passenger jets as well. Jet transports, supersonic fighters and bombers, and transcontinental jet passenger aircraft became the norms in AVIATION, as scientists worked to improve the reliability, fuel efficiency, and power of all types of jet aircraft.

The same technology that generated nuclear weapons and jet aircraft also propelled scientific endeavors in the area of space exploration. Just as ICBM missiles carried nuclear weapons, these same missiles also propelled rockets into outer space. After the SOVIET UNION launched *Sputnik,* the first artificial satellite, into outer space in 1957, the United States and the Soviet Union entered into a full-blown space race, with each country vying to be the first to perform particular feats in space. In 1958, President DWIGHT D. EISENHOWER created the NATIONAL AERONAUTICS AND SPACE ADMINISTRATION (NASA), an organi-

zation in which scientists worked to develop the TECHNOLOGY needed for space exploration. Although the Soviet Union was the first country to send a man into outer space in 1961, President JOHN F. KENNEDY stated a national goal of landing a man on the moon and returning him safely to earth by the end of the decade. Throughout the 1960s, scientists worked to meet this goal with such space program projects as the Mercury, Gemini, and Apollo missions. As scientists honed their space technology with increasing skill, the space missions involved going ever-greater distances over longer periods of time. Meeting Kennedy's goal became a reality when *Apollo 11* landed on the lunar surface on July 20, 1969.

As space technology took off in the 1950s and 1960s, so too did the computer sciences. In the early 1950s, the first commercial computers came on the market in the United States. Originally designed as powerful calculators to help with the increasingly intricate and detailed calculations of scientists, the potential for computers soon grew beyond the scientific community with the development of the ELECTRONIC NUMERICAL INTEGRATOR AND CALCULATOR (ENIAC). In 1952, computers successfully predicted the results of the presidential election and fascinated many Americans in the process. Computers made operating businesses more efficient by performing certain tasks more quickly and with fewer errors than when done by people. With the development of the transistor, computers became more compact and affordable, offering various software that appealed to a broad range of users. In the early 1960s, however, computers remained expensive and difficult to operate. This changed as scientists developed simpler computer languages such as the Dartmouth Time-Sharing System (DTSS) and the Beginner's All-Purpose Symbolic Instruction Code (BASIC). With the invention of the integrated circuit, computers that once filled an entire room could now fit into the space of a television. Despite the growing potential for computer science, there was a high level of opposition to computers among the public. Some people feared the loss of jobs that the computer revolution would bring, while others dreaded learning how to communicate in a computerized world.

While these technological advances enthralled scientists and the public alike, the biological sciences also experienced several major breakthroughs. Although very little was known about how genes functioned in the early 1950s, three scientists helped to determine the structure of DNA, the genetic code that comprises life. Rosalind Franklin, working with the Wilkins scientific group in Ireland, discovered that DNA was helical, while James D. Watson, working with Englishman Francis H. C. Crick, found that DNA was formed by two helixes wound round each other: the double helix. Building on the work of these scientists, biochemist Marshall W. Nirenberg worked to crack the code for RNA, and, in 1961, he discovered the entire genetic code. These discoveries led to a molecular revolution in science that helped to find important connections between human genes and disease and greatly benefited the medical community. Also, once scientists cracked the genetic code, they began experimenting with RNA to find out how life first started on earth.

Scientists made great advancements in the earth sciences as well. With the development of sonar in World War II, scientists studied the ocean floor in a much more detailed and thorough manner. Throughout the 1950s, oceanographers worked to map the floor of the ocean using reflected sound waves and amazed the world by what they found. Huge underwater canyons and volcanoes covered the ocean floor, and the discovery of deep ocean trenches went a long way toward explaining earthquake activity and the shape of the earth's continents.

Other scientific advances helped explain the origins of man. Before 1950, radioactive dating techniques helped date fossils, but the system was crude and unreliable. A group of geologists and physicists at the University of California at Berkeley discovered a better test to date fossils. The radioactive-potassium dating system devised during the 1950s was much more reliable than all other previous testing systems, and dating by radioactive decay became the standard in anthropology and archaeology. In 1961, Dr. Grant E. Meyer and Elwin L. Simons of Yale's Peabody Museum discovered a skull belonging to an early ape ancestor, named *Aegyptopithecus*. Using potassium-argon dating, the skull was found to be between 26 and 28 million years old, allowing scientists to learn more about the history of life on earth. Building on these fossil-dating advancements, scientists developed two new techniques to date old, nonliving material in 1960: thermoluminescence and obsidian dating. In 1968, scientists discovered the oldest amino acids known to exist in a formation of rocks in South Africa. A group of Harvard and NASA scientists established the amino acids to be 3.1 billion years old.

As scientists learned more about the physical earth, they also became aware of the delicate balance of the environment. In 1962, environmentalist RACHEL CARSON published *Silent Spring*, a best-selling book about how chemicals in the air and water, especially DDT, were killing all forms of wildlife and endangering human life. Carson's book set off a wave of reaction among the scientific and public communities alike. For the first time, a new attitude existed toward the earth, one dedicated to saving and protecting the environment. This enthusiasm set off the ENVIRONMENTAL MOVEMENT, which worked to educate and motivate people about the preservation of the earth's resources.

Global warming constituted another important issue in the environmental movement. The earth was once thought so big that it was believed small changes in the earth's temperature over extended periods of time would have little effect on the life of the planet. In 1964, this theory changed when two climatologists, Syukuro Manabe and Richard Wetherald, developed a computer model of the atmosphere to predict how water vapor and carbon dioxide would affect the climate. The effect was global warming, or the greenhouse effect, a theory that maintained that the excessive burning of fossil fuels for industrial purposes caused the level of carbon dioxide to rise and the earth's temperature to increase. Global warming carried many environmental consequences, such as the melting of the polar ice caps and the disruption of the agricultural growing cycle.

While scientists made significant discoveries in the physical, biological, and earth sciences, they also worked to improve the day-to-day lives of the American people. In the 1950s and 1960s, Americans began to look to scientists to invent ways to improve their lives in a variety of areas. Before 1950, dental drills were slow and painful. This changed with the invention of water-powered and air-powered drills that made dental visits quick and relatively painless. As scientists worked with the concept of hormone manipulation, research on oral contraceptives and synthetic hormones increased throughout the 1950s. In 1960, the U.S. Drug Administration approved THE PILL for use throughout the country. In 1950, the Aircall Corporation of New York marketed the first radio pager (beeper) for consumer use, and advancements in communication technology enabled Americans to make long-distance calls to Europe via a transatlantic cable by 1960. Technological advancements in the field of electronics made TELEVISION available to almost everyone, changing the nature of leisure time in American society and directly resulting in the development of such products as TV dinners. In order to cook TV dinners quickly, scientists introduced the first patented microwave oven by Raytheon in 1953. With increasing competition from television, MOVIES needed to find new ways to draw people to the theaters, and scientists soon developed the three-dimensional film.

A direct link existed between the growing role of science in American society during the 1950s and 1960s and the establishment of the National Science Foundation (NSF) in 1950. During and after World War II, concern about the role of the United States government in scientific endeavors led to the creation of the NSF. The foundation granted money and equipment to scientists and scientific institutions involved in basic research of importance to national security and industry. Because the NSF primarily aided basic research rather than applied research, the foundation was especially important to colleges and universities.

Further reading: John Diebold, *The Innovators: The Discoveries, Invention, and Breakthroughs of Our Time* (New

York: Dutton, 1990); Alexander Hellemans and Bryan Bunch, *The Timetable of Science* (New York: Simon & Schuster, 1988); Trevor Illtyd Williams, *Science: A History of Discovery in the Twentieth Century* (New York: Oxford University Press, 1990).

— Donna J. Siebenthaler

segregation (de facto and de jure)

Segregation involved the cultural, political, and social separation of white and black communities in the United States.

Before the emancipation of African American slaves at the close of the Civil War, there was little need for formal segregation in American society. The institution of slavery kept the white and black races separated from one another. At the close of the war, many whites, mainly southerners, were not willing to fully integrate blacks into their society. The ideology of "separate but equal," providing facilities to blacks that were equal to those facilities available to whites, made it constitutionally permissible for whites to exclude African Americans from their facilities, though such facilities were rarely, if ever, equal. Upheld in the case *Plessy v. Ferguson* (1896), this policy became the standard practice throughout the United States. Allowing this doctrine to became legally entrenched at the end of the 19th century and the start of the 20th, it was virtually impossible for the black community to integrate into society.

Segregation was prevalent in nearly every aspect of life throughout the country: stores, schools, transportation, restaurants, restrooms, and even water fountains kept blacks separated from whites. Segregation was represented in two forms, de facto, by custom, largely prevalent in the North, and de jure, by law, virtually everywhere in the South.

Segregation was a national problem. At the end of World War II, there was a massive immigration of African Americans from the southern states to the North in search of job opportunities in northern factories. Many African Americans settled in communities throughout the North. Since the economic status of these individuals was quite poor, their living conditions were substandard as well. The term "ghetto" came to describe these neighborhoods. While law did not mandate separation, it occurred nonetheless as a result of economic conditions.

In the South, the pattern was different. Rigid laws there enforced patterns of segregation that governed all contacts between the black and white races.

The black community launched its assault against segregation during the Civil Rights movement. Blacks and whites held many SIT-INS, marches, and rallies alike, protesting segregation. ROSA PARKS, an African American, refused one day to sit at the back of a bus, violating a standard practice of segregation. This event triggered a bus boycott and led to the boycotting of other businesses, such as lunch counters and restaurants. MARTIN LUTHER KING, JR., one of the most prominent civil rights leaders, was arrested in his efforts to end segregation through peaceful, nonviolent protest.

The first legislative step taken to put an end to the practice of segregation came with the unanimous decision in *BROWN V. BOARD OF EDUCATION* (1954) handed down by the WARREN COURT. This Supreme Court decision stated that the separate but equal facilities provided in schools were inherently unequal, and the ruling led to the desegregation of the public education system. This outraged leaders in many southern states, who resisted complying with the radical ruling. Arkansas governor ORVAL FAUBUS placed state military forces in front of a school building to keep blacks from entering. President DWIGHT D. EISENHOWER answered with federal troops, reaffirming the validity of the Supreme Court ruling.

The CIVIL RIGHTS ACT OF 1964 also helped advance the desegregation process. The legislation established that the commerce clause of the Constitution made segregation illegal in privately owned public facilities, such as restaurants and other public accommodations. This act was upheld with the ruling of *HEART OF ATLANTA V. UNITED STATES*, in 1965, forcing the hotel to admit African Americans at their facilities.

The VOTING RIGHTS ACT OF 1965 furthered the advancement of desegregation in guaranteeing black suffrage by removing previous restrictions placed solely on African Americans.

By the end of the 1960s, legally enforced segregation in the United States had almost completely disappeared. Even so, segregated patterns based on economically determined residential separation still persisted.

Further reading: C. Vann.Woodward, *The Strange Career of Jim Crow* (New York: Oxford University Press, 1974).

— Jennifer Howell

Servicemen's Readjustment Act   See G.I. Bill in Volume VIII

service sector

In the decades after World War II, the service sector emerged as the largest segment of the American ECONOMY, making the United States the world's first "service economy," and encompassing a wide range of economic activities that produce services rather than tangible products.

Industries that comprise the service sector include wholesale and retail trade, transportation, finance, communications, insurance, real estate, various professional services (including health care and legal services), personal services (barber and beauty shops, for example), and public services (government, including education).

The growing dominance of the American service sector in the 20th century coincided with the long-term decline of employment in AGRICULTURE and, subsequently, in manufacturing. In the late 19th century, the proportion of the American LABOR force engaged in agriculture began to decline and more Americans found employment in the manufacturing and service sectors. Manufacturing became the largest sector of employment in the early decades of the 20th century. By the 1940s, however, the service and manufacturing sectors employed roughly equal shares of the labor force. During the 1950s, the service sector surpassed manufacturing to become the largest sector of employment in the United States, accounting for the vast majority of newly created jobs. Thirteen million new jobs were created in the service sector between 1947 and 1965. In contrast, manufacturing accounted for only 4 million new jobs and agriculture suffered a loss of 3 million jobs during the same period. Thus, the service sector's share of the American labor force continually expanded. Between 1947 and 1965, the share of the American labor force employed in the service sector increased from 46 percent to 55 percent. For most of this period, wholesale and retail trade constituted the largest area of employment in the service sector. In the late 1960s, however, the rapid growth of employment in the public sector made government the largest employer in the service sector. In addition, increased demands for professional services—such as communications, legal services, and ADVERTISING—contributed greatly to the growth of the service sector in the 1950s and 1960s.

In postwar America, the service sector's share of the gross national product (GNP) changed very little, even as its share of employment increased rapidly. This disparity derived, in part, from the nature of employment in the service sector; jobs in the service sector tended to be labor-intensive positions in which output per worker increased negligibly compared to productivity gains in other sectors of the economy. Throughout the 20th century, the agricultural and manufacturing sectors increased their output levels while decreasing their need for manpower. The introduction of automation and other innovations in manufacturing, for example, dramatically increased the rate of productivity per worker and, in most cases, decreased the need for employees. In contrast, jobs in the service sector—whether in sales, MEDICINE, EDUCATION, or janitorial services—typically allowed for comparatively modest increases in worker productivity. This economic pattern accounts for the fact that even in the 1950s, when the United States was the leading manufacturing nation in the world, the service sector actually provided more jobs than did American manufacturing.

Employment patterns in the service sector that emerged after World War II differed markedly from other sectors of the American economy. Women, part-time employees, and older workers were heavily represented in the service sector. By 1960, almost half of all service sector employees were women and 71 percent of all female wage earners were employed in the service sector. Over one-fourth of all service sector workers were employed only part-time. In addition, the service sector held a high concentration of older workers; nearly 60 percent of American workers over the age of 65 were employed in the service sector (although their share of all service sector jobs was only 5 percent). The strong representation of women, part-time workers, and older Americans in the service sector contrasted sharply with their weak presence in industry. When American manufacturing was booming in the 1950s, industrial workers—mainly represented by unions—enjoyed good wages and benefits. In contrast, less than 10 percent of service sector employees belonged to unions, which could give them the instrumental means to negotiate better wages and conditions of employment. The fact that the vast majority of service sector workers were overlooked by the UNION MOVEMENT contributed to a high concentration of jobs that offered lower pay scales and fewer benefits compared to traditional blue-collar manufacturing jobs. By the late 1960s, the growing dominance of the service sector raised concerns among many Americans about the implications of such employment for the future standard of living for Americans.

Further reading: Victor R. Fuchs, *The Service Economy* (New York: Columbia University Press, 1968); Frank Levy, *Dollars and Dreams: The Changing American Income Distribution* (New York: W. W. Norton, 1987).

— Susan Allyn Johnson

sit-ins

Energizing the Civil Rights movement in the early 1960s, sit-in demonstrations proved to be a widely popular form of nonviolent protest, and they played a major role in the formation of the STUDENT NONVIOLENT COORDINATING COMMITTEE (SNCC).

While sit-ins protesting segregation occurred soon after the Supreme Court's BROWN V. BOARD OF EDUCATION decision in 1954—most notably in Oklahoma City starting in 1958—the deliberately planned protests spearheaded by four students at the North Carolina Agricultural and Technical College in Greensboro (A&T) were the first to receive national attention. On Monday, February 1, 1960, four black A&T students sat down at a whites-only lunch counter in the local Woolworth department store. When they were refused service, they quietly pointed out that they were welcome at every other counter in the store and stated they would remain seated until they were served. They did so until the store closed for the day; that night, the four recruited 20 more black students to return to the counter the next day. By the end of the week, over 400 college students, both black and white, took part in the sit-in protests, and a week after the protests began the lunch counter closed for business. By mid-July, after a 50 percent decline in profits for the Greensboro Woolworth, the store consented to serve black patrons at all its counters.

The actions by the A&T students tapped into the growing desire for bold, decisive action by black college students across the country. Less than two weeks after the first sit-in in Greensboro, over 500 black students in Nashville, Tennessee, organized sit-in demonstrations at downtown lunch counters and restaurants. Students from the elite schools of Boston, Massachusetts, picketed 12 local Woolworth stores, demanding the company adopt a nationwide policy of nondiscrimination. The CONGRESS OF RACIAL EQUALITY (CORE), local chapters of the NATIONAL ASSOCIATION FOR THE ADVANCEMENT OF COLORED PEOPLE (NAACP), and MARTIN LUTHER KING, JR., along with his SOUTHERN CHRISTIAN LEADERSHIP CONFERENCE (SCLC), all publicly supported the sit-ins. While the national office of the NAACP first criticized the protests as counterproductive student pranks, the financial and motivational backing of the SCLC, along with King's endorsement, furnished the movement with the support it needed. "American students have come of age," King said at a rally three weeks after the Greensboro protests, "You [students] now take your honored places in the worldwide struggle for freedom." Often during the sit-ins, black and white demonstrators sang gospel hymns like "We Shall Overcome," a song that quickly became synonymous with the civil rights movement.

Nonviolence was the central principle of the sit-ins, and to that end the students in Nashville created a general code-of-conduct for the demonstrations. Protesters were to be courteous and friendly at all times, not block any entrances or walkways, not hold conversations with people not at the counters, not laugh out, and not strike back if verbally or physically provoked. Nonviolence helped keep the situation from escalating out of control; four days into the Nashville protests, white hecklers burned lighted cigarettes into the backs of female protesters, and several student participants were thrown from their seats and assaulted.

While the arrests of people who attacked demonstrators were rare, police routinely arrested protesters for trespassing and disturbing the peace. In Tennessee and South Carolina, however, protesters refused to post bail and chose instead to serve the 30-day jail sentence, a practice soon dubbed "jail, no bail." Protestors who refused to post bail

overwhelmed local prisons; by April 1960, the number reached over 2,000. Even civil rights leaders took part in the routine. Martin Luther King, Jr., in October 1960, participated in a sit-in protest in Atlanta, Georgia, that resulted in his arrest and incarceration, a jail sentence terminated only after the intervention of presidential candidate JOHN F. KENNEDY.

The sit-ins popularized the concept of CIVIL DISOBEDIENCE—inviting arrest and jail time through nonviolent protest. Their most important legacy, however, was the creation of the STUDENT NONVIOLENT COORDINATING COMMITTEE, better known as SNCC. In April 1960, the SCLC, recognizing the growing power of youth protests, sponsored a conference of students in Raleigh, North Carolina. Over 200 delegates from 50 colleges and high schools participated in the conference, many of whom, including their future leader JOHN LEWIS, previously participated in sit-in protests. Inspired by the success of nonviolent demonstrations, the group met again in Atlanta and formed SNCC, which went on to play a vital role in the FREEDOM RIDES to register black voters in the South.

By late 1961, over 70,000 people had participated in sit-in protests, and they had succeeded in ending segregationist practices in 140 cities. The Supreme Court, in *Garner et al. v. Louisiana* (1961) and *Peterson v. City of Greenville* (1963), found the protests to be lawful, overturning the convictions of protesters arrested for disturbing the peace and trespassing, respectively. There were sit-ins in every southern and border state as well as in Illinois, Nevada, Ohio, and California. This method of nonviolent protest helped to engender other movements during the 1960s, including the FREE SPEECH MOVEMENT and demonstrations against the VIETNAM WAR.

Further reading: Rhoda Lois Blumberg, *Civil Rights: The 1960s Freedom Struggle* (Boston: Twayne Publishers, 1991); William H. Chafe, *Civilities and Civil Rights: Greensboro, North Carolina, and the Black Struggle for Freedom* (New York: Oxford University Press, 1980).

— Adam B. Vary

Southeast Asia Treaty Organization (SEATO)

Organized in 1954, the Southeast Asia Treaty Organization provided military defense and economic cooperation between the United States and nations in Southeast ASIA and the Pacific.

Patterned after the NORTH ATLANTIC TREATY ORGANIZATION (NATO), member countries of SEATO—the United States, Australia, France, Great Britain, New Zealand, Pakistan, the Philippines, and Thailand—proclaimed that an attack within the treaty area was to be construed as aggression against all, and they pledged to come to one another's aid. In addition to cooperation with each other, SEATO members pledged support to protect Cambodia, Laos, and South Vietnam.

Headquartered in Bangkok, Thailand, SEATO was led by a ministerial council consisting of member countries' foreign ministers or their nominated deputies. Despite a shared goal of promoting ANTICOMMUNISM, the organization's leaders often disagreed on SEATO's specific goals and how best to implement them. Some members, such as the United States, believed that SEATO served best as a tool against COMMUNISM. Others complained that SEATO frequently neglected economic issues of concern in favor of military matters alone.

SEATO comprised an important institutional linchpin of U.S. foreign policy in Asia. American involvement in Southeast Asia promoted several goals, including establishment of a containment policy, prevention of the spread of communism; protection of strategic sources of raw materials; development of secure military bases; expansion of American influence; and reduction of European economic involvement in the region. After communists defeated the American-backed government of Jiang Jieshi (Chiang Kai-shek) in China, President HARRY S. TRUMAN faced pressure from government officials and the American public to avoid the "loss" of remaining Asian countries to communist forces. The United States supported the signing of a defense treaty in an effort to stabilize the area following a disappointing failure in the KOREAN WAR. President DWIGHT D. EISENHOWER and Secretary of State JOHN FOSTER DULLES believed SEATO would serve to counterbalance the influence of communist China and the growing presence of Ho Chi Minh in Vietnam. SEATO offered a way for the United States to expand its sphere of influence and gain desperately needed allies in the region. The United States believed regional military treaties would form a united front against encroaching communist borders. Eisenhower also faced internal pressure from members of the REPUBLICAN PARTY, who saw Asia, not Europe, as America's best potential economic market and political ally.

American involvement in Southeast Asia stemmed as well from the desire to help European allies and to protect their economic interests. Both France and Great Britain possessed colonies in the region, which formed integral parts of their economy since the 19th century. In 1954, France lost its military struggle with the Vietnamese nationalist forces under the control of the communist Ho Chi Minh, finally relinquishing colonial rule. The fighting officially ended with the 1954 Geneva Convention, which divided Vietnam along the 17th parallel into northern and southern territories. France joined SEATO not just to fight the communist threat but also to protect its economic interests in Vietnam. French inclusion in SEATO created local mistrust of the organization's intentions. Newly independent countries such as Vietnam saw SEATO as an institution created to perpetuate continued colonial control.

Other problems threatened the effectiveness of SEATO. As U.S. involvement in the VIETNAM WAR intensified, internal divisions within SEATO became increasingly clear. Although the United States, New Zealand, Australia, Thailand, and the Philippines sent troops to Vietnam, other SEATO countries refused to send military support. Most SEATO members, with the exception of Pakistan and France, approved of American involvement in what some considered a civil war. In addition, a lack of participation by important countries in the region such as Japan, India, and Indonesia undermined the impact of SEATO. By 1975, France and Pakistan withdrew from the organization and communists declared victory in Vietnam. American domestic opinion had turned sharply against the war and further involvement in the region became a contentious political issue. Because of the lack of international and domestic support and loss of its primary mission, SEATO disbanded on June 30, 1977.

Further reading: John Gaddis, *We Now Know: Rethinking Cold War History* (New York: Oxford University Press, 1997).

— Lyra Totten-Naylor

Southern Christian Leadership Conference (SCLC)
Established by MARTIN LUTHER KING, JR., in 1957, the SCLC was committed to nonviolent action to achieve social and political justice for all African Americans.

The SCLC grew out of the bus boycott in Montgomery, Alabama, during 1955 and 1956. King wanted a permanent organization to carry on the successful fight in other areas. The SCLC inspired many black leaders to believe that nonviolent protests, such as the boycott, might succeed in battles against SEGREGATION. Its approach was therefore different from that of the NATIONAL ASSOCIATION FOR THE ADVANCEMENT OF COLORED PEOPLE (NAACP), which relied almost entirely on legal actions. The SCLC wanted to end segregation more quickly than seemed possible through the NAACP's methods.

While King headed the new organization, other important civil rights leaders were involved. Ralph Abernathy was an ordained Baptist minister from Alabama who was actively involved in the Civil Rights movement, and he succeeded King after his assassination as the president of the SCLC. Jesse Jackson was another civil rights activist who devoted his time to the Civil Rights movement.

The SCLC was primarily located in the South. It conducted leadership training programs, citizen education projects, and voter registration drives. In promoting desegregation, the organization continually promoted nonviolent protests. The SCLC was most noted for its many marches. The first was in Albany, Georgia, in 1961, in which activists protested the segregated public facilities in the city. This confrontation failed when the community arrested the protestors, who failed to bring about the desired change.

In early 1963, however, the protests worked in Birmingham, Alabama. While in Alabama, the SCLC encouraged children and teenagers to join in the confrontations. In response, Eugene "Bull" Connor, the local police commissioner, released dogs and used high-pressure water hoses on the protestors. TELEVISION brought these scenes of nonviolent protestors being abused into homes around the country, horrifying viewers, and helping the Civil Rights movement to gain momentum. The protestors eventually negotiated with local Birmingham officials and won their battle when the city desegregated restrooms, drinking fountains, lunch counters, and fitting rooms throughout the metropolitan area.

The biggest march that the SCLC organized came on August 28, 1963, with the MARCH ON WASHINGTON led by King and others. More than 200,000 people gathered that day to show support for the Civil Rights movement, and to press for passage of a bill mandating the integration of public accommodations that was bottled up in Congress. At this march, King gave his famous "I Have a Dream" speech, which outlined his goals for the Civil Rights movement.

Another well-known demonstration led by the SCLC occurred in March 1965, with a march planned from Selma, Alabama, to the capital of Montgomery to demand black voting rights. Just outside of Selma, the protestors were met by police and counterdemonstrators telling them to go home. When the marchers refused, the police started to beat and tear gas the demonstrators. Again, this was televised, and the event came to be known as Bloody Sunday. The upheaval prompted President LYNDON B. JOHNSON to react. In a speech televised nationwide, he spoke against the violence that the nation saw, and urged the protestors

Civil rights leaders (left to right): Martin Luther King, Jr., leader of the Southern Christian Leadership Conference; Attorney General Robert Kennedy; Roy Wilkins, executive secretary of the NAACP; and Vice President Lyndon Johnson, after a special White House conference on civil rights, 1963   *(Library of Congress)*

to continue their march. The SCLC also successfully petitioned federal district judges for an order barring police interference with their march. The marchers arrived in Montgomery five days later, to hear once again King's powerful words against segregation and restrictions on voting rights. This march influenced Johnson to sign the VOTING RIGHTS ACT OF 1965, banning the use of literacy tests and other voting restrictions against blacks, and mandating that federal registrars register voters who had previously been turned away.

In 1968, the SCLC turned its attention to the issue of poverty. King developed the Poor People's Campaign with the help of the SCLC. He and others spoke out against the economic discrimination faced by African Americans. The SCLC supported workers who had gone on strike in order to receive equal pay. The organization also pressured the Senate to approve a bill funding low-income housing.

In 1969, after King's assassination the year before, the SCLC began to encounter trouble raising money. At the same time, the organization faced internal differences about goals. Yet the organization survived, and it continues the struggle for racial equality.

Further reading: Adam Fairclough, *To Redeem the Soul of America: The Southern Christian Leadership Conference and Martin Luther King, Jr.* (Athens: University of Georgia Press, 1987); David J. Garrow, *Bearing the Cross: Martin Luther King, Jr., and the Southern Christian Leadership Conference* (New York: William Morrow, 1986).
— Megan D. Wessel

Southern Manifesto

The Southern Manifesto was a document signed by the leaders of the southern states rejecting the Supreme Court ruling that all school SEGREGATION under the "separate but equal" doctrine was unconstitutional.

On May 17, 1954, the Supreme Court handed down a unanimous decision in the *BROWN V. BOARD OF EDUCATION* case. The Court ruled that it was unconstitutional for schools to be segregated and ruled that the "separate but equal" doctrine laid down in the *Plessy v. Ferguson* ruling of 1896 was unconstitutional. Southern whites were furious at the decision and called May 17 "Black Monday." Many of the southern senators and representatives in Congress were outraged by this decision as well, and they were determined to resist it.

On May 12, 1956, 101 members of Congress, all from southern states, affirmed their opposition to the *Brown* decision in what they called the "Southern Manifesto." Signers of the manifesto declared that it was their intention to use "all lawful means to maintain segregation." Many state and local government officials in the South also sup-

ported the document. Those signing the manifesto agreed not to desegregate unless forced to by law. These southerners felt that the Supreme Court ruling constituted an attack on states' rights. They felt, too, that the Supreme Court was attempting to use its power to legislate, not interpret the law.

The support that the manifesto gained in the South gave it some respectability in the rest of the country. Many southerners rallied around the manifesto and formed such groups as the National Association for the Advancement of White People and WHITE CITIZENS' COUNCILS. There was a resurgence in the popularity of the KU KLUX KLAN, an organization that terrorized blacks and sought to prevent them from exercising their court-ordered rights. Many of these new groups used scare tactics in order to keep the supporters of desegregation quiet. Throughout the South there was a dramatic increase in bombings, lynchings, and murders.

By 1957, the manifesto had reached the national spotlight when ORVAL FAUBUS, the governor of Arkansas, refused to comply with a court ruling to desegregate Central High School in Little Rock. The governor, along with the Arkansas National Guard and several white protesters who had gathered at the scene, blocked the entrance of the school. President DWIGHT D. EISENHOWER was forced to dispatch federal troops to Little Rock so that nine black students could enter the school for classes.

Throughout the South, the Southern Manifesto encouraged efforts to stop or slow desegregation. In some communities, the public schools were shut down completely. In other places, leaders instituted student placement laws, in which local officials used nonracial criteria to delegate which schools certain students should attend. The federal courts constantly struck down these plans to keep segregation alive in the South.

The manifesto echoed once more in 1963, when Alabama governor GEORGE C. WALLACE promised in his inaugural speech, "segregation now, segregation tomorrow, and segregation forever." That same year, Wallace delivered on his promise when he blocked the entrance of the University of Alabama to stop two African American students who were trying to register. President JOHN F. KENNEDY subsequently sent in the Alabama National Guard to allow the two black students access to the school.

The Southern Manifesto encouraged violence and social discord in direct contempt of the *Brown* ruling. The chaos eventually gained the attention of government leaders in Washington, D.C. Finally, Republicans and progressive Democrats joined together and passed the CIVIL RIGHTS ACT OF 1964 and the VOTING RIGHTS ACT OF 1965. These measures, along with strict federal enforcement of the laws, quickly put an end to the demands of the Southern Manifesto and the resistance against desegregation by the South.

Further reading: Harvard Sitkoff, *The Struggle for Black Equality, 1954–1992* (New York: Hill & Wang, 1993).

— Matthew Escovar

Soviet Union (and foreign policy)

The Soviet Union, as the world's preeminent communist power, constituted the primary focus of American foreign policy during the COLD WAR that unfolded in the decades after World War II.

As the war ended, the Soviet Union, an American ally during the conflict, was one of the two remaining world superpowers. The alliance soon fragmented. Americans had long been suspicious of the Soviets, refusing to extend formal diplomatic recognition after the Bolshevik Revolution. Recognition came in the 1930s, but suspicions remained. During the wartime alliance, the Soviet Union played down rhetoric predicting the inevitable triumph of COMMUNISM over capitalism, but, after the war, the rhetoric resumed. The United States and the Soviet Union also had different priorities. The Soviets needed to rebuild their war-ravaged homeland. The United States wanted to rebuild BUSINESS that had already prospered during the war.

During the struggle, Soviet leader Joseph Stalin participated in the Teheran and Yalta Conferences, as well as the Potsdam Conference after Germany's surrender, to help determine the postwar world map. At Potsdam, Stalin infuriated his Western counterparts by asking for more than the West thought he deserved. Despite their differences, they reached agreements on boundary and occupation lines. Within a few years, however, the Soviets began to challenge what were already flexible agreements and moved further to consolidate their power in Eastern EUROPE. They also chose not to participate in the American-led MARSHALL PLAN to provide economic aid in reviving Europe.

The Soviet Union quickly concentrated its power in Eastern Europe, adding many countries to its sphere of influence and eventually forming the Warsaw Pact in 1955 to counteract the Western-inspired NORTH ATLANTIC TREATY ORGANIZATION (NATO). Within the Soviet sphere, East Germany constituted a focal point of its concerns. In 1953, the Soviets crushed a worker rebellion in Berlin, a city that would remain a potential flashpoint of American and Soviet foreign policy. In August 1961, the Berlin Wall was constructed, which divided the city, and the West and the Soviets continued to disagree over the city's fate.

East Germany was not the only satellite to cause concern for the Soviets. In 1956, just months after Nikita Khrushchev denounced Stalin and claimed that he had governed through his "cult of personality" rather than on behalf of communist ideology, Poland and, especially, Hungary posed difficulties. In the latter, demonstrations calling for independence eventually led to many deaths and the formation of a new Soviet puppet government. Twelve years later, Czechoslovakia also faced Soviet military might. After the Czechs opened the door to reform and mentioned the possibility of closer ties with the West, the Soviets began to pressure the local Communist Party to halt its activities. The Soviets were unsuccessful and finally were forced to once again engage military tactics to suppress the movement.

There was one glaring exception to Soviet rule in Eastern Europe. Under the leadership of Josip Tito, a communist, Yugoslavia steadfastly maintained its autonomy. It did not join either the military pact or COMECON, the economic counterpart to the military Warsaw Pact.

Tensions between the United States and the Soviet Union increased over the fate of the People's Republic of China. In 1949, Mao Zedong's communists defeated Jiang Jieshi's Nationalist forces, and the American-supported Jiang fled to nearby Taiwan. Relations were strained further with the KOREAN WAR. Both China and the Soviets supported North Korean forces while the United States supported South Korea. Over the next decade, the Soviet Union strongly aided China and North Korea, but by 1960 relations began to deteriorate. By the end of the 1960s, tensions were high.

Another issue of disagreement for the Americans and Soviets was the VIETNAM WAR. Throughout the conflict, the Soviets strongly supported the North Vietnamese while the United States aided the South. The relationship between the Soviet Union and North Vietnamese leader Ho Chi Minh dated back to before the Korean War, when they signed a cooperation agreement.

The Soviet Union did not ignore AFRICA during this time. Egypt was a close ally. The Soviet Union supported Egypt in 1956 during the SUEZ CRISIS, when the Suez Canal was nationalized. The Soviets contributed to the construction of the Aswan High Dam and assisted Egypt in the 1967 Arab-Israeli War.

Throughout the cold war, the specter of nuclear annihilation was never very far from many people's minds, especially after the Soviets obtained their own nuclear device in 1949. These fears came to a head in the 1962 CUBAN MISSILE CRISIS. Just three years after Fidel Castro became Cuba's leader, Khrushchev placed offensive missiles on the island 90 miles from Florida. American intelligence discovered the missiles, and President JOHN F. KENNEDY demanded their immediate withdrawal. Ultimately, Khrushchev yielded to Kennedy's demands and removed the missiles, but not before the two nations moved to the brink of nuclear war. By the end of the next year, the Soviets and Americans signed the LIMITED TEST BAN TREATY OF 1963, prohibiting all aboveground tests and agreeing to prevent the use of arms in space.

Khrushchev was removed from power in 1964 and was replaced by Leonid Brezhnev. As the 1970s approached, tensions became somewhat more relaxed between the two cold war adversaries.

Further reading: Aleksandr Fursenko and Timothy Naftali, *"One Hell of a Gamble": Khrushchev, Castro, and Kennedy 1958–1964* (New York: W. W. Norton, 1997); Vladislav Zubok and Constantine Pleshakov, *Inside the Kremlin's Cold War: From Stalin to Khrushchev* (Cambridge, Mass.: Harvard University Press, 1996).

— D. Byron Painter

space exploration

Inspired by military as well as scientific motives, exploration of the universe beyond Earth's atmosphere moved from the realm of science fiction into reality during the two decades immediately following World War II.

Space exploration traditionally relied on human powers of observation from Earth. As telescope TECHNOLOGY advanced with the development of wider reflective mirrors, it allowed for the collection of more light from space and glimpses into regions of the sky never probed before. In

Astronaut Alan B. Shepard being fitted for a space suit, 1961 *(Library of Congress)*

1948, the Hale Telescope was completed at the Palomar Observatory near San Diego, California. Equipped with a 200-inch mirror weighing 14.5 tons, the telescope was the largest instrument of its kind and allowed unprecedented visual acuity in the study of comets, asteroids, and distant galaxies. It also helped to confirm the existence of quasars, luminous high-energy objects billions of light-years from Earth, which were first classified in the 1950s using radio astronomy, a new type of space study.

Although radio observations of space began in the 1930s, the advent of large antennas after 1945 allowed dramatic advances in radio astronomy. In November 1963, the largest and most sensitive radio telescope in existence was completed at the Arecibo Observatory in Puerto Rico. It included a fixed spherical reflective "dish" 1,000 feet in diameter nestled in a natural sinkhole and was capable of studying phenomena as close as Earth's upper atmosphere or searching the distant cosmos for signs of extraterrestrial life. Among its first accomplishments was the discovery of the true rotation rate of the planet Mercury around the Sun (once every 59 days) in 1965. England's 250-foot steerable radio telescope, built at Jodrell Bank Observatory in 1957, allowed Sir Bernard Lovell, a pioneer in radio astronomy, to advance the knowledge of meteors, nebulae, and other extraterrestrial sources of radio waves.

Rapid scientific developments in rocketry during World War II made it possible to propel manmade satellites into space by the late 1950s. On October 4, 1957, the SOVIET UNION launched *Sputnik 1,* the first spacecraft to reach Earth orbit. The United States, eager to dispute Soviet scientific and potential military dominance of space, countered with *Explorer 1* on January 31, 1958, and established the NATIONAL AERONAUTICS AND SPACE ADMINISTRATION (NASA) that same year. Numerous unmanned flights followed, including: Soviet *Luna 1* (1959), the first spacecraft to escape Earth orbit and fly near the Moon; American *Mariner 2* (1962), the first to travel to another planet (Venus); and *Luna 9* (1966), the first spacecraft to land on the Moon and send back photographs.

These efforts intensified the "space race" between the Soviet Union and the United States and initiated manned flight, the most dramatic development in space exploration. On April 12, 1961, Soviet cosmonaut Yuri A. Gagarin became the first human to travel in space when his *Vostok 1* space capsule made a single orbit around the earth. On May 5, the United States successfully launched astronaut Alan B. Shepard, Jr., although his suborbital flight in *Freedom 7* took him only 302 miles and lasted only 15 minutes. John Glenn was the first American to orbit the earth when his *Friendship 7* spacecraft made three revolutions on February 20, 1962.

Less than three weeks after Shepard's success, President JOHN F. KENNEDY called for the United States to land a man on the Moon by the end of the 1960s, prompting both the United States and the Soviet Union to accelerate their manned space programs. Subsequent spacecraft designs and flight projects—Gemini and Apollo in the United States and Voskhod in the Soviet Union—experimented with lunar exploration. Several flights in the mid-1960s saw crew size increase from one to three, the first woman in space (Soviet cosmonaut Valentina Tereshkova on June 16, 1963), the first walk in space by Soviet cosmonaut Aleksei Leonov on March 18, 1965, and longer flights requiring greater maneuverability and longer distances from Earth. On December 24, 1968, *Apollo 8* became the first manned spacecraft to escape Earth's gravitational pull and orbit the Moon. This prepared the way for the successful flight of *Apollo 11,* which landed on the lunar surface on July 20, 1969.

Although manned space exploration was marked by extraordinary accomplishments, it was also set back by tragedy. On January 27, 1967, three U.S. astronauts—Virgil Grissom, Edward White, and Roger Chaffee—were killed when their Apollo spacecraft was consumed by fire during a test one month before its scheduled launch.

Further reading: Michael Collins, *Carrying the Fire: An Astronaut's Journeys* (Norwalk, Conn.: Adventure Library, 1998); John S. Lewis, *Worlds without End: The Exploration of Planets Known and Unknown* (New York: Perseus Books Group, 1999).

— Peter Robinson

Spock, Benjamin (1903–1998)

Benjamin Spock helped a generation of Americans to rethink their methods of raising children.

Benjamin Spock was born on May 2, 1903, in New Haven, Connecticut. He was the oldest child of a railroad lawyer and a homemaker. Although not deeply religious, the Spocks were strict with their children. After attending Andover Academy for two years, Spock went on to Yale University to study English literature. He joined the crew team and won a gold medal rowing in the 1924 Paris Olympics.

Spock received his medical degree from Columbia University in 1929. He completed an internship at Presbyterian Hospital and a one-year pediatric residency at New York Nursery and Child's Hospital. Believing that psychological training was necessary in order to give young mothers advice on child rearing, Spock completed a psychiatric residency at the New York Psychoanalytic Institute.

Spock opened a private pediatric practice, where questions arose that seemed to contradict the standard doctrine of child rearing that emphasized strict discipline and emotional detachment. A publisher approached him to write a book on child care in 1938, but Spock refused

on the grounds that he did not know enough about pediatrics. He taught at the Cornell University Medical College from 1933 to 1947, and he served as a navy psychiatrist from 1944 to 1946. Spock also held teaching positions at the Mayo Clinic, the University of Pittsburgh, and Case Western Reserve University throughout his career.

In 1943, Spock began work on the book that made him the 20th century's most renowned pediatrician. *The Common Sense Book of Baby and Child Care* was published in 1946, at the beginning of the post–World War II BABY BOOM. Dr. Spock urged parents to trust their instincts and cast off theories of child rearing that demanded feeding schedules, discouraged affection between parents and children, and called for strict discipline. Postwar parents followed Spock's advice. As more families moved to the suburbs and more middle-class women left jobs and colleges to stay home with their children, they embraced Spock's emphasis on family. By the time of his death in 1998, *The Common Sense Book of Baby and Child Care* had sold over 50 million copies and was translated into more than 40 languages.

Spock's other books on parenting elaborated on topics presented in *The Common Sense Book of Baby and Child Care* and underscored his belief in parenting as natural and instinctive. His works include *A Baby's First Year* (1954), *Feeding Your Baby and Child* (1955), *Decent and Indecent* (1970), and *Raising Children in a Difficult Time* (1974). His final book, *A Better World for Our Children* (1994) called for a restoration of morality and increased social activism in order to deal with the problems of violence, divorce, and mass-consumerism.

Spock's approach to child rearing was criticized in the 1960s and 1970s. Conservatives accused him of creating a generation of self-centered adults, and they blamed him for contributing to the social upheaval of the 1960s. Spock's emphasis on permissiveness, they argued, led many young people to question the actions of their government in the VIETNAM WAR. Feminists accused Spock of preaching that full-time motherhood was essential to a child's normal development. He later revised *The Common Sense Book of Baby and Child Care* to include discussions on the roles of fathers, day-care centers, and sitters in raising secure and confident children. Later editions of the book also included alternating pronouns, so that he used "he" and "she" instead of just "he" alone.

Spock became a political activist after his retirement from Case Western Reserve University in 1967. Believing it was a pediatrician's duty to inform parents of the harmful effects of radiation, he joined SANE (National Committee for a Sane Nuclear Policy). He spoke out against the Vietnam War at colleges and universities around the country. In 1968, Spock was sentenced to two years in prison and a

$5,000 fine for encouraging students to evade the draft. The sentence was later overturned, but Spock spent several nights in jail for his part in political disturbances. The national People's Party, a left-wing coalition party dedicated to peace, cooperation, and feminism, nominated Spock to be its candidate for president of the United States in 1972. Spock continued to be active in the struggle against nuclear weapons until his death in 1998.

Further reading: Lynn Z. Bloom, *Doctor Spock: Biography of a Conservative Radical* (Indianapolis: Bobbs-Merril, 1972); Thomas Mair, *Dr. Spock: An American Life* (New York:Harcourt Brace, 1998); Dr. Benjamin M. Spock, *A Better World for Our Children: Rebuilding American Family Values* (Bethesda, Md.: National Press Books, 1994).

—Angela K. O'Neal

sports

Sports in the post–World War II period underwent changes that reflected Americans' increased leisure time and eagerness to find new means of recreation and entertainment.

The world of sports experienced tremendous transformations during the decades immediately following World War II. These changes encompassed almost every aspect of the games, including who was allowed to play, where the teams played, and how audiences experienced the games. These changes, although often highly controversial, fueled the growth and prosperity of sports in America, allowing them to become even more powerful and pervasive as cultural forces.

A variety of sports vied for Americans' attention in the postwar years. While many people participated in organized sports, particularly in high school and college, they also found themselves engaged vicariously as spectators of professional sports that became increasingly popular. In 1945, baseball was the undisputed king of sports, with no real challenger. Although boxing could attract large crowds and tremendous levels of interest for isolated events, especially for charismatic fighters such as MUHAMMAD ALI, no sport could compete with baseball over an entire season. Football, basketball, and hockey lagged far behind in terms of popularity, and they were generally seen as less significant, and sometimes barely respectable, endeavors. During the postwar period, however, football came to challenge baseball's supremacy in the public eye, and the other sports took purposeful strides as well.

In the 1940s, most major professional sports teams were concentrated in the Northeast, with a few teams in the Midwest. Although the National Football League (NFL) and the short-lived All-America Football Conference fielded teams in California, not until 1958, when Walter O'Malley moved the Brooklyn Dodgers to Los Angeles, did baseball move west. During the 1950s and 1960s, as the NFL together with its rival from 1960 through 1969, the American Football League, competed for markets, they established teams in Denver, Kansas City, Oakland, Dallas, Houston, and New Orleans, among other cities. Baseball did not migrate as vigorously, but by 1968, there were teams in Los Angeles, San Francisco, Atlanta, and Kansas City, and several other teams had migrated within the East and Midwest.

More revolutionary than the expansion and migration of professional franchises were the shifts in the access Americans had to the teams and their games. Since the 1920s, American had been able to listen to sports on the radio, with the broadcasts creating strong allegiances across broad listening areas. The explosive popularity of TELEVISION in the 1950s transformed the way Americans enjoyed sports. With television, Americans could watch games from the comfort of their own homes, with a markedly better view of the action than stadium seats provided. In 1958, around 800 professional baseball games were broadcast on television, and by the 1960s, professional football was gaining prominence, largely through its appeal to television audiences. College football, also televised, became equally popular at this time. The expanded interest in and access to top-level professional teams translated into diminished crowds for the smaller, minor leagues.

An influx of new teams combined with existing ones created a professional sports landscape that more closely mirrored the demographics of the United States, as players on the field slowly began to resemble the city populations they represented. JACKIE ROBINSON earned his significant place in American history in the late 1940s as a trailblazer when BRANCH RICKEY signed him to play baseball and integrate the Brooklyn Dodgers and its all-white organization. Prior to Robinson's signing, he and other African American professional baseball players could play only in the Negro leagues on teams that supplemented their normal league schedules with barnstorming tours across the United States, Canada, and Latin America. After Robinson began his tremendously successful Dodger career in 1947, there was no denying the fact that African American ballplayers deserved opportunities to play in the big leagues. After a 13-year span in which African American ballplayers won nine National League Most Valuable Player Awards and the same number of Rookie of the Year Awards few could argue that the sport benefited from black athletes. Not incidentally, the country was better off as well, as these players provided inspiration to numerous Americans who joined the Civil Rights movement in the 1950s and 1960s. The Negro leagues, however, suffered and eventually failed as their stars and crowds flocked to the major leagues. Professional football, basketball, and tennis also integrated at roughly the same time but with much less fanfare.

By the end of the 1960s, professional baseball and professional football were in a close competition for the hearts, eyes, and wallets of the American viewing public. This shared preeminence did not occur because of a lack of alternatives. On the contrary, the National Hockey League's six teams, located in northern U.S. cities and several in Canada, secured a small television contract and intensely loyal followings by the end of the 1950s. The National Basketball Association (NBA), formed in the late 1940s with the merger of two rival leagues, did not challenge professional football and baseball for sporting supremacy in part because its owners proved too competitive. Unable to cooperate with each other, they did benefit from steady growth. During the 1950s, basketball teams in Pittsburgh, Toronto, St. Louis, and Sheboygan all failed to survive. Although some great teams and rivalries developed during the 1950s and 1960s, the NBA was not nearly as prominent as it later became. Throughout these years, professional tennis and golf provided sporting alternatives for men, and, after the elimination of the All-American Girls' Baseball League in 1954, the only real professional options for athletic women.

Further reading: Randy Roberts and James S. Olson, *Winning Is the Only Thing: Sports in America since 1945* (Baltimore: Johns Hopkins University Press, 1989).

— Brad Austin

States' Rights Party

A group that split from the DEMOCRATIC PARTY in 1948, the States' Rights Party represented a group of dissident southern Democrats who opposed President HARRY S. TRUMAN and the Democratic Party's civil rights policy, particularly its support of desegregation.

In the early 1940s, many southern Democrats argued that the national Democratic Party was too liberal in its support of African Americans and organized labor. These southern conservatives withheld their support from President Franklin D. Roosevelt in the 1944 presidential election until he dropped liberal vice president Henry Wallace from the ticket. When Truman became president in 1945, however, he alienated these same southern conservatives by using the FAIR DEAL and his Committee on Civil Rights to gain support among liberals, labor, and blacks. Although he was aware of the South's increasing alienation, Truman reasoned that southern Democrats would always remain loyal to the Democratic Party rather than support the REPUBLICAN PARTY.

Southern Democrats, angry over Truman's apparent disregard for the South, met at a conference of States' Rights Democrats in Jackson, Mississippi, just two months before the 1948 national Democratic Party convention. They urged the national party to denounce civil rights programs and support states' rights, but the conference was unsuccessful in changing the national party's platform. At the July national Democratic Party convention, the Truman administration tried to placate the South by simply restating its vague and weak platform on civil rights from the 1944 presidential election. Minneapolis mayor HUBERT H. HUMPHREY, however, led the Democratic liberal forces in insisting on a strong plank supporting specific civil rights measures. Following the adoption of this platform, the entire Mississippi delegation and half of the Alabama delegation walked out of the convention in protest.

On July 17, 1948, three days after the Democratic convention, Governor Fielding Wright of Mississippi invited anti–civil rights Democrats to Birmingham, Alabama. The States' Rights Democrats, or the DIXIECRAT PARTY as they were popularly known, officially established their own political party when 6,000 southern delegates met to nominate their own candidates for the 1948 presidential election. The Dixiecrats nominated Governor J. Strom Thurmond of South Carolina as their presidential candidate and Fielding Wright as the vice presidential candidate.

Following the nominations, the Dixiecrats crafted a platform that clearly articulated the objectives of the States' Rights Party. The Dixiecrats argued that the policies of the executive branch of the government and its control of the Supreme Court led to a totalitarian state. Only by a strict adherence to the U.S. Constitution and its system of checks and balances could the rights of the states and individuals be upheld. The Dixiecrats, therefore, supported the supremacy of the Constitution and opposed the centralism and bureaucratization of the government. They also strongly advocated all forms of SEGREGATION and opposed any federal civil rights program, including that advocated by the Democratic Party. The Dixiecrats argued that the enforcement of a civil rights program destroyed the social, economic, and political life of the South. Furthermore, they argued that the adoption of a civil rights program should be left to the discretion of the individual states, not the federal government.

Although the Dixiecrats claimed to work for southern interests, neither the majority of southern Democrats nor the rest of the country supported the States' Rights Party. The Dixiecrats hoped to win enough votes to throw the election into the House of Representatives in order to bargain over civil rights. Many southern Democrats, however, remained loyal to Truman, fearful that a Democratic split would lead to a Republican victory and the loss of federal projects and patronage. In the 1948 presidential election, the party netted only 1,169,134 votes, or 2.4 percent of the popular vote. Its 39 electoral votes came from Alabama, Louisiana, Mississippi, and South Carolina.

Immediately following the election, the States' Rights Party sharply declined as most members returned to the

Democratic Party. Thurmond became a member of the Republican Party while serving in the U.S. Senate. Although the party ran no candidates in the 1952 election, it did resurface to nominate Virginian T. Coleman Andrews for president and Californian Thomas H. Werdel for vice president in the 1956 election. This time, the party received only 107,929 popular votes and no electoral votes. The party disintegrated shortly after the election.

Further reading: Amile B. Ader, *The Dixiecrat Movement: Its Role in Third Party Politics* (Washington, D.C.: Public Affairs Press, 1955).

— Donna J. Siebenthaler

steel industry

The postwar years found the steel industry in a state of decline from its previous place of dominance in the world market.

For most of the 20th century, the American steel industry comprised a relatively small number of firms, the largest of which was the United States Steel Corporation, which carried the nickname "Big Steel." The other steel companies, including Bethlehem Steel, Republic Steel, Inland Steel, Jones & Laughlin, and Armco, were known collectively as "Little Steel." These firms historically dominated the steel market both nationally and internationally, but between 1945 and 1969 the industry fell from a position of undisputed supremacy to one of weakness. This decline resulted from a complex mix of forces that allowed foreign producers to supplant American steel to such an extent that many domestic manufacturers left the industry.

One important reason for the decline of the steel industry was its history of labor disputes in the postwar period. The steel industry was highly unionized after World War II, and over 500,000 of these workers belonged to the powerful United Steel Workers of America (USWA) union. Between 1946 and 1959, the USWA initiated five major strikes against the industry, the scale and scope of which were unprecedented in American labor history. The 1946 strike against the industry represented the largest single labor walkout ever, while the 1951 disruption constituted such a threat to the national economy that President HARRY S. TRUMAN tried to seize the steel industry, a move the Supreme Court later ruled unconstitutional. Similarly, the 116-day strike in 1959 was the longest industrial labor action at that time, and it was particularly damaging to the industry since it helped foreign steel producers gain greater access to American markets.

A second critical factor in the decline of American steel firms was the steady erosion of the traditional price advantage they held over foreign producers. Because the USWA demanded and often received wage and benefit increases during contract negotiations, management responded by consistently raising the price of steel. Between 1945 and 1959, the price of basic steel rose on average 11 percent per year, which was over three times the rate of increase for consumer prices. While higher prices generated large profits, they also allowed foreign steel companies to become more competitive, and, by 1965, imports accounted for over 10 percent of all steel consumed in America. By comparison, 1949 imports were just 0.5 percent of domestic steel consumption. The steady rise in steel prices also significantly reduced American exports over time.

A third cause of the decline involved shortsighted management decisions. Because American steel firms commanded nearly two-thirds of the world's production capacity in 1945, many managers became complacent and often inattentive to developments outside their industry. This bureaucratic atmosphere also forestalled worker initiatives and contributed to wasteful and low-quality production methods. Similarly, while the industry did spend billions on new plant and equipment, these capital investments were usually made as incremental improvements to established mills and not allocated to the construction of new facilities that incorporated the latest steel production technologies. In contrast, foreign firms, many of whose plants were destroyed during World War II, built new and more efficient facilities that gave them another competitive advantage over their American counterparts.

The fourth element of the decline was the speed with which foreign steel producers recovered from the war, due in part to the American government's help in financing the rebuilding of these companies through economic assistance tied to its COLD WAR policies. In particular, Japan and Germany were so successful in reestablishing their steel industries that by 1960 they accounted for 16 percent of world output, up from just 3 percent in 1945. With foreign countries producing more steel, the share of world steel production by American firms likewise fell from 64 percent to 26 percent between 1945 and 1960. This in turn reduced plant utilization, which further added to domestic production costs.

While American steel managers were aware of the changes in world steel markets, a number of factors prevented them from acting decisively to protect their interests. They included an underlying attitude of arrogance and indifference to competitors that was based on American dominance of the world steel market. Similarly, the federal government did not adopt a coherent industrial policy to encourage the growth and modernization of steel after the war, forcing the steel industry to fend for itself. Furthermore, because steel executives strongly supported free trade policies, they refused to seek import restrictions that would have protected their business and possibly stemmed the industry's decline. Eventually, American steel firms petitioned legislators for assistance in dealing with foreign competition, and, in 1969, the federal government enacted the first import restrictions on steel.

Further reading: Paul A. Tiffany, *The Decline of American Steel: How Management, Labor and Government Went Wrong* (New York: Oxford University Press, 1988).

— Dave Mason

Steinem, Gloria   See Volume X

Stevenson, Adlai E.   (1900–1965)

One of the leading political orators and writers of the 20th century, Adlai E. Stevenson was a successful Illinois governor and two-time Democratic candidate for president of the United States.

Born on February 5, 1900, in Los Angeles, California, and raised in Bloomington, Illinois, Stevenson grew up surrounded by famous politicians and intellectuals. His grandfather, Adlai Ewing Stevenson, was Grover Cleveland's vice president, while Stevenson's father played an active role in Illinois politics. Stevenson graduated from Princeton University in 1922 before attending Harvard Law School for two years. Instead of completing his law degree, Stevenson returned to the Midwest to work as a newspaper reporter and oversee the family-owned *Bloomington Daily Pantograph.* He then worked briefly as a reporter in Cincinnati, and he completed his law studies at Northwestern University in 1926.

Though he began a law career in Chicago, Stevenson was always more interested in performing public service than in winning legal cases. In 1933, he moved to Washington, D.C., to work for the NEW DEAL in the Agricultural Adjustment Administration. One year later, Stevenson became the chief attorney in the newly created Federal Alcohol Control Administration. While he left this position in 1935 to return to Chicago and resume his legal career, Stevenson continued to take an active role in local politics as a member, and eventual president, of the Chicago Council on Foreign Relations.

Throughout the late 1930s, Stevenson maintained ties with Washington and developed a reputation as an excellent speaker on international relations. In June 1940, he moved back to Washington, where he took a position as chair of the Committee to Defend America by Aiding the Allies, a group that worked to build alliances with European nations fighting the Axis powers following the onset of World War II. His impressive experience with foreign relations made Stevenson a strong candidate for several wartime posts. In 1941, he agreed to act as the principal

Adlai Stevenson in front of campaign poster, 1956
(Library of Congress)

attorney to Secretary of the Navy William Franklin (Frank) Knox, and then as special assistant to Secretary of State Edward Stettinius. Leading a mission to Italy in late 1943 and early 1944, he also helped determine what role the Foreign Economic Administration would play overseas. Following World War II, Stevenson headed the U.S. preparatory commission created to help establish the United Nations (UN), and he served as a UN delegate in 1946 and 1947.

After completing his second year as a UN delegate, Stevenson again went home to Illinois where he ran a successful campaign for governor in 1948. He was widely viewed as a progressive leader who brought greater efficiency to the state government. During his four-year administration, Stevenson strengthened the state police force and improved the highway systems by initiating a 10-year road building program. He also improved the state EDUCATION systems and welfare programs. Many times Stevenson had to make difficult decisions, such as sending the National Guard to Cicero in 1951 to defend a group of blacks from white rioters or vetoing a popular anticommunist measure.

Though Stevenson preferred to serve a second term as governor, the DEMOCRATIC PARTY had other plans for the popular politician. In 1952, he accepted a draft nomination by the Democratic Party as the party's candidate for president of the United States. Stevenson waged an embattled campaign as Americans blamed President HARRY S. TRUMAN for the KOREAN WAR, continued inflation, and increased government spending. As Democratic heir apparent, Stevenson appeared to be committed to a continuation of Truman's policies. Many people also believed he was too soft on COMMUNISM and too progressive on civil rights. While his campaign became famous for its emphasis on issue-oriented substance rather than on style or image, the immensely popular DWIGHT D. EISENHOWER defeated Stevenson. Stevenson won only nine states and 89 electoral votes.

Despite this defeat, the Democratic Party again nominated Stevenson as its candidate for president in 1956. Throughout the campaign, he argued for a nuclear test ban and negotiations with the Soviet Union. He also campaigned for increased federal spending to eradicate poverty, aid education, and support the elderly. For the second time, however, Stevenson misread the American public and lost to Eisenhower.

Stevenson reluctantly agreed to try for a third party nomination in 1960, but he lost to JOHN F. KENNEDY. Once elected, Kennedy appointed Stevenson ambassador to the UN, a position in which he continued to serve under President LYNDON B. JOHNSON. As ambassador, he argued for and defended American anticommunist actions such as the invasion of Cuba in 1961 and the invasion of the Dominican Republic in 1965. Ironically, it was not until Stevenson served as UN ambassador and appeared in nationally televised conferences that the American public appreciated Stevenson's international expertise and intellectual abilities. Although he never served in the top foreign policy posts, Stevenson played a significant role on the American political scene. Just as he contemplated retirement, Stevenson died of a massive heart attack in 1965.

Further reading: John B. Martin, *Adlai Stevenson and the World* (New York: Doubleday, 1977).

— Donna J. Siebenthaler

Student Nonviolent Coordinating Committee (SNCC)

The Student Nonviolent Coordinating Committee (SNCC) played a central part in the Civil Rights movement in the 1960s.

SNCC was organized in April 1960 by black students who had taken part in SIT-INS earlier that year in Greensboro, North Carolina. Instrumental in the group's formation was ELLA BAKER, a black woman working with the SOUTHERN CHRISTIAN LEADERSHIP CONFERENCE (SCLC) set up by MARTIN LUTHER KING, JR. after the MONTGOMERY BUS BOYCOTT.

Headed by chairman JOHN LEWIS, SNCC's main goal, as explained in a 1960 statement of purpose, was integration, attained through nonviolent protests. The tactic of nonviolence inspired by Judeo-Christian ideals and the teachings of India's Mahatma Mohandas Gandhi was politically shrewd. By inviting southern police brutalities in front of national TELEVISION cameras, organizers of nonviolent protests gave moral superiority to SNCC.

In May 1961, after the initial integration efforts triggered by the 1960 Greensboro sit-in, SNCC cosponsored FREEDOM RIDES to desegregate bus terminals throughout the South. It then attempted to desegregate public facilities in Albany, Georgia, through nonviolent demonstrations. As it continued direct actions and sit-ins, SNCC encouraged disenfranchised southern blacks to register to vote. In the summer and fall of 1963, SNCC organized the Freedom Ballot in Mississippi. Eighty thousand blacks voted in a mock election pitting black NATIONAL ASSOCIATION FOR THE ADVANCEMENT OF COLORED PEOPLE (NAACP) member Aaron Henry against white civil rights activist Reverend Edwin King, proving that blacks would vote if they were given the opportunity. The 1964 Mississippi Summer Freedom Project saw 800 volunteers help thousands of blacks register to vote, while the MISSISSIPPI FREEDOM DEMOCRATIC PARTY challenged the right of the all-white Democratic delegation to represent Mississippi at the national convention.

In 1965, after Jimmy Lee Jackson was killed by a state trooper in Marion, Alabama, Martin Luther King, Jr., and SNCC organized a protest march from Selma to Montgomery, Alabama. When Governor GEORGE C. WALLACE banned the march, 525 people, including SNCC Chairman John Lewis, decided to proceed anyway and walked across the Edmund Pettus Bridge on Sunday, March 7, 1965, where they were immediately dispersed and beaten by Alabama state troopers.

SNCC's struggle on behalf of integration and enfranchisement bore fruit when Congress passed the CIVIL RIGHTS ACT OF 1964, banning discrimination in public facilities and schools, and the VOTING RIGHTS ACT OF 1965, which forbade state laws aimed at disenfranchising black voters. Despite these successes, SNCC grew increasingly disappointed with the nonviolent strategy. Violence took its toll on even the most patient protesters and, as police brutality moved behind closed doors, the propaganda effect seemed limited. Impatient to see dramatic results, SNCC pursued a more aggressive stance.

The growing frustration was first evident during the August 28, 1963, MARCH ON WASHINGTON, where Lewis delivered a militant speech that contrasted with King's famous "I Have a Dream" address. Lewis declared, "We cannot be patient, we do not want to be free gradually, we want our freedom, and we want it now. We cannot depend on any political party, for both the Democrats and Republicans have betrayed the basic principles of the Declaration of Independence."

On June 7, 1966, JAMES MEREDITH, the first African American to attend the University of Mississippi, was shot as he made the "Walk against Fear," a march from Memphis, Tennessee, to Jackson, Mississippi. STOKELY CARMICHAEL, SNCC's chairman since May, organized a protest march in which he adopted the slogan "BLACK POWER." The movement, a direct repudiation of SNCC's nonviolent and integrationist ethos, advocated self-defense and black economic and political independence. Carmichael traveled abroad, denouncing the VIETNAM WAR and political and economic repression. H. Rap Brown replaced Carmichael as chairman in May 1967. The creator of the slogan "Burn, baby, burn," Brown joined the BLACK PANTHERS and was imprisoned in 1970 for armed robbery. SNCC meanwhile changed its name in 1969 to Student National Coordinating Committee and became a small, divided organization. It faded away as the Civil Rights movement splintered.

Further reading: Clayborne Carson, *In Struggle: SNCC and the Black Awakening of the 1960s* (Cambridge, Mass.: Harvard University Press, 1995); Emily Stoper, *The Student Nonviolent Coordinating Committee: The Growth of Radicalism in a Civil Rights Organization* (Brooklyn: Carlson Publishers, 1989).

— Philippe R. Girard

Students for a Democratic Society (SDS)

One of many student protest organizations established in the early 1960s, SDS for a time became the most influential of these activist groups.

Founded by activist Al Haber in 1960 at the University of Michigan, SDS remained largely unknown until June 1962, when 40 students from major universities assembled in Port Huron, Michigan. There, they rekindled the organization and delineated their beliefs, intentions, and objectives in *The Port Huron Statement*. This SDS manifesto, written by University of Michigan student TOM HAYDEN and others assembled at the meeting, spoke to a young generation of Americans who were critical of the jarring con-

tradictions they perceived between the ideals and the realities of American life, and the rampant indifference to these disturbing paradoxes on the part of most Americans. The manifesto, a document proposing wide-ranging social reforms, began with the words, "We are people of this generation, bred in at least modest comfort, housed now in universities, looking uncomfortably to the world we inherit." It declared that the world the student generation would inherit needed to be changed.

SDS members were troubled by America's pervasive racism and its high level of poverty, both of which exemplified the alarming gap between America's political rhetoric of equality and a reality that belied such proclamations. Moreover, they condemned the COLD WAR ideology that drove the nation's foreign affairs, the growing political exclusiveness that was blocking citizens' access to government, and the increasing domination of bureaucra-

University of Texas Students for a Democratic Society members protesting the war in Vietnam while other students jeer, 1965 *(Library of Congress)*

cies in universities, big business, government, the military, and political parties that was rendering the average American powerless.

In its manifesto, SDS called for "truly democratic alternatives to the present." What its members proposed was a resurrection of participatory politics, but one in which the efforts of individuals would prompt crucially needed reforms. Students would serve at the forefront of this attempt to bring about a positive shift in the status quo, or, in the words of SDS's manifesto, to "establish an environment for people to live in with dignity and creativeness." While SDS advanced many of the same reforms previously advocated by liberals, such as an end to violence, poverty, racism, and social injustice, its members sought to differentiate their politics and methods from the "Old Left" (traditional LIBERALISM together with the socialism and COMMUNISM of past decades). In contrast, SDS referred to its ideology as "NEW LEFT." It further distinguished itself from left-wing predecessors by placing emphasis on individual rather than bureaucratic efforts, grass-roots organizing on college campuses and in cities, and "participatory democracy."

An early initiative was the Economic Research and Action Project, which sought to create an alliance between workers and students in urban areas. Despite concerted efforts, the project proved unsuccessful.

The first major student protests erupted in the fall of 1964 at the University of California at Berkeley. Angered by the university's efforts to deny them their traditional venue for political activities on campus, several hundred students staged SIT-INS and occupied administration buildings. Major student organizations, including SDS, took part in the demonstration and formed the FREE SPEECH MOVEMENT. After a tense standoff, the university relented. What initially began as a protest for students' rights at Berkeley, however, quickly intensified into general criticisms of universities around the country. These included the poor quality of campuses, the lack of open and free discussions, the bureaucratic nature of college administrations, and the universities' suspiciously close ties with the government. As student protests spread, activists employed many of the tactics of nonviolent resistance they had learned from the Civil Rights movement. The growth of SDS accompanied the growth of campus unrest.

America's increasing involvement in the VIETNAM WAR changed the focus of the protests. With the nation's military escalation in Vietnam and the 1965 expansion of the military draft, student groups redirected their impassioned rage into an antiwar movement. Students began to burn draft cards and American flags and stage campus strikes and antiwar rallies. Opposition to the war, with SDS in the forefront, came to consume the energies of the student movement. By the end of 1967, SDS claimed more than 100,000 supporters and took responsibility for hundreds of protests on campuses nationwide.

By this time, however, some SDS members began complaining of the organization's increasingly authoritarian bent. Additionally, women involved in SDS criticized the group's prevailing misogynist attitudes. They accused male members of denying them egalitarian treatment, of relegating them to little more than sex objects and glorified secretaries, and of purposefully ignoring the larger issue of gender discrimination in American society. Furthermore, some SDS leaders, including Tom Hayden, began abandoning their previously espoused strategies of nonviolent protest and, instead, urged the use of more militant tactics. The year 1968 degenerated into dramatic clashes between students and police on major college campuses; and violent confrontations between police and protesters at the DEMOCRATIC PARTY's national convention in Chicago. At the same time, SDS began to break up into factions. The most extreme of these splinter groups was the WEATHERMEN, which proposed a strategy of revolutionary terrorism. By 1971, disunity and divisiveness had come to characterize SDS and led to its complete demise. The organization's New Left ideology, with its rhetoric of hope, reform, and social justice, likewise collapsed. Both were victims of SDS's rejection of its founding principles—"participatory democracy," equal opportunity, passive CIVIL DISOBEDIENCE, and moral legitimacy.

Further reading: Wini Breines, *Community and Organization in the New Left, 1962–1968* (New York: Praeger, 1982); Kirkpatrick Sale, *SDS: Ten Years toward a Revolution* (New York: Random House, 1973).

— Irene Guenther

Submerged Lands Act

The Submerged Lands Act, passed in 1953, ended a long battle between the states and federal government over the control of submerged lands along coastal shorelines.

The states initially took control of the lands submerged off their coasts in the 1920s. California, Texas, and Florida all claimed rights to fishing the waters surrounding their own respective shorelines. This soon included not only fishing but other activities as well, and the states began to grant leases to remove sand, gravel, sponges, shells, and to harvest kelp. By 1926, the states were granting leases for mineral, gas, and oil development. At this time, the amount of oil and natural gas beneath the ocean was not fully realized, and therefore the federal government had no need to challenge the states' claims to the submerged lands.

As the federal government recognized the amount and importance of the oil and minerals that lay beneath these waters, it contested the states' stake to these lands. In 1945, the U.S. government filed suit against the state of California for allowing the extraction of oil from submerged lands. The Supreme Court decided the case in favor of the federal government. The United States was awarded "paramount rights" to the submerged lands within three miles of the coast of California. In September 1945, President HARRY S. TRUMAN gave the United States all rights to the mineral resources beneath the high seas. This took away the states' rights to the submerged lands and the resources off their coasts. A statement released by the White House stated that the action was "concerned solely with establishing the jurisdiction of the United States from an international standpoint."

States did not surrender easily prerogatives which they felt were rightfully theirs. They continued to lobby for the ownership of the submerged lands off their coasts. Many inland states, most oil companies, and several interest groups were also in favor of state control of these lands. When DWIGHT D. EISENHOWER campaigned for president in the 1952 election, he promised to award the states ownership of their submerged lands.

Eisenhower won the election in 1952, and he kept his promise. On May 22, 1953, he signed a bill that gave each state ownership of submerged lands off its borders, and the mineral deposits in such lands. The submerged lands included lands extending out to sea as far as the states' historic boundaries. The exact distance varied from state to state, between three miles and 10 and one-half miles off the coast. This act allowed state governments to lease the lands to private companies and make a profit from the leasing fees. The passage of this act ended the long dispute between the federal and state governments over control of these lands, although critics called the measure a great giveaway.

Further reading: Ernest R. Bently, *Tidelands Oil Controversy: A Legal and Historical Analysis* (Austin: University of Texas Press, 1953).

— Matthew Escovar

suburbanization

Suburbanization resulted from the migration of people from inner-city dwellings to homes in the residential outskirts of cities in the 1950s.

As World War II ended, the United States was unprepared for the large numbers of returning veterans. Construction of homes had plummeted in the years before the war due to the Great Depression and continued to decline after the United States entered the war. When the soldiers returned home, there simply were not enough houses for them. Many lived with parents or other relatives until adequate housing could be built.

The FEDERAL HOUSING ADMINISTRATION (FHA) and the Veterans Administration (VA) both helped to reduce the down payments and interest rates for people buying houses. WILLIAM J. LEVITT built a new suburban community in Long Island, New York, using assembly-line techniques that lowered prices substantially and sped up the construction process. Levittown became a prototype for all suburban communities, characterized by rows upon rows of identical houses, community churches, and swimming pools.

The migration of people from the cities to the suburbs changed the face of the American landscape. Trees were cut down to provide more land, which was divided into small squares, each containing a house and a two-car garage. Folksinger Malvina Reynolds described the suburbs in a song: "Little boxes on the hillside, little boxes made of ticky tacky, little boxes on the hillside, little boxes all the same." Neighborhoods such as Levittown became notorious for containing rows and rows of identical houses with large picture windows for displaying one's material possessions. A Levittown newsletter stated, "Our lives are held closely together because most of us are within the same age bracket, in similar income groups, live in almost identical houses, and have common problems."

The population in the suburbs boomed from 31.1 million people before 1941 to 60.1 million in 1960. The move to the suburbs was also accompanied by a tremendous increase in the marriage and birth rates of Americans. The BABY BOOM prompted a 40 percent increase in the birth rate, compared to the years before and during the war, and people were getting married at younger ages. The suburbs provided a way for these couples, just starting out, to find affordable housing for their new families.

Suburbanites were largely white Americans, who left African Americans and Latinos behind in the inner cities. Levittowns, in fact, did not sell homes to blacks. While enjoying their suburban lifestyle, whites were often unaware of the problems that plagued minority groups who lived within the cities, such as poverty and racial tensions.

Suburbia also spurred growth in religious participation, which nearly doubled during the 1950s. Suburbanites looked to each other and to RELIGION to fill the sense of community that they had lost when they moved out of the city. No longer did extended families live down the hall or down the street.

Owning a house in suburbia became an integral part of the American dream. TELEVISION shows such as *Leave It to Beaver* and *Father Knows Best* all depicted the typical white family in its suburban community.

The role of women in suburban society also changed dramatically. After World War II, women were called back into the home once again as housewives. Living outside the cities, women had to drive their children to school and other programs while tending to those errands necessary to maintain their suburban homes.

Suburbanization also spurred the growth of the AUTO-MOBILE INDUSTRY. Suburbanites often worked in the cities and needed the means to travel to and from their homes. Automobiles became the preferred mode of transportation. With more drivers on the roads, the need for a highway system became apparent. The INTERSTATE HIGHWAY ACT OF 1956 allocated money for the construction of a national highway system.

Businesses soon began moving to the suburbs as well. Shopping centers, which numbered eight in 1945, jumped to 3,840 in 1960. Seventeen new centers opened in one three-month period in 1957 alone. Adequate parking and extended hours changed consumerism in the United States. Don M. Casto, designer of the Miracle Mile shopping center in Columbus, Ohio, described the people as having "path habits like ants," as he reflected on the way they headed to the strip malls that sprang up across the country.

Suburbanization also produced far-reaching effects on the environment. The rapid development of land often occurred without extensive planning. The American landscape became cluttered with neighborhoods, highways, restaurants, malls, and auto dealerships. Billboards filled any unused space.

Suburbanization changed the face of America in the 1950s and established many patterns still prevalent in society.

Further reading: David Halberstam, *The Fifties* (New York: Villard Books, 1993); G. Scott. Thomas, *The United States of Suburbia* (New York: Prometheus Books, 1998).

— Jennifer Parson

Suez crisis

The Suez crisis involved a joint Anglo-French-Israeli invasion of the Suez Canal Zone in Egypt in 1956, followed by a major international furor that resulted in the withdrawal of the invading forces and the humiliation of the invaders.

The Suez Canal had long been an important axis upon which many important themes in the modern MIDDLE EAST turned. Soon after it was built in 1869, the British obtained a controlling interest in the canal and made it the linchpin of British imperialism in the region. With the rise of Egyptian nationalism in the decades that followed, what constituted a point of pride to the British served as a mark of humiliation to the Egyptians. Despite local opposition, British control of the canal was never seriously questioned as long as British power in the region remained strong. After two debilitating world wars, however, British power waned to such an extent that the Egyptian government,

led by nationalist Gamal Abdel Nasser, threatened to end British control of the canal.

Nasser at first used the canal as a bargaining chip to gain economic aid for the construction of the Aswan Dam, which, when completed, would create thousands of new acres of fertile farmland. Egypt needed British and American economic aid, however, to carry out this project. The United States, for its part, was primarily concerned with preventing communist influence in the region as a result of the COLD WAR and maintaining access to crucial oil reserves. After Nasser negotiated an arms deal in 1955 with Czechoslovakia, a satellite of the SOVIET UNION, the United States abruptly cancelled American funding for the Aswan Dam, and Nasser, in retaliation, unilaterally nationalized the Suez Canal that same year.

Three powers had a vested interest in returning control of the canal back to the British. In addition to Great Britain, France, which still possessed colonies in North Africa, feared that the example set by Nasser would threaten control of its possessions elsewhere. ISRAEL was also deeply antagonistic toward Egypt as a result of Egypt's

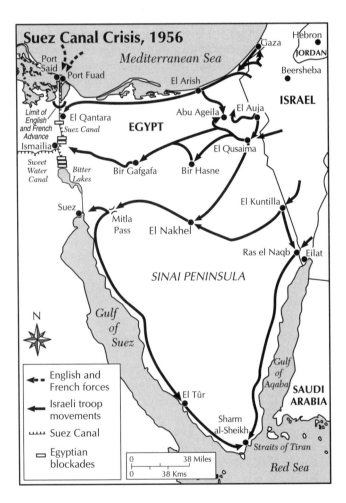

role in the war of 1948 and also because Nasser had made anti-Israeli propaganda a key component of his brand of Arab nationalism. The additional threat of arms from the Soviet bloc also struck fear in the hearts of Israeli policymakers. Although the United States opposed Egyptian nationalization, the administration of DWIGHT D. EISENHOWER chose to rely on economic as opposed to military force to return control of the canal to Britain. As a result, Britain, France, and Israel secretly formed a plan, named Operation Musketeer Revise, to regain British control of the canal by force.

Israel attacked Egypt and occupied the Canal Zone in late October 1956 followed by a joint Anglo-French invasion in early November. Although militarily successful, the matter was far from settled. Both the United States and the Soviet Union condemned the invasion of Egypt and demanded a complete withdrawal from the Canal Zone. American leaders informed Britain that it would withhold all economic aid, including crucial oil supplies, until it withdrew. Britain, still recovering from World War II, was forced to comply, which forced the French to withdraw as well. Israel withdrew from all but the Gaza Strip and Sharm al-Sheikh near the straits of Tiran, regions which military planners considered vital to Israel's national security.

Despite the fact that it had lost the battle militarily, Egypt retained control of the canal. Nasser became a national hero to Egyptians, who believed that their humiliation at the hands of Israel in 1948 and from Britain over the course of the last century had finally been reversed. Israel also enjoyed some measure of success as a result of the conflict. Despite its withdrawal, it had again demonstrated its military superiority over the Arab states, as well as its willingness to fight threats to its national security. For the United States, the Suez crisis showcased tensions within its cold war alliances. Eisenhower felt personally betrayed by the British role in the affair. The Suez crisis also enhanced the public image of the Soviets in the region. Although the Soviet Union was brutally crushing a revolt in Hungary at the time, it was still able with very little effort to portray itself as anti-imperialist in the Middle East. The French gained nothing from their intervention and confirmed the worst suspicions of nationalists in their North African colonies. The biggest loser by far, however, was Great Britain. The Suez Crisis clearly demonstrated that British power in the Middle East independent of the United States was virtually nonexistent.

Further reading: Diane Kunz, *The Economic Diplomacy of the Suez Crisis* (Chapel Hill: University of North Carolina Press, 1991); William Roger Louis and Roger Owens, eds., *Suez 1956: The Crisis and Its Consequences* (Oxford, U.K.: Clarendon Press, 1989).

— Matthew M. Davis

T

Taft, Robert A. See Volume VIII

Taft-Hartley Act

Passed in 1947, the Taft-Hartley Act consisted of a series of amendments to the National Labor Relations Act of 1935. Imposing many new restrictions on labor unions and making it more difficult for them to perform as effectively as in the past, this measure had a crippling effect on organized labor across the United States.

Before World War II, labor unions had experienced huge surges in membership. The National Labor Relations Act of 1935, part of Franklin D. Roosevelt's NEW DEAL, established the right of workers to bargain collectively for better working conditions. It set up a mechanism whereby elections could be held to determine whether workers could be unionized and, if so, which union could represent them. During the 1930s and early 1940s, there were many successful workers' strikes, and union membership more than doubled. With the close of World War II, however, business leaders grew tired of strikes, as workers tried to get their share of wartime profits. Conservative critics, most of them Republican, viewed such strikes as unpatriotic. They also pointed out that corruption ran rampant within many unions. Critics helped encourage a growing attack on union organization.

The Taft-Hartley Act, also known as the Labor Management Relations Act of 1947, was controversial. While its stated aim was to help keep commerce stable in the United States, its antilabor bias was clear, and its working-class opponents called it a "slave labor law." Congress overwhelmingly overrode President HARRY S. TRUMAN's presidential veto of the measure. Truman vetoed the act due to his large base of blue-collar support.

The Taft-Hartley Act made it illegal for labor unions to do many of the things that they had done successfully in the past. The strike was the most powerful tool that organized labor possessed to fight for workers' rights, and this act severely restricted use of the strike. The act required 60 days notice before beginning a strike, and established that the president could delay striking for up to 80 days if it was felt that the stoppage of work caused harm to the "health and safety" of the nation. This act put an end to "third party" or "sympathy strikes" by unions in other companies in support of the protesting workers. Employers were also now able to replace striking employees with people called "scabs," people who crossed striking worker lines to work, weakening the striking process.

Aside from circumscribing the strike, the Taft-Hartley Act also placed restrictions on many of the other operations of organized workers. There were heavy penalties for boycotts by another union that supported a strike. Large-scale corruption in the finances of many unions led to the production of extensive financial documentation, which became expensive. The illegal practices of some union leaders led to placing a halt to contributions to political campaigns. Labor unions were no longer allowed to demand that members be hired for certain jobs, and they were further prevented from forcing employees to become union members.

The Taft-Hartley Act caused outrage among white- and blue-collar workers. The stern regulations mandated by this measure did not allow them to fight effectively for the rights to which they believed that they were entitled. The passage of the act caused protests by workers all over the United States.

The Taft-Hartley Act severely restricted the growth of labor unions in the United States. This law did, however, reduce the corruption that occurred in unions, and eventually allowed for more honest organized labor in the future. Truman's veto also secured for him labor's political support in the election of 1948.

Further reading: Michael Yates, *Labor Law Handbook* (Boston: South End Press, 1987).

— Jennifer Howell

Teamsters Union

The Teamsters Union, officially known as the International Brotherhood of Teamsters, Chauffeurs, Warehousemen, and Helpers of America, is one of the largest trade unions in the world. Though troubled by allegations of connections to organized crime, the union remains influential.

Teamsters, or those who drove horse-drawn wagons as deliverymen, first organized themselves into 18 local unions in the Midwest in 1898. AMERICAN FEDERATION OF LABOR (AFL) leader Samuel Gompers called on the locals to create a national teamsters union under the AFL. The next year, workers chartered both the Team Drivers International Union and the Teamsters National Union. The two unions instantly became rivals with different approaches to improving teamster working conditions. As a result of the rivalry, Gompers convinced the competing unions to meet. The two unions agreed that they were stronger together and, as a result, they joined forces to create the International Brotherhood of Teamsters (IBT) in Niagara Falls, New York, in 1903.

The young IBT struggled for progress during the early and unrestricted era of American industrialization. Strikes were costly in early 20th-century America; labor laws were nonexistent and companies used antitrust laws against unions. Despite the violence and cost, however, the persistence of early IBT strikes eventually led to better working conditions and the right to overtime pay.

Under the leadership of president Dan Tobin, the IBT, like most other unions at the time, made significant progress toward the unionization of industry during World War I and the industrial boom that accompanied it. These gains, however, proved transitory and temporary in their longevity, for most union accomplishments failed after the war as America slipped into the depression of the 1930s.

After World War II, the IBT recovered from its membership and revenue recession as most industries experienced rapid growth and rejuvenation in the post–World War II ECONOMY. Seeking to curb reemerging union power, however, Congress passed the TAFT-HARTLEY ACT in 1947. Despite this political setback, the IBT persisted in its strategic efforts to create multistate bargaining units and control trucking terminals in the growing new industry of intercity trucking that developed as a result of better automotive TECHNOLOGY and the advent of the interstate highway system.

IBT president Dan Tobin retired in 1952 after leading the teamsters for 45 years and Dave Beck was elected as his successor. Beck inherited a union made large—reaching 1 million members by 1950—and powerful by the leadership of Tobin and the booming postwar industrial complex. The IBT continued to grow throughout the 1950s and 1960s.

Because of its size, the IBT wielded great economic power, and its pension fund was a significant investment resource. Throughout the 1950s, the union underwent investigation for corrupt practices, with several of its presidents facing criminal charges ranging from racketeering to fraud.

In January 1957, the Senate Committee on Improper Activities in the Labor Field—the McClellan Committee—established by the U.S. Senate, conducted investigations of labor racketeering. The committee found evidence of widespread corruption throughout the IBT, and, as a result, the AFL-CIO, the nation's largest labor organization, expelled the IBT from its membership.

The McClellan Committee, under the leadership of ROBERT F. KENNEDY as chief counsel, brought nearly every senior leader in the IBT before the committee between 1957 and 1959. Robert Kennedy and the McClellan Committee faced allegations of carrying out a vendetta against IBT president Dave Beck and his successor Jimmy Hoffa. The investigation by the McClellan Committee constituted

Jimmy Hoffa, 1959   *(Library of Congress)*

one of the most controversial congressional hearings of the century. The revelations of the Senate committee, as well as negative public attention that the IBT attracted Marxist-style leadership and control as practiced by some locals, created further public hostility toward unions. When the Senate investigations concluded, the word "teamster" became synonymous with gangster. The McClellan Committee convicted Beck of income-tax fraud and sentenced him to serve time in prison.

Jimmy Hoffa assumed the presidency in 1957 after Dave Beck went to prison. He quickly earned a reputation among his peers as a tough and effective bargainer. In 1964, he negotiated the union's first national contract with trucking companies. Under Hoffa's leadership, Teamsters Union membership grew to more than 2 million. Hoffa was long rumored to be associated with organized crime and, beginning with the 1957 McClellan Committee, was the subject of many government investigations and prosecutions. In 1967, authorities sentenced Hoffa to 13 years in the federal prison at Lewisburg, Pennsylvania, for jury tampering, pension fund fraud, and conspiracy. President Richard M. Nixon later commuted Hoffa's sentence, and on December 24, 1971, Hoffa left prison. While working to unseat Frank Fitzsimmons, his successor in the union, Hoffa mysteriously disappeared on July 30, 1975. Hoffa was declared legally dead in 1983.

The IBT remains a strong and influential force in labor relations. As the union's long history of criminal investigations and convictions suggests, the IBT has indeed suffered from corruption and involvement in illegal activities. The IBT began efforts in the mid-1980s, however, to rid itself of its mafia-oriented public image, and, in 1987, the organization was readmitted to the AFL-CIO.

Further reading: Donald Barnel, *The Rise of Teamster Power in the West* (Los Angeles: University of California Press, 1972); Steven Brill, *The Teamsters* (New York: Simon & Schuster, 1978).

— Jason Reed

technology

Technological change dramatically altered American society in the years following World War II.

Throughout the conflict, advances in military and scientific technology—largely funded by the U.S. government—helped bring about the Allied victory. Many of these efforts, such as the building of the ATOMIC BOMB, the creation of the proximity fuse, and the development of radar, stemmed from research conducted on behalf of the military. At the same time, the U.S. government spent nearly $1 billion on pure scientific research. Following World War II, federal support of technological research continued. The government established the ATOMIC ENERGY COMMISSION in 1946 to fund research and development of peacetime nuclear power uses. It also instituted the National Science Foundation in 1950 to encourage basic research and education in the sciences. By 1950, with the COLD WAR heating up, spending for basic research reached $1 billion per year, only to rise further still after the outbreak of hostilities in the KOREAN WAR.

The National Science Foundation promoted improvements in science training and revision of the science curriculum in major educational institutions that contributed to technological development. Many students reaped the benefits of government-supported funding. By 1969, fully one-third of all engineering students in the country were funded by the federal government, as was the bulk of scientific research in the academy. Universities that specialized in technological study, such as the Massachusetts Institute of Technology, the California Institute of Technology, and the Rensselaer Polytechnic Institute, brought together eminent scientists and promising students in collaborative projects. Calculators, electromagnetic computers, and a host of consumer goods—along with medical technologies—were developed at universities around the country.

Along with government support, funding from big business made possible a variety of new advancements. Corporate centers of technology combined large amounts of money and some of the best scientists in the world to further the development of myriad consumer goods and other useful technologies. The DUPONT CORPORATION had introduced nylon in 1938, followed by other synthetic fabrics that replaced high-demand natural fibers, scarce during World War II. In 1943, the IBM-funded Mark I computer was developed at Harvard. Then, in 1947, scientists at Bell Laboratories invented the transistor, which made possible further advances in computer technology. GENERAL ELECTRIC developed the world's first reactor for a nuclear-powered submarine, which was launched in 1954. Consumer goods such as hair dryers and electric ovens came from General Electric's laboratories, as did new technology for the aerospace industry.

Atomic energy provides one of the best examples of dramatic technological development. On July 16, 1945, when American scientists detonated the world's first atomic bomb, the self-sustaining nuclear fission reaction that occurred represented the culmination of years of secret research and development conducted at unprecedented cost. Within weeks of initial testing, similar bombs were dropped on the Japanese cities of Hiroshima and Nagasaki, killing hundreds of thousands. A new age dawned, one in which humanity controlled the power of the atom, and thereby possessed the power to destroy itself. These developments spawned a profound change in global thinking, though the cold war's rapid escalation ensured that atomic research would proceed first and foremost with military enhancements in mind. In 1949, the SOVIET UNION detonated its own atomic device and the superpowers began their race to construct progressively more powerful and hence more lethal nuclear weaponry, particularly the HYDROGEN BOMB. By the close of the 1960s, five nations were members of the so-called nuclear club: the United States, the Soviet Union, France, the United Kingdom, and the People's Republic of China, with several others either on the cusp of—or unwilling to admit their possession of—this most troubling weapon.

Despite its military origins, nuclear fission offered peaceful applications, such as Britain's first nuclear power plant, which opened in 1956, followed a year later by an American plant. Nuclear power promised plentiful energy at extremely low cost—"too cheap to meter"—without the environmental damage produced by coal and oil. Critics of the new technology emphasized nuclear energy's unique risks, such as radioactive by-products.

The most visible manifestation of government scientific financing at work was America's space program. Here the United States lagged behind the Soviet Union throughout the 1950s. Moscow launched the world's first manmade satellite, named *Sputnik*, in October 1957. Shocked and embarrassed by their failure to be first, American officials responded by creating the NATIONAL AERONAUTICS AND SPACE ADMINISTRATION (NASA), and, with the National Defense Education Act, boosted federal funding for scientific research and SPACE EXPLORATION. NASA launched its own satellite in 1957, and the agency pledged to put a man into space. The Soviets beat the Americans again in 1961 with the flight of cosmonaut Yuri Gagarin. American Alan Shepard quickly followed Gagarin's exploit, and astronaut John Glenn became the first American to orbit the earth in 1962. President JOHN F. KENNEDY pledged that the United States would place a man on the moon by the end of the decade, and the Apollo program was born: the largest single scientific project ever mounted to date. Its eventual success helped unify the nation in a common purpose. Kennedy stated, "We choose to go to the moon in this decade and do the other things, not because they are easy, but because they are hard, because that goal will serve to organize and measure the best of our energies and skills." Numerous scientific accomplishments derived from the Apollo program, in such areas as advanced circuitry and computing, metallurgy and plastics, all of which enhanced the country's economic position through a broadening of its technological foundation.

From 1945 to 1968, Americans made great strides in less celestial forms of transportation. This was the great age of automobility and of air travel for the masses. America's AUTOMOBILE INDUSTRY led the world in both style and quality, dominated in the 1960s by GENERAL MOTORS, the FORD MOTOR CORPORATION, and Chrysler. With gasoline cheap and plentiful (and with Americans generally prosperous), these "Big Three" produced cars of unprecedented size and bulk. Large fins and huge amounts of chrome dominated American vehicles, which by the 1960s included numerous technologically advanced innovations once considered luxuries, such as power steering, power brakes, automatic transmission, and air conditioning. Given the ready availability of automobiles, especially in western cities such as Los Angeles, mass transit networks into the suburbs frequently proved negligible at best, and across the land America's once great passenger rail network shrank dramatically as ridership declined precipitously in the postwar decades. In time the harmful environmental impact of so many vehicles became impossible to ignore, and by the late 1960s emissions standards (and safety standards) were regulated by federal and state officials alike.

Americans also enjoyed great opportunities to fly in the postwar world, due to vast technological advancements in AVIATION. Less than three generations removed from the Wright Brothers' first flight, millions of Americans traveled aboard commercial airliners that spanned the country and connected the continents while the nation's military jets circled the globe. Air travel grew at a rate of more than 15 percent a year after the war, aided by the introduction of coach class in 1948. The world's first commercial jet airliner appeared in 1952, and, by 1959, both Boeing and Douglas offered airliners capable of carrying nearly 200 passengers at more than 600 miles per hour. With its promise of speed mixed with comfort in planes that flew high above turbulent weather, jet travel (and affordable fares) lured passengers to the air as never before. Not surprisingly, many aviation innovations derived from cold war–inspired military developments. Boeing's 707, for example, was designed in conjunction with a U.S. Air Force jet tanker. Military action in both the Korean War and the VIETNAM WAR spawned rapid advances in helicopter development, just as strategic concerns drove American rocketry. Funding from NASA transformed the aviation industry into the aerospace field, but prominent as space exploration was, most American aerospace firms made the bulk of their profits from the export of arms and air-travel equipment.

These new modes of transportation altered American society. Jets whisked passengers from coast to coast in just hours, but, as with interstate automobile travel, they increasingly made transit merely the task of getting from point A to point B, without ever witnessing what lay between. Passengers flew over land; they did not experience it. Drivers grew increasingly reluctant to leave the safety and ease of the interstate for less-traveled roads. Moreover, while innovations in transit made it easier to visit scattered families and friends, they also enabled families to move farther apart, altering traditional social structures.

Coupled with military-inspired advances in aerospace technology and transportation, similar developments in the nascent COMPUTER industry took place. In 1946, the ELECTRONIC NUMERICAL INTEGRATOR AND CALCULATOR (ENIAC) was first switched on. Originally designed to deliver complex calculations needed to complete artillery ballistics tables, ENIAC's electronic circuitry could complete more than 5,000 additions or subtractions or 360 multiplications of two 10-digit decimal numbers in a single second. This constituted unprecedented speed, and the machine's successors coupled such processing strength with stored programming and data storage. Beginning in the 1950s, the vacuum tubes that drove ENIAC were replaced by solid-state transistors, arguably the most important postwar development in the realm of electronics. First developed in 1947, transistors made electronic equipment more powerful, more reliable, and far smaller. A decade later integrated circuits, or "chips," were developed to guide American missiles. These components contained the equivalent of dozens or more transistors and quickly revolutionized the computer industry once again. As the complexity of chips grew, so too did the power of computers, though they remained largely the domain of government, large businesses, and universities throughout these decades.

As computers became commonplace in American business, so too did TELEVISION dominate American culture. Though technologically feasible in the 1920s, depression and war hindered television's market success until the 1950s. The number of sets soared from 1 million in 1950 to nearly 60 million in 1970.

Technological innovations in health and MEDICINE most profoundly improved the quality and length of American lives in the years after World War II. The war itself spawned development of powerful antibiotics, or MIRACLE DRUGS, including penicillin, and, soon after, the development of drugs useful for fighting a broad range of infections, such as tuberculosis. "Broad-spectrum" antibiotics followed, although bacteria quickly developed resistance to these powerful medicines, demanding continuing drug enhancements by pharmaceutical companies. This research led to vaccines against measles and rubella, and, in 1954, Jonas Salk introduced his celebrated vaccine against polio.

Humans were healthier because of these drugs, and because of other scientific advances as well. Molecular biology began in 1952, when scientists James Watson and Francis Crick discovered the double helix structure of DNA, which contained the building blocks of human life. Crick announced, "We have discovered the secret of life." Of more immediate impact for typical Americans were advances in cardiology and oncology that lengthened the average lifespan. More controversial were advancements in birth control and fertility. In 1957 oral contraceptives first became available, and more than 5 million American women took "THE PILL" by 1966.

Ultimately, technological change influenced every aspect of American life, from countless new appliances, to the innovations in medicine and transportation. By the late 1960s, every American institution, and indeed every American, had been affected by technologies developed since 1945.

Further reading: Ruth Schwartz Cowan, *A Social History of American Technology* (New York: Oxford University Press, 1996); Thomas Hughes, *Rescuing Prometheus* (New York: Random House, 1998).

— Jeffrey A. Engel and Chris Eldridge

television

In the years following World War II, television became an increasingly important medium in American lives.

Early experimentation with television began in the United States with Russian refugee Vladimir K. Zworykin, who developed an electronic television camera in 1923, playing a leading role. His efforts, combined with those of Charles Francis Jenkins, an early pioneer of motion picture projection TECHNOLOGY, led some to believe that television would replace radio in the late 1920s. But not until the mid-1930s was television first introduced to the American public on a broader scale. Some early telecasts featured SPORTS, news, and events such as the 1939 New York World's Fair, where coverage of President Franklin D. Roosevelt's opening day speech made him the first president to appear on television. But the involvement of the United States in World War II in 1941 curtailed further experimentation with television, and not until after the end of the conflict did the new medium make its greatest impact.

In the years following World War II, television became a central part of American life. As factories made the switch from war production to civilian goods, the electronics industry geared up to turn out picture tubes and television sets. Coupled with a postwar economic boom, the number of television sets in American homes increased from 1 million in 1950 to nearly 60 million in 1970, with a set found in virtually every home.

As the number of television sets grew, so too did the variety of programs offered to viewers both young and old. By 1955, the average family spent four or five hours each day watching television programming. Dramas, comedies, and variety shows such as *The Ed Sullivan Show,* which brought ELVIS PRESLEY and the BEATLES to American homes, dominated much of early broadcasting. Young Americans were treated to *The Mickey Mouse Club, Howdy Doody Time*, and *Kukla, Fran and Ollie*, while their parents watched situation comedies such as *Father Knows Best, The Adventures of Ozzie and Harriet*, and *Leave It to Beaver.* These shows were often formulaic, depicting white middle-class, suburban family life and stereotypical gender roles: a supportive wife and mother who tended to the home and children and a father who was the family breadwinner and problem solver. Few shows broke free of these gender stereotypes and fewer still reflected a culturally diverse American population.

The introduction of color television in 1953 brought a new dimension to television shows. While slow to catch on, by 1967, color replaced black and white as the standard medium.

As Americans spent more time in front of the television, advertisers capitalized on the medium to aggressively market their merchandise. Continuing a trend begun in radio, some companies sponsored entire shows, lending their name to the title as in *The Texaco Star Theatre* and *Palmolive Beauty Box Theater*, often with the show's actors pitching the company's products in commercials. The increase in television ADVERTISING coincided with a rise in mass consumption in the postwar years, and ads for all types of products flooded the

Nelson Rockefeller (left) and Barry Goldwater (right) with host Ned Brooks on the television program *Meet the Press,* 1960 *(Library of Congress)*

screen, persuading consumers that status and happiness could be bought.

While much of television programming was dominated by variety shows and situation comedies in the 1950s and 1960s, live coverage of sporting events gave many Americans their first glimpse of baseball star JACKIE ROBINSON and boxer MUHAMMAD ALI. Viewers watched the events from the comfort of their own homes and often with a better view than most stadium seats provided, as new camera technology helped with close-up shots of baseball and football games. Both college and professional sports benefited from television broadcasts, as Americans were able to tune in to their favorite teams regardless of where the game was played.

In the 1950s, television brought politics into living rooms across the country. Vice presidential candidate Richard M. Nixon used television in 1952 to reassure a wary public in what became known as the "Checkers speech"—referring to his daughter's dog, received as a campaign gift—that he had not accepted illegal campaign funds. Two years later, millions watched as Senator JOSEPH R. MCCARTHY interrogated suspected communists in the televised broadcast of the ARMY-MCCARTHY HEARINGS. His vicious behavior combined with his disheveled appearance led to a downturn in public support for his accusations. The impact of television on the political process became fully apparent with the broadcast of the 1960 presidential debates between JOHN F. KENNEDY and Nixon. Kennedy's relaxed and composed demeanor contrasted with Nixon's agitated and nervous appearance. Those who listened to the radio declared Nixon the winner, whereas television viewers chose the unruffled Kennedy as victor. Kennedy's assassination in 1963 brought the nation together as Americans gathered around television sets to mourn the loss of the young, charismatic president.

In later years, Americans watched in horror as images of the VIETNAM WAR appeared on television sets. Burning huts, screaming children, and wounded soldiers helped transform television from a source of entertainment to one of social importance, as ANTIWAR MOVEMENT protestors used the images to further their cause and decry the government's actions.

Further reading: Erik Barnouw, *Tube of Plenty: The Evolution of American Television,* 2nd rev. ed. (New York: Oxford University Press, 1990); Cecelia Tichi, *Electronic Hearth: Creating an American Television Culture* (New York: Oxford University Press, 1991).

— Susan V. Spellman

Termination policy

Starting in 1953, the federal government adopted a "termination" policy, embodied in a series of congressional res-olutions, that proposed the elimination of tribal reservations and limited government responsibility for Native American tribes.

President DWIGHT D. EISENHOWER wanted to limit the role of the federal government in national Indian policy and to promote assimilation of Native Americans fully into mainstream society. To that end, he proposed eliminating reservations as political entities and ending the policy of self-government among American Indian tribes. He endorsed a series of resolutions in which Native Americans lost their tribal status, and, with that status, education and health programs and land that had been set aside for them on reservations, mostly in the West. Eisenhower thought that by dissolving the Native Americans' tribal status, he could bring them more easily into American society and promote their assimilation into the American mainstream.

In 1953, in Congress, House Concurrent Resolution 108 terminated Native Americans as wards of the United States, granted citizenship to Native Americans, eliminated financial subsidies, discontinued the reservation system, and distributed tribal lands among individual Native Americans. The policy further subjected Native Americans to taxation and other forms of government regulation. It also ended the supervision of the Bureau of Indian Affairs—the agency responsible for administering federal policy for Native Americans—over the tribes.

As a result of Termination, the federal government redistributed Native American land in order to provide developers with greater access to those resources once owned by American Indians. Thousands of acres of reservation land became available to non-Native Americans and was soon exploited by real estate agents, oil producers, and logging agencies. Some Native American tribes fought back by protesting the loss of tribal lands while others pursued legal action to prevent the redistribution of their territory. In the late 1950s, the state of New York sought to expand its power facilities at Niagara Falls by acquiring the lands of the Tuscarora Indians. The state condemned the property, forcing the Tuscaroras off the land. The tribe sued in an effort to prevent removal and gathered support from other Iroquois tribes, traveling to Washington, D.C., to protest. Increased American Indian activity followed in the wake of termination, as many tribes mobilized opposition to the federal program.

Meanwhile, the Eisenhower administration confronted several key issues. Chief among these included the literacy of the people, the acceptance of white institutions, the ability of tribes to have a decent standard of living once dissolved, tribal consent, and the willingness of states to assume responsibility for the well-being of their Native American citizens. Ostensibly the Eisenhower administration wanted to make certain that the Native Americans were ready for such a transition, and, after the shift had occurred, to ensure that they could provide for themselves.

From 1954 to 1960, the federal government initiated a voluntary relocation program to settle employable Native Americans in urban areas. Many moved to large cities, but jobs were often unavailable and large numbers of American Indians found themselves living in poverty, unable to adjust to the changes that assimilation entailed. In June 1954, Eisenhower signed the Menominee Termination Bill, the first bill that terminated a specific Native American tribe. It cut federal ties with the tribe, making the Menominee people accept state and federal laws, something they were unaccustomed to doing. Set adrift by the federal government, by 1961, the Menominees of Wisconsin were almost totally dependent on welfare.

Native Americans were divided on the Termination policy. Most full-blooded Native Americans did not want a termination policy, feeling they were unready to assimilate into American society and believing they were different from the average American. Reliant on government support, they were frightened of losing programs and land. On the other hand, nontraditional Native Americans, the ones who had already accepted American mainstream culture, supported the policy because they believed it would help them to improve their opportunities. Also, disliking federal officials directing their lives, they welcomed the greater individual freedom that the Termination policy meant to provide.

As Native Americans became increasingly embroiled in the controversy over the termination policy, they adopted a more activist approach. Throughout the 1960s, American Indians began to assert themselves even more, becoming increasingly vocal in demanding their rights. The policy also helped foster a sense of Native American identity, as tribes banded together to encourage awareness of the problems American Indians faced in an era of Termination. In addition, it sparked a consciousness among whites of Native Americans' right to maintain their heritage.

In the end, the Termination policy proved largely unsuccessful, as most Native Americans found it difficult to blend into American society. Moving to cities such as Minneapolis and Los Angeles, they had trouble finding or holding the jobs given to them through the relocation programs. The Termination policy was abandoned in the mid-1960s during the presidential administration of LYNDON B. JOHNSON, who referred to Native Americans as "the Forgotten Americans" in his GREAT SOCIETY. Johnson demanded a new policy of self-determination to allow Native Americans to decide their own destinies. The Indian Civil Rights Act of 1968 gave Native Americans the right to tribal governments, tribal courts, and Native American consent, limiting the ability of the states to extend their jurisdiction over Native American lands.

Further reading: Donald L. Fixico, *Termination and Relocation: Federal Indian Policy, 1954–1960* (Albuquerque: University of New Mexico Press, 1986); Kenneth R. Philip, *Termination Revisited: Americans on the Trail of Self-Determination, 1933–1953* (Lincoln: University of Nebraska Press, 1999).

—Megan D. Wessel

Tijerina, Reies López ("El Tigre") (1926–   )

Reies López Tijerina was an influential radical Chicano leader in the 1960s.

Born in Falls City, Texas, on September 21, 1926, Tijerina came from a large and poor Tejano sharecropper family. At the age of 18 he enrolled in the Assembly of God Bible Institute at Ysleta, Texas. He left the institute after three years without a degree and began to gain a following while preaching along the Texas–Mexico border.

During the late 1950s Tijerina became interested in the history of Mexican and Spanish land grants in the Southwest. He soon came to believe that many of the hardships that Mexicans Americans faced were due to the loss of these lands. Tijerina promoted aggressive actions to obtain redress. He and his supporters tried to petition the Mexican government. In New Mexico in 1963, he organized the Alianza Federal de Mercedes (Federal Alliance of Land Grants). Using his famously fiery rhetoric, he stressed the economic, political, educational, and cultural rights of Hispanic Americans.

At its height, the Alianza claimed 20,000 members. They occupied part of Kit Carson National Forest in 1966 and proclaimed it the Republic of San Joaquin del Río Chama. The next year, several Alianza members were arrested and taken to the Tierra Amarilla courthouse. Other Alianza members attempted a dramatic raid on the courthouse to free the prisoners and make a citizen's arrest of Alfonso Sánchez, the district attorney. During the raid two lawmen were wounded and a massive manhunt was launched in New Mexico's mountains for Tijerina and his followers. He was captured and charged with several offenses stemming from the raid. The incident turned him into a front-page news personality, and, while free on bail, Tijerina began to nationalize his message.

He played a leading role in the Poor People's March on Washington, D. C., and became a popular speaker on the college and university lecture circuit promoting Alianza's aims. Although acquitted of some charges, convictions for other charges stemming from both the Carson National Forest and Tierra Amarilla incidents were upheld and he began to serve his sentences. At the end of July 1971, he was released on parole under the condition that he hold no position in Alianza. Due to the absence of its leader and then his inability to resume leadership, Alianza become less organized and influential. Tijerina began to stress cooperation rather than confrontation. In the later half of the 1970s he resumed leadership of Alianza, but he focused mostly on attempting to interest two presidents of Mexico in the land grants issue. No results came from these petitions.

Further reading: Patricia B. Blawis, *Tijerina and the Land Grants: Mexican-Americans in Struggle for Their Heritage* (New York: International Publishers, 1970).

— Kerry Webb

Title VII See Civil Rights Act of 1964

Truman, Harry S. (1884–1972)

Harry Truman was a Missouri politician who succeeded Franklin D. Roosevelt as president in 1945 and presided over the start of the COLD WAR.

Truman was born in Lamar, a small farming village in Missouri, on May 8, 1884, but he later settled in Independence, Missouri, in 1890, where he completed high school. Truman then worked for several years as a farmer, until entering the U.S. Army in 1917. He was appointed an officer in the 129th Field Artillery regiment, and he was shipped to EUROPE to fight in World War I. He returned from Europe in 1919. After Truman's haberdashery business failed in 1922, he turned to politics. With the endorsement of the local DEMOCRATIC PARTY, Truman was elected an administrative judge on the Jackson County Court.

In 1934, Truman was elected to the U.S. Senate. Reelected to a second term in 1940, he persuaded the Senate to establish a special committee with him as chair to investigate waste in defense contracts. The committee proved to be successful and gained Truman considerable national exposure.

In 1944, Roosevelt accepted the recommendation of party leaders who suggested Truman for the vice presidency. Three months into his fourth term, Roosevelt died, and Truman became president of the United States.

With World War II raging, Truman stepped in as the new commander in chief. As testing on the ATOMIC BOMB took place, Truman attended the Big Three Conference in Potsdam, where the SOVIET UNION, Great Britain, and the United States discussed the terms of Germany's surrender in World War II. Once the war in Europe was over, the United States and its allies were eager to end the war against Japan. On August 6, 1945, the first of two atomic bombs was dropped on Hiroshima, Japan; the second fell on August 9, 1945, on Nagasaki. The United States thus became the first and only country to use a nuclear bomb on another country. Though Truman received criticism in later years for his use of the bomb, he defended his decision on the grounds that it saved American lives.

Truman's second major decision involved the shift he initiated in U.S. foreign policy. Ignoring the advice of

Harry S. Truman and Winston Churchill, 1952
(Library of Congress)

George Washington to stay out of world affairs, he believed that it was necessary to stand up to the Soviet Union in what were the fledgling years of the cold war. To that end, the TRUMAN DOCTRINE promised U.S. support to countries threatened by COMMUNISM. The MARSHALL PLAN soon followed, giving economic aid to struggling Western European nations. The establishment of the NORTH ATLANTIC TREATY ORGANIZATION (NATO) assured military assistance to the 12 signatory countries on the grounds that an attack against one would be considered an attack on all.

Truman's presidency was not without crisis. Between June and September 1948, Soviet forces established a land blockade of western sectors of Berlin, Germany, which were occupied by the British, French and Americans. A massive airlift became necessary in order to supply the three zones. On May 15, 1948, the state of ISRAEL was established, and Truman immediately recognized the new nation, even though Arab armies converged on Israel almost immediately. The United States, however, remained neutral during the first of these Arab-Israeli wars. On June 15, 1950, North Korean troops invaded South Korea. The United States, with the backing of the United Nations (UN), sent immediate military aid to South Korea. Because war was never declared on North Korea, Truman considered the conflict a "police action."

At home, Truman worked on three major issues: administration of the modern American presidency, a legislative program known as the FAIR DEAL, and issues of communism within the government. Truman expanded the executive office of the president, as new advisers were needed on matters of national defense and foreign policy. The NATIONAL SECURITY ACT OF 1947 and its amendments helped the president create the National Security Council, the Department of Defense, and the CENTRAL INTELLI-GENCE AGENCY (CIA). He also brought the growing federal bureaucracy under control by improving White House organization, placing more control in the hands of cabinet members and their departments, and entrusting them to do the bidding of the administration. The Fair Deal included both economic and social legislation, and it produced one significant triumph: it brought the issue of civil rights to the forefront of public issues. Even though none of his proposals regarding civil rights were enacted, Truman raised the issue before the public. In 1947, Truman established the FEDERAL EMPLOYEE LOYALTY PROGRAM for the sole purpose of eliminating suspected communists from government positions. This was a result of the pressures from Republicans that the president had made little effort to remove communists from government departments.

Early in 1952, Truman announced that he would not run for another term, though he could have done so had he wished. Truman left the office at the age of 68 with very low public regard. He lived for another 23 years after his presidency, advising all succeeding presidents until his death on December 26, 1972.

Further reading: Alonzo L. Hamby, *Man of the People: A Life of Harry S. Truman* (New York: Oxford University Press, 1995); Donald R. McCoy, *The Presidency of Harry S. Truman* (Lawrence: University Press of Kansas, 1984); David McCullough, *Truman* (New York: Simon & Schuster, 1992).

— Robert A. Deahl

Truman Doctrine

The Truman Doctrine established a policy of American support to countries fighting COMMUNISM, highlighting anticommunist fears throughout the United States.

The measure was first articulated by President HARRY S. TRUMAN in a message to Congress on March 12, 1947. In a speech designed to secure U.S. aid to Greece and Turkey, Truman embraced a policy of containment that would guide American foreign policy throughout the COLD WAR conflict with the SOVIET UNION.

At the end of World War II, the United States emerged as the sole, true superpower in a fragile global community. Despite its economic and military dominance, many Americans were fearful of the political repercussions posed by the potential spread of communism. By 1947, the Soviet Union had tightened its grip on Eastern Europe and the relationship between the United States and its former wartime ally had deteriorated considerably. Apprehension within the Truman administration was further heightened by the failure of Western Europe to recover economically after the war. One of the greatest fears of U.S. policymak-

ers was realized in 1947 as Great Britain, its empire dying and its own economy in shambles, chose to withdraw from Greece, leaving that country open to civil war. Meanwhile, Josip Tito, the communist leader of Yugoslavia, sent aid to communist insurgents in Greece. Turkey's political situation was also unstable following the suspension of British aid and, due to its access to the Mediterranean, it seemed a likely target of Soviet aggression. A communist takeover of both countries appeared imminent if the United States did not fill the political power vacuum.

Following his message before a special session of Congress, Truman succeeded in gaining $400 million to assist the governments of both Greece and Turkey in resisting communist forces. The subsequent flow of aid and military advisers soon stabilized the situation in both countries. Truman went much further, however, and promised aid to any country fighting communists. According to the Truman Doctrine, the United States would "support free peoples who are resisting attempted subjugation by armed minorities or by outside pressures." In the developing bipolar world, the United States sought to stop the spread of communism rather than challenge the Soviet Union directly. The Truman Doctrine constituted the rhetorical component of America's anticommunist foreign policy structure, the MARSHALL PLAN served as its economic embodiment, and the NORTH ATLANTIC TREATY ORGANIZATION (NATO) formed its political and military framework.

Truman's foreign policy was driven by several ideological assumptions. American officials believed that the countries of EUROPE were so weak, and their people so desperate that, without assistance from the United States, citizens in those war-ravaged nations might turn to communism even without Soviet interference. Policymakers also believed that they understood the nature of both the communist and the Soviet systems. Communism was inherently evil, and thus a fundamental and necessary choice existed between democracy and communism. According to this vision, Joseph Stalin, the Soviet leader, was completely committed to Marxist-Leninist doctrine and thus bent on world domination and never to be trusted. American leaders also assumed that all American interests were global interests. American prosperity could not be insured unless the Soviets were prevented from controlling raw materials—and American prosperity was necessary to bring peace and order to the globe.

Such global thinking led policymakers to ignore specific issues and groups in favor of fitting various conflicts into a general ideological framework. For example, despite Truman's rhetoric, the governments in neither Greece nor Turkey were democratic and, as critics pointed out, the latter had even been pro-Hitler. The Truman Doctrine also influenced America's domestic life. Motivated in part by a fear that the country would become a garrison state if it was eventually surrounded by communist nations, the United States amassed a large peacetime military force for the first time in its history. Also, in March 1947, Truman initiated the FEDERAL EMPLOYEE LOYALTY PROGRAM, under which individuals could be dismissed for their political beliefs. In order to create popular support for his assistance programs, Truman worked tirelessly to instill a fear of communism in the American citizenry.

The Truman Doctrine marked the first step in America's massive postwar military build-up. In 1949 ANTICOMMUNISM grew in intensity as the Soviets tested their first atomic bomb and Mao Zedong declared a communist government in China. Following the outbreak of the KOREAN WAR in 1950, the defense budget grew even larger.

The impact of the Truman Doctrine was indeed far-reaching, setting the tone for the cold war, establishing a model for America's new proactive role in world affairs, and serving as a rationale for later American involvement in foreign countries, including Korea and Vietnam.

Further reading: Melvyn P. Leffler, *The Specter of Communism: The United States and the Origins of the Cold War, 1917–1953* (New York: Hill & Wang, 1994).

— Douglas G. Weaver

U

union movement

The American labor union movement came to maturity in the years after World War II, bringing with it material success and stability, but also compromising many of the ideals of its youth.

In some ways the war years were good for unions. Membership rose by over 4 million to include a total of 14,322,000 Americans, over 35 percent of the nation's nonagricultural workforce. Feeling that the war had been even kinder to factory owners, unions flexed their muscles substantially at its conclusion. Almost 13 million workers went on strike at some point in the 18 months after the war's end. The situation appeared so grave to President HARRY S. TRUMAN that he ordered government seizure of several facilities affected by strikes and contemplated drafting striking railway workers into the military.

Fear of these strikes provided support for the Republican-controlled Eightieth Congress to pass the TAFT-HART-LEY ACT, over Truman's veto, in 1947. Where the NEW DEAL had put the federal government on the side of helping organize labor, Taft-Hartley erected governmental obstacles to union activity. Sympathy strikes were banned and states were allowed to prohibit the practice of closed shops, where an employee had to join a union before getting a job. Most damaging of all, the president was given power to delay strikes for an 80 day "cooling off" period.

After these initial postwar confrontations, the union movement settled into the mainstream of American society. Control of unions fell to moderate elements, as radicals were driven out in purges facilitated by the strong wave of ANTICOMMUNISM sweeping the country. Strikes declined and union leaders became almost indistinguishable from the managers with whom they negotiated. National union officials retained control over locals by setting rules, insuring that power flowed from the top down. Unions evolved into greater bureaucracies and became more centralized. The 1955 merger of the two largest unions, the AMERICAN FEDERATION OF LABOR (AFL) and the CONGRESS OF INDUS-TRIAL ORGANIZATIONS (CIO), provides the best example of this. "Tuxedo Unionism," as it was termed by disgruntled steelworkers, meant more cooperation between unions and management and less input from the union rank and file.

Even worse for the perception of unions by their members and the public, corruption among top union officials increasingly came to light in the late 1950s. TEAMSTERS UNION president David Beck went to prison for stealing union funds. The ensuing congressional investigation of the Teamsters uncovered connections to organized crime, which led to the union's expulsion from the AFL-CIO. Hollywood helped spread the perception of corrupt unions in the film *On the Waterfront,* which depicted an ex-prize fighter's struggle against union corruption along the New York waterfront. Congress tried to address union corruption with the Landrum-Griffin Act, which gave the federal government power to oversee internal union affairs to assure democracy for rank-and-file members. It also made it a federal crime to misuse union funds. The Teamsters had difficulty adjusting to this government oversight as Beck's successor, Jimmy Hoffa, also ended up in prison, thanks to aggressive prosecution by Attorney General ROBERT F. KENNEDY.

While some union members expressed outrage at their leadership's corruption and distance from the rank and file, most did not chiefly because union members could see tangible improvements in their standard of living and working conditions. Wages increased and benefit packages offering health care and paid vacations became more commonplace, even in industries that did not have significant levels of unionization. With fewer bread-and-butter issues to contest and less power within unions, active rank-and-file participation in unions declined.

Although membership rose most years, the percentage of the American labor force involved with unions declined steadily through the 1950s and 1960s. This drop resulted not only from the apathy or contentment of industrial workers but also from important changes that occurred in the ECONOMY. Manufacturing jobs were increasingly locating in the southern sunbelt states, which were historically hostile to union activity. Moreover, structural changes in the economy were diminishing the share of the LABOR force involved in sectors such as manufacturing and mining where union activity was heavily concentrated.

Established unions were initially slow to respond to these changes, but by the 1960s they had begun to come around. In 1965, the AFL-CIO recognized the UNITED FARM WORKERS, organized by CÉSAR CHÁVEZ. At the other end of the occupational spectrum, white collar unions such as the American Federation of State, County, and Municipal Employees were getting started by the late 1960s, although most private-sector white-collar employees rejected unionization.

As the union movement looked to the 1970s, it faced several challenges. Not only did it need to counter increasing public perception that it was corrupt and unresponsive it also needed to reinvigorate its rank and file. Most important, it needed to find ways to make its existence relevant to workers in a rapidly changing American economy that no longer rested on manufacturing.

Further reading: Robert H. Zieger, *American Workers, American Unions, 1920–1985* (Baltimore: The Johns Hopkins University Press, 1986).

— Dave Price

United Farm Workers (UFW)

Committed to nonviolent action for social justice and to the labor movement, the United Farm Workers sought to organize Mexican American farm workers to attain better living and working conditions.

The United Farm Workers originated in Delano, California, where César Chávez and Dolores Huerta founded the National Farm Workers Association (NFWA) in 1962. Chávez and Huerta knew intimately the difficulties facing farmworkers. Chávez had worked in the fields as a child, traveling with his family across central and northern California to pick grapes, berries, nuts, and vegetables. Huerta's father was a migrant farmworker and union activist. She had worked to improve the conditions of migrants through a community interest group during the late 1950s.

Farmworkers labored long hours for wages far below the poverty line, lived in overcrowded makeshift housing, and often lacked access to toilets, running water, refrigeration, and preventative medicine. Many children of farmworkers left school after only three or four years because migration disrupted their studies. To help support their impoverished families, children went to work in the fields, where the average life expectancy among workers was only

49 years. Labor contractors and growers relied upon workers' fears of unemployment, blacklisting, and, in the case of Mexican immigrants, deportation to stifle protest. Ethnic and racial tensions among Mexican American, Mexican, Filipino, black, and Anglo workers also made organizing difficult. Nor did farmworkers enjoy legal protection. The 1935 National Labor Relations Act (NLRA) did not cover agricultural workers. Local courts often sided with growers, limiting farmworkers' basic rights to picket, strike, boycott, and exercise freedom of speech.

Chávez and Huerta's cross-cultural grass-roots organizing emboldened Delano farmworkers and broke down some of the ethnic and racial barriers dividing them. After area growers refused a wage increase, the predominantly Mexican and Mexican American NFWA joined striking Filipino workers in a walkout in 1965. Many growers fought back aggressively with tactics that included employment of strikebreakers, police harassment of union leaders, charges of communist infiltration of the NFWA, and legal injunctions against picketers. The response of the NFWA catapulted the farmworkers' struggle to national prominence, ending the isolation that was one of the strike's greatest weaknesses. Chávez enlisted the support of university students, church leaders, trade unionists, and civil rights activists, who spread news of the farmworkers' struggle far beyond rural California. The union also launched a series of consumer boycotts against major grape producers, and stores selling nonunion grapes. Chávez's commitment to nonviolence and the emphasis he placed on human rights appealed to those sympathetic to the southern black CIVIL RIGHTS MOVEMENT. In 1966, a number of grape growers capitulated, and the NFWA merged with another agricultural organization to become the United Farm Workers.

The struggle continued. The union's focus on growers' use of pesticides helped to inspire an alliance with environmental activists. In the spring of 1967, Chávez led a march of strikers and their supporters on a 300-mile pilgrimage from Delano to Sacramento. The march vividly dramatized the fact that the issues animating the strikers involved not only labor rights but also the civil rights of Mexican Americans. Its major purpose was to battle the fear of Mexican American farmworkers, who, like southern blacks, had long experienced racial SEGREGATION, discrimination, slurs, and violence. With banners bearing portraits of the Virgin of Guadalupe—the patron saint of Mexico—and "Huelga"—the Spanish word for "strike"—marchers cut a path across the racial boundaries of the San Joaquin Valley, attracting thousands of farmworkers along the way.

Five years after the strike had begun, Delano's major nonunion growers signed a contract with the NFWA in July 1970. In 1971, the UFW affiliated with the AFL-CIO. But the union's troubles were far from over. With no input from their workers, powerful growers in the Salinas, San Joaquin, and Imperial Valleys signed "sweetheart" contracts with the TEAMSTERS UNION that allowed growers control in the fields. Between 1970 and 1974, farmworkers led by the UFW walked off the fields in protest. These strikes were marked by Teamster-sponsored violence against picketers and thousands of arrests, mostly of strikers on flimsy charges. While Huerta's forceful negotiating skills secured a favorable contract with a subsidiary of the mammoth United Fruit Corporation, the UFW otherwise struggled to survive.

As a result of pressure from the UFW, its supporters, and those growers who now sought economic stability, California passed the 1975 Agricultural Labor Relations Act (ALRA), the first law to recognize the right of farmworkers to bargain collectively. The UFW won handily over the Teamsters in most union elections throughout the 1970s and the organization surpassed 100,000 members in 1980. The union, however, faced major challenges in the following decades. The board established to enforce the ALRA lacked effectiveness due to insufficiency of funds. Conservative political forces swept the state, bitterly attacking the UNION MOVEMENT. Finally, undocumented workers, whose fear of deportation made unionization difficult, came to make up an increasingly large number of farmworkers. Still, the UFW had managed to push the agricultural industry to end many of its most egregious practices and succeeded in substantially raising the wages of its workers.

Further reading: Susan Ferris and Ricardo Sandoval, *The Fight in the Fields: César Chávez and the Farmworkers Movement* (New York: Harcourt Brace, 1997); J. Craig Jenkins, *The Politics of Insurgency: The Farm Worker Movement and the Politics of the 1960's* (New York: Columbia University Press, 1985).

— Theresa Ann Case

Urban League

Created in 1910 as a voluntary-service agency, the Urban League constituted one of the major civil rights organizations in the United States and became known as the social service agency of African Americans.

Headquartered in New York City, the Urban League brought together black and white members in an effort to promote economic self-reliance, equality, and civil rights for all African Americans. Working as a nonprofit, nonpartisan, community-based movement, the Urban League targeted education, employment, and economic stability as the main avenues to secure equal participation in mainstream society for all black Americans. With offices at the local, state, and national level, the Urban League used a variety of programs, including advocacy, policy analysis, and community mobilization, to carry out its mission.

To help further its goals, the Urban League relied on scientific social work, civil rights techniques, and pressure group tactics to open various employment and educational opportunities that had been closed to African Americans. With a majority of its members living in the northern and western states, the Urban League focused the greatest part of its efforts on the North and West.

In the years following World War II, African Americans feared a loss of economic and social gains made during the conflict. The unemployment rates among African Americans in the cities, always high, began to rise in the postwar years, and many African American veterans were unable to find work. Concerned about the threat of urban racial violence amid job discrimination, the Urban League—led by Lester Granger, a league veteran and prominent newspaper columnist—prodded the federal government to take a more active role in helping blacks achieve equality.

Driven by a desire to protect and expand job opportunities for black Americans, the Urban League sought the establishment of a permanent FAIR EMPLOYMENT PRACTICES COMMITTEE, which might guarantee that African Americans could share in policymaking and program planning while promoting unemployment insurance for domestic and agricultural workers. It also pushed for the integration of unions, using its own Industrial Relations Laboratory to secure fair employment opportunities for all black American workers. In 1948, in part because of Urban League lobbying, President HARRY S. TRUMAN banned employment discrimination in federal government agencies. In addition, efforts made by the Urban League during the war, such as the establishment of a black youth training program designed to provide young workers with the skills required to obtain blue-collar jobs, expanded in the postwar years in the form of career conferences held on the campuses of traditionally African American colleges to encourage employment in white-collar positions.

The Urban League advocated change in other areas as well. In 1952, the group created the Office of Housing Activities to deal with discriminatory housing practices. Having long supported the removal of racially restrictive covenants from all federally assisted housing, the Urban League now acted to stop racially discriminatory company-built housing. The Urban League lobbied intensively both U.S. Steel and the Levittown Corporation, companies that barred black residents from living in their housing developments.

By the late 1950s, the Urban League began to suffer from internal divisions. Its critics argued that the group had done little more than assist urban black Americans in acquiring low-skill, low-paying jobs and housing in traditionally black neighborhoods. Granger came under increasingly heavy attack by more militant members of the organization, who called for more aggressive action, much like that of other civil rights organizations of the period. Granger, however, remained focused on achieving African American self-reliance by working through social programs, insisting that the emphasis of the Urban League remained that of getting people to work and not of engaging in violent protest.

Concerned with alienating white policymakers and supporters of the Urban League, Granger limited the organization's involvement in direct action and nonviolent protest. As a result, other civil rights groups became more important to many African Americans than the Urban League. The image of the organization began to change when Whitney M. Young replaced Lester Granger as president in 1961. Chosen because of his more aggressive style of leadership, Young led the league to become an active partner with other civil rights organizations.

Support for the Urban League grew under the direction of Young due in large part to the development of its 1964 Voter Education Project. Using a grass-roots approach, league members were effective in educating and motivating black Americans to register and vote. Meanwhile, Young shifted the group's focus from its long-held goal of promoting equality of opportunity to eradicating the gap between the economic and social opportunities available to black and white citizens. In an effort to bring democracy and hope to poor, urban areas, the group supported the establishment of economic institutions by helping to develop African American-owned businesses, cooperatives, consumer unions, and franchises.

In later years, the Urban League expanded its social service efforts and supported new housing, health care, and education initiatives. Additional emphasis was placed on reducing teen pregnancy and combating crime in African American communities.

Further reading: Jesse Thomas Moore, *A Search for Equality: The National Urban League, 1910–1961* (University Park: Pennsylvania State University Press, 1981); Nancy J. Weiss, *The National Urban League, 1910–1940* (New York: Oxford University Press, 1974).

— Caryn Neumann

V

veterans

The transition between military and civilian life became increasingly difficult for veterans in the years following World War II.

The United States was involved in three major military conflicts in the period between 1940 and 1970—World War II, the KOREAN WAR and the VIETNAM WAR. Over time, the veterans of these conflicts found it increasingly difficult to assimilate back into civilian life. Significantly, this problem occurred not because the nation's citizens felt less respect for the men and women in military service or less appreciation for their service to the country. Rather, many veterans of the Vietnam War felt disconnected because they had participated in a conflict that fewer Americans agreed with.

The more than 16 million veterans of World War II enjoyed the highest level of American support and had the greatest success in reentering civilian life. Americans saw these veterans as fighting an evil enemy, and since the war took nearly four years and involved nearly 1.1 million casualties, the country treated World War II veterans as heroes. One example of this support was the G.I. Bill, passed by Congress in 1944 as a way to say "thank-you" to these veterans. Immediately dubbed the "GI Bill of Rights," this law constituted an important part of the effort to reintegrate military personnel into the civilian economy, since it established a wide array of medical, financial, and educational programs exclusively for veterans. It was also symbolic of the pride, respect, and appreciation the country felt for its servicemen and women.

The veterans of the Korean War, unlike World War II, were part of a broader United Nations military force. Their mission was to prevent the spread of COMMUNISM from North Korea into South Korea, which failed to provide the glory that defeating the Nazis brought. Additionally, fewer than 6 million men and women were in uniform during the war and total casualties were less than 150,000. The participation of American soldiers did not command as much

media attention compared to World War II. Finally, there was less tangible proof that the war was a success, since North Korea remained communist and the final two years of the conflict were mired in a slow peace process during which soldiers continued to die. Called by some "the Forgotten War," Americans did not give Korean veterans the same enthusiastic reception bestowed upon earlier veterans. Congress did, however, extend the benefits of the G.I. Bill to include Korean veterans, and, given the growing American economy, these men and women were able to assimilate with relative ease back into civilian life.

Unlike World War II, the Vietnam conflict, the longest military engagement in American history, proved problematical for many of the soldiers involved. An undeclared war, the main objective was to prevent the spread of communism from North Vietnam to South Vietnam. More than 8.7 million men and women served in the conflict, but, unlike earlier wars, they were young soldiers with an average age of just 19; by comparison, the average World War II soldier was 26. Also, because the draft deferred college students, many of those who fought in Vietnam came from the working class, and they were disproportionately African American and Latino. The Vietnam War was the most divisive conflict in American history, characterized by massive protests, social division, and contentious debate. Because many Americans did not feel that it was a war the United States should be involved in, the men and women who served in the war were denied the respect earned by combat veterans of previous wars. While they still received many of the same government benefits given to earlier veterans, their assimilation back into civilian life was far more difficult. As many as 40 percent of all Vietnam veterans developed drug dependencies or symptoms of post-traumatic stress disorder. Possibly the most revealing symbol of how difficult dealing with this war was for America and its veterans was the Vietnam War Memorial on the Mall in Washington, D.C. The series of black granite plaques containing the names of more than 58,000 soldiers who died in the conflict finally provided a way for the nation to treat those who made the ultimate sacrifice with respect.

Further reading: Jon Halliday and Bruce Cumings, *Korea: The Unknown War* (London: Viking, 1988); Richard Moser, *The New Winter Soldiers: GI and Veteran Dissent during the Vietnam Era* (New Brunswick, N.J.: Rutgers University Press, 1996); Gerald F. Linderman, *The World within War: America's Combat Experience in World War II* (New York: Free Press, 1997).

— Dave Mason

Vietnam War

America's COLD WAR against COMMUNISM led to its longest war, the controversial failure in Vietnam.

In 1945, war broke out when Vietnam declared independence from France, which had colonized the region since the mid-1800s. Battling nationalist forces, French troops continued to fight in Vietnam until 1954, when France's domestic support for the war wavered after a devastating defeat at Dien Bien Phu. Plans to allow France a peaceful withdrawal from the country took shape, and from May 8 through July 21, 1954, representatives from eight nations, including the United States, Vietnam, and France, met in Geneva, Switzerland. The agreement they drafted, known as the Geneva Accords, temporarily divided Vietnam at the 17th parallel so that both France and Vietnam had an opportunity to stand back and allow Vietnamese soldiers to return to their native regions. The nationalist (and communist) leader Ho Chi Minh retained control of North Vietnam, while the Emperor Bao Dai ruled South Vietnam. The United States refused to sign the agreement, fearing the possibility of a communist takeover of Vietnam, and instead chose to support the South Vietnamese government, soon replacing Bao Dai with Ngo Dinh Diem. Diem was a Vietnamese leader living in exile in the United States who returned to take charge. He refused to participate in the national elections called for by the Geneva Accords out of fear that the communists would prevail, and he instead declared South Vietnam's independence, a move that many communist forces saw as an attempt by the United States to interfere with the national independence that the Geneva Accords had pledged.

Throughout the 1950s, the southern government of Ngo Dinh Diem and its army (ARVN) received extensive American economic and advisory aid. The ARVN fought the National Liberation Front (NLF), a revolt within South Vietnam, along with its military arm—the Viet Cong—and received substantial aid from Hanoi, North Vietnam's capital. Democrat JOHN F. KENNEDY, elected president in 1960, took the advice of Secretary of Defense Robert S. McNamara, and he quietly increased troops in Vietnam until there were more than 9,000 in 1962.

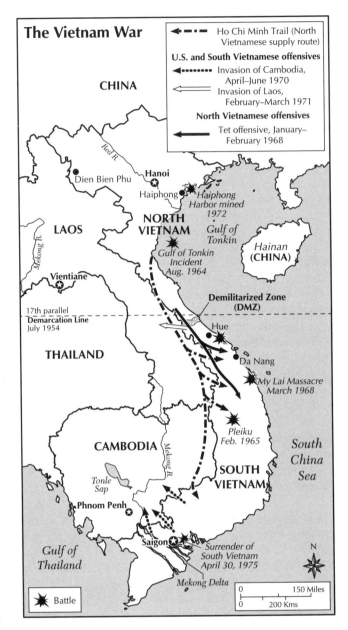

The unpopularity of Diem became obvious in June 1963, when Buddhist monks set themselves on fire in downtown Saigon, South Vietnam's capital, to protest his regime. The authoritarian Diem, a Catholic, had imposed severe restrictions on the Buddhist faith. A coup by military officers that killed Diem in October 1963 had the approval of American officials, though Kennedy was troubled by the murder. The new American president, LYNDON B. JOHNSON, took office after Kennedy's assassination, and he inherited a conflict that escalated into a full-scale war. In August 1964, open fighting between Americans and North Vietnamese in the Gulf of Tonkin led to a congressional resolution to "prevent further aggression" by North Vietnam, not merely to protect South Vietnam. China's nuclear explosion in October 1964 made American leaders more determined to subdue communism, even as NLF forces began direct attacks on American bases. By 1965, U.S. troops in Vietnam numbered 23,300, and, early that year, American planes began air strikes, using napalm, a jelly-like burning substance, on both people and land. In March, American troops entered the ground war. Nguyen Van Thieu took control of South Vietnam's government, and, by July, Johnson promised him open-ended aid against North Vietnam.

American troops heading for Vietnam in the early years of the war were composed mainly of volunteers in air force, navy, and marine combat units. But by 1965, increasing numbers of soldiers were needed to fight, and the U.S. government reinstated the draft. In the beginning, approximately 20,000 men per month were drafted. By 1968, the number of men drafted had escalated to almost 40,000 per month, with the majority young men—the average age was 19—from lower economic classes. Many found themselves in army combat units, which had high casualty rates. Unable to take advantage of the exemptions that many white middle- and upper-class citizens claimed, especially those who possessed the financial means to attend college, a disproportionately large number of draftees were African American and Latino.

Johnson, like Kennedy, intensified the action through a pliant Congress, and decided on policies and chose bombing targets without clear goals, all the while misleading the American public. TELEVISION broadcast scenes from the jungle war, and an ANTIWAR MOVEMENT grew on

U.S. helicopters airlift soldiers into battle against Viet Cong guerrillas, Quang Tri, 1965   *(United States Army)*

American college campuses. America's allies also called for restraint. American leaders, believing that military might would quickly destroy the enemy, relied on artillery and bombs. These means had little effect on Vietnamese guerrillas expert at escaping notice and enlisting popular support, who fought from an extensive underground tunnel system. By 1967, despite the presence of nearly 500,000 American soldiers, the use of more bombs than in World War II, and the expenditure by the United States of $2 million a month, the Communists, with aid from China and the Soviet Union, refused to capitulate. That year, some 2,800 Vietnamese died each month, many of them women and children. High body counts persuaded American military leaders that they were winning, but they were mistaken. By summer, more than 13,000 Americans had died in Vietnam.

Meanwhile, South Vietnam suffered runaway inflation, Americanization by consumer goods, and boom-time corruption. In America, antiwar feeling spread, joining social, racial, and cultural unrest. Popular protest flared often; even some government officials wanted to scale the war down.

Tensions came to a head during Tet, the Vietnamese New Year, on January 30, 1968. The NLF launched a major offensive in the cities, timed to occur as festivities began. While the NLF failed to hold any important positions, the Tet Offensive shocked Americans and brought to a boil questions about the war that had long been simmering. On March 31, Johnson announced both his willingness to negotiate peace and his decision not to run for president in 1968.

North Vietnam agreed to talks, but both sides continued to fight while negotiating. Republican Richard M. Nixon, elected president in 1968, listened to Henry Kissinger, his national security adviser, and tried to achieve a "peace with honor" that would keep South Vietnam independent. The effort produced massive secret U.S. bombing of neutral Cambodia to cut off sanctuaries from which, Nixon argued, the North Vietnamese were launching attacks. When Nixon sent in troops in April 1970, many American campuses erupted, and innocent students were killed by National Guardsmen in demonstrations at Kent State University in Ohio and Jackson State University in Mississippi. Congress tried to end funding, and Nixon withdrew some troops in a policy he called Vietnamization.

The two sides agreed to the Paris Peace Accords in January 1973, after more than 58,000 American and more than a million Vietnamese deaths. But Nixon's settlement provided neither peace nor honor. North and South Vietnam continued to fight. Watergate forced Nixon's resignation in 1974, and American support for the war melted away. Saigon fell to the North on May 1, 1975, and remaining Americans withdrew in chaos. More than 1.5 million

refugees from Southeast ASIA followed them in the next few years. Popular support helped Hanoi win the war and unify the country on its own terms. Protest at home helped reverse American foreign policy and eventually brought the conflict, which had lasted a quarter century, to an end.

Further reading: Philip Caputo, *A Rumor of War* (New York: Holt, Rinehart & Winston, 1977); George C. Herring, *America's Longest War: The U.S. and Vietnam, 1950–1975,* 3d ed. (New York: Knopf, 1996).

— Barbara M. Hahn

Volunteers in Service to America (VISTA)

Created in 1964 as part of LYNDON B. JOHNSON'S GREAT SOCIETY, Volunteers in Service to America (VISTA) was a program that recruited, trained, and placed full-time volunteers with nonprofit and public organizations that serviced low-income communities.

Whereas VISTA began under the presidency of Johnson, its roots lay in the administration of JOHN F. KENNEDY. Before the early 1960s, most Americans were not aware of poverty in the United States. Through media attention and books such as MICHAEL HARRINGTON's *The Other America,* awareness of poverty in the United States became increasingly evident. As a result of this visibility, in 1962, Kennedy established a study group, headed by Attorney General ROBERT F. KENNEDY, to explore the idea of creating a domestic service program whose volunteers would work in low-income communities. The committee proposed the establishment of a National Service Corps (NSC). State legislatures had several goals for the NSC. By utilizing full-time volunteers, the NSC would be able to reach those in greatest need of services. Legislatures hoped that the work and visibility of the volunteers would aid in garnering support from both the private and the public sector, promote further volunteerism by other community members, and encourage people to work in fields that provided social services.

In May 1963, hearings began in Congress on the NSC bill. Concerns over political agitation, integration, and leadership, however, prevented the legislation from moving successfully through Congress.

Seven months after Congress defeated the NSC bill, it was reformed and renamed VISTA as part of Johnson's WAR ON POVERTY programs. In March 1964, Johnson delivered an address before Congress about the seriousness of poverty in the United States, and he declared that poverty could be eradicated with help from Congress. Johnson asked for funding and for the authority to create a volunteer corps. Under the ECONOMIC OPPORTUNITY ACT OF 1964, Congress allocated almost a billion dollars for the formation of 10 different antipoverty programs, including VISTA, HEAD START, and JOB CORPS. The goals of the new VISTA were no different from those of the failed NSC. Unlike NSC, however, VISTA would function under the Office of Economic Opportunity. At the center of these policies was the assumption that solutions to poverty required direct intervention and that low-income people had a right to participate in housing, health, education, and work solutions.

VISTA volunteers served full time in one-year terms. They worked for a variety of agencies and participated in projects ranging from literacy programs to economic and community development to battered women's shelters. In addition to the experience gained during their term, volunteers received a living allowance, health insurance, and an educational award to be used toward future education or student loan debt. While volunteers had to be 18 years old to participate, there was no upper age limit set for participation. Many of the volunteers possessed college degrees, but not all positions required a degree.

VISTA changed with subsequent presidential administrations and shifting political climates. In the early 1970s, President Richard M. Nixon combined several programs, such as VISTA and the PEACE CORPS to form the ACTION agency. ACTION discouraged the community development emphasis of VISTA, and such activities declined. VISTA, however, continued to secure federal funds and maintained its community organizing initiatives. During the 1980s, ACTION administrators dismantled the recruiting and training structure of VISTA. In addition, there was a decline in the number of organizations that received volunteers. Grass-roots efforts ensured that VISTA's work in community organizing remained alive. In 1993, ACTION combined with three other groups under the National Service Trust Act to form the Corporation for National Service, and VISTA officially became Americorps ° VISTA.

By the turn of the 21st century, there were over 100,000 former VISTA volunteers. Since its founding, the effect of VISTA workers on the communities they served has been debated. Recent evaluations of the program suggest that VISTA workers do in fact have a positive impact on the neighborhoods and communities in which they work. According to the executive summary for 1997, volunteers that year each generated an average of $24,000 in funds for their sponsoring organizations and recruited more than 4 million hours of community service. Though the survival of VISTA has at times been uncertain, changes in the decades after its creation have kept it alive.

Further reading: T. Zane Reeves, *The Politics of the Peace Corps and VISTA* (Tuscaloosa: University of Alabama Press, 1988).

— Heather L. Tompkins

Voting Rights Act of 1965

Passed overwhelmingly by Congress and signed into law by President LYNDON B. JOHNSON on August 6, the Voting Rights Act of 1965 strengthened federal protection and enforcement of African American voting rights in the South.

During the early 1960s, various civil rights organizations fought to secure the constitutional right of blacks to the ballot, a right originally guaranteed by the Fifteenth Amendment. Since the era of Reconstruction, blacks were kept from the polls through literacy tests, poll taxes, intimidation, violence, and other questionable voter registration practices. The 1965 measure comprised a significant part of the federal government's legislative response to what civil rights protests laid bare—the many remaining barriers to black enfranchisement.

The drive to secure black voting rights began in earnest in 1964, when the CONGRESS OF RACIAL EQUALITY (CORE) and the STUDENT NONVIOLENT COORDINATING COMMITTEE (SNCC), two civil rights organizations, launched the Mississippi Freedom Summer Project, in which college students and local volunteers assisted southern blacks in registering to vote. Then in early 1965, MARTIN LUTHER KING, JR., and the SOUTHERN CHRISTIAN LEADERSHIP CONFERENCE (SCLC) organized a mass march in Selma, Alabama, to protest black disfranchisement. Both of these peaceful events were met with strong white resistance and violence— three Freedom Summer volunteers were murdered by local Mississippi law enforcement; many Selma marchers were beaten by police; and two white Selma marchers advocating black voting rights were murdered. The violence that erupted in the South received heavy media coverage and outraged the American public, especially northerners. Support for change in the South and for a new voting rights bill grew.

In August, just five months after the Selma march, Johnson persuaded Congress to pass the Voting Rights Act of 1965. Drafted by the administration, the act was designed to eliminate the remaining barriers to black enfranchisement. The legislation targeted specific southern states or counties known to have discriminated against black voters through registration procedures. Those with the worst records included Alabama, Georgia, Louisiana, Mississippi, many North Carolina counties, South Carolina, and Virginia. The act required these areas to submit changes in voting laws and procedures to the U.S. attorney general for approval. The attorney general could also appoint poll watchers and voting examiners as needed to ensure that blacks were able to register and vote without harassment. This provision gave real teeth to the legislation and allowed the attorney general unprecedented power and control over state elections. In addition, the act outlawed gerrymandering, or drawing lines for election districts in an unfair way for the purpose of denying the right to vote on the basis of race. Literacy tests and other ploys used in the South to limit the franchise to whites also were prohibited.

The power of the Voting Rights Act of 1965 to protect black voting rights was buttressed by two other significant federal actions. In 1964, Congress passed and the states ratified the Twenty-fourth Amendment, which outlawed the use of poll taxes in federal elections. Then in a 1966 ruling, the Supreme Court prohibited all poll taxes, including those at state-level elections. The Voting Rights Act of 1965 was successful almost immediately after it went into effect. Black voter participation in the South increased dramatically and transformed southern politics. In Mississippi, for example, the proportion of registered black voters rose from approximately 6 percent in the years before 1965 to 60 percent by the end of the decade. By the 1970s, black votes had helped to elect more blacks to political office, thus giving African Americans an even stronger voice in government. The measure also opened the polls and political offices to other minority groups. In subsequent years the provisions of the Voting Rights Act of 1965 were renewed and strengthened.

Further reading: Hugh Davis Graham, *The Civil Rights Era: Origins and Development of National Policy, 1960–1972* (New York: Oxford University Press, 1990); Steven F. Lawson, *Black Ballots: Voting Rights in the South, 1944–1969* (New York: Columbia University Press, 1976).

— Lori Creed

W

Wallace, George C.   See Volume X

Wallace, Henry A.   See Volume X

War on Poverty   The War on Poverty, part of President LYNDON B. JOHNSON's GREAT SOCIETY program, aimed to help the newly recognized poor across the United States during the 1960s.

Before his assassination in 1963, President JOHN F. KENNEDY asked his council of economic advisers to investigate poverty within the United States. Kennedy, like many others, had read MICHAEL HARRINGTON's *The Other America,* a book that in 1962, brought attention to the issue of poverty in America. Johnson, after taking over as president, felt the need to continue this effort to investigate and help the poor. In his State of the Union address in 1964, Johnson said, "This administration today, here and now, declares unconditional war on poverty in America."

In the 1960s, poverty was different than it had been in the 1930s. During the 1960s, the ECONOMY was booming and plenty of jobs were available, but the poor were often undereducated, malnourished, and unable to find decent homes and jobs. The children of the poor suffered from an inability to escape the vicious cycle of poverty. Johnson and his advisers recognized the need to research the cause and manifestations of poverty within American society and launch an integrated assault.

Johnson believed that his War on Poverty benefited not only the poor but had a positive effect on the morality and economy of the nation. Since the problem of poverty was a fairly new concern to the federal government, many, including Johnson, were not always sure how to proceed. The administration used many different approaches and techniques to combat the problem, recognizing that some would inevitably fail. The increased effort to investigate the causes and sources of poverty, many hoped, would point the government in the right direction.

The ECONOMIC OPPORTUNITY ACT OF 1964 was a key part of the program. It sought to help the poor find work through such agencies as the JOB CORPS, which provided funds for employment of the young.

The War on Poverty included many types of programs aimed at helping people out of both urban and rural poverty. Training programs prepared unskilled workers for jobs, and housing programs provided better homes and living environments, especially within slums and ghettos. Johnson's plan gave aid to schools and tried to stop poverty from impeding students' success. HEAD START was a nursery and kindergarten program for underprivileged children, while Upward Bound gave poor talented children a chance to attend college. Health programs gave medical care to those who lacked it or had received poor care in the past. The elderly received increased Social Security stipends, and the Food Stamp program provided assistance to those without enough money to buy groceries. Meanwhile, Johnson continued to push for civil rights legislation to aid African Americans and gain an equal footing in the United States.

The War on Poverty relied on local initiatives as well as federal action. The Office of Economic Opportunity supervised COMMUNITY ACTION PROGRAM projects, which fought poverty with locally controlled programs in areas including job training, community health, housing, and home management.

Johnson once said of the poor, "They have no voice and no champion. Whatever the cost, I was determined to represent them. Through me they would have an advocate and, I believed, new hope." His War on Poverty was the first coordinated national effort to combat intensively the problems of the poor, an effort that had been previously limited to charitable groups.

When Johnson left the White House in 1969, 36 percent of Americans had been lifted out of poverty. Though the success was not as great as hoped, the Johnson administration played an important role in helping those poor who needed assistance most.

Further reading: Paul K. Conkin, *Big Daddy from the Pedernales: Lyndon Baines Johnson* (Boston: Twayne, 1986); Lyndon B. Johnson, *The Vantage Point* (New York: Holt, Rinehart and Winston, 1971).

— Jennifer Parson

Wallace, Henry A.   See Volume VIII

Warren, Earl (1891–1974)
Earl Warren, chief justice of the Supreme Court between 1953–69, strongly favored the protection of civil liberties and civil rights.

Warren was born in Los Angeles, California, on March 19, 1891. He received his undergraduate degree in political science as well as a law degree from the University of California at Berkeley. Graduating near the bottom of his class with only a C average in law school, he nonetheless passed the California state bar examination at the age of 23 and began to practice law in San Francisco. He held various local political offices, and he served as district attorney of Alameda County, California, from 1925 to 1939. After moving up the state government ladder in 1939, Warren was elected attorney general of California, a position he retained for four years.

Warren next won election as governor of California in 1942. As a liberal Republican, he garnered the support of both Democrats and Republicans to win a stunning victory. During his second term as governor, Warren opposed loyalty oaths required by the Board of Regents for all state employees as a part of the anticommunist crusade, and he later saw them invalidated by the California Supreme Court.

Before he could finish his second term as governor, Republican presidential candidate THOMAS E. DEWEY selected Warren as his vice presidential running mate in the election of 1948 against President HARRY S. TRUMAN. After they were defeated in a stunning upset, Warren was elected governor by the people of California to a third term in 1950. In his own quest for the presidency in 1952, he was swept aside by the entrance of General DWIGHT D. EISENHOWER into the race. In return for Warren's support, Eisenhower promised him a seat on the U.S. Supreme Court.

When Chief Justice Fred Vinson died in 1954, Eisenhower made good on his promise and Warren became chief justice. Warren began his first term by orchestrating a decision that upheld equal rights for African Americans. In *BROWN V. BOARD OF EDUCATION* (1954), Warren pushed hard for a unanimous 9-0 vote by personally persuading all justices initially opposed that the case ending school SEGREGATION was so charged that it demanded unanimity.

Warren took a liberal stance on other cases as well. In *Galyan v. Press* (1954), the Court upheld the government's right to deport anyone who was an alleged member of the Communist Party and an alien in the United States even if the person had renounced party membership. In a change of heart, the Court began to protect the rights of communists. In *Watkins v. United States* (1957), it ruled that the efforts of the HOUSE UN-AMERICAN ACTIVITIES COMMITTEE (HUAC) would no longer be tolerated; it was subsequently dissolved in 1975 because of its abuse of congressional power. In *Yates v. United States* (1957), the Court overturned the convictions of 14 communists convicted under the Smith Act, which prohibited advocating the violent overthrow of the government, thereby reversing its decision in *DENNIS V. UNITED STATES* (1951), handed down just six years earlier.

Warren also sought to reform the criminal justice system to protect the rights and liberties of all individuals. In *MIRANDA V. ARIZONA* (1966), the WARREN COURT ruled that the police must inform a criminal suspect that he or she had the right to remain silent and the right to an attorney before any questioning could proceed. This case also guaranteed that a person who could not afford an attorney would have one appointed by the court.

In *REYNOLDS V. SIMMS* (1964), Warren helped craft a majority ruling that representation in state legislatures must be based on population. In *ENGEL V. VITALE* (1962), Warren and the majority banned prayer in public schools.

Warren also served as head of the Warren Commission, convened in November 1963 by President LYNDON B. JOHNSON to investigate the assassination of JOHN F. KENNEDY. The 15-person panel concluded that LEE HARVEY OSWALD acted alone and his murder by Jack Ruby did not constitute actions that were part of a foreign or a domestic conspiracy. Despite criticism of Warren, he stood by the conclusion of that report.

In 1968, the year Warren announced his retirement, Alabama governor GEORGE C. WALLACE accused Warren of having done "more to destroy constitutional government in this century than any one man." Eisenhower, displeased with the liberal stance Warren favored, considered his appointment of Warren as chief justice the "biggest damnfool mistake I ever made." Earl Warren died in 1974.

Further reading: Jack Harrison Pollack, *Earl Warren: The Judge Who Changed America* (Englewood Cliffs, N.J.: Prentice Hall, 1979); Mark Tushnet, *The Warren Court in Historical and Political Perspective* (Charlottesville: University Press of Virginia, 1993); John D.

Supreme Court Justices (left to right) William O. Douglas, Stanley Reed, Chief Justice Earl Warren, Hugo Black, Felix Frankfurter, and others stand with President Eisenhower on the White House steps, 1953   *(Library of Congress)*

Weaver *Warren: The Man, the Court, the Era* (Boston: Little, Brown, 1967).

— John E. Bibish IV

Warren Court

The U.S. Supreme Court experienced a profound transformation from the 1950s to the 1960s. Appointed chief justice by President DWIGHT D. EISENHOWER in 1953 to replace Fred Vinson, EARL WARREN presided over a court that protected civil liberties for all citizens in many different areas of law.

The court Warren led was initially composed of many pre–World War II liberals, such as Hugo Black, William Douglas, Felix Frankfurter, Stanley Reed, and Robert Jackson, as well as moderates and conservatives such as Harold Burton, Sherman Minton, and Tom Clark. The composition changed drastically when six of these seats were vacated by death and retirement in the 1950s and 1960s.

Justice Robert Jackson vacated the first seat in 1954, which was filled by John Harlan, a justice who served from 1955–71, while the conservative Sherman Minton's seat was vacated and filled in 1956 by William J. Brennan, who served from 1956–90. Following Minton's replacement, Stanley Reed's seat was vacated and filled first by Charles Whittaker, who served from 1957–62, and then by Byron White who served from 1962–93. Moreover, the court changed again in 1958 when Harold Burton's seat was vacated and filled by Potter Stewart, a rigid conservative, who served until 1981.

The composition of the Warren Court shifted again during the administrations of presidents JOHN F. KENNEDY and LYNDON B. JOHNSON, when new members were selected based upon their support for each president's social reform agenda. When Felix Frankfurter suffered a debilitating stroke in 1962, Kennedy appointed Arthur Goldberg to fill the seat. When Johnson called Goldberg to fill the vacant ambassadorship left in the

United Nations by ADLAI STEVENSON's death, Abe Fortas took his place and served until 1969. Lyndon Johnson was also responsible for replacing Tom Clark in 1967 with civil rights activist THURGOOD MARSHALL, who served until 1991.

One area of law that was affected by the Warren Court was civil rights. Southern states in the early 1950s insisted on a social norm dictating the general inferiority of African Americans who suffered serious and pervasive discrimination. The segregated social order came under attack in the BROWN V. BOARD OF EDUCATION case that began in 1951, when Linda Brown of Topeka, Kansas, and other black children questioned whether they could attend an all white segregated school. When the opinion for *Brown v. Board of Education* was announced as a 9-0 unanimous majority, the nine men declared the "separate but equal" doctrine unconstitutional.

The Warren Court is remembered for its groundbreaking precedents in the protection of civil rights as well as civil liberties in criminal procedure. Cases such as *ESCOBEDO V. ILLINOIS* (1964) and *MIRANDA V. ARIZONA* (1966) reflect a trend within the liberal consensus of the Court to deter all police misconduct and eliminate any unfair prosecution or conviction that may result. This was apparent in *Escobedo* when a confession of murder was excluded because the Sixth Amendment right to counsel was never granted to the defendant. In *Miranda,* the Court ruled that the Fifth Amendment's protection against self-incrimination restricted police interrogation of a suspect under arrest.

Biased apportionment of electoral districts prevailed throughout the nation and effectively diluted voting power. In *BAKER V. CARR* (1962), the issue centered on questionable apportionment of state legislature seats that ignored significant economic growth and population shifts within the state of Tennessee. The Court ruled that federal courts had the jurisdiction to scrutinize legislative apportionments. In a similar case, *REYNOLDS V. SIMMS* (1964), the Warren Court held that representation in state legislatures must be based on population rather than geographical areas so that legislatures represented people and not simply acres of land.

ENGEL V. VITALE (1962) was decided by the Warren Court, angering conservatives for its ban of prayer in school. The Court decided that authorization of a nondenominational, voluntary prayer by the New York Board of Regents violated the "establishment of religion" clause of the First Amendment because the state of New York officially approved the prayer.

By the time Chief Justice Earl Warren retired in 1969, the Supreme Court had undergone a major shift that lasted through the next generation. Not until conservatives assumed electoral power and began to change the composition of the liberal court was there an effective challenge to the changes made.

Further reading: L. A. Scot Powe, *The Warren Court and American Politics* (Cambridge, Mass.: Belknap Press of Harvard University Press, 2000); Mark Tushnet, *The Warren Court in Historical and Political Perspective* (Charlottesville: University Press of Virginia, 1993).

— John E. Bibish IV

wars of national liberation

Throughout the 1950s and 1960s, nations in Southeast ASIA, LATIN AMERICA, the Caribbean, and AFRICA engaged in wars of national liberation, independence movements against either foreign invaders or European colonial rulers in the hope of gaining self-rule, social reforms, and democracy.

In the years following World War II, many former European colonies struggled to become independent nations. Their efforts led to the dismantling of the colonial empires of Great Britain and France and the unshackling of Dutch and Portuguese colonies as well. Algeria, the Belgian Congo, Mozambique, Angola, and the Dominican Republic were among the former colonies that pushed for self-rule in the postwar years. Often, revolutionary leaders favored social reforms advocated by socialist and marxist doctrines. Many forged relations with the SOVIET UNION, which was usually more willing than the United States to support the activities of revolutionary groups with material and motivational assistance. The United States sometimes seemed more intent on maintaining stability for the benefit of American economic interests than in addressing the concerns of people struggling for political reform.

Wars for national liberation became an important part of the COLD WAR. During the cold war era, U.S. foreign policy initiatives responded to threats posed by the Soviet Union. When JOHN F. KENNEDY took office in 1961, he hoped to establish warmer relations with Soviet leader Nikita Khrushchev, but Khrushchev stated instead that he would sponsor "wars of national liberation" in Third World countries. The statement posed a threat to the containment policy the Kennedy administration favored. In response, the United States continued its effort to hold back the spread of Soviet-inspired COMMUNISM into unstable countries by initiating economic and military policies designed to thwart the advances of the Soviets.

In Southeast Asia, one such war of national liberation unfolded in Laos. An American-backed right-wing general battled with a neutralist prince and a Soviet-supported official for control of the country previously ruled by France. Lacking any strategic significance to the United States, Laos instead represented symbolic importance to Kennedy, who feared that the loss of the small, poverty-stricken nation to communist forces would represent "visible humiliation." Negotiations at the 1962 Geneva Conference staved off a Soviet takeover, making Laos a neutral country. The victory was short-lived, however, as Laos became an area of contention in the VIETNAM WAR. The CENTRAL INTELLIGENCE AGENCY (CIA) organized an army of Laotians to attack North Vietnamese supply routes along the Vietnamese-Laotian border. Political and social upheaval followed.

Another such liberation effort took place in South Vietnam. The American-supported leader, Ngo Dinh Diem, failed to win popular support with the Vietnamese people while the procommunist forces of the Vietminh took to killing village leaders throughout the country in an attempt to overthrow the corrupt regime of Diem. By 1960, an anti-Diem coalition made up of communists and Buddhists created the National Liberation Front with a military force known as the Vietcong. The United States, in the 1954 SOUTHEAST ASIA TREATY ORGANIZATION (SEATO) accord, had agreed to defend South Vietnam against communist infiltration, and Kennedy held firm to this commitment. American forces, economic aid, and political reforms in South Vietnam all comprised part of an effort to fend off the advances of the Vietnamese communist leader, Ho Chi Minh. In the years that followed, South Vietnam's war of liberation was substantially aided by the United States. Kennedy and his successor, LYNDON B. JOHNSON believed that the loss of South Vietnam to communist forces would lead to the fall of all of Southeast Asia to communism, and as a result, both administrations expended significant time and resources on the fight against communist infiltration. Their dedication to assisting South Vietnam's struggle proved costly for the United States both at home and abroad.

Wars of national liberation also occurred in Latin America. Kennedy's ALLIANCE FOR PROGRESS sought to expand the middle class in Latin American nations to create a bulwark against revolution. But runaway inflation threatened the fragile peace between rich and poor, and the Alliance for Progress failed in its objective. Revolution grew more likely, and Johnson responded with force when a rebellion broke out in Santo Domingo, in the Dominican Republic. Juan Bosch, a former president who had been overthrown by a military junta, sought to replace the military regime with one that allowed free elections and a redistribution of land benefiting a wider representation of the population. As the military regime fell apart, it asked Johnson for help. Fearful of what he felt was communist influence in the regime, he sent 22,000 American troops to the Caribbean nation under the guise of protecting American citizens. It became apparent, however, that Johnson intended to establish a pro-American government, as he claimed that the troops had prevented "the Communists . . . from taking over." The president announced the initiation of the "Johnson Doctrine," a policy that stipulated that the United States would use force anywhere in the hemisphere to keep communist forces from coming to power. Latin American wars of liberation came at a cost to both the United States and Latin America.

American policy in Africa was much like that in Latin America. In Africa, between 1945 and 1970, more than 40 nations gained their independence from European masters. Lack of funds and political experience, however, prevented many new governments from maintaining stable regimes. While the United States offered little help to many of these countries, the Belgian Congo was the exception. In 1960, Congolese leaders declared independence and Patrice Lumumba, a militant nationalist, assumed control of the nation. The United States became fearful that Lumumba, who had received training in Moscow, would halt the export to the West of valuable minerals such as copper and uranium. When civil unrest erupted in the region, the United States backed Joseph Kasavubu, the right-wing leader of the mineral-rich province of Katanga, as a potential replacement for Lumumba. Following Lumumba's assassination in 1961, Kasavubu took control of the nation. With the help of the United Nations and U.S. support, order was restored and revolution was headed off for a while. By 1964, the United States was the dominant foreign power in the Congo, but nationalist revolts threatened the region. Assistance from the CIA combined with a large-scale outlay of military aid helped quell the rebellion, but when it erupted again in 1967, the U.S. Senate forced a reduction in economic and military support. The Congolese were left to fight their own war of liberation.

Further reading: Richard J. Walton, *Cold War and Counterrevolution: The Foreign Policy of John F. Kennedy* (New York: Viking Press, 1972).

—Kim Richardson

Watts uprising (1965)

The Watts uprising of 1965 was the first of many urban uprisings that took place in the turbulent 1960s, reflecting tension and dissatisfaction among urban African Americans.

The uprising began on August 11, 1965, with the arrest of Marquette Frye, a 21-year-old black resident, by Lee Minikus, a white Los Angeles police officer. Minikus suspected Frye of intoxication and proceeded to arrest him. A crowd gathered, and a second police officer arrived on the scene. As tensions increased between the black residents of Watts and the two white police officers, the second officer began striking onlookers with his baton. Word spread about the incident. Fueled by an intense heat wave that blanketed the city, members of the Watts community spent the next two days looting and burning local stores, most of

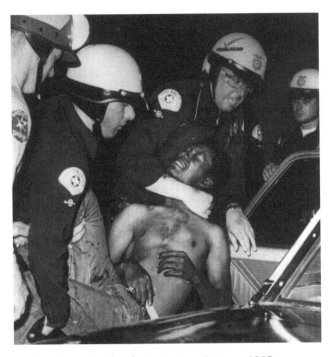

Los Angeles police hustle Watts rioter into car, 1965
(Library of Congress)

which were owned and operated by whites. An estimated 35,000 blacks—many of them teenagers—participated in the riot, which lasted five days.

In the wake of the violence, 34 people were killed, 1,000 more were injured, and over 4,000 were arrested. It took 16,000 members of the National Guard, the Los Angeles Police Department (which was almost entirely white), and county deputies to put down the revolt. Rioters caused damage estimated at $30 million, with substantial destruction to a large number of white-owned businesses. Many of the churches, stores, and homes owned by African Americans, however, were left untouched.

The Watts uprising alarmed civil rights reformers because the residents of Watts typically enjoyed a much higher standard of living than many African Americans in impoverished areas. Located in the south-central portion of Los Angeles, California, the black population of Watts at the time of the uprising numbered 250,000. African American families in Watts did not live in cramped, overcrowded apartment buildings, as was often the case in many large cities, but rather in single, detached houses with ample lawns located on tree-lined streets.

The uprising in Watts revealed a deep-rooted anti-white sentiment that was difficult for many white residents of Los Angeles to comprehend and exemplified the extreme tensions that existed within other black communities across the United States. Progress made in recent years

in promoting African American equality, and the promise of even greater opportunities, served only to raise expectations and deepen the anger of many black residents of Watts, many of whom felt that advancements in race relations had stalled in the face of high unemployment and prevailing poverty. Despite the efforts of MARTIN LUTHER KING, JR., who had visited the Watts area in the weeks before the riot and recommended a civil rights march as a way of communicating racial tensions, there remained a smoldering violence in the community.

The uprising frightened many white Americans. In the past, violence on the part of whites had been directed at African Americans in an effort to deny advancement in the area of civil rights. In Watts, the pattern had reversed with violence targeted at whites, many of whom became increasingly concerned that similar disturbances would affect other areas of the country as news of the Watts uprising spread. African Americans around the country perceived the unrest as a legitimate effort to bring attention to their cause. They resented their treatment as second-class citizens, despite advances achieved by the Civil Rights movement, and they wanted whites to recognize the legitimacy of their grievances. The differences of opinion within black and white communities caused deepening hostilities that erupted later in uprisings that occurred across the nation.

In the aftermath of the Watts uprising, the nonviolent goals of the Civil Rights movement lost ground to a growing militancy among young African Americans, who banded together to loudly express their dissatisfaction with American society. Unrest in other cities such as Newark, New Jersey, and Detroit came to a boil, as civil rights groups that favored militant action used the Watts uprising as a source of inspiration, advocating violence and destruction as a way to further their cause.

Further reading: Jerry Cohen, *Burn, Baby, Burn! The Los Angeles Race Riot of August 1965* (New York: Dutton, 1966; Horn, Gerald). *Fire This Time: The Watts Uprising and the 1960s* (Charlottesville: University of Virginia Press, 1995).

— Jennifer Parson

Weathermen

When STUDENTS FOR A DEMOCRATIC SOCIETY (SDS) began to split into hostile factions amid the violence of 1968, Weathermen won control of the organization and expelled dissenters, destroying SDS in the process.

Many members of SDS also belonged to the Progressive Labor Party (PL). A Maoist-like communist revolutionary organization, PL favored tight discipline enforced by strict leaders. In 1964, some of its members formed the May 2nd Movement to agitate against the VIETNAM

WAR on college campuses. To this end, the few hundred May 2nd movement members often adopted the COUNTERCULTURE lifestyle of campus radicals: drugs, sex, long hair, and hippie clothes. Progressive Labor Party leaders felt this style alienated the working class, vital actors in the revolution PL advocated. In 1966, they disbanded the May 2nd movement.

Some movement members, however, still admired less narrow revolutionary forms. Among them, James Mellen, a political science professor, went to teach in Tanzania. In Africa, he came to believe that Marxist revolutions in Third World countries would help destroy American imperialism. Mellen returned to America on April 4, 1968, the day MARTIN LUTHER KING, JR. was assassinated, and the riots that followed persuaded him that revolution was coming. Within weeks he joined Mark Rudd's SDS uprising at Columbia University. Rudd, a student activist, was dissatisfied with SDS, and gravitated toward more violent revolution. Bernadine Dohrn, a 25-year-old lawyer and four-year member of SDS, also fought at Columbia. The three soon created the Third World Marxists, a group of mostly white middle-class ex-college students, who called for a youth revolution to fight in the streets.

On June 5, 1968, ROBERT F. KENNEDY, running for president, was fatally shot. On August 26, the DEMOCRATIC PARTY assembled at its national convention in Chicago to nominate a presidential candidate from the remaining candidates, and diverse groups gathered to protest the war, condemn politicians, or make revolution. More than 5,000 demonstrators ranged from Yippies, who combined serious protest with playfully shocking street theater, to conservative-looking, well-behaved, older ANTIWAR MOVEMENT demonstrators. For three days, Chicago police battled rioting protestors through the streets of Chicago, releasing tear gas, employing nightsticks, and making 668 arrests.

SDS did not officially support the Chicago protests, but many of its members participated. TELEVISION news showed much of the violence, and tens of thousands of students flocked to join SDS. Meanwhile, Third World Marxists had obtained key posts in the organization. They clashed with the Progressive Labor Party, which had begun to try to take over SDS, believing that its authoritarian style would overwhelm the diffuse organization. PL leaders still thought that Third World Marxists' tactics would distance industrial workers from socialist revolution.

At the June 1969 SDS meeting, conflict turned into a showdown. The Third World Marxists took the name "Weathermen" from the BOB DYLAN lyric "You don't need a weatherman to know which way the wind blows" from his song "Subterranean Homesick Blues." The Weathermen recruited BLACK PANTHERS and introduced issues of WOMEN'S STATUS AND RIGHTS into the agenda, including collective control of sexual relationships. The Progressive Labor Party continued to argue the importance of traditional class struggle. Most students left SDS as its radical factions grappled for control, but some supported the Weathermen's violence. Kathy Boudin, for example, moved easily from SDS to the Weathermen. Her involvement in the Civil Rights movement as a Bryn Mawr student had led her to embrace lawless methods by 1963. Inspired by Bernadine Dohrn's powerful speeches, the Weathermen seized control of SDS and drove the Progressive Labor Party out. Mark Rudd became national secretary.

Weathermen planned the first revolutionary guerrilla uprising for Chicago, in October 1969, to protest the trial of radicals charged with illegal actions committed the year before. Organizers hoped that 15,000 to 20,000 revolutionaries would come to the "National Action," but only a few hundred appeared. Wearing helmets, they marched from Lincoln Park, smashing downtown windows with clubs and chains. Police fired buckshot and hit six radicals, and arrested 68 more; demonstrators bloodied several cops. The next day, Dohrn led a Women's Militia group to destroy a military induction center, but she was arrested before her group managed to do much damage. On the third day, the remaining Weathermen gathered to parade. They broke through police lines to destroy more property; 57 policemen were hospitalized. Newspapers called the action "Days of Rage."

With members facing charges, Dohrn took the Weathermen underground to begin a bombing campaign, and founder James Mellen left the group. It resurfaced on March 6, 1970, when its participants accidentally detonated a bomb, killing three members and blowing up its New York City townhouse. The Weather Underground claimed responsibility for 26 intentional explosions over the next five years. It caused much damage but no casualties, and disbanded in 1975. Rudd surrendered in 1977, and Dohrn in 1980. Each was sentenced to probation. Boudin, however, continued her career in revolutionary movements. In 1981, she participated in an armored truck robbery. Policemen were killed and she was captured and convicted, receiving a sentence of 20 years to life.

Further reading: Susan Stern, *With the Weathermen: The Personal Journal of a Revolutionary Woman* (New York: Doubleday, 1975); Milton Viorst,. *Fire in the Streets: America in the 1960s* (New York: Simon & Schuster, 1979).

— Barbara M. Hahn

White Citizens' Councils

The White Citizens' Councils were private organizations formed throughout the South in reaction to the Supreme Court's *BROWN V. BOARD OF EDUCATION* (1954), which declared unconstitutional racial SEGREGATION in public schools. The councils advocated nonviolent and lawful resistance to any and all attempts at desegregation.

A few weeks after the announcement of the *Brown* decision, Mississippi Circuit Court judge Thomas P. Brady published a pamphlet entitled *Black Monday*. The pamphlet, which espoused white supremacy, called for organized nonviolent resistance to desegregation and became the primer for the formation of the Citizens' Councils. Robert B. Patterson, a Mississippi farmer who fought in World War II, formed the first such group in July 1954 in his town of Indianola.

Patterson and the Indianola Council created a thorough plan of expansion, traveling from town to town, meeting with each community's leaders and social luminaries. By September 1954, the Mississippi legislature praised the groups in open session and they began to receive national coverage by the Associated Press. By 1956 Patterson estimated Mississippi was home to 80,000 Council members in 65 counties. The councils quickly became the most respected, powerful, and effective private antisegregation organizations in the South. Despite their rhetoric of white supremacy, both Patterson and Brady wished to disassociate their movement from the KU KLUX KLAN, a group whose methods and secrecy were unpalatable to the prominent individuals who made up the bulk of the councils' membership. Nonetheless, critics often referred to the councils as "the up-town Klan."

As increasing numbers of black men and women pushed for desegregation, more White Citizens' Councils formed across the South, especially in the deep southern states of Louisiana, Alabama, and South Carolina. The councils in states such as Texas, North Carolina, Florida, and Tennessee were often ineffectual due to weak leadership, a reluctance to adopt the councils' unremitting ideology of white supremacy, and state governments more willing to comply with federally mandated integration measures. Still, by the end of the decade, senators such as South Carolina's Strom Thurmond and governors like Alabama's GEORGE C. WALLACE ardently supported the councils.

While day-to-day administration remained at the local level, regional councils, including the Citizens' Council of America (CCA), established in early 1956, amplified the general ideology of the council movement. At first, the councils organized boycotts of pro-integration black businesses, sent out questionnaires to all possible candidates asking their positions on racial issues, and coerced voter registration officials to be prohibitively strict with black citizens registering to vote. The economic fallout from counterboycotts of white businesses, however, led President DWIGHT D. EISENHOWER, usually reticent to publicly speak about racial issues, to condemn the councils' boycotts in 1956. Abortive attempts to affect public policy and federal investigations of inequalities in voter registration stalled the councils' efforts in these arenas as well.

The use of propaganda, concentrated in the nationally circulated newspaper *The Citizens' Council,* quickly became the main method of resisting civil rights advances. The councils' literature inflamed fears of interracial marriage, using quasi-scientific research to prove the black race's inherent inferiority to whites. Cartoons aimed at elementary school-aged children were commonplace. In 1958, the CCA distributed weekly TELEVISION and radio shows featuring interviews on racial topics with U.S. senators and representatives, many of whom aided the shows' production by granting access to government-subsidized studios. The Mississippi State Sovereignty Commission subsidized many of the shows, granting almost $200,000. While the governing bodies of southern Christian churches, the Southern Baptist Convention most prominently, endorsed a policy of swift desegregation soon after the *Brown* decision, council pamphlets often appealed to readers' belief in a divinely sanctioned duty to keep the races separate.

By the early 1960s, maintaining segregation became less of a viable reality. While Mississippi kept its public schools segregated until 1964, most southern states were integrated at least in part by 1960. Attempts at transporting black families from southern states with a "surplus" black population to northern states with a "deficit" in black residents failed, due as much to a lack of funding as overwhelming criticism of the program by even publications that supported the councils in the South. When the University of Mississippi acquiesced under pressure to integration in the fall of 1962, both the regional Mississippi Council and the CCA, which played considerable roles in encouraging the protests at the university, slipped in prestige and political solvency. With the passage of the CIVIL RIGHTS ACT OF 1964 and LYNDON B. JOHNSON's landslide election to the presidency, both the number and the membership rolls of the Citizens' Councils fell irreparably. By 1968, the failed third-party presidential candidacy of antisegregationist George Wallace effectively ended the power of the councils.

Further reading: Hodding Carter III, *The South Strikes Back* (Garden City, N.Y.: Doubleday, 1959); Neil R. McMillen, *The Citizens' Council: Organized Resistance to the Second Reconstruction, 1954–64* (Urbana: University of Illinois Press, 1971).

— Adam B. Vary

White Paper (on China)

The White Paper sought to account for the imminent communist victory in 1949 in the Chinese civil war.

The White Paper, officially entitled "United States Relations with China," was a Department of State document issued August 5, 1949, under the auspices of Secretary of State DEAN ACHESON. The 1,054-page document offered a justification of American foreign policy toward China, specifically the rationale for ceasing to aid the Nationalist Chinese regime of Jiang Jieshi (Chiang Kaishek). The White Paper argued that nothing short of American military intervention would be sufficient to save Jiang's regime, as it was too weak politically, militarily, and economically to stop the communist Chinese forces under Mao Zedong from winning the war in China. Rather than heading off criticism of American policy, the White Paper was greeted with mass skepticism, and when the Nationalist Chinese forces fled to Formosa (Taiwan,) Acheson and President HARRY S. TRUMAN were widely accused of "losing China" to communist forces.

The Chinese civil war had been going on for years and continued through World War II, even as the opposing sides both actively fought Japanese aggressors. Jiang Jieshi's Nationalist regime was recognized as legitimate by not only the United States but also the SOVIET UNION. Soviet premier Joseph Stalin and his government in Moscow were primarily concerned with maintaining stability in China, and nearly until the end of the war they believed that Jiang offered the best chance to ensure that. In the aftermath of World War II, the Soviet Union called for a coalition government, but, by October 1946, fighting had resumed.

With the resumption of fighting, Jiang and the Nationalists held the advantage, as they had plundered Manchurian industry and retaken control of the Chinese eastern railway. Mao's forces were largely cleared out of north China and Manchuria, but in so doing, Jiang badly overextended his army. By the end of 1947, Communist forces were counterattacking throughout China, and the Nationalists were badly exposed. The United States initially attempted to remain aloof from the fighting, but started formally funding Jiang to fight the communists in May 1947. In spite of this aid, Mao's forces captured Peking (Beijing) and Tientsin in January 1949, and they continued their offensive into southern China.

These events prompted Acheson and the Department of State to issue the White Paper. Alleging that "nothing the United States did or could have done within the reasonable limits of its capabilities could have changed the results [of the Chinese civil war]," the officials explained in the White Paper in great detail how the Nationalists had brought their problems upon themselves. By "reasonable limits of its capabilities," the Department of State meant that only American armed intervention in China could have saved Jiang's regime, and this was not a step the American government was willing to take. The document portrayed Jiang as inefficient and surrounded by corruption, whereas it depicted Mao, although a communist, in a neutral light.

On October 1, 1949, the communists officially proclaimed the People's Republic of China. The Soviet Union recognized the new regime the next day. Jiang's forces were forced to flee to Formosa, where Jiang claimed that he remained the rightful leader of China. This debate spilled over into the United Nations, where the United States refused to allow the Communist Chinese delegate to be seated as the official representative from China.

In the United States, the fall of China to Mao and the communists constituted a foreign policy disaster. The principle of containment, as outlined by GEORGE F. KENNAN and subsequently proclaimed in the 1947 TRUMAN DOCTRINE, called for preventing the expansion of COMMUNISM. Although containment was initially conceived to be applied specifically to EUROPE, China was a gigantic loss, and Truman and Acheson received much of the blame for failing to contain communist forces in China. While the White Paper's assessment of Nationalist weaknesses was difficult to refute, many felt that an insufficient attempt had been made to aid Jiang, especially in light of the multibillion-dollar MARSHALL PLAN intended to prop up an economically devastated Western Europe and protect it from communist insurgency. Actions such as the Berlin airlift had demonstrated that the United States would go to great lengths to stop the spread of communism, so the perception that the United States had not adequately funded Jiang, whether correct or not, made Truman's and Acheson's policy toward China look weak. The timing of Mao's victory was especially bad for Truman, as it came shortly after the first successful Soviet atomic bomb test. As fears of communism at home fed the growing red scare, the fall of China to communism deepened COLD WAR animosities.

The failure of the White Paper to deflect criticism from the Truman administration became important to policy makers in 1950 when the KOREAN WAR broke out. Truman could not allow another country to fall to communism, so American forces, under the banner of the United Nations, joined the war alongside South Korea. The fallout from the fall of China and the American unwillingness to recognize the Communist regime also had a significant lasting impact, as the U.S. government did not extend diplomatic relations until the 1970s.

Further reading: Michael Schaller, *The United States and China in the Twentieth Century* (New York: Oxford University Press, 1979).

— Phil Huckelberry

Wild and Scenic Rivers Act of 1968

The Wild and Scenic Rivers Act of 1968, which sought to preserve America's wild waterways, was an important part of President LYNDON B. JOHNSON'S GREAT SOCIETY.

The act resulted from a growing environmental consciousness, and it drew on the support of the nation's conservation groups. The Outdoor Resources Review Commission, established by Congress, provided important support, as did Secretary of the Interior Stewart Udall. Johnson himself lent his considerable political skills to the effort, and, in so doing, he earned the nickname of the "Conservation President."

Water resources were important to the advocates of conservation. The Wild and Scenic Rivers Act (an addition to the NATIONAL WILDERNESS ACT OF 1964) established a system of wild rivers. While the idea of setting aside public lands for recreational use was not new, the law forced consideration of the line between public good and private property rights, and the question of how much development should occur. The act established eight segments of rivers, with provisions for more to be added to the system later.

The Wild and Scenic Rivers Act declared that "certain selected rivers of the Nation which, with their immediate environments, possess outstandingly remarkable scenic, recreational, geologic, fish and wildlife, historic, cultural, or other similar values, shall be preserved in free-flowing condition, and that they and their immediate environments shall be protected for the benefit and enjoyment of present and future generations." The law allowed a state or states to declare a river and its surrounding areas as a scenic river.

The act defined a river as "a flowing body of water or estuary or a section, portion, or tributary thereof, including rivers, streams, creeks, runs, kills, rills, and small lakes." The act specified three classes of rivers: wild rivers generally free of impoundments and inaccessible except by trail, with primitive shorelines and unpolluted waters; scenic river areas with shorelines or watersheds still largely primitive and shore lines largely undeveloped; and recreational river areas accessible by road or railroad, which might be partially developed.

The act provided that the secretary of the interior and the secretary of agriculture should oversee the management of the river systems, while working with those state governments affected by the system. Fishing and hunting regulations would remain in control of the states in which the river system existed. The Wild and Scenic Rivers Act of 1968 established a foundation for future environmental legislation. Throughout the 1970s and 1980s, new provisions added to the act protected more rivers and the areas surrounding them.

Further reading: *U.S. Statutes at Large*, vol. 82 (Washington, D.C.: Government Printing Office, 1968).

— Robert A. Deahl

Wilkins, Roy (1901–1981)

Roy Wilkins was one of America's preeminent civil rights leaders, best known for serving as executive secretary and executive director of the NATIONAL ASSOCIATION FOR THE ADVANCEMENT OF COLORED PEOPLE (NAACP).

Wilkins was born on August 30, 1901, in St. Louis, Missouri. He lived with his aunt and uncle in St. Paul, Minnesota, for much of his youth. Wilkins, although poor, was able to attend integrated schools in Minnesota. He received a B.A. in 1923 from the University of Minnesota, majoring in sociology and minoring in journalism. While at college, Wilkins joined the NAACP.

To support himself through college, Wilkins worked a number of odd jobs, including stints at the *Minnesota Daily* (the university's newspaper) and a local black weekly, the *St. Paul Appeal*. After graduating, Wilkins went to work for a leading black weekly, the *Kansas City* (Missouri) *Call*. Unlike in Minnesota, SEGREGATION in Missouri was an entrenched system largely unfamiliar to Wilkins. Wilkins's exposure to segregation in Kansas City fueled a growing commitment to the NAACP.

In 1931, Wilkins left the *Call* to work as assistant executive secretary of the NAACP under Walter White. From 1934 to 1949, Wilkins served as editor of *The Crisis*, the official magazine of the NAACP. During World War II, he also served as an adviser to the War Department on black employment, and, in 1945, he acted as a consultant to the American delegation at the United Nations founding conference in San Francisco.

Wilkins served briefly as acting executive secretary of the NAACP in 1949, and, in 1955, after the death of Walter White, Wilkins was named NAACP executive secretary. Although not as nationally visible as many of his contemporaries, Wilkins's role as the head of the largest and best-funded civil rights organization in the country put him in a critical position. Much of Wilkins's time as executive secretary was devoted to testifying before congressional committee hearings and conferring with government officials, including presidents.

Wilkins was especially interested in utilizing the power of the judiciary to dismantle segregation laws. To that end, he worked with lawyer THURGOOD MARSHALL and others in preparing for the landmark Supreme Court case *BROWN V. BOARD OF EDUCATION*, in which the Court ruled that legal segregation in American public schools was inherently unequal and therefore unconstitutional. Wilkins and the NAACP supported a series of subsequent legal actions designed to attack segregation laws using the weight of the Constitution. Under his leadership, the NAACP funded a number of civil rights organizations engaged in nonviolent direct protest against segregation. Wilkins also helped to organize and spoke at the MARCH ON WASHINGTON in August 1963.

By the late 1960s and early 1970s, Wilkins and the NAACP increasingly came under fire from more militant civil rights organizations for being too passive in the struggle for civil rights. The NAACP responded by taking a more active stand, at times engaging in nonviolent direct action, and also by funding different organizations, some more militant than others. Nevertheless, Wilkins remained steadfast in his belief in the power of the constitution and legal action to undo the injustices of segregation. Wilkins opposed any forms of racism or black separatism, believing that "there are more people who want to do good than do evil." Wilkins's insistence on the power of the American legal system to combat segregation explains both the criticism he took from many contemporaries and also his relative lack of public presence, as he concentrated less on public events like marches and more on lawsuits and government hearings.

Wilkins was forced to retire from the NAACP in 1977 due to his declining health. He died in New York City on September 8, 1981. In his final years, younger blacks began to reevaluate Wilkins's legacy, emphasizing the progress made by the NAACP under his leadership instead of the limitations of the NAACP's efforts to use the legal system to fight segregation.

Further reading: Roy Wilkins with Tom Mathews, *Standing Fast: The Autobiography of Roy Wilkins* (New York: Da Capo Press, 1994).

— Phil Huckelberry

Women's Equity Action League

Focusing on legal and economic issues, the Ohio-based Women's Equity Action League (WEAL) formed part of the moderate, women's rights–oriented wing of the American feminist movement.

In the 1960s, new federal laws against discrimination combined with increasing assertiveness among women to revive the moribund women's movement. Traditional attitudes about the appropriate roles of women had not changed, yet more and more women did not view homemaking and childrearing as their primary responsibilities. Large numbers of women had entered the labor force and pursued higher EDUCATION. Many who attended college found themselves stifled in the isolation and routine of domesticity. Women had grown disenchanted with their status as second-class citizens and began to demand recognition of sex discrimination in all areas of life.

Laws such as Title VII of the CIVIL RIGHTS ACT OF 1964, which banned discrimination in employment on the basis of sex, offered hope to women. But these laws guarding women were not enforced and, instead, were often regarded as a joke by the men responsible for guaranteeing their implementation. By treating women's concerns

with contempt and hostility, federal officials demonstrated the need for an organization dedicated to pressuring the government from the outside to end sex discrimination. The NATIONAL ORGANIZATION FOR WOMEN (NOW) was established in 1966 to fight for the equal participation of women in employment, education, government, and the family. In 1968, much to the consternation of its conservative members, NOW called for the reform of laws restricting abortion and the passage of the Equal Rights Amendment. Various groups left NOW in response to these demands, including the women who would establish the Women's Equity Action League.

Believing that a more narrowly focused group was needed to appeal to women in the nation's heartland, Elizabeth Boyer, an Ohio lawyer and NOW founder, created WEAL. According to its president, Nancy Dowding, WEAL avoided issues "that polarize people—like THE PILL, or abortion or husbands washing dishes." The new organization attracted members who viewed abortion as too divisive an issue for a women's rights organization and who wanted to focus on legal and economic issues, especially in the areas of employment and education. WEAL was also one of a number of interest groups that succeeded in defining health care as a women's issue and in placing women's health care on the national policy agenda.

For the first few years of its life, WEAL was centered in Ohio and consisted mostly of friends of Elizabeth Boyer. Members of the inner circle around Boyer served as officers, and they controlled nominations and elections. Unlike NOW, there was little input from the rank and file, and there were no demonstrations or protests. WEAL was carefully organized from the top down to keep out radicals. Members made requests, not demands; they supported "feminine" behavior; they sympathized with their opponents and with homemakers; and they sought reform and compromise. WEAL remained a small organization since many of its members were lawyers with little time to recruit new blood. They formed a loose-knit group with top officers limited to women who had the time and money to pay for their own travel.

WEAL had intended to be a small, powerful organization for professional, executive, and influential women around the country. Over time, it discovered that a significant percentage of its membership resided in Washington, D.C., and that its members elsewhere wielded varying degrees of influence on Washington politicians. Faced with these facts, WEAL redefined its primary purpose as that of a national lobbying organization.

WEAL sought to achieve success through legislation and lobbying rather than more direct pressure tactics such as picketing. Lacking a large membership, WEAL could not employ tactics that required much grass-roots participation. Instead, it addressed women's issues through public education, policy analysis, support for litigation, and advocacy. It targeted laws, institutions, discriminatory practices, and the people who could affect them. Using money raised through direct mail fundraising, WEAL also offered financial help to candidates for public office.

In time, WEAL came to exchange ideology, tactics, and even personnel with the radical wing of the women's movement. By 1972, WEAL had dropped its opposition to a woman's right to choose abortion and had declared itself in favor of "responsible rebellion." WEAL continued to work to eliminate sex discrimination throughout the subsequent decades, still focusing on eliminating gender bias in education and employment.

Further reading: Janet A. Flammang, *Women's Political Voice* (Philadelphia: Temple University Press, 1997); Susan M. Hartmann, *From Margin to Mainstream* (New York: Alfred Knopf, 1989).

— Carynn Neumann

women's status and rights

In the post–World War II period, many women reluctantly yielded to convention and returned to the home, only to wage a battle for women's status and rights in the 1960s.

The effects of the movement for women's rights and status were far-reaching, influencing legislation as much as Americans' everyday lives. With such widespread implications, the women's movement helped to alter both the way many Americans viewed women and the relationships between men and women. While the modern movement began in the 1960s, the economic, political, and social roots lie in the World War II and postwar years. Women had been working outside of the home since the early days of industrialization, but not until World War II did a large percentage of women participate in wage labor. At the war's end, while millions of women ceased working for wages, their time spent in the paid workforce carried important consequences for future generations.

Though many women did work exclusively in the home, the domestic image of the 1950s masks the growing number of women entering and remaining in the paid workforce during the decade. While working-class white women and women of color had previously worked outside the home for wages, a growing number of white middle-class married women, particularly mothers, entered the paid workforce in the 1950s. The majority of women worked in female-dominated industries. At first, women's paid work did not challenge the domestic ideal because most Americans still assumed that women derived their satisfaction from being mothers and wives. Little recognition was given either to the importance of these women's wages to the family income or to the sense of personal satisfac-

tion women derived from their jobs. Yet by the 1960s, the inequalities within the labor system could no longer be ignored. Women's organizations and governmental agencies such as the Women's Bureau of the United Auto Workers, the National Manpower Council, and the National Federation of Business and Professional Women's Clubs worked throughout the 1950s to increase economic opportunities for women. The Women's Bureau of the Department of Labor also noted shifts in women's labor force participation and began advocating policies intended to draw women into the workforce and opposing discriminatory protective legislation. In 1954, the Women's Bureau dropped its opposition to the Equal Rights Amendment (ERA), designed to give women equal legal protection under the Constitution. While these efforts often did little to change conditions for women, the networks formed and the work begun helped bring about change in the 1960s.

Other important events provided a backdrop for the movement for women's status and rights. In 1963, BETTY FRIEDAN, former journalist and housewife, published *The Feminine Mystique*. Using interviews with Smith College alumni, Friedan argued that through POPULAR CULTURE, education, and mental health services, women had been forced out of the public arena and into the home. Women described feeling isolated and unhappy in spite of their material comfort and efforts to fill their lives with volunteer activities. Friedan called these feelings "the problem that has no name." Because of its focus on white, middle-class women, the book received criticism from some activists and scholars. Yet, hundreds of women, not all of whom were middle-class, wrote to Friedan after the book's publication and told her that they identified with what she had written. While feminism existed in the United States before, even in the conservative 1950s, the conversation built around *The Feminine Mystique* provided one way for a large number of women to be exposed to a growing feminist sensibility.

At the same time, under the persuasion of the head of the Women's Bureau, Esther Peterson, President JOHN F. KENNEDY formed the PRESIDENT'S COMMISSION ON THE STATUS OF WOMEN in the early 1960s. Chaired by Eleanor Roosevelt, the commission drew delegates from a wide range of organizations that utilized networks formed in the 1960s. Published in 1963, the report of the commission amassed a large amount of data from each state and documented the legal, economic, and social discrimination faced by women. As a result of the commission's report, Congress passed the Equal Pay Act of 1963 that prohibited the differential pay of men and women for the same work. Other important legislation followed. The CIVIL RIGHTS ACT OF 1964, specifically Title VII, made it illegal for employers to discriminate on the basis of sex, religion, race, or ethnicity. This legislation had limits, but it provided an important legal basis from which activists could demand equality.

With the passage of the Civil Rights Act of 1964, activists hoped that conditions for women would improve. The EQUAL EMPLOYMENT OPPORTUNITY COMMISSION (EEOC) received a large number of sexual discrimination complaints, but it acted on few of them. After they became aware that many of the complaints to the EEOC went unaddressed and that the organization supported some exclusionary policies, Friedan and other activists formed the NATIONAL ORGANIZATION FOR WOMEN (NOW) in 1966. Created to give women the political force to ensure that antidiscrimination legislation be used, NOW, in its mission statement, called for the equal participation of women in American society. While comprised mostly of white, middle-class women, NOW did address efforts toward issues that affected working-class women. For example, NOW supported factory women who sued companies that refused to hire women. NOW worked largely within the system to change legal and social policy, but the members also protested, marched, and raised awareness about those issues affecting women.

There were rifts within the organization, however, and not all women felt comfortable in NOW. Some found the group elitist; others disagreed on the organization's stance on particular issues; and still others felt the organization did not fully critique the system. After being labeled the "lavender menace" in the late 1960s by Betty Friedan, many lesbians left NOW, upset at the implication that lesbianism compromised the legitimacy of the group. In 1973, however, NOW officially recognized the civil rights of lesbians, after those lesbians who remained in the group demanded equal protection.

While white, middle-class married women worked to end the discrimination against women in the United States, they were not the only women who comprised the women's movement. In their union activism, working-class women in several industries became a part of a growing feminist consciousness. In addition to professional and working-class women, a younger generation of women also posed challenges to the status quo. Many of these women gained activist experience in other political movements of the 1960s, such as the Civil Rights movement, NEW LEFT, and student movements. The personal experiences of subordination these women faced as part of their work in such groups led to a recognition of the systemic exploitation and discrimination American women faced.

In 1965, for example, STUDENT NONVIOLENT COORDINATING COMMITTEE (SNCC) workers Casey Hayden and Mary King critiqued the treatment of women in their position paper, "Sex and Caste: A Kind of Memo." Pointing to the way leaders relegated tasks traditionally thought of as female, such as secretarial work, to women in the groups, they argued that women were held back from full participation in the movement. They and others were also offended by civil rights leader STOKELY CARMICHAEL's sexist—and sexual—comment when asked about the role of women. "The only position for women in SNCC," he said, "is prone." The paper resonated with many women and caused discussion within SNCC about the role of women in the group. Similarly, women in New Left organizations, such as STUDENTS FOR A DEMOCRATIC SOCIETY (SDS), struggled to have their voices heard in meetings and to influence the agenda of the organization. Often, male leaders made them feel that their viewpoints were not important. Women also experienced sexual exploitation, feeling their status in the group depended on the degree of their sexual involvement. As they felt torn between the goals of the New Left and their growing awareness of their status as women, many used the networks found in SNCC, SDS, and antiwar groups to articulate their feelings about the experience of being women in these groups. Several times, women tried to give speeches about their subordination, only to be met with jeers and obscenities from the audience. For some women, these episodes proved to be the last straw. Many women left these political organizations to form their own groups. Robin Morgan described her decision to leave the movement in the 1970 paper "Goodbye to All That." In it she called for a new movement, writing that it was the job of the feminist to "build an even stronger independent Women's Liberation Movement, so that sisters in their counterfeit Left captivity will have somewhere to turn. . . . Power to all the people or none."

Often considered more radical, this "women's liberation movement" spread in part due to consciousness-raising groups. Just as former members of the New Left had gathered together to talk about their experiences, women met in groups formed with classmates, coworkers, and neighbors to discuss those issues they felt to be important. Considering their personal lives as political, these women considered the transformation of themselves and their relationships to be as much an integral part of changing society as the enforcement of antidiscriminatory legislation. "The personal is political" became their slogan. Working outside of the political and legal system, many different activist grass-roots organizations formed. They created battered women's shelters and boycotted and protested companies that discriminated against women or did not provide adequate services for women. They protested the 1968 Miss America Pageant, which they felt epitomized the objectification and commodification of women. Others, such as the New York Redstockings, held speakouts for women to talk about their experiences with illegal abortions. In Chicago, a group of feminists formed an underground abortion service called "Jane."

While African American women and Mexican American women had participated in the women's movement from the beginning, these women sometimes formed their own groups. In 1971, for example, hundreds of Chicanas met at the First National Conference of Chicanas. African Americans created the National Black Feminist Organization in 1973. Torn between the sexism they sometimes experienced within their communities and the racism they sometimes experienced within women's groups, minority women met to talk about what it meant to be a woman and a person of color. They also worked on issues that they felt most affected their communities. At the same time, African American women and Chicanas forced white activists to confront the racism that existed within the larger women's movement.

The cultural critique of the late 1960s and early 1970s resulted in the proliferation of new kinds of media opportunities for women. Interested in reaching women who were not involved in the movement, journalist Gloria Steinem founded the mainstream magazine *MS* in 1971. From the beginning, the magazine attempted to cover a wide range of issues that spoke to the diversity of experience among women. In 1973, a Boston health collective published *Our Bodies, Ourselves,* a book intended to educate women about their bodies and their health care options.

Further reading: Dennis A. Deslippe, *"Rights, Not Roses": Unions and the Rise of Working-Class Feminism, 1945–1980* (Urbana: University of Illinois Press, 2000); Sara Evans, *Born for Liberty: A History of Women in America* (New York: The Free Press, 1989); Ruth Rosen, *The World Split Open: How the Modern Women's Movement Changed America* (New York: Viking Press, 2000).

— Heather L. Tompkins

Y

Yep, Laurence (1948–)

Best known as an author of children's books, Lawrence Yep is a multitalented writer who has written historical fiction, short stories, and novels.

Yep was born on June 14, 1948, the son of second-generation Chinese Americans. He grew up in an apartment above the grocery store his parents owned in the Western Edition District, a predominantly black neighborhood in San Francisco, California. Yep left his neighborhood for school, taking the bus to Chinatown. He drew upon his feelings of isolation and his adaptation into different cultures in his writings and credited them for his love of science fiction: "In the 1950s when I was growing up, there were no books on being Chinese American," Yep later reported. "I really liked science fiction because kids from the everyday world were taken to another world, and had to learn another language, another culture. Science fiction was about adapting and that's what I was doing every time I got off the bus."

Yep discovered his love of writing while attending a predominantly white Catholic high school. A teacher encouraged him to pursue his writing, telling Yep that if he wanted an "A" in the course, he had to get his work published. Although he did not get any of his writing published at that time, the experience of applying for publication helped Yep in the future. From there Yep went to Marquette University in Milwaukee, Wisconsin. While in college, his short stories began to get published, earning him awards and accolades. He returned to California where he graduated from the University of California at Santa Cruz.

In 1973, *Sweetwater*, his first science fiction novel for children, was published. "I didn't realize it at the time, but the aliens in the book are based on the bachelor society in Chinatown," Yep explained, referring to the large number of unmarried Chinese immigrant men in the early part of the century. Much of Yep's fiction expressed alienation, recalling his childhood feelings of living between two cultures and having to adapt to unfamiliar surroundings. He enrolled in the doctoral program in literature at the State University of New York at Buffalo. In 1975, he earned his Ph.D., and he saw the publication of the award-winning *Dragonwings*. The novel for young adults, based on a true story, is about a Chinese American aviator who built and flew a flying machine in 1909. The book enjoyed wide success, receiving numerous awards, including the Newberry Honor Book award for the best children's book in 1976.

Yep has enjoyed many other literary successes, including *Dragon's Gate*, winning him his second Newberry, the wildly popular *The Rainbow People* and *Tongues of Jade*, compilations of Chinese folktales, and the production of the stage adaptation of *Dragonwings*. Yep has also taught creative writing at the University of California at Berkeley.

Further reading: Dianne Johnson-Feelings, *Presenting Laurence Yep* (New York: Twayne Publishers, 1995).

— Elizabeth A. Henke

Young Chicanos for Community Action

The Young Chicanos for Community Action was an organization that used military-style efforts to facilitate social change and fight injustice in Mexican American communities.

In the 1960s, Mexican American youth began to reject what they perceived as limited opportunities available to them in white, middle-class America. They adopted the term Chicano, previously seen as derogatory by earlier generations, as a personal and political identifier meant to exemplify ethnic pride. Chicano youth of the 1960s, often working-class Mexican Americans with better access to higher education than previous generations, challenged earlier notions of political accommodation and assimilation as the only means to achieve equal status in a racist society.

Part of the larger LATINO MOVEMENT, the Young Chicanos for Community Action, founded by David Sánchez and four Chicanos in East Los Angeles, began as a service club to assist the neighborhood. Later the organization adopted a paramilitary stance and evolved into a defensive patrol, which tried to protect local residents. It welcomed both men and women into the organization, many of whom were young Mexican Americans who sought a goal of becoming leaders in their own communities.

Formed under the name Young Citizens for Community Action in 1967, the group established headquarters for its activities at a Los Angeles coffee house, "La Peranya," using the facility as an office and meeting hall. Shortly after forming, the organization changed its name to Young Chicanos for Community Action, and shortly thereafter to the Brown Berets, after the article of clothing chosen as a sign of unity. Despite the changes in name and the closing of the coffee house in 1968, group members became leaders in the Chicano movement, effectively mobilizing their members for protest. Satellite chapters formed throughout the Midwest and Southwest.

The organization fought against inequality in both schools and mainstream white society. While in California, the Brown Berets joined school "blow-outs," or walk-outs, staged by high school students in response to inadequate teaching and facilities. Police in Los Angeles made efforts to disband the group by raiding its headquarters, slandering members, and encouraging members of counter organizations to attack Brown Beret members. The police sought to discredit the group in the eyes of both the white and the Chicano communities. Sánchez led the group at the National Chicano Moratorium on August 29, 1970, in East Los Angeles, where leaders of the Chicano movement protested against the VIETNAM WAR, citing a 19 percent casualty rate for Mexican Americans in the war compared with a 12 percent rate for all Americans. In 1972, the Brown Berets occupied Catalina Island off the coast of Los Angeles in the hope of raising awareness of the plight of Chicanos.

Further reading: Carlos Muñoz, Jr., *Youth, Identity, Power: The Chicano Movement* (London: Verso, 1989).

— Toni Nelson Herrara

Chronology

1946

George F. Kennan, U.S. ambassador to the Soviet Union, writes the "Long Telegram" urging the United States to contain the Soviet Union's current sphere of influence.

U.S. Congress creates the Indian Claims Commission to settle old disputes.

The Congress of Industrial Organizations (CIO) begins a drive to organize labor in the South known as "Operation Dixie" whose disappointing results signal the waning of organized labor's power.

President Harry S. Truman issues Executive Order 9808, which creates the President's Committee on Civil Rights.

The University of Pennsylvania introduces ENIAC, the world's first wholly electronic digital computer.

The Employment Act of 1946 creates a three-member Council of Economic Advisors. The council's purpose will be "to analyze and interpret economic developments."

Dr. Benjamin Spock publishes *The Common Sense Book of Baby and Child Care,* which encourages a generation of parents to trust their instincts and be affectionate with their children.

William Levitt uses assembly-line techniques to construct the largest housing project in American history in Hempstead, Long Island.

The Center for Disease Control (originally known as the Communicable Disease Center) is established in Atlanta.

U.S. Congress passes the Atomic Energy Act, which establishes the Atomic Energy Commission (AEC) to explore, promote, and regulate the uses of nuclear energy.

The birth rate begins the 18-year postwar surge known as the baby boom.

1947

The Rio Pact promises reciprocal military assistance if Soviet intervention threatens any Western Hemisphere country.

Jackie Robinson joins the Brooklyn Dodgers and becomes the first black baseball player in the major leagues.

Overriding President Truman's veto, U.S. Congress passes the Labor Management Relations Act of 1947, also known as the Taft-Hartley Act, which regulates the activities of organized labor.

The House Un-American Activities Committee (HUAC) accuses Hollywood film companies of infusing film scripts with communist propaganda and harboring communist sympathizers.

HUAC begins investigations to ferret out alleged communist infiltration of the film industry; the "Hollywood Ten" refuse to cooperate with proceedings.

The National Security Act of 1947 coordinates the formerly separate departments of the U.S. Army, Navy, and Air Force within a single, unified command called the National Military Establishment; the act also establishes the National Security Council and the Central Intelligence Agency (CIA).

The Truman Doctrine proclaims a U.S. commitment to help noncommunist countries resist Soviet expansion.

The Federal Employee Loyalty Program requires "loyalty investigations" for all civilian employees of the executive branch and all its job applicants to root out communist sympathizers.

The U.S. government sponsors Operation Bootstrap to industrialize Puerto Rico.

The play *A Streetcar Named Desire,* by Tennessee Williams, is produced.

The American Farm Bureau Federation advocates federal policies to allow agricultural prices to fluctuate according to supply and demand.

1948

The United States offers western European countries that reject communism the Marshall Plan, a massive program of aid for the devastated countries of Europe.

Twenty-nine North and South American nations sign the Charter of the Organization of American States, which founds an anticommunist federation of American countries, lays down its fundamental principles, and describes its structure.

Coach class air travel is introduced, making air travel more widely affordable.

The Mexican Labor Program extends the importation of Mexican farmworkers, or *braceros,* begun in 1941.

A group of Democrats who oppose Truman's hard-line approach to communism form the Progressive Party, splitting the Democratic ticket by nominating Henry A. Wallace for president.

Segregationist Democrats walk out of the Democratic National Convention and form the States' Rights, or "Dixiecrat," Party, endorsing Strom Thurmond for president.

In a close race, Republican Thomas E. Dewey loses the presidential election to incumbent Harry S. Truman.

Alfred C. Kinsey publishes *Sexual Behavior in the Human Male* to wide acclaim and condemnation, inviting discussion and further research on human sexuality.

Elijah Muhammad recruits Malcolm X to the Nation of Islam.

General Motors and the United Auto Workers negotiate a labor agreement that incorporates a cost-of-living adjustment (COLA) for union workers.

President Truman issues an order making the U.S. government an equal opportunity employer.

The United States begins the Berlin airlift to circumvent the Soviet Union's blockade of Berlin.

Norman Mailer publishes his first novel, *The Naked and the Dead.*

Former diplomat Alger Hiss is accused of passing government documents to the Soviet Union; two years later he is convicted of perjury.

Palestine is partitioned under UN supervision to form the Jewish state of Israel; one day later, neighboring Arab armies attack Israel but are repelled.

William Shockley invents the transistor, which leads to the miniaturization of many electronic devices and appliances.

1949

In his State of the Union address, President Harry S. Truman outlines an expansion of New Deal policies known as the Fair Deal.

The Soviet Union successfully detonates an atomic bomb, breaking the U.S. monopoly of the weapon.

The National Security Act of 1949 places all military service departments under the authority of the newly created Department of Defense.

The North Atlantic Treaty Organization (NATO) is formed under the guidance of Secretary of State Dean Acheson.

The United States, France, and Great Britain establish the Federal Republic of Germany.

Arthur Miller's Pulitzer Prize–winning play, *Death of a Salesman,* is produced.

The first McDonald's applies assembly-line methods to restaurant food preparation in San Bernardino, California.

Ending the Chinese Revolution, Mao Zedong's Communist forces defeat the Guomindang (Nationalists) under Jiang Jieshi (Chiang Kai-shek), driving them to Taiwan.

1950

The National Security Council drafts NSC-68, a policy paper that establishes American cold war policy for the next 20 years.

Frank McNamara offers the Diners Club card, popularizing use of credit cards for small-scale consumer purchases.

William Faulkner receives the Nobel Prize in literature.

The United States becomes involved in the Korean War.

The National Science Foundation is established to fund industrial and defensive research.

A Senate committee led by Joseph McCarthy accuses many Americans of being communists or having ties to communist organizations; many careers are ruined before McCarthy is discredited.

Actress Marilyn Monroe makes her movie debut.

Julius and Ethel Rosenberg are accused of selling secrets of atomic bomb–making to the Soviets; they are convicted and later executed.

For his role in mediating the Arab-Israeli conflict, Ralph Bunche becomes the first African American to win the Nobel Peace Prize.

Overriding the veto of President Harry S. Truman, the U.S. Congress passes the Internal Security Act of 1950 (also known as the McCarran Act), which requires all communist and communist-front organizations to register with the attorney general.

1951

General Douglas MacArthur favors expanding the Korean conflict into China, against President Harry S. Truman's policy; Truman relieves MacArthur of duty.

The Japanese Peace Treaty of 1951 and the Termination of the State of War with Germany formally end World War II.

President Truman attempts to seize the steel industry to end strike disruption, a move the Supreme Court later declares unconstitutional.

In *Dennis et al. v. United States,* the U.S. Supreme Court upholds provisions of the Smith Alien Registration Act of 1940 that prohibit advocacy of the forceful over-throw of the U.S. government.

The sitcom *I Love Lucy* is first broadcast.

1952

The U.S. tests the first hydrogen device on the Pacific atoll Eniwetok.

Ralph Ellison publishes *The Invisible Man,* a novel about the black experience in America.

Walter P. Reuther becomes president of the Congress of Industrial Organizations.

The campaign of presidential candidate Dwight D. Eisenhower runs the first political commercials on television.

On live television, the UNIVAC computer predicts the winner of the 1952 presidential election.

Democrat Adlai Stevenson, governor of Illinois, loses the presidential election to Republican Dwight D. Eisenhower.

In Richard Nixon's "Checkers" speech, the vice presidential candidate refutes accusations that he personally benefited from campaign contributions.

Overriding the veto of President Harry S. Truman, U.S. Congress passes the McCarran-Walter Act, which continues the basic quota system established by the Immigration Act of 1924 but adds new provisions to exclude possible communist sympathizers and to permit the expulsion of aliens who support the communist cause.

The first commercial jetliner offers rapid air travel to the public.

Jonas Salk develops a vaccine for polio.

1953

The Department of Health, Education, and Welfare is established.

The Bureau of Indian Affairs' relocation program (also known as the Termination policy) attempts to eliminate reservations and encourage Native Americans to move to cities.

After months of negotiations, an armistice ends the Korean War.

The microwave is patented.

The Submerged Lands Act grants ownership of submerged lands along coastal shorelines to the states rather than the federal government.

Earl Warren is named chief justice of the U.S. Supreme Court.

The Soviet Union successfully tests its own hydrogen bomb.

Novelist and essayist James Baldwin publishes his first book, *Go Tell It on the Mountain.*

President Dwight D. Eisenhower delivers his "Atoms for Peace" speech to the United Nations General Assembly, calling for international control of atomic energy.

1954

In *Brown v. Board of Education of Topeka, Kansas,* the U.S. Supreme Court unanimously rules that segregation in public schools is unconstitutional.

Bill Haley and the Comets release "Rock around the Clock," which becomes the first big hit of rock 'n' roll.

Britain, France, the United States, Australia, New Zealand, the Philippines, Pakistan, and Thailand sign the SEATO Pact of 1954 to counteract communist influence in Asia.

In televised Senate hearings, Senator Joseph McCarthy accuses the secretary of the army of covering up communist activity on a U.S. army base; the Senate formally condemns McCarthy for abusing the powers of the Senate Privileges and Elections Subcommittee.

Puerto Rican nationalists open fire on the floor of the U.S. House of Representatives.

The Atomic Energy Act of 1954 allows private companies to participate in atomic energy research, development, and production.

The first nuclear-powered submarine is launched.

After Jacobo Arbenz Guzmán, the elected president of Guatemala, nationalizes assets of a U.S. company, the CIA organizes a coup to overthrow him.

Following Communist forces' decisive defeat of the French in Vietnam, the United States sponsors the anti-communist regime of South Vietnam.

1955

The National Farmers Organization forms in Iowa to protest low agricultural prices.

The Soviet Union consolidates control over Eastern Europe with the Warsaw Pact.

The American Federation of Labor (AFL) merges with the Congress of Industrial Organizations (CIO).

Rosa Parks refuses to give up her seat to a white passenger on a bus in Montgomery, Alabama; after her arrest, Dr. Martin Luther King, Jr., organizes the Montgomery bus boycott.

1956

"Howl," a poem by Allen Ginsberg, helps inspire the "Beat Generation" of American writers.

The soil-bank program authorizes federal payments to farmers who reduce production of certain crops.

One hundred and one U.S. congressmen issue the Southern Manifesto on Integration, which denounces U.S. Supreme Court desegregation rulings.

In his influential book *The Power Elite*, sociologist C. Wright Mills argues that the concentration of power under a bureaucratic minority is endangering American democracy.

Singer Elvis Presley becomes America's most popular rock and roll star.

After Egypt nationalizes the Suez Canal, forces from Israel, Great Britain, and France seize the Sinai Peninsula in an incident known as the Suez Crisis; the United States confirms Egypt's sovereignty over the region.

The Citizens' Council of America is established to coordinate white groups' legal, nonviolent resistance to integration.

President Dwight D. Eisenhower is reelected over Adlai Stevenson.

U.S. Congress passes the Interstate Highway Act of 1956, which establishes the National System of Interstate and Defense Highways to upgrade and modernize 40,000 miles of U.S. roads.

1957

The Southern Christian Leadership Conference (SCLC) is organized; Dr. Martin Luther King, Jr., is named president.

The AFL-CIO expels the Teamsters union from its membership after the McClellan Committee, under the staff leadership of Robert F. Kennedy, finds evidence of widespread corruption within the union.

The Soviet Union launches *Sputnik*, the world's first artificial satellite.

The integrated circuit, or "computer chip," is invented.

Jack Kerouac's novel *On the Road* is published; its success prompts others to use the unstructured and chaotic "beat" style of writing.

Vance Packard's book *The Hidden Persuaders* denounces American advertisers' use of psychological manipulation.

In Little Rock, Arkansas, U.S. soldiers escort nine black children to school after Governor Orval Faubus calls out Arkansas National Guard to keep them out; it is the first time since Reconstruction that the federal government calls in military power to enforce the civil rights of African Americans.

U.S. Congress passes the Civil Rights Act of 1957 to protect the voting rights of all American citizens, especially blacks.

U.S. Congress approves the Eisenhower Doctrine, which authorizes military aid for any Middle Eastern nation requesting such assistance in order to resist communist aggression.

1958

U.S. Congress establishes the National Outdoor Recreation Review Commission to study the outdoor recreation resources available in the United States.

The State Department creates an independent Bureau of African Affairs to handle relations with emerging independent nations in Africa.

The Federal Aviation Administration (FAA) is established to regulate air travel.

The National Defense Education Act of 1958 establishes a federal loan fund for college students and a number of grants and fellowships for graduate school students, particularly in the areas of math, science, and foreign language.

The Affluent Society, a book by economist and diplomat John Kenneth Galbraith, attacks the myth of consumer sovereignty.

Democratic candidates sweep midterm elections in both houses of Congress.

Walter O'Malley moves the Brooklyn Dodgers to Los Angeles, catalyzing the migration of baseball to the western United States.

The diminutive Volkswagen Beetle is introduced in the United States, competing successfully with large American cars.

President Eisenhower creates the National Aeronautics and Space Administration (NASA) to foster research on flight and space exploration.

1959

Rebels under Fidel Castro take control of the Cuban government; to the dismay of many Americans, Castro allies Cuba with the Soviet Union.

A Raisin in the Sun premieres, making Lorraine Hansberry the first African-American woman to have a play produced on Broadway.

1960

The Food and Drug Administration approves the first oral contraceptive.

The sit-in movement begins when four black college students sit at a whites-only Woolworth's lunch counter in Greensboro, North Carolina.

The Civil Rights Act of 1960 aids blacks in registering to vote.

The Student Nonviolent Coordinating Committee (SNCC) is formed at Shaw University.

Richard Nixon and John F. Kennedy spar in the first televised presidential debates.

Democratic senator from Massachusetts John F. Kennedy is elected president by a small margin over incumbent vice president Richard Nixon.

Barry Goldwater publishes *The Conscience of a Conservative,* a popular book of political commentary.

1961

In his farewell address, President Eisenhower warns against the growing spread of communism and excessive militarization.

President John F. Kennedy's Alliance for Progress promises economic aid to Latin American countries in return for political and social reforms.

Soviet premier Nikita Khrushchev answers President John F. Kennedy's demands for the reunification of Berlin with the construction of the Berlin Wall.

President Kennedy reorganizes civil defense, setting up the Office of Civil Defense (OCD) to implement a system of fallout shelters and emergency communications.

The Congress of Racial Equality (CORE) and the Student Nonviolent Coordinating Committee (SNCC) organize the first "freedom rides" through the South on interstate buses in order to force compliance with desegregation laws.

Russian cosmonaut Yuri Gagarin becomes the first human in space, orbiting the Earth once; three weeks later American astronaut Alan Shepard achieves suborbital spaceflight.

The Peace Corps is established.

Trained by U.S. military advisers, anti-Castro Cuban rebels begin an unsuccessful invasion of Cuba at the Bay of Pigs; the U.S. government is criticized both for its involvement and for the failure of the invasion.

Folksinger Bob Dylan begins performing.

The United States sends economic aid and military advisers to South Vietnam.

Overturning a conviction by a Louisiana court, the U.S. Supreme Court rules in *Garner et al. v. Louisiana* that participants in a civil rights sit-in were not guilty of disturbing the peace.

President Kennedy appeals for a new program to put a man on the moon before 1970.

1962

Michael Harrington's book *The Other America* criticizes the inequality of income distribution and the existence of poverty in the United States.

In *Baker v. Carr*, the U.S. Supreme Court rules that legislative apportionment by the states is subject to federal court scrutiny.

In *Engel v. Vitale*, the U.S. Supreme Court rules that religious observances in the public schools are unconstitutional.

James Meredith is escorted onto the University of Mississippi campus by federal marshals; the ensuing riots kill two people and wound more than 100.

John Glenn becomes the first U.S. astronaut to orbit the earth.

President John F. Kennedy announces the Soviet Union's secret shipment of nuclear missiles to Cuba. In response, Kennedy issues Proclamation 3504: Interdiction of Delivery of Offensive Weapons to Cuba, which imposes a naval blockade of Cuba to prevent further shipments. After several tense days, the Soviets agree to remove the missiles. The incident is known as the Cuban missile crisis.

Silent Spring, a national best-seller by Rachel Carson, warns of the dangers that pesticides pose to the environment.

The Port Huron Statement of the Students for a Democratic Society condemns social stagnation and demands the decentralization of the democratic process; this ideology becomes known as the New Left.

1963

Timothy Leary is fired from Harvard's faculty for using students in his research on the effects of hallucinogenic drugs; his slogan "Tune in, turn on, drop out" becomes a rallying cry of the counterculture.

The Southern Christian Leadership Conference (SCLC) and Martin Luther King, Jr., organize civil rights protests in Birmingham, Alabama, resulting in King's arrest; while incarcerated, King writes his famous essay "Letter from Birmingham Jail."

Millions of television viewers watch as high-pressure hoses and attack dogs are turned on peaceful civil rights demonstrators in Birmingham, Alabama.

Medgar Evers, a field secretary for the National Association for the Advancement of Colored People (NAACP), is murdered in Jackson, Mississippi.

Four young black girls are killed in a church bombing in Birmingham, Alabama.

Approximately 250,000 people march on Washington to demonstrate for civil rights.

U.S. Congress passes the Equal Pay Act of 1963, which ensures that women are paid at the same rate as their male coworkers, but only in certain limited circumstances.

In *Gideon v. Wainwright,* the U.S. Supreme Court rules that states must provide legal counsel to defendants.

President John F. Kennedy is assassinated; Vice President Lyndon B. Johnson succeeds President Kennedy.

Betty Friedan publishes *The Feminine Mystique,* galvanizing women dissatisfied with their traditional roles.

The Limited Test Ban Treaty of 1963 prohibits the testing of nuclear weapons in the earth's atmosphere, in outer space, or underwater.

Alabama governor George C. Wallace personally bars three black students from the University of Alabama, vowing never to accept desegregation; the National Guard oversees the students' registration later the same day.

In *Abington Township v. Schempp,* the Supreme Court prohibits prayer in public schools.

1964

Surgeon General Luther Terry's report on tobacco and health initiates a sustained government effort to reduce smoking.

The Civil Rights Act of 1964 outlaws discrimination in public accommodation.

Civil rights workers James E. Chaney, Andrew Goodman, and Michael Schwerner are murdered near Meridian, Mississippi.

The National Wilderness Preservation Act of 1964 is signed into law; its purpose is to set aside large, federally owned tracts of land to be left undeveloped.

The Twenty-fourth Amendment to the U.S. Constitution outlaws poll taxes.

In *Heart of Atlanta Motel, Inc. v. United States*, the Supreme Court rules unconstitutional discrimination in the provision of services to anyone based on race.

Jimmy Hoffa, president of the Teamsters union, is found guilty of fraud and other charges.

Climatologists Syukuro Manabe and Richard Wetherald predict the rise in global temperatures that comes to be known as the greenhouse effect.

The U.S. Supreme Court decision *Escobedo v. Illinois* establishes that a suspect in police custody has a right to consult counsel during an interrogation.

The Congress of Racial Equality (CORE) and the Student Nonviolent Coordinating Committee (SNCC) organize the Mississippi Freedom Summer Project, which registers thousands of blacks to vote.

Cassius Clay wins the World Heavyweight Boxing Championship by beating Sonny Liston; the next day, Clay announces he has converted to Islam and taken the name Muhammad Ali.

Republican presidential candidate Senator Barry Goldwater's "Extremism in the Defense of Liberty" speech blames the Democratic Party for communist gains in Cuba, Europe, and Southeast Asia, as well as for violence and corruption in the United States.

Lyndon B. Johnson wins the presidential race against Republican Barry Goldwater in a landslide.

President Lyndon B. Johnson's "Great Society" speech outlines a plan for the most comprehensive social reform since the New Deal.

U.S. Congress passes The Gulf of Tonkin Resolu-tion, which authorizes the president to take military action in Vietnam; U.S. aircraft begin bombing raids in North Vietnam.

The Mississippi Freedom Party challenges the right of the all-white Mississippi Democratic Party delegates to represent the state in the Democratic National Convention.

The Warren Commission Report states that President Kennedy's assassin Lee Harvey Oswald acted alone.

The Civil Rights Act of 1964 is passed; it prohibits discrimination at the polls, in federally assisted programs, and in public accommodations.

The Economic Opportunity Act of 1964 establishes VISTA, the Job Corps, Head Start, and the Community Action Program (CAP).

Seventy-three million people watch the Beatles' U.S. debut on *The Ed Sullivan Show.*

1965

The Food and Agriculture Act of 1965 establishes a system of subsidies for farmers who retire land from cultivation on a long-term basis.

U.S. Congress passes the National Foundation on the Arts and Humanities Act of 1965, providing funding for the National Endowment for the Arts (NEA) and the National Endowment for the Humanities (NEH).

Black civil rights leader Malcolm X is assassinated in New York City; later that year, Alex Haley's *The Autobiography of Malcolm X* is published, inspiring young black radicals.

Dr. Martin Luther King, Jr., leads the Selma-Montgomery March; two white demonstrators are killed, and other marchers are brutally beaten. Dr. King threatens an economic boycott of Alabama.

A race riot in the Watts section of Los Angeles kills 34 people and results in the arrest of 3,400.

The Equal Employment Opportunity Commission (EEOC) is established to investigate claims of employment discrimination in violation of Title VII of the Civil Rights Act of 1964.

The House Un-American Activities Committee opens a public investigation of the Ku Klux Klan.

Students at the University of California at Berkeley sponsor rallies, sit-ins, and strikes demanding the right to organize politically on campus; the protests are the forerunners of the nationwide student revolution.

Author and playwright Leroi Jones, known after 1968 as Amiri Baraka, founds the Black Arts Repertory in Harlem.

U.S. Congress passes the Voting Rights Act of 1965, mandating that the federal government closely monitor voter registration in each state.

U.S. Congress passes the Water Quality Act of 1965, which requires the states to set standards of quality for streams within their borders.

Civil war breaks out in the Dominican Republic; the United States sends troops. The crisis produces the Johnson Doctrine, which states that an American president can use military force whenever communism threatens the Western Hemisphere.

U.S. Congress passes the Elementary and Secondary Education Act of 1965, which improves educational opportunities by providing $1.3 billion in federal aid to schools with large numbers of children from low-income families.

U.S. Congress passes the Social Security Amendments of 1965, which provide federally funded health insurance for the elderly (Medicare) and the poor (Medicaid).

U.S. Congress passes the Housing and Urban Development Act of 1965 to rehabilitate existing housing stock and create new public housing units.

U.S. ground troops land in South Vietnam; they engage in combat against North Vietnamese troops and Viet Cong guerrillas.

U.S. Congress passes the Appalachian Regional Development Act as the centerpiece of President Johnson's War on Poverty.

U.S. Congress passes the Immigration Act of 1965, which sets annual limits of 120,000 immigrants from the Western Hemisphere, but no national quotas, and sets annual limits of 170,000 immigrants from the rest of the world.

Activist Ralph Nader publishes *Unsafe at Any Speed,* a critique of automotive safety in America.

The American Association of Advertising releases a study finding that TV ads exert more influence over consumer behavior than do print advertisements.

U.S. Congress passes the Motor Vehicle Air Pollution Control Act to reduce smog.

1966

In *Miranda v. Arizona,* the U.S. Supreme Court extends federal constitutional protections to defendants in state criminal trials.

James Meredith is shot and wounded during his Freedom March.

Bobby Seale and Huey P. Newton found the Black Panthers in Oakland, California.

Organized by César Chávez, two unions merge to form the United Farm Workers.

The Alianza Federal de Mercedes occupies Kit Carson National Forest, asserting land rights granted to Mexican Americans by the 1848 Treaty of Guadalupe-Hidalgo.

The federal minimum wage is extended to farmworkers.

The National Organization for Women is founded with Betty Friedan as president.

Truman Capote publishes his "nonfiction novel" *In Cold Blood;* it is the first of its genre.

Stokely Carmichael, chair of SNCC, rallies demonstrators at a march in Mississippi around the demand for "black power."

U.S. Congress passes the National Traffic and Motor Vehicle Safety Act of 1966.

In *Reynolds v. Simms,* the Supreme Court holds that legislative districts must be apportioned on the basis of population.

1967

The Young Lords, a militant Puerto Rican group, is established in Chicago for community self-defense.

Muhammad Ali refuses to be drafted and urges other blacks to resist induction into the military.

Thurgood Marshall becomes the first African-American justice on the U.S. Supreme Court.

Sixty countries sign the Nuclear Nonproliferation Treaty.

Young Chicanos for Community Action forms in Los Angeles to fight against injustice in Mexican-American communities.

U.S. Congress passes the Air Quality Act of 1967, which establishes a regional system for the enactment and enforcement of federal and state air quality standards.

Three U.S. astronauts are killed when their *Apollo* spacecraft bursts into flames in a test prior to launching.

Rodolfo "Corky" Gonzáles publishes the epic poem *Yo Soy Joaquín* (I am Joaquin), which inspires thousands of young Chicanos to demand their civil rights.

1968

The American presence in Vietnam peaks at 550,000 troops.

The American Indian Movement (AIM) is founded in Minneapolis by Clyde Bellecourt, Dennis Banks, Eddie Benton Banai, and George Mitchell.

The National Trails Act establishes the National Trails System as part of an extended effort to preserve the U.S. landscape.

Dr. Martin Luther King, Jr., is assassinated in Memphis, Tennessee; riots erupt in more than 100 U.S. cities.

In *Epperson* v. *Arkansas,* the Supreme Court overturns an Arkansas statute prohibiting the teaching of the theory of evolution.

President Lyndon B. Johnson announces that he will not run for reelection.

Robert F. Kennedy, former U.S. attorney general and brother of John F. Kennedy, is assassinated during his presidential campaign.

Street battles break out between police and protesters outside the Democratic National Convention in Chicago.

The Indian Civil Rights Act of 1968 gives Native Americans the right to form tribal governments and limits states' ability to govern Native American lands.

In his presidential nomination acceptance speech, Richard Nixon attacks Johnson's "Great Society" program and lays out his foreign policy goals.

Republican Richard Nixon is elected president over Democrat Hubert H. Humphrey.

Viet Cong and North Vietnamese forces launch surprise attacks on U.S. and South Vietnamese units during the Tet holiday; the attacks are beaten back, but the Tet Offensive increases antiwar sentiment in the United States.

J. Edgar Hoover names the Black Panthers the most dangerous black extremist organization in America.

Under threat of federal antitrust litigation, IBM divides its programming and hardware operations.

The Wild and Scenic Rivers Act of 1968 seeks to preserve America's wild waterways.

Documents

Truman Doctrine, 1947

Public Papers of the Presidents, Harry S. Truman, 1945,
pp. 176–180
March 12, 1947

Mr. Vice President, Mr. Speaker, Members of the Congress of the United States:

The gravity of the situation which confronts the world today necessitates my appearance before a joint session of the Congress.

The foreign policy and the national security of this country are involved.

One aspect of the present situation, which I present to you at this time for your consideration and decision, concerns Greece and Turkey.

The United States has received from the Greek Government an urgent appeal for financial and economic assistance. Preliminary reports from the American Economic Mission now in Greece and reports from the American Ambassador in Greece corroborate the statement of the Greek Government that assistance is imperative if Greece is to survive as a free nation.

I do not believe that the American people and the Congress wish to turn a deaf ear to the appeal of the Greek Government.

Greece is not a rich country. Lack of sufficient natural resources has always forced the Greek people to work hard to make both ends meet. Since 1940, this industrious, peace loving country has suffered invasion, four years of cruel enemy occupation, and bitter internal strife.

When forces of liberation entered Greece they found that the retreating Germans had destroyed virtually all the railways, roads, port facilities, communications, and merchant marine. More than a thousand villages had been burned. Eighty-five percent of the children were tubercular. Livestock, poultry, and draft animals had almost disappeared. Inflation had wiped out practically all savings.

As a result of these tragic conditions, a militant minority, exploiting human want and misery, was able to create political chaos which, until now, has made economic recovery impossible. Greece is today without funds to finance the importation of those goods which are essential to bare subsistence. Under these circumstances the people of Greece cannot make progress in solving their problems of reconstruction. Greece is in desperate need of financial and economic assistance to enable it to resume purchases of food, clothing, fuel and seeds. These are indispensable for the subsistence of its people and are obtainable only from abroad. Greece must have help to import the goods necessary to restore internal order and security so essential for economic and political recovery.

The Greek Government has also asked for the assistance of experienced American administrators, economists and technicians to insure that the financial and other aid given to Greece shall be used effectively in creating a stable and self-sustaining economy and in improving its public administration.

The very existence of the Greek state is today threatened by the terrorist activities of several thousand armed men, led by Communists, who defy the government's authority at a number of points, particularly along the northern boundaries. A Commission appointed by the United Nations Security Council is at present investigating disturbed conditions in northern Greece and alleged border violations along the frontier between Greece on the one hand and Albania, Bulgaria, and Yugoslavia on the other.

Meanwhile, the Greek Government is unable to cope with the situation. The Greek army is small and poorly equipped. It needs supplies and equipment if it is to restore authority to the government throughout Greek territory.

Greece must have assistance if it is to become a self-supporting and self-respecting democracy.

The United States must supply this assistance. We have already extended to Greece certain types of relief and economic aid but these are inadequate.

There is no other country to which democratic Greece can turn.

No other nation is willing and able to provide the necessary support for a democratic Greek government.

The British Government, which has been helping Greece, can give no further financial or economic aid after March 31. Great Britain finds itself under the necessity of reducing or liquidating its commitments in several parts of the world, including Greece.

We have considered how the United Nations might assist in this crisis. But the situation is an urgent one requiring immediate action, and the United Nations and its related organizations are not in a position to extend help of the kind that is required.

It is important to note that the Greek Government has asked for our aid in utilizing effectively the financial and other assistance we may give to Greece, and in improving its public administration. It is of the utmost importance that we supervise the use of any funds made available to Greece, in such a manner that each dollar spent will count toward making Greece self-supporting, and will help to build an economy in which a healthy democracy can flourish.

No government is perfect. One of the chief virtues of a democracy, however, is that its defects are always visible and under democratic processes can be pointed out and corrected. The government of Greece is not perfect. Nevertheless it represents 85 percent of the members of the Greek Parliament who were chosen in an election last year. Foreign observers, including 692 Americans, considered this election to be a fair expression of the views of the Greek people.

The Greek Government has been operating in an atmosphere of chaos and extremism. It has made mistakes. The extension of aid by this country does not mean that the United States condones everything that the Greek Government has done or will do. We have condemned in the past, and we condemn now, extremist measures of the right or the left. We have in the past advised tolerance, and we advise tolerance now.

Greece's neighbor, Turkey, also deserves our attention.

The future of Turkey as an independent and economically sound state is clearly no less important to the freedom-loving peoples of the world than the future of Greece. The circumstances in which Turkey finds itself today are considerably different from those of Greece. Turkey has been spared the disasters that have beset Greece. And during the war, the United States and Great Britain furnished Turkey with material aid.

Nevertheless, Turkey now needs our support.

Since the war Turkey has sought additional financial assistance from Great Britain and the United States for the purpose of effecting that modernization necessary for the maintenance of its national integrity.

That integrity is essential to the preservation of order in the Middle East.

The British Government has informed us that, owing to its own difficulties, it can no longer extend financial or economic aid to Turkey.

As in the case of Greece, if Turkey is to have the assistance it needs, the United States must supply it. We are the only country able to provide that help.

I am fully aware of the broad implications involved if the United States extends assistance to Greece and Turkey, and I shall discuss these implications with you at this time.

One of the primary objectives of the foreign policy of the United States is the creation of conditions in which we and other nations will be able to work out a way of life free from coercion. This was a fundamental issue in the war with Germany and Japan. Our victory was won over countries which sought to impose their will, and their way of life, upon other nations.

To ensure the peaceful development of nations, free from coercion, the United States has taken a leading part in establishing the United Nations. The United Nations is designed to make possible lasting freedom and independence for all its members. We shall not realize our objectives, however, unless we are willing to help free peoples to maintain their free institutions and their national integrity against aggressive movements that seek to impose upon them totalitarian regimes. This is no more than a frank recognition that totalitarian regimes imposed upon free peoples, by direct or indirect aggression, undermine the foundations of international peace and hence the security of the United States.

The peoples of a number of countries of the world have recently had totalitarian regimes forced upon them against their will. The Government of the United States has made frequent protests against coercion and intimidation, in violation of the Yalta agreement, in Poland, Rumania, and Bulgaria. I must also state that in a number of other countries there have been similar developments.

At the present moment in world history nearly every nation must choose between alternative ways of life. The choice is too often not a free one.

One way of life is based upon the will of the majority, and is distinguished by free institutions, representative government, free elections, guarantees of individual liberty, freedom of speech and religion, and freedom from political oppression.

The second way of life is based upon the will of a minority forcibly imposed upon the majority. It relies upon terror and oppression, a controlled press and radio, fixed elections, and the suppression of personal freedoms.

I believe that it must be the policy of the United States to support free peoples who are resisting attempted subjugation by armed minorities or by outside pressures.

I believe that we must assist free peoples to work out their own destinies in their own way.

I believe that our help should be primarily through economic and financial aid which is essential to economic stability and orderly political processes.

The world is not static, and the *status quo* is not sacred. But we cannot allow changes in the *status quo* in violation of the Charter of the United Nations by such methods as coercion, or by such subterfuges as political infiltration. In helping free and independent nations to maintain their freedom, the United States will be giving effect to the principles of the Charter of the United Nations.

It is necessary only to glance at a map to realize that the survival and integrity of the Greek nation are of grave importance in a much wider situation. If Greece should fall under the control of an armed minority, the effect upon its neighbor, Turkey, would be immediate and serious. Confusion and disorder might well spread throughout the entire Middle East.

Moreover, the disappearance of Greece as an independent state would have a profound effect upon those countries in Europe whose peoples are struggling against great difficulties to maintain their freedoms and their independence while they repair the damages of war.

It would be an unspeakable tragedy if these countries, which have struggled so long against overwhelming odds, should lose that victory for which they sacrificed so much. Collapse of free institutions and loss of independence would be disastrous not only for them but for the world. Discouragement and possibly failure would quickly be the lot of neighboring peoples striving to maintain their freedom and independence.

Should we fail to aid Greece and Turkey in this fateful hour, the effect will be far reaching to the West as well as to the East.

We must take immediate and resolute action.

I therefore ask the Congress to provide authority for assistance to Greece and Turkey in the amount of $400,000,000 for the period ending June 30, 1948. In requesting these funds, I have taken into consideration the maximum amount of relief assistance which would be furnished to Greece out of the $350,000,000 which I recently requested that the Congress authorize for the prevention of starvation and suffering in countries devastated by the war.

In addition to funds, I ask the Congress to authorize the detail of American civilian and military personnel to Greece and Turkey, at the request of those countries, to assist in the tasks of reconstruction, and for the purpose of supervising the use of such financial and material assistance as may be furnished. I recommend that authority also be provided for the instruction and training of selected Greek and Turkish personnel.

Finally, I ask that the Congress provide authority which will permit the speediest and most effective use, in terms of needed commodities, supplies, and equipment, of such funds as may be authorized.

If further funds, or further authority, should be needed for the purposes indicated in this message, I shall not hesitate to bring the situation before the Congress. On this subject the Executive and Legislative branches of the Government must work together.

This is a serious course upon which we embark.

I would not recommend it except that the alternative is much more serious.

The United States contributed $341,000,000,000 toward winning World War II. This is an investment in world freedom and world peace.

The assistance that I am recommending to Greece and Turkey amounts to little more than 1/10 of 1 percent of this investment. It is only common sense that we should safeguard this investment and make sure that it was not in vain. The seeds of totalitarian regimes are nurtured by misery and want. They spread and grow in the evil soil of poverty and strife. They reach their full growth when the hope of a people for a better life has died.

We must keep that hope alive.

The free peoples of the world look to us for support in maintaining their freedoms.

If we falter in our leadership, we may endanger the peace of the world—and we shall surely endanger the welfare of this Nation.

Great responsibilities have been placed upon us by the swift movement of events. I am confident that the Congress will face these responsibilities squarely.

Marshall Plan, 1947

Henry Steele Commager, ed., *Documents of American History*, 8th ed. (New York: Appleton, Century, Crofts, 1968, pp. 531–532) ADDRESS [BY GEORGE C. MARSHALL] AT HARVARD UNIVERSITY
June 5, 1947

I need not tell you gentlemen that the world situation is very serious. That must be apparent to all intelligent people. I think one difficulty is that the problem is one of such enormous complexity that the very mass of facts presented to the public by press and radio make it exceedingly difficult for the man in the street to reach a clear appraisement of the situation. Furthermore, the people of this country are distant from the troubled areas of the earth and it is hard for them to comprehend the plight and consequent reactions of the long-suffering peoples, and the effect of those reactions on their governments in connection with our efforts to promote peace in the world.

In considering the requirements for the rehabilitation of Europe the physical loss of life, the visible destruction of cities, factories, mines, and railroads was correctly estimated, but it has become obvious during recent months that this visible destruction was probably less serious than the dislocation of the entire fabric of European economy. For the past 10 years conditions have been highly abnormal. The feverish preparation for war and the more feverish maintenance of the war effort engulfed all aspects of national economies. Machinery has fallen into disrepair or is entirely obsolete. Under the arbitrary and destructive Nazi rule, virtually every possible enterprise was geared into the German war machine. Long-standing commercial ties, private institutions, banks, insurance companies and shipping companies disappeared, through loss of capital, absorption through nationalization or by simple destruction. In many countries, confidence in the local currency has been severely shaken. The breakdown of the business structure of Europe during the war was complete. Recovery has been seriously retarded by the fact that 2 years after the close of hostilities a peace settlement with Germany and Austria has not been agreed upon. But even given a more prompt solution of these difficult problems, the rehabilitation of the economic structure of Europe quite evidently will require a much longer time and greater effort than had been foreseen.

There is a phase of this matter which is both interesting and serious. The farmer has always produced the foodstuffs to exchange with the city dweller for the other necessities of life. This division of labor is the basis of modern civilization. At the present time it is threatened with breakdown. The town and city industries are not producing adequate goods to exchange with the food-producing farmer. Raw materials and fuel are in short supply. Machinery is lacking or worn out. The farmer or the peasant cannot find the goods for sale which he desires to purchase. So the sale of his farm produce for money which he cannot use seems to him an unprofitable transaction. He, therefore, has withdrawn many fields from crop cultivation and is using them for grazing. He feeds more grain to stock and finds for himself and his family an ample supply of food, however short he may be on clothing and the other ordinary gadgets of civilization. Meanwhile people in the cities are short of food and fuel. So the governments are forced to use their foreign money and credits to procure these necessities abroad. This process exhausts funds which are urgently needed for reconstruction. Thus a very serious situation is rapidly developing which bodes no good for the world. The modern system of the division of labor upon which the exchange of products is based is in danger of breaking down.

The truth of the matter is that Europe's requirements for the next 3 or 4 years of foreign food and other essential products—principally from America—are so much greater than her present ability to pay that she must have substantial additional help, or face economic, social, and political deterioration of a very grave character. The remedy lies in breaking the vicious circle and restoring the confidence of the European people in the economic future of their own countries and of Europe as a whole. The manufacturer and the farmer throughout wide areas must be able and willing to exchange their products for currencies the continuing value of which is not open to question.

Aside from the demoralizing effect on the world at large and the responsibilities of disturbances arising as a result of the desperation of the people concerned, the consequences to the economy of the United States should be apparent to all. It is logical that the United States should do whatever it is able to do to assist in the return of normal economic health in the world, without which there can be no political stability and no assured peace. Our policy is directed not against any country or doctrine but against hunger, poverty, desperation, and chaos. Its purpose should be the revival of a working economy in the world so as to permit the emergence of political and social conditions in which free institutions can exist. Such assistance, I am convinced, must not be on a piecemeal basis as various crises develop. Any assistance that this Government may render in the future should provide a cure rather than a mere palliative. Any government that is willing to assist in the task of recovery will find full cooperation, I am sure, on the part of the United States Government. Any government which maneuvers to block the recovery of other countries cannot expect help from us. Furthermore, governments, political parties, or groups which seek to perpetuate human misery in order to profit therefrom politically or otherwise will encounter the opposition of the United States. It is already evident that, before the United States Government can proceed much further in its efforts to alleviate the situation and help start the European world on its way to recovery, there must be some agreement among the countries of Europe as to the requirements of the situation and the part those countries themselves will take in order to give proper effect to whatever action might be undertaken by this Government. It would be neither fitting nor efficacious for this Government to undertake to draw up unilaterally a program designed to place Europe on its feet economically. This is the business of the Europeans. The initiative, I think, must come from Europe. The role of this country should consist of friendly aid in the drafting of a European program and of later support of such a program so far as it may be practical for us to do so. The program should be a joint one, agreed to by a number, if not all European nations.

An essential part of any successful action on the part of the United States is an understanding on the part of the people of America of the character of the problem and the remedies to be applied. Political passion and prejudice should have no part. With foresight, and a willingness on the part of our people to face up to the vast responsibility which history has clearly placed upon our country, the difficulties I have outlined can and will be overcome.

George F. Kennan's "Sources of Soviet Conduct," 1947

Harry S. Truman Library, Book Collection
(Foreign Affairs, pp. 53–63)
July 1947

The political personality of Soviet power as we know it today is the product of ideology and circumstances: ideology inherited by the present Soviet leaders from the movement in which they had their political origin, and circumstances of the power which they have now exercised for nearly three decades in Russia. The outstanding features of Communist ideology as it existed in 1916 may be summarized as follows: a) the central factor in the life of man, the factor which determines the character of public life and the "physiognomy of society," is the system by which material goods are produced and exchanged; b) the capitalist system of production is a nefarious one which inevitably leads to the exploitation of the working class by the capital-owning class and is incapable of developing adequately the economic resources of society or of distributing fairly the material goods produced by human labor; c) capitalism contains the seeds of its own destruction and must, in view of the inability of the capital-owning class to adjust itself to economic change, result eventually and inescapably in a revolutionary transfer of power to the working class; d) imperialism, the final phase of capitalism, leads directly to war and revolution.

The circumstances of the immediate post-revolution period—the existence in Russia of civil war and foreign intervention, together with the obvious fact that the Communists represented only a tiny minority of the Russian people—made the establishment of dictatorial power a necessity. This, together with the abrupt attempt to eliminate private production and trade, had unfortunate economic consequences and caused further bitterness against the new revolutionary regime. While the temporary relaxation of the effort to communize Russia, represented by the New Economic Policy (1921), alleviated some of this economic distress and thereby served its purpose, it also made it evident that the "capitalistic sector of society" was still prepared to profit at once from any relaxation of governmental pressure and would, if permitted to continue to exist, always constitute a powerful opposing element to the Soviet regime and a serious rival for influence in the country. Somewhat the same situation prevailed with respect to

the individual peasant who, in his own small way, also was a private producer. Lenin, had he lived, might have proved a great enough man to reconcile these conflicting forces to the ultimate benefit of Russian society, though this is questionable. But be that as it may, Stalin and those whom he led in the struggle to succeed Lenin were not the men to tolerate rival political forces in the sphere of power which they coveted. From the Russian-Asiatic world out of which they had emerged they carried with them a skepticism as to the possibilities of permanent and peaceful coexistence of rival forces. There were to be no forms of collective human activity or association which would not be dominated by the party. No other force in Russian society was to be permitted to achieve vitality or integrity. Only the party was to have structure. All else was to be an amorphous mass.

And within the party the same principle was to apply. The mass of party members might go through the motions of election, deliberation, decision and action; but in these motions they were to be animated not by their own individual wills but by the awesome breath of the party leadership and the overbrooding presence of "the word." Now the outstanding circumstance concerning the Soviet regime is that down to the present day the process of political consolidation has never been completed and the men in the Kremlin have continued to be predominantly absorbed with the struggle to secure and make absolute the power which they seized in November 1917. They have endeavored to secure it primarily against forces within Soviet society itself. But they have also endeavored to secure it against the outside world. For ideology, as we have seen, taught them that the outside world was hostile and that it was their duty eventually to overthrow the political forces beyond their borders. Finally, their own aggressive intransigence with respect to the outside world began to find its own reaction. It is an undeniable privilege of every man to prove himself right in the thesis that the world is his enemy; for if he reiterates it frequently enough and makes it the background of his conduct he is bound eventually to be right.

It lies in the nature of the mental world of the Soviet leaders as well as in their ideology that no opposition to them can be officially recognized as having any merit or justification whatsoever. Such opposition can flow, in theory, only from the hostile and incorrigible forces of dying capitalism. As long as remnants of capitalism were officially recognized as existing in Russia, it was possible to place on them, as an internal element, part of the blame for the maintenance of a dictatorial form of society. But as these remnants were liquidated, little by little, this justification fell away; and when it was indicated officially that they had been finally destroyed, it disappeared altogether. And this fact created one of the most basic of the compulsions which came to act upon the Soviet regime: since capitalism no longer existed in Russia it became necessary to justify the retention of the dictatorship by stressing the menace of capitalism abroad. But the quest for absolute power, pursued now for nearly three decades with a ruthlessness unparalleled (in scope at least) in modern times, has again produced internally, as it did externally, its own reaction. The excesses of the police apparatus have fanned the potential opposition to the regime into something far greater and more dangerous than it could have been before those excesses began.

So much for the historical background. What does it spell in terms of the political personality of Soviet power as we know it today?

Of the original ideology nothing has been officially junked. Belief is maintained in the basic badness of capitalism, in the inevitability of its destruction, in the obligation of the proletariat to assist in that destruction and to take power into its own hands. But stress has come to be laid primarily on a few concepts which relate most specifically to the Soviet regime itself: to its position as the sole truly socialist regime in a dark and misguided world and to the relationships of power within it.

The first of these concepts is that of the innate antagonism between capitalism and socialism. We have seen how deeply that concept has become imbedded in foundations of Soviet power. It has profound implications for Russia's conduct as a member of international society. It means that there can never be on Moscow's side any sincere assumption of a community of aims between the Soviet Union and powers which are regarded as capitalist. It must invariably be assumed in Moscow that the aims of the capitalist world are antagonistic to the Soviet regime and therefore to the interests of the peoples it controls. If the Soviet government occasionally sets its signature to documents which would indicate the contrary, this is to be regarded as a tactical maneuver permissible in dealing with the enemy (who is without honor) and should be taken in the spirit of *caveat emptor*. Basically the antagonism remains. From it flow many of the phenomena which we find disturbing in the Kremlin's conduct of foreign policy: the secretiveness, the lack of frankness, the duplicity, the wary suspiciousness and the basic unfriendliness of purpose. These phenomena are there to stay for the foreseeable future. There can be variations of degree and of emphasis. When there is something the Russians want from us, one or the other of these features of their policy may be thrust temporarily into the background; and when that happens there will always be Americans who will leap forward with gleeful announcements that "the Russians have changed," and some who will even try to take credit for having brought about such "changes." But we should not be misled by tactical maneuvers. These characteristics of Soviet policy are basic to the internal nature of Soviet power and will be with us, whether in the foreground or the background, until the internal nature of Soviet power is changed.

This means that we are going to continue for a long time to find the Russians difficult to deal with. It does not mean that they should be considered as embarked upon a do-or-die program to overthrow our society by a given date. The theory of the inevitability of the eventual fall of capitalism has the fortunate connotation that there is no hurry about it. The forces of progress can take their time in preparing the final *coup de grace*.

The second of the concepts important to contemporary Soviet outlook is the infallibility of the Kremlin. The Soviet concept of power, which permits no focal points of organization outside the party itself, requires that the party leadership remain in theory the sole repository of truth. For if truth were to be found elsewhere, there would be justification for its expression in organized activity. But it is precisely that which the Kremlin cannot and will not permit.

On the principle of infallibility there rests the iron discipline of the Communist party. In fact the two concepts are mutually self-supporting. Perfect discipline requires recognition of infallibility. Infallibility requires the observance of discipline. And the two together go far to determine the behaviorism of the entire Soviet apparatus of power. But their effect cannot be understood unless a third factor be taken into account: namely, the fact that the leadership is at liberty to put forward for tactical purposes any particular thesis which it finds useful to the cause at any particular moment and to require the faithful and unquestioning acceptance of that thesis by the members of the movement as a whole. This means that truth is not a constant but is actually created, for all intents and purposes, by the Soviet leaders themselves. It may vary from week to week, from month to month.

The accumulative effect of these factors is to give to the whole subordinate apparatus of Soviet power an unshakable stubbornness and steadfastness in its orientation. This orientation can be changed at will by the Kremlin but by no other power. Once a given party line has been laid down on a given issue of current policy, the whole Soviet governmental machine, including the mechanism of diplomacy, moves inexorably along the prescribed path, like a persistent toy automobile wound up and headed in a given direction, stopping only when it meets with some unanswerable force.

But we have seen that the Kremlin is under no ideological compulsion to accomplish its purposes in a hurry. Like the Church it is dealing in ideological concepts which are of long-term validity, and it can afford to be patient. Thus the Kremlin has no compunction about retreating in the face of superior force. And being under the compulsion of no timetable, it does not get panicky under the necessity for such retreat. Its political action is a fluid stream which moves constantly, wherever it is permitted to move, toward a given goal. Its main concern is to make sure that it has filled every nook and cranny available to it in the basin of world power. But if it finds unassailable barriers in its path, it accepts these philosophically and accommodates itself to them. The main thing is that there should always be pressure, unceasing constant pressure, toward the desired goal.

These considerations make Soviet diplomacy at once easier and more difficult to deal with than the diplomacy of individual aggressive leaders like Napoleon and Hitler. On the one hand it is more sensitive to contrary force, more ready to yield on individual sectors of the diplomatic front when that force is felt to be too strong, and thus is more rational in the logic and rhetoric of power. On the other hand it cannot be easily defeated or discouraged by a single victory on the part of its opponents. And the patient persistence by which it is animated means that it can be effectively countered not by sporadic acts which represent the momentary whims of democratic opinion but only by intelligent long-range policies on the part of Russia's adversaries—policies no less steady in their purpose and no less variegated and resourceful in their application than those of the Soviet Union itself.

The main element of any U.S. policy toward the Soviet Union must be that of a long-term, patient but firm and vigilant containment of Russian expansive tendencies. It is important to note, however, that such a policy has nothing to do with outward histrionics: with threats of blustering or superfluous gestures of outward "toughness." While the Kremlin is basically flexible in its reaction to political realities, it is by no means unamenable to considerations of prestige. Like almost any other government, it can be placed by tactless and threatening gestures in a position where it cannot afford to yield even though this might be dictated by its sense of realism. It is a *sine qua non* of successful dealing with Russia that the foreign government in question should remain at all times cool and collected and that its demands on Russian policy should be put forward in such a manner as to leave the way open for a compliance not too detrimental to Russian prestige.

The Soviet thesis not only implies complete lack of control by the West over its own economic destiny, it likewise assumes Russian unity, discipline and patience over an infinite period. Let us bring this apocalyptic vision down to earth and suppose that the Western world finds the strength and resourcefulness to contain Soviet power over a period of 10 to 15 years. What does that spell for Russia itself?

The Soviet achievement has been carried out at a terrible cost in human life and in human hopes and energies. It has necessitated the use of forced labor on a scale unprecedented in modern times under conditions of peace. It has involved the neglect or abuse of other phases of Soviet economic life, particularly agriculture, consumers' goods production, housing and transportation.

To all that the war has added its tremendous toll of destruction, death and human exhaustion. In consequence of this, we have in Russia today a population which is physically and spiritually tired. The mass of the people are disillusioned, skeptical and no longer as accessible as they once were to the magical attraction which Soviet power still radiates to its followers abroad. There are limits to the physical and nervous strength of people themselves. These limits are absolute ones and are binding even for the cruelest dictatorship, because beyond them people cannot be driven. The forced-labor camps and the other agencies of constraint provide temporary means of compelling people to work longer hours than their own volition or mere economic pressure would dictate; but if people survive them at all they become old before their time and must be considered as human casualties to the demands of dictatorship. In either case their best powers are no longer available to society and can no longer be enlisted in the service of the state.

Meanwhile a great uncertainty hangs over the political life of the Soviet Union. That is the uncertainty involved in the transfer of power from one individual or group of individuals to others.

This is, of course, outstandingly the problem of the personal position of Stalin. We must remember that his succession to Lenin's pinnacle of pre-eminence in the Communist movement was the only such transfer of individual authority which the Soviet Union has experienced. That transfer took 12 years to consolidate. It cost the lives of millions of people and shook the state to its foundations. The attendant tremors were felt all through the international revolutionary movement, to the disadvantage of the Kremlin itself.

But this is not only a question of Stalin himself. There has been, since 1938, a dangerous congealment of political life in the higher circles of Soviet power. The All-Union Party Congress, in theory the supreme body of the party, is supposed to meet not less often than once in three years. It will soon be eight full years since its last meeting. During this period membership in the party has numerically doubled. Party mortality during the war was enormous, and today well over half of the party members are persons who have entered since the last party congress was held. Meanwhile the same small group of men has carried on at the top.

Who can say whether, in these circumstances, the eventual rejuvenation of the higher spheres of authority (which can only be a matter of time) can take place smoothly and peacefully, or whether rivals in the quest for higher power will not eventually reach down into these politically immature and inexperienced masses in order to find support for their respective claims? If this were ever to happen, strange consequences could flow for the Communist party: for the membership at large has been exercised only in the practices of iron discipline and obedience and not in the arts of compromise and accommodation. If consequently anything were ever to occur to disrupt the unity and efficacy of the party as a political instrument, Soviet Russia might be changed overnight from one of the strongest to one of the weakest and most pitiable of national societies.

It is curious to note that the ideological power of Soviet authority is strongest today in areas beyond the frontiers of Russia, beyond the reach of its police power. This phenomenon brings to mind a comparison used by Thomas Mann in his great novel *Buddenbrooks*. Observing that human institutions often show the greatest outward brilliance at a moment when inner decay is in reality farthest advanced, he compared the Buddenbrook family in the days of its greatest glamour to one of those stars whose light shines most brightly on this world when in reality it has long since ceased to exist. And who can say with assurance that the strong light still cast by the Kremlin on the dissatisfied peoples of the Western world is not the powerful afterglow of a constellation which is in actuality on the wane? It is clear that the U.S. cannot expect in the foreseeable future to enjoy political intimacy with the Soviet regime. It must continue to regard the Soviet Union as a rival, not a partner, in the political arena.

But the possibilities for American policy are by no means limited to holding the line and hoping for the best. It is entirely possible for the U.S. to influence by its actions the internal developments, both within Russia and throughout the international Communist movement. It is a question of the degree to which the U.S. can create among the peoples of the world generally the impression of a country which knows what it wants, which is coping successfully with the problems of its internal life and with the responsibilities of a world power and which has a spiritual vitality capable of holding its own among the major ideological currents of the time. By the same token, exhibitions of indecision, disunity and internal disintegration within this country have an exhilarating effect on the whole Communist movement. At each evidence of these tendencies, a thrill of hope and excitement goes through the Communist world; a new jauntiness can be noted in the Moscow tread; new groups of foreign supporters climb on to what they can only view as the bandwagon of international politics, and Russian pressure increases all along the line in international affairs.

It would be an exaggeration to say that American behavior unassisted and alone could exercise a power of life and death over the Communist movement and bring about the early fall of Soviet power in Russia. But the U.S. has it in its power to increase enormously the strains under which Soviet policy must operate, to force upon the Kremlin a far greater degree of moderation and circum-

spection than it has had to observe in recent years and in this way to promote tendencies which must eventually find their outlet in either the breakup or the gradual mellowing of Soviet power. For no mystical, Messianic movement—and particularly not that of the Kremlin—can face frustration indefinitely without eventually adjusting itself in one way or another to the logic of that state of affairs. Surely there was never a fairer test of national quality than this. In the light of these circumstances the thoughtful observer of Russian-American relations will find no cause for complaint in the Kremlin's challenge to American society. He will rather experience a certain gratitude to a Providence which, by providing the American people with this implacable challenge, has made their entire security as a nation dependent on their pulling themselves together and accepting the responsibilities of moral and political leadership that history plainly intended them to bear.

"Letter from Birmingham Jail" (April 12–20, 1963)
Reverend Dr. Martin Luther King, Jr.

Courtesy of the King Center, Atlanta, Georgia.

Birmingham, Alabama
My Dear Fellow Clergymen:

While confined here in the Birmingham city jail, I came across your recent statement calling present activities "unwise and untimely." Seldom do I pause to answer criticism of my work and ideas. If I sought to answer all the criticisms that cross my desk, my secretaries would have little time for anything other than such correspondence in the course of the day, and I would have no time for constructive work. But since I feel that you are men of genuine good will and that your criticisms are sincerely set forth, I want to try to answer your statement in what I hope will be patient and reasonable terms.

I think I should indicate why I am here in Birmingham, since you have been influenced by the view which argues against "outsiders coming in." I have the honor of serving as President of the Southern Christian Leadership Conference, an organization operating in every southern state, with headquarters in Atlanta, Georgia. We have some eighty-five affiliated organizations across the South, and one of them is the Alabama Christian Movement for Human Rights. Frequently we share staff, educational and financial resources with our affiliates. Several months ago the affiliate here in Birmingham asked us to be on call to engage in a nonviolent direct-action program if such were deemed necessary. We readily consented, and when the hour came we lived up to our promise. So I, along with several members of my staff, am here because I was invited here. I am here because I have organizational ties here. But more basically, I am in Birmingham because injustice is here. Just as the prophets of the eighth century B.C. left their villages and carried their "thus saith the Lord" far beyond the boundaries of their home towns, and just as the Apostle Paul left his village of Tarsus and carried the gospel of Jesus Christ to the far corners of the Greco-Roman world, so am I compelled to carry the gospel of freedom beyond my own home town. Like Paul, I must constantly respond to the Macedonian call for aid.

Moreover, I am cognizant of the interrelatedness of all communities and states. I cannot sit idly in Atlanta and not be concerned about what happens in Birmingham. Injustice anywhere is a threat to justice everywhere. We are caught in an inescapable network of mutuality, tied in a single garment of destiny. Whatever affects one directly, affects all indirectly. Never again can we afford to live with the narrow, provincial "outside agitator" idea. Anyone who lives inside the United States can never be considered an outsider anywhere within its bounds.

You deplore the demonstrations taking place in Birmingham. But your statement, I am sorry to say, fails to express a similar concern for the conditions that brought about the demonstrations. I am sure that none of you would want to rest content with the superficial kind of social analysis that deals merely with effects and does not grapple with underlying causes. It is unfortunate that demonstrations are taking place in Birmingham, but it is even more unfortunate that the city's white power structure left the Negro community with no alternative.

In any nonviolent campaign there are four basic steps: collection of the facts to determine whether injustices exist; negotiation; self-purification; and direct action. We have gone through all these steps in Birmingham. There can be no gainsaying the fact that racial injustice engulfs this community. Birmingham is probably the most thoroughly segregated city in the United States. Its ugly record of brutality is widely known. Negroes have experienced grossly unjust treatment in the courts. There have been more unsolved bombings of Negro homes and churches in Birmingham than in any other city in the nation. These are the hard, brutal facts of the case. On the basis of these conditions, Negro leaders sought to negotiate with the city fathers. But the latter consistently refused to engage in good-faith negotiation.

Then, last September, came the opportunity to talk with leaders of Birmingham's economic community. In the course of the negotiations, certain promises were made by the merchants—for example, to remove the stores' humiliating racial signs. On the basis of these promises, the Reverend Fred Shuttlesworth and the leaders of the Alabama Christian Movement for Human Rights agreed to a moratorium on all demonstrations. As the weeks and months went by, we realized that we were the victims of a broken promise. A few signs, briefly removed, returned; the others remained.

As in so many past experiences, our hopes had been blasted, and the shadow of deep disappointment settled upon us. We had no alternative except to prepare for direct action, whereby we would present our very bodies as a means of laying our case before the conscience of the local and the national community. Mindful of the difficulties involved, we decided to undertake a process of self-purification. We began a series of workshops on nonviolence, and we repeatedly asked ourselves: "Are you able to accept blows without retaliation?" "Are you able to endure the ordeal of jail?" We decided to schedule our direct-action program for the Easter season, realizing that except for Christmas, this is the main shopping period of the year. Knowing that a strong economic-withdrawal program would be the by-product of direct action, we felt that this would be the best time to bring pressure to bear on the merchants for the needed change.

Then it occurred to us that Birmingham's mayoralty election was coming up in March, and we speedily decided to postpone action until after election day. When we discovered that the Commissioner of Public Safety, Eugene "Bull" Connor, had piled up enough votes to be in the run-off, we decided again to postpone action until the day after the run-off so that the demonstrations could not be used to cloud the issues. Like many others, we waited to see Mr. Connor defeated, and to this end we endured postponement after postponement. Having aided in this community need, we felt that our direct-action program could be delayed no longer.

You may well ask: "Why direct action? Why sit-ins, marches, and so forth? Isn't negotiation a better path?" You are quite right in calling for negotiation. Indeed, this is the very purpose of direct action. Nonviolent direct action seeks to create such a crisis and foster such a tension that a community which has constantly refused to negotiate is forced to confront the issue. It seeks so to dramatize the issue that it can no longer be ignored. My citing the creation of tension as part of the work of the nonviolent-resister may sound rather shocking. But I must confess that I am not afraid of the word "tension." I have earnestly opposed violent tension, but there is a type of constructive, nonviolent tension which is necessary for growth. Just as Socrates felt that it was necessary to create a tension in the mind so that individuals could rise from the bondage of myths and half-truths to the unfettered realm of creative analysis and objective appraisal, so must we see the need for nonviolent gadflies to create the kind of tension in society that will help men rise from the dark depths of prejudice and racism to the majestic heights of understanding and brotherhood.

The purpose of our direct-action program is to create a situation so crisis-packed that it will inevitably open the door to negotiation. I therefore concur with you in your call for negotiation. Too long has our beloved Southland been bogged down in a tragic effort to live in monologue rather than dialogue.

One of the basic points in your statement is that the action that I and my associates have taken in Birmingham is untimely. Some have asked: "Why didn't you give the new city administration time to act?" The only answer that I can give to this query is that the new Birmingham administration must be prodded about as much as the outgoing one, before it will act. We are sadly mistaken if we feel that the election of Albert Boutwell as mayor will bring the millennium to Birmingham. While Mr. Boutwell is a much more gentle person that Mr. Connor, they are both segregationists, dedicated to maintenance of the status quo. I have hoped that Mr. Boutwell will be reasonable enough to see the futility of massive resistance to desegregation. But he will not see this without pressure from devotees of civil rights. My friends, I must say to you that we have not made a single gain in civil rights without determined legal and nonviolent pressure. Lamentably, it is an historical fact that privileged groups seldom give up their privileges voluntarily. Individuals may see the moral light and voluntarily give up their unjust posture; but as Reinhold Niebuhr has reminded us, groups tend to be more immoral that individuals.

We know through painful experience that freedom is never voluntarily given by the oppressor, it must be demanded by the oppressed. Frankly, I have yet to engage in a direct-action campaign that was "well timed" in view of those who have not suffered unduly from the disease of segregation. For years now I have heard the word "wait!" It rings in the ear of every Negro with piercing familiarity. This "Wait" has almost always meant "Never." We must come to see, with one of our distinguished jurists, that "justice too long delayed is justice denied."

We have waited for more that 340 years for our constitutional and God-given rights. The nations of Asia and Africa are moving with jetlike speed toward gaining political independence, but we still creep at horse-and-buggy pace toward gaining a cup of coffee at a lunch counter. Perhaps it is easy for those who have never felt the stinging darts of segregation to say, "Wait." But when you have seen vicious mobs lynch your mothers and fathers at will and drown your sisters and brothers at whim; when you have seen hate-filled policemen curse, kick, and even kill your black brothers and sisters; when you see the vast majority of your twenty million Negro brothers smothering in an airtight cage of poverty in the midst of an affluent society; when you suddenly find your tongue twisted and your speech stammering as you seek to explain to your six-year-old daughter why she can't go to the public amusement park that has just been advertised on television, and see tears welling up in her eyes when she is told that Funtown is closed to colored children, and see ominous clouds of inferiority beginning to form in her little mental sky, and see her beginning to distort her personality by developing an unconscious bitterness toward white people; when you have to concoct an answer for a five-year-old son who is asking, "Daddy, why do white people treat colored people so mean?"; when you take a cross-country drive and find it necessary to sleep night after night in the uncomfortable corners of your automobile because no motel will accept you; when you are humiliated day in and day out by nagging signs reading "white" and "colored"; when your first name becomes "Nigger," your middle name becomes "boy" (however old you are) and your last name becomes "John," and your wife and mother are never given the respected title "Mrs."; when you are harried by day and haunted by night by the fact that you are a Negro, living constantly at tiptoe stance, never quite knowing what to expect next, and are plagued with inner fears and outer resentments; when you are forever fighting a degenerating sense of "nobodiness" then you will understand why we find it difficult to wait. There comes a time when the cup of endurance runs over, and men are no longer willing to be plunged into the abyss of despair. I hope, sirs, you can understand our legitimate and unavoidable impatience. You express a great deal of anxiety over our willingness to break laws. This is certainly a legitimate concern. Since we so diligently urge people to obey the Supreme Court's decision of 1954 outlawing segregation in the public schools, at first glance it may seem rather paradoxical for us consciously to break laws. One may ask: "How can you advocate breaking some laws and obeying others?" The answer lies in the fact that there are two types of laws: just and unjust. I would be the first to advocate obeying just laws. One has not only a legal but a moral responsibility to obey just laws. Conversely, one has a moral responsibility to disobey unjust laws. I would agree with St. Augustine that "an unjust law is no law at all."

Now, what is the difference between the two? How does one determine whether a law is just or unjust? A just law is a man-made code that squares with the moral law or the law of God. An unjust law is a code that is out of harmony with the moral law. To put it in the terms of St. Thomas Aquinas: An unjust law is a human law that is not rooted in eternal law and natural law. Any law that uplifts human personality is just. Any law that degrades human personality is unjust. All segregation statutes are unjust because segregation distorts the soul and damages the personality. It gives the segregator a false sense of superiority and the segregated a false sense of inferiority. Segregation, to use the terminology of the Jewish philosopher Martin Buber, substitutes an "I-it" relationship for an "I-thou" relationship and ends up relegating persons to the status of things. Hence segregation is not only politically, economically and sociologically unsound, it is morally wrong and sinful. Paul Tillich has said that sin is separation. Is not segregation an existential expression of man's tragic separation, his awful estrangement, his terrible sinfulness? Thus is it that I can urge men to obey the 1954 decision of the Supreme Court, for it is morally right; and I can urge them to disobey segregation ordinances, for they are morally wrong.

Let us consider a more concrete example of just and unjust laws. An unjust law is a code that a numerical or power majority group compels a minority group to obey but does not make binding on itself. This is *difference* made legal. By the same token, a just law is a code that a majority compels a minority to follow and that it is willing to follow itself. This is *sameness* made legal.

Let me give another explanation. A law is unjust if it is inflicted on a minority that, as a result of being denied the right to vote, had no part in enacting or devising the law. Who can say that the legislature of Alabama which set up that state's segregation laws was democratically elected? Throughout Alabama all sorts of devious methods are used to prevent Negroes from becoming registered voters, and there are some counties in which, even though Negroes constitute a majority of the population, not a single Negro is registered. Can any law enacted under such circumstances be considered democratically structured?

Sometimes a law is just on its face and unjust in its application. For instance, I have been arrested on a charge of parading without a permit. Now, there is nothing wrong in having an ordinance which requires a permit for a parade. But such an ordinance becomes unjust when it is used to maintain segregation and to deny citizens the First-Amendment privilege of peaceful assembly and protest.

I hope you are able to see the distinction I am trying to point out. In no sense do I advocate evading or defying the law, as would the rabid segregationist. That would lead to anarchy. One who breaks an unjust law must do so openly, lovingly, and with a willingness to accept the penalty. I submit that an individual who breaks a law that conscience tells him is unjust, and who willingly accepts the penalty of imprisonment in order to arouse the conscience of the community over its injustice, is in reality expressing the highest respect for law.

Of course, there is nothing new about this kind of civil disobedience. It was evidenced sublimely in the refusal of Shadrach, Meshach, and Abednego to obey the laws of Nebuchadnezzar, on the ground that a higher moral law was at stake. It was practiced superbly by the early Christians, who were willing to face hungry lions and the excruciating pain of chopping blocks rather than submit to certain unjust laws of the Roman Empire. To a degree, academic freedom is a reality today because Socrates practiced civil disobedience. In our own nation, the Boston Tea Party represented a massive act of civil disobedience.

We should never forget that everything Adolf Hitler did in Germany was "legal" and everything the Hungarian freedom fighters did in Hungary was "illegal." It was "illegal" to aid and comfort a Jew in Hitler's Germany. Even so, I am sure that, had I lived in Germany at the time, I would have aided and comforted my Jewish brothers. If today I lived in a Communist country where certain principles dear to the Christian faith are suppressed, I would openly advocate disobeying that country's anti-religious laws.

I must make two honest confessions to you, my Christian and Jewish brothers. First, I must confess that over the past few years I have been gravely disappointed with the white moderate. I have almost reached the regrettable conclusion that the Negro's great stumbling block in his stride toward freedom is not the White Citizen's Councilor or the Ku Klux Klanner, but the white moderate, who is more devoted to "order" than to justice; who prefers a negative peace which is the absence of tension to a positive peace which is the presence of justice; who constantly says, "I agree with you in the goal you seek, but I cannot agree with your methods of direct action"; who paternalistically believes he can set the timetable for another man's freedom; who lives by a mythical concept of time and who constantly advises the Negro to wait for a "more convenient season." Shallow understanding from people of good will is more frustrating that absolute misunderstanding from people of ill will. Lukewarm acceptance is much more bewildering than outright rejection.

I had hoped that the white moderate would understand that law and order exist for the purpose of establishing justice and that when they fail in this purpose they become the dangerously structured dams that block the flow of social progress. I had hoped that the white moderate would understand that the present tension in the South is a necessary phase of the transition from an obnoxious negative peace, in which the Negro passively accepted his unjust plight, to a substantive and positive peace, in which all men will respect the dignity and worth of human personality. Actually, we who engage in nonviolent direct action are not the creators of tension. We merely bring to the surface the hidden tension that is already alive. We bring it out in the open, where it can be seen and dealt with. Like a boil that can never be cured so long as it is covered up but must be opened with all it ugliness to the natural medicines of air and light injustice must be exposed, with all the tension its exposure creates, to the light of human conscience and the air of national opinion, before it can be cured.

In your statement you assert that our actions, even though peaceful, must be condemned because they precipitate violence. But is this a logical assertion? Isn't this like condemning a robbed man because his possession of money precipitated the evil act of robbery? Isn't this like condemning Socrates because his unswerving commitment to truth and his philosophical inquiries precipitated the act by the misguided populace in which they made him drink hemlock? Isn't this like condemning Jesus because his unique God-consciousness and never-ceasing devotion to God's will precipitated the evil act of crucifixion? We must come to see that, as the federal courts have consistently affirmed, it is wrong to urge an individual to cease his efforts to gain his basic constitutional rights because the quest may precipitate violence. Society must protect the robbed and punish the robber.

I had also hoped that the white moderate would reject the myth concerning time in relation to the struggle for freedom. I have just received a letter from a white brother in Texas. He writes: "All Christians know that the colored people will receive equal rights eventually, but it is possible that you are in too great a religious hurry. It has taken Christianity almost two thousand years to accomplish what it has. The teachings of Christ take time to come to earth." Such an attitude stems from a tragic misconception of time, from the strangely irrational notion that there is something in the very flow of time that will inevitably cure all ills. Actually, time itself is neutral; it can be used either destructively or constructively. More and more I feel that the people of ill will have used time much more effectively than have the people of good will. We will have to repent in the generation not merely for the hateful words and actions of the bad people, but for the appalling silence of the good people. Human progress never rolls in on wheels of inevitability; it comes through the tireless efforts of men willing to be co-workers with God, and without this hard work, time itself becomes an ally of the forces of stagnation. We must use time creatively, in the knowledge that the time is always ripe to do right. Now is the time to make real the promise of democracy and transform our pending national elegy into a creative psalm of brotherhood. Now is the time to lift our national policy from the quicksand of racial injustice to the solid rock of human dignity.

You speak of our activity in Birmingham as extreme. At first I was rather disappointed that fellow clergyman would see my nonviolent efforts as those of an extremist. I began thinking about the fact that I stand in the middle of two opposing forces in the Negro community. One is a force of complacency, made up in part of Negroes who, as a result of long years of oppression, are so drained of self-respect and a sense of "somebodiness" that they have adjusted to segregation; and in part of a few middle-class Negroes who, because of a degree of academic and economic security and because in some ways they profit by segregation, have become insensitive to the problems of the masses. The other force is one of bitterness and hatred, and it comes perilously close to advocating violence. It is expressed in the various black nationalist groups that are springing up across the nation, the largest and best-known being Elijah Muhammad's Muslim movement. Nourished by the Negro's frustration over the continued existence of racial discrimination, this movement is made up of people who have lost faith in America, who have absolutely repudiated Christianity, and who have concluded that the white man is an incorrigible "devil." I have tried to stand between these two forces, saying that we need emulate neither the "do-nothingism" of the complacent nor the hatred and despair of the black nationalist. For there is the more excellent way of love and nonviolent protest. I am grateful to God that, through the influence of the Negro church, the way of nonviolence became an integral part of our struggle.

If this philosophy had not emerged, by now many streets of the South would, I am convinced, be flowing with blood. And I am further convinced that if our white brothers dismiss as "rabble-rousers" and "outside agitators" those of us who employ nonviolent direct action, and if they refuse to support our nonviolent efforts, millions of Negroes will, out of frustration and despair, seek solace and security in black-nationalist ideologies—a development that would inevitably lead to a frightening racial nightmare.

Oppressed people cannot remain oppressed forever. The yearning for freedom eventually manifests itself, and that is what has happened to the American Negro. Something within has reminded him of his birthright of freedom, and something without has reminded him that it can be gained. Consciously or unconsciously, he has been caught up by the Zeitgeist, and with his black brothers of Africa and his brown and yellow brothers of Asia, South America, and the Caribbean, the United States Negro is moving with a sense of great urgency toward the promised land of racial justice. If one recognizes this vital urge that has engulfed the Negro community, one should readily understand why public demonstrations are taking place. The Negro has many pent-up resentments and latent frustrations, and he must release them. So let him march; let him make prayer pilgrimages to the city hall; let him go on freedom rides—and try to understand why he must do so. If his repressed emotions are not released in nonviolent ways, they will seek expression through violence; this is not a threat but a fact of history. So I have not said to my people, "Get rid of your discontent." Rather, I have tried to say that this normal and healthy discontent can be channeled into the creative outlet of nonviolent direct action. And now this approach is being termed extremist.

But though I was initially disappointed at being categorized as an extremist, as I continued to think about the matter I gradually gained a measure of satisfaction from the label. Was not Jesus an extremist for love: "Love your enemies, bless them that curse you, do good to them that hate you, and pray for them which despitefully use you, and persecute you." Was not Amos an extremist for justice: "Let justice roll down like waters and righteousness like an ever-flowing stream." Was not Paul an extremist for the Christian gospel: "I bear in my body the marks of the Lord Jesus." Was not Martin Luther an extremist: "Here I stand; I cannot do otherwise, so help me God." And John Bunyan: "I will stay in jail to the end of my days before I make a butchery of my conscience." And Abraham Lincoln: "This nation cannot survive half slave and half free." And Thomas Jefferson: "We hold these truths to be self-evident, that all men are created equal. . . ." So the question is not whether we will be extremists, but what kind of extremists we will be. Will we be extremists for hate or for love? Will we be extremists for the preservation of injustice or for the extension of justice? In that dramatic scene on Calvary's hill three men were crucified. We must never forget that all three were crucified for the same crime—the crime of extremism. Two were extremists for immorality, and thus fell below their environment. The other, Jesus Christ, was an extremist for love, truth, and goodness, and thereby rose above his environment. Perhaps the South, the nation, and the world are in dire need of creative extremists.

I had hoped that the white moderate would see this need. Perhaps I was too optimistic; perhaps I expected too much. I suppose I should have realized that few members of the oppressor race can understand the deep groans and passionate yearnings of the oppressed race, and still fewer have the vision to see that injustice must be rooted out by strong, persistent, and determined action. I am thankful, however, that some of our white brothers in the South have grasped the meaning of this social revolution and committed themselves to it. They are still all too few in quantity, but they are big in quality. Some—such as Ralph McGill, Lillian Smith, Harry Golden, James McBride Dabbs, Ann Braden, and Sarah Patton Boyle—have written about our struggle in eloquent and prophetic terms. Others have marched with us down nameless streets of the South. They have languished in filthy, roach-infested jails, suffering the abuse and brutality of policemen who view them as "dirty nigger-lovers." Unlike so many of their moderate brothers and sisters, they have recognized the urgency of the moment and sensed the need for powerful "action" antidotes to combat the disease of segregation.

Let me take note of my other major disappointment. I have been so greatly disappointed with the white church and its leadership. Of course, there are some notable exceptions. I am not unmindful of the fact that each of you has taken some significant stands on this issue. I commend you, Reverend Stallings, for your Christian stand on this past Sunday, in welcoming Negroes to your worship service on a nonsegregated basis. I commend the Catholic leaders of this state for integrating Spring Hill College several years ago.

But despite these notable exceptions, I must honestly reiterate that I have been disappointed with the church. I do not say this as one of those negative critics who can always find something wrong with the church. I say this as a minister of the gospel, who loves the church; who was nurtured in its bosom; who has been sustained by its spiritual blessings and who will remain true to it as long as the cord of life shall lengthen.

When I was suddenly catapulted into the leadership of the bus protest in Montgomery, Alabama, a few years ago, I felt we would be supported by the white church. I felt that the ministers, priests, and rabbis of the South would be among our strongest allies. Instead, some have been outright opponents, refusing to understand the freedom movement and misrepresenting its leaders; all too many others have been more cautious than courageous and have remained silent behind the anesthetizing security of stained-glass windows.

In spite of my shattered dreams, I came to Birmingham with the hope that the white religious leadership of this community would see the justice of our cause and, with deep moral concern, would serve as the channel through which our just grievances could reach the power structure. I had hoped that each of you would understand. But again I have been disappointed.

I have heard numerous southern religious leaders admonish their worshipers to comply with a desegregation decision because it is the law, but I have longed to hear white ministers declare: "Follow this decree because integration is morally right and because the Negro is your brother." In the midst of blatant injustices inflicted upon the Negro, I have watched white churchmen stand on the sideline and mouth pious irrelevancies and sanctimonious trivialities. In the midst of a mighty struggle to rid our nation of racial and economic injustice, I have heard many ministers say: "Those are social issues, with which the gospel has no real concern." And I have watched many churches commit themselves to a completely otherworldly religion which makes a strange, un-Biblical distinction between body and soul, between the sacred and the secular.

I have traveled the length and breadth of Alabama, Mississippi, and all the other southern states. On sweltering summer days and crisp autumn mornings I have looked at the South's beautiful churches with their lofty spires pointing heavenward. I have beheld the impressive outlines of her massive religious-education buildings. Over and over I have found myself asking: "What kind of people worship here? Who is their God? Where were their voices when the lips of Governor Barnett dripped with words of interposition and nullification? Where were they when Governor Wallace gave a clarion call for defiance and hatred? Where were their voices of support when bruised and weary Negro men and women decided to rise from the dark dungeons of complacency to the bright hills of creative protest?"

Yes, these questions are still in my mind. In deep disappointment I have wept over the laxity of the church. But be assured that my tears have been tears of love. Yes, I love the church. How could I do otherwise? I am in the rather unique position of being the son, the grandson, and the great-grandson of preachers. Yes, I see the church as the body of Christ. But, oh! How we have blemished and scarred that body through social neglect and through fear of being nonconformists.

There was a time when the church was very powerful—in the time when the early Christians rejoiced at being deemed worthy to suffer for what they believed. In those days the church was not merely a thermometer that recorded the ideas and principles of popular opinion; it was a thermostat that transformed the mores of society. Whenever the early Christians entered a town, the people in power became disturbed and immediately sought to convict the Christians for being "disturbers of the peace" and "outside agitators." But the Christians pressed on, in the conviction that they were "a colony of heaven," called to obey God rather than man. Small in number, they were big in commitment. They were too God-intoxicated to be "astronomically intimidated." By their effort and example they brought an end to such ancient evils as infanticide and gladiatorial contests.

Things are different now. So often the contemporary church is a weak, ineffectual voice with an uncertain sound. So often it is an arch-defender of the status quo. Far from being disturbed by the presence of the church, the power structure of the average community is consoled by the church's silent—and often even vocal—sanction of things as they are. But the judgment of God is upon the church as never before. If today's church does not recapture the sacrificial spirit of the early church, it will lose its authenticity, forfeit the loyalty of millions, and be dismissed as an irrelevant social club with no meaning for the twentieth century. Every day I meet young people whose disappointment with the church has turned into outright disgust.

Perhaps I have once again been too optimistic. Is organized religion too inextricably bound to the status quo to save our nation and the world? Perhaps I must turn my faith to the inner spiritual church, the church within the church, as the true ekklesia and the hope of the world. But again I am thankful to God that some noble souls from the ranks of organized religion have broken loose from the paralyzing chains of conformity and joined us as active partners in the struggle for freedom. They have left their secure congregations and walked the streets of Albany, Georgia, with us. They have gone down the highways of the South on tortuous rides for freedom. Yes, they have gone to jail with us. Some have been dismissed from their churches, have lost the support of their bishops and fellow ministers. But they have acted in the faith that right defeated is stronger than evil triumphant. Their witness has been the

spiritual salt that has preserved the true meaning of the gospel in these troubled times. They have carved a tunnel of hope through the dark mountain of disappointment.

I hope the church as a whole will meet the challenge of this decisive hour. But even if the church does not come to the aid of justice, I have no despair about the future. I have no fear about the outcome of our struggle in Birmingham, even if our motives are at present misunderstood. We will reach the goal of freedom in Birmingham and all over the nation, because the goal of America is freedom. Abused and scorned though we may be, our destiny is tied up with America's destiny. Before the pilgrims landed at Plymouth, we were here. For more than two centuries our forebears labored in this country without wages; they made cotton king; they built the homes of their masters while suffering gross injustice and shameful humiliation—and yet out of bottomless vitality they continued to thrive and develop. If the inexpressible cruelties of slavery could not stop us, the opposition we now face will surely fail. We will win our freedom because the sacred heritage of our nation and the eternal will of God are embodied in our echoing demands.

Before closing I feel impelled to mention one other point in your statement that has troubled me profoundly. You warmly commended the Birmingham police force for keeping "order" and "preventing violence." I doubt that you would so quickly commend the policemen if you were to observe their ugly and inhumane treatment of Negroes here in the city jail; if you were to watch them push and curse old Negro women and young Negro girls; if you were to see them slap and kick Negro men and young boys; if you were to observe them, as they did on two occasions, refuse to give us food because we wanted to sing our grace together. I cannot join you in your praise of the Birmingham police department.

It is true that the police have exercised a degree of discipline in handling the demonstrations. In this sense they have conducted themselves rather "nonviolently" in public. But for what purpose? To preserve the evil system of segregation. Over the past few years I have consistently preached that nonviolence demands that the means we use must be as pure as the ends we seek. I have tried to make clear that it is wrong to use immoral means to attain moral ends. But now I must affirm that it is just as wrong, or perhaps even more so, to use moral means to preserve immoral ends. Perhaps Mr. Connor and his policemen have been rather nonviolent in public, as was Chief Pritchett in Albany, Georgia, but they have used the moral means of nonviolence to maintain the immoral end of racial injustice. As T. S. Eliot has said, "The last temptation is the greatest treason: To do the right deed for the wrong reason."

I wish you had commended the Negro sit-inners and demonstrators of Birmingham for their sublime courage, their willingness to suffer, and their amazing discipline in the midst of great provocation. One day the South will recognize its real heroes. They will be the James Merediths, with the noble sense of purpose that enables them to face jeering and hostile mobs, and with the agonizing loneliness that characterizes the life of the pioneer. They will be old, oppressed, battered Negro women, symbolized in a seventy-two-year-old woman in Montgomery, Alabama, who rose up with a sense of dignity and with her people decided not to ride segregated buses, and who responded with ungrammatical profundity to one who inquired about her weariness: "My feets is tired, but my soul is at rest." They will be the young high school and college students, the young ministers of the gospel and a host of their elders, courageously and nonviolently sitting in at lunch counters and willingly going to jail for conscience' sake. One day the South will know that when these disinherited children of God sat down at lunch counters, they were in reality standing up for what is best in the American dream and for the most sacred values in our Judaeo Christian heritage, thereby bringing our nation back to those great wells of democracy which were dug deep by the founding fathers in their formulation of the Constitution and the Declaration of Independence.

Never before have I written so long a letter. I'm afraid it is much too long to take your precious time. I can assure you that it would have been much shorter if I had been writing from a comfortable desk, but what else can one do when he is alone in a narrow jail cell, other than write long letters, think long thoughts, and pray long prayers?

If I have said anything in this letter that overstates the truth and indicates an unreasonable impatience, I beg you to forgive me. If I have said anything that understates the truth and indicates my having a patience that allows me to settle for anything less than brotherhood, I beg God to forgive me.

I hope this letter finds you strong in the faith. I also hope that circumstances will soon make it possible for me to meet each of you, not as an integrationist or a civil-rights leader but as a fellow clergyman and a Christian brother. Let us all hope that the dark clouds of racial prejudice will soon pass away and the deep fog of misunderstanding will be lifted from our fear-drenched communities, and in some not too distant tomorrow the radiant stars of love and brotherhood will shine over our great nation with all their scintillating beauty.

Yours for the cause of Peace and Brotherhood, Martin Luther King, Jr.

"I Have a Dream" Speech (August 28, 1963)
Reverend Dr. Martin Luther King, Jr.
Courtesy of the King Center. Atlanta, Georgia.

I am happy to join with you today in what will go down in history as the greatest demonstration for freedom in the history of our nation.

Five score years ago, a great American, in whose symbolic shadow we stand today, signed the Emancipation Proclamation. This momentous decree came as a great beacon light of hope to millions of Negro slaves who had been seared in the flames of withering injustice. It came as a joyous daybreak to end the long night of their captivity. But one hundred years later, the Negro still is not free; one hundred years later, the life of the Negro is still sadly crippled by the manacles of segregation and the chains of discrimination; one hundred years later, the Negro lives on a lonely island of poverty in the midst of a vast ocean of material prosperity; one hundred years later, the Negro is still languishing in the corners of American society and finds himself in exile in his own land.

So we've come here today to dramatize a shameful condition. In a sense we've come to our nation's capital to cash a check. When the architects of our republic wrote the magnificent words of the Constitution and the Declaration of Independence, they were signing a promissory note to which every American was to fall heir. This note was the promise that all men, yes, black men as well as white men, would be guaranteed the unalienable rights of life, liberty, and the pursuit of happiness.

It is obvious today that America has defaulted on this promissory note in so far as her citizens of color are concerned. Instead of honoring this sacred obligation, America has given the Negro people a bad check; a check which has come back marked "insufficient funds." But we refuse to believe that the bank of justice is bankrupt. We refuse to believe that there are insufficient funds in the great vaults of opportunity of this nation. And so we've come to cash this check, a check that will give us upon demand the riches of freedom and the security of justice.

We have also come to this hallowed spot to remind America of the fierce urgency of now. This is no time to engage in the luxury of cooling off or to take the tranquilizing drug of gradualism. Now is the time to make real the promises of democracy; now is the time to rise from the dark and desolate valley of segregation to the sunlit path of racial justice; now is the time to lift our nation from the quicksands of racial injustice to the solid rock of brotherhood; now is the time to make justice a reality for all God's children. It would be fatal for the nation to overlook the urgency of the moment. This sweltering summer of the Negro's legitimate discontent will not pass until there is an invigorating autumn of freedom and equality.

Nineteen sixty-three is not an end, but a beginning. And those who hope that the Negro needed to blow off steam and will now be content, will have a rude awakening if the nation returns to business as usual. There will be neither rest nor tranquillity in America until the Negro is granted his citizenship rights. The whirlwinds of revolt will continue to shake the foundations of our nation until the bright day of justice emerges.

But there is something that I must say to my people, who stand on the worn threshold which leads into the palace of justice. In the process of gaining our rightful place, we must not be guilty of wrongful deeds. Let us not seek to satisfy our thirst for freedom by drinking from the cup of bitterness and hatred. We must forever conduct our struggle on the high plain of dignity and discipline. We must not allow our creative protests to degenerate into physical violence. Again and again we must rise to the majestic heights of meeting physical force with soul force. The marvelous new militancy, which has engulfed the Negro community, must not lead us to a distrust of all white people. For many of our white brothers, as evidenced by their presence here today, have come to realize that their destiny is tied up with our destiny. And they have come to realize that their freedom is inextricably bound to our freedom. We cannot walk alone. And as we walk, we must make the pledge that we shall always march ahead. We cannot turn back.

There are those who are asking the devotees of Civil Rights. "When will you be satisfied?" We can never be satisfied as long as the Negro is the victim of the unspeakable horrors of police brutality; we can never be satisfied as long as our bodies, heavy with the fatigue of travel cannot gain lodging in the motels of the highways and the hotels of the cities; we cannot be satisfied as long as the Negro's basic mobility is from a smaller ghetto to a larger one; we can never be satisfied as long as our children are stripped of their selfhood and robbed of their dignity by signs stating. "For White Only;" we cannot be satisfied as long as the Negro in Mississippi cannot vote and a Negro in New York believes he has nothing for which to vote. No! No, we are not satisfied, and we will not be satisfied until "justice rolls down like waters and righteousness like a mighty stream."

I am not unmindful that some of you have come here out of great trials and tribulations. Some of you have come fresh from narrow jail cells. Some of you have come from areas where your quest for freedom left you battered by the storms of persecution and staggered by the winds of police brutality. You have been the veterans of creative suffering. Continue to work with the faith that unearned suffering is redemptive. Go back to Mississippi: Go back to Alabama: Go back to South Carolina: Go back to Georgia: Go back to Louisiana: Go back to the slums and ghettos of our Northern cities, knowing that somehow this situation can and will be changed. Let us not wallow in the valley of despair.

So I say to you, my friends, that even though we face the difficulties of today and tomorrow, I still have a dream. It is a dream deeply rooted in the American dream, that one day this nation will rise up and live out the true meaning of its creed, "we hold these truths to be self-evident, that all men are created equal." I have a dream that one day on the red hills of Georgia, sons of former slaves and the sons of former slave owners will be able to sit down together at the table of brotherhood. I have a dream that one day even the state of Mississippi, a state sweltering with the heat of injustice, sweltering with the heat of oppression, will be transformed into an oasis of freedom and justice. I have a dream my four little children will one day live in a nation where they will not be judged by the color of their skin, but by the content of their character.

I Have a Dream Today!

I have a dream that one day in Alabama—with its vicious racists, with its Governor having his lips dripping with the words of interposition and nullification—one day right there in Alabama, little black boys and black girls will be able to join hands with little white boys and white girls as sisters and brothers.

I Have a Dream Today!

I have a dream that one day every valley shall be exalted, every hill and mountain shall be made low. The rough places will be plain and the crooked places will be made straight "and the glory of the Lord shall be revealed, and all flesh shall see it together."

This is our hope. This is the faith that I go back to the South with. With this faith we will be able to hew out of the mountain of despair, a stone of hope. With this faith we will be able to transform the jangling discords of our nation into a beautiful symphony of brotherhood. With this faith we will be able to work together, to pray together, to struggle together, to go to jail together, to stand up for freedom together, knowing that we will be free one day. And this will be the day. This will be the day when all of God's children will be able to sing with new meaning, "My country 'tis of thee, sweet land of liberty, of thee I sing. Land where my father died, land of the pilgrim's pride, from every mountain side, let freedom ring." And if America is to be a great nation, this must become true.

So let freedom ring from the prodigious hilltops of New Hampshire; let freedom ring from the mighty mountains of New York; let freedom ring from the heightening Alleghenies of Pennsylvania; let freedom ring from the snow-capped Rockies of Colorado; let freedom ring from the curvaceous slopes of California. But not only that. Let freedom ring from Stone Mountain of Georgia; let freedom ring from Lookout Mountain of Tennessee; let freedom ring from every hill and mole hill of Mississippi. "From every mountainside, let freedom ring."

And when this happens, and when we allow freedom to ring, when we let it ring from every village and every hamlet from every state and every city, we will be able to speed up that day when all God's children, black men and white men, Jews and Gentiles, Protestants and Catholics, will be able to join hands and sing in the words of the old Negro spiritual: "Free at last. Thank God Almighty, we are free at last."

Bibliography

Acuña, Rodolfo. *Occupied America: A History of Chicanos.* 4th ed. New York: Addison Wesley Longman, 2000.

Allen, Craig. *Eisenhower and the Mass Media: Peace, Prosperity, and Prime-Time TV.* Chapel Hill: University of North Carolina Press, 1993.

Ambrose, Stephen E. *Eisenhower: The President.* New York: Simon & Schuster, 1984.

———. *Eisenhower: Soldier and President.* New York: Simon & Schuster, 1990.

Anderson, Terry H. *The Movement and the Sixties: Protest in America from Greensboro to Wounded Knee.* New York: Oxford University Press, 1995.

———. *The Sixties.* New York: Addison Wesley Longman, 1999.

Appy, Christian G. *Working-Class War: American Combat Soldiers and Vietnam.* Chapel Hill: University of North Carolina Press, 1993.

Barnouw, Erik. *Tube of Plenty: The Evolution of American Television.* 2d rev. ed. New York: Oxford University Press, 1990.

Baughman, James L. *The Republic of Mass Culture: Journalism, Filmmaking, and Broadcasting in America since 1941.* Baltimore: The Johns Hopkins University Press, 1992.

Blake, Peter. *God's Own Junkyard: The Planned Deterioration of America's Landscape.* New York: Holt, Rinehart & Winston, 1979.

Boyer, Paul. *By the Bomb's Early Light: American Thought and Culture at the Dawn of the Atomic Age.* New York: Pantheon, 1985.

Branch, Taylor. *Parting the Waters: America in the King Years, 1954–1963.* New York: Simon & Schuster, 1988.

———. *Pillar of Fire: America in the King Years, 1963–1965.* New York: Simon & Schuster, 1998.

Brands, H. W., Jr. *Cold Warriors: Eisenhower's Generation and American Foreign Policy.* New York: Columbia University Press, 1988.

Brennan, Mary C. *Turning Right in the Sixties: The Conservative Capture of the GOP.* Chapel Hill: University of North Carolina Press, 1995.

Burner, David. *Making Peace with the 60s.* Princeton, N.J.: Princeton University Press, 1996.

Carson, Clayborne. *In Struggle: SNCC and the Black Awakening of the 1960s.* Cambridge, Mass.: Harvard University Press, 1981.

Carson, Rachel. *Silent Spring.* Boston: Houghton Mifflin, 1962.

Chafe, William H. *Civilities and Civil Rights: Greensboro, North Carolina, and the Black Struggle for Freedom.* New York: Oxford University Press, 1980.

Chalmers, David. *And the Crooked Places Made Straight: The Struggle for Social Change in the 1960s.* Baltimore: The Johns Hopkins University Press, 1991.

Dallek, Robert. *Flawed Giant: Lyndon Johnson and His Times, 1961–1973.* New York: Oxford University Press, 1998.

———. *Lone Star Rising: Lyndon Johnson and His Times, 1908–1960.* New York: Oxford University Press, 1991.

Divine, Robert A. *The Sputnik Challenge: Eisenhower's Response to the Soviet Satellite.* New York: Oxford University Press, 1993.

———, *Exploring the Johnson Years.* Austin: University of Texas Press, 1981.

———. *The Johnson Years, Volume Two: Vietnam, the Environment, and Science.* Lawrence: University Press of Kansas, 1987.

Evans, Sara. *Personal Politics: The Roots of Women's Liberation in the Civil Rights Movements and the New Left.* New York: Vintage Books, 1979.

Farber, David. *The Age of Great Dreams: America in the 1960s.* New York: Hill & Wang, 1994.

Ferrell, Robert H. *Harry S. Truman and the Modern American Presidency.* Boston: Little, Brown, 1983.

Foreman, Joel, ed. *The Other Fifties: Interrogating Midcentury American Icons.* Urbana: University of Illinois Press, 1997.

Fursenko, Aleksandr, and Naftali, Timothy. *One Hell of a Gamble: Khrushchev, Castro, and Kennedy.* New York: Norton, 1997.

Gaddis, John Lewis. *The Long Peace: Inquiries into the History of the Cold War.* New York: Oxford University Press, 1987.

———. *We Now Know: Rethinking Cold War History.* New York: Oxford University Press, 1997.

García, Mario T. *Mexican Americans: Leadership, Ideology, and Identity, 1930–1960.* New Haven, Conn.: Yale University Press, 1989.

Garrow, David J. *Bearing the Cross: Martin Luther King, Jr., and the Southern Christian Leadership Conference.* New York: William Morrow, 1986.

Giglio, James N. *The Presidency of John F. Kennedy.* Lawrence: University Press of Kansas, 1991.

Gitlin, Todd. *The Sixties: Years of Hope, Days of Rage.* New York: Bantam Books, 1987.

———. *The Whole World Is Watching: Mass Media in the Making and Unmaking of the New Left.* Berkeley: University of California Press, 1980.

Grant, Joanne. *Ella Baker: Freedom Bound.* New York: John Wiley and Sons, 1998.

Greenstein, Fred I. *The Hidden-Hand Presidency: Eisenhower as Leader.* New York: Basic Books, 1982.

Halberstam, David. *The Fifties.* New York: Villard Books, 1993.

Hamby, Alonzo L. *Man of the People: A Life of Harry S. Truman.* New York: Oxford University Press, 1995.

Harrington, Michael. *The Other America: Poverty in the United States.* New York: Macmillan, 1962.

Hartmann, Susan M. *The Home Front and Beyond: American Women in the 1940s.* Boston: Twayne Publishers, 1982.

———. *The Other Feminists: Activists in the Liberal Establishment.* New Haven, Conn.: Yale University Press, 1998.

Haynes, John Earl, and Harvey Klehr. *Venona: Decoding Soviet Espionage in America.* New Haven, Conn.: Yale University Press, 1999.

Hays, Samuel P. *Beauty, Health, and Permanence: Environmental Politics in the United States, 1955–1985.* New York: Cambridge University Press, 1987.

Herring, George C. *America's Longest War: The United States and Vietnam, 1950–1975.* 3d ed. New York: McGraw Hill Higher Education, 1995.

———. *LBJ and Vietnam: A Different Kind of War.* Austin: University of Texas Press, 1994.

Hine, Darlene Clark, and Kathleen Thompson. *A Shining Thread of Hope: The History of Black Women in America.* New York: Broadway Books, 1998.

Hogan, Michael J. *A Cross of Iron: Harry S. Truman and the Origins of the National Security State, 1945–1954.* New York: Cambridge University Press, 1998.

———. *The Marshall Plan: America, Britain, and the Reconstruction of Western Europe.* New York: Cambridge University Press, 1987.

Horowitz, Daniel. *Betty Friedan and the Making of* The Feminine Mystique: *The American Left, the Cold War and Modern Feminism.* Amherst: University of Massachusetts Press, 1998.

Hoxie, Frederick E., ed. *Indians in American History.* Arlington Heights, Ill.: Harlan Davidson, 1988.

Iverson, Peter. *"We Are Still Here": American Indians in the Twentieth Century.* Wheeling, Ill.: Harlan Davidson, 1998.

Isserman, Maurice, and Michael Kazin. *America Divided: The Civil War of the 1960s.* New York: Oxford University Press, 2000.

Jackson, Kenneth T. *Crabgrass Frontier: The Suburbanization of the United States.* New York: Oxford University Press, 1985.

Jones, Jacqueline. *The Dispossessed: America's Underclasses from the Civil War to the Present.* New York: Basic Books, 1992.

———. *Labor of Love, Labor of Sorrow: Black Women, Work, and the Family from Slavery to the Present.* New York: Basic Books, 1985.

Kaledin, Eugenia. *Mothers and More: American Women in the 1950s.* Boston: Twayne Publishers, 1984.

Karnow, Stanley. *Vietnam: A History: The First Complete Account of Vietnam at War.* New York: Viking Press, 1983.

Kaufman, Burton I. *The Korean War: Challenges in Crisis, Credibility, and Command.* New York: Alfred A. Knopf, 1986.

Kelley, Robin D. G., and Earl Lewis, eds. *To Make Our World Anew: A History of African Americans.* New York: Oxford University Press, 2000.

Kimball, Jeffrey P. *Nixon's Vietnam War.* Lawrence: University Press of Kansas, 1998.

LaFeber, Walter. *America, Russia, and the Cold War, 1945–1996.* 8th ed. New York: McGraw Hill, 1996.

———. *Inevitable Revolutions: The United States in Central America.* 2d ed. New York: W.W. Norton, 1993.

Leffler, Melvyn P. *A Preponderance of Power: National Security, the Truman Administration, and the Cold War.* Stanford, Calif.: Stanford University Press, 1992.

Lewis, John, with Michael D'Ors. *Walking with the Wind: A Memoir of the Movement.* New York: Simon & Schuster, 1998.

Linden-Ward, Blanche. *Changing the Future: American Women in the 1960s.* New York: Twayne Publishers, 1993.

Malcolm X, with Alex Haley. *The Autobiography of Malcolm X.* New York: Grove Press, 1965.

Matusow, Allen J. *The Unraveling of America: A History of Liberalism in the 1960s.* New York: Harper & Row, 1984.

May, Elaine Tyler. *Homeward Bound: American Families in the Cold War Era.* New York: Basic Books, 1998.

May, Ernest R., and Philip D. Zelikow, eds. *The Kennedy Tapes: Inside the White House during the Cuban Missile Crisis.* Cambridge, Mass.: Harvard University Press, 1997.

McCullough, David. *Truman.* New York: Simon & Schuster, 1992.

Meyerowitz, Joanne, ed. *Not June Cleaver: Women and Gender in Postwar America, 1945–1960.* Philadelphia: Temple University Press, 1994.

Murray, Charles. *Losing Ground: American Social Policy, 1950–1980.* 10th anniv. ed. New York: Basic Books, 1995.

Oshinsky, David M. *A Conspiracy So Immense: The World of Joe McCarthy.* New York: The Free Press, 1983.

Pach, Chester J., Jr., and Elmo Richardson. *The Presidency of Dwight D. Eisenhower.* Lawrence: University Press of Kansas, 1991.

Parmet, Herbert S. *Jack: The Struggles of John F. Kennedy.* New York: Dial Press, 1980.

———. *JFK: The Presidency of John F. Kennedy.* New York: Dial Press, 1983.

Patterson, James T. *America's Struggle against Poverty in the Twentieth Century.* Cambridge, Mass.: Harvard University Press, 2000.

Patterson, Thomas G. *Meeting the Communist Threat: Truman to Reagan.* New York: Oxford University Press, 1988.

Perlstein, Rick. *Before the Story: Barry Goldwater and the Unmaking of the American Consensus.* New York: Hill & Wang, 2001.

Piven, Frances F., and Richard A. Cloward. *Regulating the Poor: The Functions of Public Welfare.* New York: Vintage Books, 1993.

Polenberg, Richard. *One Nation Divisible: Class, Race, and Ethnicity in the United States since 1938.* New York: Viking Press, 1980.

Powaski, Ronald A. *The Cold War: The United States and the Soviet Union, 1917–1991.* New York: Oxford University Press, 1997.

Radosh, Ronald, and Joyee Milton. *The Rosenberg File: A Search for Truth.* New York: Holt, Rinehart, & Winston, 1983.

Rampersad, Arnold. *Jackie Robinson: A Biography.* New York: Alfred A. Knopf, 1997.

Reeves, Richard. *President Kennedy: Profile of Power.* New York: Simon & Schuster, 1993.

Reeves, Thomas C. *The Life and Times of Joe McCarthy: A Biography.* New York: Stein & Day, 1982.

Rose, Lisle A. *The Cold War Comes to Main Street: America in 1950.* Lawrence: University Press of Kansas, 1999.

Sale, Kirkpatrick. *The Green Revolution: The American Environmental Movement, 1962–1992.* New York: Hill & Wang, 1993.

Schlesinger, Arthur M., Jr. *A Thousand Days: John F. Kennedy in the White House.* Boston: Houghton Mifflin, 1965.

Schor, Juliet B. *The Overworked American: The Unexpected Decline of Leisure.* New York: Basic Books, 1991.

Schrecker, Ellen W. *No Ivory Tower: McCarthyism and the Universities.* New York: Oxford University Press, 1986.

Sheehan, Neil. *A Bright Shining Lie: John Paul Vann and America in Vietnam.* New York: Random House, 1988.

Sitkoff, Harvard. *The Struggle for Black Equality, 1954–1992.* Rev. ed. New York: Hill & Wang, 1993.

Sorensen, Theodore C. *Kennedy.* New York: Harper & Row, 1965.

Takaki, Ronald. *A Different Mirror: A History of Multicultural America.* Boston: Little, Brown, 1993.

Weart, Spencer R. *Nuclear Fear: A History of Images.* Cambridge, Mass.: Harvard University Press, 1988.

Weinstein, Allen. *Perjury: The Hiss-Chambers Case.* Rev. ed. New York: Random House, 1997.

Weinstein, Allen, and Alexander Vassiliev. *The Haunted Wood: Soviet Espionage in America: The Stalin Era.* New York: Random House, 1999.

Winkler, Allan M. *The Cold War: A History in Documents.* New York: Oxford University Press, 2000.

———. *Life under a Cloud: American Anxiety about the Atom.* New York: Oxford University Press, 1993.

Zieger, Robert H. *American Workers, American Unions.* 2d ed. Baltimore: The Johns Hopkins University Press, 1994.

Index

Boldface page numbers denote extensive treatment of a topic. *Italic* page numbers refer to illustrations; *c* refers to the Chronology; and *m* indicates a map.